SERBIE
WASHINGTON
GEORGES
AUTRICHE HONGRIE
COMMÉMORATION
de la Conférence de la PAIX
la HAYE · mai-Juillet · 1899

THE INTERNATIONAL COURT OF JUSTICE
1946-1996

PAX CVM IVSTITIA FORA TEMPLA ET RVRA CORONAT.

DEO

PROXIMO

ARTHUR EYFFINGER

The International Court of Justice 1946-1996

With Contributions by
ARTHUR WITTEVEEN

Foreword by His Excellency
MOHAMMED BEDJAOUI
President of
The International Court of Justice

Photography by
BERT AND LILIAN MELLINK

Kluwer Law International
THE HAGUE / LONDON / BOSTON

LIBRARY OF CONGRESS
CATALOGING-IN-PUBLICATION DATA

Eyffinger, Arthur.
The International Court of Justice, 1946-1996 / Arthur Eyffinger, with contributions by Arthur Witteveen.
p. cm.
Includes indices.
ISBN 90 411 0221 3 (HB: alk. paper)
1. International Court of Justice--History.
I. Witteveen, Arthur. II. Title.
JX1971.6.E98 1995
341.5′52--dc20 96-12015
CIP

Published by Kluwer Law International,
P.O. Box 85889, 2508 CN The Hague,
The Netherlands

Sold and distributed in the USA and Canada
by Kluwer Law International,
675 Massachusetts Avenue, Cambridge,
MA 02139, USA

In all other countries, sold and distributed
by Kluwer Law International,
P.O. Box 85889, 2508 CN The Hague,
The Netherlands

PRINTED IN THE NETHERLANDS

Opposite page:

The Bench of the International Court of Justice in January 1996.
First row from left to right: Judge C. G. Weeramantry from Sri Lanka, Judge G. Guillaume from France, Judge S. M. Schwebel from the United States (Vice-President), Judge M. Bedjaoui from Algeria (President), Judge S. Oda from Japan, Judge M. Shahabuddeen from Guyana and Judge R. Ranjeva from Madagascar;
Second row from left to right: Mr E. Valencia-Ospina from Colombia (Registrar), Judge V. S. Vereshchetin from the Russian Federation, Judge R. Higgins from the United Kingdom, Judge C.-A. Fleischhauer from Germany, Judge G. Herczegh from Hungary, Judge Shi Jiuyong from China, Judge A. G. Koroma from Sierra Leone and Judge L. Ferrari Bravo from Italy

Dustjacket photograph (front): Sitting of the Court on 8 March 1996.

021096 - 1000 ts
First reprint 1996

Foreword

This year, the International Court of Justice is celebrating the first half-century of its existence. An indisputable though tenuous triumph over the precariousness of existence, the celebration of a fiftieth anniversary is a great event in the life of an individual, as it is in the life of an institution. However, that event assumes particular importance when it concerns an international institution, for this institution carries a genetic heritage rendered vulnerable by the chromosome of State sovereignty, and therefore, by its very nature, seldom spared by the crises, convulsions and maladies which affect inter-State relations.

The celebration of the jubilee of the International Court of Justice, principal judicial organ of the United Nations, is therefore one of those events which required a certain splendour. Commemorated quietly nevertheless, in a sobriety which, moreover, well befits a judicial institution, albeit an international one, the fiftieth anniversary of the Court is marked by this Jubilee Book produced by Dr Arthur Eyffinger and offered in respectful tribute to our Institution.

Like every fiftieth anniversary, that of the International Court of Justice is an occasion, and a pre-eminent one at that, for a handsome family photograph, for a kind of frozen image, at the same time offering a retrospective look at the Institution. The *Jubilee Book* has clearly brought off this delicate exercise with aplomb. Essentially the product of the elegant penmanship of Mr Arthur Eyffinger, Chief Librarian at the Registry of the Court, with contributions from Mr Arthur Witteveen, Secretary in charge of information matters in the Registry, both of them Dutch nationals, this splendid publication is not only the work of two staff members sensitive to the life of the Court, but also perfectly epitomizes the links which have gradually been forged between the Court and the native country of the two authors.

Since its birth the guest of the Kingdom of the Netherlands, and comfortably housed in the serene setting of the Peace Palace in the heart of the peaceful city of The Hague, the International Court of Justice is fortunate in being the object of the solicitude of the Dutch people, who have always set great store by the values of international peace and justice. From the vantage point of its fifty years, the Court therefore expresses its gratitude to the Dutch people and to its noble Sovereign for the generous hospitality extended to it. The Court regards this hospitality as a particular privilege since the Netherlands, where international justice has its roots, is also the birthplace of Grotius, Asser, van Vollenhoven, Verzijl, Röling, Loder and van Eysinga, to name just some of the Dutch internationalists with us no more.

Well documented and richly illustrated, Mr Eyffinger's work covers the whole spectrum of the activities of the International Court of Justice from its origins to the present day. The genesis and gestation of what is sometimes justly called the *World Court* are related in minute detail. The composition and functioning of the Institution are also covered in depth. Nor has the author fought shy of a commendable and painstaking attempt to summarize when considering the complex question of the principal legal systems forming the substratum of the law applicable by the Court. However, one of the most evocative parts of this book is that devoted by the author to individuals, to the guiding spirits, past and present, of the Court; this portrait gallery, comprised of photographs accompanied by brief but accurate biographies of former or present Members of the Court, is a moving one. For many, it will bring back memories of those no longer with us after contributing so much to international justice.

Published in French and English, the two official languages of the Court, embellished with a great many black and white and coloured plates, and pleasant to read, this work, in its own way, makes a noteworthy contribution to the attainment of one of the objectives of the United Nations Decade for International Law, which is *'to encourage the teaching, study, dissemination and wider appreciation of international law'*. This contribution is all the more welcome since it does not come from an institution, since all the credit for it must go to a writer for whom history is a passion and whose special field is Hugo Grotius. The International Court of Justice, to which this work is devoted, has indeed played no part in its conception and realization. As the passive subject of this study, the Court has no desire either to approve or gainsay the views expressed in it, which are those of the author and co-author alone, drawing on the strength of the experience they have gained in the Registry of the Court.

Though now fifty years old, the International Court of Justice nevertheless would still appear to be in the springtime of its life if the many cases currently entered in the General List are anything to go by. The Sword and the Scales thus appear, more than ever, to be the best guarantors of the international peace born during the last century in the tree-lined freshness of this charming city of The Hague. A happy event, if ever there was one, and one which has today earned this city the much-coveted title of judicial capital of the world. May the pages of this *Jubilee Book*, a respectful tribute to the International Court of Justice, presage many a fine new page in the history of international judicial settlement, to the writing of which the Court will bring all the authority of the experience and age it has now acquired.

MOHAMMED BEDJAOUI
President of
The International Court of Justice

Message to the President of the Court from the Chief Justice of Canada

The following resolution, which was passed unanimously, was sent in a message to the President of the Court from the Chief Justice of Canada.

BE IT RESOLVED THAT we, the delegates of the Seventh International Appellate Judges Conference held in Ottawa, Canada in September 1995, hereby wish to extend our greetings to the International Court of Justice in the Hague, the Netherlands, on the occasion of its 50th anniversary in 1996. Committed as we are to the establishment of the rule of law in the international as well as the national arena, we congratulate the Court on its accomplishments to date, and offer our best wishes for continued success in the future.

Acknowledgments

This book celebrates a jubilee. First and foremost it tells the fascinating story of an institution. Yet, more than that, it relates the genesis of an idea, or should one say an ideal, from the first dawning of the concept of peaceful settlement up to the day its embodiment was given The Hague as a permanent abode. Finally, the book ventures to show, in a nutshell, the development of the law, from the early notions of justice and equity as they originated within the various municipal spheres of a wide, wide world up to their first assembling in a brave effort to function on the international level and within one, multicultural society.

To be sure, international law is a unified discipline. There is no such thing as Eastern or Western international law, for international law must, by very definition, be international. The law, as we have inherited it, has developed in the modern era mainly from Western sources. However, especially through the work of the Court in the past fifty years, the mainstream of the law is being continuously enriched by contributions from all quarters of the globe. The bench of the International Court of Justice, bound in terms of its Statute to be representative of the main forms of civilization, reflects these multiple strands of global influence. Those influences shaped the nascent discipline as it evolved in many cultures and must continue to nourish it as it grows to meet the needs of the richly textured international society of the future. This book ventures to do justice to these many contributory sources, highlighting the stages by which they made contact with the Court at The Hague.

To the many who have come to appreciate his work in past years it will not come as a surprise that the *auctor intellectualis* of this book's concept is Judge Christopher Weeramantry. It is with him that the project originated and it is due to his persuasive qualities that it materialized. If anything, the book itself must serve as a token of my acknowledgment to him. It should also be seen as an expression of my gratitude to the Court and the Registrar for generously allowing me to accept this challenging commitment.

Obviously, a publication like the present one cannot be produced without the active support of many. First of all, I must say a special word of thanks to the President of the Court for the warm and generous Foreword which he has so kindly contributed to the book. I owe deep gratitude to Alan Stephens, and through him Kluwer Law International, for their steadfast optimism throughout. I am indebted to the Director of the Carnegie Foundation for the facilities provided in the production of this book. I thank Arthur Witteveen, the Court's Secretary in Charge of Information Matters, for having enriched the book by generously putting twenty years of experience with the Court into the appraisal of its case-law and the conclusions to be drawn therefrom.

Bert and Lilian Mellink made a dream of mine come true with their detailed reproduction of the magnificence of the Peace Palace, thus paying tribute to the visionaries of the peace ideal. The exacting lay-out of this book has been completed with a discerning eye, meticulous care and infinite patience by Antoon J. van Vliet. Annebeth Rosenboom, Teun de Graaf and Anneke Zoutendijk were ever approachable. Finally, among the many colleagues and friends who went out of their way to serve my numerous claims for help I must mention Mrs Doreen Bloemendaal, Ms Maureen Sullivan, Mrs Pavan Sodhi and my dear Loes.

I have felt privileged and strengthened knowing all of you were around at all times.

A. E.

Contents

7. The Bench

8. The Principal Legal Systems

10. *A Review of the Court's Case-Law*
BY ARTHUR WITTEVEEN

11. *The Role of the Court*
BY ARTHUR WITTEVEEN

Statistics

Bibliography

Indices

CHAPTER ONE

The World Court:
Towards the Twenty-First Century

This book is about the Highest Court on earth, a Bench from which there is no appeal. It is about the principal judicial organ of the most representative body politic of mankind, the embodiment of an ideal that has held humanity spellbound for centuries, the outcome of a long and faltering process. The Court came into being when the nightmare of the First World War made the dream of pacifists for a fleeting moment reach out, as if in Michelangelo's fresco, and touch the utter despair of the pragmatists. What had long been considered the ultimate panacea by some, had now become the last resort of others. At the dawn of the international era, it was the first military confrontation on a global scale that stimulated the first serious attempt at worldwide organization.

However, idealism and despair, while both having their legitimate place in the psyche of man, both attest to his perplexity at the human condition and the failure to face reality. Both are escapist and all too simple and inadequate responses to the infinitely more complex fabric of life. Moreover, they are not exactly the pillars and keystones upon which the framework of modern society can rest. By these standards, therefore, the projected World Court, when put to the test in the turmoil of international politics, was almost bound to fail – and so it did, almost, in the 1930s. The wreck was salvaged by the pragmatism of hard-boiled realists who anchored the Court in a firm political setting by making it an intrinsic part of the UN Organization and turning it into the cornerstone of a multi-faceted structure of dispute settlement.

This is the role of the International Court of Justice, to which both the Bench itself and the world at large have increasingly accustomed themselves. While being the pinnacle (and therefore in a sense the symbol) of man's response to lawlessness, it operates, above all, as a very practical mechanism to prevent and counteract the use of force: *pacis tutela apud judicem* (the judge is the guardian of peace) – so reads the legend on the main facade of its seat, the Hague Peace Palace. In this, the International Court of Justice has succeeded fairly well in the past decades, in its modest way. It is true that the competence of the Court is limited. While it serves as the world's highest judicial organ, its reach is not all-embracing. Unlike the image suggested by the many depictions of its patron goddess, Justice, which in a great variety of techniques embellish the walls and ceilings of the Peace Palace, its rays do not reach into all the crevices of international conflict. In fact, even within the area of dispute settlement the province of the Court is fairly limited, for a number of reasons.

Firstly, its role extends to judicial settlement only. Adjudication in itself – as will be shown in greater detail in the next chapter – is but the last phase of dispute resolution and in many parts of the world traditionally not the most preferred or most practised of a whole chain of options for the amicable settlement of disputes. These range from negotiation and consultation, through mediation and conciliation, to arbitration among others.

Secondly, even within its proper province of adjudication, the Court's jurisdiction is not comprehensive. It is restricted to inter-State disputes and excludes any disputes in the private or mixed spheres or with respect to that new phenomenon in international relations, international organizations. However, with respect to some UN organs and agencies as specified below, the Court does have a certain competence (albeit within certain restrictions), through its advisory function.

The above may have given the reader an outline of the aspirations and limitations of the World Court, and its confinement within comparatively narrow boundaries. It may also have drawn the reader's attention to the fact that the cherished idea of an International Court took a long time to materialize. Before reviewing the genesis and operation of the Court, we do well, therefore, to walk back a little along the long and winding road that finally brought mankind to The Hague, where its time-honoured ideal became reality.

The International Court of Justice operates in the sphere of international relations. In this, its angle of approach is strictly limited to the legal aspects of the issues it deals with. Its function is to analyse and apply the existing law and, wherever possible, to render clear-cut judgments and opinions. Obviously, this approach represents a rather narrow basis on which to tackle the variety of problems and conflicts posed by complex modern society. The Court applies the law in two different ways. One of them is to furnish Advisory Opinions in response to requests from the General Assembly, the Security Council and other organs of the UN and specialized agencies authorized by the General Assembly to request such Opinions. The second is to determine legal disputes between States. Thus, in these months of its golden jubilee, the Court is preoccupied with the references made to it by the General Assembly of the UN and the World Health Organization regarding the legitimacy of nuclear weapons. In fact, it is precisely the Court's focus on the legal aspects of an issue which makes its opinion the welcome counterpart to approaches from different angles, e.g., political, social, or ethnographical studies.

The Court, in deciding disputes referred to it, is required by its Statute to apply treaties, customary international law and universally recognized general principles of law. Judicial decisions and the teachings of the most highly qualified jurists may also be used as subsidiary means for the determination of rules of law. It is from these sources that the Court draws the law it applies. Cases sometimes come to the Court heavily laden with emotional overtones but the Court is confined to its duty to apply to the dispute the law drawn from the sources stipulated in its Statute. There may sometimes be a dramatic gap, for this, reason, between findings resulting from a strict application of the law and general notions of justice as conceived by the public at large.

Today, as we look forward to the opening of the third millennium, there are as yet no worldwide legislative and executive bodies even remotely similar in competence and authority to their counterparts on the national plane. In fact, this is perhaps the most unsatisfactory aspect of the present state of international law, for it lacks mechanisms to make new laws or to enforce it – mechanisms always available within a domestic system. For this reason, which is often not commonly understood, international lawyers are sometimes faced with scepticism in relation to their discipline. Another problem is the absence of a written international code of law such as there often is in domestic jurisdictions. Nor are there sanctions or means of enforcement. It is only through the eventual recognition of these principles by all nations and the option of collective sanctions that trespassers against the code may be isolated or brought to book. As it is, the Charter of the UN, for all its merits, is but the first draft of a future World Constitution. Similarly, the Statute of the ICJ is still a relatively tentative instrument. For one thing, the Court is not competent to render judgment on nations who have not consented to its jurisdiction.

The best instrument developed thus far by the legal world to enable nations, by their united efforts, to augment the authority of the Court, i.e., the rule of law in international affairs, is the so-called

optional clause formula. Throughout the history of the Hague Courts, covering seventy-five years, this formula has not commanded an adequate level of acceptance. By adhering to this clause – the signing of which is optional, hence its rather puzzling name – States bind themselves to accept the jurisdiction of the Court in advance, irrespective of the issue concerned.

To date, the majority of States adhering to the UN Charter and ICJ Statute have not bound themselves under this clause, or have done so only conditionally, by making substantial reservations. During the entire Soviet period, East-European Socialist States, shrinking from any acceptance of interference with their sovereign rights, rejected the idea of the clause on principle. In fact, they went so far as to emphasize that it was precisely the advisory function of the Court in matters of legal theory, much more than the judging of contentious cases, which had to be regarded as the primary occupation of the Court and in fact constituted its specific contribution to the building of the international legal system. Other major powers such as the USA and France, at some stage and for different reasons, withdrew their previous acceptance of the clause. All this serves to show that – a full century after the opening of the First Hague Peace Conference – which optimistically set out to make short shrift of the armaments race, ban war from the face of the earth, and impose the rule of peace through law – the international legal order is still far from being established.

The Genesis of Modern International Law

The study of public international law is a relatively young discipline. Until fairly recently, its comparatively short period of experience was reflected in the apparent imprecision of its terminology and the lack of clarity regarding its sources. In the Western world, the theory of international law was developed in the era which saw the establishment of the modern State system, that is to say during the century leading up to the Peace of Westphalia (1648). However, the systematic and in-depth study of international law is, in many respects, the product of the last century only. Indeed, its full development on a global scale was not reached until well after World War II. The very history of the Peace Palace Library attests to this. Projected in 1903, it was envisioned by its ambitious initiator, Andrew Carnegie, as the world's leading collection of literature in the field. Despite relatively modest resources, the Library comfortably managed to retain its prominent position until well into the 1950s. By then, however, the world had started to change rapidly, and the literature of international law proliferated in many new directions such as environmental law, space law, human rights and the law relating to development. A spate of publica-

The Napoleonic Wars were terminated in the Vienna Congress of 1815 which formulated a new European system. Without perhaps fully appreciating the nationalist and democratic tendencies of the day, for a full century its terms - including the freedom of international rivers and the abolition of slavery - did restrict wars to short and localized outbursts of violence.

tions and an avalanche of books were the natural result. Within a decade the Carnegie Library lost its grip on the field.

The complete transformation of the world's political configuration in the UN era, the awakening of the Developing World, the explosion of mass communications along with the expansion of technology and transnational industries on an unprecedented scale – all within a span of less than fifty years – have dramatically changed the map and the power blocks of the earth. This circumstance has given acute urgency to the need for a true international order. An international order which, if it is to become salutary to mankind, must be based on the rule of law, provided that this legal code is the true reflection and the common denominator of all the 'principal legal systems and civilizations of the world', as so aptly stipulated in the Statute of the ICJ. This wording is by no means a coincidence for it was precisely the ICJ which was intended by its founding fathers to become a mirror for the laws of mankind. There can be no doubt that this international law of the future, if it is to become a workable instrument in the century ahead, will be of an altogether different nature from the law which up to the 1960s was ambitiously, yet erroneously, called the Law of Nations.

How came this early Law of Nations into being? The traditional answer to this, one which was never questioned really until the 1950s, was provided by the historians of international law. Their discipline, as practised over the past two centuries, was very much a product of the European mind. It was developed, characteristically, in the era of the Vienna Congress (1815), the age of the Enlightenment. An offshoot of law and history, it arose out of the encyclopedic spirit of that time. Throughout the 19th century it produced a whole series of comprehensive studies which with broad strokes of the pen ambitiously dealt with the full span of time from Pericles to Metternich.

Yet, for all their merits, these works were blatantly uncritical; they showed a disdain for anything from outside the European sphere of influence and a complete disinterest in the attainments of research into the sources of the law as revealed by other disciplines. They also shared one other characteristic. Irrespective of the practice of law as exemplified by custom

An early 19th century allegory of the heydays of colonialism. Queen Britannia, the lion at her feet, magnanimously bestows the olive branch of peace on the submissive deputies from the four quarters of the globe.

or treaty, they depicted the period up to what is generally called the rise of the Modern Era, around the 16th century, as a mere sequence of political events. That is to say, they restricted themselves to international relations and diplomacy during that period without any specific reference to the existing laws of the time.

From the Modern Era on, they shifted perspective and proceeded along altogether different lines, describing the period from the days of Grotius in terms of purely legal theory, as reflected in the successive schools of legal thought, yet again without any reference to international State practice. In short, all extra-European or European but pre-Grotian concepts were disregarded. In fact, the major debate among these authors during the whole of the 19th century concerned the issue whether Macchiavelli, Bodin and the Spanish late scholastics such as Vitoria, Suarez and Ayala were to be included or if international law was to be considered to start with Grotius only. As Wolfgang Preiser rightly concludes:

> A general history of international relations in combination with a history of the science of international law restricted to the modern era, each executed without links to the other, was no conceptual basis for fruitful developments in this new area of legal history.

Surprisingly enough, these narrow, essentially Eurocentric views only deepened as, towards the second half of the 19th century, the contacts with non-Western civilizations intensified with the rise of modern means of communication. Due to their superior technology and military supremacy, the colonizing powers simply imposed their laws wherever they went. Precious little attention was paid to the non-Western customs and law traditions they intruded upon. Latin America was opened to the Western sphere of influence and law traditions in the 17th century; the Indian subcontinent, East Asia, and Africa followed later. Still, neither the contacts with the pre-Colombian American traditions, nor the time-honoured Islamic, Hindu or Buddhist law traditions, let alone African or Pacific customary law, received any attention in the development of international law in the West up to the early 20th century. These traditions were largely treated condescendingly as 'isolated inconsequential curiosities' (Preiser).

The first cracks in that attitude appeared only when, around 1900, and more particularly during the Second Hague Peace Conference of 1907, the Latin American nations came to impress their ideas of what they called a 'New International Law' on the Western world, especially through their ample experience with arbitration as a means for the settlement of disputes. From then on, regional law concepts forced their way into the textbooks and manuals. Still, it is only from 1960 onwards, when the process of decolonization gained real impetus, that previously prevailing tenets about the exclusivity and predominance of European theory lost their relevance to the debate in an increasingly multicultural world. Since then, Western scholars and diplomats have come to realize, some reluctantly at first, that their discipline should henceforward be put on a different footing.

Until fairly recently, the classical argument of European doctrine against non-Western law traditions has been that the latter failed to have an impact on the constitutive phase of international law as it developed over the last three centuries and that they did not make any substantial additions to its accepted 'general principles'. In fact, this is precisely why most of these scholars also excluded any European law traditions previous to 1500 or outside the scope of the dozen 'civilized nations'. Around 1950, it became obvious that this attitude needed modification. The simple and decisive answer to this attitude was, clearly, that if international law was expected to remain functional, let alone become pivotal in the constitution of the international order for the next millennium, this could only be achieved on the basis of an essentially multicultural approach in which each component found its own traditions reflected in the discipline it was expected to accept. No longer could any single legal tradition prevail over all others.

It is equally obvious that it is the study of the history of international law which, by broadening its focus, may contribute considerably to the acceptance of this new rule of law. One has only to review the role and record of the early years of the ICJ and its immediate predecessor, the Permanent Court of International Justice of the inter-war years, to become aware of the fallacy of the pretension of their founding fathers that these Benches represented the world of international law. Until the late 1960s, huge parts of the Developing World were either underrepresented or not represented at all on the Bench of the World Court and consequently had no opportunity to make any mark on its case-law.

Once these areas came to be better represented, the Judges from these regions may well have felt some inhibitions, initially, in injecting into the jurisprudence of The Hague some of the insights gained from their own legal traditions. To put it in a more concrete way: civilizations like those of Africa and the Pacific, which for the settlement of disputes traditionally and throughout many centuries had relied on negotiation, conciliation, mediation or other extra-forensic solutions, could hardly be expected wholeheartedly to embrace, overnight, procedures which were perfectly alien to them, merely as a result of being given the privilege of access to or representation on the Bench of the World Court.

As we argued at the outset, adjudication is just one way of settling disputes, a formalized technique which happens to have had special appeal to the Western mind and which, with the prolonged political and economic supremacy of this part of the world, has gradually imposed itself on the developing international structures. Significantly, one of the persistent debates

Clio, the Muse of History, riding the lion backwards seated.

among the Judges on the Bench in recent decades has been precisely the way in which an element such as equity should come into play.

In the past few decades, in response to the inadequate use of the Court by the Developing World, the ICJ itself and the UN, notably within the framework of its Decade of International Law (1990-1999), have introduced quite a number of practical changes. The seats on the Bench have been regionally redistributed, the option of a Chamber procedure has facilitated access, the establishment of a special trust fund has eased the financial burdens involved in retaining counsel. And yet, helpful as these facilities may be, it would seem that they remain secondary to the need for a full scrutiny of these other sources which could enrich the totality of international law. This is the precondition for developing the new international legal order. Relevant to this new rule of law will be such sources as the early Chinese international law traditions, as exemplified by the periods of Spring and Autumn and Warring States (covering the period from the 8th to the 3rd century BC), as well as the substantial contribution to the law of treaties of the Russian schools of law, as exemplified by the impressive Russo-Sino system of treaties concluded at Nerchinsk in 1689 and at Kiakhta in 1727. This applies also to deep-rooted Hindu traditions of *dharma* (righteousness), State equality and sovereignty, Buddhist ecological considerations, Islamic notions of chivalry, African customary rules or for that matter classical and medieval European traditions.

Part of the Bench in 1995, adequately reflecting the regional distribution. From left to right Judges Ferrari Bravo (Italy), Koroma (Sierra Leone), Shi Jiuyong (China), Ranjeva (Madagascar), Aguilar-Mawdsley (Venezuela).

In the analysis of historical legal concepts, yet another persistent phenomenon should be taken into account, namely the frequent clash of day-to-day State practice with official legal theory, as may be observed in all cultures. This is reflected in the attitude of the Greek commonwealth of City-States of the early 4th century BC with regard to the so-called barbarians in the establishment of the second Attic Maritime League, as well as in the Islamic 'capitulations' or treaties with the Crusaders in the 12th century or, for that matter, Ottoman foreign policy during the Napoleonic era. Over and over again, practical understandings run counter to strict doctrine. With respect to such instances as those recalled here, it is apposite to recall Plato's view that the parties involved were 'by nature' in a state of war with each other. Again, how were trade negotiatons between Muslims and Christian merchants influenced by the principle laid down by the Council of Constance that one was not obliged to keep one's word to the non-believer?

We have still much to gain from a comparison of legal systems and epochs, along chronological as well as regional lines, on a truly global scale. 'What is here at issue is a comparative examination of independently developed, functional international legal orders which helped influence the legal character of their respective eras' (Preiser).

What may clearly help us at the present juncture, is the inventory of legally ordered inter-State systems which persisted over a longer period of time alongside the mere use of force. The generally accepted criterion for the existence of an international legal system as such is the co-existence of sovereign States treating each other respectfully as independent entities of equal rank. To be sure, one does not observe this phenomenon all too often and rarely indeed for any considerable period in the history of mankind, or beyond a well-defined area. It was certainly not a feature of the martial empires of Assyrians or Persians. And whatever may have been the privileges Hammurabi's laws attributed to his subjects, these certainly did not apply to foreigners.

In the Western world, within certain limits, one may perhaps regard as a true international legal system the Greek Commonwealth of autonomous and sovereign city-States that prevailed from about 600 BC until, in 338 BC, the Macedonians took over – albeit a system that excluded the foreign 'barbarian' States.

The norm certainly did not apply to the Romans from the days of the final subjugation of the Hellenistic kingdoms at Pydna (168 BC) until their confrontation, five centuries later, with the Persian Sassanids. The term *fœdus æquum*, meaning a treaty on equal terms, remained reserved for Rome's relations with early Italian competitors and the first Punic wars. Symptomatic of the position of Rome with regard to its relations with foreign nations was its attitude towards arbitration panels, which is fairly illustrative of the status of international relations. The concept had indeed achieved a considerable acceptance in the Greek Commonwealth, but was never accepted by the Romans.

The international relations within the feudal system of the Middle Ages were complex and unspecified and have as yet not been exhaustively analysed to allow an overall interpretation. Around 1200, when the first contours of a new State system were dimly emerging, it was, significantly, the Pope who was acknowledged as the highest arbitrator in the settlement of disputes.

What of the non-Western traditions? Within the Chinese world, the norms of an international legal system, if presumed for a previous period, certainly did not apply any longer with the creation, in 221 BC, of the Empire as the exclusive cultural centre of the world, and they would not come back into focus until the 19th century. Yet, the norms did apply to some extent to the Islamic world; the idea was very much alive within the Indian world, at different periods and to varying extents, for the subcontinental region had many principalities and rulers who had a variety of dealings with each other.

State sovereignty is perhaps the keyword for the interpretation of international relations through the centuries. The hard-won respect for borderlines and territorial integrity and the persistent fear of conquest or intervention in the political as well as the economic sphere, have turned the nations of the world into forceful defenders of a concept which, ironically, now constitutes a major barrier to the development of the supranational rule of law.

Be that as it may, the acknowledged absence of true international legal systems during many phases of the history of mankind does not imply that the basic concepts and general principles of international law were completely absent during those periods. On the contrary, several of these concepts are more or less common to mankind. The notion of just war occurs almost everywhere, the immunity of diplomatic envoys was respected by numerous cultures, respect for the concept of observance of good faith and the given word is practically universal. Other concepts are typically regional, often on account of special circumstances, which will be discussed at greater length in the review of regional law traditions (Chapter 8). The Latin American *uti possidetis* principle and the development of arbitration clauses are readily explicable from the genesis of these former Spanish colonies. The concentration on fishing rights and issues of the law of the sea is only bound to occur in coastal areas. Still other concepts, such as the insistence on universalism in Hindu law, are probably due to the moulding of various civilizations, whereas the Buddhist eye for environmental issues has definite philosophical roots. In similar vein, the period of slavery, followed by colonization, followed finally by economic dependency, inevitably left its mark on the African outlook regarding issues of human rights.

The marble throne of Zeus, a copy of the one excavated in Knossos and presented by Greece in 1913.

The Secularization of the Law

This brings us to another aspect of international law as practised in the Western world in the past few centuries. As we have seen, international law as a discipline in its own right is considered to have had its origins in Europe from the days of Grotius. Only then was the prerequisite fulfilled which is essential to Western legal thought, namely the secularization of the law and its detachment from the sacred sphere, from moral theology and scholasticism.

This phenomenon in itself was one of the outcomes of a complex process, in the course of which the prevailing medieval system of the two, often rivalling powers of Emperor and Pope was gradually replaced by the modern State system. Columbus and Luther – or in other words the change in man's outlook on the world as a result of the discovery of new continents as well as the disruption of the *Respublica Christiana* by the Reformation following the Peace of Augsburg of 1555 – had shattered the body of custom evolved

over ten centuries of European history. The world as it had been known up to then did not just grow larger, it became internally divided. Religion became an issue of high politics. From then on, the creed was *cuius regio, eius religio* (rulership determines religion). Political loyalty became firmly linked to religious conformity or, vice versa, if need be, politics conformed to religious realities: *Paris vaut bien une messe!* Yet, this was only the first phase in a long process of attitudinal change. Initially, growing sectarianism gave rise to increased longing for restoration of the *Una Sancta*. Then, despair and disillusion brought about the loosening of religious bonds and large-scale secularization.

The demise of former certainties also compelled a reconsideration of the human condition. Gradually, the static view of a world that was preordained by Divine Revelation was replaced by a more dynamic one in which man himself was taken as the measure of all things. Dogma was replaced by reason, mystery by experiment and in the unravelling of the secrets of nature man went self-confidently in search of happiness. In the sphere of the exact sciences, the upheaval was most dramatic. Somewhere between Galileo and Brahe, Keppler and Pascal 'the Old Heavens exploded'. Within a century, virtually the whole universe seemed reducible to quantitative norms and appeared observable through either microscope or telescope. It took the sobering genius of Leibniz, Locke and Vico to reduce to reasonable proportions the unlimited optimism suggested by Cartesian reason and Newtonian empiricism – for, however astounding the successes of science, these did not provide any answers to issues in the moral sphere.

It was precisely these issues which soon came to matter in the social sciences. In political terms, the former absolute claims of Papacy and Empire, as expressed by Boniface VIII or in the acknowledgment by such a prominent lawyer as Bartolus de Saxoferrato that the Emperor was above the law (*legibus solutus*), were gradually taken over by sovereign princes. For their claims to power, these monarchs did not rely on providence or divine ordination, but on intrinsic authority, as vested in the people or senate. The basic issue of the time was whether the execution of this authority was to be based on force and sheer power or on the rule of law.

Bartolus de Saxoferrato (1314-1357).

It was the answer to this elementary question which was to determine the constitutions of the respective nations. Political and legal theorists readily provided the new rulers with these answers. Macchiavelli, Bodin, Grotius, Bossuet, Pascal, Locke and Hobbes all formulated answers of their own. More often than not, in this phase of transition, civil strife was the outcome of the debate. First noticeable in the France of Francis I in the early 1500s and gradually spreading all over Europe, the prolonged process had first to pass through an extremely turbulent and painful catalytic phase before it crystallized into fixed new patterns. The Bartholemew Night and the Edict of Nantes in France, the Arminian and Gomarist troubles in the Netherlands, the Thirty-Years War in the German States and the Glorious Revolution in England bear witness to this strife. These upheavals were the stepping-stones to the desired goal, to which nations were guided by their prominent political thinkers.

For our purposes the essential feature of the Thirty-Years War is that, in the course of that contest, the religious blocs of reformatory and contra-reformatory powers that opposed each other at the outbreak of war, were gradually replaced by political blocs which, irrespective of religious conviction, were guided by the *raison d'état – tout court*. The pact concluded between France and Sweden, the early champions of each side, in 1635 is the first testimony to this remarkable evolution. Another one is that the papal nuncio, who had presided over the negotiations resulting in the 1598 Peace of Vervins between France and Hapsburg Spain, played a distinctly less prominent part at Munster fifty years later. It was indeed in the Pact of Westphalia (1648) that these new structures took concrete shape. It is this treaty which for three hundred years – with adjustments effected at Utrecht (1713) and Vienna (1815) – was to govern inter-State relations in Europe.

It remains one of the most striking phenomena of European history that the same nations which, around 1600, were still bitterly and emotionally engaged in religious battles, around 1700 unanimously embraced the *droit de convenance* as it was called at the time, an extremely pragmatic and business-like approach to international relations. One may even say that the generation of the Peace of Utrecht, in its search for the 'balance of power' and the maintenance of the *status quo* and collective security in Europe, stood at the cradle of a new international order – or rather, the new European international order.

It was precisely the long years of internal rivalry and the widening of horizons through the discovery of new continents, that had caused the European nations to become aware finally of their essential unity – a unity which, in the absence of a centralized political authority, was understood to rest if anything on their common legal traditions. A century later, at Vienna, the cement of these concepts proved solid enough to cope with the apocalypse of the Napoleonic wars. It was Count Bismarck who, in the second part of the 19th century, was to expand and optimize the system of alliances introduced by Metternich in Vienna. Summarized here in a few words, this process of change marks one of the great milestones in the evolution of a new world order.

In the West, this process of secularization of the law proved an irreversible one, never to be seriously questioned any more. To other cultures, however, the secularization of the law has been much less self-evident. In fact, the process described above is quite exceptional when viewed in a global perspective. Within the world of Islam such a process has been virtually unthinkable, while in the Indian and other Asian cultures law is equally embedded in social structures, in accordance with Hindu and Buddhist religious thought. The same holds good (to take an example even more akin and close to the Christian world) for the Judaic legal system.

The vast corpus of Hindu jurisprudence contains the *Sruti* – its sacred texts based on revelation – and their interpretation in the *Smritis* or learned commentaries of legal scholars based on human experience. Together they represent a continuous tradition of juristic interpretation in the Hindu world extending over twenty centuries and more. The world view of Buddhism, so universalistic that it encompasses all living creatures, transmitted into legal systems governed by Buddhistic thought a dimension so far-reaching that modern law has many concepts to learn from it. In the Islamic world likewise the different juristic interpretations of *Sunnis* and *Shias* and the four schools of *Hanbali*, *Shafi*, *Maliki* and *Hanafi* are to be noted. In this context reference should also be made to the astonishing achievement of the Jewish juristic system. This system, too, functions harmoniously within the ambit of the sacred law as expounded in the successive phases of *Soferim*, *Mishnah*, the *Talmuds* and – to call to mind one of Grotius' inspiring sources – Moses Maimonides' *Mishneh Torah*. And, to extend the parallel, in its disputations within the stringent and more lenient schools of *Shamai* and *Hillel*, Jewish law brought the issues of justice and legalism into sharper focus.

The purpose of this narrative is of course clear: international law, as shaped by the

The Temple of Peace raised up on the two columns of Church and State and held together by the chains of religion and the Peace of Westphalia. Pope and Emperor, surrounded by cardinals and electors, valiantly face agnostics and atheists.

exclusively Eurocentric approach which prevailed until the early 1960s, was based on the strictly legalistic premises of just one cultural tradition. The international law of the next millennium, however, must of necessity be an amalgam of concepts representative of the whole world's legal legacy. In order to attain the worldwide recognition which will condition its social relevance, it must include ethical notions from all available cultural sources.

The achievement of such an international legal system will be a huge task, no doubt. At the same time, it constitutes one of the great challenges for the decades ahead. Perhaps the most reassuring and confidence-inspiring thought for those embarking on this quest is the virtual certainty that there are precious few alternatives. In these respects at least, the progress of international society has brought mankind to the point of no return.

Let us once more turn to a review of certain aspects of the Eurocentric approach to the law. The Western mind, in the past few centuries, has concentrated on practicalities. It has consequently been inclined, more readily perhaps than the more speculative Eastern mind, to permit traditions to pass into oblivion when they no longer seemed to serve any practical purpose or promise immediate profit. This matter-of-fact approach has been a blessing to society in many respects. It has brought about the industrial revolution, wrought wonders in technology and put us on the moon. However, political and cultural predominance during so many centuries has also made the Western legal mind less susceptible to other expressions and forms of law which are innate to other cultures. It is particularly the religious and literary connotations of these other sources of law which are puzzling to the modern Western mind and tend to be dismissed as mere curiosities. It is to be feared that in coming to terms with the Islamic, Indian and Chinese law traditions in the search for a new legal order, Western scholarship can no longer afford such an attitude.

But there is more to it than this. Intimately conversant as the Western mind is with this practical approach to the law, it is easily lured into regarding this approach as representing the mainstream of European thought through its full history. That would be a fallacy. This specific approach was the outcome of a revolutionary change which took place in Europe in the second part of the 17th century, and is best characterized as the rationalization of man's outlook to reality and the mechanization of his *Weltanschauung*. The high-tech innovations of the present day are no more than the latest products, as it were, of this mental change.

One of its first effects had been the rise of specialized branches of learning. This implied the cutting up into separate disciplines of the previous unity of learning as exemplified in the curricula of *quadrivium* and *trivium*, which had governed the medieval and humanist schools and early academic centres. A second, no less consequential change, was the reorientation of all learning. Hugo Grotius is a good example of man at a crossroads, at this juncture of European history. By virtue of his authority to the present-day international lawyer, his example may serve to illustrate the final point we wish to make in the opening chapter with respect to the quest for a new international legal order. The aim of this excursus will be to highlight some of the roots of European (international) legal thought in order to reveal some parallels with non-Western traditions.

Grotius' principal title to fame in the present-day world is his work in the international field. The tragedy of his life, however, was the consequence of his politico-religious treatises. The first of these came within the national context, due to Grotius' prominent position in the quarrels between Arminians and Gomarists, the reformatory doves and hawks in the constitutive phase of the Dutch nation. The later works, produced in exile after his escape from Loevestein Castle, gave expression to his so-called unionistic programme, his efforts to remedy the schism within the Christian world. The deep relevance for the period of these works, which have now virtually passed into oblivion, can be easily demonstrated by the fact that the major tract, *On the Unity of the Christian Religion*, was by far his most frequently reprinted work. In England, where Grotius' renown up to the early 19th century was primarily based on this specific tract, this apology of the Christian faith saw reprints either in the original Latin or in English translation literally every third year over a full two centuries.

In the best humanist tradition in which he was raised, Grotius – who insisted on the requirement of ample literary, theological and historical training for the accomplished legal scholar – in fact embedded his international legal studies in a wider social programme. What he aimed at, basically, was to establish an international legal order, and regulate conflict. In his world, which was so disrupted by religious wars, he could think of no other concept but the rule of law as a common denominator to achieve unity.

On the other hand, he realized that the first and foremost threat to peace was the persistent religious quarrels throughout Europe. In order to solve these conflicts, he turned back, in a manner which typifies the humanist outlook, to the basis of Christian religion as exemplified by the teachings of the Church Fathers and the patristic commentaries on Bible and Gospel. He effectively sought to re-establish the *Una Sancta* by analysing the essence of Christian doctrine and by erecting, on this firm basis, a charter which could be endorsed by all religious denominations. This painstaking research, which took the better part of the last twenty years of his life, entailed studies into the Old and New Testaments which are perhaps the finest products of his analytical mind. The fact that his ideals, which for that matter were shared by Leibnitz, never materialized – mainly for lack of political expediency – do not necessarily detract from their value.

However, the Christian tradition, as Gro-

The Concise Catalogue of the works of Hugo Grotius housed in the Peace Palace Library, published in 1983 on the occasion of the quatercentenary of Grotius' birthday.

Members of the ICJ assembled in Loevestein Castle to pay homage to Hugo Grotius in May 1987.

tius understood it, was just one of the two components of European civilization. The other component was of course the classical tradition, taken in its broadest sense and encapsulating the Near Eastern, Jewish, Greek and Roman social concepts, ethical norms and cultural legacy. As a complement – the third step as he put it – to his comprehensive social programme, he therefore undertook the selection and rendering into contemporary Latin of all basic material from the classics that had any relevance to the ethical concepts which he wished to imprint on his time. Among various other tracts is his selection of *Dicta* from the Greek playwrights. This work, another proof of his exquisite learning and eminent stylistic genius, was produced in the same period (the mid-1620s) in which *De jure belli ac pacis* came into being.

The basic thesis underpinning all these works was a thought which was so typical of the humanist mind and became so rare in Europe later on, while remaining so common to most non-Western cultures to the present day. This thesis is that the cumulation and repetition of ideas as manifested through the ages in the works of prominent minds, be this in the literary, theological or legal spheres, constituted the core of what should be called civilization, its very intellectual legacy and the essence of human conscience.

It is typical of the modern Western mind to dismiss the numerous quotations from Greek playwrights and other non-legal sources in *De jure belli ac pacis* as irrelevant embellishments and inconsequential flourishes. To Grotius, who in this respect was just another exponent of the culture of his times, the law was not operating in the abstract, not as an exclusive system in its own right, but as the reflection, indeed the sublimation of European civilization.

It is this understanding which brings us closer to appreciating the much more socially embedded legal systems of the Islamic, Indian and Eastern cultures. It may also open our eyes to better appreciate yet another aspect, namely the manifold literary forms in which these legal sources from non-Western cultures present themselves to us – be this the Gilgamesh epic, representing the polity of the early Sumerian city state, or the *Bhagavad-Gita* and *Mahabharata,* or the discourses of the Buddha as examples of Indian sacred texts or the *Qu'ran* for Islam. European legal culture, too, started along these lines. Here too, the transfer of ethical precepts was closely linked to ritual formulas, and as a rule expressed in verse.

Grotius' De jure belli ac pacis, ed. Leipzig 1758.

The Literary Element

The stained glass windows of the Great Hall of Justice by Douglas Strachan were presented by Great Britain. Two panels of the third window feature the exponents of Science and Philosophy offering relief from the horrors of war.

It was Shelley who, with rare insight and inspiration, called poets 'the unacknowledged legislators of mankind'. Michelet maintained that 'le prêtre, le poète, le jurisconsulte, sont primitivement le même homme. Toutes les choses se confondent d'abord dans le sein de la religion'. The theme is a stock in trade of the *Ars poetica* from Scaliger to Boileau. Jakob Grimm, the most prominent representative of the German *Dichtung und Recht* movement – the circle of scholars around Klemenz von Brentano, Achim von Arnim and Friedrich Karl von Savigny who in the surge of German nationalism in the wake of the Napoleonic wars compiled the *Deutsche Rechtsalterthümer*, put it this way: 'Das Recht und Poesie miteinander aus einem Bette aufgestanden waren .... Was aber aus einer Quelle springt, das ist sich jederzeit auch selbst verwandt'.

To highlight a few landmarks from classical antiquity, most of the legendary legislators of Greece were poet-philosophers. This is true of Thales (Crete), Draco (Athens), Lycurgus (Sparta) and notably Solon of Athens. Classical historians such as Aelianus and Strabo emphasize that nearly all primitive codes, notably those of Crete and Spain, were put into verse. A first explanation of this striking phenomenon which is common to nearly all oral traditions is of course the mnemo-technical aspect. A second aspect is no doubt the didactic one, as exemplified by poets such as Lucretius, a quote from whose poem *On the Nature of Things* ('Unnoticed, Nature by her vital force herself puts an end to the grim works of Mars') even found its way into Douglas Strachan's stained-glass windows of the Great Court Hall of Justice at the Peace Palace, which were gifts from the United Kingdom.

A third aspect is probably the literary-aesthetic one, in that the ring of poetry carried convincing force by its very beauty. Ancient Greece knew two expressions for justice, *themis* and *nomos*, the first one being the reflection of divine revelation, the second of customary norms of mankind. *Nomos* is the Greek noun not just for law but for any form of harmony and melody. Its patron was Apollo, the god of law and order (in this he was the counterpart of Dionysus, the embodiment of the unfettered emotions) as well as of letters. Apollo was the leader of the band of Muses, whose mouthpiece par excellence was the Pythian oracle at Delphi which, it will be remembered, rendered its ritual formulas in versified form. In most general terms, ritual formulas and lyrics were supposed to suppress the animal in man. 'La lyra significava la legge', as the great Giambattista Vico put it concisely in his *La Scienza Nuova*. The Latin noun for poem, *carmen*, carries the same connotation of strict observance of rules and formulas.

Most of the wisdom of ancient Greece passed on from generation to generation in the sublimated form of the axioms and *dicta* expressed by the playwrights. It is on these grounds that the *auctoritas poetarum* was emphasized by humanist scholars. Guillaume Budé, in his *Annotations* to the *Pandectæ* expresses what Walter Scott would repeat: 'A lawyer without history or literature is a mechanic, a mere working mason; if he possesses some knowledge of these, he may venture to call himself an architect'. Even around 1600 scholars expressed themselves in Latin didactic poetry on legal, theological or historical themes, Grotius among them. In his neo-Latin drama *Adam in Exile* of 1601, which was the primary source for Milton's *Paradise Lost*, Grotius enlarges on natural philosophy. In similar vein, he ingeniously renders Psalm 81/82, the *Canticum Asaph* and prophecy of the Lord's Judgment over all earthly powers into a Horatian ode addressing the Judiciary:

> Judges, you must learn to live in awe of the Lord, for He attends your great assemblies of leaders, tosses the votes of the lords into the debate and presides, be it from afar, over your counsels.

In the sphere of legal learning it was Pufendorf who first criticized the 'communis error de divino in poesi'. In 1639, Guez de Balzac in a letter to Jean Chapelain referred to Grotius' attempt in his late teens at versifying Justinian's *Institutes*:

> S'il n'avait point mis les Institutes en vers, et débité quelques autres pièces de mesme nature, je l'estimerois encore davantage. (If he had not put the Institutes in verse – and several other pieces of the like nature – I would have even esteemed him the more for it.)

Criticisms such as these accentuated the trend towards the detachment of law from its philosophical and literary sources of inspiration.

In contemplating the World Court of the future it is clear that its jurisprudence will reflect the multicultural composition of the Court and draw upon the global cultural inheritance. It will be practically oriented without losing touch with the moral underpinnings on which just law is based. It will draw inspiration from all the socially related disciplines rather than depend upon law alone. It may, through the elegance of expression in which it will clothe international legal wisdom, become part of the cultural inheritance of all of humanity.

Marble figure of Pax, presented by Poland in 1930.

CHAPTER TWO

The Peaceful Settlement of Disputes

PAX UNA TRIUMPHIS INNUMERIS POTIOR
VENIT PAX AUREA CÆLO; de GULDE VREEDE KOMT van den HEMEL
Liefde Overwind
HET SCHOUW TOONEEL DER VREEDEN geopend te Aken den 10e Octob'.

The obligation of settling international conflicts by pacific means is the first law of human society. Léon Bourgeois

There are two views on the method of settling international disagreements: that of pious wishes, and that of the existing order of international relations. F. F. de Martens

The search for the peaceful settlement of disputes has a long history. It took a process of intellectual growth towards political consciousness before man's views on the issues of war and peace became more sophisticated. In the beginning was war. It was considered the natural state of man. Peace, if defined at all in early times, constituted the sparse intervals between inevitable outbursts of violence. Inter-State relations were taken to be necessarily hostile and, consequently, military accomplishments the sublimation of man's virtues. Only step by step was order wrenched from chaos, and emotion – leading inevitably to war – replaced by logic which would finally result in law. In this chapter, some of the intricacies of this process will be highlighted. In this, we may discern two different historical processes.

The first is the path of high politics and State practice. This asserted itself in the gradual expansion of an international legal order through the efforts of diplomats. It invited the establishment of ever more sophisticated means as tailor-made responses to the various forms of dispute. Within this process, through the ages, two main categories can be discerned: the settlement of disputes through the channels of diplomacy, as exemplified by the various forms of negotiation, mediation and conciliation, and settlement through the judicial process, notably by arbitral tribunals and international courts. This latter, more complicated process naturally took the longest to attain full maturity. It was only perfected around the turn of the century in what is called *l'Œuvre de la Haye*, and the institution of procedures of which the ICJ is perhaps the most sophisticated exponent. It is proposed in the present chapter to deal with the different, 'classical' means of settlement of inter-State disputes as attempted up till the 1899 First Hague Peace Conference.

In appreciating the growth of the international legal order one must however take account of the fact that, side by side with the 'official' process of State practice in international relations, goes the history of peace studies, as exemplified in the various efforts made by idealists, pacifists and anti-war movements to impose their tenets on State policy. It took many centuries before these two processes were reconciled. It was only towards the close of the 19th century that, with the intensification of worldwide communications and international organization, the two processes were effectively linked in any fruitful way. In fact, the two Hague Peace Conferences of 1899 and 1907 were the major outcome of this achievement. As the genesis of the World Court has in so many ways been determined by the *Œuvre de la Haye* – including the Hague Conferences, the conventions agreed upon by parties on those occasions, the ensuing establishment of the Peace Palace and the various institutions that have since been operating on its premises – in our survey this second process will also be briefly reviewed. If only for pragmatic reasons, our review of this specific line of thinking will be restricted to its ideals with respect to international tribunals.

The Various Means of Dispute Settlement between States

Today, the principle of the peaceful settlement of disputes is well founded in the UN Charter, Article 2 of which states that, in pursuit of the primary purposes of the UN, to maintain international peace and security:

> All Members shall settle their international disputes by peaceful means in such a manner that international peace and security, and justice, are not endangered.

In Article 33, which focuses on the Pacific Settlement issue, the text of the Charter is even more specific:

> The parties to any dispute, the continuance of which is likely to endanger the maintenance of international peace and security, shall, first of all, seek a solution by negotiation, enquiry, mediation, conciliation, arbitration, judicial settlement, resort to regional agencies or arrangements, or other peaceful means of their own choice.

Opposite page: An ornate allegorical print of the 1748 Peace of Aachen. Mars left behind, Peace rises like the Phoenix out of the ashes of war.

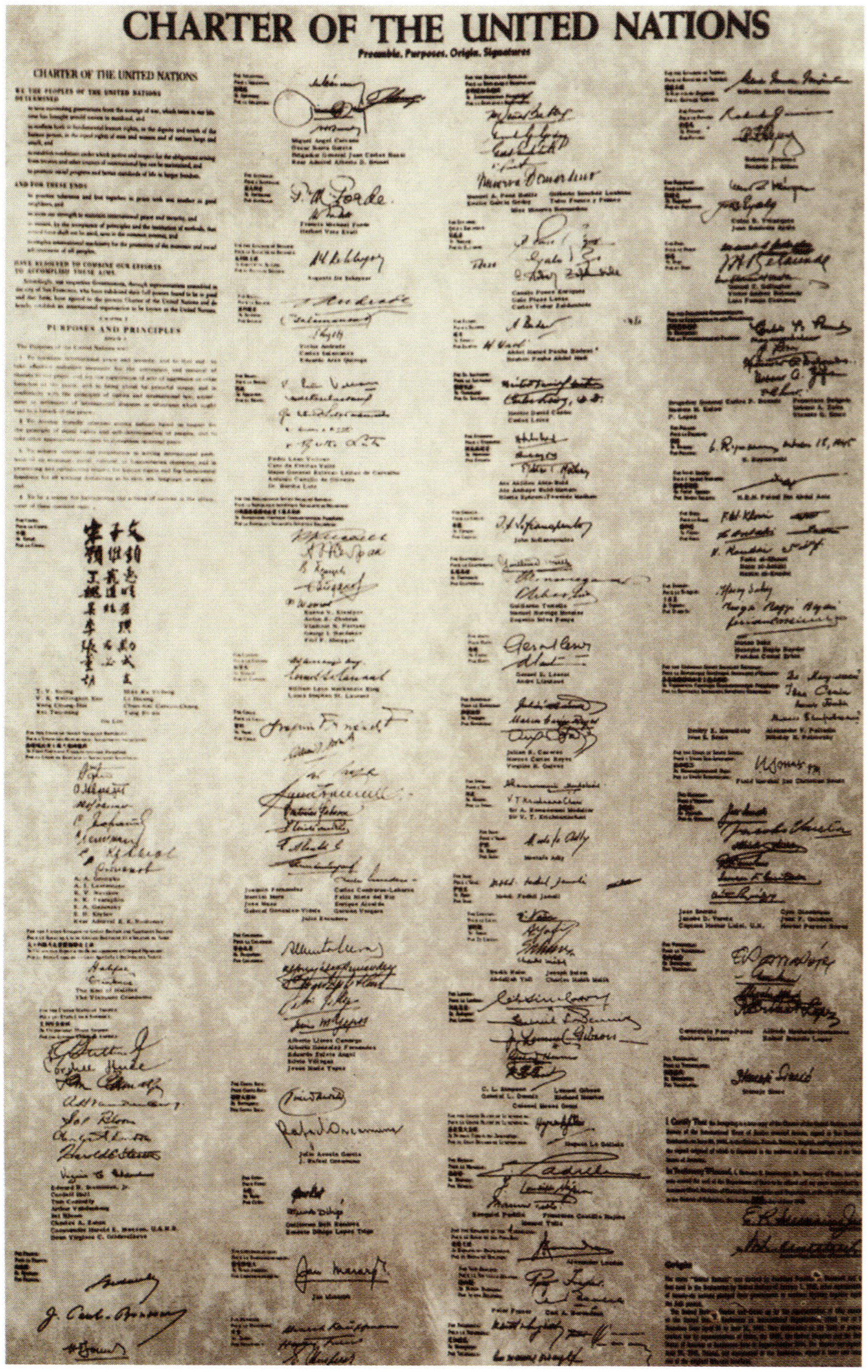

In past decades, this principle has repeatedly been reaffirmed by declarations and resolutions of the UN General Assembly, notably in 1970 and 1985. It features likewise in such documents as the 1970 Declaration on Principles of International Law concerning Friendly Relations and Cooperation among States, and the 1982 Manila Declaration on the Peaceful Settlement of International Disputes. In the Manila Declaration the General Assembly reaffirmed the obligation of States to seek in good faith and in a spirit of cooperation an early and equitable settlement of their international disputes by such peaceful means as may be appropriate to the circumstances and the nature of the disputes. The Declaration also expanded on the role which the respective organs of the UN could play in assisting parties to resolve their controversies.

Again, in 1988, the Assembly adopted the *Declaration on the Prevention and Removal of Disputes and Situations Which May Threaten International Peace and Security and on the Role of the UN in this Field.* In this, the Assembly only reflected ideas that were entertained from the early 1970s onwards in the circles of the International Law Association and, later, the Movement of Non-Aligned Countries, as exemplified in The Hague Declaration on Peace and the Rule of Law in International Affairs, adopted by the Movement during its 1989 Hague Meeting. In this Declaration, the Movement also suggested the idea of a Decade of International Law, which was to culminate in a Third Hague Peace Conference in 1999. Moreover, it strongly advocated an enhanced role for the ICJ and recommended the drawing up of a draft universal convention on peaceful settlement of disputes, the idea of such a universal legal instrument being first suggested by Romania. In 1989, the UN General Assembly declared the period 1990-1999 as the UN Decade of International Law. Universal concern at the frequency of international conflicts, the tendency to resort to force and indiscriminate intervention in the internal affairs of nations could not have been better expressed.

Traditionally, the principle of peaceful settlement of disputes is closely linked to the principle of the non-use of force. This may be seen from the texts of the 1945 Pact of the League of Arab States, the 1948 American Treaty on Pacific Settlement (the Pact of Bogota) and the Final Act of the 1975 Helsinki Conference on Security and Cooperation in Europe. In the latter text, the principle is significantly put in the context of ('and to be interpreted taking into account') all other principles set forth in the Declaration on Principles Guiding Relations between Participating States. Acknowledged as such are:

Sovereign equality, respect for the rights inherent in sovereignty; refraining from the threat or use of force; inviolability of frontiers; territorial integrity of States; non-intervention in internal affairs; respect for human rights and fundamental freedoms, including the freedom of thought, conscience, religion or belief; equal rights and self-determination of peoples; cooperation among States; and fulfilment in good faith of obligations under international law.

An interesting aspect of the above-quoted Article 33 is its final clause, in which it is stipulated that parties are in fact left free to agree on such peaceful means as they think may be appropriate to the circumstances and the nature of their dispute. Given the various prevailing traditions in the world, this would seem a most appropriate clause. Nonetheless, through the ages, a number of mechanisms have been developed, each of which – time has taught – lends itself to application subject to both the nature and the phase of the dispute. The most prominent of these are the following: negotiations and consultations; inquiry; good offices; mediation; conciliation; arbitration; judicial settlement; resort to regional agencies or arrangements; other peaceful means. We will now briefly review these mechanisms, highlight their main characteristics and interpret their interrelationship. The regional aspects will be dealt with in a later chapter within the context of the various regional law traditions (Chapter 8). Similarly, more recent forms of dispute settlement as developed in the UN era will be dealt with later, within the context of the ICJ. The present chapter serves mainly to introduce the classical mechanisms which came to bear on the constitution of the Hague Courts.

Negotiation

The first, and indeed one of the foremost means of dispute settlement is through the channel of negotiations. It is perhaps the only universally accepted means of settlement and both the PCIJ and ICJ in successive Judgments (*Free Zones of Upper Savoy*, *North Sea Continental Shelf*) have stressed its value. In fact, negotiation is the normal way of transacting business between States and governments. Technically speaking, it is more than mere deliberation, in that it serves the purpose of achieving agreed solutions. It appears in bilateral as well as multilateral form, in which latter case it often takes the form of conferences.

The process normally includes contacts through diplomatic channels, the appointment of representatives, and the exchange of documents and texts of statements throughout the process, as the history of negotiations may be of value to later interpretation, the more so if they lead to an international treaty. In case of eventual dispute, recourse may be had to the preparatory work, which in turn often prompts mutual consultation and exchanges of views between parties.

The Manila Declaration highlights flexibility as one of the main characteristics of direct negotiations within the context of dispute settlement. It can indeed be applied to all kinds of disputes, whether political, legal or technical. Yet preferably

Frontispiece of B. Picart, Traitez de Paix, 1726.

not in the way Talleyrand used it, when he referred to negotiation as *l'art de laisser les autres suivre votre propre voie*.

In contrast to other forms of peaceful settlement such as conciliation and mediation, arbitration or judicial settlement, negotiation is distinguished by the absence of a neutral third party which can suggest or even impose a solution. Just because it involves only the States parties to the dispute, those States can themselves monitor the whole process and conduct it in the way they deem most appropriate, which has often enhanced its effectiveness. Accordingly, in the reality of international life, it is this means of settlement which is most often resorted to by States. However, the absence of third parties is at the same time the weakness of the process. Negotiation, therefore, is often the first phase in a process of settlement. In fact, many treaties include clauses providing for negotiation as a prerequisite prior to the submission of the dispute to other forms of (third party) settlement. In practice, this negotiating phase is now generally considered, *inter alia* on the basis of Article 2 of the UN Charter, as a duty. This 'duty to negotiate' also involves the obligation to promote *meaningful* negotiations. However, in practice this is at times frustrated by either the denial by a party of the very existence of a dispute or, the other way round, its assertion that certain conditions must be met prior to its entering into meaningful negotiations. Obviously, if one side, or both, remain adamant, the continuation of the discussions is a meaningless process, as the PCIJ and ICJ have experienced in the *Mavrommatis* case and the *South West Africa Cases* (Preliminary Objections). In all such cases, recourse must be had to other means.

The League of Nations Commission of Enquiry into the Greco-Bulgarian Incident at work (1925).

Inquiry

The function of inquiry may in a sense be regarded as a subsidiary one in the process of dispute settlement; it often has a technical character. When, in a dispute, a difference of opinion arises between parties as to points of fact, they may agree on initiating an inquiry in order to investigate the disputed issue and determine whether violations of international commitments or treaty law come into play. Inquiry may also facilitate the collection of additional information which may – if not solve the dispute – at least elucidate the facts that gave rise to it. The Conventions that were agreed upon during the 1899 and 1907 Hague Peace Conferences specifically refer to the institution of international commissions of inquiry (whose competence may vary) to facilitate the solution of disputes. The method is an accepted and indeed current tool within the organizations of the UN system.

Essentially, inquiry is an impartial third-party fact-finding and investigation procedure, although the third-party element, while customary, is not imperative. The process may be initiated by mutual consent of parties or evolve from the terms of an applicable treaty. Treaties may specifically provide for the establishment of permanent commissions of inquiry, fact-finding or investigation, whose jurisdiction is to be accepted in advance by the States parties to the treaty in question. Parties may also suggest a commission of their own accord, or ask one person alone to investigate the dispute. They may, for example, approach the Secretary-General of the UN to appoint a special representative or a mission to carry out inquiries.

The composition of such a commission depends, of course, on the technical nature of the dispute. However, legal expertise has often proved to be indispensable. In terms of procedure, and depending on the nature of the dispute and its subject-matter, the investigation may involve the hearing of parties, the examination of witnesses or fact-finding visits, in fact the techniques of gathering evidence which are customary in the arbitral and judicial processes. Normally, the person or commission making the inquiries is allowed latitude as regards the procedure preferred, though there have been cases where parties have laid down detailed regulations in advance. At the conclusion of the process, as a rule, a report is submitted to parties, including factual findings and recommendations, again depending on the competence of the inquirer.

To conclude, inquiry may have a prophylactic function in reducing tension, and this is why the General Assembly, in a 1967 resolution, explicitly stressed its relevance within the complex system of settlement procedures. The method happily combines the benefits of diplomacy and legal techniques to obtain an impartial report on the facts or suggestions for resolving the issue. The latter aspects connect the functions of commissions of inquiry with those of commissions of conciliation. This resemblance was appreciated by the UN General Assembly when in 1949 it created the *Panel for Inquiry and Conciliation*, which for that matter has never been used thus far.

Good Offices

In case States prove unable to solve a dispute between them, a third party may offer assistance to prevent further deterioration of relations and to help find solutions. Such an offer of 'good offices', whether by a State, an individual or an Organ, is of course subject to its acceptance by all parties to the dispute. The basic role of the third party is to provide parties with a channel of communication and encourage them to resume negotiations. At times, however, third parties proceed further and start taking an active part in the process of dispute settlement by making actual proposals for the solution of the controversy. This goes a long way in the direction of another means of settlement, namely mediation. With the latter method, good offices share the aspects of facilitating the dialogue between the parties to the dispute and scaling down hostilities and tensions.

A distinction must be drawn between technical and political good offices. Technical good offices are basically of a conditioning nature, in providing parties with means and facilities to restore contact and diplomatic relations. Political good offices, on the other hand, include appeals for peace or an armistice. Here, States that render good offices interfere in the substance of the conflict in order to facilitate its solution, and actually suggest procedures of settlement.

The basis for the rendering of good offices is found in customary international law and the sovereignty of States, though explicit provisions have also been included in such diverse arrangements as the 1907 Hague Convention on the Settlement of Disputes, the UN Charter, the 1948 Bogota Pact and the 1961 Vienna Convention on Diplomatic Relations.

Throughout history, the procedure of good offices has been a common means of dispute settlement. Its results have varied, in accordance with the precarious method and susceptibilities involved. Strict impar-

Design of the main entrance of the Peace Palace by H. Th. Wijdeveld.

tiality is of course imperative, as confidence in the reliability of the third party is of the essence. Major powers may carry more prestige and influence, yet are generally more inclined to pursue their own interests to the detriment of parties, whereas smaller States in their turn carry less influence. This is also why, generally speaking, technical assistance has the best chances of success. The permanent neutral status of Switzerland has in the past made this nation a likely candidate to perform the role succesfully. Yet even Switzerland failed in rendering technical good offices in the Indo-Pakistan conflict concerning Bangladesh in the early 1970s. In recent years good offices have been increasingly entrusted to the UN Secretary-General, as has been the case in the Cyprus and Kampuchea dilemmas, the Arab-Israeli conflict, in Afghanistan and in matters concerning East-Timor.

The major advantages of the procedure are the breaking of a stalemate, the removal of psychological inhibitions and the introduction of new elements into negotiations. Yet, as Bindschedler correctly concludes, its basic condition 'is always the existence of a certain willingness of parties to reach a solution of the conflict, regardless of the public stances they may have adopted, which might appear to be irreconcilable'.

Mediation and Conciliation

Neither in the primary sources nor in secondary literature is a clear distinction drawn between the terms 'mediation' and 'conciliation'. They would seem to be interchangeable in many respects. Both terms are found in the relevant articles of the UN Charter and the Bogota Pact; however, the 1907 Hague Convention only refers to mediation, whereas for instance the 1928 General Act for the Pacific Settlement of International Disputes and the 1957 European Convention only refer to conciliation. Be that as it may, both terms describe the intervention of third parties in a dispute.

This third party can be a State, an international organization or a private person. It would seem that the term conciliation is sometimes reserved for the intervention of a private person. Obviously, States have better facilities at their disposal than private persons, and major States can also bring their influence to bear on the issue. The possible negative aspects of this feature we have already discussed. Examples of fortunate mediation were the role of Germany during the 1878 Berlin Congress, of the Soviet Union in the 1966 Indo-Pakistan conflict and of the USA in the 1978 peace talks between Egypt and Israel. As for international organizations, the UN has on various occasions been involved in mediation efforts, be it through the Secretary-General, the General Assembly or the Security Council.

Mediating activity is essentially an extension of the function of good offices. Here too, the suggestions made by the intervening party to narrow the gap between the points of view of the parties to a dispute may be either of a strictly technical and procedural nature or also include the substance of the dispute. Of a more compelling nature than inquiry or good offices, conciliation and mediation are not binding on parties as is the case with arbitral awards and judicial procedures. In other words, while the activities of the mediating agent are subject to the acceptance of parties, his findings are presented as recommendations and advice. The voluntary acceptance of a proposed settlement can however considerably strengthen its effectiveness and durability: there are no outright winners and losers here. Moreover, an *ad hoc* solution is rarely considered to set a precedent for future behaviour, and this also enhances the chances of acceptance by parties. Pragmatism, rather than legal justification, governs the proceedings.

Again, this specific means of settlement has the advantage of introducing a neutral new element into a dispute. As stated earlier, proceedings are very flexible, the wishes of parties can to a large extent be taken into account, and their autonomy is as a rule left intact. Proceedings can be either voluntary or compulsory and may be initiated by the mediating agent or (one of the) parties. In the latter case parties have the right unilaterally to appeal to a competent body, that is if they have in advance agreed upon such a body of appeal, on the basis of special or general treaty provisions. The advantage of pre-arranged mediation is the absence of oversensitivity in moments of acute stress, the disadvantage is often seen in the lack of a free choice.

There are no strict rules as to the procedure of mediation itself, which basically consists of a negotiating process under the direction of the mediator, be this bilateral or unilateral. Proceedings normally include a written and an oral phase. The services rendered may be of a conciliatory, a technical or even a financial nature, as exemplified by the mediation of the World Bank in the *Indus Water Dispute* between India and Pakistan in the 1950s. Also, the mediator will as a rule supervise the execution and continued observance of the arrangements.

The interesting aspect of the procedure for the mediating agent is that he is not restricted to basing his recommendations on existing law, but can make proposals *ex æquo et bono*, based on norms of equity. For this very reason, mediation is a highly suitable alternative to judicial proceedings in cases of a politically delicate nature and with respect to other non-justiciable disputes. This is why, under present political circumstances, conciliation enjoys a wider popularity than other more binding procedures.

Detail of the drawing for a tapestry in the Small Hall of Justice presented by France. The tapestry itself never materialized as the artist died in the First World War.

Experience has also shown the weakness of the method: impartiality is hard to attain. In fact, the mediator runs the risk of imperiling his own relations with either one or both parties, notably in armed conflicts. The primary requirements of the procedure are therefore informality and confidentiality. Psychological factors have often made States reluctant to accept the role, just as political sensitivities have often made parties as well as mediators reluctant to place on record the details and nuances of the procedure they went through. Publicity and public statements rarely add to the chances of success in this sphere and indiscretion may be termed one of its major hazards. More often than not, mediation or conciliation may start with secret informal talks for the purpose of simply drafting an agenda for formal negotiations. Therefore, the situations best suited to this kind of interference are deadlocked situations, situations where the threat of escalation is imminent or, conversely, where military activities have settled matters, and what remains to be done is to work out the consequences.

As with good offices, mediation and conciliation are considered a mode of settlement which, after being tried unsuccesfully, should give way to other, usually more formal means. However, one of its major attractions is precisely the avoidance of the repercussions on the prestige of parties which arbitral or judicial proceedings may entail. On the other hand, from the

Major works on arbitration by La Fontaine, Moore, Scott, Wetter, Stuyt, Coussirat-Coustère, the Systematic Survey of the League of Nations and the UN Reports.

standpoint of the establishment of a uniform legal order, the compromise that is sought, by virtue of the very nature of the conciliatory method in particular, constitutes a distinctly unbalancing element. Consequently, conciliation and mediation seem particularly inappropriate in the context of multilateral conventions.

Arbitration

Proceeding now from mediation and conciliation to the idea of arbitration, we must appreciate that we pass a distinct borderline. So far we have reviewed means of settlement of disputes which come within the sphere of diplomacy. Turning to arbitration and, later on, judicial settlement, we leave this sphere and enter an area in which disputing States, having accepted the failure of other means, agree upon submitting the dispute to procedures over which they can no longer exercise full control. Having familiarized ourselves by now with the paramount position of State sovereignty in the relations between nations, we may appreciate the psychological barrier that is to be crossed in the course of this process. As will shortly be seen in greater detail, judicial settlement of disputes by international benches is an even more advanced step towards renouncing sovereignty than is arbitration. Accordingly, even when the historical process of dispute settlement had reached the point of more or less general acceptance of the concept of arbitration – though not, as yet, compulsory arbitration – the majority of nations at that juncture were by no means as yet disposed to consider the idea of judicial settlement.

Professor T. M. C. Asser, surrounded by staff members of the Bureau of the PCA. Asser was sole arbitrator in the dispute between Russia and the USA over whaling ships that came before the Court in 1900-1902.

This acceptance of voluntary arbitration became general only towards the end of the last century, and in this process the Hague Peace Conferences definitely functioned as a clearing house. Still, at the time, most leading politicians considered the idea of an International Court of Justice absolutely inconceivable in the near feature. The establishment of the Permanent Court of International Justice within only 25 years after the 1899 Hague Conference is therefore truly a major achievement. Three factors helped to accelerate this process: first the tremendously salutary impact of the build-up of international legal arrangements in the last two decades of the 19th century; secondly, the ample experience with arbitration through the Permanent Court of Arbitration in the subsequent two decades, from 1900 onwards; thirdly, the overwhelming impact of the First World War in conditioning minds to the absolute urgency of more compulsory mechanisms of dispute settlement.

It is now proposed first to discuss the basic characteristics of arbitration as compared to the diplomatic means of settlement which have been reviewed above and then to review the practice of arbitration leading up to the Convention that was signed at the 1899 First Hague Peace Conference. It is precisely this Convention for the Pacific Settlement of International Disputes and its complement that was signed in 1907, during the Second Hague Peace Conference, which constitute the basic documents for modern arbitration procedure.

International arbitration, in principle, is the settlement of disputes between States, and only between States. This concept must be strictly distinguished from the settlement of civil disputes by what is also known as arbitration, as practised notably by the Court of Arbitration of the International Chamber of Commerce. Neither does the concept include the mixed arbitral tribunals dealing with claims by private individuals or legal persons which were established in great numbers after both World Wars.

In the process of international arbitration, the settlement of the dispute is attempted by judges chosen by the parties themselves on the basis of respect for the law. Recourse to the procedure implies submission in good faith to the award of the tribunal. Accordingly, the procedure results in decisions binding upon the parties to the dispute. Unlike diplomatic procedures, arbitration is therefore a compulsory means of settlement. In this it resembles judicial settlement through international courts. In its method, however, it is much different. Arbitration takes place by mutual consent of the parties to a dispute and such parties retain considerable control over the process through the power of appointing arbitrators of their own choice. By contrast, judicial settlement relies upon pre-constituted international courts or tribunals, the composition of which is not to the same extent subject to control by the parties to the dispute, as will be discussed in fuller detail in the next chapter. Again, arbitral tribunals are often *ad hoc* panels, constituted to hear a particular case. They do not, as a matter of principle, determine their own jurisdiction, and they make their awards in accordance with rules especially adopted for that purpose by agreement of parties.

Consent of parties to arbitration may be expressed prior to or after the occurrence of a dispute. Again, such commitment may be made in treaties entirely devoted to settlement of disputes or, and this is the more common method, by inclusion of a so-called 'compromissory clause' in a treaty. This clause provides for the settlement by arbitration of disputes that may arise in regard to the interpretation or application of that treaty. All the aspects of the operation of such an arbitral tribunal (its specific rules of establishment, its size, method of work, applicable law, the place of its seat) are usually dealt with in lesser or greater detail by a special agreement between parties, the so-called *compromis*, which also provides for the representation of parties by agents and the nomination of advisers, counsel and staff.

Arbitration may be performed by one individual as a sole arbitrator or umpire, or by a group of individuals who form a tribunal. In the latter event, provision is made, usually, for odd numbers. Three members is the most common practice, although five is not unusual either. Each party appoints one of the three (or as the case may be two of the five) arbitrators, while the chairman of the tribunal is normally appointed by joint decision, either of the parties or of the appointed arbitrators. Eventual vacancies are usually regulated in the same manner. Nationality and personal qualifications are of course essential elements, and specific requirements in this respect on the part of parties are often stipulated in the arbitration agreement.

Early design of the ante-chambers of Parties.

The rules of procedure are either left to the tribunal or requested by parties to be determined following the instructions by the agents of the governments involved. The same holds good in regard to the application of the law. As a rule the application of public international law and more particularly the general principles of international law are stipulated in the agreements. Still, other arbitration agreements have specifically chosen principles of equity, justice, or equitable solution as applicable to the dispute.

As a rule, parties to the dispute file written pleadings (memorials and counter-memorials) within certain time-limits to be determined by the Tribunal. The Tribunal also regulates the procedure of oral proceedings and documentary evidence and the hearings of experts and witnesses. To this end, it is usually assisted by a secretariat or registry. This organ serves as a channel of communication between parties and Tribunal, provides for interpreters and translators and conducts all administrative matters. The major function of the so-called Permanent Court of Arbitration that was established in 1900 was precisely to serve as a permanent secretariat readily available to parties. Its Bureau acts as an impartial source of assistance, *inter alia* by keeping a list of arbitrators from which parties compose the panel to help solve their specific disputes. In a sense, therefore, it is somewhere between an *ad hoc* and a permanent tribunal. It constitutes a permanent basis for facilitating immediate reference to arbitration by enabling parties to readily set up *ad hoc* tribunals.

As stated above, parties in the *compromis* undertake to abide by the decision of the tribunal which is binding upon them. As for the execution of the award, which is often also stipulated in the agreement, parties may agree upon the establishment of further commissions. Any dispute concerning the execution or interpretation of the award is submitted to the Tribunal that pronounced the award.

Genesis of the Idea of Arbitration

We will now briefly review some historical aspects of this specific means of dispute settlement. In reviewing the history of arbitration, scholars of previous generations have often insisted on the relevance of classical and medieval parallels. While the reference to earlier notions of arbitration is of course appropriate in very general terms, in as much as it instils in one's mind the patterns of thought which have governed man's search for a better world, it must be pointed out at the outset that no such parallels played any significant role in the establishment of the procedures and Courts that came into being in the first quarter of the present century. Ancient practice did not influence international arbitration as we know it. The increased consciousness of earlier parallels is the result of research into the sources of international law in the last half-century.

Still, it may be maintained that the settlement of disputes by arbitrators occurred from pre-classical antiquity down to the late Middle Ages, with varying importance at different periods. Herodotus tells us of King Darius presiding as arbitrator; Solon and Themistocles acted similarly. Inscriptions and early treaties such as that of Athens with Megara and Mytilene at about 600 BC, bear witness to arbitration, as do certain aspects of the *Amphyktyony*, the regional religious organizations within the Greek Commonwealth. The thirty-year armistice of 445 BC between Athens and Sparta featured a 'compromissory clause', making any future quarrel subject to arbitration; however, these provisions were never applied. During the period of Macedonian hegemony (338-168 BC), territorial disputes were settled through arbitration, but clearly under Macedonian control. The latter aspect held good for the Romans as well: arbitral awards were made in exercise of Roman sovereignty over other political bodies.

During the Middle Ages, arbitration occurred between the Italian city-States as between the Swiss Cantons and the German Hanse. In most cases arbitration was a substitute for decisions by courts, or jurisdiction claimed by emperor or pope. Several popes sought unsuccessfully to introduce a system of compulsory arbitration under their umpireship; in practice, their role rather resembled that of the conciliator. In the 16th century, the medieval system collapsed. Although one would expect that the subsequent rise of the system of independent, sovereign nation-States would further the use of arbitration, it was not until the end of the 18th century that any such impartial bodies, taking decisions according to objective rules, are found. It is to this point that the origin of modern arbitration can be traced.

Around 1800, the urge for a more durable form of peaceful coexistence and a firmer foundation of society gave rise to the idea of applying arbitration to the *prevention* of disputes, rather than to *end* hostilities. The best way to do so, it was felt, was

John Jay (1745-1829), one of the founding fathers of the USA, first chief justice of the Supreme Court and negotiator of the Jay Treaty of 1794 which settled major grievances with Great Britain.

by concluding treaties which made provision for arbitration. The interesting thing is, that this idea was not born in Europe but on the American continent. Of pivotal importance in that respect was the so-called *Jay Treaty* concluded in 1794 between Great Britain and the USA, which regulated a range of heavily contested issues between the two nations.

In subsequent years, numerous treaties of this kind were concluded between the USA and South American States. As is discussed in fuller detail in the chapter on the Latin American international law component, it was particularly within the ambience of the young Latin American republics that, in the course of the 19th century, the concept of arbitration was brought to full maturity. The 1826 Panama Conference and the 1880 *General, Permanent and Absolute Arbitration Treaty* between Colombia and Chile were major stepping stones to the 1899 Hague Conference. Other interesting awards of the period were in the *Behring Sea* (1873), *Delagoa Bay* (1875) and *Costa Rica Packet* (1897) arbitrations.

Still, undoubtedly the most influential specimen of the period was the so-called *Alabama Treaty*, negotiated in Geneva in 1873 between Great Britain and the USA. This treaty defined the rights and obligations of neutrals in the wake of incidents which had occurred during the American Civil War. The issue gave rise to much parliamentary consideration of the adoption

EXTRACT FROM THE SPEECH OF THE ATTORNEY-GENERAL IN THE *Alabama* CASE, published in the *London Times*, 14 May 1864

That is the course which the Government have taken; that is the course to which they will adhere; and, in view of the difficulties I have mentioned, I think it is a course which is fully justified. (Hear.) There is one other consideration of importance which I wish to mention; and here again, I hope that what I say will not cause offence in the United States, for I state it because it is true, and because it is important that the matter should be understood. [...] *The House well knows that I refer to the extraordinary demands arising out of the case of the* Alabama. *(Hear, hear.) I have no hesitation in saying, that the United States' Government, by advancing such demands, and by seeking to make our Government responsible for pecuniary compensation for prizes taken by the* Alabama *upon the high seas, and never brought within our ports or in any way whatever under our control, are making demands directly contrary to the principles of international law laid down by their own jurists, and thereby render it infinitely more difficult for us, at their request, to do any thing resting on our own discretion, and which we are not bound to do in law. (Hear, hear.) What we may fairly say is this: 'We will adhere to the rules laid down by your own authorities. We will execute our own law. We will allow no asylum to prizes or to property unjustly captured. If any such are brought in, any demand for their reclamation shall be investigated. But we will not undertake to recognize claims going beyond these limits. We will not undertake to interfere between belligerents in any other way than that in which by the rules of international law we can fairly be called upon to interfere.' (General cheering.)*

ADMIRAL RAPHAEL SEMMER
Captain of the Alabama

The commerce raider *Alabama*, built in British shipyards, was the most formidable cruiser of the Confederacy during the American Civil War. Under its legendary Captain Raphael Semmer, and supported by the British, it sank, burned, or ransomed some seventy ships of the Union before being destroyed. The *Alabama*-case was of significance for the development of international law with respect to questions relating to neutrality and the competence of arbitral tribunals.

of arbitration clauses in treaties. The USA and several European nations voted in favour of their adoption. From then on arbitration also gained a foothold in multilateral treaty practice, such as the *Congo Act* of 1885 and the *Anti-Slavery Act* of 1890. The first provision for compulsory arbitration was contained in the Constitution of the Universal Postal Union.

Another indirect outcome of the *Alabama* dispute was the following. Two of the major learned societies that were to govern the sphere of public international law to the present day were both founded in 1873. The first was the *Institut de Droit International* (IDI). At its founding conference in 1873, the IDI reviewed the Washington Rules of 1871, on which the *Alabama* award was based and then went on to discuss questions of procedure in international arbitral tribunals. These debates resulted in the famous *Projet de règlement pour la procédure arbitrale internationale,* which later constituted one of the major sources at the 1899 Hague Peace Conference.

The second was the Association for the Reform and Codification of the Law of Nations, which in 1895 was renamed the *International Law Association* (ILA). It was the first gathering of its kind of international lawyers. The ILA saw the drafting of a code of international law as its first priority and the preliminary to the creation of a new system of arbitration.

Statue of Desiderius Erasmus of Rotterdam (1469-1536) by Hildo Krop, unveiled in 1938 and bearing the motto Dulce bellum inexpertis.

We now see that the notion of arbitration and the idea of a permanent court of arbitration that was to be launched at the 1899 Hague Conference did not arrive out of the blue. In a way, they emerged quite naturally from the thinking of the day. The last quarter of the 19th century has rightly been called the era of the 'legal internationalists'. It would seem that, at that juncture, all the strings that had been woven in the previous half-century were pulled together. The idea of international organization through arbitration procedures was advocated from different angles and for different purposes by activists from government, business circles and the professional world alike – through endless streams of meetings, public lectures, magazines, pamphlets and journals. It became a general feeling that the useless and extravagant investments on armaments should, with the passage of time, be replaced by a code of international law, in the same way as law had superseded feudal violence at the dawn of modern times. It was perhaps primarily the progressive enlightenment of public opinion that forced all concerned into taking some kind of action. During the 1890s, the pressure on politicians grew rapidly to the point of saturation.

If anything, it was the Peace Movement which, during these last decades of the century, helped to mould and direct public opinion. Arbitration had been a prominent issue for the peace movement ever since its Brussels, Paris and Frankfurt Peace Congresses of the 1840s. Yet, from the 1890s onwards, it focused all its hopes on arbitration as a short-term means of stopping warfare. The idea was much furthered also by the efforts of the Interparliamentary Union that was founded in Bern in 1889. It organized periodic conferences for members of national electoral bodies. Men like Henri La Fontaine, Fredrik Bajer and Albert Gobat devoted much of their lives to this institution. In London, in 1890, the Union agreed upon the arbitration clause as a *sine qua non* of any treaty. Again, in Bern in 1892, during the very meeting that saw the founding of the International Peace Bureau and the Interparliamentary Bureau, its President, Schenk, expressed the opinion that a general treaty to prepare a Permanent Court would not be long in coming. Morelli and Mancini in Italy, Passy, Noyet and Victor Hugo in France, Descamps in

Belgium, Cobden and Richard in Great Britain and Hodgson Ladd in the USA helped to pave the way.

The first reaction to these developments from official government circles came in 1887, when the US Government invited European nations to discuss the launching of an 'international court'. Such a plan, still ridiculed in the 1894 *Reichstag* and looked upon with much reserve by Gladstone, was effectively outlined during the 1895 Brussels and 1896 Budapest meetings of the Interparliamentary Union. On those occasions, they were championed by the Belgian Minister Beernaert and by William Randal Cremer of London, the Secretary of the International Arbitration League of 1870 and co-founder with Frédéric Passy of the Union. The scheme that was submitted to the *Comité d'Examen* of the Third Commission at the Hague Conference (the Commission that dealt with matters of Arbitration) was based on a previous proposal of the Union and a famous *Mémoire* drafted by Descamps.

On 10 November 1896, the USA and Great Britain signed an arbitration treaty which only excluded vital interests. Although never ratified, it was yet another stepping stone towards the Hague Convention.

These were the circumstances surrounding the 1899 debate in The Hague as, in its opening sessions, the Conference was confronted with Russian, British and American schemes for a Court of Arbitration and various proposals for obligatory arbitration on the basis of a so-called permanent treaty. The outcome of this debate in the competent *Comité d'Examen* under the stimulating guidance of the French tactical genius, Léon Bourgeois, will be the subject of the next chapter. However, before turning to those events, if only to do justice to the raison d'être of the Hague Conference, notably with respect to the proposal of an International Court, we must briefly review the tradition of this time-honoured ideal.

Eternal Peace through Federations and Tribunals

In the West, the first glimmerings of diplomacy are only to be found within the context of the Greek Commonwealth. These *proxenia*, as they were called, in turn predate by centuries the first known formal

William Randal Cremer (1828-1908), founder of the Interparliamentary Union of 1889, was awarded the Nobel Peace Prize in 1903.

interrelations of States on terms of peaceful coexistence, the *amphictyones*. What we would now call humanitarian concepts only came into being much later, as the grim effects of increasingly sophisticated armaments made themselves felt. Warfare was then humanized by restricting its most abasing atrocities. Reason, morals, the very preservation of orderly life called for peace, as was then felt. Thucydides was the first to point out the generally brutalizing impact of war. The Erasmian adage *bellum dulce inexpertis* (war is sweet to him who has never experienced it) dates back to the lyrics of Pindar. Influential schools like the Cynics, Stoics and Epicureans advertised the senselessness of weaponry. Still, to Plato war was but the predictable outcome of the natural growing process of States; Aristotle characterized conquest as just another means of acquisition.

Rome did not do much to further the cause of peace either. Preconditioned, in Virgil's words, to rule mankind by sheer power, it saw the doors of Janus' Temple closed only twice in half a millennium. To the strict Roman, growth and expansion were essential to survival. The *Pax Romana* provided political and social stability, but did not much alter the theory as summarized in the *dictum* of Vegetius, its most authoritative military commentator: *qui desiderat pacem, præparet bellum*, let him who desires peace, prepare for war.

Theory as well as attitude changed with the coming of Christianity. But even the followers of Christ were soon led to victory *in hoc signo*. As the Roman Empire collapsed, and amidst the barbaric onslaught, the Church set out to preserve moral values. Since lasting peace proved unattainable, as war would always claim

its place, St Augustine, among others, helped develop the theory of the just war. To him, war was the price to be paid for peace, and this goal its very justification. Christian warriors were accordingly ordered to fight for the dawning of peace on the far horizon. Still, the devastating effects of wars were reduced by all possible means, in exempting whole categories of men from service to protect trade and agriculture in what was called the Peace of God, or by forbidding violence on certain days in the Truce of God. At the edge of this debate, alleged radical heretics such as the Cathars and Hussites persisted in their rearguard insistence on the stricter observance of humanitarian principles. Mostly in vain, of course, for man has always been more resourceful in checking the impact of his shortcomings than in anticipating them.

Or has he? It was also during this Medieval period that the first attempts to create a proper world organization as a means of ensuring lasting peace were made. It is here that we first meet a striking phenomenon which from then on would remain a persistent under-current in European society right up to the time of the Hague Peace Conferences, namely the projects for eternal peace. We should review some of the more prominent of these peace proposals as, from early on, they invariably contained at least one of the two elements of a League of Nations and an International Court. It is on this account also that, in retrospect, these projects were hailed by 19th and early 20th century legal historians as the alleged forerunners of the League of Nations and the World Court.

Clearly, the latter interpretation is a gross overestimation. In most cases the parallel between these projects and the League of Nations are purely external and superficial. Most of these projects were no more than vagaries of thought or deceptive political schemes. Also, not a single one of these numerous proposals ever had any direct demonstrable bearing on the higher politics of their day – nor is there so much as a clue from the early days of the League to suggest that any of these projects were slumbering even in the back of the minds of its founding fathers. In fact, their interest within our context is precisely in that they suitably illustrate the wide gap that had to be bridged over the centuries between the lofty notions of these apostles of peace and the grim reality of everyday politics. Gratuitous outpourings of political fantasy as most of these schemes were, they may still serve as an adequate introductory note to the review of the much more pragmatic methods of dispute settlement that were developed through the ages within the various strictly legal cultures.

In 1306, the French lawyer Pierre Dubois, 'the greatest journalist of the Middle Ages' as he was once called and indeed a man gifted with a lively style and given to brilliant propositions, launched a pamphlet *On the Recovery of the Holy Land*. In this tract, he postulated the establishment of universal peace throughout Christendom as a prerequisite for a new crusade. As Nussbaum recapitulates, what Dubois proposed was a general council of all prelates and secular Christian princes, to be convoked and presided over by the Pope. War among its members would be outlawed and disputes were to be settled by arbitral tribunals with three prelates and three secular princes for each party. The arbitrators were to be chosen from a large panel set up by the Council and appeals against their decisions would be referred to the Pope. A violator of the peace would be duly subdued by the joint armies of the Council – and banished to the Holy Land! Still, it was not sheer idealism that prompted this project. Dubois quite frankly envisaged a hegemonic position for France – at the cost of the Hapsburg Emperor. Also, his Council of a United Europe was primarily intended to better face the Musulman. Still, the author may gain credit for having been the first to think of the idea of compulsory arbitration based on a political organization.

Clearly, with Dubois, fresh ground was broken. In subsequent decades we find similar ideas in such varying works as Dante's *De monarchia*, Honoré Bovet's *Arbre de batailles* and Paduan Marcilius' *Defensor pacis*. To be sure, most of the proposed confederations were designed to better coordinate the defence against Turkish oppression. Thus, in 1462, King

Peace by Justice and Right by Stephen Reid (1907)

George Podebrad (1420-1471), King of Bohemia from 1458, tried to organize an anti-Turkish League of Christian States (1462).

Maximilien de Béthune, Duke of Sully (1560-1638), was the trusted Minister of King Henry IV of France. His memoirs, the Economies royales (1638), include the famous Grand Dessein of a European Confederation or 'Christian Republic'.

Jeremy Bentham (1748-1832), English philosopher and theoretical jurist. Early expounder of Utilitarianism. Some of his ideas were included in his 'Plan for a Universal and Perpetual Peace' (1789).

George Podebrad of Bohemia approached Louis XI of France with yet another, rather fantastic scheme. It provided for a permanent council with broad compulsory powers over the federal States, and for a permanent federal tribunal. Again, the French king was to be in a hegemonic position, which may be regarded as another token of the waning prestige of the Emperor.

A kindred idea was incorporated in a Treaty concluded in 1518 between Henry VIII of England and Francis I of France. This plan also envisaged a league against the Turks. However, as Nussbaum argues, at the same time it was yet another move in the subtle diplomatic game of Cardinal Wolsey to thwart a similar idea promoted by Pope Leo X. The scheme was soon abandoned.

The Wars of Religion barred any similar peace proposals in the 16th century, but at least three new and interesting proposals for political reconstruction to secure universal peace are documented over the next century. In 1623, a Paris writer, Emeric Crucé, published his *Le nouveau Cynée; ou, Discours d'état représentant les occasions et moyens d'établir une paix générale*, in which he sought to persuade princes of the absurdity of war and sought its abolishment through arbitration. In this connection, he recommended that the princes maintain – preferably in Venice – a permanent assembly of Ambassadors which would sit as a court to resolve disputes between member princes dispassionately. He, too, granted France precedence over mighty Spain. This plan also fell quickly into oblivion.

This did not hold completely true for the quite interesting scheme found in the memoirs of the Duke of Sully (1560-1638), a former minister of Henry IV of France. Although this project was also based on wishful thinking, the very reputation of its author, who was a leading statesman of his day, obviously lent it more credibility. The plan is known as the *Grand Dessein* and was ascribed by Sully to his King in order to enhance its prestige; it dates from after Henry's assassination in 1610. The plan envisaged a federation on the basis of a redistribution of European territory. It also outlined in full detail how best to expel the Turks from Europe. The Federation was to consist of fifteen members, among whom were six hereditary monarchies, six elective monarchies and three republics. It would operate through a General Council with supreme political and judicial functions, and through six provincial councils. Its crucial feature, in Nussbaum's analysis, was the weakening of the prominent position of Austria and Spain, the Hapsburg adversaries of France – hence the egalitarian structure of the Federation. Among the territories the Hapsburgs would lose were Spanish Belgium and Tyrol.

To be sure, the century abounded with scholars who tried their hand at similar proposals. Campanella, Richard Zouche and Comenius are just three of the more prominent names. Towards the close of the century we also find the first proposal of the kind from the Anglo-Saxon world – and its typically British features are unmistakably clear from the very different nature of the project. We refer to the *Diet* of William Penn, the able administrator of Pennsylvania. One singular aspect of his project, which was published in 1693, was that he wished the Turks and Muscovites to be included in his scheme of a Supreme Council. To this end, he had contrived an elaborate parliamentary structure. Thus, the votes of its delegates were to be determined by the yearly revenues of the foreign trade of member-States.

Perhaps the most influential among the numerous speculations on eternal peace through a European confederation over the centuries is the *Projet pour rendre la paix perpétuelle en Europe* by the Abbé de St Pierre, a comprehensive scheme for international relations that was launched in 1713 and effectively inspired by the Treaty of Utrecht. What its author, who had himself attended the peace conference, had in mind was to freeze the political *status quo* in Europe and thus perpetuate the settlement that was effected at the conference table in Utrecht. His Federation, which was to consist of some nineteen sovereign States, was to preclude foreign as well as civil wars, *inter alia* by guaranteeing the existing forms of government. It was intended also to cover the field of private international law – so as to promote international trade. Supreme authority would be vested with a permanent assembly of delegates of the federated sovereigns, called the Senate. This Senate, in which the major States would have a vote and the smaller ones would vote in groups, would settle disputes and force recalcitrant parties into submission by war. In principle, non-Christian powers were not excluded from this Federation, which would have its permanent seat in Utrecht. The Abbé himself, with admirable foresight, ventured that it would probably take the world two more centuries to accept the notion of an international court. Leibniz, having experienced the political failure of the project outlined in his *De jure suprematus*, agreed with him, as did Rousseau, reluctantly.

The close of the 18th century saw two more projects developed by prominent thinkers. The first originated with the British lawyer Jeremy Bentham. It was devised in 1789 but published posthumously in 1849. Its most typical feature is its seeking to avoid the scourge of war by means of a permanent congress that should sit as an international court of justice and to which all nations should send two delegates. Public opinion, Bentham maintained, would enforce obedience. Eventual non-compliance would be dealt with by banning the refractory State from the congress.

The second plan came from no less an authority than Immanuel Kant who, in 1795, published his *Zum ewigen Frieden* (Towards Perpetual Peace). Kant, with his superior reasoning, argued that perpetual peace was by no means a chimera but indeed an attainable goal, if attempted by a well-defined process of gradual approximation (for which he provided the blueprint) and under certain conditions that were well within human power. Among these imperative conditions he mentioned the abolishment of armies and the conclusion of unconditional peace treaties. The prerequisites for being welcomed into his confederation of States were definitely more strict than in the case of Bentham. Firstly, his league of nations would include republics only, which were, in his terminology, any form of government that was typified by popular representation and the separation of the executive and legislative powers. It was Kant's feeling that, if the citizens of a republic were themselves made responsible for the burdens and calamities of war, they would be less readily inclined to rush into combat. Secondly, he insisted that the public law of Europe should be founded upon a Confederation of Free States, which he later called the General Congress of Nations. As compared to St Pierre's and so many other schemes, the striking element of Kant's project is that it proceeded from just the reverse premiss: he did not expatiate upon the structure of his confederation but, on the contrary, pointed out that perpetual peace was conditioned by the establishment of such a federation, in whatever form.

It may be concluded that, if the implementation of perpetual peace had amounted to the mere application of theoretical schemes, several alternative models were readily available at the beginning of the 19th century, to ensure the durable unification of Europe and the final elimination of war. One could opt for the Anglo-Saxon judicial schemes, as exemplified by Penn's Diet and Bentham's Court, or rather for the continental, political designs of de Sully, Saint-Pierre or Kant. As Frederick the Great is said to have written to Voltaire with respect to the project of St Pierre: 'The Abbé's peace plan is very practical but for the fact that it needs for its success the consent of Europe, and some other bagatelles'. It was, evidently, due to the absence of this political willpower that these and all later schemes collapsed. Neither William Ladd's *Congress of Nations* (1840) on the model of the American Confederation, nor Blüntschli's *Federation* (1878) along the lines of the German *Reich*, nor again the scheme for an International Government in Geneva as suggested by one of the co-founders of the Institut de Droit International, James Lorimer from Edinburgh (1818-1890), whatever their merits may have been, invited any serious debate.

However, if initially these peace projects were isolated phenomena, launched at the private initiative of either visionaries or idealists, and as often prompted by political opportunism as by firm conviction, from the start of the 19th century onwards the curtain went up on a new scene. From that moment on, the intellectual progress of mankind towards a legal order became manifest in the serious attempts at international organization, in the sphere both of academic research and peace studies. In this venture, all previous arguments aimed at curbing the arms race and the atrocities of war were combined: the religious convictions of Quaker and Mennonite as much as the socio-economic arguments put forward by sociologists; the short-term goal of putting an end to an ongoing conflict or preventing an impending one as well as the long-term objec-

Tommaso Campanella (1568-1639), Dominican, sought to reconcile humanism with Roman Catholic theology. In prison he wrote the utopian La città del sole on the ideal commonwealth.

William Penn (1644-1718), a prominent Quaker, son of a British admiral and founder of Pennsylvania. He was perhaps the first to envisage a Supreme Council of States (General Diet, mainly a judicial body), also including non-Western powers.

The author of the Projet de paix perpétuelle, (1712-1716), the idealist Abbé de St Pierre, sought to perpetuate the arrangements of the 1713 Treaty of Utrecht. He profoundly influenced Rousseau and was backed by Voltaire, Swift and Hume.

Left: Frédéric Passy (1822-1912), the 'dean' of European pacifists and colleague of Cremer in the Interparliamentary Union and the Universal Peace Congress. As a member of the Chamber of Deputies he attacked the French colonial policy as violating the most basic human rights.

Right: Alfred Hermann Fried (1864-1921) was a leading figure in the central European peace movement. From disparate intellectual sources, he forged an ideological synthesis, for which he claimed scientific certainty and which was appealing to German pacifists. During 1899-1921 he was editor of Die Friedens-warte.

tives for the betterment of the world order.

It was the carnage of the Napoleonic Wars that prompted the sudden emergence of these peace societies throughout continental Europe, Great Britain and the USA. In 1829, Sellon launched the first *Société de la Paix* in Geneva. Seventy years later, on the eve of the First Hague Peace Conference, hundreds of flourishing peace societies from all over the world were registered at the *Bureau International de la Paix* in Bern. Initially, they were idealistic dens of resistance to violence on principle. However, having witnessed the tragedies of the Crimean War and the struggles for unification in Italy, Germany and the USA, they had changed course and grown into well organized institutes, expertly staffed and often operating from a very pragmatic and realistic angle.

William Stead (1849-1912), in the 1880s editor of the Pall Mall Gazette and editor of the monthly Review of Reviews in the 1890s, launched the slogan 'Always Arbitrate Before You Fight'. In 1899, at The Hague, he proclaimed an International Peace Crusade.
During the Conference of 1907 he edited a daily Courrier de la Conférence.

Prominent publicists had helped reform their opinions, men such as Victor Hugo or Alexis de Tocqueville. Accordingly, they had developed new lines of argument which attested to their political maturity. No longer were total and instant disarmament their main goals, but rather the gradual outlining of a new system of international law and a network of international agreements which would provide lasting security by means of tribunals, neutrality treaties and – the keyword of the period – the settlement of disputes through arbitration. Frédéric Passy, who in 1867 launched the *Ligue internationale et permanente de la paix* in Paris, took it for granted that, until this long awaited system prevailed – which he thought would take another century – arms were the acceptable instruments for enforcing peace.

After early clashes with other, more radical social movements, such as nihilists, socialists and Marxists, pacifists closed ranks and joined forces with these factions in the positive bid for unified action. French pacifism was reorganized in the *La Paix par le Droit* movement. In Great Britain, the *English International Arbitration and Peace Association* was established in circles run by Hodgson Pratt, William Stead and G.H. Perris.

Meanwhile, impressive publications served to draw worldwide attention and warranted ample exposure in the media. The movement produced spellbinding literature as readily as academic masterpieces or scientific analyses of military techniques and arms expenditure. In 1889, the Austrian Bertha von Suttner published her *Die Waffen Nieder*, which was translated into sixteen languages. Jean de Bloch's *Der Zukunftkrieg* (1892) and Alfred Fried's *Friedens-Katechismus* (1895) were followed by Norman Angel's best-selling *The Great Illusion* (1910). In Tsarist Russia, Leo Tolstoy and Ivan Novikoff, from different angles, did much to support the idea.

The enormous coverage and publicity even drew the attention of undisputed champions of capitalism such as Andrew Carnegie, Alfred Nobel and Henry Ford. It was Nobel's *Will* of 1896, Carnegie's *Gospel of Wealth* of 1900 (and later *Endowement* of 1911) and Ford's *Peace Mission* which lent added prestige to the peace movement. In short, around the turn of the century, international pacifism could no longer be ignored.

We have now reviewed the various sources from which inspiration could be drawn in the establishment of an international legal order. On the wave of this tide, in 1898, in the highest circles at St Petersburg, the initiative was taken to develop what has become known to the world at large as *l'Œuvre de La Haye*. Here the machinery was set in motion which, within a quarter of a century, would result in the opening of a World Court in the Peace Palace at The Hague.

Le progrès de la paix.

Left: Jean Bloch (1836-1902), the author of 'The Future of War'.

Right: Baroness Bertha von Suttner (1843-1914), the founder and president of the Austrian Peace Society. A pacifist journalist, she wrote the epoch-making Die Waffen Nieder, a novel vividly and effectively portraying the horrors of war. An advocate of arbitration, she successfully headed the lobby of peace leaders at the 1899 Hague Peace Conference.

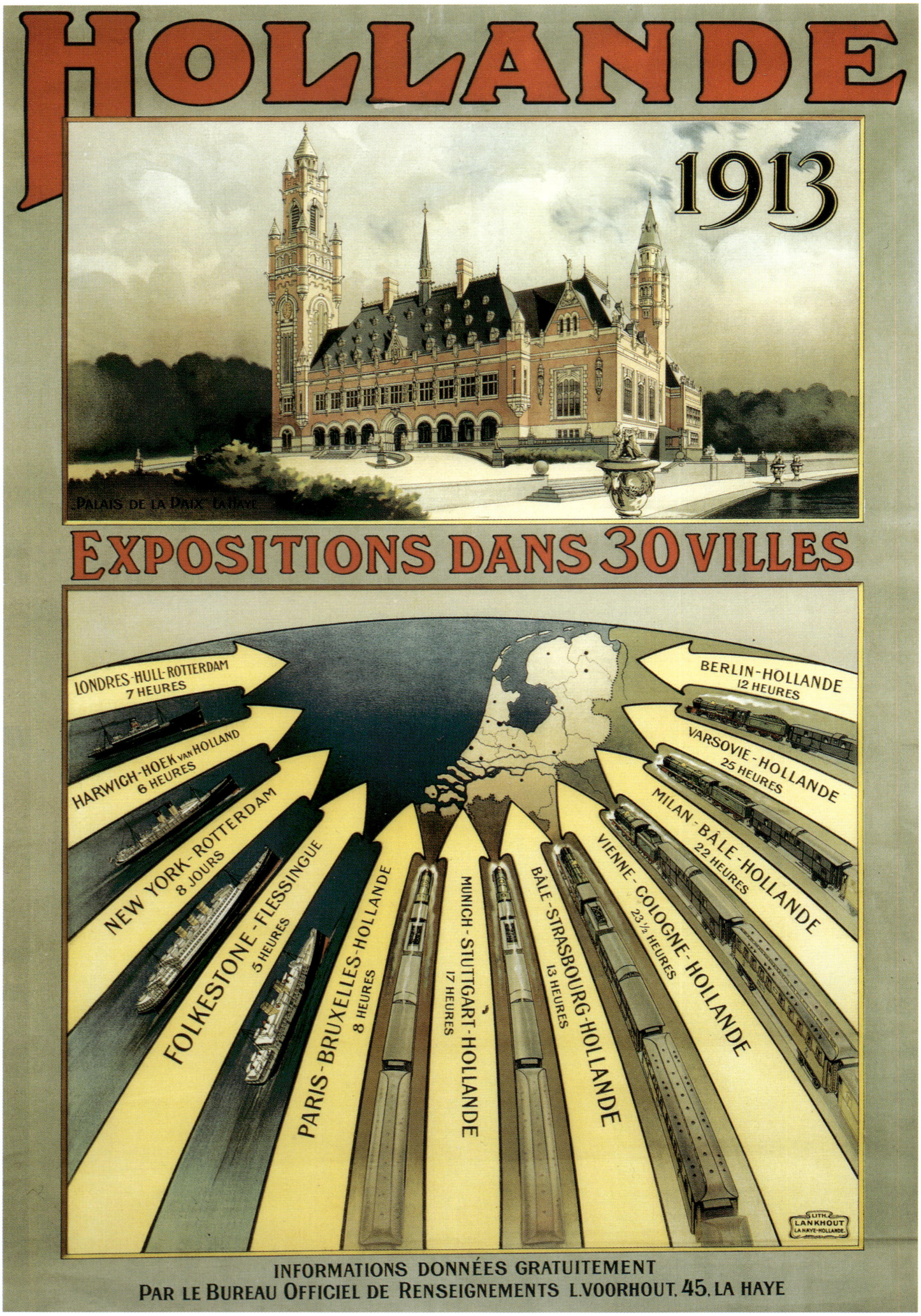
HOLLANDE
1913
"PALAIS DE LA PAIX" LA HAYE
EXPOSITIONS DANS 30 VILLES
LONDRES-HULL-ROTTERDAM
7 HEURES
HARWICH-HOEK VAN HOLLAND
6 HEURES
NEW YORK-ROTTERDAM
8 JOURS
FOLKESTONE-FLESSINGUE
5 HEURES
PARIS-BRUXELLES-HOLLANDE
8 HEURES
MUNICH-STUTTGART-HOLLANDE
17 HEURES
BÂLE-STRASBOURG-HOLLANDE
13 HEURES
VIENNE-COLOGNE-HOLLANDE
23½ HEURES
MILAN-BÂLE-HOLLANDE
22 HEURES
VARSOVIE-HOLLANDE
25 HEURES
BERLIN-HOLLANDE
12 HEURES
LITH. LANKHOUT LA HAYE-HOLLANDE
INFORMATIONS DONNÉES GRATUITEMENT
PAR LE BUREAU OFFICIEL DE RENSEIGNEMENTS L.VOORHOUT, 45. LA HAYE

CHAPTER THREE

L'Œuvre de La Haye

The First Hague Peace Conference

Czar Nicholas' Circular Letter

On 30 July 1898, Count Otto von Bismarck, the unchallenged master of European politics during the second half of the 19th century, passed away. It was the end of an era. Merely three weeks later, on Wednesday, 24 August 1898 to be precise, a new era opened, an era of international law. On that day Czar Nicholas II astounded the world by the issuance of a circular letter, in which he convoked the nations to an international conference which would concern itself with the problems of world peace and disarmament. The steady increase, the letter stated, of ever more sophisticated armaments and the financially excessive burdens that went along with it, had placed an intolerable check on the upward march of humanity and the social and intellectual development of the nations. Armament itself had become the primary threat to peace. Swords had to be beaten into ploughshares and spears into pruning hooks, or rather quick-firing artillery into locomotives and bridges.

The message prompted a mixture of disbelief, scepticism and joy. To be sure, the initiative fitted into a certain tradition of Romanov politics. In 1804, in the midst of the Napoleonic turmoil, Alexander I had suggested that after Napoleon's downfall the nations of Europe should unite in a treaty which would determine 'the positive rights of nations ... and assert the obligation of never beginning war until all resources which the mediation of a third party could offer have been exhausted'. On such principles, he maintained, one could proceed to a general pacification, and give birth to a league of which the stipulation would form 'a new code of the law of nations'. Again, pacifism went back a long way in Russian history. Tolstoy had been just another exponent of this time-honoured tradition. Indeed, one of the most eloquent and best documented assaults on the armaments race had come from Count de Bloch, a Russian banker and pacifist, who in 1892 had published an impressive and widely influential six-volume protest (*Future War*) against the barbarity of modern warfare. In 1896, Count de Basily, one of Nicholas cabinet ministers had been much impressed by the call for disarmament at the 1896 Budapest conference of the Interparliamentary Union.

Still, no pressure whatever from public opinion made itself felt in the austerity of Nicholas' palace and *Realpolitiker* were quick in detecting the circumstances that prompted this peace crusade. Andrew White, then American Ambassador in Berlin and destined to become one of the architects of the Hague Courts, expressed reservations with regard to the motives of the Czar: 'A kindly man ... wishing in a

Czar Nicholas II (1868-1918). This portrait hangs in the Small Court Room of the Peace Palace.

See previous page: One of the vases of precious Rozenburg porcelain in remembrance of the First Hague Peace Conference of 1899. It represents the Huis ten Bosch, the summer residence of the Dutch Royal Family in the woods near The Hague and venue of the conference.

languid way the good of his country ... but the indifference to everything about him evident in all his actions, his lack of force even in the simplest efforts for the improvement of his people and, above all, his yielding to the worst elements in the treatment of the Baltic provinces and Finland, did not encourage me to believe that he would lead a movement against the enormous power of the military party in his vast empire'.

His reservations were understandable. Even nowadays, it is not easy to disentangle the blend of self-interest and humanitarian objectives which prompted the call at the time. The burdens of the armaments race did exhaust the Russian treasury. Anxiety regarding the impressive war machine that was steadily building up along Russia's western borders dominated political debate at St Petersburg. In less than thirty years Bismarck had succeeded in rallying the former petty kingdoms of Germany into a military, naval and colonial power of the first order. A new potent force had manifested itself in the person of Emperor Wilhelm II, who in 1890 had forced Bismarck to resign. Bismarck's genius and his network of treaties and alliances were being replaced by an impulsive *Wille zur Macht*. The delicate political equilibrium of previous decades was no longer to be relied upon.

Not surprisingly, the first remonstrance to the Russian circular letter came from Berlin, protesting that no armament could be called excessive which would guarantee peace and that no German felt its burden. The USA, then close to entering the concert of nations, in a first oral answer by White, accepted the invitation in the most cordial terms. After an early impromptu reaction of warm sympathy by Lord Balfour, leader of the House of Commons, Britain's Prime Minister, Lord Salisbury, in the most prudent and circumspect terms, promised Great Britain's support to a conference intent on discussing 'the most effective means of securing the continuance of general peace and of putting some limit on the constant increase of armaments'.

In general, diplomats deemed the proposal 'visionary and Utopian, if not partaking of Quixotism', in the language of the time. In fact, nothing obscured the thrust of the initiative in high political circles as much as the unequivocal support of the world peace movement. Undue enthusiasm for the humanitarian aspect of the

'Dropping the Pilot'. At variance with Bismarck's policy, the Imperial and imperious young Wilhelm II had virtually forced 'the Pilot Who Weathered the Storm' to resign (Punch, March 1890).

armament problem, it was felt by politicians, might well obscure the gravity of the economic problems involved. In a reaction to all this, a leading journal in St Petersburg hastily announced that what the Czar had in view was not so much a general and instantaneous disarmament, to which there were insurmountable obstacles, but rather a united effort finally to bring about some de-escalation, at least in the yearly increase in expenditure on weaponry. Still, as we have seen in the previous chapter, Czar Nicholas's initiative was carried on the wave of a changing tide. The convocation of the First Hague Peace Conference implied the formal acceptance in the world of high politics of an issue hammered at for decades by the peace movement.

The Second Circular Letter

On 11 January 1899, Count Muraviev, Russia's Foreign Minister, despatched a second circular letter. In the letter, melancholic reference was made to the recent outbreak of violence which had clouded the political horizon since the issuing of the first circular letter. France and Great

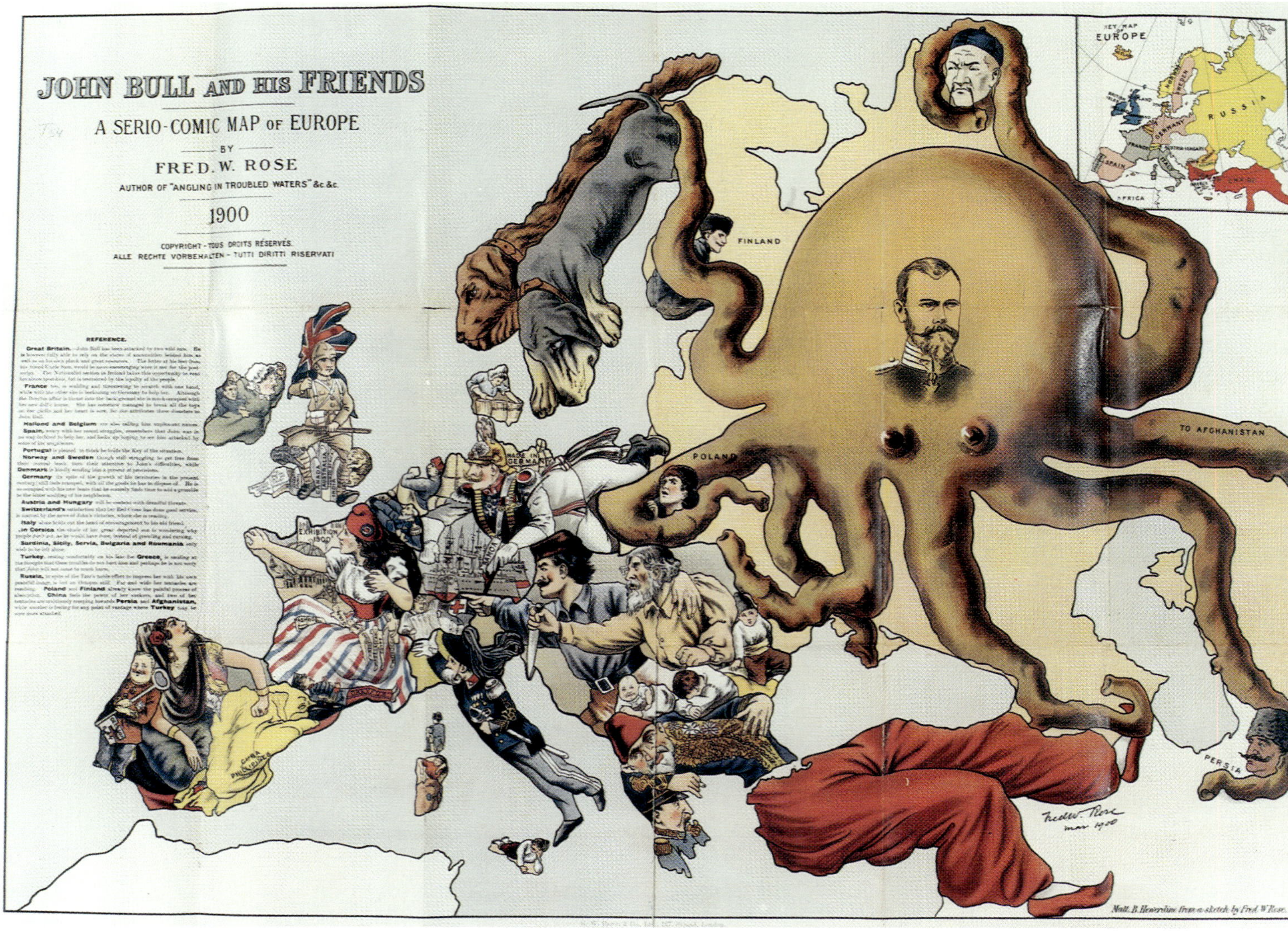

John Bull and his Friends, a cynical portrayal of Europe around the turn of the century.

Britain had been on the brink of war over the Fashoda incident in Africa, there was the Khalifa in revolt, and so much more. The objectives of the proposed conference were outlined: first to set a limit to the progressive increase of armaments and second to discuss the prevention of armed conflict by the pacific means of settlement at the disposal of international diplomacy such as mediation and arbitration.

Eight issues were to be considered, including the freezing of military effectiveness and budgets; the prohibition of new types of arms; the restriction or prohibition of explosives, bombs dropped from balloons and submarine torpedo-boats, the extension of the attainments of the 1864 Geneva Convention to the area of naval warfare; the revision of the unratified 1874 Brussels Declaration on the laws and customs of war; and, lastly, the acceptance of the principles of mediation and optional arbitration as a means of preventing or settling international disputes, and the establishment of a model and uniform practice in these respects.

From early on, it was thought advisable by its backers that the Conference should not sit in St Petersburg or any other capital of a great power. Even the slightest partiality, it was generally felt, might impede the progress of work. Brussels was taken into consideration; Leopold II keenly advocated the idea. Geneva was never really considered, as Andrew White claims in his memoirs: 'the number of anarchists and nihilists who had taken refuge there, and the murder of the Empress of Austria by one of them shortly before, at Geneva, in broad daylight, had thrown discredit over the ability of the Swiss government to guarantee safety to the conference'. By mid-February, it was announced that the young Queen of the Netherlands, Wilhelmina, had formally accepted the suggestion of The Hague as the seat of the Conference. The Hague was easy to reach; Holland was neutral at the time; it had a strong parliamentary tradition; it was the native country of Hugo Grotius and Cornelis van Bynkershoek; it had been the scene of many international conferences, from Nymegen, Ryswyck and Utrecht to the 1893-1894 meetings in The Hague of the Interparliamentary Union and the Conference of Private International Law, initiated by Tobias Asser. Also, the kinship of the Dutch royal family to the Romanovs may have been a factor. The Dutch King William III (1849-1890) was the son of William II and Anna Pavlovna, the daughter of Czar Paul I.

Queen Wilhelmina placed at the disposal of the Conference one of the most charming historic sites in the Netherlands, the summer residence of the royal family, the palace Huis ten Bosch (House in the Woods), not far from the city centre. On 7 April, the Dutch Ministry for Foreign Affairs formally invited the nations to the opening of the Conference on 18 May, this being the birthday of Czar Nicholas II.

The issue of invitations was a thorny one and provoked much comment. In order to prevent debate over the status of the younger States in the continents overseas, whose very legitimacy and independence were questionable, only the nations accredited to the St Petersburg Court were invited, with the addition of Luxembourg, Montenegro and Siam. The Dutch much resented the exclusion of the young South African Republics as the USA did the absence of Central and South American representatives, the authoritative international lawyer from Argentina, Carlos Calvo, among them. The American and Mexican delegates were to represent the whole of their hemisphere. Another noticeable absentee was the Holy See, due to Italy's obstinate protests. Conflicts of the kind are hard to avoid, no matter what course is steered. The way Russia handled the affair was probably the only practical way open to save the Conference. About mid-May, some one hundred delegates from twenty-six nations registered in the more fashionable hotels of The Hague.

The Work of the Third Commission

After the ceremonial opening of the Conference on 18 May, the delegates set to work a few days later. Mr de Staal, elected President of the Conference, outlined the programme, which provided for three Commissions. The First Commission was to consider the limitation of armaments and the humanizing of war. The Second Commission was to discuss the adaptation of the principles of the 1864 Geneva Convention to the area of maritime warfare, and the laws and customs of war. The Third Commission was to review the maintenance of general peace, good offices and mediation, international commissions of inquiry and international arbitration. During a period of ten weeks work was done in the various committees and subcommittees with regular plenary meetings intervening. Before final decisions were to be taken, delegates were given the opportunity to consult their governments.

The outcome of the Conference will not be discussed in full detail here. Our main concern is with the findings of the Third Commission. The First Commission became the scene of hot-tempered debate. The views on the points at issue differed

The Peace of Utrecht (1713-1714), a series of treaties which concluded the War of the Spanish Succession (1701-1714). The settlement, which was to govern international politics for the next few decades, also established Great Britain as the leading colonial and maritime power.

Cornelis van Bynkershoek (1673-1743), influential Dutch author of works on the position of ambassadors, the sovereignty of the seas, prizes and neutrality, contraband and blockade. A positivist who placed greater emphasis on actual usage than on deduced precepts.

widely. Inevitably, the discussion had to be limited to a preliminary exchange of ideas, some recommendations and a few expressed desires. The Second Commission put together sixty articles of impressive impact and accomplished more with respect to naval warfare and the wounded than all the previous Red Cross Conferences combined. Still, this was no more than another milestone along the road to the 1949 Geneva Conventions.

The tasks of the Third Commission, less technical than those of the other Commissions, were essentially of a diplomatic nature and touched most directly on the issue of State sovereignty. Clearly, it was the *pièce de résistance* of the Conference. Most delegates were experts in the field. The presidency was entrusted to Léon Bourgeois, a former French Prime Minister. Count Nigra of Italy and Lord Pauncefote of Great Britain were elected honorary presidents.

The full Commission convened nine times and, on the suggestion of its President, installed a Special Committee of Examination (*Comité d'Examen*), to which were appointed Asser of Holland, Descamps of Belgium, d'Estournelles of France, Holls of the USA, Lammasch of Austria-Hungary, de Martens of Russia, Odier of Switzerland and Zorn of Germany. The Committee soon became the centre of interest of the whole Conference.

THE OPENING OF THE 1899 PEACE CONFERENCE

The opening of the International Peace Conference on 18th May was welcomed by a perfect spring day; The Hague presented a stirring and picturesque spectacle. The flags of many nations were flying in the wind from public buildings, hotels, embassies and many private houses. At 10 a.m. the members of the Russian delegation, in full uniform and with a splendid escort, attended mass in the tiny Orthodox Chapel near Scheveningen to pray in honour of the Czar's birthday. Interestingly enough, this chapel was situated on the very spot where, eight years later, the founding stone of the Peace Palace was to be laid.

The opening ceremony of the Conference was set for 2 p.m. From noon onwards, shining varnished open carriages drawn by four in hands could be seen traversing the two miles from the city centre. They passed by the drill field or Malieveld, then through the woods, skirting the ponds, up to the simple but striking beauty of the tiny summer palace. The brilliant caparisons of the horses and the colourful dress of the delegates were a sight to see in the beaming sun.

Through the ages, the charms of the Hague Woods have inspired poets and statesmen alike. The humanist scholars Hugo Grotius and Constantine Huygens both wrote poems of considerable length in a eulogy of the park. On 15 July, G. H. Perris, publicist and attender at the Peace Conference, jotted down the following lines in his notebook:

Between the Hague and the palace is the Bosch - a splendid park nearly two miles long, divided lengthwise by a series of lakes, embowered by magnificent trees, in whose shade one may walk or rest and think. All around reigns not indeed dead silence - for unseen birds are flitting ceaselessly in their leafy heights, and a rumble of human life is faintly audible from the nearest boulevard - but perfect tranquillity.

The face of the long water, a brown mirror except where it is covered with a cream of weed, is hardly disturbed by a ripple in these burning days; the swans, lazily majestical, alone break the picture of over-arching branches. Brave old beeches and towering elms shake themselves gently in the sun, and the limes throw out the last wealth of their intoxicating perfume. A fairy network of leaves against the azure sky is repeated in shadow on the grass and soil. A place in which to forget old passions and prejudices and the grosser forms of selfishness; a place for good consideration, courtesy, patience and the philosophic mind. Yes, decidedly, it was an inspiration to hold here the first parliament of peace; and The Hague has its appropriate reward, for has not this tiny capital become the juridical metropolis of the world? What capital can boast a prouder title?

Of the Palace itself he said: '... this is a mere shooting box compared with the palaces at Moscow and St Petersburg, and yet it is already one of the world's historical buildings, and the cradle of an idea that might, if anything could, reconcile us to that singular institution, the Russian Tsardom.'

The hundred representatives filled the Oranjezaal to capacity. The seats had been arranged along four rows of concentric semi-circular tables, covered with green baize. In this way all the delegates enjoyed a clear view of the President's chair in the bay window and of the adjoining tables of secretaries and attachés.

Seats had been allotted in alphabetical order of the States; only minor adjustments of protocol had been made in a stealthy way. Thus, seats of honour for the American delegates had been provided for by arranging them under the heading A of Amérique, next to Allemagne. On this the veteran diplomat Count Munster, head of the German delegation, in jest inquired of his American neighbours, with a reference to the Spanish war, whether this arrangement formed part of their new imperialistic policy. On their protesting their innocence he remarked: Surely innocence has always been your drawing card in diplomacy.

Munster, indeed, was a character. White felt 'he was saturated with the ideas of fifty years ago.' He thought telegraphs and telephones a curse and at a reception spoke of bacteria and microbes as all a modern humbug.

No space whatever was reserved, or for that matter could be spared, for spectators and journalists. The delegates agreed that the character of the negotiations did not call for open discussion. Only a handful of invited guests were admitted to attend the ceremony from the narrow gallery in

The gathering of delegates in the Oranjezaal of the Huis ten Bosch.

the cupola; apart from them, all outsiders were strictly excluded from the Conference. In this way the privacy of the deliberation was duly guaranteed - only it meant war with the press, who insisted on being informed of the proceedings daily and in detail. No Conference of the sort had ever been held before, so no one exactly knew how to handle this problem.

At the second meeting of the Conference, on 20 May, the delegates agreed upon the maintenance of secrecy for the full duration of the deliberations. The President and the bureau alone were authorized to communicate to the members of the press, a summary of the proceedings of each committee. Embittered journalists and representatives of all sorts of peace organizations, who had crowded into the premises, spat venom on this pretended secrecy of the proceedings. Although strict regulations were somewhat relaxed later, no satisfactory solution was found. In the end, this would very much hamper the general acceptance abroad of the results of the sessions. In view of the widely spread misunderstandings regarding the goal of the Conference and the ensuing scepticism and mistrust, the scenario decided upon did not testify as to the tactical genius of the organizing committee.

The American delegate Frederic W. Holls, who in 1914 edited a very capable survey of the proceedings, vividly remembered the opening ceremony. At two o'clock sharp, he noted, an impressive silence came over the assembly, in which every member doubtless realized that a great and solemn historic moment had arrived. In this atmosphere, the Dutch Minister for Foreign Affairs rose to call the meeting to order.

Standing in front of the huge allegorical panels by Jordaens, commemorating the Peace of Westphalia of 1648 and representing among others the entrance into the room of the Goddess of Peace about to close the Temple of Janus, de Beaufort gave a welcoming address. In it he referred to the lofty initiative of Czar Nicholas II, but also called to memory Nicholas' predecessor Alexander and the latter's desire to see all sovereigns and all the nations of Europe united for the purpose of living as brethren, aiding each other according to their reciprocal needs.

He read the text of a congratulatory telegram which he proposed to despatch to the Czar and amidst unanimous applause conferred the presidency of the Conference on the Russian Ambassador, Mr de Staal. In his address, this veteran diplomat promised the assembly to employ all the efforts which the sad privilege and feeble auxiliary of his advanced age offered to justify the confidence placed in him. He then recalled the historic importance of The Hague and for that matter The Netherlands, in the development of international law and proposed to send a telegram to its young Queen Wilhelmina, their hostess Queen.

He then proceeded to the appointment of the honorary and vice-presidents, Mr de Beaufort and the clearheaded and straightforward (White) van Karnebeek, the Foreign Minister and first delegate of the host country respectively, and to the election of the secretariat. The assembly passed a resolution declaring all meetings of the Conference and its Committees to be absolutely secret and was then adjourned to Saturday, 20 May.

Frederic Frommhold de Martens (1845-1909), veteran diplomat and prominent internationalist from St Petersburg. He chaired the Second Commission of the Hague Conference and played a distinguished role in the early years of the Institut de Droit International and Permanent Court of Arbitration.

'It was felt' as Holls put it in his report, 'that the question of success or failure of the Conference depended almost entirely upon the chance of unbroken harmony in this Committee'. As he saw it, these men eventually saved the Conference from failure. Their absorbing interest in the issue under discussion and their common endeavour to accomplish the noble goals set, as difficult as these might seem at first, became in his opinion the most memorable feature of the entire Conference. Its members soon dropped all diplomatic reserve, and 'sincere personal esteem as well as genuine good fellowship, appeased even the most serious differences of opinion'.

Memoirs of the period, without exception, give credit to the Russian Frederic de Martens as having been the very soul of the Committee and, if only due to his patience, as having contributed most to its success. De Martens himself, while being one of the prominent international lawyers of the period, was a sober realist. In his *Treatise on the Law of Nations*, a few years before the Conference, he made the following observation regarding the idea of a Court of Arbitration:

> There are two views on this method of settling international disagreements: that of pious wishes, and that of the existing order of international relations. It is essential to avoid illusions on this matter for the future of a court of arbitration itself. Reality shows that there exist many such disputes and occasions in international conflicts which are impossible to clarify with the assistance of legal analysis. Many of them have grown up over the historical life of peoples and can be eliminated only by force and by violating the existing law and order. It is difficult to imagine that the parties would agree to hand over their historical dispute for resolution by any arbitration tribunal or that the latter could find any legal basis for settling it.

As is well-known, one of the central issues of the debate within the Third Commission was to concentrate on the very idea of such a Court of Arbitration. The Germans firmly resisted the idea, the Kaiser having declared himself categorically opposed to any intervention in his affairs of State. In the midst of debates, the sessions were suspended. Zorn, the German representative, and Holls left for Berlin to consult Count von Bülow, the German Foreign Minister, so as to avert imminent crisis. All in all, the Committee held eighteen sessions, usually three a week. It first convened in the famous Chinese Room of the summer palace, but then moved to the *Salle de Trèves* at the Binnenhof, in the centre of The Hague.

The Third Commission of the 1899 Hague Conference, presided over by the inspiring Léon Bourgeois, the first French delegate.

The Idea of an Arbitral Tribunal

Among the problems discussed, the issue of arbitration was generally felt to be the most efficacious and equitable means of settling disputes. Still, the Russian circular letter did not provide for any arbitral tribunal. This idea was brought up, to general surprise, by Lord Pauncefote.

When the British delegate first announced the idea of a Permanent International Tribunal, as the pacifist William Stead put it in the *Manchester Guardian*: 'One could have heard a pin drop in the Conference. Members looked at one another for a moment in blank amazement, and not a few felt for the first time that they were face to face with serious business put forward by practical statesmen in grim earnest'.

The surprise was heightened by the subsequent announcement of de Staal that the Russian Government was to submit a proposal of very similar purport and that the American delegates were likewise preparing such a scheme. Then it turned out that the Italians had some amendments to offer, too. In the first days of June, the Drafting Committee of the Arbitration Commission found itself overwhelmed by six proposals:

1. the Russian scheme, including a code of arbitral procedure;
2. the British scheme for a permanent tribunal;
3. the American scheme for a permanent tribunal;
4. an American project for special mediation;
5. an Italian amendment to the Russian scheme for mediation and arbitration;
6. the Russian supplementary scheme for a permanent tribunal.

The British and American proposals soon proved much the same in essence. They provided for a permanent bureau which would summon the court whenever litigants so demanded. The court itself was to be chosen by the litigants from a list to which each contracting power contributed names, though in the English proposal the litigants might also choose one or more judges not listed. Decisions of the tribunal would go by majority. The Russian supplementary scheme provided for a court to be established at The Hague and made up of five arbitrators to be designated by as many powers, and possibly two arbitrators appointed by litigants. The court was to be controlled by a secretariat with adequate staff, that would render a yearly account of its operations. The main object of the Italian amendment was to restrict the obligatory element in the Russian proposal.

The Committee agreed upon the acceptance of the British scheme as a basis for further discussion. It was at this juncture that Zorn interfered to point out that the German Emperor held arbitration as dangerous and derogatory to the monarch's sovereignty and the nation's independence. Reaction was firm and violent. Lord Pauncefote himself suavely replied that the view of statecraft as exposed by Wilhelm was 'perhaps not altogether modern'. Still, the scheme was slightly modified to oblige the German Emperor, which Holls and the conciliative Zorn took it upon themselves to defend at Berlin. By July, it became apparent that an obligatory clause would never pass German opposition. On 4 July, this clause was cut out and the principle of optional arbitration adhered to. It was at this juncture, later critics have argued, that by far the best opportunity to achieve something really spectacular was missed.

Be that as it may, the final scheme agreed upon passed the full Third Commission without much opposition. It also included a widely discussed French idea concerning the proposed court, which was raised and ingeniously defended by Bourgeois and d'Estournelles. It was meant to authorize the Secretary-General of the court to draw the attention of the conflicting parties to the court as a peacemaking institution and, in its final wording in the Convention (Article 27 in the old, 48 in the new num-

An artist's impression of the Hague Conference by Charles Toché. Against the cupola of the Huis ten Bosch in the back the delegates are portrayed amidst the statues of Peace (left) and War (right), Hugo Grotius, Czar Nicholas II and Queen Wilhelmina on raised platforms and Mercury as the harbinger of peace. In the ornamental border feature prominent politicians, internationalists and peace leaders who had been instrumental to the convening of the conference.

bering), 'reminded the contracting parties of their duty to draw the attention of parties to the Court'. As Descamps, the rapporteur of the Committee would comment, the principle of arbitration had definitely penetrated into international practice. It had 'all the sympathies of the present and the richest promise for the future'. The institution of a Permanent Court had been unanimously agreed to. The Court would have jurisdiction in all matters, its members having a mandate fixed at six years. On 25 July, a Convention comprising sixty-one articles was laid before the Conference. The Commission proved a fine showcase: Great Britain's scheme for arbitration, Russia's Commissions of Inquiry, France's duty-clause, and the mediation plan to the credit of the USA.

An Appraisal of the Conference

On Saturday 29 July, a fair summer day, the members assembled for the last time in the Huis ten Bosch for the signing of the Final Act of the Conference and the various conventions and declarations, beautifully engrossed documents with the seals of the plenipotentiaries affixed to them. As the *Times* observed: 'Two and a half months ago the atmosphere at the House in the Woods was one of frigid reserve, not to say mutual mistrust; yesterday was like a breaking-up for holidays at school. Everybody was pleased with everybody in general, and with the president in particular'. Or, as Holls reported home, 'Any one who would have predicted, even as late as July 1898, that a Conference would meet and accomplish even a fraction of the results attained at The Hague, – that the subject of a federation of the civilized world for justice would even be discussed, not by enthusiasts and private individuals, but by leading diplomats of all civilized nations, called together for that purpose by the most powerful autocrat of the world, – would have been regarded as a dreamer, if not as demented'.

Public opinion on the whole has been less sympathetic towards the results of the Conference. As Zorn declared in the *Deutsche Rundschau* in 1900: 'There have been severe critics who have characterized the labours of the Conference as 'threshing out Russian straw'. To say the least, the Hague Conference was a unique experiment, the first Conference of its sort ever attended by representatives of so many nations. It constituted the priceless precedent of a meeting at a time of profound peace to discuss durable means of settling conflicts. In this, it was essentially different from the conferences held at Wesphalia (1648), Utrecht (1713) Vienna (1815), Paris (1856) or Berlin (1878), which all owed their convocation to a specific war. Perhaps it most resembled the preventive vocation of the Congo and Pan-American Conferences.

Nothing utopian had been aimed at by these diplomats, nothing quixotic was worked out, nothing miraculous had been accomplished. A piece of solid workmanship in the field of international law had been produced. Dimly, on the far horizon, the first glimmerings of an international code could be perceived. But the wheels of progress grind slowly, as statesmen are among the first to appreciate. In 1899, as at any other juncture of history, too many, often conflicting, forces had been at work to really ask for more.

Certainly, the Conference did not prevent war: before long, Russia, its very initiator, would come to grips with Japan, as Great Britain went to war with the Boers. Still, in 1904 the Dogger Bank Incident between Russia and Great Britain, which involved the 'honour and vital interests' of both parties, was resolved by a Commission of Inquiry set up under Article 9 of the 1899 Convention on Pacific Settlement. Only a few months later, President Theodore Roosevelt, with the same article in hand, initiated the negotiations which ended the Russo-Japanese conflict with the 1905 Treaty of Portsmouth. By that time, too, the greatest achievement of the Conference, the Permanent Court of Arbitration, had earned itself a secure place in international affairs.

The Permanent Court of Arbitration

In the 1899 Hague Convention on the Pacific Settlement of International Disputes, the Permanent Court of Arbitration is treated under the second and third parts of the fourth title, more specifically in Articles 20 to 29 (Articles 41-50 in the revised but not essentially altered text of the 1907 edition). Discussed in succession are the purpose of the Court, its competence, its judiciary aspects, its secretarial and administrative bodies – these latter being the International Bureau, headed by the Secretary-General, and the Administrative Council – and the cost.

In the Convention, the initiative for the constitution of the Court was left to the President of the Administrative Council, the Dutch Minister for Foreign Affairs *qualitate qua*, subject of course to the formal ratification of the treaty by the nations. In September 1900 Minister De Beaufort deemed the number of nations that had joined the Treaty as satisfactory. On 19 September the Administrative Council was installed, and on 9 April 1901 a first meeting was convened to appoint functionaries. Accommodation was found in one of the typical Hague manor-houses on the Prinsegracht, former habitat of the aristocracy.

The rooms and salons were stylish and fashionable and breathed a quiet dignity. Well furnished with all sorts of souvenirs of the Peace Conference and the symbols of peace and international law, they were the natural venue for the decorous diplomats and eminent scholars who were meant to frequent them. A photograph of the day shows the elegant Professor Asser seated among his staff members. It is in these first quarters that the Court would enjoy what in retrospect must be considered the heyday of its existence, the period leading up to the opening of the Peace Palace in August 1913 and the outbreak of World War I, just a year later. It was a modest building or, as William Stead put it in his typically uncompromising way: 'The prudent Dutch Government and the somewhat sceptical members of the Council decided to proceed tentatively, and so they have provided for the headquarters of the tribunal modest premises which can be procured at a minimum cost, but are in singular contrast to the hopes entertained by those who founded the Hague Tribunal'. It was Carnegie's generous donation that would soon lend them the never anticipated prospects of much loftier premises.

The housing of the Permanent Court of Arbitration during the years 1901-1913 at the Prinsegracht in The Hague.

In its opening years, the Court was welcomed by the public at large and news media with the same mixed feelings that had surrounded the 1899 Conference. Obviously, the idea of the Court, never really anticipated before the summer of 1899, had not yet settled in the popular mind. Overblown expectations on the one hand were faced with total disbelief on the other, sheer ignorance in one place contrasted with a lack of deeper interest in another. Numerous were the newspapers predicting that the silver inkstands would never see proper use, that any money spent on the project was wasted, or that submitting a conflict was much too costly. However, numerous too were those who had expected the Court to put an end to the Boer War overnight. Clearly, both groups missed the point completely. Vested with the power agreed to by the signatory States, which was non-compulsory arbitration only, the Court was merely a first step towards a truly international judicial body. If anything, it was a sign to the world that a new era of law had dawned upon mankind. It was not at all the World Court itself, long-awaited by many for centuries, that was authorized, prepared and able to intervene of its own accord in conflicts in the name of Law and Righteousness. Indeed, in 1900, no one familiar with international law even took such a body seriously for a long time – in 1907 Beernaert, for one, called it a *'redoutable utopie'*.

More alarming to the young institution, in those early days, was the disavowal of its very existence by the signatories to its Convention in moments of conflict. France chose to have its conflict with Britain over African matters settled through the mediation of a single arbitrator, to the fury of its prominent senator, Baron d'Estournelles, one of the most militant advocates of the Court in those early days. Downright embarrassing to its British partisans, who had been so instrumental in drawing up the 1899 Convention, was Great Britain's flat refusal to have the issue of the Boer War submitted to the Court.

However, these setbacks were soon far outweighed by the signal successes of the Court. Also, the tendency, from 1900 onwards, to stipulate specific reference to the Hague Court in the compromissory clauses of treaties proved to be persistent. Permanent arbitration treaties were agreed upon in ever greater numbers by ever more nations. Pursuant to the 1901 Pan-American Conference in Mexico, all South American nations that had been banned from the 1899 Conference became signatories to the Hague Convention *en bloc*. Before turning to an appraisal of the functioning of the Court in the context of international society over the past century, a brief description of its nature, sphere of action and procedure is called for.

CONFÉRENCE DU DÉSARMEMENT

Avec la conférence du désarmement de La Haye. Pensant avec raison qu'ils ont bien mérité de leurs peuples et peuvent songer à eux-mêmes, les Souverains décident à l'unaminité de venir complimenter HIGH-LIFE TAILOR, 112, rue Richelieu (coin du boulevard) sur son merveilleux complet sur mesure à 69 fr. 50 et de lui faire leurs commandes en vue de l'Exposition de 1900.

The Nature and Province of the Court

As is well known, the most striking feature of the PCA is its very name. In fact, it is neither a Court nor an arbitral tribunal – and if a Court at all, it is certainly not a Permanent Court. The organization can perhaps best be characterized as 'an institutional framework open to the parties to a dispute to avail themselves of at their choice' (Butler), 'a permanent arbitration service' which is rendered by the backbone of the institution, the International Bureau. It is this Bureau which compiles a list of legal authorities ('Members of the Court' as they are termed, although they are in actual fact only potential arbitrators), who have declared themselves available for a (renewable) term of six years to serve as arbitrator in the event of a dispute. This list is compiled on the basis of a selection of candidates made by the Contracting Powers. Each of these Powers is entitled to submit the names of up to four candidates of known competency and the highest moral reputation, who are disposed to accept the duties of arbitrator. These may be of their own nationality or foreign. In fact, not all nations have four appointees serving at all times.

In the event of a dispute an *ad hoc* arbitral tribunal is constituted from the candidates on the general list, or in certain cases from outside the list. In practice, three different systems have been used: single arbitrators (Asser in the *Island of Palmas* Arbitration, Lardy in the *Timor Island* Arbitration), panels of three and panels of five arbitrators. The differing nations are to agree upon a single arbitrator or, in the case of a panel of three, each to appoint one or, in the case of a panel of five, two arbitrators from the list. These arbitrators proceed by joint effort to appoint their umpire or head arbitrator (this being the third or fifth member of the panel), if need be with the help of one or two other nations, eventually by drawing lots among candidates. Parties then notify the Bureau of their intention to apply to the Court, and submit the names of the arbitrators. The Bureau then makes the requisite arrangements and the Court convenes at a date agreed upon by the parties. When performing duties out of their country, members of the tribunal enjoy diplomatic status.

As can be seen, the role of the Court is in many respects a passive one. The sovereignty of the conflicting parties is respected in every way. Any 'permanency' of the Court is to be found in the list of names – of arbitrators who actually never meet in plenary session. This procedure is, obviously, a very deliberate one and a compromise in itself. It suitably reflects the widely differing views maintained at the Hague conference table. As we have seen, the choice of the British proposal was made on account of its conciliatory qualities in the midst of widely varying views. In fact, during the negotiations within the Committee, the elastic was stretched to breaking point. In retrospect, the major accomplishment of the Commission was perhaps not so much the acceptance of the idea of the Court, which – as we saw – was an achievement in itself, but the realization of a generally accepted, workable instrument. In appreciating this we may call to mind an observation made by the current Judge Fleischhauer of the ICJ with respect to the progress of the law:

> Very careful consideration must be given to the appropriate balance, in a given field, between making substantial progress and achieving wide acceptance. If the latter is to be accomplished, it is necessary to negotiate a consensus at whatever the highest common denominator of agreement may be – which may be very low – but then insist that no deviations from the standard are permissible. Alternatively, if more substantial

The inkpots of the PCA.

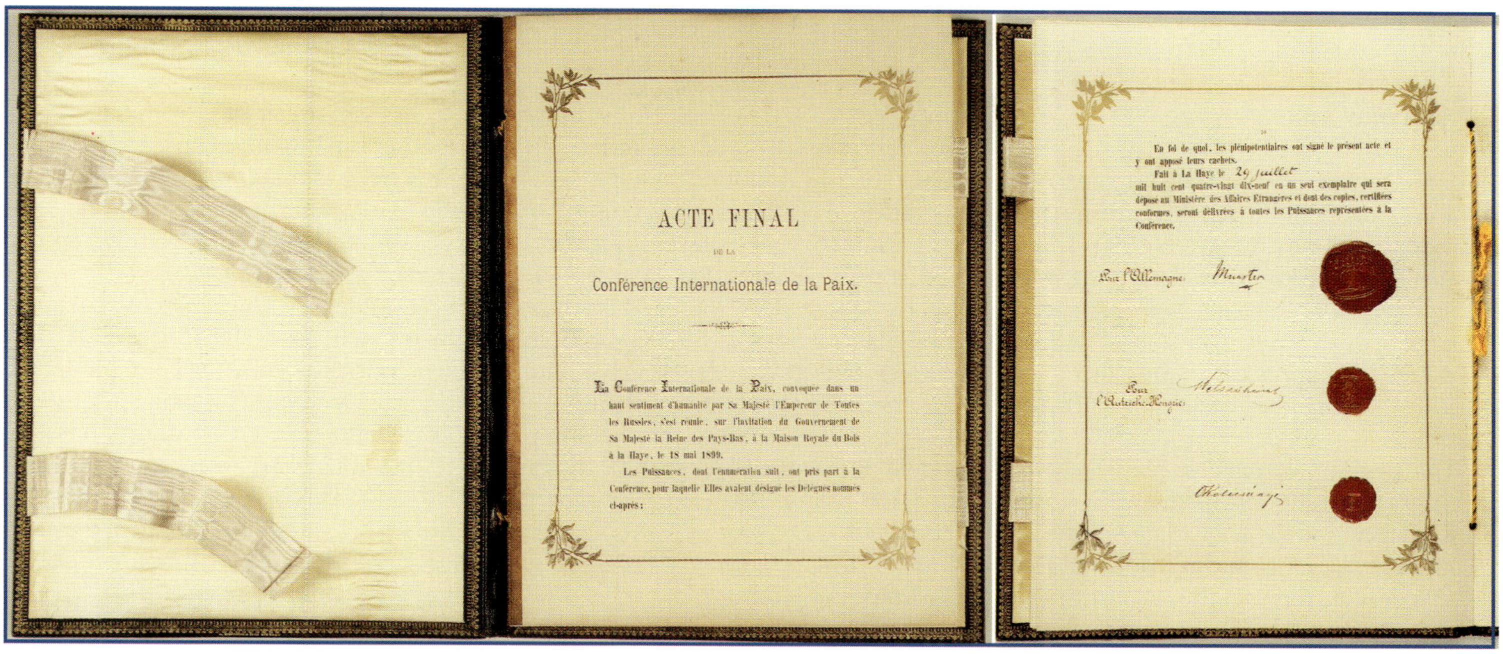

The Final Act of the First Hague Peace Conference signed on 29 July 1899.

> progress is to be achieved and yet wide participation is desired, it may be necessary to permit extensive reservations or the choice between a number of options. Other relevant variables may be the minimum number and importance of the States required for bringing a treaty into force. (*Indian JIL* 1985, at p. 7)

This observation held good to the highest degree for the constitution of the text of the 1899 Convention in relation to the establishment of the Permanent Court. The body to be installed was to be vested with legal authority but with very few plenary powers, far less political influence. The utmost care was to be taken not to deter parties by infringing their autonomy. The very idea of arbitration was adhered to, and preferred to judicial settlement, in view of the nations' fear of surrendering their sovereignty. States not wishing to accept a permanent court, incidentally, preferred to object officially to the idea on what they called practical grounds, arguing that it would make little sense to have the world's top international lawyers picked from all over the globe for six years at a stretch, only to settle a case once in a while.... Eight years later, during the Second Hague Peace Conference of 1907, a United States proposal put forward by its delegate Choate, for the formation of a fixed Court, thus better to establish international jurisprudence, was defeated.

The PCA is competent to settle all arbitration cases between the Contracting Parties, and may under certain conditions even include a non-contracting power. On request, it offers facilities for differences between a State and a private party. The competence of the tribunal created within the framework of the PCA is set out by the parties in their *compromis*, and the procedure to be agreed upon is extremely flexible. In general terms it follows the principles governing international arbitration as reviewed in the previous chapter.

Pursuant to the 1899 and 1907 Conventions, the Bureau is also empowered to function as a registry for Commissions of Inquiry. Thus, Commissions of Inquiry have been set up four times (in 1904, 1912, 1921 and in 1961, concerning the well-

The office of the Secretary-General of the PCA.

THE PERMANENT COURT OF ARBITRATION

Procedure of Arbitration

In the Articles 30–57 of the Hague Convention of 1899, the rules of arbitration are outlined. For the greater part these were taken from current treaties, but they were adapted to the specific needs of the Court. They were amended in 1907, the creation of a summary procedure being the most conspicuous change.

The first act of parties, actually preceding the initiation of the arbitration proceedings, is the submission of the so called Compromis, stating the issue and the competence of the arbitrator(s). Proceedings fall into two parts: written pleadings and oral discussions.

During the first phase, the agents and barristers of parties submit and exchange relevant documents corroborating their case. In the second phase, these are verbally explained and commented upon by the arbitrators. The Court then retires to deliberate and conclude the case by a simple majority of votes.

The verdict on the writ, possibly including the dissenting views of a minority of arbitrators, is then undersigned by president and secretary (previous to 1907 by all arbitrators) and read at a public session to which the agents and lawyers of the parties are summoned. The award is binding on the parties and no appeal is allowed. However, under certain conditions, the parties can reserve in the *compromis* the right to demand revision of the award.

The Administrative Council

In a way, the Council is the chief executive body of the institution. It has mainly an administrative function in supervising the International Bureau, salaries and budgetary matters, and the editing of a yearly report on the activities to the Contracting Powers.

However, in some instances the Council has taken far-reaching decisions, e.g., by extending the jurisdiction of the PCA to State versus non-State disputes in 1935, by authorizing the International Bureau, in 1937, to put its offices and organization at the disposal of Conciliation Commissions, and in 1992, 1993 and 1996 to establish a number of sets of new optional procedural rules for various types of dispute settlement.

The Council is composed of the diplomatic representatives accredited to The Hague of the nations which have adhered to the Hague Conventions of 1899 and 1907, eighty-one at present.

The council is presided over by the Foreign Minister of the Netherlands, the depository State of the Hague Conventions. It is this body which nominates the Secretary-General, being the chief executive, as head of the International Bureau and Registrar to the Court. His term is five years, which can be renewed.

The Members of the Court

The Contracting Powers together also create the Court proper. To this end, each power is entitled to select a maximum of 4 arbitrators. Their names are put on the list, which is drawn up by the Bureau, for a period of 6 years, after which their term can be renewed. Parties may select their arbitrators from this list, or from outside it. On 1 January 1996, the number of arbitrators on the list was 265.

On the founding of the PCIJ, it was provided in the Statute of the League of Nations, that candidate-Judges for this Court were likewise to be elected from the list submitted by the national groups (the maximum 4 arbitrators selected by each Contracting Power) in the PCA. And the same holds good for the ICJ, whose members are likewise chosen by the General Assembly and the Security Council from a list submitted by the national groups in the PCA. The members of the Court can also propose candidates for the Nobel Peace Prize.

The International Bureau

The Bureau is the very premise to the functioning of both Court and Council. According to its regulation, drawn up on 8 December 1900, the Bureau's chief functionary is the Secretary-General. He is assisted by a First Secretary and four other functionaries.

The Bureau is responsible for the day-to-day operations of the institution and serves as registry in proceedings conducted under its auspices.

This double function is reflected in the Bureau's activities, the functioning of which is also basically twofold. First, of course, it is secretarial, looking after the routine matters of daily affairs, handling inquiries and communications. This aspect also covers the preservation of the Court's archives, being the universal storehouse of arbitrage projects and of great value to arbitrators.

Parties are under an obligation to submit copies of any laws proceeding from the Court's awards or of measures subsequently taken to the International Bureau. This lends the Bureau a check mechanism of its own as regards the observance of awards by parties.

Pursuant to an arrangement concluded between the PCA and ICSID the International Bureau from time to time undertakes the organisation of hearing sessions of this institution. The same applies to hearing sessions under the auspices of the Arbitration Court of the International Chamber of Commerce and other arbitral tribunals.

When the Court is in session the Bureau becomes a registry, taking care, through its Secretary-General, of the exchange of documents between parties and agents (such as memoirs, conclusions, claims and counter-memoirs), its functionaries attending sessions, assisting arbitrators, drawing up interlocutory judgments and performing intermediary tasks between the Court and the respective parties.

The vignette of the Permanent Court of Arbitration (1899). The scene in front of the Peace Palace (the ara pacis *and the idea of* pacta sunt servanda*) was taken from a print by B. Picart of 1726. The stamp was never officially used by the Court until 1990.*

known *Red Crusader Incident*), all involving naval incidents. In 1937 the Administrative Council of the PCA authorized the International Bureau to put its offices and organization henceforth at the disposal of Conciliation Commissions. This has taken place on three occasions, in 1937, 1954 and 1955.

History of the Court

The history of the Court can be divided into four main periods. The first covers the years till the amendment of the Statute in 1907 (four cases), the second the period up to the outbreak of the First World War (11 cases); the third spans the inter-war period (eight cases), and the fourth extends over the UN period (four cases). Undeniably, as far as the caseload goes, the second period (1907-1914) was the heyday of the institution. At that juncture, most governments were fully satisfied with the machinery as it was: optional, but morally authoritative. Arbitration had become firmly rooted. Important awards were given in the *Casablanca*, the *North Atlantic Coast Fisheries*, and the *Savarkar* cases.

However, the outbreak of war in 1914 meant the bankruptcy of the political system. Inevitably, it also left its traces on the credibility of the notion of pacific settlement, including the Court. The subsequent wave of optimism led to the establishment of a more reliable and far-reaching security system, pinnacled by the League of Nations. One of the tentacles of this post-war global network soon spread to The Hague, the Permanent Court of International Justice. Ever since, there have been international lawyers who have advocated either the abolition of the Arbitration Court or its retreat to areas of mixed or private, commercial or financial conflicts. The Court went through a gloomy period (1938-1954) during which no appeal was made to it.

All in all, twenty-eight arbitral tribunals have been set up within the framework of the Court. They included technical matters such as claims, indemnities, damaged interests and financial questions; also, land concessions, border disputes and fishery differences. A few had a distinct political impact, such as the *Casablanca* case and the *North Atlantic Coast Fisheries* case, or concerned intricate juridical problems, as in the *Orinoco*, *Savarkar* and *Island of Palmas* cases.

New Directions

In 1959, the Administrative Council of the Court made an appeal to the Contracting Parties to resort to the Court more extensively and instructed its Bureau to examine how best to increase the role of the Court. This call has met with some response and, in recent years, the Bureau itself, too, has taken an active part in seeking to fulfil this objective.

In 1968, the Secretary-General of the PCA concluded a cooperation arrangement with the International Centre for the Settlement of Investment Disputes (ICSID). ICSID arbitral tribunals have held hearings at the seat of the PCA in 1988, 1992, 1993 and 1994. Pursuant to the rules on international commercial arbitration adopted by the United Nations Commission on International Trade Law (UNCITRAL) in 1976, the Secretary-General of the PCA is empowered to designate an 'appointing authority' to break certain deadlocks that may arise in connection with the appointment and challenge of arbitrators.

In line with its auxiliary role as established in the 1899 and 1907 Conventions, the PCA in 1981 placed its offices and staff at the disposal of the Iran-USA Claims Tribunal. The Tribunal was the outcome of

The coat of arms of the PCA.

an agreement reached with the help of the Algerian Government to solve the problems that had arisen from the occupation of the US Embassy in Tehran in 1979. The tribunal later moved into its own buildings in The Hague, but the Courtroom of the PCA is still used as a venue for hearings of the full tribunal.

In 1987, a dispute between Somalia and the UN Development Programme was submitted to the PCA, but proceedings were soon suspended. During 1989-1994 the International Bureau of the PCA acted as the secretariat of a Tribunal dealing with the US/UK Arbitration concerning *Heathrow Airport user charges*. In recent years, and in similar vein, various international commercial arbitration institutions have made use of the facilities of the Court. In 1995, the Bureau became actively engaged in the fulfilment of its international role as registry for several arbitral tribunals.

One of the most promising outcomes perhaps has been the increase, between 1960 and 1995, of the number of Contracting Powers from sixty to eighty-one. Still, in the light of the authority the Hague Conventions have on the customary rules of international law to the present day, this number is surprisingly small. One may guess at the reasons for this situation, as well as why the Court came to be underutilized in recent decades. Is it the notion of arbitration itself which is less attractive to nations; is it the procedure of the PCA; do the qualifications of the arbitrators on the list come into play; should the Court extend its province; should one still distinguish between the public and private spheres?

In recent years, and within the framework of the UN Decade of International Law leading up to the centenary of the creation of the Court, the Bureau has taken several new initiatives to revitalize the role of the Court. In 1991, a Working Group for Improving the Functioning of the Court was established; the following year the Expert Group on the Revision of Some Aspects of the PCA became operational. Since then, two new sets of optional procedural rules have been adopted regarding disputes between two States and cases where only one State is involved. Invariably, procedural flexibility and party autonomy remain the keywords of the policy adopted. In 1996 new sets of procedural rules for International Commissions of Inquiry, for conciliation and for arbitration in which intergovernmental organizations are involved have been submitted to the Administrative Council for approvement.

Again, in September 1993, the first ever Conference of the Members of the PCA took place. It adopted a resolution concerning the establishment of a Financial Assistance Fund for qualified States, and one inviting its Secretary-General to appoint a Steering Committee to consider the possible revision of the 1907 Convention. In view of the UN Decade of International Law and the coming Centenary of the 1899 Convention, the PCA also strengthened its links with the UN. In October 1993, the Court was granted Permanent Observer Status in the General Assembly, while in January 1994, UN Secretary-General, Mr Boutros Boutros-Ghali, paid a visit to the PCA Bureau.

The review of the nature, procedure and early history of the Permanent Court of Arbitration served the purpose of showing the process of gradual evolution towards an international legal order. The summary of recent developments with respect to the PCA, and more particularly its search for revitalization is indicative of the present-day attitude of sovereign States towards the legal process of dispute serttlement, be this through arbitral tribunals or a Standing Court such as the ICJ. In this respect, the analysis of the motives for under-utilization of the PCA as recently attempted by its International Bureau, runs parallel to the efforts made by the ICJ in recent years to improve its grip on international affairs. In this quest, perhaps the most essential issue is to establish whether it is primarily the very idea and the underlying principles of arbitration and adjudication respectively which make nations shrink from more frequently and less hesitantly submitting their conflicts to the Hague institutions, or rather the practical elements of procedure and the like. In other words, are these motives intrinsic or external, essential or circumstantial, and is it for the Courts to adjust their law, or for the nations to change their attitude?

Before attempting to analyse the functioning of the International Court, the tale of its genesis has to be rounded off in a description of the two decades that link the constitution of the PCA to the establishment of the PCIJ.

The Second Hague Peace Conference

The American Initiative

In 1903, the American Peace Society presented a petition for an international peace conference to the Massachusetts Legislature. This body, in turn, passed a resolution requesting the Congress 'to authorize the President of the United States to invite the governments of the world to join in establishing ... a regular international congress to meet at stated periods to deliberate upon the various questions of common interest to the nations and to make recommendations thereon to the governments'. In September 1904 this request was taken up by the Interparliamentary Union gathering at St Louis.

President Theodore Roosevelt showed little reserve to further the cause. On 21 October 1904, his Secretary of State John Hay addressed a circular note to the representatives of the USA accredited to the governments signatory to the acts of the Hague Conference of 1899 in which the plan was defined. The Hague was again suggested as the meeting place, *inter alia* – as it was stated – in view of the 'undying memories which cling around it'. No categorical programme was proposed, but the issues relegated to a future conference in 1899 were to be included. Also, a procedure was suggested to have States absent in 1899 made co-signatories.

The response to the call was favourable. Only Russia made its participation dependent on the cessation of hostilities in the Russo-Japanese war. On 16 December 1904, a second circular invited the nations to propose specific subjects for the conference. Subsequently, the International Bureau of the PCA was requested to work out the agenda.

On 5 September 1905, the Treaty of Portsmouth, New Hampshire, USA, put an end to the conflict in the Far East, due to the mediation of President Roosevelt. Within a week, Russia, through its ambassador in Washington, declared itself prepared not only to attend, but 'to assume the responsibility of summoning a Second Hague Peace Conference'. Roosevelt, with characteristic chivalry, renounced the honour to the Czar, subject to the condition of having all American States invited.

On 12 April 1906, Russia presented an elaborate programme for the Conference, including the following topics: additions and improvements to all 1899 conventions, namely regarding the Court of Arbitration and the international commissions of inquiry; regarding the laws and customs of war; and regarding the adaptation to maritime warfare of the principles of the 1864 Geneva Convention. As well, revision of the 1899 declarations and the framing of a convention relative to the laws and customs of maritime warfare.

However, in the formal invitation, distributed on 4 April 1907, which established the opening date of the Conference at 15 June, reference was made to claims by several nations to raise other issues as well. The Conference was to be held at the Binnenhof, the former residence of the Counts of Holland and currently seat of the Houses of Parliament in the centre of The Hague. Plenary sessions were to be held in the 13th-century Knights Hall (*Ridderzaal*).

Theodore Roosevelt (1858-1919), President of the USA over 1901-1909. In 1906 he won the Nobel Peace Prize for his mediating role in the Russo-Japanese War. He initiated the summoning of the Second Hague Peace Conference.

The Second Conference assembled in the 13th-century Hague Knights Hall.

The Conference

The conference lasted a full four months, from 15 June till 18 October. The number of delegates, too, was more than doubled from 100 to 256. Together, they represented forty-four out of the fifty-seven nations which at the time claimed sovereignty. The present Conference could justly claim the title of 'Confederacy of the World' and 'Parliament of Man' bestowed upon it. Of the nineteen States of the Western Hemisphere, seventeen were represented. However, Africa was no more represented in 1907 than it had been in 1899. Asia was represented by the same four governments that attended in 1899. An embarrassing diplomatic problem was posed by Korea. Invited to the Conference in 1904, it had in the meantime been virtually absorbed by Japan, its Emperor being held captive. Despite all this, a delegation of three, nominated before the crisis, arrived at The Hague, vainly claiming admittance. The Old World was represented by the same twenty governments as in 1899, Norway now operating as an independent nation.

The Conference was divided into four commissions, the first one being the Arbitration Commission. It held ten reunions and was split into a commission on arbitration plans and warfare, attended by 103 members which met 47 times; and a second on maritime prizes, constituted by 89 members and meeting six times. The first task of the Commission was to review the 1899 Convention. In years gone by the Convention and the Court that resulted from it, had been succesfully tested in issues susceptible to judicial settlement, notably the *Dogger Bank* incident. Also, within a decade, over fifty treaties including compromissory clauses had been negotiated. Portugal had concluded ten such treaties, France eight, the USA and Great Britain seven.

If nations were prepared, as Bourgeois argued in his opening address to the Conference, to conclude compulsory arbitration treaties on concrete subjects with specific nations, then why not with all nations on all differences that might arise? In fact, many nations were prepared to sign such a general treaty – showing that by now the idea of arbitration was universally endorsed. Optimism prevailed until, within a few days, it appeared that Bismarck's 'era of blood and iron' was not over yet. The examination *'sans parti pris'* by the stern and austere German delegate Kriege resulted in the rejection of 'literally every proposed subject of arbitration, be it large or trivial' as Brown Scott recalled in gloomy detail. Drago from Argentina, who was sitting next to Scott, handed the American a slip of paper on which was written 'This is the death of arbitration'. And so it was. The idea of compulsory arbitration was buried that very day. For weeks the Conference spoke of the *Elephas Germanicus*, that formidable and prudent animal which, though 'thirsting for a Permanent Court' and 'starving from sheer

Left: John Bassett Moore (1860-1947), probably America's foremost international legal scholar of the inter-war period. Moore distinguished himself in national and international public service and was through his publications instrumental in the codification of international law. He was Assistant Secretary of State (1898-1899), a member of the PCA (1912-1938) and Judge of the PCIJ (1921-1928).

Right: James Brown Scott (1866-1943), Secretary-General of the Carnegie Foundation for International Peace, Member and President of the Institut de Droit International, President of the American Society of International Law and first editor of the American Journal of International Law.

lack of obligatory arbitration' – as was sneered -, could not be induced to cross the bridge to peace so fitly built for it by the Conference.

Undeterred, the First Commission brought up two other issues in the sphere of dispute settlement. The first one, initiated by the American delegation, concerned the institution, at The Hague, of a *Permanent Court of Arbitral Justice*. This would consist of a team of expert, salaried judges who would be permanently at the disposal of nations willing to present controversies of any kind. Both Germany and Great Britain favoured the proposal, which was adopted by the Conference and embodied in thirty-five articles. These, however, only proposed the establishment of the Court as such; no agreement was reached in regards to its composition. At that time, it was thought that this obstacle would be overrun in due course, to all appearances well before the Third Conference would meet....

A similar issue was the establishment of an International Prize Court. Both Germany and Great Britain had made proposals to this effect, although these differed widely. Britain opted for a permanent court composed of judges representing the major merchant marines. Germany sought a court which was only to be constituted upon the outbreak of war and would include among its five members a representative of the belligerent nations and three judges selected from the permanent court. It was the American representative, Choate, who managed to reconcile the parties. The outcome was a Permanent Court of Arbitral Justice in which the great maritime powers were to be permanently represented and the minor ones proportionally. However, 'the wits had their jest here too', as the keen observer from the State Department, James Brown Scott, did not fail to notice. Whereas the Court of Arbitral Justice agreed upon lacked judges, the Prize Court was a court without law. However, the British Government took it upon itself to summon the leading maritime nations to London for a conference to codify maritime law and custom some time in 1908.

The Convention regarding the Prize Court remained unratified, whereas the draft concerning the Judicial Arbitration Court never passed beyond the stage of a recommendation. Still, at the time it was felt by most participants that with the amendment of the 1899 convention, the unanimous recognition of the principle of obligatory arbitration and the foundation laid for no fewer than two courts of justice, the First Commission had made an essential contribution to the progress of world order.

The Outcome

Like its predecessor, the second Conference was hailed as a success and condemned as an utter failure. The small margins of progress only confirmed the

STATEMENTS BY ELIHU ROOT (1845-1937). Secretary of War, Secretary of State, Senator, and Nobel Peace Prize laureate (1912). A politician rather than a philosopher, Root commanded widespread respect among scholars, peace leaders and philanthropists, also witness his Presidency of the ILA and the Carnegie Endowment. He was a member of boundary tribunals, of the PCA (1910-1937) and of the 1920 and 1929 advisory Committees on the PCIJ.

On the 1907 Peace Conference

If you set up one idea, no matter how good it is, and make it paramount over all other, it leads to destruction. Did you ever see a man carrying an armful of oranges and drop one? He reaches to pick that one up and then another drops, and so on until he has lost them all. The important thing is to get something that will hold two oranges and then improve it until it will carry three, and then, on the basis of your experience, improve it still further until it will carry four and then five. That is the way you get on with oranges. (From Philip C. Jessup, *Elihu Root*, 1938, Vol. 2, at p. 70)

Not only the conventions signed and ratified, but the steps taken toward conclusions which may not reach practical and effective form for many years to come, are of value. Some of the resolutions ... do not seem to amount to very much by themselves, but each one marks on some line of progress the farthest point to which the world is yet willing to go. They are like cable ends buoyed in mid-ocean, to be picked up hereafter by some other steamer, spliced, and continued to shore.... Each necessary step in the process is as useful as the final act which crowns the work and is received with public celebration. (*Ibid.*, Vol. 2, at p. 75)

It is important to remember that the object of the conference is agreement, and not compulsion. If such conferences are to be made occasions for trying to force nations into positions which they consider against their interest, the powers can not be expected to send representatives to them.... Comparison of views and frank and considerate explanation and discussion may frequently resolve doubts, obviate difficulties, and lead to real agreement upon matters which at the outset have appeared insurmountable. It is not wise, however, to carry this process to the point of irritation. After reasonable discussion, if no agreement is reached, it is better to lay the subject aside, or refer it to some future conference in the hope that intermediate consideration may dispose of the objections. (*Ibid.*, Vol. 2, at p. 82)

On Arbitration and Adjudication

The method in which arbitration can be made more effective, so that nations may be more ready to have recourse to it voluntarily and to enter into treaties by which they bind themselves to submit to it, is indicated by observation of the weakness of the system now apparent. There can be no doubt that the principal objection to arbitration rests not upon the unwillingness of nations to submit their controversies to impartial arbitration, but upon an apprehension that the arbitrations to which they submit may not be impartial.

It has been a very general practice for arbitrators to act, not as judges deciding questions of fact and law upon the record before them under a sense of judicial responsibility, but as negotiators effecting settlements of the question brought before them in accordance with the traditions and usages and subject to all the considerations and influences which affect diplomatic agents. The two methods are radically different, proceed upon different standards of honorable obligation, and frequently lead to widely differing results.

It very frequently happens that a nation which would be very willing to submit its differences to an impartial judicial determination is unwilling to subject them to this kind of diplomatic process. If there could be a tribunal which would pass upon questions between nations with the same impartial and impersonal judgment that the Supreme Court of the United States gives to questions arising between citizens of the different States, or between foreign citizens and the citizens of the United States, there can be no doubt that nations would be much more ready to submit their controversies to its decision than they are now to take the chances of arbitration.

It should be your effort to bring about in the Second Conference a development of The Hague Tribunal into a permanent tribunal composed of judges who are judicial officers and nothing else, who are paid adequate salaries, who have no other occupation, and who will devote their entire time to the trial and decision of international causes by judicial methods and under a sense of judicial responsibility.... (*Ibid.*, Vol. 2, at p. 75-76) impression gained from 1899 that no miracles should be expected. Still, as Brown Scott remarked during one of the meetings: 'We must not reject the minimum solely because it is not the maximum of our desires' and 'experience shows that the voeux of one Conference are the conventions of its successor'.

The Dutchman Tobias Asser, one of the more prominent members of both conferences, was realistic in these respects. While highly critical as to its results, he was fully satisfied with the critical urgency of this and subsequent conferences, if only for the advancement of mutual understanding by personal contacts. Mr Elihu Root, the American Secretary of State, while not necessarily less realistic, was less critical as he concluded:

> The work of the Second Hague Conference, presents the greatest advance ever made at any single time towards the reasonable and peaceful regulation of international conduct, unless it be the advance made at the Hague Conference of 1899. ... The achievements of the Conferences justify the belief that the world has entered upon an orderly process through which, step by step, in successive Conferences, each taking the work of its predecessor as its point of departure, there may be continual progress toward making the practice of civilized nations conform to their peaceful professions. ... The question about each international Conference is not merely what it has accomplished, but also what it has begun and what it has moved forward.

It will now be reviewed in which way the two ideas for the Constitution of Courts that were launched during the 1907 Conference were fostered in subsequent years and influenced contemporary developments.

Nº. 69. MARDI 3 SEPTEMBRE 1907

Courrier de la Conférence

DE LA PAIX

Rédigé par WILLIAM T. STEAD

Prix d'abonnement par semaine:
pour la Hollande fl. 0.65
" l'Etranger fl. 0.75
Prix du numéro:
fl. 0.15.

Collaborateurs:
Mme la Baronne BERTHA VON SUTTNER,
M. ALFRED H. FRIED,
M. FRÉD. PASSY,
M. FELIX MOSCHELES.

Directeurs-Editeurs: MAAS & VAN SUCHTELEN

BUREAUX: Princessegracht 6A, La Haye. — Téléphone No. 287. — Adr. Télégr. MAASSUCHTELEN.

La délégation de Russie.

Assis: 1. M. le Comte Prozor, 2. M. de Martens, 3. M. de Nelidoff, 4. M. Tcharikoff, 5. Major-Général Yermoloff.
Debout: 1. Col. Ovtchinikoff, 2. M. le Baron Nolde, 3. M. le Comte Schouvalow, 4. M. Basili, 5. M. Michelson, 6. M. le Capt. Behr, 7. M. le Capt. Wonlarlarsky, 8. M. Mandelstamm, 9. M. Melikoff, 10. M. Mouravieff.

AVIS.

Au Cercle International du Princessegracht, 6A, où se trouveront le Prince

sera: „Le système politique de la Corée à l'avenir."

Le Prince Yi se déclare fort satisfait des résultats de sa visite aux Etats-Unis.

pourront donner lieu en aucun cas à l'agression militaire ni à l'occupation matérielle du sol des nations américaines. Nous faisons cette réserve d'accord avec

un autre Etat pour infraction de contrats, seront soumis à la Cour Permanente d'Arbitrage de La Haye quand les Parties elles-mêmes n'auraient pas stipulé dans

The Russian delegation at the 1907 Conference. A page from William Stead's Courrier de la Conférence.

Towards a 'World Court'

The Central American Court of Justice

On 14 November 1907, only a few weeks after the adjournment of the Hague Peace Conference and its discussion of the project for the creation of a Permanent Court of Arbitral Justice, the five Central American Nations which, under Spanish control, had formed the Captaincy-General of Guatemala, assembled in Washington for a Central American Peace Conference. On that occasion, the delegation of El Salvador, freshly back from The Hague, presented to the Conference a plan for an arbitral court of justice for Central America.

The plan was yet another in a long tradition of attempts to establish an enduring Central American unity. In our chapter on regional developments in international law, this tradition is discussed at greater length. Suffice it to recall to mind that ever since their independence from Spain, in 1821, the five Central American States had been seeking unity and solidarity. In spite of frequent friction, this persistent tradition had led to attempts at some form of federation. In 1823, the Republic of the United Provinces of Central America was formed, but foundered within a few years. Repeated attempts at reunion were made throughout the 19th century. All were abortive, as unanimity proved hard to attain. Also, at the time, communications in the area were still difficult and distances were considerable; in fact, no practical imperative for unity was felt to support the idea.

The creation of a judicial agency to handle dispute resolution was a persistent strain among the forms of cooperation considered. In 1902, in Corinto, Costa Rica, Honduras, Nicaragua and El Salvador signed a treaty providing for obligatory arbitration and the constitution of a permanent tribunal of arbitration. This tribunal was meant to deal, in particular, with the various boundary problems. Each State was to nominate an arbitrator and an alternate to serve for a one-year term. The Tribunal was installed in San José in October 1902.

However, the system provided for was rather artificial. In early 1907, the Tribunal failed to solve difficulties which had arisen between Honduras and Nicaragua, at which point the President of Honduras declared the Corinto Treaty null and void. These problems led the USA and Mexico – whose Presidents had the year before intermediated to resolve very similar problems which had arisen between Guatemala and El Salvador – to propose the aforementioned 1907 peace conference. At that conference, the proposal to revive the union gave rise to sharp divisions. Still, on 20 December 1907, a general treaty of peace and amity was signed, including a convention establishing the Central American Court of Justice.

Except for the actual conception, in constituting the Court only few ideas were taken from the Hague Arbitral Court project. The Central American Court, which was to represent the 'national conscience of Central America', consisted of five justices (*magistrados*) who were appointed for five years, one by each Republic. Its seat was in Cartago, Costa Rica. At its inaugural session the proud announcement was made of a substantial gift by the American Andrew Carnegie, to provide for a permanent home for the Court – a striking parallel to what occurred in The Hague during the same period.

The Court was ill-starred. Even before its opening, the newly erected Court House was destroyed by an earthquake. The seat of the Court was transferred to San José and Andrew Carnegie made a second gift for a new Court House, which was completed late in 1917. However, in March 1918 the Court ceased to exist. The Treaty of 1907 had provided that the Court should continue to function for a period of ten years, which was to be extended unless timely notice of the desire to terminate the Treaty was given by signatories. In March 1917, Nicaragua effectively gave notice of its intention to terminate the Convention. It ceased to be in force by April 1918, after gallant attempts to revive the idea had failed.

In fact, the Court was doomed from the outset. The first obstacle to its success was the method of election and the lack of independence (including in terms of salaries) of what were in fact 'national' justices, Secondly, the Court's jurisdiction was too broad; *inter alia*, it allowed individuals to bring lawsuits against governments. As Hudson observes (*Permanent Court*, at p. 70), contemporary opinion in Central America regarded the Court not just as a judicial institution, but also as a political agency for conciliation and mediation and for the maintenance of peace. Indeed, it was soon involved in politics; in 1917, it was accused by Nicaragua of having 'degenerated ... into a center of lively intrigues'. Thirdly, the Court never developed a satisfactory procedure.

Consequently, the Court never exercised any great influence. Of the ten cases it handled, five involved individuals and were all declared inadmissible. Of the five cases between States, three were instituted on the Court's own initiative and were of no jurisprudential importance. The other two 'presented problems of a legal nature which might have given tests of its usefulness except for the fact that in both the ambitions of an overshadowing outside State deprived the action of the Court of reality' (Hudson).

Nonetheless, it was the first international court in modern history to be endowed with continuing functions; in this respect, it represented a tradition of solidarity in Central America which at the time was unique in the world. Towards the end, around 1917, the justices themselves, from their accumulated experience, made sound suggestions for reform, which might have prompted a fresh start. Unfortunately, political unrest, both worldwide and in the regional sphere, prevented the extension of this fascinating experiment. Still, the lessons learned from San José were taken into consideration shortly afterwards in The Hague.

The Proposed International Prize Court

The 1907 Hague Convention for an International Prize Court never came into force. Even so, it was the first international agreement intended to create a permanent international tribunal of the kind. To be sure, the idea of prize courts in itself was not new. From their early beginnings, States had set up national prize courts to adjudicate the legality of the capture of ships and goods by navies or commissioned privateers. However, in those courts national rules, obviously, prevailed.

In the 1856 Paris Declaration on neutrals, prevailing 18th century concepts were revived. One of the first comprehensive studies undertaken by the *Institut de Droit International* immediately after its foundation in 1873 concerned precisely this issue (1875). In 1887, the *Institut*, in its *Règlement international des prises maritimes*, envisaged the creation of an international tribunal for prize appeals by each belligerent at the very opening of hostilities; however, this plan was never acted upon by the States.

The concept gained new impetus with the rising interest in arbitration between States. The proposals submitted by the British and German delegations at the 1907 Hague Peace Conference were reflected in Convention XII of the Conference. This Convention was meant to remain in force for twelve years, then to be tacitly renewed for six years at a time, unless denounced. It was eventually signed by thirty-three nations and 30 June 1909 was set as the date for the deposit of ratifications, that is, if the States could furnish the Court with nine

The nations adhering to the 1899 and 1907 Hague Conventions have their chairs in the Japanese Room (being the venue of the Administrative Council of the PCA) embellished with their coats of arms. These are the coats of arms of Guatemala (left) and Colombia (right).

judges and nine deputy-judges. This condition, however, was never met; accordingly, the deposit never took place.

The most interesting aspect for our purposes is that – as with the Central American Court – the Convention for the Prize Court reviewed some fundamental problems concerning the constitution of international courts. The permanent institution it envisaged and its obligatory competence would have made this Court a true international judicial tribunal, as distinct from a mere arbitral forum. It anticipated a Bench of fifteen Judges, seven to be appointed by the governments of the leading maritime nations of the world, six others through a scheme of rotation within six groups. The term of office of Judges was to be six years.

The scheme also provided for national Judges *ad hoc*, to replace sitting Judges when a party to a case happened at the time not to be represented on the Bench. This concept was new at the time; it was adopted later on in the Statute of the PCIJ, albeit in a modified form. The Court was equally meant to serve as a Court of Appeal against decisions of national courts. Also, the Convention opened the way for claims by individuals, which went against prevailing doctrine of the day. Again, the Convention gave the Court a creative law-making role. In the absence of a legal foundation for its judgments in international rules, it was to follow the principles of justice and equity. At the time, this idea met with lively criticism.

Accordingly, in February 1908, the British Government suggested a conference to agree upon the generally recognized principles of international law within the field of maritime economic warfare which the proposed Court was to observe. During December 1908-February 1909, a number of States attended this London Naval Conference and drew up the so-called London Declaration. From the outset, the Declaration met with strong opposition, notably by Great Britain and the USA. To quench opposition, an additional protocol was drafted in September 1910; still, ratifications were never deposited. This effectively sealed the fate of the Prize Court. The idea has never been revived. Nonetheless, the obstacles it faced – for instance regarding the appointment of Judges and Deputy-Judges – helped to crystallize the concept of an International Bench.

The Proposed Court of Arbitral Justice

In spite of all the controversy during the 1907 Conference over so many issues, numerous still were the delegations at The Hague who voiced their conviction that the triumph of the 1899 Conference, the Permanent Court of Arbitration, for all its merits, was inadequate as a judicial institution. The Russian and American delegations launched projects aimed at converting the PCA into a truly permanent body. To some, this was still unacceptable; to others, it did not go far enough. Their criticism of the process of arbitration was that it was difficult, time-consuming and expensive.

More valid was their criticism that the tribunal afforded no basis for the cumulation of a body of jurisprudence. It was precisely for these reasons that the nations deemed the creation of a more permanent agency with truly judicial characteristics a next, imperative step in the establishment of an international legal order. Their wish found expression in the following recommendation which was adopted by the Conference almost unanimously:

> The Conference recommends to the signatory Powers the adoption of the annexed draft convention for the creation of a Court of Arbitral Justice and the bringing it into force as soon as an agreement has been reached respecting the selection of the judges and the constitution of the Court.

The draft convention (*projet d'une convention*) which was annexed to this *vœu* in the Final Act of the 1907 Conference called for the creation of a court 'of free and easy access, composed of judges representing the various judicial systems of the world'. The new court was to sit in The Hague, as an extension of the PCA. It was to meet at least annually and be administered by the International Bureau of the PCA. It was to have competence to deal with all cases submitted to it, in virtue of either a general treaty or a special agreement. Only contracting States were to be allowed access to the Court. No specific directions were given in regard to which law the Court should apply. The Convention was to be concluded for a period of twelve years, with a provision for automatic renewal subject to denunciation.

However, the major obstacle at the Conference had proven to be not so much the idea of the creation of the Court itself but rather how to find an acceptable method by which the judges should be elected. A more detailed review of this thorny problem is given in the chapter on the election of Judges of the ICJ (Chapter 7). Suffice it to say that the 1907 draft was silent on this point, although numerous proposals were elaborated at the time, including possibilities of direct or indirect appointment or election, and systems of rotation.

Thus, a Bulgarian proposal called for the appointment of a competent person by each State. The Brazilian delegation agreed to this but preferred a division of judges into three groups, which were to sit in rotation. American, British and German schemes proceeded upon the basis of population and allowed certain States permanent representation, while others would follow a system of rotation. The concept of judges *ad hoc* was brought up again, too. Efforts to arrive at an immediate agreement were abandoned after a last-ditch American attempt had failed to drum up adequate support. This was a proposal for an open election of fifteen judges, with one nomination by each State and a vote by correspondence conducted by the PCA Bureau.

The first initiative to resolve the deadlock was again taken by the US Government during the 1909 London Naval Conference. Its proposal was to insert in the Convention a stipulation that the Prize Court should also be competent to deal with arbitral cases submitted to it. In such cases the Court would follow the provisions of the 1907 draft convention. The Conference, however, pronounced itself incompetent to deal with the proposal.

Later that year the USA repeated its proposal in a circular letter. However, at the time the procedure suggested was clearly deemed unsatisfactory, as various replies reveal. The German, French and British governments suggested holding a conference to deal with the problem. During informal negotiations in Paris in March 1910, a draft convention was formulated, which was revised in July in The Hague. It envisaged the selection of a judge by each party to the Convention and included a system of rotation. However, being linked to the plan for the Prize Court, the project foundered upon the failure to create the latter Court.

Nonetheless, all these protracted efforts did have their impact on world opinion. By 1914 there was a general conviction that a new judicial institution of this kind was really needed. Also, the contours of this Court and its general lines of procedure were gradually taking shape. It was left to the Third Hague Peace Conference, scheduled for 1915, to iron out the controversies regarding particulars and finalize the Convention. This was not to be.

One other interesting event during the 1907 Hague Peace Conference should be called back to memory. It occurred in the afternoon of 30 July 1907. In the presence of delegates and other dignitaries, the first stone of the Peace Palace was laid. The festive ceremony inspired a resolution proposed by Baron d'Estournelles that each Government represented should contribute to the erection of the 'temple and symbol of peace'. The Contracting Powers were to send materials of construction and ornamentation representing the purest example of their national production, so that the Palace, an expression of universal good will and hope, might be built of the very substance of all peoples. How this Palace of Peace, the present home of the International Court of Justice, came into being will be described in the next paragraph.

The Peace Palace at The Hague

In the year 1900, Andrew Carnegie, one of the most fascinating figures of his day and the archetype of the business tycoon of the

The laying of the first stone by Count de Nelidow. With a silver hammer the Russian First Delegate thrice tapped the founding stone in the names of Czar Nicholas II, Queen Wilhelmina and the Conference, thus inaugurating as he called it the construction of the perfect counterpart of Rome's Temple of Janus, whose belfry would stand out as another Alexandrian Pharos, guiding the nations towards justice.

Andrew Carnegie (1835-1919), portrayed by B. J. Blommers in 1913.

period, retired from affairs – promptly to pass on to what he deemed the natural second phase of his life. His *Carnegie Steel Company* having reached a record annual profit of about 40 million dollars and with prospects even more dazzling, Carnegie decided 'to stop accumulating and begin the infinitely more serious and difficult task of wise distribution', as he put it in his *Carnegie's Gospel of Wealth*, the epoch-making book that appeared that very year. The *Company* and its holdings were sold to Pierpoint Morgan for 480 million dollars – leaving Carnegie presumably the richest man on earth. He left for Europe to ponder on what became known as 'Mr Carnegie's Conundrum', how best to discharge the stewardship of his wealth.

Andrew Carnegie, the emigrant son of a humble Scotch weaver's family from Dunfermline, was a man of his time in seizing the vast opportunities the new land offered. He amassed his huge fortune through the construction of railroads and the development of oil, iron and steel industries. It must be said that he applied the same shrewdness, cunning and common sense in the distribution of his 'surplus wealth' that he had displayed in the process of accumulating it. His gifts could hardly be characterized as pure charity, and he never donated unconditionally. 'There is nothing that robs a righteous cause of its strength more than a millionaire's money', he once observed. He was careful in examining the ultimate implications of his involvements, making ample inquiries in advance. However, once satisfied of the importance of a goal, he allotted his money very generously, making sure of the proper administration of the capital.

Carnegie's gifts came mainly under three headings: education, welfare and peace. Being a self-made man of vast, though perhaps not too profound learning, the author of several books (among them a monograph of merit on James Watt), he considered a free library the best gift imaginable to any community. In all, he established some 3,500 public libraries, always provided the community would accept the maintenance of the building and the upkeep of the collection. 'I do not give, I make others give', he frequently stated.

His projects, on a global scale, extended to art galleries, museums, music-halls (the Carnegie Hall in New York), swimming-baths and, notably, 7,600 organs to churches and public halls all over the world. A second category was science and research 'to be applied to the improvement of mankind' and including the foundation of minor colleges and special chairs. In this sphere, Carnegie-Mellon University, the Carnegie Endowment in Washington and the Carnegie Trust Funds for the Universities of Scotland are probably the best known projects of his.

Gradually, a shift of interest became noticeable towards the field of the international peace movement. To be sure, Carnegie had shown himself an opponent of war at an early stage. He fiercely opposed the growing imperialism in the USA and particularly the acquisition of the Philippines. At one stage owning eighteen British newspapers, he made them all cry out his fairly radical views – on home rule for instance.

Being on friendly terms with writers like Mark Twain and Matthew Arnold, he was positively influenced by his contacts with Herbert Spencer and Darwinism. Also, he counted leading English politicians like Gladstone, Chamberlain and Lord Rosebery among his correspondents. Again, through his intimate friend Elihu Root, he had access to the inner circles in Washington and got to know Cleveland, Hay, McKinley, Roosevelt and Wilson personally. Several of these men featured on the boards or as trustees of his Foundations and Trusts. It was through these contacts that his one and only political appointment ever came about. In 1891 he was among the American delegates to the Second Pan-American Congress.

Between 1904 and 1919 Carnegie donated over 25 million dollars to the promotion of peace, although he long withstood the pressure from activists such as William Stead to actively join the peace movement. Once convinced, his pacifism had a very personal stamp which did not always endear him to everyone: 'Peace at any Price', it has been described cynically. Still, he dedicated himself and his fortune unconditionally to this cause.

Not all his projects were successful. A curious move was his founding of The Simplified Spelling Board. It emerged from his conviction that unification of the nations would emerge quite naturally from the undoing of the 'babel of tongues'. Theodore Roosevelt joined the advisory council of the Board and indeed ordered the adoption of the new spelling in all White House documents. But Swinburne called it a monstrous absurdity, Mark Twain spoke of a capital crime, Carnegie's own British Trusts refused to adopt it and cynics heaped ridicule on the idea. The movement soon lost impetus and, at last, Carnegie withdrew disillusioned. A very similar project was the Church Peace Union, founded in 1914. It rallied men of all religions, aiming to bring their ethical influence to bear on the political and economic decision-making process.

His most significant endowment was the Carnegie Endowment for International Peace, founded in 1910. Its Deed expressed its aim 'to hasten the abolition of war, the foulest blot upon our civilization'. It was ex-Secretary of State Elihu Root who persuaded Carnegie, reluctant at first, to have the Trust established; Root himself accepted the responsibility of becoming its first President. Remarkably, during the First World War, the Endowment took a firm stand against German oppression. It opted in favour of the American war policy, stating in November 1917 that Germany's blind reliance on military power must be broken 'before any other effective steps can be taken to secure international peace'. It published a monumental 155 volume *Economic and Social History of the War*. In later years, the *Endowment* was instrumental in fashioning the 1928 Kellogg-Briand Pact.

Of major concern in this context are Carnegie's three Temples of Peace. The first was the Pan-American Union Building, advocated by Theodore Roosevelt and completed in 1907. It was to function as the international home for the union of all the republics of the hemisphere. The second one, inspired – like the first one – by Elihu Root, was the ill-fated Court House of the Central American Court of Justice in Cartago, Costa Rica, the gift which resulted from the 1907 Central American Peace Conference in Washington. As will be recalled, it was destroyed by an earthquake shortly after its completion, rebuilt in San José – to be closed soon after its completion due to the failure of the Court project. The third Temple, and Carnegie's favourite, was the Hague Peace Palace.

In the summer of 1899 William T. Stead, the energetic British journalist and pacifist, paid a visit to *Skibo Castle*, the princely summer residence of Carnegie in the Scottish Highlands, to discuss 'Carnegie's Conundrum', the problem which Carnegie had put to the public at large as to how best to spend his money in the interest of

The prize contest among architects from all over the world was won by Louis Cordonnier of Lille. His prize-winning design featured inter alia two belfries at the front, two library turrets at the back and baroque ornamentation throughout. These were cut down to the final design shown in this watercolour.

1913: THE OPENING CEREMONY

The summer months of 1913 were heydays of social life in Holland. The opening of the Peace Palace coincided with the first centenary of Dutch liberation from French rule in Napoleonic times. The year 1813 had marked the restoration of independence, the return of the House of Orange and the drawing up of the constitution. Accordingly, in August-September 1913, The Hague was literally inundated with ceremonies. Historical pageants crowded the squares, sparkling fireworks were let off every night, and people feasted their eyes upon dignitaries in ceremonial dress being driven in coaches and pairs to splendid balls and receptions. The opening of the palace was to take place on 28 August, the new cabinet was to be installed on 29 August, and 31 August was the Queen's birthday – that year being the fifteenth of her reign. Together these events gave rise to perfectly justified exultancy.

The impression of the mondain capital was heightened too by the presence of hundreds of celebrities attending one of the many conferences that were held at The Hague during those weeks, precisely because of the imminent opening on 28 August. From 18 to 23 August some 500 pacifists from all over the world, headed by De Louter and Lafontaine, attended the XXe Congrès Universel de La Paix held in the Ridderzaal by the Dutch society *Vrede door Recht* and the Roman Catholic peace movement, while on 5 September the Interparliamentary Union planned to convene here for its eighteenth conference.

These conferences, in their turn, had evoked other events. Thus, for one, Dutch suffragettes had arranged exhibits on the status of women through the ages. All in all, it looked very much as if the whole Universe of pacifism had gravitated to The Hague – indeed the atmosphere around the Binnenhof and the Hofvijver was that of a joyful world reunion. The very presence of Bertha von Suttner, Alfred Fried, Bourgeois, Constant d'Estournelles, Renault, and so many veterans of the Second Hague Conference recalled the summer of 1907. This idea was also strengthened by the programme of the current peace congress, which featured high on its agenda the drawing up of issues for the Third Hague Peace Conference. This conference was projected for somewhere in 1915.... Little did one know at the time that history was to play tricks on man once more.

Carnegie leaving the grounds after the opening of the Palace.

But even so, amid all the cheers there was cause for sadness too: if only in the personal sphere. The reunion could not hide the absence of the many combatants for peace that had died in the past years. De Martens, Asser, and then William Stead, one of the many who (one and a half years previously, how time did fly!) had expectantly stepped aboard the *Titanic*. 'Expectantly' was the word indeed, for had not this medium himself prophesied his drowning?

On 27 August, Dutch science paid homage to three men who, by their work for international organization, had made the world their debtor: Fried, Renault and Elihu Root were granted the honorary doctor's degree by Leiden University through Professor van Eysinga. The following day then, finally, the world of politics, learning and pacifism crowded together within the Palace walls.

The two-minute 70 mm movie that recorded the opening, shows Carnegie and his wife upon entering the Palace: a grey, small figure, but cheerful and resolute, and proudly wearing the decoration of the Grand Cross of Orange-Nassau. Inside, the couple was heartily welcomed by cheers from the four hundred guests, who from half past one had rapidly filled the Great Court Room, which that day seemed great in name only. It was a splendid sight! The silk, satin and lace, and the ostrich feathers, towering coiffures and jewelry of the ladies *en grande toilette* rivalled the sparkling uniforms of military men and colourful dress of foreign diplomats. Scholars and politicians, among whom were the members of the two cabinets in cheerful conversation, looked definitely sober in their ceremonial dress. The sun beamed through the four stained glass windows, reflecting a myriad of colours on the light oak panelling. Six brass and crystal crowns of light illuminated the polychromic ceilings. Then, at half past two sharp, and announced by the national anthem, in came the royalty.

The ceremony itself was succinct and mainly symbolic. It consisted of Van Karnebeek's handling over of the key to the palace gates to the president of the *Conseil Administratif* of the PCA, the Dutch Minister of Foreign Affairs van Swinderen. This ceremony was placed in a setting of speeches and musical interlude. The choir opened with Palestrina and Valerius; then van Karnebeek rose. In his address, which was as witty and polished as ever, the aged President of the Carnegie Foundation expanded on the Court of Arbitration, discussed its successes and handicaps and reminded the audience of the call for obligatory measures, an armed coercive force, and permanent and special tribunals. He switched from French to English in order to address some personal words to Carnegie, which evoked warm applause, paid homage to the architects and proudly mankind. In subsequent months, Stead interviewed men of prominence to assist him in collecting sound ideas to serve Carnegie who for that matter received an average of some three hundred suggestions a day. It was the Russian Counsellor of State and prominent delegate at the 1899 Hague Conference, Frederic de Martens, who first proposed having Carnegie create a fund for the building of adequate headquarters for the recently established Hague Court of Arbitration.

In June 1900, to promote his idea, De Martens himself arranged a meeting in Berlin with Andrew D. White, the former head of the American Delegation at The Hague and currently US Ambassador in Germany. White was one of Carnegie's 'old shoes', as Carnegie once put it. The two of them had toured the world in 1878, visiting China and India and travelling together from Singapore to Lapland. In response to the request by De Martens, White promptly wrote to Carnegie. Within a week, on 23 June, he received a formal reply, inviting him to spend some days in the Highlands. White was in no position to leave Germany that year and invited Carnegie to Berlin instead. Carnegie declined, and due to all sorts of complications of a personal nature the contact was never made. However, in August 1901, a mutual acquaintance signed the *Skibo Castle* visitors book, Frederic W. Holls. Admittedly, Holls interest was first awakened through White. Still, there was more to it

listed the many gifts from foreign nations the Foundation had already received. His last words had a ring of prophesy as he said: 'This Palace will be a Temple of Peace, in which, even if waves of war arise on the horizon, better sentiments can find a resort in order to resume their flight after the gale like the doves of Noah's Ark'.

On behalf of the Permanent Court of Arbitration, van Swinderen in his response paid compliments to van Karnebeek and likewise had some words for the grey Scot: 'By the cooperation of the world powers, your initiative has got the sanction which you deemed necessary.... That is the check, Mr Carnegie, which I beg you to accept from my hands, that means through my words, from the entire complex of Europe, Asia and America here represented at Her Majesty's Court. It's a draft on the future, but I trust you will consider the drawer good for it.' In his autobiography Carnegie would call his 'Temple of Peace ... the most holy building in the world ... because it has the holiest end in view. I do not even except St Peter's, or any building erected to the glory of God, whom, as Luther says, 'we cannot serve or aid; He needs no help from us....' The highest worship to God is service to man. At least I feel so with Luther and Franklin.'

After the ceremony the Board's secretary, Mr Patijn, led the audience on a guided tour of the premises. Royalty and diplomats in a cavalcade visited the Japanese and Bol rooms, the gardens and rosarium. In the evening, the

special guests and the *Corps diplomatique* were entertained by the Dutch Government at a gala dinner in the Ridderzaal and were received by the Queen at the Royal Palace.

On the following day Andrew Carnegie came over to the Palace once more to unveil a bust of William Randal Cremer, presented to the Carnegie Board by the International Arbitration League, of which Cremer had been the founding father as far back as 1870. On that occasion Carnegie and Lord Weardale, Chairman of the Interparliamentary Union expounded on the merits of the British pacifist who, in 1888 and along with Frédéric Passey, also had taken the initiative towards the establishment of Weardale's Union. Afterwards a garden party was held in honour of the 18th Interparliamentary Conference. The fair weather allowed the guests, among whom was the landscape architect Mawson in person, to have a closer look at the gardens. These were, of course, still *in statu nascendi*, but the box-wood hedges made the groundplan plain to the eye. With its pond down in the centre and its rosariums near the terrace, the garden layout was in the natural English style. If anything, the overall impression was one of quiet stateliness. Whatever the years might add to its splendour, it was thought that the time-honoured oaks and beeches on the slopes in the background made a perfect setting for the Palace.

than this. On 2 March 1901, Holls had been appointed a Member of the Permanent Court of Arbitration. In April, the Secretary-General of the PCA had despatched a circular letter to the arbitrators to sound out their ideas on the launching of an international law library in The Hague. It was precisely to defend this project, rather than supporting the idea of a Court House, that Holls came to plead with Carnegie. As Holls wrote White promptly after his return from Scotland, Carnegie had shown keen interest in the idea of the library – much more, actually, than in the other project which, as Holls wrote, the Scottish American deemed premature and presumptuous to a degree that could only hamper the authority of the Court itself.

At that juncture, White decided to interfere; he went to see Carnegie personally at *Skibo Castle*. It then proved that with Carnegie the original idea of a book collection had developed into something far grander, namely 'the creation of a centre and symbol of a world's desire for peace and goodwill to men'. On 30 October Holls and White discussed this project over lunch in New York. In November, a confidential communication from Holls was received at the office of the Secretary-General of the PCA, notifying the Bureau that an American millionaire, who wished to remain unnamed, had asked him, Holls, 'to find out whether an offer from him to supply the Court with a first-class library of international law and diplomacy, and possibly too, with a building in which to house it, would or would not be received with favor'. In March 1902 Holls received the reply from The Hague that no government had raised any objections on principle, always provided that no increase in expenditure on their part was involved.

Carnegie, notified by Holls, reacted with circumspection. In August Holls paid a second visit to Scotland and here secured the solemn promise that Carnegie would provide an ample sum for the procurement of the 'best obtainable library on international law and diplomacy', subject to the condition that the idea was acceptable to the Court and a proper site could be found. But then once again events took a sudden turn following a new twist introduced by Andrew White.

During August, and in the course of a busy correspondence with Carnegie, White once more pleaded in favour of the De Martens project of a 'temple of peace, of which the doors, unlike those of the Temple of Janus, shall be kept wide open in time of peace and closed in time of war ... as a solemn and silent reminder to the nations that there is at last, after all these weary centuries, a court for the peaceful settlement of international questions, open to all'.

In glowing rhetoric and bold allegory, White outlined a true gallery of heroes of international law, culminating in Grotius – his perennial idol. He pictured artists from all over the world adorning the temple, thus testifying to the progress of mankind. His great persuasive power and love of architecture did not fail in their effect on Carnegie. Meanwhile, the Dutch Government showed reserve. In these official circles, the offer from a private donor was deemed somewhat *infra dignitatem* for the Court. It was felt that the Contracting Powers had to provide adequate accommodation for themselves. De Martens, however, once more pleaded in favour of the idea.

In October Andrew White was awarded

'Wijdeveld's turret', one of the last minute modifications to the Peace Palace. This turret came to replace the northern belfry; as a consequence, the great and small court rooms of the original design were interchanged. The turret is now situated behind the Great Hall of Justice.

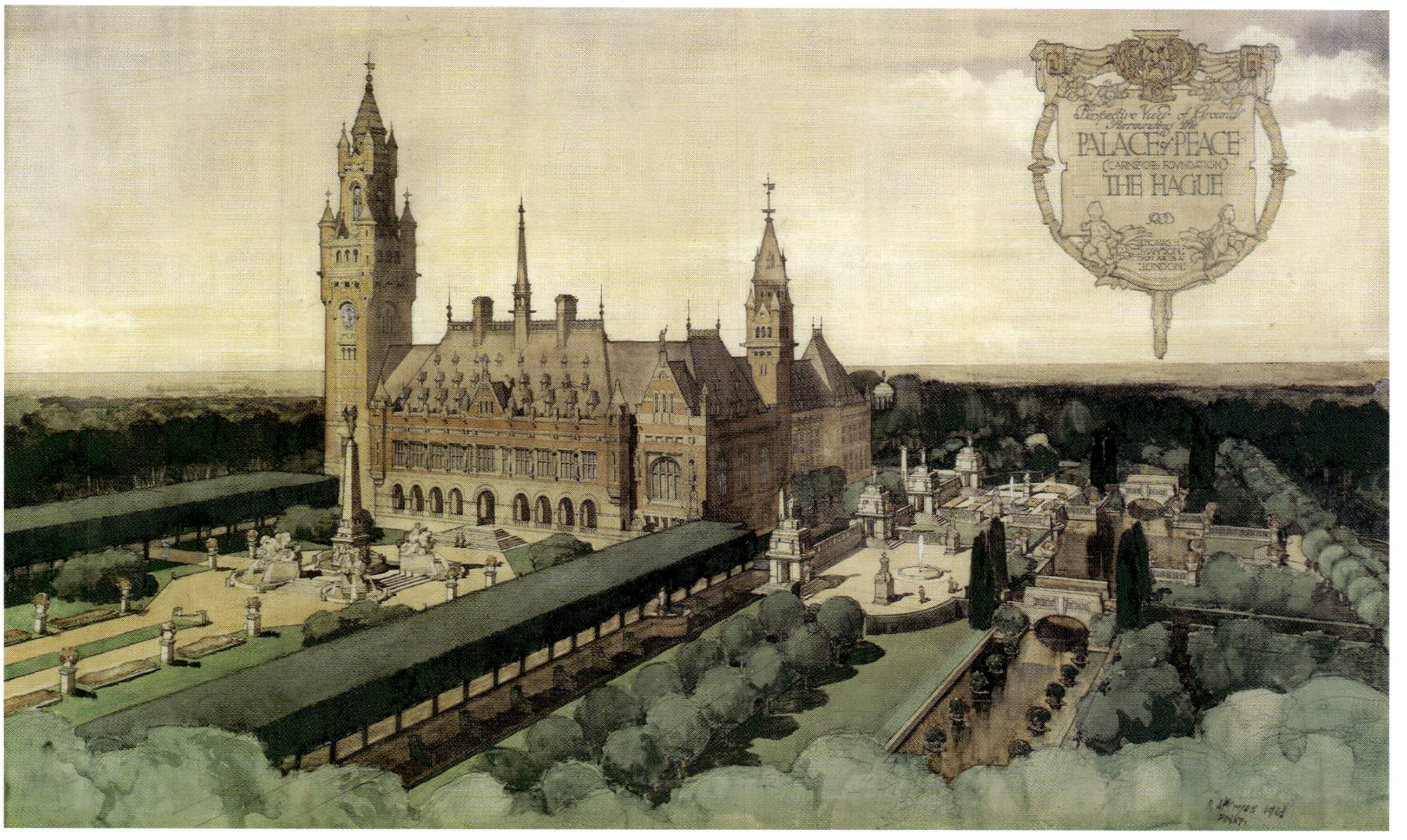

The winning design of the layout of the park by Thomas H. Mawson of London. Again, most of the sculptures and fountains were dispensed with for financial reasons. The back of the Palace features the tiny Temple of Peace, an echo of the Roman Temple of Vesta in the best Palladian tradition. Along with much of the rich peace imagery, this cupola succumbed to the economizing forces.

an honorary doctorate at St Andrews, while Carnegie was installed as Lord Rector. The following January Holls discussed the project with the Scotsman, and then again in February, in The Hague. In March, the Dutch Government finally agreed to the idea, provided that certain legal conditions could be fulfilled. These were to be met through the creation of a Foundation. Eventually, Carnegie, who would have preferred to have the donation put at the disposal of the young Queen Wilhelmina, gave in to this idea. On 22 April 1903, he instructed his Hobden banker 'to pay the draft of one and one-half million dollars drawn by the accredited officials of the Dutch Government, on account of the Temple of Peace in The Hague'. On 11 June, Queen Wilhelmina, the 'Guardian Angel of Peace' as Carnegie called her, sent her heartfelt thanks to Carnegie. On 23 July, Frederic Holls was called away by death in the midst of his active life.

The genesis of the project has been reviewed here in some detail, to illustrate the various threads from which the fabric of peace was woven. Pacifists and private entrepreneurs such as William Stead and Andrew Carnegie joined forces with international lawyers and diplomats like Frederic De Martens, Elihu Root, Andrew White and Frederic Holls. Together they broke the deadlock to promote an ideal which, if left to official government channels, would have taken a considerably longer period to be realized. In this, the Peace Palace – being at once the symbol of peace, a research centre and an international court house – is if anything typical of the period in which the international legal order first took shape.

CHAPTER FOUR

The Permanent Court of International Justice

You are about, Gentlemen, to give life to the judicial power of humanity. Philosophers and historians have told us of the laws of the growth and decadence of Empires. We look to you, Gentlemen, for laws which will assure the perpetuity of the only empire which can show no decadence, the empire of justice, which is the expression of eternal truth

Léon Bourgeois, 1920

The First World War marked a watershed in man's thinking on the settlement of disputes. The general feeling that more drastic steps were needed to forestall a repetition of the nightmare, aptly fulfilled the premise for the launching of a first international organization on a global scale. From that moment on, previous thinking about the constitution of an international judicial body was put on a different footing as well. Obviously, such a bench was inconceivable outside the framework of the League of Nations. In fact, it was the constitution of the League which opened new opportunities for determining the system of election of Judges, which in 1907 had posed an insurmountable problem to the projected Court of Arbitral Justice.

The creation of an international court was envisaged in the first unofficial drafts of the Covenant of the League, although not too emphatically. An early British proposal in 1918 provided for arbitration only, as did General Smuts' plan. While a 1918 French concept did include a tribunal and the assurance of the execution of its decisions by an international council, President Wilson's first draft for a League made only passing reference to 'judicial decision or arbitration'. As later drafts confirmed, Wilson did not deem the idea very opportune at the time. Prior to the Paris Peace Conference, more detailed provisions for a Court are found in a Scandinavian draft only.

However, in Paris, in January 1919, Lord Robert Cecil circulated a British 'draft sketch of a League of Nations' which referred to a judicial body, meant to be 'the existing Hague organization, with any additions or modifications made by the League, or by the Peace Treaties'. A later version even referred in explicit terms to 'the creation of a permanent court of international justice'. Interestingly, its de-

See previous page: The emblem of the Permanent Court of International Justice.

'Map of Europe in 1914' designed by W. Trier.

cisions were supposed to 'have no force or effect unless it is confirmed by the Report of the Conference or Council'. This Court was provisionally to be manned by the arbitrators of the PCA.

It was Lord Cecil who, at that juncture, on behalf of his Government, emphasized the need for the creation of a new court. In his outline (*Notes on a Permanent Court*), five out of the proposed nine Judges were to be nominated by the Principal Allied and Associated Powers. These five were in turn to select the remaining four Judges from a list of candidates nominated by other members of the League. Cecil wisely foresaw objections to this idea from the small States, but asserted that, once within the League, these States 'must and will abandon the doctrines of Barbosa'. Mr Ruy Barbosa of Brazil had in 1907, at The Hague, insisted that each State must be represented on the Bench.

In February 1919, a Commission of the League set to work on the basis of three draft proposals. First, an Italian draft, submitted by V. E. Orlando. It envisaged a court composed of Judges appointed by all contracting States. This Court was to sit in sections, each consisting of a President, one Judge chosen by each litigant, and four Judges elected by the Court. Secondly, a French proposal, submitted by L. Bourgeois and, thirdly, the American Hurst-Miller draft. The latter project (in its Article 12, which became the basis for later reviews) explicitly spoke of a Permanent Court of International Justice, 'competent to hear and determine any matter which the parties recognize as suitable for submission to it'.

Essentially, this is the text that appeared in the Draft Covenant of the League of February 1919, following a meeting of President Wilson with Lord Cecil. It also embodied the concept – which had appeared in earlier British, French and Italian proposals – of what was later called an Advisory Opinion. The textual addition read: 'and also any issue referred to it by the Executive Council or Body of Delegates'.

Numerous exchanges of views followed. German and Austrian counter-proposals were submitted, with F. Larnaude of France arguing in favour of the selection of Judges by the Council rather than by the Assembly. However, no substantial textual amendments were incorporated in the final draft of the Covenant that became Part I of the Peace Treaties concluded at Versailles (28 June 1919), St Germain-en-Laye (10 September 1919), Neuilly-sur-Seine (27 November 1919) and Trianon (4 June 1920). The text of Article 14 reads:

> The Council shall formulate and submit to the members of the League for adoption plans for the establishment of a Permanent Court of International Justice. The Court shall be competent to hear and determine any disputes of an international character which the parties thereto submit to it. The Court may also give an Advisory Opinion upon any dispute or question referred to it by the Council or by the Assembly.

The Article is indeed fundamental to the proper understanding of the Court's proceedings. Here, in a nutshell, are the bare essentials of the Court's functioning over the years up to the present day, namely its judicial duties towards States and its advisory functions vis-à-vis international organizations.

By now, the name of the court was fixed, too. In months gone by earlier variants had been circulating before the Conference, e.g., 'High International Court of Justice', 'International Tribunal', 'Court of International Law' and 'International Court of Justice' (as found in an Italian proposal). In the final analysis, they were all dismissed in favour of the name first suggested in the British draft convention of 20 January 1919: Permanent Court of International Justice.

The name aptly emphasized both the international and the permanent nature of the new institution. As discussed in the previous chapter, the specific wish for a permanent Court was not exactly incidental. It reflected the idea of a definite step forward from the PCA. Also, the name duly stressed the judicial nature of the court, as compared to the concept of arbitration. As Hudson observes (*op. cit.*, at p. 104), perhaps the order of words was not altogether appropriate. What was intended was in fact not so much a 'permanent court of international justice' but rather a 'permanent international court of justice'.

In Paris, clearly, the PCIJ was envisaged as a creature of the League of Nations and its members were to take part in that organization. Article 415 of the Treaty of Versailles refers explicitly to the 'Permanent Court of International Justice of the League of Nations'. Or, as the Committee of Jurists was to report in 1920: 'The new Court, being the judicial organ of the

The ornamental key to the entrance gates of the Peace Palace that was presented by Van Karnebeek to the Administrative Board of the Permanent Court of Arbitration.

League of Nations, can only be created within this League. As it is to be a competent part of the League, it must originate from an organisation within the League, and not from a body outside it'.

The 1920 Committee of Jurists

At its second session, in February 1920, the Council of the League proceeded to discuss a memorandum submitted by the Secretary-General. It contained a list of jurists to be invited 'to form a committee to prepare plans for the Permanent Court of International Justice and to report to the Council'. During May-June the Council sent invitations to a number of jurists. The projected Committee's attention was drawn to the plans prepared by various States. Prominent among these was the plan of the so-called 'Five Powers'. The reference was to the Scandinavian nations, the Netherlands and Switzerland, States which had not participated in the World War and which, from 1917 onwards, had set up national committees to prepare the creation of a court. Late in 1919, the Dutch Government had invited these nations to a conference for joint consideration of their individual plans. The Five Powers Conference held in The Hague in February 1920, had adopted a *projet* of 55 Articles. This draft was to prove another valuable instrument to the League's Committee.

The Committee consisted of ten jurists, five of them nationals of the Great Powers, five of smaller Powers. Some were veterans of the Hague Peace Conferences, others would shortly take a prominent part in the work of the Court itself:

Mr Adatci (Japan)
Mr Altamira (Spain)
Baron Descamps (Belgium), *President*
Mr Fernandes (Brazil)
Mr Hagerup (Norway)
Mr De Lapradelle (France)
Mr Loder (The Netherlands)
Lord Phillimore (Great Britain)
Mr Ricci-Busatti (Italy)
Mr Root (USA)

Baron Descamps, Hagerup, Ricci-Busatti and Root had played an active role in one or the other of the Hague Conferences; Fernandes in the Paris Peace Conference; Lord Phillimore in the drafting of the Covenant. Loder, the former president of the Five Power Conference, was to become Judge and President (1922-1924) of the Court, as was Adatci (1931-1933); Altamira would serve as a Judge on both benches of the PCIJ.

The Committee of Jurists assembled in the Japanese Room. In June-July 1920, at the Peace Palace, this Committee worked out a first draft scheme for the Permanent Court of International Justice.

The Secretariat of the Committee, too, was composed of illustrious names: it was headed by Commendatore Anzilotti, Under-Secretary-General of the League and later Judge and President of The Court, and included Nippold, Winiarski, later Judge and President of the ICJ, and Åke Hammarskjøld, later Registrar and Judge of the PCIJ.

This authoritative Committee of Jurists met in the Peace Palace at The Hague in 35 sessions from 16 June to 24 July 1920. During its first, public meeting, held on 16 June, speeches were delivered by Jonkheer van Karnebeek, the Dutch Minister for Foreign Affairs, Léon Bourgeois, the founding father of the Court, and Baron Descamps, the President of the Committee of Jurists.

Van Karnebeek first greeted Bourgeois:

> May he be welcome to Dutch soil! In him I greet the statesman who has presided over the labours of the chief Committee of each of the two Hague Conferences and whose services to the cause of international justice have entitled him to a position of authority and imperishable merits, which are universally recognised.

He went on in high spirits:

> Gentlemen, events have not been able to arrest the onward march of ideas. The League of Nations has taken up again the thread which for a long time seemed abandoned, and has entrusted to you the task of assisting it, by your advice, to formulate the important decisions to be taken in the near future. The grandeur of this task is apparent when, above the conflicts of interests and passions of mankind, is seen the guiding star of the noble idea of governing the future by the laws of justice. In a world which has passed through one of the greatest trials which history has ever known, in an international society shaken to its fundations, and almost at the end of its resources, the work of justice which is to be carried on in this Palace appears like an awakening, like a promise of moral reconstruction, like the message of a better future worthy of the League of Nations.

Then Léon Bourgeois took the floor. The speech he delivered was to become famous. Both as a tribute to this advocate of the Court and a testimony to the prevailing atmosphere of the period, part of his speech will be reproduced here. Bourgeois opened by paying tribute to Elihu Root as

one of the champions of the great undertaking:

> ... the great jurist and eminent American statesman, whose presence permits us to affirm that in the work which has called us together the old world and the new world, in spite of passing difficulties, cannot be separated by a durable barrier, and that indeed the two words 'old world' and 'new world' can now have no other meaning than the world of the past and the world of the future. For it is nothing less than humanity as a whole which will form the new world of tomorrow.

He then reviewed the accomplishments of the past two decades:

> It is fitting that The Hague has been designated for the meetings of your Committee. The recollection of the Conferences of 1899 and 1907 can never pass from the memory of those who had the honour – and there are some of them amongst you – to take part in them. It would be unjust to allow these first steps in the organisation of justice and peace to be forgotten. It is true that the artisans of these times had not the power and did not even dream of establishing at a single blow and at once the sovereign power of right. They knew that the force of special interests and of passion remains and will

Léon Bourgeois (1851-1925), the 'spiritual father' of the League of Nations. Statesman, scholar, reformer and peace leader, he held ministerial positions in various French cabinets. He was the author of a famous book Solidarité *(1897). A most persuasive and sincere man, he chaired the French delegations to the 1899 and 1907 Hague Conferences, and both times chaired the Arbitration Commissions. He was a long-standing member of the PCA. In 1920, he became President of the French Senate, was unanimously elected first President of the Council of the League of Nations, and was awarded the Nobel Peace Prize.*

> remain always formidable. It took three centuries for Christianity to establish its empire in the world, and no one could have imagined that an international convention, however solemn, could suffice to realise what must be nothing less than a universal revolution.
>
> The work, however, is far from having been useless. Roads were opened. Methods were laid down. That generous idea which, since the time of Henry IV, thanks to the labours of the philosophers of the eighteenth and nineteenth centuries, has succeeded in winning the support of all superior intellects, took for the first time at The Hague a concrete form in a series of international acts which were countersigned by the representatives of more than forty nations.
>
> It has, alas, needed the horrors of four years of war, of accumulated ruins, of millions of dead and of crimes which were inexpiable, to open the eyes of the greater number of men, and if in some countries the mad ambition of politicians can still contemplate a return to similar catastrophes, it would arouse immediately in the soul of innumerable simple people the open revolt both of feeling and of conscience.

Subsequently, he enlarged on the essence of the proposed Court:

> The Court of Justice must be a true Permanent Court. It is not simply a question of arbitrators chosen on a particular occasion, in the case of conflict, by the interested parties; it is a small number of Judges sitting constantly and receiving a mandate the duration of which will enable the establishment of a real jurisprudence, who will administer justice.
>
> This permanence is a symbol. It will be a seat raised in the midst of the nations, where Judges are always present, to whom can always be brought the appeal of the weak and to whom protests against the violation of right can be addressed. Chosen not by reason of the State of which they are citizens, but by reason of their personal authority, of their past career, of the respect which attaches to their names known over the world, these Judges will represent a truly international spirit which is by no means, as some people pretend, a negation of the legitimate interests of each nation, but which is, on the contrary, the safeguard of these interests, within the very limits of their legitimacy.

To him the difference between the Court of Arbitration and the Court of Justice was crystal clear:

> This Permanent Court will not be, as I have said, a Court of Arbitration, but a Court of Justice. The Court of Arbitration, whose eminent services we all remember, will certainly not cease to function in all the cases for which it was set up. But it has a special character and its range of action is already determined. There is between the sentence in an arbitration and the judgment of a tribunal an essential difference, a difference as profound as that which exists between equity and justice. Arbitration can take account of a thousand elements of fact and a thousand contingencies, and often of certain necessities of a political kind. The decrees of justice take account only of a rule defined and fixed by law.

Bourgeois was a visionary man, an idealist with a firm understanding of social processes:

> Justice follows necessarily the organisation of life itself. In the interior of a State the Courts can only give decisions in any real and useful sense, if precise laws have already determined the relations between men, fixing in consequence their rights and obligations and offering to the representatives of law the means of confronting the facts with the law so defined and of representing the violations of it.
>
> In other words life precedes law. In so far as it is unorganised, in so far as the functioning of its different forms, political, social or economic, have not been determined, the action of equity can be exercised between conflicting forces and tendencies, but the true action of law has not yet been born.
>
> Between States it cannot be otherwise. International life tends to develop every day with an intensity which no one a century ago could have foreseen or dared to estimate. The interdependence of matters of every order, political, economic, financial, social, makes felt at the very extremities of the world the repercussion of the needs and activities of everyone. The creation of an international organ through which, in the higher interest of all, the flux and the reflux of all these forces shall be regulated, is indispensable to the peace and prosperity of each and all.

He realized that:

> What would be the efficacy, what would be the reality of a sentence of justice, if it did not find in a strong organisation of international institutions what one calls in a technical term the executory of these decisions? The Covenant foresees several degrees of sanction, and as a last resort and, within limits very closely confined, military sanction.
>
> It is much to be desired that we should not be obliged to have recourse to that, but it is impossible to think that all tendencies towards violence will disappear from the world and that in consequence the opposition of the force of right to the force of violence will not be, alas, still for a long time necessary.

In this way, he both encouraged and advised the Committee that was about to start its work. He concluded with a solemn *vœu*:

> Speaking in the name of the Council of the League of Nations I have wished simply to show what a large place in our eyes the Court of Justice must take in the international organisation of the world. We wish to see it armed with the highest moral power and organised for a penetration as deep as possible into all the points of contact in the life of nations.
>
> We are ready to assure as completely as possible the extent of its competence and the execution of its judgements, and it is just because of the confidence that we place in its beneficent action that we wish to establish between the general powers of the Council and the Assembly and the special powers of the Court the closest solidarity and the most profound harmony.

His last words to the Committee were those quoted at the opening of this Chapter. In response to Bourgeois, Baron Descamps reviewed the work of the Hague Conferences and the Permanent Court of Arbitration.

Then the Committee commenced its work. The Secretariat of the Committee prepared an analysis of all previous drafts submitted by States (the Italian, German and British proposals of 1907; the Five Powers plan of 1919) as well as of the Convention establishing the Central American Court of Justice, and of drafts prepared by the *Interparliamentary Union* and the *Union juridique internationale*. Predictably, it was the thorny problems of the election of Judges and compulsory jurisdiction on which the Committee dwelt longest. However, on 24 July, a draft scheme was adopted unanimously.

The first sitting of the Court, in the Bol Room of the Peace Palace, on 30 January 1922.

In August, this scheme was defended by De Lapradelle before the Council in San Sebastian. It invited much comment, as is shown by the subsequent letter to the members of the League, warning them in advance that it would regard 'an irreconcilable difference of opinion on the merits of the scheme as an international misfortune of the gravest kind ... and probably irreparable'. Among the issues debated was the question of the languages to be used. Mr Balfour objected to the proposal that the sole official language should be French. L. Bourgeois, who acted as rapporteur throughout, and D. Caclamanos of Greece, submitted reports which were then communicated to the League's Assembly. The Argentine, Colombian and Panamanian delegations submitted further amendments.

The Assembly in turn referred the *Draft Scheme* to its Third Committee. Headed by Bourgeois, this Committee convened ten times between 17 November and 16 December 1920. It also set up a sub-committee of ten, presided over by Hagerup and including five former members of the Committee of Jurists. Inevitably, the central issues within the sub-committee were the question of obligatory jurisdiction and the constitution of the Court.

The first official meeting of the Court, February 1922.

By mid-December, the plan was adopted unanimously by the Third Committee and reported to the Plenary Assembly. Here, Bourgeois once more took a leading role. The suppression in the plan of the earlier provisions for obligatory jurisdiction as proposed by the Committee of Jurists provoked severe criticism; it was attributed to the influence of the Great Powers. As Fernandes of Brazil maintained: 'I was once enthusiastic; to-day I am barely confident. I am waiting'. Upon which Loder exclaimed: 'You are fighting against time; you will do so in vain'.

Still, on 13 December, the Assembly declared its unanimous approval of the draft Statute as amended. The term Statute, incidentally, replacing the terms 'draft-scheme' or 'constitution' as the plan had been referred to before, was first used by Bourgeois in December. In fact, it was a novelty in international legislation; it was a practical one, though, and it stuck. The *Statute* was recorded three days later in a so-called *Protocol of Signature*, an idea suggested by Fromageot. The document thus obtained the status of an international convention, the entry into force of which was subject only to its ratification by the necessary majority of nations.

However, the Protocol itself also contained a novelty. Attached to it was a draft of a so-called *Optional Clause*, along lines developed by the Swiss delegate Max Huber on the spur of a suggestion first made by Mr R. Fernandes of Brazil that a member of the League be permitted to adhere to either of two texts regarding the extent of jurisdiction of the Court. During the debates in the sub-committee Huber once had argued that, in his view, to reach a universal agreement on compulsory jurisdiction would constitute 'almost as great a step in advance as the establishment of the Court'. Surprisingly enough, the Optional Clause was approved by the Council. It was opened for signature as a separate protocol on 17 December 1920. Thus, in this roundabout way, one of the most controversial aspects of the jurisdiction of the Court was woven into the Statute. This was just another token of the persistence shown by the advocates of compulsory jurisdiction – notably Huber, Fernandes, Loder, LaFontaine (Belgium) and Blanco (Uruguay) – in promoting their cause.

On 25 February 1921 – twenty-seven members had signed the Protocol by then – the Secretary-General was authorized to take steps to proceed with the nomination of candidates. On 1 September 1921, twenty-two of the forty-one signatories had deposited ratifications. The Statute of the Court could be regarded as having entered into force – and the constitution of the Court as assured.

One setback, however, was to make itself felt throughout the working life of the PCIJ. Among the forty-eight nations which finally came to ratify the Protocol of Signature and endorse the Statute, the very nations which rapidly became the leading Powers in international affairs, the USA and the USSR, were the signal absentees. Though the United States duly signed the Protocol, the two-thirds majority in the Senate was never obtained. The USA refused to approve the Paris Peace Treaties; it returned to its traditional Monroe doctrine and policy of 'splendid isolation'. Nonetheless, throughout the years of the PCIJ, a Judge of American nationality served on the Bench.

As for the Soviet Union, until 1934 it did not take part in the League. It was never involved in any litigation before the PCIJ, be it directly or indirectly, and never signed the Statute. Again, it never had a Judge on the Bench. Marxist-Leninist ideas concerning the role and nature of law were considerably different from those held by other political and social philosophies. This led inevitably to a different assessment of the Court, as shown by the formal rejection of the competence and authority of the Court in the *Eastern Carelia* case.

The Statute of 1922 proved a workable scheme indeed. Only once was it amended, pursuant to a Resolution of the Assembly of December 1928. After some years of experience with the operation of the Court, it became evident that the Statute had not foreseen all eventualities. A new Committee of eleven experts was set up, consisting of renowned international scholars (e.g., Van Eysinga, Fromageot, Sir Cecil Hurst, Ito, Politis, Root). One of its main tasks was to review the conditions laid down by the United States for its acceptance of the Statute.

The Committee held fifteen meetings in Geneva during March 1929. It decided on the inclusion of four new articles and the amendment of nineteen existing articles. The major points involved were the abolishment of the institution of Deputy-Judges; the extension of participation in elections to non-members of the League; and the decision to keep the Court in permanent session to better meet the pressure of work. One goal was not achieved: in January 1935, the US Senate again refused its consent to the ratification of the 1920 and 1929 Protocols that had been duly signed by its representative on 9 December 1929.

The findings of the Committee were submitted to a Conference, approved by the League Assembly and embodied in a Protocol of 14 September 1929, which came into force in February 1936. Side by side with the body of 'Rules of Court', a growing set of Resolutions of Council and Assembly, and a range of hundreds of international agreements supporting the reference of disputes to the Court, the Statute has remained the main instrument of the Court's functioning in the broadest sense of the term.

A few lines may be devoted here to the Rules of Court. Their drafting was left to the Court's own discretion. The original Rules were adopted in March 1922. They were thoroughly revised in July 1926. In February 1931, new (and considerable) changes were introduced. In May 1931, following the revision of the Statute, the Court decided to undertake a general revision of the Rules. This procedure took a full five years. In March 1936, the final version was promulgated.

The Installation and Composition of the Court

As Hudson observes, 'the provisions of the Statute which deal with the election of members of the Court represent the greatest triumph achieved in 1920'. The 1907 proposals for the projected International Prize Court and the Permanent Court of Arbitral Justice had been utterly dissatisfactory. The greatest obstacle had been the irreconcilable views of the greater and smaller Powers. By 1920, however,

The Geneva 1929 Committee that revised the Statute of the Court.

The fountain made of Copenhagen porcelain, a gift from the Danish government, in the inner court yard of the Peace Palace.

a similar difficulty had been surmounted with the creation of the League of Nations. Availing itself of this analogy, the Committee of Jurists, by entrusting the election to the League Assembly and Council, was able to break the deadlock. One may argue, therefore, that it was the creation of the League which was the prerequisite for the successful launching of the Court.

A detailed review of the complex system of nomination and election of Judges will be reserved for Chapter 7. Suffice it to say that, until the revision of the Statute in 1929, the Court was composed of eleven Judges and four Deputy-Judges, elected simultaneously for a term of nine years. The system of rotation, as it is applied during the UN period, which provides for the replacement of a third of the Bench after three years, had not yet been developed at that stage.

The election of the first Bench of the PCIJ

had begun on 14 September 1921. It took the Council and Assembly no less than three days, thirteen ballots and the interference of a joint conference to agree upon its composition. The outcome was a happy one, though. In experience and geographical representation the roster was as satisfactory as any system of election might have produced. Of the eleven Judges and four Deputy-Judges, no fewer than ten were members of the PCA.

The Opening Ceremony

At the request of the Secretary-General, the panel of Judges met for the first time on 30 January 1922. Nine Judges and three Deputy-Judges attended the meeting. On 3 February, the Court elected Judge Loder as its President and Mr Hammarskjøld as Registrar.

On 15 February, the public inaugural meeting of the Court took place. In the presence of the Queen of the Netherlands, the Queen Mother and the Prince Consort, the members of the Court in turn made their solemn declarations. Speeches were made by a representative of the Council, the Secretary-General of the League, the Dutch Minister for Foreign Affairs, the Mayor of The Hague and the President of the Court.

On behalf of the Council, Mr de Cunha, the Brazilian delegate, declared that:

> I feel an indescribable emotion in speaking before so august an assembly. For the first time in the course of history, men have finally succeeded, after many efforts, in establishing the Permanent Court of International Justice. This is an event of such great importance that it is at first sight difficult to estimate its full significance. The 15th of February 1922 will be one of the greatest days in the annals of human justice. ... In the great, young, American Continent, which has no doubt suffered much less from war than gallant Europe, the idea of international justice is perhaps stronger and more living than in any other part of the earth. The people of the New World feel instinctively attracted towards this high ideal, which is to-day accomplished before our eyes, and through which we hope to find protection from the terrible catastrophes with which the pages of history are filled.

He then paid explicit homage to 'the champion of human justice and international morality, Léon Bourgeois of France'.

Sir Eric Drummond, Secretary-General of the League of Nations, reminded his audience of the various difficulties that had been overcome in the previous quarter of a century, and of the gloomy prognosis by those familiar with the international system, until the last moment:

> Some of my collaborators at the last Assembly warned me that the election of the Judges was likely to continue for at least ten days or a fortnight, and the most sanguine expected that there would be a full week of elections. I am happy to say that these prognostics were completely falsified, and that all the Judges and the Deputy-Judges were elected in the space of two days. This constitutes a great tribute to the ingenuity of those who devised the present plan.

In his capacity as Secretary-General he declared:

> The relation between the Court and the League is similar to that which exists between the Courts and the Government in England, and elsewhere. The Judges are appointed by the State, but the State cannot remove them. There can be no dictation or interference by the Government with Courts. Indeed, the Courts can give decisions on what the State itself has done, though ultimately the authority of the Courts derives from that very Government....

He concluded on a note of high expectation:

> The path of world progress lies at the present time enshrouded in fog, but here and there glimpses of light are breaking through and illuminating the way. The definite foundation of this Court is such a ray, and when the gloom is finally dispersed, this ray, since it emanates from the sun of justice, will only shine the more brilliantly on all civilised nations.

The Dutch Minister of Foreign Affairs, Van Karnebeek, expressed the pride and gratitude of his Government, recalled the Conference of the Five Powers, and of the 1920 Committee of Jurists, and traced the history of the Court back to the Hague Conferences and to Grotius and Bynkershoek:

> The hour of universal justice is striking.... In a world shaken to its foundations as the result of a gigantic disaster, the

Robert Bannatyne Finlay, First Viscount (1842-1929).

Henri-Auguste Fromageot (1864-1949).

Dionisio Anzilotti (1867-1960).

establishment of the Court of Justice appears like a bright star in the darkness which hides from our eyes the uncertainties of the future. ... In the midst of the economic and political dislocation which still prevails, we raise to-day the standard of moral solidarity between the nations. It is an act of faith!

Dr J. Patijn, Burgomaster of The Hague fell in with him:

> The greater the event, the greater the difficulty which attends its birth. We do not despair, especially at this moment; for we believe that from the general upheaval which we are now experiencing, from the fundamental changes which are taking place in the economic, financial and social relations of the world, from this new grouping of nations, there will arise a new order, more harmonious and, may be, happier than the old.

The last speech was reserved for the newly elected President of the Court, Judge Loder. The eminent Dutch jurist made a gem of it. First addressing his Queen, he made the simile:

> The gardener who is about to plant a valuable seedling which he tends with devotion and which he desires should grow strong, selects with care a soil which combines the qualities most favorable to its development. The Permanent Court of International Justice is like this precious plant; its gardener is the whole world, which expects from it a new era of happiness, when right and justice shall flourish on the earth. But if the roots of this plant are to strike deep, if it is to develop and become a tree with solid trunk, with strong, wide-spreading branches and with thick foliage beneath which the peoples may find rest, it requires a fertile soil, permeated by long centuries of order and of freedom; freedom of mind and of conscience, freedom of action for all, and order which respects the rights of others, so that this freedom may be no empty form of words but a living reality. It is in this corner of the earth which we call Holland that just such a soil is to be found.

In response to Mr de Cunha, Loder enlarged on the comparison between the Court and the League on the one hand and national Governments and their Judicature on the other:

> The field of activity of the Permanent Court is still wider. It is not only accessible to members of the League of Nations, but also, in accordance with its Statute, to States which, although they are not as yet members of the League, recognize the authority of that body in regard to the settlement of their disputes. Thus the organ itself will be enabled to contribute to the development of the power of its creator.

In his turn, he paid due homage to Léon Bourgeois:

> I desire to say how much I deplore his absence, for he is in spirit the very creator of this Court, and it is, in a great measure, owing to him that we are gathered here to-day. He has been devoted for many years to this noble work; his eloquence has been heard throughout the world and his arguments have stirred the hearts and minds of men. It is to his perseverance, to the untiring efforts of his creative and constructive energy that the Court owes its existence. He has succeeded because he possesses the faith which refuses to doubt that right will be triumphant. The victory of to-day is his victory; to him is therefore due the homage and respect of more than forty nations.

Loder also paid his respect to the Leyden University Board, which had presented the Court with:

> ... a gift which is both generous and appropriate – a Presidential hammer. Science, free by nature, recognises that freedom can only exist under the reign of order, and of this order the hammer is a symbol. The Court has not failed to appreciate the true value of this gift. ... The hammer is inscribed with the noble motto of the first Prince of Orange: *sævis tranquillus in undis* ('at rest on the choppy sea', the well-known emblem of the nestling halcyon or kingfisher). May we be ever inspired by it in the accomplishment of our task.

In his *Peroratio*, the Court's President enlarged on the history of international law:

> Since the commencement of history force has ever in the end gained the mastery over right and justice. The impious sophism that right is after all nought but force, organised and controlled – force sometimes even intentionally brutal – will henceforth be rejected, and in its place will reign the divine principle that all existence in this world must be based on order and on harmony, an emanation

of the Deity himself, imposed by Him upon mankind. ... The establishment of the Permanent Court marks in fact the arrival of a new era in the civilisation of the world. It is of the greatest importance that the true significance of this fact should be realised. We must not regard it with the disdainful smile of the sceptic who believes in nothing, because all loftiness of spirit in him is lacking, and yet at the same time we must also avoid exaggerating or misinterpreting the significance of this new institution, lest we suffer disillusionment in the future. Nothing enters this world in a state of perfection, neither man himself nor the institutions which he creates. Evolution, often slow and painful, is the law of the universe.

The inaugural session was followed by a preliminary session which ended with the adoption of the Rules of Court. The first official session took place on 15 June, 1922.

The First Bench

A brief survey of the members of the First Bench may serve to show the variety of backgrounds and experience.

Its President, the Dutchman Loder, had been one of the founders of the International Maritime Committee. He had been instrumental in the creation of the Court, more precisely in his capacity as President of the Hague Five Powers Conference of 1920 and as Vice-President of the Committee of Jurists.

Judge André Weiss was a French internationalist and Professor at Paris from 1896 onwards. He became Member of the prestigious *Institut de France* in 1914, Member of the PCA in 1920, President of the IDI in 1922 and of the International Academy of Comparative Law in 1923. His works on international law, notably his *Traité de droit international privé* in six volumes, were recognized as authoritative.

Robert Bannatyne Finlay, First Viscount had a medical training at Edinburgh, where he was Lord Rector before entering politics in 1885. He had been Solicitor-General, Attorney-General and Lord Chancellor (1916-1919) before returning to the legal and political work in the House of Lords. He was elected to the PCA and elected Judge to the PCIJ in 1921.

Didrik Nyholm of Denmark was a former Judge at the Copenhagen Court of Appeal and Counsellor of State. He was from 1861 to his election in 1921 first Judge at the mixed courts in Egypt and then President of the Court of Cairo. He was Member of the PCA from 1913 and submitted a draft plan for a World Court to the 1920 Committee of Jurists.

John Bassett Moore had been professor of international law at Columbia University for some thirty years. He had broad experience at the State Department and in international arbitrations, on which he wrote his authoritative *History and Digest of International Arbitrations* (six volumes), which, along with his eight-volume *Digest of International Law* had won him international repute.

Judge de Bustamante, professor of international law in Havana, had represented Cuba at the 1907 Hague and the 1919 Paris Peace Conferences. His reputation rested on the famous Bustamante Code of Private International Law of 1908. He was to be re-elected in 1930.

Judge Rafael Altamira of Spain, former professor in Oviedo and Madrid, was an expert in comparative law and international arbitration. A former Member of the 1920 Committee of Jurists, he was to be re-elected in 1930.

Judge Yorozu Oda of Japan had been professor at Kyoto University and was an expert in Japanese and Chinese administrative law.

The Italian Dionisio Anzilotti was a celebrated professor of international law, formerly of Florence, Palermo, Bologna and Rome Universities, and a legal adviser to his Foreign Ministry. He was Assistant Secretary-General of the League of Nations during 1920-1922, Judge (1922-1939) and President (1928-1930) of the PCIJ. Among his works, notably on international responsibility, features his *Corso di Diritto Internazionale*, which has been translated into French and German.

Max Huber of Switzerland was Professor at Zurich University, with historical and sociological leanings, before being called to the bench of the PCIJ (1921-1930). He was its President from 1925-1927 and its Vice-President during the following term, and left a deep and lasting imprint on the Court. He was a long-standing member of the PCA, known for his impartiality, and President (1928-1944) of the International Committee of the Red Cross.

Ruy Barbosa of Brazil had been one of the

Frank B. Kellogg (1856-1937).

Cecil J.B. Hurst (1870-1963).

Max Huber (1874-1960).

Mineitciro Adatci (1869-1934).

prominent scholars attending the 1907 Hague Conference. He was one of the great figures in the development of Latin American international law and cooperation. He died without ever having attended a session of the Court.

During its nine-year term the Bench underwent various changes. On 1 March 1923 Judge Barbosa passed away. By a special election on 10 September 1923 he was replaced by Judge Pessõa, who had been instrumental in the codification of Brazilian law, had served as Procurator-General, Minister of Justice and finally President of Brazil. He had attended the 1919 Paris Peace Conference.

In April 1928, Judge Moore submitted his letter of resignation, which was accepted with regret – and provisionally, as no such a step had been anticipated in either the Statute or the Rules. On 8 September, Judge Hughes was elected. Charles Evans Hughes had been Governor of New York, Justice of the Supreme Court and Secretary of State. In February, 1930, he offered his resignation, after his appointment as Chief Justice of the Supreme Court of the United States. On 17 September of the same year he was replaced by Judge Kellogg.

Frank B. Kellogg had been Senator, Ambassador, Secretary of State and President of the American Bar Association. A jurist by profession, Kellogg turned towards diplomacy after World War I, to help abolish 'the scourge of war'. A man of vision and cautious optimist, urging patience in the quest for peace, Kellogg became instrumental in the US grand scheme to renounce war as national policy (the Kellogg-Briand Pact of Paris). He was awarded the Nobel Peace Prize in 1929.

Two more vacancies occurred as Judge Weiss passed away in August 1928 and Lord Finlay in March 1929. On 19 September 1929, these vacancies were filled by Henri Fromageot and Sir Cecil Hurst respectively.

Henri-Auguste Fromageot, a quiet practising internationalist, trained at Paris, Leipzig and Oxford, was a specialist in maritime law and an authority on arbitration. He served his country at virtually all of the international conferences from 1907 onwards and throughout the inter-war period, notably at Locarno. He was a member of the Prize Court and was on the 1920 Committee of Experts. Elected Judge in 1929, he sat throughout the existence of the PCIJ. He left his personal library to the Court.

Sir Cecil J.B. Hurst, a Cambridge man, was a Legal Adviser to the Foreign Office before becoming Member of the PCIJ (1929-1946). He presided over the Court during 1934-1936. He was a member of the PCA from 1929-1950. Hurst was an expert on multilateral negotiations and a highly skilled and influential diplomat during the Versailles to Locarno years. He served on the committees which drafted the Statute of the PCIJ and the Constitution of the ILO, chaired the League Commission on War Crimes and was editor of the *British Yearbook of International Law*.

The four Deputy-Judges of this period were Michailo Yovanovitch, the Yugoslavian former Minister of Justice and President of the Courts of Appeal and Cassation at Belgrade; Beichmann, the Norwegian former President of the Court of Appeal at Trondheim; Demètre Negulesco, the Romanian professor who was to be elected as a titular Judge in 1930; and Wang Ch'ung-hui, the Chinese former Minister of Justice and Foreign Affairs who was known for his English translation of the German Civil Code. Elected as a Judge in 1930, he resigned in 1936.

The Second Bench

At the general election in 1930, in pursuance of the revised Statute, the number of Judges was increased to fifteen. Judges Kellogg, Fromageot, de Bustamante, Altamira, Anzilotti and Hurst were re-elected. Judges Huber and Pessõa declined to stand for re-election. Following formal demands from the Latin American world, the seven newly elected Judges produced a wider geographical distribution. The Latin American component was increased from two to three. However, this time the Scandinavian region was not represented.

Mineitciro Adatci of Japan, was doctor of law, veteran Ambassador and Judge (1930-1934) and President (1931-1933) of the PCIJ. His career spanned the period from the Meiji era to the 1930s. Adatci was a prominent representative of the internationally oriented Japanese scholarship. He attended the 1919 Paris Peace Conference, was on various League committees and was widely respected as a conscientious, fair-minded and skilled parliamentarian. He resigned as President in 1933, died the following year and was given a

State funeral by the Dutch government in recognition of his services.

Another newcomer was Gustavo Guerrero of El Salvador, an experienced diplomat and former Minister for Foreign Affairs. He had played a prominent role in the Council and Assembly of the League and had presided over the Tenth Assembly of the League. He was to become President of the PCIJ as well as of the ICJ, and indeed one of the most prominent characters in the history of the International Court.

Baron Rolin-Jaequemyns of Belgium had served as a judge in the Congo, had been a delegate to the 1899 Hague Conference, and had played an active role in the League. He died in 1936.

Count Michel Rostworowski of Poland was a former professor of Cracow University and a codifier of Polish law. He served for many years in the League Assembly. Prior to his election as a titular Judge, he had served four times as Judge *ad hoc*. He died in March 1940.

Judge José Urrutia had been a diplomat, Foreign Minister and President of the Senate of Colombia. An active member of the League Assembly during the 1920s, he had served on the 1929 Committee of Jurists. He resigned in January 1942.

Judge Walter Schücking of Germany was a prolific author, who had held chairs at various prominent university centres and had been a member of the *Reichstag*. Prior to his election he had served twice as Judge *ad hoc*.

Jonkheer Willem van Eysinga of the Netherlands, Member of the PCA from 1926 and of the PCIJ from 1931 to 1946 and its Vice-President during its final years, had been Professor at the Groningen and Leyden Universities and legal adviser to the Dutch Foreign Ministry. He was a member of the 1929 Committee of Jurists and Dutch delegate at many conferences, including the 1930 Hague Codification conference. He wrote an authoritative work on the history of international law in the Netherlands, Grotian studies, and tracts on international rivers and on chemical warfare.

The second Bench, understandably, also underwent several changes. Pursuant to the death of Judge Adatci in December 1934, Judge Harukazu Nagaoka was elected on 14 September 1935. Judge Nagaoka was a veteran diplomat and had served the League in various capacities. He resigned in January 1942.

The death of Judge Schücking in August 1935 and the resignation of Judge Kellogg in September created two vacancies; the resignation of Judge Wang in January 1936 created another. The projected elections were complicated by the requests of Brazil, Germany and Japan to participate in the elections. These nations, while Parties to the Statute, had withdrawn from the League. Finally, as a result of two separate elections, both held in October 1936, Judges Hudson, Hammarskjøld and Cheng were elected.

Judge Manley O. Hudson a Harvard Law School Professor and pupil of Roscoe Pound, was Judge of the PCIJ from 1935-1939 and later (1948-1953) chaired the ILC. A peace crusader in his early years, Hudson made a durable contribution to international law. He was close to Eric Drummond and in numerous articles advocated his nation's acceptance of the membership of the League. A champion of the PCIJ, he wrote the authoritative history of the Court. Unwilling to leave The Hague in spring 1940, he eventually made a perilous exit through Italy. He was influential in the drafting of the Statute of the ICJ. Later on, he initiated the Harvard Research in International Law.

Åke Hammarskjøld of Sweden, Registrar (1922-1936) and Judge (1936-1937) of the PCIJ, was a former foreign service officer. His untimely death cut short a promising career. His major work, *La juridiction internationale*, was published posthumously in Leiden in 1938.

Judge Cheng Tien-Hsi of China had been a judge of the Chinese Supreme Court and had served as Vice-Minister of Justice.

Soon yet another vacancy had to be filled following the death of Baron Rolin-Jaequemyns in July 1936. In May 1937, Charles De Visscher of Belgium was elected. Judge De Visscher, former professor of international law at Ghent and Louvain universities, had served as Secretary-General of the *Institut de Droit International*. Prior to his election he had appeared before the Court as counsel on several occasions.

In July 1937, Judge Hammarskjøld died. It was only in September 1938 that Judge Erich came to replace him. Rafael Erich had served as professor of international law in Helsinki, as a diplomat and as Prime Minister of Finland. He had attended the League Assemblies from 1921 to 1932, and had been Deputy-Judge from 1930.

The four Deputy-Judges that were elected

Jonkheer W.J.M. van Eysinga (1878-1961).

Manley O. Hudson (1886-1960).

Åke Hammarskjøld (1893-1937).

in 1930, Joseph Redlich of Austria, José Caeiro da Matta of Portugal, Mileta Novacovitch of Yugoslavia and the aforementioned Rafael Erich were never called upon for active service in that capacity prior to February 1936, when their posts ceased to exist.

At the close of 1939, as the second nine-year period expired, the Court found itself exposed to perils not just from without but also from within. Quite apart from the overall political situation, which became more disquieting every day, as early as 1937 the Peruvian delegation informed the League Assembly that it had proposed to the Latin American nations 'that they should take concerted action with a view to obtain for American jurists a larger number of seats'. What Peru aimed at, apparently, was no fewer than six seats instead of the two allocated up till then. Then, in announcing its support for Peru, the Chilean delegation raised the threat of an alternative American Court of International Justice.

Soon afterwards, the Egyptian Foreign Minister, in agreement with Turkey, Iran and Iraq, suggested that the Court should 'include a jurist representing Islamic civilization and Moslem law'. These criticisms can be seen as the first signs that the surface of the League system was cracking. After the upheaval of the Second World War, a return to the previous system would be virtually impossible.

In December 1939, the election was postponed and Members of the Court were requested to 'continue to discharge their duties' until their places had been filled. Then, in March 1940, Judge Rostworowski died. Again, due to the international tension, nothing much happened until, in January 1942, Judges Urrutia and Nagaoka resigned. By then, however, it had become clear that Court and League were no longer in a position to undertake any purposeful action. The Third Bench was never constituted.

PUBLICATIONS OF THE PCIJ

Between 1922 and 1946 the PCIJ published the following series:

Series A (Nos 1-24):	*Collection of Judgments* (up to and including 1930)
Series B (Nos 1-18):	*Collection of Advisory Opinions* (up to and including 1930)
Series A/B (Nos 40-80):	*Judgments, Orders and Advisory Opinions* (beginning in 1931)
Series C (Nos 1-19):	*Acts and Documents relating to Judgments and Advisory Opinions given by the Court* (up to and including 1930)
Series C (Nos 52-88):	*Pleadings, Oral Statements and Documents* (beginning in 1931)
Series D (Nos 1-6):	*Acts and Documents concerning the Organization of the Court*
Series E (Nos 1-16):	*Annual Reports*
Series F (Nos 1-4):	*General Indexes*

The first Bench of the PCIJ during its first case, the Wimbledon case (1923).

A Survey of Cases

During the years of its active existence, i.e., from 1922 to 1940, the PCIJ handled 66 cases, 36 of a contentious nature, and 28 advisory requests. Twelve of these were settled out of Court. In all, the Court rendered 32 Judgments and delivered 27 Advisory Opinions, all of these at the request of the Council of the League. The *Eastern Carelia* case of 1928 was the only advisory request to be rejected. With nearly four cases a year filed on average, the Court functioned in a practical and effective manner and easily demonstrated its superior value to the international community as compared to any prior experience with arbitral panels. It helped to resolve some serious international disputes, and in so doing threw light on some previously grey areas of international law. At the same time, it developed a true judicial technique and steadily built up a sophisticated internal procedure.

The subject-matter of the cases varied, as did their political background. Numerous cases looked backwards, so to speak, and revolved around the interpretation of the 1919 Peace Treaties. This was true of no fewer than eleven Judgments and eighteen Advisory Opinions. Among them were the disputes between Greece and Bulgaria over the interests of the latter's nationals, which were brought up in 1924, 1930 and 1932, and the conflict between France and Switzerland over the Free Zones of Upper Savoy. As Schlochauer observes:

> ... in this respect the activities of the PCIJ differed considerably from those of its successor. The significance of the pronouncements of the PCIJ may be seen in the further development of rules of procedure, in its contributions in the field of treaty interpretation and in the establishment of recognized sources of international law. It also contributed indirectly towards the general development of international law.

Another set of issues – the ones most hotly debated – looked ahead, centering on the tensions in the German-Polish-Lithuanian area, which in the end led to the outbreak of the Second World War. They involved problems regarding the treatment of German minorities (settlers, interests, schools, taxes) and the position of the Free City of Danzig (Gdansk). Between 1923 and 1935, these issues cropped up no less than seventeen times.

During the first year of its existence, the PCIJ acted mainly in its advisory capacity. The first three cases submitted to it were requests for Advisory Opinions on matters concerning the ILO: the conditions of agricultural labourers, methods of production, and the appointment of delegates to conferences.

The first contentious case, brought in 1923, was a really burning issue. It was in this very first case, concerning the *Wimbledon* dispute, that the Court built itself a reputation. It stands as a milestone like the *Alabama Award* in the sphere of arbitration. In March 1921, the British vessel *S.S. Wimbledon*, carrying munition on behalf of a French company, was refused access to the Kiel Canal by the German authorities who, to justify their conduct, referred to the German Neutrality Regulations. However, in the Treaty of Versailles, free access for the vessels of all nations at peace with Germany was stipulated. Eventually, the German authorities were ordered to pay indemnities.

In the course of the following two decades, the disputes submitted to the Court varied from questions concerning Brazilian and Serbian loans issued in France to Palestine concessions; from frontier disputes between Czechoslovakia and Poland, Albania and Yugoslavia, and Turkey and Iraq, to lighthouses awarded to France on the Greek coasts in the wake of the Balkan wars. International river disputes came in as well: the contested jurisdiction of the European Commission of the Danube, or the River Oder Commission, and the incident between Belgium and the Netherlands over the waters of the River Meuse.

Interestingly, well over two-thirds of all cases were filed in the first decade of existence of the PCIJ, the years 1922-1932, the heyday of the League and the era of the Locarno agreements. This record in itself is suggestive of the susceptibility of international litigation to a general climate of stability and détente within the international community. The increasing unrest and dissatisfaction resulting from the financial crisis in the early thirties made itself felt here as everywhere else. Under the ensuing tide of nationalism and radicalism which engulfed Italy and Japan and swept away Germany's Weimar Republic, the authority of the weakened League of Nations soon came to be held in contempt. This effectively prevented League and Court from acting as the planned 'Great Bulwark of Peace'.

Rosenne concludes his assessment of the Court in the following way:

> ... what the Court, as the other organs of the League (and often in cooperation with them) really succeeded in doing, was for a time to keep a tense situation under some form of control. Given other political conditions, the League would have enjoyed greater long-term success, and the Permanent Court with it. As things were, the major disputes with which the Court dealt were connected with that very situation which sparked off the Second World War. None of the skills of statesmanship and diplomacy available at the time succeeded in avoiding that disaster, and it is too much to expect more of the Court Procedure. (*Law and Practice* 1985, at pp. 13-14)

The Court made a very significant contribution to the development of international law:

> From its experimental beginnings it established the point that a permanent international judicial organ integrated with the political organization of the international community is both feasible and necessary, even without going so far as to be accompanied by any true compulsory jurisdiction. ... The exper-

Left: Judge B.C.J. Loder, first President of the Court (1922-1925), leaving the Peace Palace, 1922.

Right: The Judges André Weiss and Didrik Nyholm chatting at the entrance of the Peace Palace, 1922.

ience of the Permanent Court, its dispassionate and unhurried consideration of the issues brought before it, the high standards of personal integrity and professional competence, and worldly wisdom, of its members, the fact that the judicial pronouncements were endowed with strong moral authority in addition to their formal finality, provided the foundations for the reconstituted system of international adjudication after the dust of the Second World War had started to settle.

Still, in the final appreciation of most commentators, the Court's nadir was reached in 1931 when it was persuaded to render an Advisory Opinion on the heavily charged political issue of the Customs Union between Germany and Austria. Although the Court took a firm stand against Germany's arguments, this decision highlighted the weakness of the judicial process in the current legal order. Despite all the precautions taken, politicization had brought the Court down. The last public sitting was held on 4 December 1939, when the Court dealt with the request for interim measures of protection in the *Electricity Company of Sofia* case. After that, no further business was dealt with, and no new Judges were elected. The last case to be submitted to the Court, on 17 June 1939, between Liechtenstein and Hungary, remained unsettled. The last official function of the Court was the ordering, on 26 February 1940, of interim measures in the *Sofia* case. Oral proceedings were scheduled for 16 May. However, well before Germany overran the Netherlands, during the first days of May 1940, the Court had been moved to Geneva, leaving behind its Vice-President, Van Eysinga, and a few Dutch Registry officials. It was a new Court, with new promises and under the auspices of a new political organization, that would return in 1946. The Judges of the PCIJ resigned on 30 January 1946. On 18 April the PCIJ was dissolved by a Resolution of the Assembly of the League, convened to wind up its last business. On the same day, the ICJ was inaugurated.

The Palace in winter apparel.

CHAPTER FIVE

The International Court of Justice: Genesis, Registry, Premises

The Genesis of the International Court of Justice

> *In the last resort, recourse to international justice depends on the will of governments and on their readiness to submit for legal decision all which can and should be preserved from the arbitrament of violence. As for the Court, it means to accomplish to the full the duties incumbent upon it; and it will not weaken in that resolve.*

With this stirring peroration, the President of the PCIJ, Gustavo Guerrero of El Salvador, concluded the last public session of the Court on 4 December 1939. As Rosenne recalls: 'It was an eerie moment of history. Poland, partitioned, lay prostrate after the Blitzkrieg. On the Western front the three great European Powers of that epoch were locked in the grim struggle of the misnamed phoney war' (*Law and Practice* 1985, at p. 23).

The Bench, it must be said, showed its will-power and determination to the last. It did its utmost to prevent politics from interfering with its administration of justice. Indeed, it made a point of demonstrating this. Meanwhile, it appreciated the urgency of the situation and had read the writing on the wall. In November 1939 it had discussed eventualities with the Dutch Government and, as a matter of precaution, had dispatched part of its archives to Geneva. Early in 1940, the evacuation *en bloc* of all personnel of the Court was considered.

Even so, surprise attack and early surrender foreclosed all options. Mid-May saw the Registrar pleading with German authorities to secure promises of non-molestation. Two months later, with the abolition of all diplomatic immunities in the occupied Netherlands, the foreign personnel of the Court were granted leave for departure. The Dutch remained, headed by Vice-President Van Eysinga, to deal with current affairs. Meanwhile, in Geneva, the President and Registrar, assisted by three officials only, watched over the Court's long-term interests. As President Guerrero recalled six years later, on the occasion of the inaugural session of the new Court:

> I shall never forget that day - 16 July 1940, when, in the early hours of a morning veiled with a mist of sadness and grief, we slowly left the station of this martyred city, with tears in our eyes and our hearts full of anguish. We asked ourselves what would become of this people so full of indignation against the invader, and of the moral, intellectual and artistic treasures here patiently assembled through many centuries of civilization.

Oddly enough, at this juncture, the exact legal standing of the staff was not perfectly clear, neither to the Germans nor to the Board of the Carnegie Foundation. The premises became German property but the Courts were international institutions and the staff of the PCA remained in office at The Hague throughout the war. In negotiating with the Board and the German occupier, Van Eysinga argued that the German Government had never questioned the international standing of the Court. At length, the Germans agreed to respect the status of the Palace if only for its symbolic stature, a pledge they kept throughout the war years.

All through the years of enforced inaction, the Court formally maintained that, being an independent organ, its existence was not really affected by the political situation. Accordingly, in 1945 it resumed work. At this point, however, it was overtaken by reality. A new world had emerged from chaos; it was soon to impose its will on the Court.

See previous page: Justitia, one of the four brass medallions in the ornamental entrance gates, also featuring: Amicitia, Pax and Concordia, gifts of the German Government.

José Gustavo Guerrero of El Salvador (1876-1958), who was President both of the PCIJ and the ICJ.

Early Thoughts

The exchange of views in regard to the post-war world order started quite early, in official circles also. Actually, the Washington State Department considered plans well before the United States even entered the war. The Atlantic Charter of August 1941 and the Washington Declaration of the United Nations of January 1942 paved the way for the Four Nations Declaration on General Security which was signed in Moscow in October 1943 by the Soviet Union, the USA, Great Britain and China. At this juncture, the establishment 'at the earliest practicable date' of a general international organization was advocated. The sovereign equality of all peace-loving States was to be the guiding principle of the organization envisaged.

A first step towards international judicial reorganization was taken by the Foreign Ministers of the South American Republics. In January 1942, they instructed the Inter-American Juridical Committee to make recommendations in this sphere, which were submitted in September of the same year. Similar concerns preoccupied Washington in those days. However, as the USA had been neither a Member of the League nor a party to the Permanent Court's Statute, the American approach needed to be a cautious one. Eventually the proposal was approved in principle. In July 1942, Secretary of State Hull announced the acceptance by the USA of the establishment of an International Court after the War. Meanwhile, within the Soviet Union, parallel ideas were being developed, in which M. Krylov, later to be a Judge of the Court, took a prominent part.

Interestingly enough, the thinking within British official circles took a different course during this period. Initially, the continuance of the Permanent Court was taken for granted. As early as October 1941, the British Government invited the USA Government to discuss the future of the Permanent Court in London, but the offer was declined. The initiative was resumed early in 1943, as representatives of ten governments, not including the Soviet Union and the United States, agreed on nominating a group of experts, assuming that 'an international court in some form would be needed in the future'.

The gist of this tale is that, however different the views regarding the implementation of the idea may have been, the sheer necessity of a Court was never seriously doubted. Whatever the institutional shortcomings of the League of Nations and the Permanent Court may have been, it was primarily thanks to them that such thoughts were now generally entertained throughout the international community. What had been a virtual impossibility around 1900 and had been attempted on an experimental basis in 1920, was no longer really questioned in 1940.

Malkin's Committee of Experts

In February 1944, the Informal Inter-Allied Committee of Experts, under the chairmanship of Sir William Malkin, published a stimulating report on the future of the International Court. The Committee had a purely informal status and its members were appointed on the basis of personal capacity without binding their governments. Their sole object was to make recommendations to the United Nations as a whole. Among its members were three future Judges of the ICJ: Gros, Winiarski and Fitzmaurice, who acted as secretary.

The Committee reached the sound conclusion that the Statute of the PCIJ was a highly workable instrument for any future Court and should be retained as such. In terms of jurisdiction, it held that essentially political matters should be excluded from the competence of the Court. It also reasoned that the advisory jurisdiction of the Court should be maintained in the new set-up. The issue regarding the creation of a new Court or the continuance of the old one was deemed to be outside its terms of reference and was left to the policy-makers to settle.

The report of the Committee was a highly valuable contribution to future thinking regarding the Court. Apart from this, as Rosenne concludes:

> It is, indeed, a tribute to the ideals which the very notion of international justice inspires, that at the height of the War this group of men, from eleven different countries, most of them temporarily exiled from their homes, could spare the time from their engrossing official and national duties, to consider these problems. (Rosenne, *Law and Practice*, 1985, at p. 28)

Dumbarton Oaks

An informal exchange of views on the establishment of an international organization for the maintenance of peace and security, agreed upon in Moscow in October 1943, took place at Dumbarton Oaks in August-September 1944. The proposals it produced were intended to be of assistance to a full conference of the United Nations to be held at a later stage. With regard to the projected Court, Chapter Four of the Proposals envisaged an International Court of Justice as one of the principal organs of the Organization. In Chapter Five, the election of Judges was entrusted to the General Assembly of the Organization.

In Chapter Seven, the Court was described as the principal judicial organ of the Organization. It should function in accordance with a Statute - be this the Statute of the PCIJ or a new Statute based thereon - which should be annexed to and be a part of the Charter of the Organization; all members of the Organization should *ipso facto* be parties to the Statute and it was left to the General Assembly, upon the recommendation of the Security Council, to decide on the admittance of parties not members of the Organization.

In Chapter Eight, the competence of the Court was to be defined as comprising justiciable disputes, with the explicit exclusion of any such disputes which according to international law came within the domestic jurisdiction of a State. Legal questions connected with non-justiciable disputes should be referred to the Court for advice through the channels of the Security Council.

Unlike Malkin's Committee of Experts, the Dumbarton Oaks conference formally recognized the organic connection between the Court and the Organization. Also, it inclined to the view that the Statute of the PCIJ should be retained as a constituent instrument of the Court. The issues still outstanding at this stage were whether to establish a new Court or retain the old one, the number of Judges, the method of election, and finally, the matter of compulsory jurisdiction. This was not really a coincidence; these were, essentially, the very problems which for so long had prevented the establishment of an International Court in the first place. However, it was the full appreciation of these problems at this stage and the general desire to solve them which led to the establishment of a new committee on a broad footing to examine the bones of contention.

An informal meeting in the library at Dumbarton Oaks. Cadogan, Stettinius, and Gromyko are seated second, third and fourth from left.

The Washington Committee of Jurists

In March 1945, the US Government issued invitations to the members of the wartime anti-Nazi coalition to send delegates to a Committee of Jurists to meet in Washington in April and to prepare a draft of the Statute. In all, no less than forty-four nations were represented on this Washington Committee of Jurists; only India and South Africa declined to attend. The Committee was chaired by Green Haywood Hackworth, an official of the US State Department, Member of the PCA since 1937, and later Judge (1946-1960) and President (1955-1958) of the ICJ. Jules Basdevant, the distinguished French jurist became its Rapporteur. He was later to serve on the ICJ for twenty years and preside over the Bench from 1949 to 1952. Actually, quite a number of jurists assembled here were to become Judges of the Court at a later stage. The PCIJ was represented through Judge Manley Hudson, acting as an observer.

The meetings of the Committee had a reconnoitering character only. It was not empowered to take any definitive action; its conclusions were to be considered as the recommendations of experts. The Committee managed to finish its work just before the opening of the constituent meeting of the Organization, the San Francisco Conference, on which the Allied Powers had decided at Yalta. During its meetings, the

Committee carefully scrutinized the Statute of the PCIJ and proposed a number of amendments, most of them of a technical nature. What it left open was whether the planned Court was to be considered a new institution or an extension of the Permanent Court, as well as the recurrent issues of elections and compulsory jurisdiction. With regard to the latter aspect, the question was raised whether the acceptance of the Court's compulsory jurisdiction was to be a condition for membership of the Organization itself.

The San Francisco Conference

At the San Francisco Conference, which was attended by fifty States and was in session during April-June 1945 to prepare the Charter of the United Nations on the basis of the Dumbarton Oaks Proposals, the drafting of the Statute of the Court was entrusted to a special, technical committee. This Committee IV/1 invited two members of the PCIJ, President Guerrero and Manley Hudson, to attend in a consultative capacity. It established four subcommittees, one on the question of continuity, one on the issue of nominations, one on elections, and one on matters of jurisdiction. The Committee delivered a Report to Commission IV of the Conference which, after being verified by the Coordinating Committee and the Advisory Committee of Jurists of the Conference, was incorporated into the Charter. It was adopted as its Chapter Fourteen (Art. 92-96), to which the Statute of the Court was then annexed.

Jules Basdevant (1877-1968), member of the 1945 UN Committee of Jurists, Judge (1946-1965) and President (1949-1952) of the ICJ.

The results of the Conference were far-reaching. The first major decision taken was that the new Court should be a component part of the newly launched Organization, the United Nations, and constitute its principal judicial organ, on the same footing as the General Assembly, Security Council, Economic and Social Council, Trusteeship Council and Secretariat. The Statute of the Court was to be annexed to and form part of the Charter. The reason for not integrating the two documents into one was merely a practical one, i.e., to avoid unbalancing the 111 articles of the Charter through the addition of the 70 articles of the Statute. Besides, this procedure also facilitated access to the new Court for States which were not members of the United Nations.

Obviously, despite all the technicalities involved, the preference for a new Court rather than for a continuance of the old one was primarily a political decision. Essential to the outcome had been the agreement reached on these matters by the two States which had emerged from the war as the world's leading powers. Major considerations had been that thirteen States represented at San Francisco were not signatories to the Statute of the PCIJ - including both the Soviet Union and the United States - and that sixteen signatories of that same Statute were not participants in the Conference. A further consideration was that, as the Court was to form part of the United Nations, it seemed inap-

Green Haywood Hackworth (1883-1973), the chairman of the 1945 UN Committee of Jurists, Judge (1946-1961) and President (1955-1958) of the ICJ.

The Soviet delegation at San Francisco: First row on the left Professor S. A. Golunsky (1952-1953 Judge) and on the right Professor S. B. Krylov (1946-1952 Judge).

propriate for this role to be filled by the PCIJ, which was closely linked to the League of Nations, then on the point of dissolution. Also, the proposed structure was more consistent with the provision in the UN Charter that Members of the United Nations would *ipso facto* be parties to the Court's Statute.

A factor which was important, though it did not directly contribute to the outcome, was the feeling in some quarters that the PCIJ represented the old world, the previous world order, in which European States had enjoyed political as well as legal predominance in the international community. A fresh start and a new institution, it was felt, would make it easier and more attractive for non-European powers to join and make their influence felt. Time has definitely confirmed the truth of this assumption. Within the sub-committee, out of ten votes, France, Great Britain and Brazil were the only nations to advocate the continued existence of the PCIJ, although it must be said that some other nations voted in favour of the converse decision on practical grounds only.

In contrast to this, and a major source of future controversy, was the decision taken at San Francisco to maintain a degree of continuity in the administration of international justice. This decision merely reflected the political reality of the time.

In general terms, at San Francisco, the draft of the Washington Committee of Jurists was followed. The Conference did not write into the Charter any provisions making compulsory any specific method for the pacific settlement of disputes. In terms of the faculty of requesting Advisory Opinions, the General Assembly, in a departure from the Dumbarton Oaks Proposals, was put on the same footing as the Security Council. On the other hand, the arrangement retained the PCIJ tradition of entrusting the election of Judges to both Council and Assembly.

Also in San Francisco, a Preparatory Commission of the United Nations was established, on which each Contracting Power was represented, to make provisional arrangements regarding each principal organ of the new Organization. In spite of reservations made by some nations, it was decided to have the elections to the Court take place at the earliest opportunity, that is during the first part of the First Session of the Council and Assembly in London.

The Transfer

On 26 June 1945, together with the Charter, the Statute of the ICJ was adopted. Both came into force on 24 October of the same year. In October, too, the PCIJ met for the last time to take all appropriate steps to ensure the transfer of its archives and effects to the new Court. On 31 January 1946, in London, the Old Bench resigned. On 6 February, still in London, the first Bench of the ICJ was elected. The Secretary-General issued instructions to summon a first meeting of the Court to be held at The Hague as soon as could conveniently be arranged and authorized the

Publications related to the San Francisco Conference.

conduct of negotiations with the Board of the Carnegie Foundation at The Hague regarding the premises.

During a first meeting of the Judges in London, presided over by the senior Judge, Gustavo Guerrero, administrative and organizational matters were discussed with the Acting Secretary of the Court, Dr E. Hambro. On 3 April the Court met for the first time; it had discussions with the Registrar of the PCIJ, Mr Lopéz Olivãn, who then recruited temporary staff, made preliminary financial arrangements and dealt with the question of the premises.

The Court's first session in The Hague took place from 6 April to 6 May 1946. The Court started by electing Gustavo Guerrero as its President, and Jules Basdevant as its Vice-President, Mr Hambro as Registrar and Mr Garnier-Coignet as Deputy-Registrar. It arranged the conditions of service of the Registry staff, dealt with diplomatic and budgetary matters, and elected the Chamber of Summary Procedure.

The Inauguration of the Court

On 18 April 1946, on the very day the League of Nations and the PCIJ voted themselves out of existence, the International Court of Justice held its solemn inaugural sitting at the Peace Palace. In the presence of Princess Juliana and Prince Bernhard of the Netherlands, the President of the General Assembly of the United Nations, representatives of the Security Council, the Economic and Social Council and the UN Secretariat, and members of the Dutch Government and the Diplomatic Corps, the President of the ICJ made the Solemn Declaration provided for in the Statute and then invited his colleagues to do the same.

In his opening address to her Royal Highness, President Guerrero observed:

> To-day, as in 1922, on the occasion of the inauguration of the Permanent Court of International Justice, the Royal Family is present. This is symbolic of the desire for justice which has animated the Dutch nation throughout the centuries.

In his impressive speech, he enlarged on the continuity of the principle of international adjudication as exemplified by the Old and the New Bench:

Publications related to the UN Charter and the ICJ.

> I would for a moment summon up a few past memories and remind you of the ties that bind the Court of to-day to that of yesterday. In the long chain of institutions created to secure the pacific settlement of international disputes, the Permanent Court of International Justice was the most important link. The establishment of a really permanent system of rendering justice between States dates only from its creation. ... The place of the Permanent Court of International Justice, which left The Hague in 1940, is now taken by the International Court of Justice. But between the old and the new Courts the bonds have remained so close that it is hard to believe that there has been a change. The United Nations, indeed, have never sought to minimize the services rendered by the old Court; their aim has been simply to adapt the machinery of international justice to the new conditions of the international order established to safeguard peace. For this reason, though the International Court of Justice is one of the principal organs of the United Nations Organization, its Statute is based on that of the Permanent Court of International Justice. For this reason, the new Court to-day begins its work in the same city, in the same palace and in the same hall in which the previous Court delivered its judgments which constitute the most remarkable collection in the field of international law. This work will be continued by us in the same spirit which animated our predecessors. We shall preserve its continuity and devote ourselves to maintaining its prestige and authority.

Mr Henri Spaak, the then President of the

Edvard Isak Hambro of Norway, Registrar of the ICJ during 1946-1953 and President of the UN General Assembly during 1970.

J. Lopéz Olivãn of Spain, Registrar of the ICJ during 1953-1960.

General Assembly of the United Nations, stressed the peculiar place of the Court in the international system:

> Members of the Court, I would not venture to assert that the International Court of Justice is the most important organ of the United Nations; but I think I may say that in any case there is none more important. Perhaps the General Assembly is more numerous; perhaps the Security Council is more spectacular; perhaps the activities of the Economic and Social Council would be more constant and more varied. Your work will perhaps be less in view, but I am convinced that it is of quite exceptional importance. And if I could personally express a hope, it is that in the years to come, your duties may become every day more important. If I might express another hope, it is that one day your jurisdiction may become compulsory for all countries and for all disputes without exception. For I am deeply convinced that peace will not finally be established until all countries have recognized the truth that there can be no civilized world nor any lasting peace, if there be not complete and absolute respect for international jurisdiction and its judgments.

Most speakers referred to the past miseries of the war. Mr Henri Spaak called to mind that:

> A ceremony like this enables us to realize the dangers we have been through and the rewards of our sufferings and of the victory we have achieved. If we had had the misfortune to lose the war, would there ever have been an International Court of Justice? It is certain that, within a few months of a victory won by our adversaries, we should not have witnessed, in a hall like this, the rendering of a solemn tribute to the cause of law and justice by fifty-one victorious nations. At this solemn moment, let us think once again of those who gave their lives that such an hour as this might be possible.

Dr Ivan Kerno, Assistant Secretary-General of the United Nations stated:

> It is with great emotion that I find myself once more in the city of The Hague, which has remained the seat of the Court and where I have spent several years of my life in various capacities. Since then, the tide of war and the terrible enemy

The inauguration of the International Court of Justice on 18 April 1946.

occupation have passed over it. We still see the sad scars here, as in many other countries throughout the world. I have myself lived under occupation; it is perhaps one of the means best calculated to enable one to appreciate the immensity of the task of reconstruction and re-adaptation which awaits all those who devote themselves to international activities.

Mr van Royen, the Dutch Minister for Foreign Affairs, addressing the Court, reminded the Judges of the words on the pedestal of the statue of Erasmus in the rosebeds of the Peace Palace gardens:

Dulce bellum inexpertis. The horrors of war, of which this statue has been a silent witness, have still further emphasized the truth of these words. But what were the miseries of war in the time of Erasmus, or even the disasters of the second world war, compared to the catastrophe which, as a result of the invention of new and more effective means of destruction, would menace the world if a new war broke out? With you, Gentlemen, lies the task of contributing to the banishment of this nightmare.

With reference to Montesquieu's *Esprit des lois*, he spoke of:

... the strict impartiality with which a Judge must perform his duty and the inflexibility which he must manifest - not indeed in regard to the law, which is ever developing and renewing itself - but in regard to the particular wishes and claims of parties, which cannot be taken into account when judgment has to be rendered according to law. In such a case, indeed, a Judge must show himself to be a completely disinterested authority which can modify neither the force nor the rigour of the law.

Mr De Monchy, Burgomaster of The Hague, sketched for his audience a vivid picture of the immense losses Holland had recently suffered, only to conclude:

But we must not despair. A few months only have passed since there was established an organization comprising all the nations of the planet. Let us bear in mind the words of Anatole France: 'Slowly but surely mankind fulfils the dreams of the sages'. The existence of your Court is an appeal to the conscience of the nations, telling them that force of arms is not the only, nor the best, way of securing what they consider to be their rights.

On 5 May 1945, the Court adopted the Rules, which in substance corresponded to those of the PCIJ in their revised version. They were to stand in this form until 1972. They served to emphasize continuity in matters of jurisprudence as well as procedure which was deliberately intended, as well as a new departure in terms of organizational structures. To be sure, the reconstruction of the machinery of adjudication was much facilitated by the presence of many who had served the Permanent Court in various capacities, whether as Judge, Judge *ad hoc*, Counsel or Registry staff member.

On 22 May 1947, the first case was brought before the Court, namely the *Corfu Channel* case.

THE RULES OF COURT

In pursuance of powers conferred upon it by the Statute, the ICJ has drawn up its own *Rules of Court*. These Rules are intended to supplement the general rules set forth in the Statute and to make detailed provision for the steps taken to comply with them. Since the Rules have been drawn up in pursuance of the Statute, they may not contain any provisions that are repugnant to the Statute or which confer upon the Court powers that go beyond those conferred by the Statute. The Rules of Court thus amplify the provisions of the Statute concerning the Court's procedure and the working of the Court and of the Registry, so that on certain points it is necessary to consult both documents. The ICJ is competent to amend its Rules of Court, and can thus incorporate into them provisions embodying its practice as this has developed.

On 5 May 1946, the ICJ adopted rules largely based on the latest version of the *Rules of Court* of the PCIJ, which dated from 1936. In 1967, in the light of the experience it had acquired and of the need to adapt the Rules to the changes that had taken place in the world and in the pace of international events, it embarked upon a thoroughgoing revision of its Rules and set up a standing Committee for the purpose. On 10 May 1972, it adopted certain amendments which came into force the following 1 September. On 14 April 1978 the Court adopted a thoroughly revised set of Rules which came into force on 1 July 1978. The object of the changes made was to increase the flexibility of proceedings, making them as simple and rapid as possible, and help to reduce the costs to the parties, so far as these matters depended upon the Court.

From: *The International Court of Justice 1946-1986*, by the ICJ, The Hague, 1986)

THE FERDINAND BOL ROOM

On entering, in 1922, the PCIJ took possession of several rooms which had hitherto belonged to other institutions. Among these was a salon on the first floor with a 17th century Dutch style interior, the Ferdinand Bol Room, after the artist who painted the three masterpieces that cover the walls. It was used for deliberations by the PCIJ and ICJ until the mid-seventies. From then on its function was taken over by the modern facilities offered in the new wing.

The name of Ferdinand Bol has a ring, mainly due to his affinity with Rembrandt, whose pupil he was. Bol was born in Dordrecht in 1616, a barber's son. At twenty he moved to Rembrandt's bustling studio in Amsterdam to become 'a man of his own' about 1640. However, the problem with Bol is precisely that he never really became a master of his own. In his younger years, understandably, he was virtually overwhelmed by the genius of Rembrandt. Later on, the Flemish painters Rubens, van Dyck and Jordaens won him over. He then proceeded to copy their styles with the same virtuosity and gentle ease that is typical of his style throughout. His heydays were the fifties and sixties when he was literally overloaded with commissions and showered with compliments by the Amsterdam regent class.

With Bol, lucrative portraits and groupings of dignitaries alternate with fashionable, huge historical pieces, on biblical and mythological themes in a classicist mood with increasingly baroque overtones. The four examples found in the Peace Palace are part of the collection of the *Rijksmuseum* and in all respects are representative of the artist's style. Three of them are found in the Bol Room, the fourth in the Board's Administration Room downstairs.

The first panel represents the finding of Moses (based on Exodus 2:5-7), but has more of a sensual pastorale in the classical tradition of the goddess Diana and her nymphs taking a bath. The second panel probably represents the *Offering of presents at the building of Solomon's Temple* (based on I Kings 9:11,14 and 10:25). The third panel represents *Aeneas receiving through Venus his new armour from Vulcan's Smithy* (Virgil, *Aeneid* VIII: 370-385). As regards the dating of the pieces nothing much can be ascertained. All four of them are by all means from Bol's later years, the 1660-1670s.

The Ferdinand Bol Room also contains a triptych on the ceiling by Gérard de Lairesse. It was bought on the strength of an interpretation which afterwards proved wrong. The paintings do not represent an allegory on the 'Triumph of Peace' or the 'Munster Peace Treaty' as was thought. In the middle panel a maiden sits on a throne high on the clouds, holding the hat of freedom and flanked by Mercury. She represents Amsterdam's mercantile liberty and is about to be crowned by *putti* with the *corona navalis*. At her feet a roaring lion with flaming sword and heavy shield, on which feature the town's emblem of the three St Andrew crosses, stands ready to defend the lady's honour atop rocks which feature date and signature. On the left panel Concordia tramples down the enchained Mars, whereas on the right panel the helmeted Minerva is seen vanquishing the three Harpies: Violence, Envy and Fraud. The river gods of Y and Amstel, imperative to Amsterdam's prosperity, feature in the right and left bottom corners.

And finally, above the doors we find carved in light oak panels, the busts of Hugo Grotius and Cornelis van Bynckershoek, the two renowned Dutch international lawyers of the 17th and 18th centuries.

The Ferdinand Bol Room, the deliberations room of the Court in the Peace Palace until the mid-1970s.
Above: The first session of the International Court of Justice in this room.
Left: Detail from the large painting 'Offering of Presents at the Building of Solomon's Temple' by Ferdinand Bol (1618-1682).

The Registry

The 1922 Statute of the Court provided for the appointment of a Registrar, who was to reside at the seat of the Court. Though numerous articles of the Statute referred to the Registrar, it seems that at the time of the drafting there was little appreciation of the importance of the post. Apparently the later developments which made the office so vital to the functioning of the Court, were not foreseen. From a clerk of the Court, the Registrar developed into the head of an institution called the Registry - which surprisingly enough was not mentioned in the Statute.

Article 21(2) of the present Statute empowers the Court to provide for the appointment of such officers, other than the Registrar, as may be necessary. Still, the appointment of a Registrar is the only statutory duty imposed upon the Court. Over the recruitment and appointment of 'other officers', the Court has complete discretion.

The paramount consideration in the employment of the staff and in the determination of the conditions of service should, according to Article 101(3) of the Charter, be the necessity of securing the highest standards of efficiency, competence and integrity. The other consideration referred to in the same article of the Charter, and which undoubtedly holds good for the Secretariat itself, namely that due regard shall be paid to a wide geographical distribution of recuitment, is perhaps more difficult to apply in view of the small number of staff involved in The Hague and its very specific duties.

Meanwhile, this power of the Court to appoint its own staff, distinguishes it sharply from the other principal organs of the UN Organization. The amplification given in Article 17 of the Rules of Court to the skeleton provisions provided by the Statute only corroborate this difference. It states that the officials of the Registry shall be appointed by the Court on proposals submitted by the Registrar. Again, in the declaration to be made by new officials, to the effect that they will perform their

The staff of the Registry in 1996.

The Registry

REGISTRAR

DEPUTY REGISTRAR

LEGAL MATTERS
Principal Legal Secretary
First Secretaries
Secretaries
Legal Officers
Associate Legal Officers

LINGUISTIC MATTERS
First Secretary

English Section	*French Section*
Translator/ Interpreter	Translator/ Interpreter

INFORMATION MATTERS
Secretary
Associate Officer

ESTABLISHMENT DEPARTMENT
Head (Accountant)

– *Finance* –
Associate Officer
Salary Administration Clerk
Finance/System Assistant
Accounting Clerk

– *General Services* –
Senior Registry Clerk
Registry Clerk
Senior Driver
Telephonists
Security Guards
Messengers

PRINTING DEPARTMENT
Head
Second Officer

DOCUMENTS DEPARTMENT
LIBRARY OF THE COURT
Librarian
Associate Librarian
Library Clerk
Stack and Reference Clerk

TYPEWRITING AND
REPRODUCTION DEPARTMENT
Head
Typing Pool
Typists
Documents Reproduction Clerks

ARCHIVES AND
DISTRIBUTION DEPARTMENT
Archivist
Assistant Archivist
Distribution Clerks
Indexer/Researcher

SECRETARIES OF
MEMBERS OF THE COURT

duties as officials of the ICJ with all loyalty, discretion, and good conscience, no reference at all is made to the United Nations. This creates a distance between the staff of the Registry and the staff members of the Secretariat of the United Nations. This discrepancy is indeed quite intentional and harks back to the days of the PCIJ. As Rosenne concludes, 'the maintenance of this system is probably essential if anything like an independent judiciary is to exist in the international sphere' (*Law and Practice*, 1985, at p. 255).

The differentiation of the Registry staff from the Secretariat Staff is thus to be seen as a question of principle. In general, however, the conditions of employment of Registry officials, their emoluments and their pension rights correspond to those of UN officials of equivalent category and grade and their costs are borne by the United Nations. They enjoy the same privileges and immunities as members of comparable rank on diplomatic missions at The Hague.

In 1946, the Court in its policy of appointments, gave preference to those staff members of the PCIJ who showed interest in being enlisted in the new Organization. Both the preservation of continuity and the advantage of highly technical experience came into play here. The *Staff Regulations* for the Registry of the new Court were approved by the Court in March 1947. It was stipulated that any question relating to rights or duties of staff members not covered by the Regulations was to be dealt with by the Registrar, having regard to the rules in force in the UN Secretariat. Any disputes arising between the Registrar and a staff member should be submitted either by the Registrar or the person in question to the Court for settlement according to a procedure which the Court may decide. In recent years, the issues relating to this procedure have been given increasing attention.

The most essential duties of the staff and of the different departments of the Registry are outlined in the *Instructions for the Registry* which were adopted in March 1947 and slightly amended in September 1949.

The Registry is the administrative organ of the ICJ. It is responsible to the Court alone. Since the ICJ is both a Court of Justice and an international organ, the Registry's tasks are both those of a service helping the administration of justice and

Registrar Eduardo Valencia-Ospina from Colombia signing the Order of the Court of 10 January 1996 in the Law and Maritime Boundary *case between Cameroon and Nigeria.*

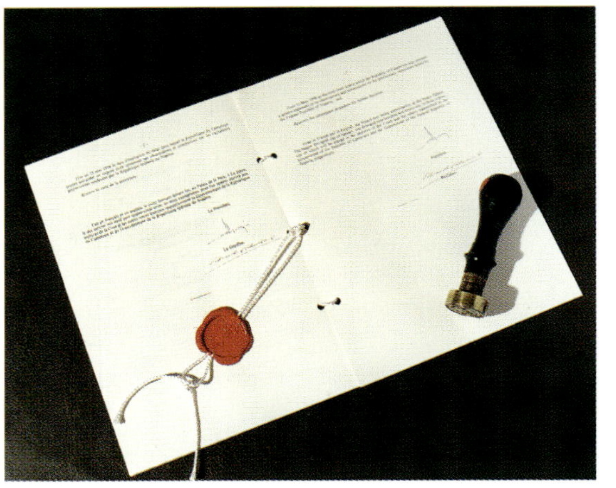

those of the secretariat of an international institution. Its activities are officially classified under four aspects, which in practice partly overlap. They are, on the one hand, of a judicial and diplomatic nature, including the maintenance of the Court's General List and the preparation of cases for hearing and related correspondence. On the other hand, they include linguistic activities and correspond to the work of the legal, administrative and financial departments and of the conference and information services of an international organization.

The administrative aspects cover personnel and financial administration, office organization and the printing of the Court's publications, which are considerable indeed. However, it is precisely the contact with the judicial work of the Court which distinguishes the Registry Staff from the general international civil service and which justifies its afore-mentioned exclusive status.

Apart from the administrative work, all communications are entrusted to the Registry, be this with the United Nations or other international organizations, with governments of States parties to cases, or with respect to extra-judicial activities, e.g. matters concerning privileges and immunities. The Registry staff also looks after contacts with universities, the media and the general public.

The Office of Registrar and Deputy-Registrar

The Registrar is the chief administrative officer of the Court. He is appointed by the Court, by secret ballot and by absolute majority, from among candidates proposed by Members of the Court. He is elected for a term of seven years and may be re-elected, provided that his candidature is proposed again. The present Registrar of the Court, Mr Eduardo Valencia-Ospina of Colombia, who was appointed in 1987, was the first official from the Latin American world to be elected to the office. The Registrar has the status of an Assistant Secretary-General of the United Nations.

The Court also appoints a Deputy-Registrar under the same conditions and in the same way as the Registrar. Both officials make a solemn declaration before taking up their duties. As regards the distribution of duties between the Registrar and Deputy-Registrar no special provisions are made. In principle, the latter official is the assistant of the former, acts as Registrar in his absence and, in the event of the office becoming vacant, exercises the functions of Registrar until the office has been filled. In the absence of both officials the President of the Court appoints an official of the Registry to replace the Registrar. Given the international civil service character of the Registry, the Registrar is not disqualified from acting as such in cases where he is the national of one of the States parties.

The duties of the Registrar relate both to the administration of the Court and to the conduct of its judicial business. Under the Rules of Court and Instructions for the Registry, 'the Registrar is responsible for all departments of the Registry. The Staff is under his control and he alone is authorized to direct the work of the Registry, of which he is the head'. He is required to reside at The Hague. He normally serves as the channel for communication between the ICJ and States or Organizations, attends the meetings of the Court and ensures that minutes are drawn up. He countersigns the Court's decisions and has custody of its seal.

Registrars of the ICJ
E.I. Hambro (Norway), 1946-1953
J. López-Oliván (Spain), 1953-1960
J. Garnier-Coignet (France), 1960-1966
S. Aquarone (Australia), 1966-1980
S. Torres Bernárdez (Spain), 1980-1986
E. Valencia-Ospina (Colombia), 1987-present

Deputy-Registrars of the ICJ
J. Garnier-Coignet (France), 1946-1960
S. Aquarone (Australia), 1960-1966
W. Tait (Great Britain), 1966-1976
A. Pillepich (France), 1977-1984
E. Valencia-Ospina (Colombia), 1984-1987
B. Noble (Great Britain), 1987-1994
J.-J. Arnaldez (France), 1994-present

Pursuant to the *Rules of Court*, the Registrar has also to 'deal with enquiries concerning the Court and its work' and 'ensure that information concerning the Court and its activities is made accessible to governments, the highest national Courts of justice, professional and learned societies, legal faculties and schools of law, and public information media'. Accordingly, he arranges the publication of information concerning the composition, jurisdiction and work of the Court, and the cases before the Court. In this task he is assisted by one of the Registry's Secretaries who is especially entrusted with information matters.

One aspect of the Registrar's function may be highlighted here in greater detail, as it serves both to illustrate the status of the office and its importance to the independent functioning of the Court itself. It concerns the performance of the function of transmitting the various documents and notices to the Parties and other States concerned. As Rosenne observes:

In performing such functions there is little room for discretion. The Statute, Rules and Instructions are mandatory in most cases. ... The Registrar is thereby required to bring to the notice of the party from whom the document emanates any failure to conform with the directions of the Statute or of the Rules noted by him in the document instituting proceedings or in a pleading.
In performing functions of this character, it is submitted that, as the Registrar is carrying out ministerial functions in which he has no discretion, his action therefore does not bind the Court. ... Nevertheless, in the performance of these ministerial functions, the Registrar may be faced with problems of considerable delicacy. ... The Registrar must satisfy himself that he is legally correct in undertaking the specific task required of him. ... In solving problems of this character, the Registrar in fact has recourse to what is an implied power to make summary and provisional decisions of an international character. ... The existence of this aspect of the Registrar's work provides justification for the argument that his position bears such a close resemblance to that of the Secretary-General. The creation of a post such as this in independence of the similar post of Secretary-General is one of the guarantees for the independence of the Court (Rosenne, *Law and Practice*, 1985 at pp. 258-259).

The formal provisions of the Statute and other instruments are enhanced by the dignity with which the office has been invested - the solemn declaration made in open Court, the judicial robes worn by the Registrar in Court, and the assimilation of the Registrar to the Status of Head of Diplomatic Mission (a status also enjoyed by the members of the Court). All these aspects, which have their influence also on the Registry staff, are considered absolutely essential for the proper performance of the functions of the Court.

In the Netherlands, therefore, the Registrar is, in a general way, accorded the same treatment as heads of diplomatic missions accredited to Her Majesty the Queen of the Netherlands. On official missions, the Registrar enjoys all the privileges, immunities and facilities granted to diplomatic envoys. By an General Assembly Resolution of 1946, the Members of the United Nations are also called

The Deputy-Registrar, Mr J.-J. Arnaldez from France (right) and the Principal Legal Secretary, Mr Ph. Couvreur from Belgium (left).

From top to bottom: the Registrars Mr J. Garnier-Coignet, Mr S. Aquarone and Mr S. Torres Bernárdez.

Left: The bench of Secretaries of the Registry.

Right: The interpreters of the Registry in the booth of the Great Court Hall.

upon to recognize and accept the UN *laissez-passer* issued to the Registrar (and officials of the Registry) by the Court.

The Staff of the Registry

Apart from the Registrar and Deputy-Registrar, the Staff at present consists of permanent officials and officials on fixed or short-term contracts appointed by the Court or the Registrar. The total number varies acording to the case-load and peculiar aspects of a case (this applies, in particular, to the linguistic staff of interpreters and translators). In 1996 the Court comprises of fifteen Judges and thirteen Judges *ad hoc*; the Registry Staff includes 24 officials in the Professional category and 37 in the General Service category. According to the *Rules of Court*, 'the Staff of the Registry shall be subject to Staff Regulations drawn up by the Registrar, as far as possible in conformity with the UN Staff Regulations and Staff Rules, and approved by the Court'.

Adopted in its present form in 1979, these *Staff Regulations* are amended and updated at regular intervals. They contain the standard provisions governing professional relations, conditions of work and matters of discipline and leave. Any question not covered by the Regulations is left to the Registrar to decide in conformity with the prevailing norms and rules within the UN Secretariat. As stipulated above, disputes between the Registrar and staff members are submitted to the Court and left to its discretion.

Hierarchically prominent among the Staff are the Principal Legal Secretary, three First Secretaries, and one Secretary. The Registry comprises of eight Departments whose officials are divided in the categories of Professionals and General Service Staff. These Departments are:

Legal Matters
This Department's duties include the drafting of the Orders of the Court and the formal parts of Judgments; the assisting of the Drafting Committees of the Court in the preparation, drafting and editing of Judgments; the drafting of correspondence with the Agents of Parties; the conducting of legal research required by cases; participation in the preparation of case documents for publication; finally, responding to outside enquiries of a legal nature. The Principal Legal Secretary acts as Secretary to the Court's Rules Committee, and stands in for the Registrar and Deputy-Registrar when necessary.

Linguistic Matters
This Department provides drafting and editing assistance to Judges, revises translations of judicial decisions and opinions, and writes minutes.

A few words must be said about the languages of the Court. The ICJ has two official languages, French and English. Before the constituting of the PCIJ, the 1920 Committee of Jurists had pronounced itself in favour of French alone. However, from the outset, the Council and Assembly of the League of Nations decided in favour of a

The translators section.

Left: The computer desk in the Establishment Department.

Right: The telephone operators at the switching board.

bilingual system which was also maintained throughout its Organization.

In 1954, this interwar principle was maintained by the United Nations in respect of the ICJ, although the UN Organization itself adopted no less than five official languages. Consequently, Members of the Court, whatever their background, work in French or English. Likewise, all official documents of the Registry are bilingual and all correspondence is conducted in these two languages. Again, Parties must file their pleadings and deliver oral arguments in either of these languages and the Registry provides interpreters and translators to render the spoken or written word in the other official language. Parties may also agree between themselves to employ other languages, provided that they themselves furnish translations and interpretations into one of the official languages of the Court.

Consequently, a considerable volume of the Registry's activity is of a linguistic nature. Also for this reason, all officials within the Registry are required to be proficient in both official languages. Officials in the higher categories, or whose work involves linguistic responsibilities, must have one of these official languages of the Court as their first language.

Information Matters

Responsibilites include apprising Members of the Court of the developments in international disputes, of proceedings and appointments in international organizations and organisms devoted to international law, and of reactions to and the aftermath of Court decisions. The Department also informs the outside media of developments in proceedings and performs protocol functions with respect to visiting Heads of State and the Host Government. It further co-ordinates the preparation of the Court's *Yearbook* and drafts the Court's *Annual Report*, provides talks on the Court, answers public enquiries and corresponds with the scholarly world.

Establishment Department

This Department deals with the general administration, including programme budgeting, maintenance of accounts, financial reporting to UN Headquarters; development and upkeep of management information systems; purchase of equipment; processing the payroll of salaries, allowances and benefits; vendor and travel disbursements; staff medical insurance; purchasing services; telecommunications and electronic data services, including the network management and the computer help desk; audio recording of public sittings; liaison with local authorities. It is responsible for the supervision of messengers, security guards, drivers and telephone operators.

The Department is headed by the Accountant. This officer assists the Registrar in executing the budget. The Registrar himself bears sole responsibility for the

The official Yearbook of the Court.

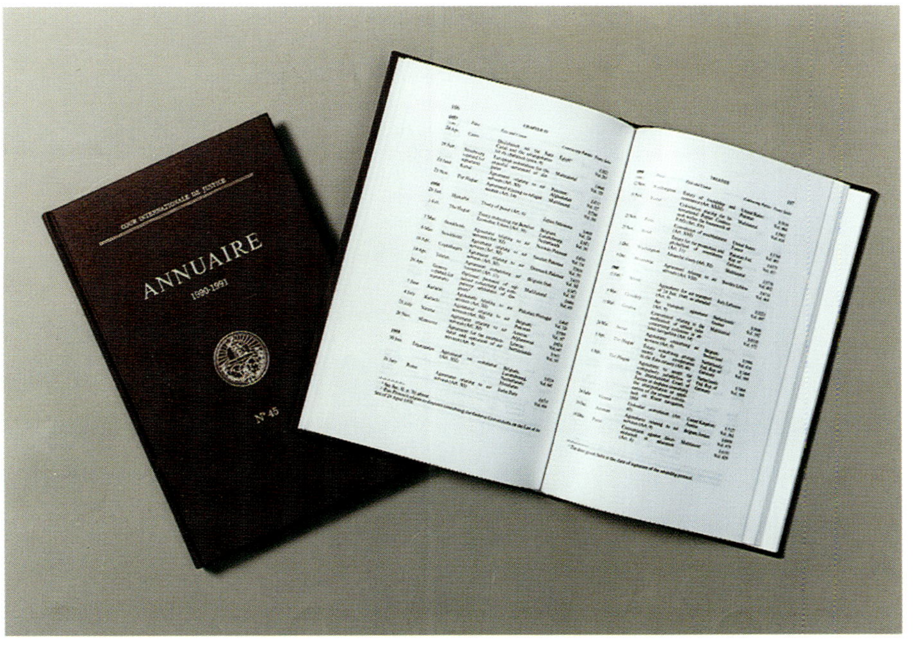

PUBLICATIONS OF THE ICJ

In general, the system of publications developed by the PCIJ was maintained in 1946. The *Rules of Court* are not very specific in these respects. They merely provide for the printing and publishing, under the responsibility of the Registrar, of 'a collection of the Judgments and Advisory Opinions of the Court, and also of such Orders as the Court may decide to include therein'.

In addition to this, the *Instructions for the Registry* provide for a special series containing the minutes of public sittings and other documents relating to cases submitted to the Court. It is left to the discretion of the Court to decide upon other publications. One such publication is, traditionally, an annual *Bibliography*. The Registrar's responsibilities include the publication of a *Yearbook*, which in no way involves the responsibility of the Court.

Copies of the Court's publications are supplied officially to governments and certain international organizations and institutions. Publication and sale is carried out through the Sales Agents and Booksellers of the United Nations in various countries. As a matter of policy prices are kept low to secure the widest possible distribution. The official publications of the Court are:

- *Reports of Judgments, Advisory Opinions and Orders*, containing full texts in French and English on opposite pages.
- *Pleadings, Oral Arguments, Documents*, containing full documentation of cases in the original language of submittance, that is English or French, and including the document instituting proceedings, the written pleadings and their annexes, the verbatim record of the oral proceedings, any documents submitted to the Court after the closure of the written proceedings, and the correspondence.
- *Acts and Documents Concerning the Organization of the Court*. Five volumes have appeared so far in this bilingual series, including *inter alia* the Charter of the UN, the Statute and the Rules of Court.
- *Yearbook*, giving an account of the work of the Court during the preceding year (running from 1 August to 31 July annually) and including chapters on the Organization of the Court, Biographies of Judges, matters of Jurisdiction and documents related thereto, the Functioning and Practice of the Court, Publications and Finances. This publication appears in separate English and French versions. The *Yearbook* is prepared by the Secretary entrusted with information matters.
- *Bibliography*, an annual publication, with indexes in French and English, listing works and documents relating to the Court as have come to the attention of the Registry during the previous year. Until 1964, these Bibliographies were included in the Court's *Yearbook*.

An annually updated French and English catalogue, listing sales numbers and prices, is available.

Documentation available on the Court

The documentation on the functioning of the Court and its Registry other than the official publications of the Court, and available in at least the two official languages of the Court, French and English, consists of:

- *Press Communiqués*.
- *Background Notes*, including synopses of cases referred to the ICJ, and *Notes* by the Registrar on the Rules of Court.
- *Collected Unofficial Summaries* of decisions concerning the law of the sea (1946-1986).

Also obtainable are the following publications:

- *Summaries of Judgments, Advisory Opinions and Orders of the International Court of Justice* (1948-1991), prepared within the framework of the UN Publications Programme of the Office of Legal Affairs, Codification Division, and available in French and English.
- *The International Court of Justice*, a popular handbook published in Arabic, Chinese, English, French, Russian, Spanish and German.
- A booklet on the Court published by the UN Department of Public Information in English, French, Spanish and Dutch.
- Unofficial editions in Arabic, Chinese, Russian and Spanish of the *Rules of Court*.
- A film on the Court produced by the UN Department of Public Information.

These publications and the film are issued within the framework of the UN Programme of Assistance in the Teaching, Study, Dissemination and Wider Appreciation of International Law.

proper use of the funds made available and for the expenses incurred. Within the Registry he alone is entitled to incur liabilities in the name of the Court, subject to delegations of authority. The accounts of the Court are audited every year by the Board of Auditors appointed by the General Assembly and by the auditors of the Secretariat of the United Nations at intervals. At the end of each biennium, the closed accounts are forwarded to the Secretariat of the United Nations.

Archives and Distribution Department
This Department is responsible for the maintenance of the Court's archives, including the General List, and the despatch and distribution of documents. Archives will contain complete files of all Court proceedings, correspondence with the United Nations and its Special Agencies, personal files of Staff Members, and all general correspondence. Neither the archives of the Court itself nor those of the PCIJ are open to the public.

Printing Department
This Department is responsible for the preparation, correction and examination of all Court publications (for which see *Publications of the Court*). In addition to the preparation of manuscripts for printing and of indexes included in publications and the correction of proofs, it comprises the preparation of estimates, the checking of accounts for printing and, in general, complete supervision of the printers' work, including the contract negotiation.

Library of the Court / Documents Department
This Department is responsible for the purchase, processing, storing and maintenance of books, serial works, periodicals and documents. It produces the annual *Bibliography* of books and articles relating to the Court, carries out research on behalf of the Court and Registry and prepares lists, indexes and bibliographies for internal purposes regarding current cases and advisory requests. The Library is not a public library but exclusively serves the Court and the Staff of the Registry. It also houses a collection of League of Nations and UN Documents. Like other Departments of the Registry, the Court Library is currently in the midst of the process of computerization.

Noteworthy within the Court Library are the archives of the Nuremberg War Crimes Tribunal, which were entrusted to the Court, pursuant to a decision of the Tribunal. The archives relate solely to the trial of the major war criminals tried in 1945-1946 and may be consulted on written application to the Registrar. They include film material and the verbatim transcripts of hearings.

At the Typewriting Department.

Typewriting and Reproduction Department
This Department handles all wordprocessing and document reproduction for the Court and Registry, such as the minutes, verbatim records of sittings, draft Judgments, official correspondence etc. It includes the Reproduction Section, which prints all Court and Registry documents for internal as well as external purposes that are not delivered to external printers for official publication.

Judges have private secretaries. Officials of the Registry in the higher and professional categories are appointed by

The reading room of the Library.

the Court on proposals submitted by the Registrar. Promotion of Staff in the Professional category also requires the approval of the Court, upon the recommendation of the Registrar. Decisions regarding the recruitment, appointments and promotion of staff in the General Service category are taken by the Registrar on the approval of the President. Similar actions with regard to short-term staff are taken by the Registrar.

The Dutch skeleton staff of the PCIJ during the war years, together with Vice-President Van Eysinga

Library Relations

Within the body of the Registry the Court Library takes a singular position in that it is not an independently functioning Department. In fact, it is an offshoot of the Carnegie Library and in many ways related to it. The Carnegie Library, being (as reviewed in a previous chapter) a major instrument of the Deed concluded in 1903 between Andrew Carnegie and the Dutch Administrative Board, was opened in the months following the inauguration of the Peace Palace in August 1913. Its first objective was to serve the needs of the Permanent Court of Arbitration. One of the main reasons, in 1922, for the League of Nations to have the PCIJ situated in the Peace Palace, was the reputation of the Carnegie Library, which during the previous decade had served the Permanent Court of Arbitration to full satisfaction. In 1923, library facilities on behalf of the PCIJ were put on the same footing. A formal arrangement to this effect was concluded in February, 1924.

However, from the very beginning, Members of the newly installed Court gave voice to their concern regarding the rather limited collection and conservative acquisition policy of the Carnegie Library, more in particular with regard to the field of foreign municipal law. As Mr Asser put it at the time:

> All national law should be represented. For with numerous international problems it is only a question of the application of the national law.

Repeated complaints on the part of the Court from 1924 onwards led to new arrangements, notably in 1926, which, however, only gave temporary relief, as may be seen from the Sixth Annual Report of the Court, in which the following Resolution of August 1929 is reproduced (at pp. 51-52):

> The Court has realized for some time that the Peace Palace Library ... does not, as at present constituted and organized, afford the instrument of work which the Court requires. The lacunae in the Library are very considerable, more especially as regards law other than international law properly so-called, and a definite desire has been expressed on the part of the Court that the Library should obtain at all events the works which are authoritative in the various countries and relating to the law of such countries.

The incident is noteworthy as another footnote to the gradual development of the law of nations. In launching the Peace Palace Library, the Board of Directors of the Carnegie Foundation had duly anticipated the acquisition of books within the developing discipline. What they had not perceived was the adequate representation of the world's municipal laws, the very prerequisite for the PCIJ to live up to its ambition to represent all legal traditions and a genuine premise for the further elaboration of the international legal system.

Negotiations with the Carnegie Foundation made it clear that the funds at its disposal would not allow it, within a reasonable period of time, to satisfy the needs of the Court. By May 1930, the Secretary-General of the League of Nations had come to the conclusion that 'there was no other solution except to request the Assembly to vote an additional item to enable the Court itself to make the necessary purchases'.

The Assembly, at its Eleventh Session, agreed to this. As the Report of its Supervisory Commission put it:

> ... the time had come for provision to be made in the Court's budget for the purchase of further books and for the salary of an official who, under the control of the Court, would be

The binding entries at the Library.

> responsible for their acquisition. While it is understood that the books purchased out of League funds may be kept in the Library of the Peace Palace and entered in its catalogues, they will of course remain the property of the League.

Jacob ter Meulen, the well-known Peace Palace Librarian at that time, Grotian scholar and great historian of peace studies, had outspoken negative feelings about the bipartition. In his annual reports, we find ample proof of the urgent needs of the Court, of his lengthy talks with Mr Hammarskjøld, the Court Registrar, and of his repeated requests to the Board of the Foundation to have the budget raised to meet the Court's requirements.

However, in 1930, Ter Meulen's fears came true and the unity of the collection was lost. Early in 1931, a formal Agreement was signed. The League of Nations voted a yearly credit to have the Court establish a library of its own with the exclusive purpose of serving the Court and the Staff of the Registry. The Court formed a Library Committee to ensure the purchase of relevant literature, contracted a staff member of the Carnegie Library and in February 1931 this new official, Mr Douma, took up his duties.

In December 1946, following the exchange of notes between the Registrar and the Director of the Carnegie Library, the General Assembly of the United Nations approved two new Agreements concerning the relations between the Court and the Carnegie Foundation. In regard to the library, these relations were specified in a Covenant, the so-called *Modus Vivendi*, which basically confirmed the 1931 Agreement and governs the relations between the libraries to the present day.

Gifts from private collections such as from the late Judge Fromageot helped to gradually extend the collection of the Court Library to the present 35,000 volumes, comprising monographs, serialized works and periodicals in the strict sphere of public international law.

Still, despite all its expertise and primary source material, the Court Library, in its day to day functioning, is, obviously, very much dependent on the Carnegie Library. This Library currently amounts to some 800,000 volumes covering the areas of private and public international law, comparative and municipal law. Quite naturally, over the decades, there has been much debate about the (dis)advantages of the split (or twin) libraries. Puzzling to the world outside, the idea has also been questioned at several instances from within, by functionaries of both institutions, the ICJ and the Carnegie Foundation. Judge Baxter took it for yet another proof of the innate particularism of librarians!

The transfer of the Neurenberg files.

The Court's Premises

The Peace Palace

Undeniably, the Hague Peace Palace is a most interesting place to visit. Its reputation in the world at large is fully justified. The *fin-de-siècle* atmosphere, the stylish halls and rooms, the wealth of decorative elements, the sheer craftmanship applied in such a variety of techniques, the many gifts from all over the world, are indeed a feast to the eye. In the production of this book, efforts have been made to pay tribute to this aspect, so representative of the period which brought about the *Œuvre de la Haye*.

To modern eyes, two elements in particular draw attention as typifying this unseemingly remote past and world long gone by. These are, first, the integration of the decorative and functional elements and, second, the classical, humanist imagery. Not a single wood or window panel, not a single wall or floor tile meets the eye which is not either a decorative element in itself or part of a larger decorative pattern. The blond oak of the dove-tail ceiling of the small Court Room, put together with perfect disdain for nails, rivals the ceiling in adjoining rooms in which the most elaborate paintings summarize the time-honoured *adagia* of the peace movement. The foliage of the acanthus leaves in the stained glass windows match those of the gold leaf timbering of the Japanese room and recall Morris' *Arts & Crafts* movement.

The Rozenburg tile pannel presenting a panorama of the grounds with explanatory legends. The ornamental border highlights the successive steps in the genesis of the Peace Palace.

While this first element, despite all the exuberance, captures one's imagination to say the least, the second element is definitely less satisfactory to the late 20th century beholder. The reference is to the lavish appliance and cryptic entwining of the allegorical, the mythical, the astrological and the historical elements. Most of the messages depicted by the wall panels plainly beat modern interpretation. Symbolism pervades all outpourings in this building. Original drawings left by the interior architect Herman Rosse (the young genius from the Kensington School of Art who was as much enchanted by the commission of the Peace Palace as he was enamoured by the charming assistant of Thomas H. Mawson, the English landscape architect) reveal that in the rich imagery and the application of colours there was no room for coincidence.

And yet, in some places, the classical patterns are shattered and the cake of custom broken - as in the waiting rooms for the parties in the main hall. Here, mythical allegories of Oceanus and Neptunus and flowery Latin legends are linked to locomotives and steam-ships, to attest to the coming of a new age. Just as the cannelures of the early Greek marble columns echo the plane-marks of their wooden predecessors, throughout the Peace Palace the products of the new century are represented in the imagery of the previous one. In the province of the arts, as much as in the field of law, the Peace Palace stands at the crossroad in time. One has only to recall the

THE JAPANESE ROOM

The Japanese Room is considered by many the most decorous and elegant chamber of the Palace. The room owes its name to the gift presented by the Japanese Imperial Government, which is found there. This precious gift consists of a series of superb silk tapestries, named *Hundred flowers and hundred birds in late spring and early summer*, designed in the tradition of the *Tsuzure-Nishiki* style by Jimbei Kawashima II.

The work represents a fine specimen of the Japanese tradition, linking creativity with craftsmanship. Indeed, the Tsuzure style is considered by intimates 'the art of arts', the most refined and the most laborious technique of silk tapestry. The art was recreated in the 1840s by Kawashima I, a court artist who travelled extensively through France. It was his son who was commissioned, in the summer of 1909, with what would become the ultimate endeavour of his life.

Kawashima managed wonderfully, applying only the best of products: brilliant alizaline tinctures of rich coloration to dye the precious Goshu silk, and gold threads in dozens of shades. The scenes of the six major panels represent a landscape of an exceptional vivacity and naturalness; among a lustre of Oriental trees, beds of flowers and plants in full bloom in late spring (cherries, azaleas and magnolias in between oaks and Japanese cedars), a myriad of birds are chirping and twittering next to pigeons and pheasants in many varieties, swallows and peacocks proudly spreading their magnificent feathers. The work is probably the most noteworthy among the treasures to be found in the Palace.

Apart from the Japanese tapestry, gifts from two other nations decorate the room: four cloisonné vases of gold-plated copper from China and a set of elephant tusks on a pedestal presented by Siam. Finally, the room is remarkable for its rosewood panels (a gift of Brazil) featuring intricate intarsia with golden geometrical patterns, and its delicately painted ceilings.

Palais des Nations in Geneva to perceive the worlds apart.

Still, to contemporary esthetics, the clash of styles in the Peace Palace, being the inevitable result of the basic concept to invite gifts from all over the world, was painfully disturbing. The most outspoken critics of the time were directed at the central staircase, a true copy of the French classicist staircase of the Paris *Opéra*, also in its inclusion of candelabras of Bohemian crystal - yet put within a context of a Byzantine coppola from Ravenna and a gothic apsis from Chartres. To top this came the provocative modernist statue of *Peace* generated by a non-conformist American artist. Less conscious of classical styles than his grandparents, modern man, luckily, feels less resentment at this 'blasphemy' than did, for instance, the Dutch Queen Wilhelmina at the time. In fact, to him, the spot appears to breathe the solemn austerity that suits the background for a photograph of the World Court.

Surely, if Andrew Carnegie himself wished for a Temple and Symbol of Peace, the outcome must have satisfied him to the full. Still, the benefactor wanted more than this. The Peace Palace was also meant to harbour a modern machinery for the settlement of disputes. Unfortunately, soon enough it was to become painfully clear, that in this respect the designers had not exactly been visionaries.

To make a long story short, the history of the International Courts at The Hague has been one of endless struggle to beat the persistent lack of space and lack of finances. From the very outset, and for all its charms, the Peace Palace has offered accommodation in many respects inadequate to the rapidly expanding world of international law. Time has definitely belied the words of the first President of the Carnegie Foundation when, on the occasion of the laying of the cornerstone in 1907, this dignitary observed: 'the Peace Palace will worthily shelter the Permanent Court of Arbitration and will be equally able to serve for any other international judicature.

If perhaps worthily, it has not always been comfortably; indeed one must admire the inventiveness and creativity mustered by all parties over the decades to meet the recurring problems. In this jubilee year of the ICJ, the Dutch Government through the Carnegie Foundation, owner and administrator of the Palace, as a befitting present, has committed itself to the reconstruction of yet another part of the Old Building, the attics this time, and to building yet another new wing in the grounds to serve its prominent tenant. We will now briefly recapitulate this tale of seventy-five years.

In one of his first communications to the Carnegie Foundation, on 15 November

An early design of the Small Court Room.

1921, Sir Eric Drummond, the Secretary-General of the League of Nations, drily stated that:

> Should the Court be established in the Palace, the League of Nations would be able to place at the disposal of the Foundation the annual sum of 50,000 Dutch guilders so as to indemnify it for the expenses arising out of the use of the Palace by the Court. Moreover, the League of Nations would reimburse the Carnegie Foundation any expenditures incurred by it for necessary modifications of the Peace Palace in order to make the premises suitable for the Court's use.

Three months afterwards, the PCIJ moved into the Palace. However, less than a year later, it was followed by a competing institution. In 1913, in The Hague, the Academy of International Law had been founded, the brainchild of the *Institut de Droit International*. It was intended to be established in the premises of the Palace in 1914. Owing to the outbreak of war, this project had to be suspended. In 1920, the Committee of Jurists, had expressed its wish 'that the Academy ... may be set in operation in as near a future as possible side by side with the PCA and the PCIJ, at the Palace in The Hague'. At length, the Academy was installed in 1923.

In 1913, critics had ridiculed the sheer size of the Palace which they thought was bound to remain half-empty for most of its superfluous existence. Now, within a few years, the increased activities of both PCIJ and Academy saw the two institutions rivalling for any spare rooms. Inadequate to meet the requirements of its occupants, the Palace soon underwent repeated modification. But there was more rivalry than just between the PCIJ and the Academy.

On its arrival in 1922, the PCIJ in a way impaired the privileged position which the Permanent Court of Arbitration had enjoyed during the previous decade. The arrangements suggested to the newcomer by the Board of Directors of the Carnegie Foundation included the transfer of rooms which - although left unoccupied until then - had formally been put at the disposal of the PCA.

At first, the Administrative Council of the PCA was disposed to give up these rooms on the assumption that the newcomer would enjoy the Court's hospitality, rather than that of the Foundation. At the root of this lay a prolonged financial dispute between PCA and the Carnegie Foundation, harking back to the early years. On the occasion of the opening of the Peace Palace the President of the Foundation had symbolically transferred the key of the Palace to the Court's Secretary-General. Some of the Contracting Nations, notably France and Great Britain, had seen in this more than just a ceremonial gesture. Sharp memoranda were exchanged to settle the issue as to which institution was the effective Administrative keeper of the building and was to bear the expenditure for the upkeep.

At length, in the summer of 1923, it was agreed that the Carnegie Foundation would take full responsibility for the upkeep of the Palace, including the cost of heating, lighting and maintenance. These regulations have remained unaltered to the present day.

Soon after its arrival, it proved that the PCIJ needed considerably more space than had been anticipated. The first major action taken by the Carnegie Foundation, after earlier adaptations, was the removal of the book stacks and the transfer of rooms previously allotted to the Academy. In 1929, part of the Palace was reconstructed anew, to provide more room for the ever-

One of the typical style rooms of the Palace. The canvas, a gift from France, in a time-honoured commonplace glorifies the peaceful country-side as compared to the hectic life of the metropole.

The precision bombardment of the German Registers Office by the RAF on 11 April 1944.

expanding Court. This time, the Court had applied for individual offices for its Judges.

In 1930, to oblige the Court, a new building was opened on the premises, adjoining the Palace and connected to the main building by a passage, to serve as book storage for the Peace Palace Library, which then vacated some of its rooms in the main building. Less than two years later, another new building had to be constructed adjacent to the Library stack building, this time to lodge the Academy. Its former offices were now occupied by Judges of the PCIJ. All these modifications were made at the expense of the Carnegie Foundation and reimbursed by the League in annual instalments. Even so, the Foundation's financial means were stretched to the outer limits in these years. The perennial shortage of funds is manifest throughout the Board's records.

Shortly after the Second World War, with the arrival of the ICJ, similar problems occurred, and again not just temporarily. The Peace Palace had suffered much from the war. In 1944, launching-pads for the experimental V-weapons had been installed nearby in the dunes. Every now and then projectiles flew over the Palace with high-pitched, whistling screams. The frequent near-hits and imminent explosions held all in constant fear. Twice, in November 1944 and in January 1945, hundreds of (stained-glass) windows were shattered as wooden panels came tumbling down with the shock of untimely exploded rockets. Another exploding V-weapon hit and destroyed the house of librarian Ter Meulen in the nearby Archipelbuurt.

Ironically, more damage was done by the Allied Forces, who kept bombing the German launching installations and often lacked precision. In March 1945, a nearby area was hit with enormous casualties. However, in Mid-April 1944, a RAF precision bombardment, in response to urgent requests from the Dutch underground movement, utterly destroyed the despised German Registers Office, right opposite the Palace, where identity cards were kept (at the site of the present headquarters of *Kluwer Law International*). The raid had been minutely prepared;

The Impression of The Hague Court by a President's Wife

I would like to ... write a few words about the International Court of Justice, of which far too little is known to the general public of most countries who are members of the United Nations.

Perhaps, too, some of the impressions of a wife of a man who has been one of its Judges for nine years, three of them as President, may be of interest. There are, after all, only fifteen permanent Judges of this Court at any given time, so by the rule of mathematics there cannot be too many Judges' wives. Since my husband is the only Australian who has ever been elected to the Court, I am the only Australian wife to have participated in this uncommon way of life. It has had great rewards and some drawbacks.

It is important where one lives: the climate, the people, the conditions of life. My own experience of Holland, where the permanent seat of the Court is, had been very brief. In the year 1947, when my husband was in opposition in the Australian Parliament, we had spent a little time there. We had been most kindly received, entertained, and seen something of the country.

We had also been received at the summer palace by Queen Juliana, an intelligent, knowledgeable woman, beloved by her people. Apart from these contacts, however, and those in Washington and New York with Dutch diplomats, we did not know the people of Holland or the country.

From its inception in 1946 the International Court of Justice has sat in the Palace of Peace, a vast, somewhat whimsical, overdecorated structure with wonderful gardens; this building is not, alas, occupied solely by the Court and its Registry staff, for the Court is but the lessee of certain parts of the building, which has become a national monument of sorts.

In my experience the two terms into which the year is divided range, at a rough estimate, from three and a half to four months each. This sounds as though the Judges have considerable leisure, but this is by no means so. As a rule the cases before the Court are long and heavy, demanding much examination of documents, the law, transcripts of oral pleading and the individual Judge's own contribution. There is a lot of 'homework' to get through during the recesses, as well as preliminary readings of the next case coming up.

From: Jean Spender, *Ambassador's Wife* (1968)

nearby London the geographical situation had been carefully simulated, including hardboard models of the Peace Palace.

On 21 February 1946, the United Nations and the Carnegie Foundation signed an Agreement, approved by the General Assembly by Resolution of 11 December 1946, for the use by the ICJ of the premises previously occupied by the PCIJ. It stipulated a payment of 48,000 Dutch guilders on an annual basis. In 1951, this sum was increased to 68,500 Dutch guilders, in 1958 to 100,000 Dutch guilders.

However, by 1950, owing to wear and tear, leakage and sinking of floors, the ageing building badly needed major repairs. Endless lists of complaints were submitted by the Court, including rust-eaten gates and conduit-pipes, poorly fitting windows and loose-fitting swinging doors causing insufferable drafts. Cracked walls, flaking ceilings, outdated technical installations and elevators, insufficient heating and ventilation, poor illumination as well as lack of book storage space did not exactly make the Palace the proper entourage to house the International Court, as the Registrar kept politely yet insistently pointing out to the Carnegie Foundation.

On top of this came the ever-increasing number of tourists (up to 2000 per day at the time) and coaches blocking the entrance gates and causing congestion on the driveways. In a major restoration, which lasted more than four years, the Foundation appeased the complaints and put a halt to the rumours of the Court's imminent migration to Geneva.

Even so, the ever greater need of space for the Court prompted new measures. The most pressing needs of the mid-1960s concerned offices for temporary language personnel, improvements in the typing pool area and additional space for the Library. It was suggested that existing offices be modified; to have additional rooms created in the attics; to have a new wing built; to transplant the Peace Palace Library to the Academy building and to have new headquarters for the Academy designed. As usual, the costs involved posed insurmountable problems.

New Buildings

In 1964, during his term of Presidency, Sir Percy Spender approached Secretary-General U Thant with a list of complaints regarding the Court's accommodation, in which he also applied for additional funds. Sir Percy proposed to have a new

Prestige and Protocol of the International Court of Justice

Back in Holland, one final matter my husband put in train for the International Court was the acquisition of their own premises. Striking and beautiful as the Palace of Peace is, from the practical point of view it is not very suitable. In truth the building has become a great tourist attraction.

Under the supervision of guides, sightseers are not permitted into those parts set aside for the Judges, but the fact remains that they flock around en masse at the rate, at the height of the season, of over two thousand people a day.

While the President and Vice-President have very fine rooms indeed, those allotted to the Judges, though handsomely appointed, are far from adequate. A man just has not the room for the masses of documents and books that most of the cases demand. Translators, typists, archives, all have to be housed. Space presents a very real problem, apart from the fact that there is a lot of scattering about of the office accommodation.

Rather than be tenants of part of the building, my husband and his colleagues believed that the needs and prestige of the Court demanded its own premises. Through discussion with the Dutch authorities, the Secretary-General of the United Nations (U Thant), and some of his officials, a little pressure here and there, the stage has now been reached when Holland, desirous of retaining the Court in this country, has agreed to provide a suitable site and to assist generously the erection of the building.

In fact, my husband received a letter from U Thant thanking him for the part he played in bringing all this about. My fervent hope is that, whoever may be the next President, he will make very sure that the building erected for the Court will provide the necessary dignity of background and the spaciousness that the World Court should have.

The thorny question of protocol on the relative precedence of Judges and ambassadors was another matter needing attention. It had been a question which, up till then, had evaded any solution. It did not prove insoluble. In conjunction with the Dutch protocol department and the Dean of the diplomatic corps a sort of way of living together was worked out. A perfect solution between heads of diplomatic missions and Judges of the International Court probably does not exist, particularly in a small capital, but a vast improvement has been effected, noticeably at official functions.

I understand that in recent months the precedence of the President of the Court has in the United States been dealt with at an official level. Together with the President of the Security Council and the General Assembly, the President of the Court ranks above ambassadors.

During his time on the Court, and particularly during his Presidency, my husband did, I believe, a great deal to raise the stature and prestige of this third organ of the United Nations. Others must, from early 1967, carry on this work.

From: Jean Spender, *Ambassador's Wife* (1968)

A view of the new wing with the offices of the Judges. The building, designed by Deurvorst and Schriecke, was opened in 1978.

wing built and suggested to that end applying the designs dating from the mid-1950s for the so-called Schumann Court, the present European Court of Human Rights at Strasbourg. This Court had originally been planned to have its seat in The Hague in a building to be erected in the grounds of the Peace Palace.

In 1965 it was concluded that a new building would be provided for the Court at the earliest convenience. In view of the financial crisis of the United Nations cost were to be borne by the Dutch Government - in similar vein as the Swiss Government had renovated and extended the old *Palais des Nations* in Geneva. However, apparently the idea was dismissed and for many years nothing was heard of the project. Then, in November 1968, the Court insisted on having at the least the most urgent repairs carried out. In the early 1970s a major renovation project was executed; walls were aligned, bookstorage areas dug out in the cellars all along the front side of the Palace, while electrical equipment was modernized.

Then, in the autumn of 1971, another Committee was raised to investigate the feasibility of additional buildings. In October 1972 the ICJ submitted specifications as to staff and rooms required. A year later, during a meeting on 30 October 1973, it was finally decided to have a new building erected in the grounds. Three models being submitted, at length, in October 1975, the entry *Hortus Nato* was elected. In December 1976 the top of the new building was reached and the 'panne-bier' poured, in the summer of 1977 the interior decorating began, and on 4 April 1978, during a chilly morning ceremony, the wing was inaugurated by H.M. Queen Juliana of the Netherlands - just as her mother had opened the Old Building sixty-five years earlier.

In the presence of the Dutch Prime Minister Mr van Agt, the Secretary-General of NATO Mr Joseph Luns, former Dutch Minister of Foreign Affairs, and a bevy of diplomats and dignitaries, the President of the Carnegie Foundation, the former Dutch Minister of Foreign Affairs Mr van Royen, transferred the building to Dr Kurt Waldheim, Secretary-General of the United Nations. The new wing, a stylish modern design featuring large windows and Brazilian marble panelling, harboured conference and chambers for the Judges, in particular the Deliberations Room on the third floor. During the ceremony, a plaquette was unveiled by the Court's President, Judge Jiménez de Aréchaga of Uruguay, bearing a quotation from Cicero: *Fundamentum est justitiæ fides, id est dictorum conventorumque constantia et veritas*. That day put an end to decades of justified lamenting.

Nonetheless, from then on, restoration and reconstruction of the Old Palace never ceased. In years to follow most of the staff rooms of the Registry were redecorated, cloakrooms renewed, and the old restaurant (*Refectorium*) renovated. Even so, in the past decade, also due to the sharp increase in the caseload of the Court and the ensuing expansion of staff, the accommodations of the Court proved to be less and less suitable for the Court's purposes.

Social Aspects of the International Court of Justice

For some years past official entertaining by the President of the Court had taken place in hotels. Pleasant, but there is always something a little anonymous about such functions. My husband and I decided on a different course. The official receptions we gave were held in the Palace of Peace itself: a wonderful setting with its dignity, space and gardens.

Instead of confining these entertainments to those directly concerned with the Court and the case before it, we decided to throw our net wider to include Dutch officials, members of the Government, of protocol, the diplomatic corps, and private friends: the point of the exercise being not only to make our parties more enjoyable, but to bring the International Court and its members out into the public eye as much as possible so that people should at least be aware of their existence. With the Palace lighted up, its garden and façade illuminated, one could not have a more imposing background for the representatives of many nations.

For a considerable time before Percy took his seat on the International Court of Justice, Queen Juliana of the Netherlands had not entertained the members of the Court. The story as related to me by the wife of a Judge who had been on the Court for some years before we arrived at The Hague, and had served a term as President, was that the reason for this lay at the door of a certain past President who could not be bothered with the social obligations of his position.

It seemed that, on one occasion, without consulting his colleagues, he refused, on behalf of them all, an invitation from the Queen on the plea that the Court would be in recess and, therefore, its members would be absent from The Hague. As it happened, the Court had not adjourned when the date mentioned came round. Given their choice, I cannot but help feeling that, if only as a matter of courtesy, the Judges would readily have remained in or returned to The Hague.

I admit to being highly pleased when, early in my husband's first year as President, Queen Juliana and Prince Bernhard gave a dinner for the Court. The dinner fell on one of those exquisitely soft late April evenings that can bless this country. Driving to the royal palace, 'Het Huis ten Bosch', the palace in the woods, about fifteen minutes from the city, the trees, parks and gardens were gay and fresh in their new green.

There were about sixty guests: the members of the Court and their wives, the Registrar of the Court, members of the Royal Court and the Queen's household. I sat on the right of Prince Bernhard at the horseshoe-shaped table, and found him a cheerful and attractive companion. The Queen, with Percy on her right, sat opposite us. The two of them appeared to get along famously. Queen Juliana and Prince Bernhard are two people who have a strong hold upon the affection and esteem of the people of the Netherlands. They are unaffected, devoid of pomposity and remarkably informal in a very pleasant fashion.

In September 1964, we attended a magnificent banquet, given by Queen Juliana and Prince Bernhard, in honour of the State visit of King Olav of Norway to Holland. This was a rare occasion, for it was held in the world-famous Rijksmuseum in Amsterdam. When we went in to dinner we sat at a long, narrow table seating a hundred guests in a room hung with priceless pictures. My husband and I, the ambassador of Norway, the Dean of the diplomatic corps, Baron van der Straten-Waillet and his wife, appeared to be, apart from members of the King's entourage, the only foreigners present. Seated near the centre of the table, I had a perfect view both ways of the marvellous treasures upon it; the china, silver, candelabra, et cetera, belonging to the museum had been brought out. I was told that an entertainment of this nature in the museum was unusual, and had not taken place for twenty years or so.

We had met the handsome widower King at a reception the previous evening, and found him an approachable, likeable, human, rather shy I thought, person. This night he appeared thoroughly to enjoy himself.

After dinner and coffee had been served, we were all free to wander around this wonderful museum at will. I had often visited it before, but never been there in these circumstances: a private show, as it were. To be able to stroll without haste, sit and chat without disturbing anyone, go where one wanted, was an ideal way to see the fine collection of paintings it houses.

From: Jean Spender, *Ambassador's Wife* (1968)

The work in process for the construction of another new building and the reconstruction of the attics in the main building of the Palace.

The Peace Palace itself became physically incapable of further transformation to meet the needs of the Court in the years ahead.

Again, after prolonged negotiations, action was taken. In this jubilee year of the Court a new extension to the 1978 wing will be opened, harbouring more chambers for Judges, conference rooms, storage space and a dining room. Also, new offices are under construction in the upper floors and attics of the Palace. The space originally occupied by the ICJ in the Old Building (some 50 rooms) amounted to some 3,300 m^2; the extension with the new wing in the mid 1970s added some 40 rooms (3,800 m^2). Additional space after completion of the new facilities will again amount to some 4,000 m^2 (50 rooms). In all, the space and number of rooms available to the Court from 1997 onwards (140 rooms covering 12,000 m^2) will have tripled, as compared with fifty years earlier. It is hoped that in terms of facilities the Court and the Foundation are ready to face the new century.

In the past fifty years five Secretaries-General of the United Nations visited the Hague Court: Mr Trygve Lie (1946-1952), Mr U Thant (1961-1971), Mr Kurt Waldheim (1972-1981), Mr Javier Perez de Cuellar (1982-1991), and Mr Boutros Boutros-Ghali (1992-present).

POSTAL SERVICES AND PCIJ/ICJ SERVICE STAMPS

The UN postal service, which was established in 1948, does not extend to the Court. From the outset of the ICJ, special issues of Dutch postage stamps 'dienstzegels' – service stamps) have been used for the Court's official correspondence, in accordance with earlier practice for the PCIJ. It is the Archivist's duty to ensure that all outgoing mail is provided with the ICJ service stamps. The stamps are affixed not by the Registry, but by Dutch postal officials, namely the staff of the post office on the premises of the Peace Palace.

As of 1934, service stamps for the mail of the PCIJ were issued: overprints with the name 'COUR PERMANENTE DE JUSTICE INTERNATIONALE' in gold on previously issued Dutch stamps: on two stamps of 'the flying dove'-series, designed by Chris Lebeau, on four values of the Queen Wilhelmina stamps, design of Professor Jan Veth, and on the peace-stamp, designed by P.A.H. Hofman. The original peace-stamp was issued on 18 May 1933, League of Nations Day; the design represents a dove in front of a sword in a star with rays.

On 1 April 1940, a new series of four values was issued bearing the portrait of Queen Wilhelmina, in the new design by W.A. van Konijnenburg. Unfortunately, the overprint in gold was erroneously spelt '... INTERNATIONALF'. In the reissued version soon after, this mistake was corrected.

After World War II, on 10 February 1947, a series of five values was issued with the overprint 'COUR INTERNATIONALE DE JUSTICE' in gold on the Queen Wilhelmina stamps of 1940.

In 1950, for the first time, special stamps in two values were designed by Jan van Krimpen. These were discontinued on 18 March 1951 and replaced by a new series of two different designs by Sem L. Harz and Jan van Krimpen: the lower values of this series (in total six) bearing the image of the Peace Palace, the higher values (in total eight) the portrait of Queen Juliana, and the scales as the symbol of justice. In 1977 three additional values were issued.

Between 1989 and 1994, and anticipating the 50th anniversary of the United Nations and the Court, a new set of stamps with different designs by Walter Nikkels was issued bearing the image of the Peace Palace. On these stamps the name of the Court is mentioned in French and English. Until now fifteen values have been issued. Since 1989, the Dutch ICJ service stamps can also be obtained in mint condition.

In 1985, the Peace Palace was the host of the national stamp exibition, 'unofil85'.

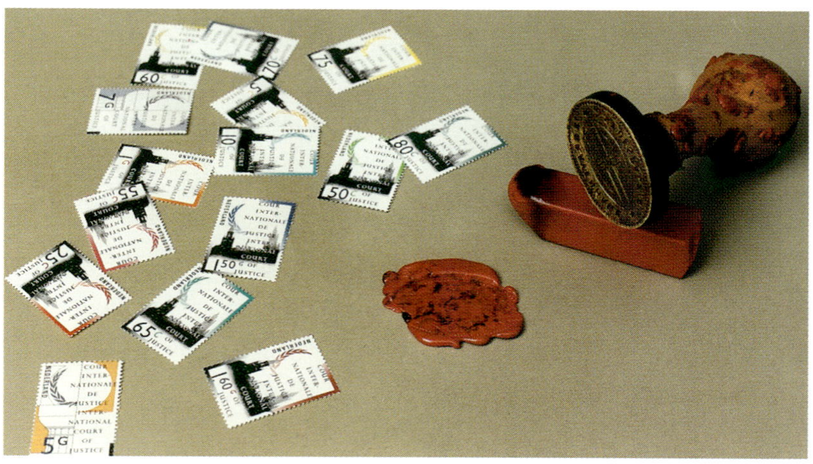

CHAPTER SIX

Matters of Jurisdiction and Procedure

Contentious Cases

In the opening chapter, the jurisdiction and procedure of the Court were touched upon in the most general terms. It is now intended to take a closer look at the functioning of the Court within the international machinery of dispute settlement. For practical reasons, the contentious jurisdiction and procedure will be dealt with first.

The International Court of Justice is the principal judicial organ of the United Nations. In this capacity, its main objective is to help to achieve one of the primary aims of the United Nations, namely to bring about the peaceful settlement of disputes in conformity with the principles of justice and international law. It follows, therefore, that its province and main occupation is with legal disputes.

An international dispute has once been described by the PCIJ as 'a disagreement on a question of law or fact, a conflict, a clash of legal views or of interests'. As stated earlier, the competence of the Court is restricted to legal disputes between States only. International organizations, whether governmental or non-governmental, cannot appear before the Court in contentious cases. Private persons cannot appear in their own right either, but their interests may be served in an indirect way. Their State may bring a case on their behalf and maintain a claim against another State on account of wrongs allegedly suffered by its nationals at the hands of that other State. Expressed in technical terms, such a State renders 'diplomatic protection' to its nationals. The *Nottebohm* and *Barcelona Traction* cases are good examples of where States have attempted to exercise 'diplomatic protection' on behalf of their nationals.

Access to the Court

If the Court is accessible to States only, it is indeed open to literally every State in the world – or, put differently, every independent State that so wishes has ample means of access to the Court. Basically, there are two ways open to a State to have access to the Court.

First, Member States of the United Nations, by signing the Charter on being admitted to membership, simultaneously and *ipso facto* become Parties to the Statute of the Court and have access to it. To date 186 States come under this category.

States which are not Members of the United Nations can also obtain access to the Court, on an equal footing, after having satisfied certain conditions. This was the case at one stage with Switzerland, Japan, Liechtenstein and San Marino. In principle, the specific conditions for access are to be determined in each case by the General Assembly upon the recommendation of the Security Council. Up until now, however, the conditions laid down at the first occurrence, namely in response to the request by the Swiss Federal Council of December 1946, have been maintained. These conditions are acceptance of the provisions of the Statute of the ICJ and compliance with the decisions of the ICJ. States in this position are also requested to contribute to the expenses of the Court. Japan, San Marino and Liechtenstein having become regular Members of the United Nations, only two States are at present in this category, Switzerland since 1948 and Nauru since 1988.

However, before actually becoming a party to a case – as contrasted with being Party to the Statute of the Court – one other essential condition has to be complied with, and indeed one which is entirely up to the States themselves: they have to give their consent thereto, whether generally with regard to certain classes of disputes or particularly in respect of a given dispute. No State to which the Court is open can be made a party to contentious proceedings against its express will or, put in positive wording, unless it has in some manner so consented. A State must agree to the Court dealing with the dispute in question, whether generally or specifically. Put more technically, it must agree to the jurisdiction of the Court *ratione personae* as well as *ratione materiae*.

While this provision of previous consent to the jurisdiction of the Court might induce States to drop initial hesitations to adhere to the Statute, the coin has its reverse side. The second basic principle underlying international adjudication is the binding nature and finality of the Court's decision. Once consent is given,

Parties are bound without appeal and obliged to comply with the judgment. In fact, consent to jurisdiction on the one hand and binding force of the Court's judgment on the other are the two cornerstones of the system of judicial settlement as practised by the ICJ.

One may say that the advanced techniques developed within the international community during the past seventy-five years of conferring jurisdiction on the Court reflect the natural tension experienced by States between their express wish to avail themselves of the facilities, and protection, of judicial recourse, and their reluctance to put their interests in the hand of third parties. The various ways in which States may confer jurisdiction on the Court are reviewed below.

Jurisdiction

Jurisdiction is the authority conferred on the Court to decide a case. A title of jurisdiction may be conferred in two ways, basically: bilaterally or unilaterally. First, States may bilaterally agree to submit an existing dispute to the Court and thereby accept the jurisdiction of the Court. This is called the *Special Agreement* or *Compromis*, which term for a particular kind of treaty was first met within the context of the arbitral procedure. The *Compromis* explicitly states the subject of the dispute and the Parties. Eleven disputes were referred to the PCIJ in this way; to date the ICJ has received twelve cases through such an agreement.

The second way is the submission by one Party of a *Unilateral Application*, a written notification of the institution of proceedings. This is actually the most common way of applying to the Court, as this is the way in which disputes arising out of the interpretation of treaties (as well as under the 'Optional Clause') are often brought before the Court.

It has long been a general practice among States to include in international agreements, be they bilateral or multilateral, provisions known as compromissory clauses. These clauses provide for reference of disputes emanating from the interpretation or application of the treaty in question to certain methods of pacific settlement. As noted earlier, many treaties contain arbitral clauses, or references to forms of mediation or conciliation. Nowadays, recourse to the ICJ is one of the more common provisions, either as a direct method of settlement or after the exhaustion of other means. The wording of these clauses may differ considerably. Model clauses have been prepared, *inter alia*, by the *Institut de Droit International* in 1956.

Among the numerous treaties conferring jurisdiction on the Court in case of dispute are a number of older treaties (approximately some four hundred involving some sixty States) conferring jurisdiction on the PCIJ. To prevent these treaties from losing their effectiveness, the Statute of the Court stipulates that any such reference to the PCIJ shall be interpreted as referring to the ICJ.

In the event of a dispute arising out of such a treaty, States are of course at liberty to discuss and agree upon a Special Agreement with the contesting Party. However, the Treaty provisions allow them to file a unilateral application. In other words, the provisions put in the compromissory clause make the jurisdiction of the Court compulsory for the respondent State, provided that the dispute is found to arise out of the interpretation or application of the treaty. Like the Special Agreement, this unilateral application must indicate the subject of the dispute and the Parties involved. In addition, however, it must specify the treaty provision on which the applicant State bases the jurisdiction of the Court.

Instead of concluding a treaty with a compromissory clause, States may also work the other way round and conclude treaties specifically for the settlement of disputes, in which the elaboration of the arbitral or judicial procedure is the very substance of the agreement. This provision, too, has a long tradition and harks back to the 19th century.

A singular procedure (known as 'forum prorogatum'), attesting to the flexibility of the Court, is when the Court agrees to assume jurisdiction when consent by one Party is given only after the proceedings have been started by the other. In this way procedural irregularities or jurisdictional voids in the institution of the proceedings may be waived to afford the Court jurisdiction on the substance of the case.

Right: An early design of the Great Court Hall.
Below: The original designs of the entrance door of the Great Court Hall and the antechambers for the Parties.

THE GREAT HALL OF JUSTICE

The Great Hall of the Hague Court is an impressive room, if only for its dimensions. It is decorated with exquisite oak panelling, colourful rugs and sparkling chandeliers of Bohemian crystal. Its walls are embellished by lofty latin maxims and notably by a French gift, the painting by Albert Besnard representing *Peace through Justice* and featuring the goddess separating belligerents beneath a scene in which lawyers and philosophers are disputing. The most striking element of the Hall are four stained glass windows by Douglas Strachan, presented by Great Britain.

The central theme of these highly elaborate and allegorical windows is the evolution of the peace ideal, and this theme is developed throughout in its four phases (from left to right): the Primitive Age, the Age of Conquest, the Present Age and the Achievement of Peace. In the successive windows one discerns the gradual development of human intelligence and civilization based on the firm belief of a World Force greater than man: from self-preservation, through fallacies of military power and industrial supremacy, man is led into an age that sees war as a monstrous folly. The colour schemes of the windows express the mood of the period concerned. The windows each consist of four main panels and separate upper parts.

The first panel of the uttermost left window, representing the *Primitive Age* features Mother Earth at the First Dawn with the Hunter in the foreground. The second panel contains the Keeper of Sheep, who first abstained from killing. Hunter and Shepherd are archetypes of Warrior and Pacifist.

The third panel represents the Tiller of the ground and the Harvesters of the fruits of the earth. The mid-distance of the second and third panels compare the cave-dwelling and early cultivation on the left to the discovery of fire on the right, not unlike the bases where the ship of the adventurous wanderer is put next to the nesting bird typifying the home-loving man.

The fourth panel introduces metal working and the strife and slaughter caused by migratory movements. The signs of the Zodiac at the top parallel man's progress on earth to the larger progression through space. The upper lights represent the mental outlook of the Primitive Age, typified successively in Terror and Worship of natural phenomena, the four elements, the four seasons and the four phases of man.

The first panel of the *Age of Conquest* contains the energetic Conqueror with bloodthirst and greed in the lower sections. The second and third panels are linked again: huge walls protect the Conqueror against invaders. On the barren fields all industry has vanished and Peace and Love are held in bonds. On the fourth panel, amid ruins of architecture and utter desolation, up comes the Constructive Spirit visionary of Justice and Peace. In the upper lights Bellona, the war goddess, and her hordes preceded by Hunger and Death redden the heavens.

In the first panel of the *Present Age* an optimistic view is expressed. Vital Energy and Construction are key words here, representing Industrial Revolution and man's insight that war and massacre stand in the way of production and may be replaced by peaceful settlement of disputes. The second panel stands for Finance and Labour, the brain and the body that determine the issue of war and thereby man's progress. Finance is depicted scrutinizing the globe and keeping his finger on the telegraph machine; Labour holds Bellona enchained.

The third panel illustrates the Enlightenment through Science. By conceiving dreadful war engines of destruction science is the best deterrent of war, as by providing medical care it alleviates suffering. The fourth panel represents the Philosopher and Arts as Peacemakers. The beauty of life they reveal is expressed in the crystal, ivory and silver fountain and the crystal image of Peace they have fashioned. The minor upper panels represent the four quarters of the earth seeking mutual understanding, though balancing between a peaceful spirit (on the left) and distrust (on the right).

The fourth window, *Peace Achieved*, announces a new age of human development. In the upper panels the Order, Harmony and Immensity of the Universe are depicted hiding the mystery of Man's destiny. The main panels tell a story on three levels from left to right. Below, the Peoples of the Earth, guided by the Phoenix, migrate from the ruined fortress on the left to the New City on the right under the aegis of the Gryphon.

In the middle section figure the Swordbreaker and Plenty on the left, Destiny weaving a tapestry of increasingly white patterns in the middle, and leading Statesmen, Scientists and Philosophers on the right. In the upper portion of the second panel Arbitration can be discerned with the Four Quarters of the Earth, North and South holding the balance, East and West abiding by the verdict. In the third panel Bellona dies in the arms of Peace.

The windows represent the best of cultural traditions. Typical of the atmosphere are the Latin legends which run along the windows in banderoles: *Non galeae, non enses erant: sine militis usu / mollia securae peragebant otia gentes* read the hexameters on the first window: *Helmet nor sword were found; man lived in peace without any need of the military*. The words echo the nostalgia for the pastoral ages when lamb and lion lived in perfect harmony. The idea is repeated in the legends of the fourth window which are, significantly, taken from Virgil's Fourth Eclogue: *Redeunt Saturnia Regna*, 'The Golden Age Returns'.

But in between, no doubt about it, the laws of the Iron Age rule. The second panel, again taken from Virgil, echoes Juno's address to Allecto in *Aeneid* VII 335-338: *Tu potes unanimos armare in proelia fratres / atque odiis versare domos, tu verbera tectis / funereasque inferre faces, tibi nomina mille / mille nocendi artes...* ('You know well how to set brothers, united in love, at armed conflict one against the other. You can wreck homes by hate and bring scourges and firebrands of death within their walls. You have a thousand types of mischief, a thousand artful ways of doing harm'. W.F. Jackson Knight).

The legends of the third panel, which have a Lucretian ring, are: *Sensim vis efficit ipsa vivida naturae, ut cessent fera moenera Martis...* ('Unnoticed, Nature by her vital force herself puts an end to the grim works of Mars...').

The sculptured figures representing *Veritas* and *Justitia* were sculptured by Toon Dupuis. The six chandeliers were designed by B. Ingenhousz and produced by Braat of Delft.

The 'Optional Clause'

A provision for conferring jurisdiction to the Court in advance of a particular dispute resembling the compromissory clause, yet of a more general nature, is the so-called *Optional Clause*. As discussed above, the name is somewhat deceptive. By this provision States reciprocally accept the jurisdiction of the Court for all legal disputes as compulsory, and this either unconditionally or with certain reservations. The signing of such a clause is an 'option' open to all States, hence its name. The Clause, an idea that was advocated from the days of the First Hague Peace Conference, was the furthest application of the concept of compulsory jurisdiction ever reached.

The history of the Clause, as discussed in an earlier Chapter, can be traced back to the review by the League of Nations of proposals made by the 1920 Committee of Jurists. Given the importance of the provision and the controversy it has prompted, the relevant paragraphs 2 and 3 of Article 36 of the Statute of the ICJ are reproduced here in full:

> 2. The States parties to the present Statute may at any time declare that they recognize as compulsory *ipso facto* and without special agreement, in relation to any other State accepting the same obligation, the jurisdiction of the Court in all legal disputes concerning: (*a*) the interpretation of a treaty; (*b*) any question of international law; (*c*) the existence of any fact which, if established, would constitute a breach of an international obligation; (*d*) the nature or extent of the reparation to be made for the breach of an international obligation.
>
> 3. The Declarations referred to above may be made unconditionally or on condition of reciprocity on the part of certain States, or for a certain time.

These Declarations, which take the form of a unilateral act by the State concerned, are known as Declarations of acceptance of the compulsory jurisdiction of the Court. They are deposited with the Secretary-General of the United Nations and published in the UN Treaty Series and the ICJ Yearbook. The effect of declarations under the optional clause is that States which so subscribe to it acknowledge their mutual rights to bring each other before the Court by filing an application instituting proceedings and agree, in advance, to appear before the Court if any application is filed against them.

After a promising start, the formula ultimately fell short of success. In 1925 no less than 23 States out of 36 Parties to the Statute accepted the compulsory jurisdiction of the PCIJ in this way, in 1935 it was 42 out of 49 States. However, during the UN years, the number hardly ever passed the fifty mark. To date, out of the 186 member States of the United Nations, only 60 subscribe to the clause.

A complicating element are the manifold reservations to the scope of the clause, the very tolerance of which some commentators consider as having nullified the effectiveness of the formula. At present, some three-quarters of the Declarations by States are limited by reservations. These may relate to aspects of time, to certain types of disputes and to certain Parties. They may, for instance, restrict the observance of the clause to specific periods (such as five years with tacit renewal), stipulate termination by simple notice (sometimes taking immediate effect) or exclude disputes from before the date of acceptance of the clause. They may exclude from the clause disputes for which other means of settlement are provided, matters concerning the declarant's vital interests, or falling within the domestic jurisdiction of the State or arising out of hostilities. Again, they may exclude certain treaties, certain areas of law or certain nations, such as those with which the State in question has no diplomatic relations.

Most undermining of the jurisdiction of the Court are 'self-judging' reservations,

Mr Ramsey MacDonald from Great Britain announcing his Government's adherence to the optional clause, in the 10th Assembly, September 1929.

by which States reserve from the Court's jurisdiction disputes involving their domestic jurisdiction or national defence as determined not by the Court but by the declarant State.

Another circumstance confining the effect of the clause is the reciprocity which expressly or by implication attaches to these Declarations. In other words, a reservation made by one Party to a dispute may nullify the effect of the broader Declaration made by the other Party. In this way the Court's compulsory jurisdiction is effectively reduced to those disputes in which Declarations of both Parties coincide. In view of the limited number of States accepting the clause in the first place and the numerous reservations appended to their Declarations by the great majority of States, the ultimate meaning of the clause should not be overestimated.

The qualified success of the formula serves to illustrate the modest measure of progress made in this specific respect over the past hundred years and the general reluctance of States to entrust their interests to third party settlement. None of the permanent members of the League Council nor any of the permanent members of the Security Council ever accepted the Clause unconditionally, and several of them did not ever accept the Clause at all; today, only the United Kingdom accepts it, with substantial reservations.

I.4: I.C.J. — Declarations under Article 36 (2)

4. Declarations recognizing as compulsory the jurisdiction of the International Court of Justice under Article 36, paragraph 2, of the Statute of the Court

Declarations under Article 35, paragraph 2, of the Statute of the Court as implemented by Security Council Resolution 9 (1946) of 15 October 1946 are deposited with the Registrar of the Court. For those declarations, see United Nations, *Treaty Series*, or the *Yearbooks* of the Court.

Note: The declarations recognizing as compulsory the jurisdiction of the International Court of Justice deposited with the Secretary-General by the Governments of Bolivia, Brazil, Guatemala, Thailand and Turkey were made for specified periods of time which expired. For the text of those declarations, see United Nations, *Treaty Series*, vol. 1, p. 49 (Guatemala); vol. 15, p. 221 (Brazil); vol. 16, p. 207 (Bolivia); vol. 65, p. 157 (Thailand), and vol. 191, p. 357; vol. 308, p. 301; vol. 491, p. 385, and vol. 604, p. 349 (Turkey).

In a communication received by the Secretary-General on 12 April 1967, the Government of South Africa gave notice of withdrawal and termination, with effect from that date, of the declaration of 12 September 1955. For the text of the said declaration, which was deposited with the Secretary-General on 13 September 1955, and for the notice of termination, see United Nations, *Treaty Series*, vol. 216, p. 115, and vol. 595, p. 363, respectively.

A declaration recognizing as compulsory the jurisdiction of the International Court of Justice had been deposited on 26 October 1946 with the Secretary-General on behalf of the Republic of China (for the text of that declaration, see United Nations, *Treaty Series*, vol. 1, p. 35). In a communication received by the Secretary-General on 5 December 1972, the Government of the People's Republic of China indicated that it does not recognize the statement made by the defunct Chinese government on 26 October 1946 in accordance with paragraph 2 of Article 36 of the Statute of the International Court of Justice concerning the acceptance of the compulsory jurisdiction of the Court.

In a notification received by the Secretary-General on 10 January 1974, the Government of France gave notice of the termination of the declaration of 20 May 1966. For the text of that declaration and for the notice of termination, see United Nations, *Treaty Series*, vol. 562, p. 71 and vol. 907, p. 129, respectively.

In a notification received by the Secretary-General on 7 October 1985, the Government of the United States of America gave notice of the termination of its declaration of 26 August 1946.[1] For the text of the declaration see United Nations, *Treaty Series*, vol. 1, p. 9.

In a notification received by the Secretary-General on 21 November 1985, the Government of Israel gave notice of the termination of the declaration of 17 October 1956.[2] For the text of the declaration see United Nations, *Treaty Series*, vol. 252, p. 301.

States which have made declarations under Article 36, paragraph 2, of the Statute of the International Court of Justice or whose declarations made under Article 36, paragraph 2, of the Statute of the Permanent Court of International Justice are deemed to be acceptances of the compulsory jurisdiction of the International Court of Justice[3]

Australia	Denmark	India	Netherlands	Somalia
Austria	Dominican Republic[4]	Japan	New Zealand	Spain
Barbados	Egypt	Kenya	Nicaragua[4]	Sudan
Belgium	El Salvador	Liberia	Nigeria	Suriname
Botswana	Estonia	Liechtenstein	Norway	Swaziland
Bulgaria	Finland	Luxembourg[4]	Pakistan	Sweden
Cambodia	Gambia	Madagascar	Palau	Switzerland
Cameroon	Greece	Malawi	Panama[4]	Togo
Canada	Guinea-Bissau	Malta	Philippines	Uganda
Colombia[4]	Haiti[4]	Mauritius	Poland	United Kingdom
Costa Rica	Honduras	Mexico	Portugal	Uruguay[4]
Cyprus	Hungary	Nauru	Senegal	Zaire

Texts of the declarations

(The date shown after the name of the State indicates the date of deposit of the declaration.)

(a) ***Declarations made under Article 36, paragraph 2, of the Statute of the International Court of Justice***

AUSTRALIA

17 March 1975[5]

"*Whereas* on the first day of November one thousand nine hundred and forty-five Australia ratified the Charter of the United Nations of which the Statute of the International court of Justice is an integral part; and

"*Whereas* Australia made a declaration under paragraph 2 of Article 36, of the said Statute on the sixth day of February, one thousand nine hundred and fifty-four; and

"*Whereas* Australia desires to withdraw the said declaration;

"The Government of Australia hereby *withdraws* the said declaration and *declares* for and on behalf of Australia that it recognises as compulsory *ipso facto* and without special agreement in relation to any other State accepting the same obligation, the jurisdiction of the International Court of Justice, in conformity with paragraph 2 of Article 36 of the Statute of the Court, until such time as notice may be given to withdraw this declaration.

"The Government of Australia further *declares* that this declaration does not apply to any dispute in regard to which the parties thereto have agreed or shall agree to have recourse to some other method of peaceful settlement.

"*In witness whereof*, I, Edward Gough Whitlam, Prime Minister acting for and on behalf of the Minister of State for

Proceedings

Contentious proceedings before the International Court of Justice, as also with its predecessor, are governed by fundamental principles and specific rules found in the Statute and Rules of Court. However, when envisaging the future role of the Court, in 1922, the founding fathers of the PCIJ wisely foresaw that, in seeking to satisfy the sense of justice of the greatest possible number of potential litigants among nations conversant with widely differing legal systems, flexibility was of the essence. Indeed, it was a virtual prerequisite for the success of the Court to gain the confidence of all potential Parties.

Consequently, in order to equally satisfy diverse legal traditions represented in the Court, civil and common law traditions of procedure were combined. To this end, proceedings before the Court were divided into two stages, a written phase to be followed by an oral phase. In this way it was left to the States involved in a dispute to take their own legal traditions as a measuring-rod for laying greater emphasis on either the one or the other phase of the proceedings. Thus, it was felt, the Court was best ensured of being adequately informed by Parties before reaching its final decision.

In one other respect, the founding fathers of the PCIJ must be commended. They managed to attain a workable equilibrium between theory and practice, revealing respect for the rule of life as much as for the rule of law. Wisely enough, the ICJ has acted with extreme circumspection in attempting to change the rules laid down by its predecessor. As a result, the Court maintains the same combination of simplicity in laying down the rules as it shows flexibility in their application.

For this attitude there are ample reasons. International litigation is essentially different from procedures in national courts, if only because the Court's very authority derives from the litigants. The legal relations between States are immensely complex. Sovereign States are sensitive to interference with their ways of conducting their affairs. The issues at stake are often momentous.

One other element asserts itself. Disputes often have a long history and contesting

The opening of a session of the Court in the Great Hall of Justice.

States an intense and sometimes frustrating experience with other procedures of settlement (negotiation, mediation, arbitration) before the ICJ comes into play. It attests to the complexity of the cases brought before the Bench that, even so, more often than not, they require lengthy study on the part of the litigating States before they are ready for submission to the Bench. In this perspective, the average duration of less than thirty months for a case to be adjudged by the ICJ is certainly not a bad record, compared to major national and international arbitral procedures. Earlier cases of extreme length such as the *Barcelona Traction* case (11 years) and the *South West Africa* case (6 years) – both of which date from prior to the revision of the Rules in these respects – are no longer a measuring-rod of the Court's functioning.

Representation of Parties

States have no permanent representatives accredited to the Court. When they become engaged in a dispute before the Court, they usually communicate with the Registry through their Minister of Foreign Affairs or their Ambassador in The Hague. Upon becoming a Party to a case they are represented by an Agent, normally an Ambassador or a legal adviser to the Ministry. The status of this Agent may be compared to that of a head of a special diplomatic mission, which is to say that he is empowered to bind his country, in word and writ, during all stages of the case concerned. This Agent takes care of all formal acts, the Application of the case to begin with, and as a rule opens (and often directs most of) the argument during the oral proceedings.

States may also appoint Deputy-Agents and, of course, counsel, advocates and other experts as required – not necessarily of their own nationality. There are no formal qualifications for these officials. In practice, however, the number of qualified and experienced lawyers in the international sphere is limited, even nowadays.

The Institution of Proceedings

As stated above, proceedings before the Court may be instituted basically in two ways, that is either through the notification of a Special Agreement concluded between Parties, or by means of a unilateral application by one Party. Obviously, in the choice between these options the state of the relations between the two States and their attitude as regards the dispute are reflected. The filing of a unilateral application is sometimes suggestive of the lack of agreement between contesting Parties as for instance to the very existence and/or the contents of the dispute. For this reason the Applicant must submit to the Court explicit information not only as regards the Party challenged, but also with respect to the nature of and the grounds for the claim. Normally, in these cases the first issue to be settled by the Court is the matter of its jurisdiction. Clearly, where there is a Special Agreement, it is the acceptance in advance by both Parties of the jurisdiction of the Court which constitutes the major difference as compared to the unilateral application and often considerably simplifies the task of the Court.

Once a case has been filed with the Court, the Registrar commences carrying out a series of statutory duties. He assigns the case a number in the General List and communicates the application to the Respondent State, to all members of the Court, to each State Party to the Statute of the Court and, through the Secretary-General, to all member States of the United Nations, so that such States may consider whether they wish to seek to intervene in the case.

The Registrar, in consultation with the President of the Court, also furnishes a provisional name to the case, indicating its contents in non-prejudicial terms. In adding the names of the States Parties, he avails himself of a form by which the names of States in cases introduced by *Compromis* are presented as A/B, while in unilateral applications these are presented as A v. B.

The next obligatory step taken by the President consists of the summoning of Agents of Parties in order to review, in a private meeting, the time-limits for the first round of written pleadings. In case of disagreement between Parties, the Court, or the President himself, is entitled to decide the matter of its own accord so as not to cause unjustified delay. The Court embodies this decision in an Order. In principle, the case is then ready for the major procedural phases to commence. These are of a twofold nature.

The Written Pleadings

Between the organization of the written and oral phases distinct differences are to be noted. First, written documents are submitted by Parties unilaterally to the Court. Unlike arbitral procedures, in adjudication before the Court there are no direct communications of pleadings and documents between Parties. In other words, it is only in the second, oral stage of the process, the hearings, that opponents meet face to face. Also, the written pleadings remain confidential until after the conclusion of the first phase, whereas oral hearings are as a rule carried on in public.

The first phase of the procedure opens with the submission of written pleadings by Parties, signed by their Agents and delivered in 125 copies to the Registrar for distribution to the other Party, the Members of the Court and interested governments and persons. The Registry provides an unofficial translation of the pleadings in the other official language of the Court.

Pleadings contain a detailed statement of the points of fact and law and answers to allegations by the other side. They tend to be fully documented.

Pleadings may be filed either consecutively or simultaneously. The latter procedure is the normal one in cases brought by *Compromis*. It serves to stress the full equality of Parties and the absence of the idea of a plaintiff and defendant. The pleadings consist of rounds of Memorials and Counter-Memorials, the latter documents serving to refine earlier statements or add to previous information.

In cases submitted by unilateral application the Applicant first files his Memorial, followed by a Counter-Memorial by Defendant. These are followed by a second round, consisting of a Reply responded to by a Rejoinder. Parties are granted equal spans of time to prepare their documents, normally three to six months for each pleading. Even so, Parties have often requested the extension of the time-limit to be in a position to set forth their case with due and proper care. During the 1960s, the latitude granted to Parties led to extremes which were at the time severely criticized.

In these consecutive pleadings following a unilateral application, the second round is often the more momentous one. The main purpose of this second round of pleadings is to establish and define more precisely the issues still outstanding in the dispute. It is only at this stage that the Defendant is able fully to react to the claims made by the Applicant. On the other hand, Parties are requested to keep these documents as short as the character of the case permits. This condition was added to the Rules after experience with the *Barcelona Traction* case in which no less than thirty-seven bulky volumes of documents were filed.

Once this written stage is completed, new documents in the case can be submitted only in exceptional circumstances and provided the Court is satisfied that there is adequate justification for the request. At this stage, too, always provided that Parties agree, pleadings are made available to the press and the public at large. To this end, copies are sent to the UN information centres and libraries.

The pleadings of Parties are concluded and summarized in the so-called 'submissions', a very practical concept from the Civil Law tradition. This is a concise statement by Parties of what exactly they demand the Court to adjudge and declare on the basis of the factual data presented and the legal grounds adduced. The Court in turn deems itself bound not only to reply to these questions to the best of its abilities, but also not to enlarge on points not specifically requested by Parties in their final submissions.

Hearings

After an average interval of three months following the submission of the last pleadings, the case is ready for hearing. Unlike the sittings of arbitral tribunals and unless otherwise agreed by Parties, these oral proceedings are public; they usually take two to three weeks. Here again, the lengthy hearings in the *Barcelona Traction* and *South West Africa* cases of the 1960s, which took 64 and 102 sittings and provoked criticism at the time, were exceptions to the rule.

Hearings are held in the dignified setting of the Great Hall of Justice and are an impressive sight, featuring the Bench of Judges in their black gowns and white jabots, flanked by the Registrar in black gown and white bands (and assisted in his turn by his professional staff of Secretaries) and faced by the Agents and counsel in their national legal robes, Applicants seated on the President's left, Defendants on his right. (In case of a Special Agreement the order is alphabetical.)

Depending on the public interest aroused by the case, the opening session of the hearings is often electric. At the appointed hour, with counsel nervously inspecting their drafts; the press and news media intrusively crowding all over the place; interpreters ready at hand in their booths; the audience – equipped with electronic head phones – expectantly awaiting events, and law students peering over the balcony, the Court's usher, in ceremonial robe, announces 'La Cour'.

All rise when, entering through the passage from the robing room, the Judges, among flashing cameras and buzzing television lenses, proceed to take their places on the Bench, according to seniority. At the request of their President 'Please be seated', the fifteen Judges take their seats – and so does the undulating mass of heads in front of them.

Essentially, proceedings consist of rounds of speeches by counsel, hearings of witnesses and experts, and questions by Judges. Applicants start and each Party normally has two rounds. Parties are granted latitude as regards the organization and presentation of their defence. The Court avoids a legalistic approach to the admission of evidence. Parties are requested to refrain from repeating points adequately dealt with in the written phase. They are to keep their oral statements as succinct as possible, and confine themselves to the issues that essentially divide Parties.

Counsel almost always deliver texts prepared in advance. There is little rhetoric involved, and almost no improvisation. Even so, in most instances, the oral statements are the true *pièce de résistance* of the contest and one should never underestimate the importance of what is called intertextuality – or, as Rosenne sums it up:

> Skillful pleading may not win a bad case, but it can mitigate the effect of a negative decision. While clearly there is no room for flamboyant advocacy appropriate for a trial by a jury, the effect of intonation, of inflexion, of command of language and a cultivated presentation of the case, of personal integrity and candour, mastery

A cartographer at work.

of complicated issues and, where appropriate, a touch of humour, of drama, a well-timed quotation – all this is concealed in the lifeless printed version of the oral pleadings which is subsequently circulated and published. Above all, it is in the hearings that the two Parties first meet face-to-face. Their cases emerge from the remote tranquillity of Counsel's chambers and clash head-on in the hands of highly skilled lawyers, each of whom knows the strength, and the weakness, of his own and of his opponent's cases, and before a Court of equally skilled and experienced personalities'. (Rosenne, *The World Court*, 1995, at p. 129)

Counsel addresses the Court in either of its official languages. The Registry provides simultaneous interpretation. It also provides a provisional verbatim record, the so-called *compte-rendu* (C.R.), which is distributed a few hours later, and an unofficial version in the other language which follows some two days later. These drafts constitute the basis for the formal minutes of the proceedings which are afterwards published in the series of *Pleadings, Oral Arguments and Documents*.

There is no flourishing tradition within the Hague Court of the presentation of oral evidence by either witnesses or experts. Instances of examination and cross-examination resembling Anglo-American procedure have been rare. The same holds true for the 'playing to the gallery', as known in the meetings of the political bodies of the United Nations. In fact, heated debate and pungent polemics are vir-

A bathymetric chart illustrating the 1982-1985 Continental Shelf dispute (Libya/Malta).

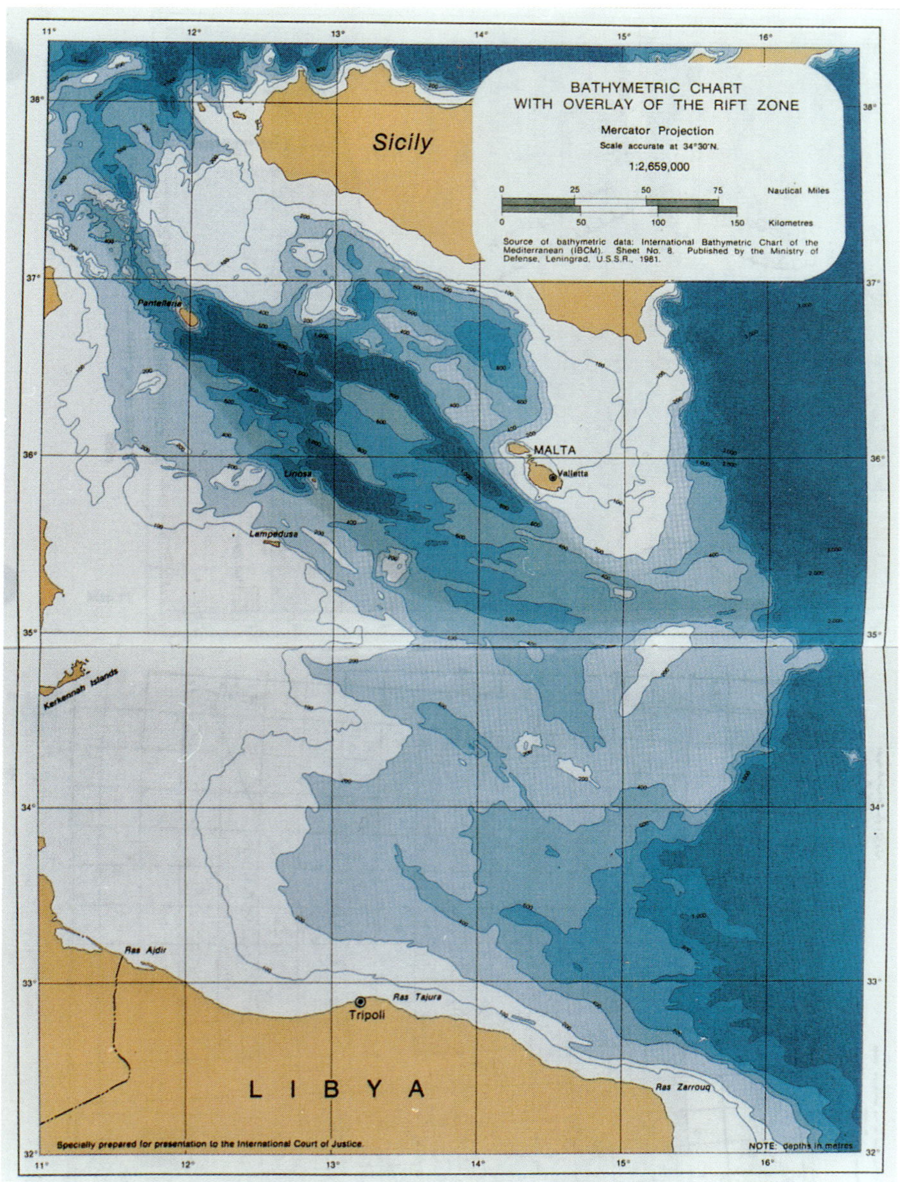

8 CONTINENTAL SHELF

Volume III

Maps

Map 1. Map showing area where exploration by Malta has been carried out, with Texaco well marked "X".
Map 2. Map showing Malta's baselines.
Map 3. Map showing area covered by Maltese concessions giving details of concessions to the south, and showing also Libyan concessions overlapping Maltese concessions or extending beyond the median line.
Map 4. Map showing *Kannizzati* lines as drawn by Maltese fishing authorities for allocation to Maltese fishermen.
Map 5. Map showing area covered by certain Maltese fishing activities (long-line fishing and trawling).

Counter-Memorial of the Libyan Arab Jamahiriya

Volume I

Map 1. British Admiralty charts. (Mediterranean Sea. Isola di Lampedusa to Capo Passero, including Malta. No. 2124.)
(14) Map 2. Maltese baselines.
Map 3. Bathymetric map of the Central Mediterranean.
Map 4. General geomorphological setting.
Photograph of the sea-bed model. North/south view showing northern and southern units of the Pelagian Sea.
Map 5. Saudi Arabia-Sudan delimitation.
Map 6. Geological map. (*Source:* Institut français du pétrole (IPP) - Centre national pour l'exploitation des océans (CNEXO).)
Figure 1. Schematic geological cross-section - Sirt to Ionian Abyssal Plain.
Table 1. Gross national product per head for middle income countries - World Bank 1981. (*Sources:* IBRD, *World Development Report 1983*, pp. 148-149; *Economic Survey*, Economic Division, Office of the Prime Minister, Malta, 1981.)
Table 2. Contributions to foreign exchange earnings by tourism 1979-1981. (*Source: Economic Survey*, Economic Division, Office of the Prime Minister, May, 1982, pp. 62, 26.)
Table 3. Contribution to GDP by industrial origin, Malta 1979-1981. (*Source: Economic Survey*, Economic Division, Office of the Prime Minister, Malta, 1981, p. 16.)
Table 4. Landings of fresh fish in Malta. (*Sources:* Colonial Office, *Blue Books*, Government Printing Office, Valletta, 1938; Government of Malta, *Department of Agriculture*, Government Printing Office, Valletta, 1951, 1952; *Malta Handbook*, 1980; Department of Fisheries, Valletta, 1982.)
Table 5. Fishing labour force. (*Sources:* Colonial Office, *Annual Reports*, Government Printing Office, Valletta, 1928-1929; *Malta Handbook*, 1980, p. 84; Department of Fisheries, Valletta, December 1982.)

tually absent and singularly contrasting to the courteous and businesslike atmosphere maintained throughout. The Court itself has to date never availed itself of its right to call witnesses of its own accord.

The Court is also empowered to request experts, as it did in the *Gulf of Maine* case and, in the *Libya-Chad* dispute, by engaging cartographers. It may order the preparation of a technical report or an investigation on the spot, as it did in the *Corfu Channel* case. It may even proceed itself to an inspection *in loco* (*'descente sur lieu'*), as the PCIJ did in the *Diversion of Water from the Meuse* case. Invitations by Parties to that purpose have more than once been declined by the Court. At the moment, the Court is considering an invitation by Slovakia and Hungary for a *descente* in the matter of the *Gabčíkovo-Nagymaros Project* case.

The same holds good for the right of the Court or individual Judges to put questions to counsel and ask for clarification or additional information to clear up a point at issue. Such questions are not the integral and ordinary part of the process of cases as they are in common law courts. In this aspect, the ICJ is closer to continental practice. In fact, this cautious attitude of the Court has caused criticism on the part of some commentators. In interpreting the Court's attitude one must, however, bear in mind the delicate position of an international tribunal as well as the civil law tradition. Nevertheless, in recent years, active interchange of views between Members of the Bench and counsel has distinctly increased.

The oral phase of the pleadings is concluded by the reading by Agents of their final submissions and the handing of a signed copy thereof to the Registrar. The President then declares the hearings closed and invites Agents to remain at the disposal of the Court.

Incidental Procedures

In the preceding pages the overall framework of proceedings before the ICJ has been reviewed. In general terms, the above is the normal procedure of pleadings in contentious cases, the main proceedings. However, as often as not, this 'natural' flow of events is interrupted by circumstances which may indeed seriously affect the course of proceedings. They may lead to what are called incidental procedures. Basically, these procedures of an incidental character come under five different headings; they will be reviewed

The descente sur lieu (on-the-spot investigation) of the PCIJ in 1937, in the Belgian-Dutch dispute on the Diversion of Water from the River Meuse.

successively. One essential element with respect to these incidental procedures must be borne in mind. Whereas the main procedure cannot be instituted without the express consent of Parties, incidental jurisdiction derives directly from the provisions of the Statute of the Court, irrespective of the consent of Parties.

Preliminary Objections

Preliminary objections are a common phenomenon in the Court's practice over the years. Obviously, preliminary objections are often advanced by Respondents in cases of unilateral applications. By raising its objections, the defendant Party seeks to prevent the Court from judging on the merits of the case. To this end, the Party may advance various arguments.

Firstly, the Party may allege that the Court lacks jurisdiction. It may contest the terms of the jurisdictional clause of the treaty upon which the Applicant State has founded its claim or question its acceptance of the optional clause with which it is being confronted or the scope of that acceptance. Thus, it may argue that the treaty in question is null and void or, on the contrary, that the dispute does not fit within the terms of the treaty – for instance by antedating its conclusion. In similar vein, it may direct the Court's attention to a reservation it attached to its acceptance of the compulsory jurisdiction of the Court, as for instance regarding disputes which it considers as falling within its domestic jurisdiction.

Secondly, it may contest the very existence of the dispute and declare the application inadmissible. It may argue that the essential provisions of Statute and Rules have not been complied with; that the dispute no longer serves an object or that a Judgment would be without practical effect; again, that the dispute is not of a legal nature and therefore exempted from the province of the Court; that the Applicant lacks the capacity to act, either due to lack of legal interest in the dispute or because another formal prerequisite has not been fulfilled, such as the prior exhaustion of local remedies or other forms of settlement.

Thirdly, Defendant may argue that the dispute is not covered by the subject-matter of which it is seized by the Applicant and indispensably involves other aspects – or other Parties – not challenged by the Applicant; finally, that the dispute is basically of a political nature and should rather be put before a political organ of the United Nations.

All these eventualities have been duly anticipated and are adequately covered by the Statute and Rules. In this, clearly, the committees and conferences that drafted these documents in their successive versions availed themselves of the experience which had been gained through arbitral procedures of the last 200 years.

Preliminary objections must be submitted by a Party in writing within the time-limit fixed by the Court for the delivery of its Counter-Memorial. The proceedings on the merits are then suspended and a kind of trial within a trial commences, which constitutes a distinct phase of the case. By an Order of the Court time-limits are fixed for Parties to submit their observations and a series of public sittings is held. Interestingly enough, the respondent Party who has introduced the objections in this phase becomes the Applicant, as it is the burden of this State to prove the merits of its contentions.

After the hearings the Court deliberates and a Judgment is delivered on the preliminary issue. For, in the final analysis, it is the Court itself that settles the issue. According to its Statute: 'In the event of a dispute as to whether the Court has jurisdiction, the matter shall be settled by the decision of the Court' (Art. 36.6).

As far as the Court is concerned, three outcomes are possible: first, it can uphold (at least one of) the preliminary objections and the case is removed from the roll, possibly to be resumed later, once additional conditions are fulfilled; secondly, the objections are formally rejected and the proceedings on the merits are resumed; thirdly, the Court declares that the objections are possibly valid but are not of an exclusively preliminary nature. It then joins the issue to the consideration of the merits of the case and proceeds to that phase and to review all issues at stake together.

However, other options are open to the discretion of Parties, which may either cut short or, on the contrary, complicate preliminary proceedings. All of the following variants have occurred once or twice in the practice of both Courts. Firstly, the Respondent State may decide to withdraw its objections. Secondly, it may decide to contest the jurisdiction of the Court or the admissibility of the claim, but prefers to do so in due course and within the context of the normal flow of proceedings. Thirdly, Parties of their own accord agree to request the Court to join the objections to the merits – which the Court is then bound to do, given its prevailing rule to grant Parties utmost latitude. Fourthly, the Applicant State in its turn, and within the due time-limits for the delivery of its Memorial, also raises objections. In that eventuality, the same preliminary procedure as described above is repeated.

One other option also exists. The Court, on its own initiative, may consider preliminary issues that have not been brought up by Parties. Prior to the revision of the Rules in 1972, the Court was also empowered to decide to join preliminary objections to the merits, but this possibility has now been waived.

The raising of preliminary objections has occurred more frequently and met with more success before the ICJ than before the PCIJ. It should be stressed that the option of raising preliminary objections, although on average delaying the final decision of the Court with little less than a full year, is not primarily to be seen as an obstruction to the speedy administration of justice, but as a safeguard available to litigants. To quote Rosenne again:

> ... preliminary objections play an important role and should not be dismissed as technical playthings. ... Given the political ambience in which much international litigation is conducted, a Government which loses a case on technical jurisdictional grounds is likely to have an easier task in explaining its position to its constituency. (Rosenne, *The World Court*, 1995, at p. 125)

Non-Appearance

One of the ways by which a Party may show its rejection of the jurisdiction of the Court – or the admissibility of the claim advanced against it – is by refusing to appear before the Court. Non-appearance has occurred in certain phases of a case and in all successive phases.

While complicating affairs, non-appearance does not prevent proceedings from taking their course. However, before proceeding to the merits, the Court must be satisfied that it does indeed have jurisdiction in the matter. It must then proceed to examining the factual and legal foundations of the Applicant's claim. If satisfied, the Court brings the written and oral phases to conclusion and renders judgment. However, non-appearance has at times induced the Applicant to discontinue its case altogether, or from a certain moment, as for instance when the Court is to proceed to determine the amount of compensation.

Interim Measures of Protection

As stated above, many disputes that are submitted to the Court have a long history. Whether this is the case or not, they may also have acute urgency. Old quarrels may cause spontaneous outbursts of violence, as much as newly developing disputes may commence to constitute an acute threat to the rights or possessions of a Party – or the lives of its subjects. In any such case a Party may request the Court to indicate interim measures of protection.

To date it has always been the Applicant itself that has asked for protection, although of course the Respondent State is equally entitled to do so (as is for that matter the Court; however, the Court has

never seen fit to do so). In some instances, Respondent States, challenged by these urgent proceedings, have questioned or contested the jurisdiction of the Court or failed to appear. As with normal procedures, the Court is not stopped by this action from deciding upon the issue.

The situation described above requires prompt action on the part of the Court. Accordingly, the President may immediately call upon the Parties to refrain from any acts that may jeopardize the effectiveness of any decisions to be taken by the Court. All other business is temporarily postponed and urgent hearings are held, taking priority over all others. Normally, a decision is reached within three weeks. The Order, embodying the Court's findings, is read by the President during a public sitting. In several cases the Court has found reason to decline the indication of measures of protection.

Joinder of Proceedings

In past decades both PCIJ and ICJ have on several occasions felt themselves confronted by parallel cases submitted by different Parties against a common opponent on issues which, on closer inspection, the Bench concluded to be related to identical subject-matter. In those circumstances the Court is empowered, and at various instances saw fit, to order a joinder of the proceedings. Parties are then invited to submit joint pleadings and oral argument.

This measure, taken on practical grounds, also has practical consequences; for instance as regards the number of Judges *ad hoc* allowed to sit on the Bench. It has happened that the Court decided not to join cases but to proceed with parallel and similar Judgments resulting in decisions rendered on the same day.

In the Deliberation Room of the New Wing.

Intervention

A last element which may intervene with normal procedure is the request for intervention by third Parties. The decisive issue as regards the legitimacy of this request is whether this third Party has any interest of a *legal* nature in the case and whether this interest may be adversely affected by the decision of the Court. It is for the Court to decide upon the admissibility of the request. In the *Land, Island and Maritime Frontier* case between El Salvador and Honduras, Nicaragua was given a standing of 'non-Party intervener', which meant that its rights were secured but that it was not bound by the Judgment of the Court.

In cases where the dispute related to the interpretation of a treaty or convention to which more States than the Applicant and Respondent were Parties, this required legal interest is self-evident. In any such event, States in question possess the right to intervene and may exercise this right by submitting to the Court a Declaration to that purpose. Conversely, the interpretation of the treaty in question by the Court will also become binding upon these intervening Parties.

The Court's Deliberations

The Court represents the world's major legal traditions. To inspire general confidence in its Judgments and in the concept of impartial administration of international justice, it must ensure that these traditions come to bear on the final Judgment. To ascertain this in such a diverse body is no small matter and demands a collaborative effort. Rules to this end were gradually developed. Indeed, the Rules prevailing since 1978 are the outcome of three revisions (put through in 1936, 1968 and 1976) ever since the first Resolution concerning the Internal Judicial Practice of the Court was adopted in 1931. Even so, it is at all stages left to the discretion of the Court to adjust procedure according to circumstances surrounding a certain case. The essential element in all this is that, as is the accepted rule in all judicial systems and international arbitration, the Court's deliberations are conducted in secrecy.

In their present form, deliberations include five phases, covering on average some three months.

Immediately after the hearings are completed, the President proceeds to draft a list of relevant issues of the case requiring decision, for his colleagues to comment upon. These deliberations take place in the so-called Deliberation Room. Prior to the construction of a new wing to the Peace Palace in the mid-seventies, these deliberations took place in the Bol Room of the main building. The new, spacious and stylish room on the third floor of the new wing, equipped with modern electronics, is a most appropriate venue for these meetings. During these deliberations, the Court is only aided by the Registrar, some of the Secretaries and interpreters. Minutes are drawn in a very succinct way and only meant as reference source for the internal use of the Court alone.

Following the adoption of the President's list of issues, each Judge prepares a written Note stating his tentative views with regard to the issues of the case. These Notes are translated by the Registry into the other official language of the Court and distributed among the members of the Bench in that case. From these Notes, which serve at that stage only and are later destroyed, a first indication will be provided as to where the majority opinion may lie.

At this juncture, plenary deliberations are resumed. In a free and detailed exchange of views, Judges now express their personal conclusions in reverse order of seniority, that is commencing with any Judges *ad hoc* and ending with the Vice-President and President. This is designed to prevent undue influence by more authoritative Members of the Bench. The general direction of the discussion and the first contours of the decision-in-the-making now start to become apparent.

At the end of this round of meetings, a Drafting Committee of three members of the Bench is constituted. It is the task of this Committee to try and formulate the majority opinion. To this end, two Judges are elected by secret ballot from among the Judges whose views seem to reflect most closely the apparent majority view. In principle, the President chairs the Committee *ex officio*. Essential to the functioning of the Committee, however, is that its chairman joins the majority feeling. Therefore, if the President feels unable to support this view, he is replaced.

The Drafting Committee prepares a preliminary draft Judgment in English and French, which is then circulated to the Members of the Court. In the drafting of the introductory passages summarizing the proceedings and in the verification of references the Committee is provided with

A deliberation of the Court before a public session.

The authenticized copy of the first Judgment of the Court in the Corfu Channel case.

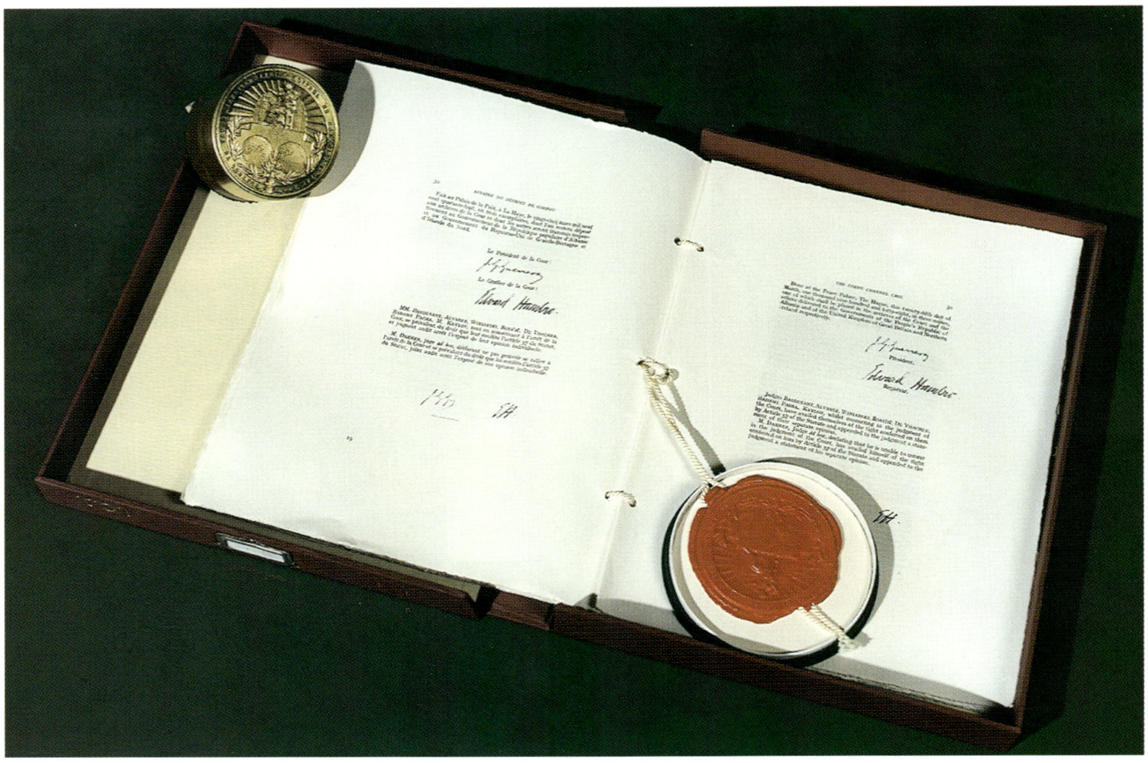

assistance by Registry officials. Emendations of Judges having been incorporated, the revised draft is submitted for what is called 'first reading' and discussion at successive private meetings. An amended draft is then circulated anew for shorter 'second reading', this time not paragraph by paragraph but page by page.

After this second reading a final vote is taken – again in inverse order of seniority and by simple 'yes' and 'no' – on the answers proposed to points formulated in the submissions of Parties. Decisions are taken by absolute majority and no abstentions are allowed. Should the votes be equally divided, the President (or acting President) has the casting vote. The results of the vote are recorded in the minutes.

The Judgment

The delivery of a Judgment of the International Court of Justice during a public sitting in the Great Hall of Justice of the Peace Palace is surrounded by maximum publicity. In the presence of Parties, dignitaries and mostly a capacity crowd, the President reads the Judgment or parts of it – depending on its length – in one of the Court's official languages. Once he has started reading, Agents of Parties are each handed a copy of the provisional issue of the text signed by President and Registrar and sealed with the Court's seal. Together with a third copy, retained in the Court's archives, these constitute the official copies of the Judgment.

When the President has concluded, the Registrar reads the translation of the operative provisions. Then the text is distributed to the press and public at large, together with an unofficial press release summarizing the Judgment in both languages. While journalists telefax the texts to their editors and television crews hasten back to the studios, the official text of the Judgment is, by the most expeditious means, sent to the United Nations in New York.

Thus, in a matter of an hour, a procedure which may have covered years is concluded and a dispute which may have lasted decades brought to – in principle – an irrevocable end. During the following weeks the Judgment is published in printed form in a fascicle of the *Reports of Judgments, Advisory Opinions and Orders*, put on sale to the public and sent to the governments of all States entitled to appear before the Court. Later on, all documents and annexes related to the case, the verbatim records of the public sittings, any new or additional documents submitted by Parties and the principal correspondence between Registrar and Agents are published – in their original language only – in the volumes of the *Pleadings, Oral Arguments, Documents* series for the learned world to study and digest.

What does a Judgment look like and how is it construed?

A Judgment of the ICJ is a document with an average length of fifty pages. It bears the official date of the day on which it was delivered. The document is issued in a bilingual version, with the authentic language on the left-hand pages and the other official language of the Court on the right. The decision as to whether the French or English version is to be authoritative is taken by the Court immediately after its final vote. The text of the Judgment is divided into paragraphs which, since 1966, bear consecutive numbering. The style is kept as simple as the nature of things allows and pains are taken to avoid any terminology too closely connected with any particular legal system.

Following Civil Law practice the Judgment falls into three main sections. First comes a formal introductory part, stating the names of Judges, representatives of Parties, a summary of proceedings and the Parties' submissions. This is followed by a careful exposition of the arguments of Parties and an enlargement on the matters of fact and law that have guided the Court towards its conclusion leading up to the precise grounds for the decision. The third section is the operative paragraph, introduced by the phrase 'For these reasons' and spelling out the decision on the requests as formulated by Parties in their submissions.

> The Court considers that the Norwegian Government is entitled, by virtue of the condition of reciprocity, to invoke the reservation contained in the French Declaration of March 1st, 1949; that this reservation excludes from the jurisdiction of the Court the dispute which has been referred to it by the Application of the French Government; that consequently the Court is without jurisdiction to entertain the Application.
>
> In view of the foregoing it is not necessary for the Court to examine the first ground of the first Objection, or to deal with Objections 3 and 4 presented by the Norwegian Government, or with the Submissions of the Parties other than those upon which it is adjudicating in accordance with the reasons stated above.
>
> For these reasons,
>
> THE COURT,
>
> by twelve votes to three,
>
> *finds* that it is without jurisdiction to adjudicate upon the dispute which has been brought before it by the Application of the Government of the French Republic of July 6th, 1955.

Declarations, Separate and Dissenting Opinions

Until 1978, it was difficult, if at all possible, to establish the names of the Judges that constituted the majority in a given Judgment. It is only since the last revision of the Rules of Court that the number and names of Judges have to be explicitly indicated and this with respect to the final vote on the operative clause of Judgment, Opinion or Order only. Again, this is the outcome of a gradual process of fifty years during which the internal judicial procedure as well as the terminology and phraseology were gradually standardized. Anyone familiar with the voting procedures of the early years of the PCIJ will appreciate the improvements made upon the original system.

However difficult it might have been to form the majority, to identify the minority has often proved much less complicated. Judges who voted against the prevailing opinion have more often than not – and this from the very outset of the Court – felt the urge to expound their points of view. On several occasions we have discussed the various reasons that led Judges to append a Declaration or Opinion to the operative part of the Judgment. The varying ways in which commentators have reacted to this practice has also been reviewed. Suffice it to say that the continental approach tends to favour the single, anonymous Judgment – as in the practice of the Court of Justice of the European Communities at Luxembourg – whereas the common law tradition allows every Judge to voice his own opinion. To be sure, Judgments of the Court are themselves collective.

Declarations and Opinions are printed in the two languages directly following the text of the Judgment. In this, Separate Opinions precede Dissenting ones; the internal arrangement within each category follows the seniority of their authors.

The most simple expression of a personal view is the *Declaration*, which more often than not is nothing more than a brief indication of concurrence or dissent. It is a tradition that Judges may join efforts in writing these brief statements, the so-called *Joint Declaration.*

The second way in which Judges air their personal views on the case, or certain aspects of the decision, is by way of an Opinion. These may be brief. However, Opinions running into hundreds of pages, and indeed into twice to three times the length of the Judgment itself, are no exception. Although Judges are instructed to restrain the tone as well as the contents of their Opinions, and should not introduce matters not covered by the Judgment itself, the all-time record is an

Publications of the Court.

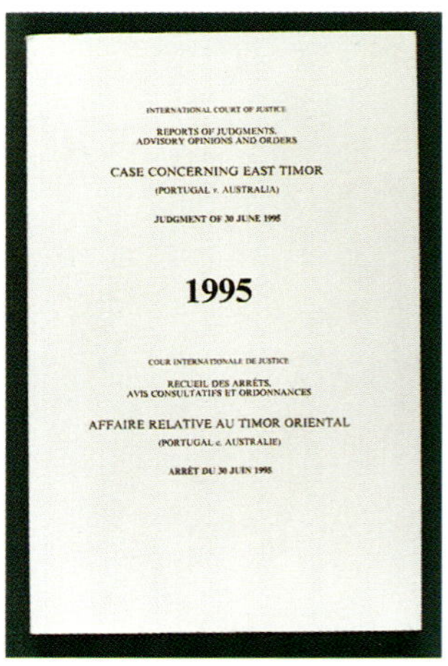

Publications of the Court.

Opinion of 454 pages, that is ten times the length of the Judgment, in the *South West Africa* case. Even nowadays, as Rosenne argues, individual Opinions are at times prolix and often read 'more like articles than as expressions of judicial opinion' (*The World Court*, 1995, at p. 139).

These Opinions fall into two categories. The first is the *Separate Opinion*, the second the *Dissenting Opinion*. In former days, the term Individual Opinion was used, which could sway either way. As with Declarations, Judges may join together and write a 'Joint Opinion'. Judges who wish to file Opinions are required to do so between the first and second reading in the phase of deliberations, in order to allow the Drafting Committee to take these Opinions into account when completing the Judgment. Thus those Opinions may markedly influence the final content of the Judgment.

In a *Separate Opinion* a Judge indicates that, whereas he has voted in favour of the majority decision and its operative provisions, he either disagrees in full or in part with the Court's reasoning, or has reached the same opinion by a different line of thought or on different or additional grounds. These Judges form part of the majority in their voting.

The latter is not the case with Judges who append a *Dissenting Opinion*. The Dissenting Opinion states the reasons for the Judge's disagreement – in full or in part – with the majority view and the operative provisions and elaborates the underlying reasoning which has caused the Judge to vote against the Judgment as a whole, or against vital aspects of its operative provisions.

Although most of these Opinions open with a polite statement of regret, there is no lack of collegiality in submitting a dissent. While many Judges, and most Benches at the instance of their successive Presidents, have tended to seek unanimous decisions, arguing that too great a dissent would weaken the authority of the Judgment, other Judges have maintained that unanimous Judgments may conceal the defects of the Court's reasoning or conclusions.

As Rosenne recalls (*The World Court*, 1995, at p. 137), in 1929 President Max Huber voiced his opinion that this right of dissent was 'a guarantee against any subconscious intrusion of political considerations' and that through its existence 'Judgments were more likely to be given in accordance with

DECLARATION OF VICE-PRESIDENT ODA

My view, as appears in my separate opinion, is that the Danish Application was misconceived and that the case should have been dismissed. As this view did not prevail, the Court has taken a decision on the substance of the case, drawing a particular line of delimitation the choice of which does not appear to me to be founded on any justifiable reasoning. Considering, however, that the line in question does lie within the infinite range of those possibilities which could have been selected by the Parties if they had reached agreement, I have decided that it is proper for me to vote with the majority despite my difference of opinion on several points.

(Signed) Shigeru ODA.

the real force of the arguments submitted'. In fact, he later declared that he would probably not have accepted a seat on the Bench if this Anglo-American system had not prevailed.

Clearly, these differences in viewpoint are hard to reconcile. Yet there is no need to do so. Indeed, both approaches may be deemed perfectly legitimate – from different perspectives. Undoubtedly, the objective of the Court's Judgments in the long run, is to strengthen the international legal order and help perfect the mechanisms for the peaceful settlement of conflicts. From this perspective, the ultimate goal may be well served by the most detailed exposition of conflicting views, being the reflection of the state of the art, so to speak.

Another way to serve these ultimate ends, is the continuity of approach sustained by the Court in its successive decisions. It would not serve the development of international law for the ICJ to adopt conflicting approaches to similar problems in successive cases. Nor would this conduce to confidence among the actors in the international arena – or strengthen the authority of the Court itself. Obviously, the ultimate aim of the Court is to clear the road to international harmony, concordant with justice.

All this being said, the immediate and paramount purpose of a Judgment is to settle a very specific dispute by a decision based on law which is binding upon very specific Parties. These Parties are States which, at times, have not yet quite come to terms with the idea of international adjudication and compliance with external authority. Beyond doubt, within the precarious equilibrium of international politics, a clear-cut and if possible unanimous decision of the full Court carries more weight than a split decision, 'weakened' as Parties may feel by all sorts of conflicting considerations. Be this as it may, given the course steered by the Court over the years, the presentation of separate and dissenting views may enhance the understanding of the judgment and contribute to the progressive development of international law.

Compliance with the Court's Decisions

Any Judgment of the ICJ is binding upon Parties, final and without appeal. This holds equally for Chamber Judgments. Conversely, a decision of the Court has no binding effect with respect to disputes other than the one decided, nor between States other than those who were Parties to the case.

Throughout the League and UN periods the Court has emphasized that non-compliance by Parties with its Judgments would be incompatible with the letter if not the very spirit of its Statute. It is not to be left to Parties to challenge the Judgments, grant them latitude for interpretation or waive the practical consequences of the Judgments as regards their legal rights and obligations. By signing the Charter and acceding to the Statute, States have agreed to comply with the Court's Judgments. Implementation of the Court's Judgments therefore seems self-evident.

Still, there are situations imaginable in which the Court's Judgment is not the final word. A Party may maintain that the other Party has failed to perform the obligations incumbent upon it under the Court's decision. It may then submit the matter to the Security Council, which is authorized by the Charter to recommend or decide upon appropriate measures to give effect to the Court's Judgment.

The only other authority capable of questioning, interpreting or revising its Judgments is the Court itself. At the request of a Party, the ICJ may interpret its Judgments in cases where a difference of opinion has arisen between Parties as regards its meaning. On a few occasions, the Court has been requested to exercise this function.

Possible revision of a Judgment comes into play when, subsequent to a Judgment, new facts are brought to the attention of the Court by a Party, which put its earlier decision in a decisively different perspective. In any such circumstances the allegedly prejudiced Party may request revision of the Judgment. However, this right of Parties is not an unconditional one. The Party in question must itself also have been unaware of this new fact – and this not through its own negligence – and must submit its request within six months of its discovery of the new piece of evidence or information and within ten years of the delivery of the Judgment.

As Rosenne concludes: 'The cases on interpretation and revision indicate that [attacks] on the finality of the *res judicata* will not be easily entertained'.

INTERNATIONAL COURT OF JUSTICE

1985
10 December
General List
No. 71

YEAR 1985

10 December 1985

APPLICATION FOR REVISION AND INTERPRETATION OF THE JUDGMENT OF 24 FEBRUARY 1982 IN THE CASE CONCERNING THE *CONTINENTAL SHELF (TUNISIA/LIBYAN ARAB JAMAHIRIYA)*

(TUNISIA *v.* LIBYAN ARAB JAMAHIRIYA)

Single application combining requests for revision, interpretation and "correction of an error" – Procedure.
Request for revision of a judgment – Admissibility – Article 61 of the Statute – Discovery of "new fact" – Whether "new fact" known to party claiming revision – Means available to that party to ascertain fact, which it was in its own interests to do – Whether fact was "of such a nature as to be a decisive factor".

Request for interpretation of a judgment – Article 60 of the Statute – Whether jurisdiction affected by existence of Special Agreement providing for recourse to the Court by Parties jointly to request "explanations and clarifications" – Admissibility of request for interpretation – Real purpose of request – Existence of dispute as to meaning or scope of judgment – Significance of principle of res judicata.

Request for correction of an error found to be without object.
Request for interpretation concerning reference to "the most westerly point on the shoreline (low-water mark) of the Gulf of Gabes" – Irrelevance of presence of wadi at approximately latitude referred to.
Request that the Court order an expert survey.

JUDGMENT

Present: *President* NAGENDRA SINGH; *Vice-President* DE LACHARRIÈRE; *Judges* LACHS, RUDA, ELIAS, ODA, AGO, SETTE-CAMARA, SCHWEBEL, MBAYE, BEDJAOUI, NI; *Judges ad hoc* BASTID, JIMÉNEZ DE ARÉCHAGA; *Registrar* TORRES BERNÁRDEZ.

Advisory Opinions

The Jurisdiction of the Court

As stated above, apart from deciding contentious cases between States, the ICJ has a second competence, namely an advisory one. One must realize from the outset that this function is not a self-evident one for a court. In fact, in various legal systems the idea is unknown or unpalatable. Although the concept somewhat resembles British practice as employed within the context of the Privy Council and while several other legal systems do allow the executive to request high courts for advisory opinions, the governments are numerous who maintain that a court should restrict itself to dealing with disputes and to rendering binding decisions. As Rosenne observes, 'the introduction into the Covenant of the League of Nations of a discretionary power for the Permanent Court to render Advisory Opinions was thus a controversial innovation' (*The World Court*, 1995, at p. 107).

Accordingly, it was with considerable hesitation that the idea was adopted by the Court in the early 1920s – and was surrounded by very definite restrictions. The right to request such Opinions was retained by the Council and Assembly of the League, which could be reasonably relied upon to keep in mind the interests of the whole, not only of particular member States. Also, the Court on its part, in rendering the Opinions, remained faithful to the pivotal requirements of its judicial character and the principles governing its contentious jurisdiction; in fact, it assimilated the rules governing its advisory procedure to that jurisdiction. The Court reserved the power to decline any request which it considered contrary to its judicial character.

Three aspects mainly distinguish the Advisory Opinion from the Contentious case, i.e., the absence of Parties, the absence of a binding decision and the different class of international actors involved, namely International Organizations and not States.

Over the decades, suggestions have been made to extend the Advisory competence of the Court to States. These proposals, however, have been rejected. This is not to say that States are not at all involved in advisory procedures – on the contrary. At all events, they usually supply most of the necessary information to the Court.

Moreover, the Organs of the League of Nations that were entitled to request Advisory Opinions were the Council and Assembly exclusively. In both these Organs, States were the exclusive representatives. Within both bodies, decisions were taken by unanimous votes. Consequently, in the final analysis, it was States who initiated any Advisory procedure – only this time not individually or by bilateral agreement, as in contentious cases, but through general agreement. Conversely, one may say, and contrary to what was maintained at some stages by commentators, for this very reason the granting of advisory competence to the Court did not essentially run contrary to the concept that the Court was developed by and for States and should serve them.

However, the most essential element of the concept of an Advisory Opinion to be borne in mind as compared to contentious decisions is that, unlike Judgments, Opinions have no binding effect upon the requesting Organization. The Organization remains at liberty to give effect to the Opinion or not, and if so by what means. This aspect, incidentally, also distinguishes the ICJ from Supreme Courts of certain countries in their capacitiy as interpreters of the nations' constitutions. Still, the authority of an Opinion by the ICJ within the international community should not be underestimated. In practice, the authority of an Opinion rendered by the Court, based on priniples of international law, gives it great weight.

In San Francisco, the prevailing concepts with regard to the Advisory Opinion during the inter-war period were not substantially altered, although a few technical adjustments were put through. The most striking departure from the original concept was that the right to ask Opinions from the Court was substantially extended.

Today, the advisory jurisdiction of the Court is governed by Article 65 of the ICJ Statute and Article 96 of the UN Charter. By virtue of Article 65 of its Statute the Court 'may give an Advisory Opinion on any legal question at the request of whatever

body may be authorized by or in accordance with the Charter' to make such a request. The wording 'may give', incidentally, suitably reflects the discretionary power of the Court.

Which are these bodies referred to in the Statute? According to the text of the Charter, Opinions may be asked of the Court by the General Assembly and the Security Council on any legal question; to this is added that:

> Other organs of the United Nations and specialized agencies which may at any time be so authorized by the General Assembly, may also request Advisory Opinions of the Court on legal questions arising within the scope of their activities.

At present, no less than 22 organs are authorized to request Advisory Opinions, including all the principal organs and Specialized Agencies of the United Nations with the exception of the Secretary-General. In recent years, extending the right to the latter official – an idea prompted by the Secretary-General himself in his 1992 *Agenda for Peace* – has been widely advocated, but remains controversial.

Nevertheless, in past years, only a few Organs and Agencies have seen fit to exercise their right to request an Advisory Opinion. In fact, over the twenty-five years of its existence, the PCIJ dealt with more requests than the ICJ in twice the number of years, though 21 out of the 27 Advisory Opinions of the Court that were delivered between 1922 and 1935 related to the consequences of the First World War. The ICJ delivered only 3 Opinions related to the Second World War.

So far, the ICJ has dealt with 21 Advisory Opinions, no fewer than 11 of which were submitted during its first decade. By the General Assembly 13 requests were made, resulting in 12 cases, only 1 was made by the Security Council (the 1970 *South West Africa* Opinion), 1 by the Economic and Social Council and 3 by the Committee on Applications for Review of Administrative Tribunal Judgements.

Of the Specialized Agencies, 2 requests were made by the World Health Organization, 1 request was made by the Executive Board of UNESCO and 1 by the Assembly of the International Maritime Organization.

The most recent requests came in 1994 and 1995: questions from the World Health Assembly and from the General Assembly concerning the legality of the threat or use of nuclear weapons, on which the Court gave Opinions in the very weeks of its golden jubilee.

The Deliberation Room of the Court in the New Wing. In the background the interpreters booth.

As Rosenne argues, what has most influenced the work of the ICJ as compared to that of the PCIJ in this sphere were the political and institutional changes made in San Francisco. It may be argued that the PCIJ was perhaps more inclined to reject requests that were made without the consent of States directly involved; at any rate, it did decline to give an opinion in the *Eastern Carelia* case over the vigorous objection of one of the States immediately concerned.

Within the United Nations, the idea of unanimity was abandoned and replaced by two-thirds majority in the General Assembly and a majority of nine out of fifteen in the Security Council. In the Specialized Agencies a regular majority voting is the norm. Accordingly, the ICJ has not felt itself blocked by the opposition from certain quarters to the request, even from Parties directly involved.

The most effective advisory proceedings have been requests concerning legal questions of general international concern, the binding character of awards rendered by Administrative Tribunals, legal obligations arising under Security Council Resolutions, claims with respect to damages suffered by the United Nations, and the interpretation of the UN Headquarters Agreement – in short, issues of a general interest and which did not lend themselves to contentious proceedings.

Advisory Procedure

Organs or Agencies considering asking for an Advisory Opinion will embody this request in a resolution or decision. Before submitting the request to the Court they will as a rule have a legal advice. As regards the General Assembly, for instance, in an Annex to its *Rules of Procedure* previous advice by its Sixth (Legal) Committee is recommended; most other Organs and Agencies have similar provisions.

The next step is the formal submitting of the exact statement of the question upon which the Advisory Opinion is sought accompanied by all documents likely to turn light on the question. The Court at once informs States to which the Court is open of the request received.

As for the composition of the Court, in several advisory proceedings, Members of the Court have refrained from sitting. Conversely, provisions are made in the Rules of Court for the inclusion of Judges *ad hoc*. This is left to the discretion of the Court, and comes into play when an Advisory Opinion relates to a legal question actually pending between two or more States. In practice, Judges *ad hoc* have sat only rarely, six times with the PCIJ, twice with the ICJ.

As in contentious procedures, the Court may decide to hold written and oral proceedings. It may invite States to file written statements within a certain time-limit, which is two months on average. Normally, the written submissions are far less extensive than in contentious cases.

More than once, the Court has felt impelled to consider whether the issue was a legal question and whether it was appropriate for the Court to pronounce upon the matter. So far, the Court has not found reason to decline to answer a request for an Advisory Opinion.

The written proceedings completed, the requesting Organization and States are invited to present statements during the phase of oral proceedings. Normally, hearings are held within two months from the filing of the written statements and they are much shorter than those in contentious cases.

Oral procedure in Advisory Opinions nevertheless resembles that of contentious cases. Written and oral statements are published in their original language in the *Pleadings* series of the Court.

Advisory Opinions are delivered in the same manner as Judgments and may also include Declarations and Opinions by Judges. Signed and sealed copies are sent to the Secretary-General of the United Nations and to the Organization in question. The Opinion is published in the two official languages of the Court in its series of *Judgments, Advisory Opinions and Orders*.

To conclude, a few words may be said on the Advisory Opinions on applications for the review of Judgments of the UN and ILO Administrative Tribunals. Four instances of such requests have been brought to the ICJ, three of which through the UN Administrative Tribunal (UNAT). These two Tribunals deal with disputes between international organizations and their staff members with respect to conditions of appointment and contracts of employment.

If the validity of the Tribunal's Judgment is contested, the Court may be requested to give a binding opinion. In the case of the UNAT, the request is framed by a special committee, the Committee on Applications for the Review of Administrative Tribunal Judgments, an organ of the General Assembly. As regards the ILO, the request is made by its Governing Body or its Executive Board. Since staff members have no standing to appear in person before the Court, the officer may submit written observations through the chief administrative officer of his organization. In 1995, the General Assembly revised the Statute of the UN Administrative Tribunal to eliminate recourse to the Court.

CHAPTER SEVEN

The Bench

Some Preliminary Remarks

I solemnly declare that I will perform my duties and exercise my powers as Judge honourably, faithfully, impartially and conscientiously.

By making this Solemn Declaration, at the opening of the first public session he or she attends, a newly elected Member on the Bench of the world's highest international Court takes up his duties. The simplest of formulas and the briefest of ceremonies thus conclude what is indeed an elaborate procedure and a protracted process of nomination and election. In the next few pages we will review this intriguing and complicated subject.

To understand and appreciate these complexities, one must bear in mind that three elements have contributed to the establishment of the system of elections as we know it today and effectively influence the outcome of the process. These are the legal, or substantial element; the political factor, which is bound up with national pride and State sovereignty; and, finally, the historical element, relating to the way in which opinion was shaped by practical experience with international tribunals - and notably arbitration panels - until about 1920.

There is no need for us to review the genesis of the system of elections in full detail. For our purposes it will suffice to highlight its basic philosophy, its successive phases of refinement, and some controversial elements. In passing we will illustrate a few aspects with references to historical anecdotes and incidents. However, this may well be the main consideration which the student of the Court has to deal with when examining the complexities which underly the election and composition of the Bench, namely that these are in many ways a compromise, obtained over a long period, between sometimes dramatically opposite views and often contrasting objectives.

A final preliminary consideration asserts itself. If the 'World Court' is bound, in its composition, procedure and actual functioning fairly to reflect the main forms of civilization and principal legal systems of the world, and to do so through representatives who are eminently qualified both morally and intellectually, it is the course of history during the past half century and the dramatic changes it has brought about or, in other words, the shifting socio-political environment itself which has imposed continuing readjustment and reformulation.

The map of the world has changed considerably since the days when the San Francisco Charter and the Statute of the Court were drafted - and so has thinking about the functioning and relevance of international law and adjudication. Time has taught us to accept that there is no such thing as a single, irrefutable formula readily approved by all parties. Likewise, there will never be a basis for the composition of the Court which is enduringly endorsed to by all States as the ideal formula. Conflicting views in the personal, national and regional spheres will inevitably be manifest at every stage, and it follows that the system of nomination and election of Judges cannot possibly satisfy everyone in each and every detail.

As an example one can point to the fact that, although critics have indeed been numerous throughout the years, their recommendations have themselves been as contradictory as they have been frequent. By aiming to remedy apparent or alleged shortcomings, they never failed to introduce new pitfalls. If anything, their efforts serve to illustrate the complex and sensitive subject-matter in hand. To date, no

Judge Rosalyn Higgins making her Solemn Declaration, 1995.

adequate substitute for the prevailing system has been found.

The International Court of Justice is a highly prestigious body. Accordingly, the competition for seats on the Court has always been keen. This holds true at literally every level at which the process unfolds: at the personal level; at the national level, in the rivalry between the academic, diplomatic and judicial spheres to submit candidates; at the intra-regional level of 'National Groups' that nominate candidates, in the competition within a group of nations that are jointly to fill a single seat on the Bench of the Court; at the inter-regional level, in the relative distribution between the groups and continents of the fifteen available places on the Bench; and finally, at the international level in the obvious interplay of the legal and the political elements at UN Headquarters. Without detracting from the strictly judicial functioning of such an eminent body, it remains an undeniable fact that the Court operates in a politicized society and is indeed the principal judicial organ of an otherwise political organization. In the end if not the beginning, election to the Court is a political act.

Perhaps there is not so much, intrinsically, to distinguish the international Judge from his counterpart at the national level, in that the basic qualifications required for both are essentially the same, i.e. a high moral standard and professional competence. Admittedly, at the ICJ this holds true to the highest degree. Still, the reference to the national sphere in Article 2 of the Statute of the Court, which is the authoritative provision in these respects, is in itself illustrative:

> *The Court shall be composed of a body of independent Judges, elected, regardless of their nationality from among persons of high moral character, who possess the qualifications required in their respective countries for appointment to the highest judicial offices, or are jurisconsults of recognized competence in international law.*

However, what makes all the difference at the international level is not so much the Judges as the composition of the Bench. It is here that both in its assumptions and in its very wording the Statute of the Court, in Article 9, has over the decades provoked discussion and critical comment which we shall have to look at in greater detail. Still, it is to be feared that, for the time being, most shortcomings are virtually inevitable, for those that have given cause for criticism relate not so much to the phraseology of the Statute itself as to the still imperfect state of international organization:

> *At every election, the electors shall bear in mind not only that the persons to be elected should individually possess the qualifications required, but also that in the body as a whole the representation of the main forms of civilization and of the principal legal systems of the world should be assured.*

The wording of Article 9 is not in itself

Manley O. Hudson, the historiographer of the PCIJ.

exclusive and is indeed paralleled by the Statutes of other international legal organs. It dates back to the 1920s - and thus reflects the state of international affairs during the inter-war period of the Permanent Court of International Justice. What is more, it also reflects the way of thinking and doctrine of that period, in as much as it starts from the assumption of a static society and of neatly defined legal systems, an approach which typifies the Eurocentric views of the time. It makes no allowance for future changes in the system, let alone for the processes of decolonization and self-determination or the changes in the socialist system which the world has witnessed in the past half-century.

Consequently, as far as the 'legal systems' are concerned, the phraseology of 1945 has been overtaken by events. What about the second requirement? Does the present composition of the Court reflect the 'main forms of civilization', if this expression is taken to mean a fair regional distribution or - to use the formula applied by the UN Charter to the allocation of elective seats in most UN Organs – an 'equitable geographical distribution'?

The composition of the Court has changed dramatically in recent decades. Many of these changes in the distribution of seats have resulted from the admission to the United Nations of some 130 new Members, most of them newly independent States, and from the campaign launched by those new Members to promote more equitable distribution. We shall see what these results were and whether they can be considered satisfactory. However, one must begin by clarifying the point of departure and the prevailing criteria at the very beginning of this historical process, around 1900, as these left their mark on the text of the Charter and Statute of 1946.

The statue of the first President of the PCIJ, the Dutchman B. C. J. Loder (1849-1935), in one of the corridors of the Peace Palace.

The Number of Judges

The creation of an independent International Court of Justice, that time-honoured ideal of mankind, had long been effectively frustrated by the primitive state of the international community. Around 1900 this was illustrated by the virtual deadlock arising from, on the one hand, the persistent demands by the Great Powers that they should be permanently represented on such a body and, on the other, the equally determined insistence by the 'lesser lights' on the strict application of the principle of equality of States large and small.

For all the diplomacy brought to bear on the question during the two Hague Peace Conferences of 1899 and 1907, this political riddle was not solved. The problem of how to elect the Judges, and on what criteria, had baffled the Second Hague Peace Conference in 1907 in its efforts to create a Court of Arbitral Justice, which at the time was the only acceptable compromise between the by then generally approved concept of arbitration and the still widely resisted idea of adjudication. Its proposal for an International Prize Court had effectively encountered the same difficulties.

The controversy included the issue of the number of Judges. Initially, and for obvious reasons, each State wished to be allowed to appoint its own Judge. In retrospect, it is hard to conceive that this idea was ever taken seriously, if only on account of the practical problems it would have posed. Still, the demands of nations could not be so easily disregarded, and much thought was given to the problem of how to solve this dilemma. Accordingly, the 1907 Prize Court Convention envisaged the appointment of a Judge and a Deputy-Judge by each State, but with only fifteen Judges actually sitting at any one time; an obvious compromise, but one that is interesting as the number fifteen was suggested for the first time.

This number likewise features in proposals made in connection with the Paris Peace Conference. Thus, a Swiss proposal of 1919 envisaged a Court of fifteen Judges, yet allowed each Party the right to challenge five, so that only five Judges would actually sit at any one time. Again, the original Statute of the PCIJ, based on the draft of the 1920 Committee of Jurists, provided for eleven Judges and four Deputy-Judges, empowering the Assembly of the League of Nations, on the proposal of the Council, eventually to increase the number to fifteen Judges and six Deputy-Judges, once the Court's jurisdiction had been extended. Its general idea - as Manley Hudson, eventually the last American Judge on the PCIJ and the foremost commentator of the period rightly observed - was to create a Court 'large enough to represent the various systems of legal thought, yet small enough to include only persons of eminence; large enough to admit of challenges and to offset inevitable absences, yet small enough to enable effective conferences to be held'. (Hudson 1943, at pp. 147-148).

In fact, the leading international lawyers of the day had something to say on the matter. The Root-Phillimore plan suggested 11 Judges and 4 supplementary Judges, and the 1920 Committee itself proved to be divided, with the Dutch jurist Loder insisting on 9, the Japanese Adatci on 13, Lord Phillimore on 15, whereas the French representative de Lapradelle took 11 as a bare minimum. A British proposal to restrict the number to 9 was opposed on the ground that, as the Great Powers would always be represented on the Court, other States could not so easily agree on the distribution of fewer places.

The issue remained a subject of discussion until long after the establishment of the PCIJ. The 1929 Committee of Jurists would not hear of any later increase 'to avoid the risk of an exaggeration which might cause misconception'. As late as 1936, the Court's Vice-President, the Dutchman Van Eysinga, expressed his view that 'ideally speaking, ... the best composition for an international tribunal' was five Judges, including two of the nationality of the Parties; but he admitted that 'for political considerations', this was impossible for a World Court. One may gather from these lines how deeply the early experience with arbitration panels had imprinted itself on the minds of contemporary international lawyers.

Reference has been made to Deputy-Judges. The idea of including Deputy-Judges, first conceived in the 1907 Hague Project, was intended to serve a threefold purpose, as De Lapradelle put it, i.e., the practical purpose of filling vacancies in the event of the death or resignation of sitting Judges; the political purpose of satisfying States that had no nationals among the Judges; and the idealistic notion of imbuing future Judges with the spirit which must pervade the Court, by admitting young Judges who could from time to time serve for a while on the Bench of the Court and keep in constant touch with it. The British and Italians never believed in the idea, as they plainly stated at the First Meeting of the League Assembly - but they found no support.

It was the 1929 Committee of Jurists which finally tipped the balance, by proposing the abolition of Deputy-Judges on the ground of practical experience over the past decade. As Hudson observes, the Commission seems to have feared that Judges would feel less obliged to attend the sessions if Deputy-Judges were on hand to take their places. After the 1930 elections, the Deputy-Judges of the first term did not return and the idea was abandoned. Ever since, the Bench of the World Court has been composed of fifteen Judges.

The Distribution of Seats

It was only with the constitution of the League of Nations that the long-standing controversy over the election of Judges was resolved. The matter was settled by analogy with the solution found in the distribution of seats in the Council and Assembly of the League. The 1920 Committee of Jurists which prepared the Statute of the Court-to-be, was the first body that could avail itself of this opportunity created by the League, in allowing the presumptive Permanent Members of its Council each to have a Judge of its nationality elected to the Bench.

It was this understanding, greeted at the time with general satisfaction and relief, which accounted for the distribution of seats on the PCIJ, and on the first Bench of the ICJ. In 1946, this distribution was as follows: the so-called 'Western' States (Western Europe, Great Britain, 'Old Commonwealth' and USA) 6 seats, Latin America 4 seats, the Socialist States 3 seats, the Afro-Asian group (including China) 2 seats. At that time, the former Axis Powers were not members of the United Nations.

The world then started to change rapidly. By 1965 the number of States represented in the General Assembly had increased

The Chinese Wang Ch'ung-hui (1881-1958), Deputy-Judge of the PCIJ during 1922-1925 and titular Judge during 1930-1936. At various stages of his career Mr Wang Ch'ung-hui held the Premiership and the Ministerships of Justice and Foreign Affairs of his nation. He was also Chief Justice of the Supreme Court of China.

from 45 to 118. General dissatisfaction among the newly independent nations occasioned the expansion of the Security Council from 11 to 15 members, in order better to reflect changing political structures (and implicitly weaken the dominance of the Permanent Members). At that juncture, the composition of the Court still remained unaffected, but it too responded to the admission of large numbers of newly independent States, especially from Africa. The regional distribution of the Court was brought roughly into line with that of the Security Council. At the 1964 elections, the 'Western' States received 5 seats, the Socialist States 2, Latin America 2 and the Afro-Asian group 6, i.e., 2 for African and 4 for Asian States. Four years later, the distribution among the Afro-Asian group was equalized. The only noteworthy change since that time has been the 'seizing', in 1987, of a seat by the Caribbean Community, at the expense of the Latin American representation. It is fair to say that, at present, the ICJ is representative, if perhaps not of the main legal systems, at least of the main forms of civilization and ethical and religious convictions in our multicultural world.

But can one speak of a fair distribution? This issue is still a bone of contention, notably among the Asian group, which is representative of so large a part of the world population. Some commentators maintain that it is the Court's lack of sufficient regional balance which accounted for the relative under-utilization of the Court. As Rosenne argues, this is hard to prove:

> In fact there are usually found amongst the Members of the Court at any given moment Judges who are highly qualified and experienced international lawyers as such, Judges who have had considerable

A Nomination

Mr Menzies thought it unthinkable that Percy should go back to private life, and suggested that he should consider being nominated for election to the International Court of Justice, sometimes referred to as the World Court, which sits in The Hague and deals with cases brought before it by sovereign States. It would be of considerable prestige to Australia, and the Prime Minister believed that my husband was the one man who could bring it off.

I am still rather ashamed that, at the time, I knew very little about this high judicial body and was to learn that the general public knew less, seldom having been given, through Press or radio or television, much information about it, a fact that struck me strongly with the knowledge of experience at a later date. If the civilized world was ever going to forsake the barbarism of war and live by the rule of law, surely the peoples of it should know that, as an organ of the United Nations, this Court had been established for the purpose of dealing with international quarrels.

After many discussions between my husband and myself, and a good deal of careful thought, he decided to accept the suggestion put forward by our Prime Minister. As a lawyer the idea had considerable appeal; as a man who believed deeply in the rule of law, and that, unless it could be accepted generally, humanity would destroy itself through future major wars - to say nothing of the human suffering and sorrow, waste, sacrifice and destruction war brings in its wake - it seemed to him that here might be an opportunity to play a part in the furtherance of peace between nations.

So eventually the die was cast. Percy made his decision to permit his nomination for election as a judge of the International Court of Justice. On the personal side the appointment, if he won, would bring a great blessing. As a judge of the Court it would be possible for him to return to Australia once a year during either the summer or the winter recess. Life is too short to cut oneself off from family, the friends of a lifetime, one's own country, and our elder son in America and our younger son when he returned home.

The International Court elections were held towards the end of 1957. The first step was to obtain the nomination of a country and other countries, submitted not by governments but by national groups of distinguished lawyers. At the appropriate time, when the General Assembly is in session, the elections take place, held separately, but simultaneously, in both the General Assembly and the Security Council.

Australia had never before had one of its citizens on the International Court, though twice Australians had been nominated - Professor K. H. Bailey (now Sir Kenneth) in 1946 and Dr H. V. Evatt in 1948 - but they had failed to be elected.

There are fifteen judges on this Court, five vacancies occurring every three years. All member nations of the United Nations, at

that time numbering somewhere in the eighties, have the right to nominate a judge. When once elected to the Court, a judge does not sit as an Australian or Frenchman or Greek or whatever his nationality may be, but as a member of the Court, presumably removed from any pressure from his own country or Government, or any other country or Government. He is there to administer justice between those sovereign nations coming before the Court.

The decision to allow himself to be nominated having been made, there was little to do but wait. The elections which would decide our future for some years to come would not take place until close to the end of the year. Meantime we turned our attention to present duties.

From: Jean Spender, *Ambassador's Wife* (1968)

> diplomatic experience at a high level of responsibility (including one or two former Foreign Ministers), and Judges whose main experience has been in domestic judicial and administrative spheres. ... It is not necessary that every Judge be highly familiar with the whole of present-day international law (a virtual impossibility!). ... The practical experience of the judicial function undoubtedly requires a high level of statesmanship and practical wisdom in addition to knowledge of the law, and this mixture of talents is generally speaking adequate and meets the international requirements. (Rosenne, *The World Court* 1995, at pp. 60-61)

Meanwhile, the debate about numbers and distribution continues. As early as the mid-1950s both the *Institut de Droit International* and the General Assembly discussed the possibility of increasing the number of Judges on the Bench to 18, to ease the intense political competition to secure a seat on the Court. The obvious disadvantages, notably the further hampering of the decision-making process by enlargement of the body, account for the hesitant reaction to those proposals. As for the required qualifications of Judges, it can be maintained that this primary responsibility rests not so much with the electors, who proceed on the basis of a previously constituted list of candidates, as with the nominators who constitute the list. We will now consider this process of nomination and election of Judges.

The Nomination of Judges

The system of nomination of Judges of the ICJ is an intriguing one. In a way it is an anomaly and virtually outdated; it can only be explained in historical terms. It is a reminder, and this cannot be sufficiently emphasized, that the ICJ, by following in many respects the intellectual wake of the PCIJ, is perhaps as much the brainchild of the Hague Peace Conferences as it is of the League and the United Nations. The procedure for the nomination of Judges in fact derives from the one developed in 1899 in relation to the Permanent Court of Arbitration, which has survived to the present day. As this well-established procedure for nominating arbitrators was the only readily available instrument at the time, the 1920 Committee, in an obvious attempt to play down the political element, was glad to have recourse to it.

The crucial feature of this procedure is the idea of *indirect* nomination, that is to say not by Governments directly but through so-called National Groups. The idea was well suited to the PCA, as this is not a standing court properly speaking, but in fact consists of a Secretariat in The Hague which administers a list of aspirant arbitrators, from which list contending parties are free to compose a panel. The list itself is drawn up by the Parties adhering to the 1899 (and subsequently the 1907) Conventions. Each party is entitled to nominate four members of its National Group in the PCA.

The idea conceived by the 1920 Committee of Jurists that drafted the Statute of the PCIJ was that each National Group would nominate no more than four candidates for the PCIJ, only two of whom could be its nationals, after consultation with representatives of the national supreme courts, law schools and learned academies. During the full 20 years of the PCIJ the system functioned adequately and despite some opposition it was maintained in the 1946 Statute. The anomaly, however, concerns the transplantation of an idea developed for one Court, the PCA, to another institution, the PCIJ/ICJ which operates on altogether different principles. To date, 81 nations adhere to the Hague Conventions and the PCA, whereas 186 nations are parties to the Statute of the Court. That is to say, that a hundred or more nations 'artificially' constitute National Groups for the sole purpose of nominating Judges. However, in the final analysis, this anomaly was, and still is, deemed to counterbalance the disadvantages of entrusting the nomination to Governments directly. It is the general feeling that both the qualifications and the independence of Judges are better promoted in this way.

The Election of Judges

The independence of the judiciary is acknowledged worldwide to be a precondition for the sound administration of justice. However, at both national and international level the same striking feature is to be observed, namely that the independence of the judiciary has to be safeguarded through procedures which are usually entrusted to a political organ. At the national level it is ultimately the executive branch - through whatever procedure, and this may differ considerably - that effectively authorizes appointments. At the international level matters are more complicated, and understandably so, as at this level there is nothing to parallel the authority of the executive branch in the national sphere. It is precisely the absence of such an authoritative body that accounts for much of the elaborate and circumspect procedure surrounding the election of international tribunals.

As we have seen, Judges of the International Court of Justice are elected from the list of candidates submitted by the nominating groups. These elections take place at UN Headquarters in New York, normally at special public meetings during the November sessions. The candidates are elected by the Parties to the Statute of the Court, that is the States Members of the United Nations (at present 186) plus States that are non-Members but are parties to the Statute - at present 2, i.e., Switzerland and Nauru. Elections are held in both representative organs of the United Nations, the Security Council and the General Assembly, by secret ballot during independent and simultaneous meetings of these bodies.

In order to be elected a candidate must obtain an 'absolute majority' in both

An Election

On 1st October my husband and I had the curious experience of being at the opening of the United Nations with Percy there in the role of onlooker. It had been decided that, with his name coming up as a nominee for the International Court, it would not be correct for him to take an active part in the debates of the General Assembly. This was the day of the election of judges to seats about to fall vacant on the Court. A number of countries had nominated my husband early in the piece, and more nominations had continued to come in as the date of election came nearer. It was exciting, getting news of his nomination by far-distant countries. Rather flattering, to my mind, that so many came rolling in until, when nominations closed, they numbered over twenty.

But now the elections of judges to the International Court of Justice were upon us. The date was 1st October. We had been assured again and again that Percy was a certainty. He had received nominations from countries of North and South America, of Europe, the Middle East and Asia: by far the greatest number of nominations of any of those standing for election. But an election is not unlike a horse race; one never knows until the numbers go up.

The election was to commence at ten-thirty both in the General Assembly and the Security Council. We were in place in the General Assembly Chamber well before that hour. The foyer and corridors were, as usual, crowded with every nationality under the sun. Men from widely separated parts of the globe came up to wish Percy luck. Some of them he had more than once crossed swords with during debates. There was no doubt now, however, of the warmth of their good wishes. It gave you rather a nice feeling to realize that behind so many of the sometimes tempestuous debates there remained a pool of goodwill and personal liking. Let there be no sentimentality about this, however. There were other delegations, some representing nations of great power, others at that time vociferously raising their voices in denunciation of every western nation in sight, from whom friendly warmth for my husband was unlikely to radiate.

At ten-thirty the door at the side of the dais opened and the President, Sir Leslie Munro of New Zealand, made his appearance. He took his place behind his desk, flanked by the Secretary-General and his deputy. Silence fell when Sir Leslie brought down his gavel and announced that the first item on the agenda of the Assembly would be the election of five judges to the International Court of Justice. The names of those standing for election were read out: in all there were forty, each name representing a man from a different country, for the five vacant seats. Some of the names were known in most parts of the world, others in academic and legal circles only. Among them were ex-presidents of States, ex-ambassadors and foreign ministers, men whose interests had ranged widely through the world.

The voting was by secret ballot, and unless a man obtained a clear majority in both the Security Council and the General Assembly on the first ballot his chances were considerably dimmed. One by one, as the names of their countries were called, the leaders of the delegations came down the carpeted laneway in front of us and put their little piece of paper in the ballot box.

The counting took a long time. While it was in progress, a whisper came to us that

Sir Percy C. Spender (1897-1985), Judge (1958-1967) and President (1964-1967) of the ICJ

Percy had won an excellent majority in the Security Council. Our good friend Mr Shann, as enthusiastic on my husband's behalf as a man could be, had his efficient news commentary running well. I gave a sigh of relief: one hurdle over.

At last some papers were laid before the Secretary-General. He read out the results of the first count. Percy's name headed the list, with an overwhelming majority in both Chambers. So the next nine years of our lives were decided. It turned out that he had received the largest majority ever accorded to any man standing for a seat on the International Court of Justice. For the other four seats a greater struggle was in evidence. Voting had been too diverse to give any man a victory on the first count.

From: Jean Spender, *Ambassador's Wife* (1968)

Organs. In the inter-war years this was interpreted as 50 percent plus one of the votes cast at the meeting. Within the United Nations this is taken more strictly to mean 50 percent plus one of all Members of the respective Organs, regardless of whether they actually attend the elections and vote or not. Within the Security Council Permanent and non-Permanent Members vote on equal terms, that is to say that there is no power of veto, and decide by a simple majority of eight, not the statutory majority of nine which governs all other votes.

The procedure of double elections as outlined here is understandable on historical grounds. Both Organs in their own way lay claim to global representation. However, in the past 75 years the balance between the two bodies has shifted considerably, mainly due to the tremendous increase in the number of nations operating on the international scene. Within the League of Nations the Council dominated the scene, as it represented the Great Powers and other leading nations. Obviously, within the modern United Nations it is just as naturally the General Assembly which has taken over this claim to be the Organ representing the opinion and conscience of the world, if only because in recent decades it has so dramatically come to outnumber the fixed number of the Council, and is in fact currently more than twelve times as large.

To illustrate the expansion of the Organization: during the latest elections, in 1993, the number of votes required to obtain an absolute majority in the Assembly was three times the number needed to form a majority in the first elections of 1946. Still, suggestions made as early as the San Francisco Conference that elections should be a matter for the Assembly alone were rejected, and the League system still prevails. A recent tendency is, however, that in the case of an imminent deadlock the candidate clearly preferred by the Assembly takes precedence in the final ballot.

The elaborate provisions contained in the Statute and the scrupulous observance of a host of rules are designed to ensure due process. In the Security Council votes cast (15) are not counted until all votes in the General Assembly (in 1993: 186+2) have been cast, and this is just another example. The whole process of nomination and selection, which may theoretically cover the full interval of three years between elections is, from its very beginning, characterized throughout by diplomatic manoeuvring.

The initiative is sometimes taken by a candidate himself. He may start sounding out his chances among colleagues in the field and, once reassured, approach his National Group, or it may be the National Group that approaches him. A Government, too, often initiates diplomatic overtures well in advance, if only to assess probabilities, if not for the next, then perhaps with a view to later elections. Once the full list of candidates has been published, diplomatic activity intensifies:

> ... and there is little doubt that at times a delegation is instructed to vote for a given candidate in return for promises of support on another matter of close concern to it, whether its own candidature in another election or a matter

The election of six Judges to the ICJ by the General Assembly and the Security Council on 16 November 1960. Mr Mongi Slim of Tunisia, at the time President of the Council, deposits his vote in the ballot box.

The modern electronic voting procedure in the General Assembly.

of substantive concern. It is difficult to see why such bargains should be deprecated (except out of an exaggerated regard for legal purism), because both the General Assembly and the Security Council are political bodies and it is not expected of them, or of the States of which they are composed, to exclude political considerations when they come to perform the very important function of electing the Members of the Court. These diplomatic contacts are also valuable in maintaining the desired professional standards of the Court. Through them, influential governments are able discreetly to indicate their view whether a given candidate is qualified for the duties, and there is reason to believe that this too is a factor which influences the final outcome of the elections. (Rosenne, *The World Court* 1995, at p. 67).

These are perceptive observations by a keen commentator on the life of the Court.

More often than not the elections are a protracted process, even with the introduction of electronic equipment. It is not exceptional for at least half a dozen ballots to prove necessary for an adequate number of candidates to obtain an absolute majority in both Organs. If the vacant places have not yet been filled, and con-

The Presidency

My husband was on the International Court of Justice for nine years, for the last three years of which he was President of the Court. During these years we saw many changes both in the membership of the Court and its functioning. For certain changes in the latter he was, as President, largely responsible. When we came to Holland, the Court sat on the mornings and afternoons of every weekday, Saturday mornings, frequently Saturday afternoons and even, occasionally, on a Sunday. Sunday sittings came to an end when my husband informed the then President, Judge Klaestad from Norway, that he was not prepared to attend meetings on that day. He did have a wife around, with whom he thought, as I did, he was entitled to spend the sabbath. On 9th March 1964 my husband was elected President of the International Court of Justice; a signal honour accorded him, he felt, by his fellow judges and one which I know he did not seek. After all, to be elected a member of the highest court of law in the world is no small distinction; to be chosen as its President a tribute of which a man may well be proud.

He promptly introduced several innovations which, for some time past, he had felt were much needed. The first and, in my own opinion as an onlooker at the Court proceedings, the most important was simultaneous translation. Hitherto, during the oral proceedings, the Court had been addressed by counsel in either French or English. Counsel would speak in whichever language he chose for twenty or thirty minutes, then sit down and let the translator take over for about the same length of time. A tedious and time-consuming performance, unrealistic when witnesses were called by the parties, examined and cross-examined. With simultaneous translation, sittings were confined to half of each day, leaving the rest of the day for private research and study. Despite this lessening of time devoted to public hearings, the Court was able to cover more ground in the week than the twice-daily sittings under the old system. Apart from the additional time given to judges to devote their attention to the details of argument and so on, there was the relief from the tedium of listening to the same address twice over.

There was some demur when the new President gave instructions that a notice in English, French and Dutch should be displayed at the entrance to the Palace of Peace setting forth the times of the public sittings of the Court. Hitherto few members of the public had ever ventured to put their noses inside the courtroom, nor had they been encouraged so to do except on opening day which, in any case, is somewhat official. To the general public the International Court was just one of those esoteric mysteries not intelligible to the layman.

Remarkably enough, once it was realized that the sittings of the Court during the oral hearings were open to the public, people flocked to them. It is no uncommon sight now to see the courtroom filled, even to the galleries, with visitors from any parts of the world. Heartening, too, to see how many young people will sit for an hour or so and quietly listen, able through hearing aids to follow the argument in French or English.

To me this influx of interested people completely changed the atmosphere of the oral hearings. There was life and interest in a room which used to be sadly empty. I would have thought it depressing for the judges and counsel to survey rows of empty seats. We are all human. An audience is a stimulant. As an American woman who had lived in this city for some years and, before her departure, had become almost an habitué at the sittings remarked to me, 'Sir Percy has brought the Court into the twentieth century'.

A custom, or duty, which appeared to have fallen somewhat into disuse was that the President of the Court should go to New York around the time of the opening of the General Assembly of the United Nations to confer with the Secretary-General and other permanent officials of the United Nations on administrative matters concerning the Court. My husband revived this custom, and found it very well worthwhile.

From my observation it appears to me that a President of the International Court of Justice, if he is to fulfil his administrative as well as judicial duties, needs to be an active man with a deep interest in all that pertains to his office.

It was for such reasons that he agreed, from time to time, to arduous undertakings, such as the acceptance of an invitation to attend the twentieth anniversary of the United Nations in 1965. For this he allowed himself five days, leaving Holland on a Thursday for San Francisco, returning the following Tuesday, to preside over the Court on the Wednesday: something of a physical strain. The administrative side of the Court takes up a great deal of time. Gone were the days when we could slip away for the odd weekend for our own pleasure and enjoyment, to come back refreshed by change of climate, scene and people. It just was not possible. Much of what my husband accomplished was carried out with the aim of modernizing and arousing public interest in this instrument of international peace.

From: Jean Spender, *Ambassador's Wife* (1968)

sensus is unlikely, after numerous ballots in three successive meetings of Council and Assembly, then and only then may a special machinery be put into operation to break the deadlock. However, to date this has never happened.

A few words should be said about the independence of the Judges as stipulated in the Solemn Declaration. Understandably, the first and major concern of the 1920 Committee was to make the Judges, as far as possible, independent of the Governments of which they were the nationals. At the time it was generally felt that the failure to bring about this degree of independence had helped to wreck the Central American Court of Justice a few years previously.

The second safeguard was the explicit prohibition of the simultaneous exercise of 'any political or administrative function', or engagement in 'any other occupation of a professional nature' (Article 16). The obvious intention is to exclude conflicts of interest, political and financial. This does not of course place a bar on all activities. Judges are often invited to lecture or chair conferences; they may write professionally (with due discretion); they may even sit on arbitral panels. The latter activity is deemed acceptable as long as the subject-matter of the dispute is not susceptible of being brought before the Court (in which eventuality a Judge can be deemed to have disqualified himself from sitting on the Bench) and on the understanding that membership of the Court is considered a full-time and supervening occupation which at all times takes precedence over other activities.

A third provision is that a Judge may never sit in a case with which he had any previous connection before his election to the Court. In any such eventuality he has to excuse himself. Conversely, a Judge is bound to participate in each and every case unless prevented by illness or requested by the President to stand down for some special reason, and States may anticipate that a full Bench will examine their case. A Judge can of course resign in mid-term of his own accord and for personal reasons. The only way to be dismissed from office is by a unanimous decision of his colleagues, if the Bench is of the opinion that he no longer fulfils the required conditions.

From the early days of the PCIJ Judges have been elected for a term of nine years. On the bench of the PCIJ, however, they were elected simultaneously, to be replaced or re-elected simultaneously, so that the first Bench served in 1921-1930, and the second in 1931-1939, apart from interim elections to fill a casual vacancy. The third elections were postponed due to World War II, and a third Bench never materialized - serving Judges remained in office until the dissolution of the PCIJ. At San Francisco it was felt by the Committee of Jurists that this system, while preserving continuity during the term of nine years, did not maintain this element beyond the nine-year period, and a new system was accordingly developed. In 1946 nine Judges were elected, three to be replaced after 3, three after 6, and three after 9 years. This system has been maintained and, ever since, elections are triennial, a third of the Bench being replaced on each occasion.

The Presidency

Following each triennial election the Members of the Court elect their President and Vice-President for a period of three years. The office of President is no sinecure. His official duties include many of a diplomatic and representative nature. He is responsible for supervising the internal administration of the Court as well as for external contacts, both with the host country, The Netherlands, and with the UN Organs, notably the General Assembly. He also confers on procedural matters with Parties in pending cases and takes necessary procedural steps. In the case of a request for interim measures of protection submitted by a Party, he may call upon both Parties to refrain from taking any steps that may jeopardize the outcome of the examination of the case by the Court.

The President personally chairs all public sessions of the Court (provided he is not a national of one of the Parties, in which case the Vice-President takes over). He also presides over the Court's internal deliberations and is *ex officio* a Member of the Drafting Committee, if he shares the majority opinion. The President personally signs all Orders, Judgments, Opinions and any other formal documents for external purposes, his signature being countersigned by the Registrar for purposes of authentication. In all these functions, the Vice-President is his deputy, and after him

The Court during its deliberations in the Ferdinand Bol Room on 19 February 1969.

the most senior Judge, that is senior by priority of election or, if this is inconclusive, in terms of age.

Among the tasks of the President that involve the greatest responsibility is his casting vote in the event of an equality of votes among the Judges. Sir Percy Spender was put in a difficult position in 1966 in the controversial *South West Africa Case*'s judgment. Another incident, with a different outcome, is related by Hudson from the days of the Permanent Court. In the *Lotus* case, with the Court still consisting of eleven Judges (complemented in that particular case by a single Judge *ad hoc*), the Bench of twelve was evenly divided. The President in his casting vote favoured the opinion of among others the Judge *ad hoc*, whose voice was seen by some as having been decisive to the Judgment, which is altogether exceptional.

The President chairing deliberations in the New Wing.

A few words on the diplomatic status of the Judges. The Members of the Court and the Registrar enjoy full diplomatic privileges and immunities. However, from the early days of the Permanent Court, a bone of contention had been the relative precedence of the Members of the Court and the Diplomatic Corps accredited in The Hague. This delicate issue was finally settled in the mid-1970s, during the Presidency of Judge Lachs, when it was agreed that the President of the Court was to take precedence over the Dean of the Corps, who in his turn takes precedence over the Court's Vice-President. This pattern continues, so that precedence proceeds alternately and according to seniority between the Heads of Missions and the Members of the Court.

Chambers

So far we have spoken of the Court, meaning the full Bench of fifteen, of which nine constitute a quorum. However, a full Bench is not the only option in the operation of international tribunals. The establishment of smaller bodies, known as Chambers, is another generally accepted phenomenon. For example, the European Court of Justice in Luxembourg sits either in plenary session, for which the quorum is seven, or in Chambers of three or five.

At the ICJ, there is no long-standing tradition of Chamber procedure. However, from the early days, the Statute of the ICJ did make provision for Chambers. The procedure envisaged is basically identical to that of the full Court, although a more simplified form may be agreed upon by Parties. Thus, written pleadings may be limited to one pleading by each party and oral pleadings, by agreement, dispensed with altogether. The autonomous status of the Chamber as compared to the full Bench is emphasized by the fact that requests for revision or interpretation of its Judgments are to be dealt with by the same Chamber.

Chamber of Summary Procedure

We may discern three different types of Chambers. The first is the *Chamber of Summary Procedure*, composed of the President and Vice-President *ex officio* and three other Members plus two substitutes, and set up annually, as the text reads 'with a view to the speedy despatch of business'. Its Members are elected by the full Court, by secret ballot and absolute majority. The Chamber procedure was intended to deal with cases that lent themselves to ready solution in a simplified procedure. Curiously enough, States have never availed themselves of this procedure since the Chamber was first employed, in 1924, for a case relating to the *Interpretation of the Treaty of Neuilly*, which case resulted in two Judgments (1924-1925).

One reason for the evident lack of interest in this option may be gathered from the following incident. In 1928, the Serbian Government, in the *Serbian Loans* case, seriously considered the idea but then thought better of it 'as this course would be unacceptable to its public in view of the importance of the case'. Technically speaking this is a fallacy, as a Judgment of the Chamber is formally identical to a Judgment rendered by the Court itself, and there is no appeal from a Chamber to the full Court. However, psychological considerations prevailed in that case.

Special Chamber

The second type is the so-called *Special Chamber*, designed to deal with specific categories of cases, mostly of a technical nature, and in which Parties could avail themselves of the technical expertise of certain Judges. Originally, and until 1936, the Rules of Court even provided that in the elections regard should be had 'to any preference expressed by the Judges'. In other words, Judges could of their own accord state their areas of individual preference, and the Chamber would thus be a body of true experts in those fields. Provision was made for such a Special Chamber to sit outside The Hague. Only Advisory Opinions were excluded from this procedure from the outset.

This second type of Chamber has an interesting history, which can be seen as the natural reflection of the issues that were foremost in the public mind during certain periods. Initially, the Court had in mind two Special Chambers that would deal with Labour cases and with Transit and Communications cases. The Chambers were to be constituted for a three year period and composed of five Judges, two substitutes, and technical assessors with no right to vote.

The initial response seemed promising. In the early 1930s specific reference to the use of a Special Chamber was made in Treaties, notably by Denmark. Proposals were made for the creation of a Vacation Chamber and in 1930 Denmark suggested a Special Chamber for international commercial disputes. Still, nothing came of it and the Chambers were never used. This is a remarkable fact, particularly in view of the special provisions on the Court's jurisdiction contained in the Constitution of the ILO and the five Advisory Opinions rendered by the Court on labour-related matters during the period 1922-1932. Similarly, in 1927 and 1931 the PCIJ issued Advisory Opinions which definitely fell within the sphere of communications, namely in relation to the Danube and to railway traffic between Lithuania and Poland. However, as Rosenne observes:

> ... it is difficult to see what is the particular advantage of these specialized Chambers, or the Chamber of Summary Procedure, over the more orthodox type of arbitration, which is always useful when what is required is expert and perhaps technical knowledge in a limited sphere rather than broad general competence in international law and practice as a whole, which is the special attribute of the Court. (Rosenne, *Law and Practice*, 1985, at pp. 200-201)

In the early 1940s the Informal Inter-Allied Committee put forward a proposal for a new type of Regional Chambers, which was given particular support by the Latin-American nations. The idea never materialized, although the later provision that Chambers may sit outside The Hague can be seen as reflecting these discussions.

In 1993 the Court itself took the initiative of forming a Special Chamber of seven Members to deal with 'any environmental case falling within its jurisdiction'.

Ad hoc Chambers

The idea of *Chambers* constituted *ad hoc* was alien to the PCIJ. It was introduced in the revised Statute of 1946, but hardly mentioned in the Rules until these were revised in 1972 and 1978 successively. These revisions were specifically intended to facilitate recourse to the Chamber pro-

Session of the PCIJ of 12 October 1927: Alexandre Millerand (1859-1943), ex-President of France, during his pleading in favour of the Rumanians in the Danube case. The Dutch text of an unknown journalist, published in a newspaper, gives an impression of the oral pleading Millerand and the atmosphere in the Court Room.

Millerand spreekt.

De Fransche staatsman voor het Internationale Hof.

De macht van het goed gesproken woord.

Millerand.

In de hedenochtend gehouden zitting van het Permanente Hof van Internationale Justitie, die door een zeer talrijk publiek, waaronder de oud-commissaris der Koningin in Utrecht, mr. dr. graaf van Lynden van Sandenburg en staatsraad mr. Limburg, verscheidene gezanten en vele dames werd bijgewoond, heeft de oud-president der Fransche republiek, de heer Millerand, als vertegenwoordiger van Roemenië, gepleit in de zaak van de bevoegdheid der Europeesche Donaucommissie.

In de groote plechtige rechtzaal, waar het grijze licht van den bewolkten dag door de drie hooge glas-in-loodramen slechts spaarzaam binnendrong, waren boven het podium de groote kronen ontstoken. Recht tegenover de zwart-getogade en witgebefte, meerendeels grijzende leden van het hooge college, stond de katheder, waarachter Millerand zich verhief, wiens sneeuwwitte haar een even fel contrast vormde met het zwarte juristenkleed, als de witte, van de schouders neerhangende bontzoom.

Markant is de kop van den ex-president der Fransche republiek. Forsche, krachtige trekken, dwingende oogen en een stem waar gezag van uitgaat. Het is een levende stem, een die het gesprokene aan zich ondergeschikt maakt, die het al naar de eischen van het oogenblik omvormt, opvoert of waar het moet, wegvoert en te dempen weet.

Millerand is een redenaar van ras, een die de kunst van het woord verstaat, te vaak helaas, in onzen tijd en in ons land vooral, verwaarloosd.

Een redevoering zoo in grooten stijl gehouden, hoort men niet vaak. Nu eens krijgt het ferm geluid van den spreker een stijgende kracht, zoodat de klanken elkaar in de haast te beperkte ruimte achterhalen, dan weer vraagt die zelfde stem in hooge verbazingstonen, of stelt zij in klaar en helder timbre een probleem zóó eenvoudig, dat een ontvankelijke jury hem onverwijld gelijk gegeven had.

Doch een jury is hier niet, integendeel, een oud en wijs, een vast in 't recht verankerd college, waarvan de leden zoo minitieus en individueel hun oordeel vellen, dat elke meerderheidsbeslissing van verschillende aparte, afwijkende meeningen vergezeld gaat.

Toch, aan de bekoring van zoo'n welsprekend betoog ontkomt men niet. Een ieder zit in eigen aandachtspose te luisteren, geboeid ook door de harmonieuse gebaren, die het woord een troon schijnen te bouwen in de lucht.

De aandacht zinkt ineen, als de tolken, weergaloos knap, maar vanzelfsprekend, zonder een spoor van het oorspronkelijke talent, den feitelijken inhoud in 't Engelsch weergeven. Dat is de glans van het bezielend woord, welke nu ontbreekt. Of zou het misschien toch voor een rechter, die onpartijdig blijven wil, beter zijn naar die vertaling te luisteren, naar de nuchtere zakelijke mededeeling der feiten?

Opnieuw richt de pleiter zelf het woord weer tot het hooge rechtscollege en ieder luistert weer, de rechters zelve zoo goed als de Roemeensche delegatie, die haar rechten hoort verdedigen en de vertegenwoordigers der drie andere mogendheden, w.o. de Engelschen met hun typisch gekrulde juristenpruikjes. Zij hebben een geduchten tegenstander aan Millerand!

Met klem en groote zekerheid tevens betoogt spreker tenslotte, dat hij in het volste vertrouwen het advies afwacht van het Hof, dat immers geen kleine of groote mogendheden kent, maar alleen het recht.

A session of the Chamber in the ELSI dispute between the USA and Italy (1987).

cedure in appropriate circumstances. The new provisions responded to the requests of States, as specifically voiced in the General Assembly in previous years, and followed discussions concerning the underemployment of the Court in the wake of the *South West Africa* Case. Among their other proposals, it was suggested that the Court take account of the wishes of the Parties in the composition of an *ad hoc* Chamber.

It is interesting that on this occasion there was a swift response. In 1981 Canada and the USA jointly referred to a Chamber their long-standing dispute over their maritime boundary in the Gulf of Maine. Burkina Faso and Mali followed in 1983, with the matter of their land frontier. El Salvador and Honduras were next in 1986, with their multi-faceted delimitation issues. Again, in 1987, Italy and the USA submitted their dispute over the requisitioning of certain American assets in Sicily to a Chamber (the *ELSI* case). The very variety of these cases would serve to bear out the suggestion that *ad hoc* Chambers can now be expected to deal adequately with disputes in almost any sphere.

Judges ad hoc

Unlike the idea of *ad hoc* Chambers, the notion of Judges *ad hoc* is well entrenched in the tradition of the Hague Courts. The reason for this is obvious. One of the major differences between the arbitral procedure that was developed under the aegis of the 1899 Hague Peace Conference and given concrete expression in the PCA, and the judicial procedure formulated twenty years later for the PCIJ, was the virtual absence in the latter procedure of any direct and effective influence by Parties on the composition of the Bench. It was perhaps this element which inclined States to shrink from submitting their cases to the new institution.

As we have seen before in matters of the distribution of seats on the Bench, much intellectual effort was devoted to solving this conundrum in order to bring about a readier acceptance of the institution. This gave rise, among other suggestions, to the idea of the Judge *ad hoc*, which opened the way for a Party that found itself confronted with a Bench on which it was not represented by a Judge of its nationality - while the other Party was so represented - to choose an additional Judge.

The issue has a psychological aspect as well, of course, but there is more to it than that. A few scientific points come to mind. Firstly: it has been argued that such a situation puts the State in question at a disadvantage and actually creates an

'inequality'. However, is this truly the case? Surely not in the strict legal sense, as Judges do not represent their nations. For this reason, as explicitly laid down by the Statute, a Judge is fully entitled to sit in all cases, and is never disqualified by his nationality. Secondly: the psychological 'disadvantage' could simply be met by having the other Judge stand down in the case and refrain from participating. Thirdly: if each Party assures itself of a Judge for the sole purpose of 'securing' a vote, it will be seen that, in the voting process, the two Judges are bound to cancel each other out. (In fact, national Judges from the outset have voted on occasion against the positions of the State of their nationality.)

There are, however, substantial arguments in favour of *ad hoc* Judges. Firstly: a national Judge may rightly be deemed to be better informed of the socio-cultural,

In order to illustrate the functioning of the Judges *ad hoc*, it may be worthwile to add a few statistics which can be distilled from the appearance of these Judges on the Bench of the Court.

Nations

- In the past fifty years, and with respect to 45 cases out of a total of 71, 48 nations found occasion to appoint a Judge *ad hoc*.
- Of these 48 nations, 16 have appointed Judges in more than one case.
- Of these latter 16 nations, 7 called in Judges in related issues: Colombia and Peru in the *Asylum case*, the ensuing case on the *Interpretation* of that Judgment, and the *Haya de la Torre* case; Albania in the different phases of the *Corfu Channel* case; Belgium in the *Barcelona Traction* cases; South Africa and Ethiopia/Liberia in the *South West Africa* cases; Albania and Belgium used different Judges, whereas the other five nations made use of the same Judges.
- Cameroon, Greece, Honduras, India, Nicaragua, Portugal and Tunisia twice called in Judges *ad hoc* in different cases; Denmark and Iran on 3 occasions, Libya on no less than 5 occasions.
- In 22 cases both Parties made use of their right to appoint a Judge *ad hoc*, in 21 cases only one of the Parties availed itself of a Judge *ad hoc*, the other Party being duly represented by a titular Judge. In most cases the latter Party was a Member of the Security Council and as if by gentlemen's agreement permanently represented on the Bench.
- In quite a number of cases, however, Parties did not avail themselves of their right to appoint a Judge *ad hoc*: Lebanon in the 1953 *Electricité de Beyrouth Company* case and the 1959 *Compagnie du Port* case; Turkey in the *Aegean Sea Continental Shelf* case; Hungary in the *Aircraft* case; Czechoslovakia in the *1953 Aerial Incident* case; Iceland and the Federal Republic of Germany in the 1972 *Fisheries Jurisdiction* cases; Iran in the *Diplomatic and Consular Staff* case. In the recent *Fisheries Jurisdiction* case, Canada which is not currently represented on the Bench, has, to date, not appointed a Judge *ad hoc*, whereas Spain has.
- In some cases, in which neither of the two Parties was represented on the Bench, both Parties declined to exercise their rights: in the 1959 *Temple of Preah Vihear* case both Cambodia and Thailand declined their rights, as did Nicaragua, Costa Rica and Honduras in the *Border and Transborder Armed Actions* cases and Nauru and Australia in the 1989 *Nauru* case.

Judges

- In the past fifty years 59 Judges ad hoc have sat on the Bench of the ICJ.
- There is no noticeable change in the frequency of use of Judges *ad hoc* by Parties through the decades.
- Judges *ad hoc* have appeared on the Bench in 45 contentious cases out of a total of 71, and in 1 advisory proceeding (*Western Sahara*) out of 22 advisory requests.
- Judges *ad hoc* have been called in by 48 nations and represented 36 nationalities.
- 31 Judges have represented their own nation, whereas 28 have been called in by countries of whom they were not a national.
- The assistance of Judges of French nationality was enlisted most by foreign nations: five different Judges by five different nations.
- 47 Judges *ad hoc* have appeared in one case (the *Lockerbie* cases are taken as one in this respect), whereas 12 Judges have been called in on more than one occasion.
- Judge Valticos from Greece was called in three times by three different foreign nations (Malta, El Salvador and Bahrain) in three different cases.
- Judge Jiménez de Aréchaga from Uruguay was called in three times by the same foreign nation (Libya) in three cases, the third of which concerned the appeal for review of the first case.
- Judge Abi-Saab from Egypt was called in twice by different foreign nations, Mali and Chad respectively.
- Judge Skubiszewski from Poland was called in twice by different foreign nations, Portugal and Slovakia respectively.
- Judge Mbanefo from Nigeria was called in twice by the same foreign nations (Ethiopia and Liberia), and in successive cases in regard to the same issue (South West Africa).
- Judge Torres Bernardez from Spain was called in twice, once by his own nation and once by Honduras.
- Judge Mbaye from Senegal was called in twice, once by his own nation, once by Cameroon.
- Judges Alayza y Paz Soldén from Peru and Caicedo Castilla from Colombia were called in three times by their own nations in three cases which were closely related, the second of which concerned the appeal for revision of the first case.
- Judges Fischer from Denmark, Ganshof van der Meersch from Belgium and Van Wyk from South Africa were called in twice by their own nation. In the cases of the Belgian and South African Judges, their activities concerned in fact successive cases or phases of the same dispute, the *Barcelona Traction* and *South West Africa* issues respectively.

legal, geographical or technical intricacies that gave rise to the case. Secondly: in appointing a Judge *ad hoc* a Party assures itself of a voice not just during the public hearings, but more particularly during the later phase of private deliberations. Although this may not change the outcome of a case, it may certainly influence the wording of the Judgment. This is precisely why the Statute also makes provision for the appointment of Judges *ad hoc* if neither of the Parties is represented on the regular Bench. In a way the Court, too, may take advantage of their presence. In most cases Parties do agree to choose Judges *ad hoc*, although there are numerous exceptions to this.

In the past, voices have been raised against this procedure, asserting that 'national' Judges jeopardize the 'international' character of the Bench. This was a bone of contention during the 1907 Conference, when the majority of nations represented advanced the *nemo judex* rule to object to the inclusion of national Judges on the Bench. Conversely, the 1920 Committee defended their participation on the ground that this would protect the character of the Court as a World Court, and would avoid 'ruffling national susceptibilities'. It did, however, admit that the Court so envisaged 'more nearly resembles a court of arbitration than a national court of justice'. All in all, the point seems a minor one in view of the sheer number of Judges and the fact that the *ad hoc* Judges serve to increase that number, which may then amount to seventeen.

A more pertinent objection, however, is based on the afore-mentioned principle that no one should be a judge 'in his own case', *casu quo* a case involving his country. Strictly speaking this is true. However, here as elsewhere, one must appreciate that strained concepts of legal theory do not always apply in this sphere. As Rosenne rightly observes, allowances must be made for the tradition of 'national arbitrators' in the international arena (Rosenne *The World Court*, 1995, at p. 73). Around 1920, as perhaps even today, the appointment of Judges *ad hoc* was a *conditio sine qua non* for the success of the whole idea of third-party adjudication. One could perhaps have named them 'assessors' instead of Judges *ad hoc*, but why not indulge diplomatic sensitivities? This is another aspect which awakens one to the fact that international litigation has distinct features of its own and raises problems which cannot be solved by strict analogy or by a mere reference to municipal proceedings.

An interesting feature to be observed in the recent practice of the Court is that Parties to cases increasingly tend to choose as Judges *ad hoc* lawyers who are *not* of their own nationality. One might speculate on the balancing of the psychological and substantial elements that prompts this gesture. All in all, and given the still 'fragile foundations of international adjudication', as Rosenne puts it, the upholding of the idea of Judges *ad hoc* seems fully justified.

As can be seen from the previous survey, Judges *ad hoc* are in a somewhat different position from the regular Judges. The essential element is not so much that they serve just for one case, but that they are chosen by Parties, not elected by 'the world's legal conscience'. In all other respects, they enjoy the full rights and status of the titular Judges. Conversely, Judges *ad hoc* are required to possess the same personal qualifications, and it is for the Court to settle any doubts in this respect. They make the same Solemn Declaration and they come after the titular Judges in the order of precedence. Logically, they are not asked to give up the other positions they hold, but they are expected to give priority to the work of the Court on all occasions. At the time of the PCIJ, Judges *ad hoc* were supposed to be appointed from among previously nominated candidates, and for this purpose a cumulative list of nominees was published annually. However, in practice States hardly paid attention to the list and the idea has long since been abandoned.

An interesting point is, of course, how Judges *ad hoc* have acted in terms of voting over the years. While one may expect such a Judge to vote in favour of the Party that chose him or her, and accordingly voice dissent when the majority of the Bench votes differently, this does not always hold good. For example, Madame Bastid, the first female Judge *ad hoc* on the Bench, in the 1985 Judgment on *Application for Revision* of the 1982 *Continental Shelf* Judgment in the Tunisia/Libya dispute, voted with the majority to dismiss the Tunisian requests. It is true that this has been the only example in recent times, but it serves to show that the independence of the Judge *ad hoc* may certainly lead to similar results on other occasions as well.

Interestingly, Judges *ad hoc* who support the majority Judgment have not always done so unreservedly. Although there is as yet no example in the annals of the ICJ of a Judge *ad hoc* dissenting from the majority that upheld his Party's case, there are numerous instances of Judges *ad hoc* who appended Separate Opinions to the Judgment, to indicate that they reached the same conclusion on different grounds or following different lines of reasoning. As Rosenne argues, appending to the Judgment a Declaration or Opinion in any form by Judges *ad hoc* may be in the long-term interests of the Court itself, as it 'lends reality to the dictum that justice must not only be done but that it must be *seen* to be done. It makes it easier for a government to decide to entrust its affairs to the International Court' (Rosenne, *The World Court*, 1995, at p. 74).

National Judges

The questions we raised with respect to the Judges *ad hoc*, are no less pertinent with respect to the so-called 'national' Judges, that is titular Members of the Bench who are to sit in cases where their nations are involved. One is struck by the fact that they have been much less outspoken in favour of their nations. In fact, there have been some notable instances of national Judges who found against their countries. In the very first case of the PCIJ, Judge Anzilotti voted against the position of Italy. Judge Weiss voted with the majority to find against France, as Lord Finlay did against Great Britain. The voting of the Polish Judges in the numerous cases dealt with by the PCIJ in which their nation was involved, is interesting. From the record of the ICJ, it can be seen that Lord McNair found with the majority against Great Britain in the *Anglo-Iranian Oil Co.* case, while Judge Schwebel was, on several occasions during the *Nicaragua* case, very critical of the American position against which he repeatedly voted. He also voted against the position of the USA in the *Gulf of Maine* case, as well as in the advisory proceeding on the *Applicability of the Obligation to Arbitrate* (the 'PLO' case).

On the ICJ no national Judge has as yet dissented from a majority decision in favour of his nation. On the other hand, and to conclude this review, the mere fact that a national Judge is in a minority, or even alone, in upholding arguments asserted by his nation, does not in itself justify the conclusion that his views are attributable to national bias. Only the careful examination of a Dissenting or Separate Opinion can establish the merits of his position - which brings one to an additional argument in favour of individual Opinions appended to a Judgment, however firmly it is maintained by some commentators that such Opinions tend to impair both the homogeneity of the Bench and the authority of a Judgment. However, these matters have been discussed in the previous chapter. We will now turn to the various legal traditions as represented on the World Court during the 75 years of its existence.

Personal Qualifications of Judges

The Statute of the ICJ lays down two requirements for the proper functioning of the Court. The first concerns the personal qualifications of Judges in the moral and professional spheres, the second the adequate representation on the Bench of the world's prevailing legal and cultural traditions. Before reviewing these regional requirements in the next Chapter, we will conclude the present Chapter by reviewing the personal requirements of Judges.

Since no formal criteria to be met by a Judge of the ICJ were ever formulated, the best approach in seeking to define the apparent requirements for a Judge is perhaps

Robert Bannatyne Finlay, First Viscount (1842-1929), Judge of the PCIJ during 1922-1929.

The Polish Judge Count Michal Cezary Rostworowski (1864-1940), Member of the PCIJ from 1930-1940, and four times Judge ad hoc.

to deduce his profile from the 80 odd examples at hand over the past fifty years.

Inevitably, the careers of Judges prior to their election to the ICJ will differ in many ways. However, in reviewing their biographies, a few congruencies may be noted - some more surprising, others less so - which apply to a vast majority of Judges from whatever region of the world they came. It will be obvious too that, once the Judges-to-be are set on an international career and have entered what we might call the inner circle, their 'itineraries' inevitably tend to run parallel to a large extent. As in all fields, there are venues where they are likely to meet and committees and courses to which they cannot help being invited at some stage. We may, therefore, now venture to describe the most likely avenues to the Bench in The Hague and some of the ports of call along the way.

With very few exceptions, Judges are recruited from the academic, diplomatic and political fields, or the judiciary. Not surprisingly, only very few Judges had a military background (Baxter, Dillard and Moreno Quintana), though quite a few Judges are known to have served bravely during the two World Wars, were recruited for intelligence work or indeed helped to organize national resistance movements (Basdevant, Evensen, De Visscher). Some later declared that it was the wartime horrors that brought them to the field of international law in the first place (Jessup, De Visscher).

However, it stands to reason that a firm legal schooling is the first requirement and indeed a *sine qua non* for the Judge. Nearly all Judges held degrees and later occupied lecturerships and chairs in the legal departments of, in most cases, prominent university centres. Some of them pursued their academic efforts for decades, replacing one professorship by a more senior one and becoming Rector, Dean or Vice-Chancellor of their universities, as was the case with Judges Elias, Ranjeva and McNair.

Most of these Judges were productive authors and several of them served many years on editorial boards, and often as Editor-in-Chief of prominent Journals, as did Judges Baxter, Dillard and Schwebel on behalf of the *American Journal of International Law*, Golunsky for the *Soviet State and Law*, Jennings, McNair and Waldock for the *British Year Book*, de Castro for the Spanish *Anuario*, Ferrari Bravo for the *Italian Yearbook*, Morelli for the *Rivista* and Pathak for the *Indian Journal*.

Alongside their academic careers, quite a number, notably in the Anglo-American world, practised law. Some ten Judges took silk to become King's or Queen's Counsel. The majority of Judges were, often at a fairly early stage, recruited by their Ministry of Foreign Affairs to serve their government as a Legal Adviser. Also, no less than seven Judges were intensively involved in the drafting of the Constitution of their nation.

At some stage in their career Judges had to make up their minds to combine parallel careers or to make a choice. In many cases this meant the end of their academic career, though not of all scholarly pursuits. Some turned to the Judiciary and made impressive careers in this sphere. Among its Members, the ICJ saw three former Attorney-Generals, four Procuror-Generals, a President, a Chief Justice and four Judges of High Courts, along with six Judges, four Chief Justices and one President of a Supreme Court and a number of Presidents of District and Appeal Courts.

More surprising perhaps than our findings in the academic and judicial spheres is the number of Judges with a diplomatic or political background. No less than sixteen Judges had experience as an Ambassador, while as many as twenty-one served (at least once) as a Cabinet Minister, most of them naturally as Minister of Justice or Foreign Affairs.

The Belgian Judge Charles De Visscher (1884-1973) with his wife, attending a meeting on 16 February 1930.

Sooner or later, their diplomatic expertise or legal advisorships to their governments enabled Judges to bring their expertise to bear on the international law circuit. They were often invited to represent their nations during international conferences, on boards of international organizations, and notably at Sessions of the United Nations. In fact, all major international conferences from the 1919 Paris Peace Conference up to the 1993 Rio Conference are reflected in the biographies of Judges. Recurrent items of the first generation of Judges are the 1929 Conference of Jurists, the 1930 Hague Codification and London Naval Conferences, the 1938 Lima Conference and the Constitutive Conferences of the post-war world: Bretton Woods, Dumbarton Oaks, the Washington Conference of Jurists, San Francisco and the 1946 Paris Peace Conference.

Similarly, one is not surprised to find that the majority of the next generation of Judges took part in the 1958-1959 Geneva Conferences on the Law of the Sea and the 1968 Vienna Conference on the Law of Treaties. In the same vein, quite a number of Judges from the latest generation played an active part in the 1973-1982 UNCLOS Conference, the 1973-1975 Helsinki CSCE Conference and various Diplomatic Conferences.

Quite a few Judges had intensive dealings with Specialized Agencies of the United Nations and similar bodies: ten Judges were in particular active at ILO Conferences, five at UNESCO, and a few at UNCTAD, ECOSOC and IMO. Apart from this, some Judges were very active in Regional Organizations, be this in the Pan-American Movement, the Non-Aligned Movement, the Organization of African Unity or Commonwealth venues.

As a rule, these activities reflect both the specialized field of interest and the personal background of Judges. For example, among the Judges who served on the Bench in recent years, Judges Mbaye, Aguilar-Mawdsley, Higgins and Weeramantry are known to be experts in matters of human rights and quite naturally served on a number of Committees. However, Judge Aguilar, while serving from 1968 to 1972 as a Member of the UN Commission on Human Rights, also served several terms as President of the Inter-American Commission on Human Rights and participated in a number of on-the-spot investigations in several countries of the region. Judge Mbaye, for his part, while serving on the Board of the International Institute of Human Rights of the René Cassin Foundation and being former President of the International Academy of Human Rights, was also on the Special Committee to investigate the treatment of the Palestinians and a member of the Working Group on human rights violations in Southern Africa. He was General Rapporteur at the Organization of African Unity when it adopted the African Charter on Human and Peoples' Rights. Judge Higgins, for her part, served from 1984 until her election to the ICJ in 1995 as a Member of the Human Rights Committee monitoring the Covenant on Civil and Political Rights. Again, Judge Weeramantry published extensively on the subject, notably for the South East Asian area, and produced a theoretical study (1990) and a set of global case-studies (1993) on the impact of technology on human rights.

Arnold Duncan McNair (1885-1975), Judge (1946-1955) and President (1952-1955) of the ICJ.

A majority of Judges took part in Sessions of the General Assembly (particularly its Sixth or Legal Committee), fourteen of them in the capacity of Permanent Representative of their nation. Two Judges had served as Vice-Presidents of the General Assembly (Spender and Aguilar-Mawdsley), one as a Temporary President (Ajibola) and two as President (Padilla Nervo and Zaffrulla Khan).

Having entered the international circuit, Judges-to-be soon find themselves eligible for membership of more technical entities, in particular the International Law Commission (ILC), a select body of 34, to which much of the codification of international law within the United Nations is entrusted. At this stage, too, they may expect invitations in a private capacity from the *Institut de Droit International* (IDI), a time-honoured and very respectable association of public and private international lawyers, which operates in the same field as the ILC, but on a private and informal footing. From the biographical notes that follow the reader will see that, along with the PCA, the ILC and IDI are recurrent *sigla* in the *curricula* of the Judges. For that reason we have included a separate description of the functioning of these two prominent bodies of experts.

By this time most Judges, also through

INSTITUT DE DROIT INTERNATIONAL

The *Institut de Droit International* (IDI) is a private and rather less formal association of scholars in the fields of public and private international law. It has no international secretariat or similar permanent apparatus. The Institut meets alternate years at different venues to discuss topical issues with a view to the codification of international law, during sessions which normally take two weeks. At present, its membership is limited to 132 coopted titular members and associates. The IDI was founded in 1873 in Ghent on the initiative of a dozen prominent internationalists, among whom were Asser, Bluntschli, Calvo, Lorimer and Rolin-Jaequemyns. The Institut was intended as an academy, ambitiously aimed at becoming the judicial conscience of the civilized world by helping to define the principles of international law, promote its codification and clarify its interpretation through teaching and publications, together with peace-keeping efforts and the furtherance of justice and humanity in international relations generally.

Initially, the IDI concentrated primarily on codification, though never in a systematic manner and rather on the spur of current events. Still, through the expertise of its members, it was able to make considerable contributions to the further development of the law. Thus, the topical issue of the 1875 *Alabama* case led the IDI to elaborate rules for arbitral procedures that were later to serve the Hague Peace Conferences. In similar vein, matters of land warfare were tackled, which materialized in the so-called Oxford Manual (1880) on which the Hague rules of 1899 and 1907 were to be based. In 1913 a similar manual for sea warfare was launched. Again, it was the IDI that first drew up a code for the anticipated Prize Law Court and it was similarly instrumental in preparing the 1930 Hague Codification Conference.

On the whole, however, one may say that the activities of the IDI became less pivotal and its influence, notably in the sphere of international politics, distinctly less impressive after the turn of the century and once international organization had come to take a more professional turn with the increase of diplomatic conferences, the institution of the League of Nations and the steady growth of literature and reviews in the field. Similarly, its idea of an academy was in the mid-1920s effectuated at the Hague Academy of International Law, whose links with the IDI have traditionally been close.

The launching of codifying activities within the UN initially met with scepticism within the IDI, whose majority members rejected codification by collective treaty as being too readily adaptable to State interests. Its criticism indirectly furthered the installation of the International Law Commission in 1947, which soon came to appreciate the dangers envisaged by the IDI. In the course of time, the work of the ILC has supplanted much of the codifying function of the IDI, which now seeks to steer a different course. In historical perspective, however, its successes have been impressive. The IDI was of eminent influence upon the solving of major colonial issues during the 1880s and during the Berlin Conference, and played a decisive role in advocating freedom of navigation and neutralization of the Suez Canal.

Very few Judges on the Bench of the International Court have not at some stage been member of the Institut, and no less than seven of them have actually presided over it: Ago, Fitzmaurice, Gros, Jennings, Jessup, McNair and Morelli. Three others (Alvarez, Basdevant and Waldock) served as Vice-President. In its turn, the Institut has been instrumental to the functioning of the Court when, during its 1954 Session, it proposed amendments to the Statute of the ICJ in which it expressed its concern over political influences on the election of Judges. It favoured the expansion of the term of office of Judges, strongly opposed their re-election, and emphasized the importance of the personal qualities of a Judge *vis-à-vis* regional representation. Though widely discussed at the time, the suggestions were never implemented.

To conclude, one may say that the informal meetings and open debate of scholars at the Institut invariably tends to germinate new ideas which at times anticipate political realities by decades. Thus, its members tackled matters of human rights as early as 1929. For the same reason, however, its resolutions never gained the official status of source of international law, though they must certainly be regarded as an authoritative collective expression of contemporary doctrine. Its *Annuaire*, and the resolutions contained in it, remain at all times very much representative of the state of the arts.

their reports and publications, have made a name for themselves as experts in certain areas of the law. They will be invited to lecture at universities and other research centres, including the prestigious Hague Academy of International Law, that true stamping ground of international lawyers. All in all, 37 Judges gave 72 lectures at the Hague Academy (among them Ago and De Visscher five times; Jessup, Lachs and Lauterpacht four times; Fitzmaurice, Jiménez de Aréchaga and McNair three times). Honorary doctorates may follow.

From the description of the procedure for nomination and election of Judges it can be seen that the list of arbitrators of the Permanent Court of Arbitration is frequently a distinguished way station. Having arrived at the stage just described, Judges are extremely likely to be nominated by their nations to this list. They may expect to find themselves appointed

THE INTERNATIONAL LAW COMMISSION

The International Law Commission (ILC) is a permanent organ for the codification of international law, operating under the auspices of the United Nations. It may be seen as the 20th century institutionalization of an idea which originates from the days of the Vienna Congress of 1815, when the need for codification of prevailing rules, notably in the spheres of international rivers, slave trade and diplomacy, was first generally felt. Initially, the idea was much furthered by private societies and institutions such as the *Institut de Droit International* and the *International Law Association* (both founded in 1873) and by diplomatic conferences such as the Hague Conference in the domain of private international law (1894-1895) and, in the public sphere, the 1899 and 1907 Hague Peace Conferences, all of which produced a number of codifying conventions.

By 1907 the need for more intense preparation of such conventions was expressed, but initiatives towards this end with a view to a Third Hague Peace Conference were frustrated by the First World War. After the war, however, the Assembly of the League of Nations launched the first permanent organ called the Committee of Experts for the Progressive Codification of International Law, created to discuss issues considered 'sufficiently ripe' for regulation through agreements, and to develop adequate procedures thereto. In 1930, three such issues (nationality, the territorial sea, and aspects of State responsibility), previously selected by a special Preparatory Committee, were considered during the Hague Codification Conference. Due to inadequate preparation, this conference failed to make a landmark.

At the drafting of the United Nations Charter during the 1945 San Francisco Conference, the idea to directly invest the United Nations with full legislative powers was rejected. However, the General Assembly was invited to initiate studies to 'encourage the progressive development of international law and its codification'. To this end, the Assembly created a Committee, whose report led to the establishment, in November 1947, of the International Law Commission by Assembly Resolution 174 (II). It was explicitly stipulated by Parties that members of the Commission should serve not as representatives of governments but in their individual capacities and should be elected on the basis of their recognized competence. The work of the ILC was to be decided by the General Assembly.

By Statute, members of the ILC were elected by the Assembly from candidates nominated by UN Members, actually in much the same way as the Members of the ICJ are nominated, i.e. by national groups who each propose four names, among whom two candidates of their own nationality only. In the same vein, electors had to bear in mind that the 'main forms of civilization' and the 'principal legal systems of the world' should be adequately represented.

The membership, initially provided for 15, was in 1956 increased to 21, in 1961 to 25 and again in 1981 to 34, to reflect the growing number of States Members of the United Nations. With these changes, the concept of 'geographical distribution' became an ever more prevailing criterium in the election of members. At present the regional distribution provides for 8 seats for African States, 7 for Asian States, 3 for East-European States, 6 for Latin American States, 8 for West-European and other States and 2 more seats rotating between Africa and Eastern Europe, and between Asian and Latin American States respectively. The term of office of the members, initially provided for three years, was in 1955 increased to five years. Members are eligible for re-election and some members served for 20 years or more, thus ensuring an element of continuity.

The ILC sits at Geneva and meets annually in open session for a period of some twelve weeks. From its ranks, it elects a Chairman, a First and Second Vice-Chairman, a Drafting Committee Chairman and a Rapporteur. These officers constitute the Bureau and, together with former Chairmen and Special Rapporteurs, they form the Enlarged Bureau which meets in private and has an overall recommendatory function. The organization also provides for a Planning Group of 11 and a Drafting Committee of 14 members, and is supported by a Staff provided by the UN Secretariat. The ILC's major characteristic through the years has been the flexibility and adaptibility of its organization and procedures, maintained also by virtue of the considerable degree of independence the Commission enjoys within the framework of control set by the General Assembly.

Interestingly enough, and despite its general guidelines, which are to promote 'the progressive development of international law and its codification', the ILC has consistently restricted its province to the field of *public* international law, never even touching upon the *private* sphere. In its task, 'codification' is defined as the more precise formulation and systematization of rules, whereas 'progressive develop-

arbitrator in a particular arbitral tribunal, in the public or private sphere. Accordingly, through the decades, we find Judges as Members or Presidents of a number of arbitration panels, as in the *Beagle Channel* case. However, they are also found in the Paris ICC and London LCIA Arbitration Courts, at the ICSID Tribunal of the World Bank, in mixed, claims and compensation tribunals and commissions, in UN and other Administrative Tribunals and in International Military Tribunals and War Crimes Commissions (Golunsky, Gros, Lachs, Wellington Koo).

Another aspect should be noted here. Parties to cases before the Court tend to include among their legal teams promising young lawyers who may thus learn the intricacies of the Court. At a later stage these lawyers may return as counsel themselves. Actually, many a Judge-to-be first entered the Hague Courtroom in this

ment' in practice implies the preparation of draft conventions on subjects not yet adequately regulated. The procedure aimed at the drafting of these conventions is rather complex and involves an interplay and exchange of views between the ILC, the General Assembly, governments and (as a rule) international organizations which operate in the field under consideration.

Also, a Special Rapporteur is appointed for each topic under study, whose role is crucial in as much as he first aims at a general review of the issue and suggests general lines of study and methods of procedure to the Commission. Guided by the Commission, the Special Rapporteur will submit successive reports, normally constituted of draft articles with explanatory comments, which are best seen as proposals on his part enabling the Commission to attain its final conclusions.

Having reached agreement in principle on the substance, the Commission refers further examination and elaboration of the draft texts to a Drafting Committee. The in-depth study and frank exchange of views within this body result in conclusions which are then referred back for evaluation by the Plenary Commission. Approved 'on first reading', these drafts are then submitted to the General Assembly and, supplemented by the observations of Governments and other interested parties, reviewed by the Commission in 'second reading', upon which the final text is submitted to the Assembly, normally to serve as a basis for the drafting of a convention on the topic.

In the past fifty years the ILC has submitted final drafts on seven such topics, namely the high seas, territorial waters, nationality, law of treaties, diplomatic and consular intercourse and immunities, and arbitral procedure. Other topics under study are succession of States in respect of treaties and of State property, State Responsibility, the non-navigational uses of international watercourses, international liability for injurious consequences arising out of acts not prohibited by international law, and a draft code of crimes against the peace and security of mankind. The work of the ILC has formed the basis for the Vienna Conventions on Diplomatic Relations (1961) and on Consular Relations (1963), and notably for the 1969 Vienna Convention on the Law of Treaties, including the aspect of *jus cogens*.

The ILC is a centre of excellence for internationalists and, not surprisingly, a very high percentage of recent Judges of the ICJ have been members of the ILC at some stage of their career. Eight Judges were Chairman of the Commission (R. Ago, A. F. El-Erian, T. O. Elias, G. G. Fitzmaurice, J. Sette-Camara, Shi Jiuyong, J. Spiropoulos and V.S. Vereshchetin), three more served as Vice-Chairman (A. Gros, Nagendra Singh and Sir Benegal Rau) and several others have contributed considerably to the drafting of conventions, notably in their capacity of Special Rapporteur. In 1951, Judge Cordova was Special Rapporteur on the issue of Nationality including Statelessness. From 1961-1966 Judge Waldock was Special Rapporteur on the Law of Treaties (6 reports), and from 1968-1972 on Succession of States in Respect of Treaties (4 reports); these reports were perhaps his most impressive publications. Judge Lauterpacht served as Special Rapporteur on the Law of Treaties, being succeeded on his election to the Court by the future Judge Fitzmaurice.

Judge Ago produced 8 reports on State Responsibility (1969-1979). Judge El-Erian was on the Commission almost without interruption for twenty years (1957-1978), was Expert Consultant at the Conference on the Representation of States in their Relations with International Organizations (1975) and produced 8 reports as Special Rapporteur on this issue (1963-1978). Judge Schwebel was a member of the International Law Commission from 1977-1981, chaired its Drafting Committee and was Special Rapporteur on International Watercourses. Judge Evensen acted as Special Rapporteur on the Law of the Non-Navigational Uses of International Watercourses.

The major achievements of the ILC over the past decades have also been due to the wise course the Commission has steered and the prudence it has shown - in cooperation with the General Assembly – in selecting appropriate topics for research. A sound sense of reality has governed its policy throughout. Obviously, the Commission of 34 members is not equipped to undertake huge tasks comprizing the whole field of public international law. Neither is it to interfere with all too technical matters which are obviously better left to technical experts or to the Specialized Agencies of the United Nations.

Maybe the best token of success of the ILC has been the way this commission of legal experts - whose authority rests on intrinsic merits rather than on any legal power formally conferred on it - has been able to solve issues with serious political connotations. Thoroughness rather than velocity has been its characteristic feature throughout. In this, it is perhaps unique in an area of law that is to such a large extent subject to the whimsicalities of international politics. Long-winding though its procedures may seem to some, the Commission has, through its many Reports, special studies and Yearbooks, been a symbol and indeed the true measuring-rod of the slow, but steady development and codification of the law.

capacity, Judges Evensen and Schwebel being good examples. Some ten Judges were Counsel before the Court, five more served as Agent to a Party. The ultimate stage in this respect is of course the position of Judge *ad hoc*. Ten Judges were called in as Judge *ad hoc* before being elected, while some others served thereafter as Judges *ad hoc*.

Several Judges also served on other international tribunals prior to being elected to the ICJ or after having served in The Hague. Thus, Judges McNair and Waldock were President of the European Court of Human Rights at Strasbourg, where Fitzmaurice and Mosler were Judges, and Jennings was Judge *ad hoc*. Judge Evensen served in Strasbourg as Counsel, while Judges Ferrari Bravo and Guillaume served as Agent both at the ECHR and at the Court of Justice of the European Communities in Luxembourg. Judges Petrén and Waldock also served as President of the European Commission of Human Rights.

THE HAGUE ACADEMY OF INTERNATIONAL LAW

Probably the first mention ever of an 'international academy' was made in 1898 by the German Carl Ludwig von Bar (1836-1913), a later member of the Permanent Court of Arbitration. However, what von Bar had in mind was a quite different institution from the later Hague Academy. He proposed the founding of a consultative body of eminent scholars which could render services to the governments in cases of interstate conflict. Invested with high moral prestige, this Academy, through its advisory role would facilitate mediation and thus further the process of conciliation.

Protest was raised at this idea by the man who may be justly called the father of the Hague Academy, Otfried Nippold, the Bern professor (1864-1936). The role assigned to the Academy by von Bar, he argued, could as well be provided by the Court, even if no provisions to this extent were made by the 1899 Hague Convention. If, however, one wished to create a true academy of international law, in the sense of a permanent study centre and nursery for future scholars and diplomats, this institution could indeed fulfil a very welcome task complementary to the Court of Arbitration in developing an international code of law. In this way at The Hague theory and practice would go side by side.

It was this proposal which was submitted to the President of the Second Hague Conference, de Nelidow. De Nelidow referred to the idea in the third plenary meeting of the Conference. He also called on private initiative to raise the required funds. A fortnight afterwards de Nelidow received a letter from Mr Sturdza, Prime Minister of Romania, who pleaded 'the linking of the achievement of the First Hague Conference, to wit arbitration, and the task set to the present gathering, international jurisdiction, by means of science, to be vested in an Academy'. Enclosed in the letter Sturdza submitted the Statutes of such an institution providing for a permanent seat at The Hague, for the appointment of ten prominent scholars and for courses to be held between May and July in German, English, French and Italian. Nations would be permitted to send numbers of young diplomats, scholars, military men and officials to attend courses on all aspects of law in proportion to the governments' contributions.

Nothing much was heard of the idea in 1907. In the midst of debate on matters of obligatory arbitration and the proposed court of jurisdiction, de Nelidow righteously anticipated that any sideline would be welcomed only too happily by the opponents of arbitration to obstruct the main issue of the Conference. Three years later, Nippold submitted a plan for a two-year course covering a wide range of subjects to be taught by ten scholars of standing assisted by a competent staff. Internationalists such as Oppenheim of Cambridge and Bisshop of London in their turn enlarged on this idea and Barclay, Fiore, von Bar and Huber expressed their approval of the enterprise.

Elihu Root insisted on scholarly independence and Léon Bourgeois suggested submitting the idea to the *Institut de Droit International* for further examination. In August 1910, at its 26th meeting in London, the International Law Association supported the idea in a resolution which was reaffirmed in Paris the following year. Oddly enough, from then on the plan collapsed; the project proved far too ambitious.

Again the torch was seized. In 1910 Tobias Asser, the grey eminence of Dutch legal science, co-founder of the *Institut de Droit International* in 1873,

Increase in the Number of UN Members During the Last Fifty Years

1945	1955	1965	1975	1985	1995
50	76	118	141	159	185

We now have some idea as to what, in very general terms, are the requirements and types of curricula that in the past fifty years may have at least increased a person's expectations of being put forward as a possible candidate to eventually become a titular Judge on the Bench of the World Court.

Nationality of Judges

Before we proceed to review the regional distribution of the Bench, one more preliminary observation has to be made, with respect to the linking of Judges and nations. Judges on the Court possess their

stimulating patron of four Hague Conferences of Private Law (1893-1904) and veteran of two Peace Conferences, took the lead of a Dutch 'Provisional Committee' for the furtherance of an academy of international law. When sharing the Nobel Peace Prize with Alfred Fried in 1911, Asser voted part of it to the projected Academy. In 1911 Asser contacted the Board of the newly founded Carnegie Endowment for International Peace.

Carnegie had put some dear friends of his at the head of the Endowment. Among these were Elihu Root, former Secretary of State and member of the Permanent Court of Arbitration and Joseph Choate, former American Minister in London and head of the American delegation at the 1907 Conference. Other members were Nicholas Murray Butler and James Brown Scott, founder of the *American Journal of International Law*. Asser and Scott may be deemed the godfathers of the Academy. Scott sympathized with the idea from the first. During the Academy's opening ceremony it was said of him that to advance peace one would sooner find him prepared to cross the ocean than another man to drive from Paris to Versailles. What he did insist on, however, was a strict organization and a well-balanced programme of courses. Scott's main concern in all this was the purely scientific character of the projected Academy.

In September 1912 the said Consulting Committee lent its support to the project of an Academy. This appraisal was formally reaffirmed by the Institut during its 26th conference in Oxford in August 1913. The Academy was to be founded in the Peace Palace and the Board of the Carnegie Foundation was to serve *qualitate qua* as its Administrative Council. It was to be inaugurated in October 1914.

From 16 June to 24 July 1920 most men involved were found together at The Hague, to draw up the Statute of the Court of Justice which was to be seated alongside the pre-war Arbitration Court within the walls of the Peace Palace. It was from this committee that the new call came for the installation of the Academy. In September 1921 in Rome, at its 28th meeting, the Institut proceeded to replace the board of the Curatorium that had lost 4 out of 12 members. The president elected was Charles Lyon-Caen of Paris, to be assisted by Walter Schücking of Marburg, Catallani of Padova and Knut Hammarskjøld of Upsala, the former Swedish Prime Minister. The new Curatorium first met in September 1922 in Grenoble at the next plenary meeting of the Institut. In the spring of 1923 a brochure in 6 languages was sent over the world. The opening session took place on 14 July 1923.

The Academy's organs are the Administrative Council, the Curatorium of seventeen (of different nationalities), which is responsible for the academic management, the programme of courses and the contracting of lecturers, and the Secretary-General (at present Prof. D. Bardonnet of Paris).

The Academy's objective is to constitute a centre of advanced studies for international law (public and private) and connected sciences and it aims at facilitating the thorough and impartial examination of problems concerning international juridical relations. In order to ensure the cooperation of eminent academics, the courses are held in the summer months. Admission is open to all university graduates, subject to selection by the Administrative Council. Teaching is intended to be both highly practical and academically advanced.

Until 1940, lectures were given in French only. Since the resumption in 1947 French and English courses are given and simultaneous translation is provided for. Courses are held in two sessions (one devoted to public international law, one to private international law) of approximately three weeks. They deal with theoretical and practical aspects, including legislation and case law. The lectures are published, in the language in which they were delivered, in the prestigious green series of the *Recueil des Cours / Collected Courses*, which over the decades has developed into an authoritative source of information on basic and current legal problems in the international field. By March 1996, over 250 volumes were published by Martinus Nijhoff Publishers.

Apart from general courses on the principles of international law, special courses are given on topical subjects from within the lecturers' fields of interest. Special seminars are organized for diploma candidates, teachers and diplomats. They are divided into English- and French-speaking sections.

Since 1958, the Rockefeller Foundation sponsors a Study Centre of the Academy, which undertakes research projects. Since 1968, the Academy also organizes colloques, workshops on particular topics; papers are subsequently published. Since 1969, the Academy has developed an 'external programme', which provides for courses in developing countries on topics which are of special regional interest.

As old as the Academy is its Association of Attenders and Alumni (AAA), consisting of national groups. The AAA organizes annual conferences; their proceedings are published, along with other articles, in a Yearbook (*Annuaire A.A.A.* which in 1988 was renamed into the *Hague Yearbook of International Law*).

Left: Rafael Altamira y Crevea from Spain, Judge of the PCIJ from 1922-1942.

Right: Dionisio Anzilotti (1867-1960), Judge (1922-1939) and President (1928-1930) of the PCIJ.

THE INTERNATIONAL LAW ASSOCIATION

The International Law Association (ILA) is the oldest and largest international organization of lawyers. Like the *Institut de Droit International*, the ILA is a private non-governmental organization. Unlike the *Institut*, however, it is not a purely scientific body and its province covers a wider area, including public and private international law. Moreover, its members, some 4000 to date, are not only jurists, but include representatives from the commercial sphere, and the worlds of banking and industry. The ILA also welcomes delegates from affiliated bodies such as the Chambers of Commerce and Shipping, Arbitration, and Peace Societies - in short, to quote its Constitution: 'all who, from whatever point of view, are interested in the improvement of international relations'.

The primary object of the ILA is 'the study, elucidation and advancement of international law, public and private, the study of comparative law, the making of proposals for the solution of conflicts of law, and for the unification of law, and the furthering of international goodwill and understanding'. The ILA was founded in Brussels in 1873 (the very year the *Institut* was founded), largely through the efforts of American publicists and peace advocates like Elihu Burritt and David Dudoley Field. At the time it was felt that a code of international law should be prepared to serve as a basis for international jurisprudence and especially of international arbitration, the latter idea reflecting a topical issue of the period.

The Association's original name was 'The Association for the Reform and Codification of the Law of Nations'; it was renamed in 1895. The ILA Headquarters are in London. Also, it has some forty active national branches - the first ones having been created in the Netherlands and Germany in 1910 and 1912.

The main activity of the ILA focuses on a series of biennial conferences, held worldwide. Through the years, its discussions between lawyers, politicians and businessmen have resulted in resolutions which have often considerably furthered the development of international law. The Conference elects its President, usually a lawyer from the host country, for a two-year term, along with a vice-president as well as a chairman and a vice-chairman of the Executive Council. It is this Executive Council which supervises most of the work of the ILA and which has full powers during the span of time between conferences. The organization also provides for a treasurer, director of studies, secretary-general and secretary.

Most of the purely academic work of the ILA is performed by special international committees under the guidance of the director of studies. These committees consist of specialists in the topic of law under consideration. The selection of topics which are deemed ripe for review and study is made by the Executive Council. Reports which after ample discussion during the conference have reached their final form are published in the *Conference Reports*, the major biennial publication of the ILA. They may take the form of a restatement of law, a draft treaty or convention, or a review of current law and practice. Over the years, some of the major contributions of the ILA concerned the area of shipping, in particular with regard to bills of exchange and affreightment, but they also include the Rules for the Enforcement of Foreign Judgments, the Helsinki Rules on the Use of the Waters of International Rivers and draft conventions on International Commercial Arbitration (1950), International Traffic Accidents (1976) and State Immunity (1982).

nationalities, but do not represent their nations. They do not receive instructions from the legal departments of their Foreign Offices and are in no way bound by the policy of their country or the prevailing doctrine of its academic centres.

This having been said, it is quite impossible for any Judge to blot out his legal training and the perspectives of his previous national and international experience. Nor should he, to be sure. He has been elected on the basis of his legal standing, accumulated knowledge and specific reputation in the field. Nobody can expect him to deny his own past achievements, nor would that make him any better able to live up to his own reputation. In other words, no Judge is supposed to become a neutral actor, once he enters the Court. If that were the case, the Court would not represent the world's principal legal systems and forms of civilization, but would turn into the very opposite of what it was intended to be and would impose a common denominator with which each Judge would have to comply and against which each case would be tested. In short, a Judge, when being elevated to The Hague, is expected to bring with him as much as possible of his own stock of knowledge and wisdom and as little as possible of his political persuasions. This is the *proviso* we have to make when speaking loosely and inaccurately of 'Indian' or 'Chinese' Judges or 'France's representative on the Bench'.

The 81 Judges that have sat on the Bench during the 50 years of activity of the ICJ have represented no less than 36 nationalities. The 31 Judges of the Permanent Court represented 18 nationalities. All in all, and spanning three quarters of a century, 43 nationalities out of the 188 nations that are currently Parties to the Statute of the Court have been represented on the Bench of one of these Courts. Some of them have been represented just once, others more than once, sometimes parenthetically and sometimes on a regular basis. By this, of course, we are making particular reference to the Permanent Members of the Security Council (and, in the PCIJ, of the Council of the League of Nations) that always have a national on the Bench if they nominate one.

With respect to this latter group of UN Members, we may rightly speak of a truly national tradition in relation to the Court, and it is precisely on account of this virtually permanent representation that it is interesting to see what these nations' attitudes to the Court have been over the years, and in what ways their legal and cultural concepts have been reflected in the Court's activities and judgments. The States in question are China, France, the Union of Soviet Socialist Republics, the United Kingdom and the United States. Each of these Great Powers has an interesting - and in some cases a positively eventful - record in its relationship with the Court.

Nations that have been represented for a considerable period of time and by a number of Judges, and which could for that reason claim a *quasi-permanent* status are not numerous. Cuba and the Netherlands were represented throughout the life of the PCIJ (1922-1945), by Bustamante y Sirven, and Loder and Van Eysinga respectively, but have not had a national judge since that time. Conversely, India

Left: Bohdan Stefan Winiarski (1884-1969), Judge (1946-1967) and President (1961-1964) of the ICJ.

Right: Manfred Lachs (1914-1993), Judge (1967-1993) and President (1973-1976) of the ICJ.

and Pakistan, which were never represented on the PCIJ, have between the two of them been represented throughout almost all the 50 years of the ICJ. With regard to Spain and Italy, their traditions were represented throughout on the PCIJ, by Altamira y Crevea and Anzilotti respectively, and on the Bench of the ICJ for 25 and 10 years respectively, by Morelli, Ago and recently Ferrari Bravo for Italy; and De Castro for Spain. Together they fairly represent the Latin legal tradition. The Latin American countries, on the other hand, have been evenly represented over the decades, as can be seen from the statistics.

Among the older European Powers, Germany had three representatives, Schücking on the Old Bench, and Mosler and Fleischhauer on the New, although they together cover less than 20 years, whereas Poland, also represented by three Judges - Rostworowski on the PCIJ and Winiarski and Lachs on the ICJ - can boast a total of almost 60 years.

Of the Asian countries, Japan is to be singled out for special mention. It was represented on the Old Bench throughout 1922-1942 by Judges Oda, Adatci and Nagaoka, returning in 1961 and remaining, virtually without interruption, through Judges Tanaka and Oda (unrelated, incidentally, to his namesake of the inter-war years) - thus achieving a total record of some 50 years.

The African nations, of course, are in a class of their own. Never represented on the PCIJ, under-represented until 1966 and fairly represented only since 1969, they now share, in their French- and English-speaking traditions, a quarter-century of experience on the Bench, enough to enable us to review their contributions to international adjudication.

In the next Chapter we will review the aforementioned traditions, in so far as they can be said to have contributed in a specific way to the *Œuvre de la Haye* and the jurisprudence of the Court, drawing on legal traditions that can be deemed typical.

Judges who die during their term of office lie in state in the Japanese Room.

CHAPTER EIGHT

The Principal Legal Systems

If we seek to evaluate the implementation of the second requirement stipulated in the Statute of the Court, namely the representation on the Bench of *the main forms of civilization and the principal legal systems of the world*, we must obviously first look at the nationalities represented on the World Court during its 75 years of activity. The next concern will be to establish to what degree the characteristic elements of these legal and cultural entities have actually left their mark on the Court. Inevitably, our research must not only encompass the past 75 years but also include, in very general terms, the genesis of the idea of a World Court and its constitutive years – in short *l'Œuvre de La Haye* from the 1890s onwards.

To be sure, the procedure proposed here does not give an overall view of the involvement of the nations in question with the Court. To arrive at such a view, we must also inspect the other side of the coin, as it were, and supplement our investigation with one undertaken from the opposite angle, namely by examining the records of nations in their capacity as parties to contentious cases. This is attempted in the Chapter devoted to Parties and Cases. In the present review, we shall try broadly to corroborate our findings with the help of general observations derived from that other research.

In the present chapter the various other regional traditions will be highlighted in successive reviews of the European, Asian and Pacific, the Islamic, the Latin American and the African traditions. In doing so, we will engage in nothing more ambitious than a far from comprehensive survey, in the most general terms, of these rich and time-honoured traditions, which will also provide support for the biographical sketches of Judges that follow.

Reproductions of sixteenth century Portuguese maps, presented to the ICJ by the Portuguese Government.

DIOGO HOMEM, 1563
Mediterrâneo e Europa
Biblioteca Nazionale, Firenze

The European Component

Set justice aside, and what are kingdoms but robberbands writ large.
Augustine, *City of God*

General Notions

In the genesis of modern international law, and consequently in the establishment of the system of adjudication as we know it today, the European component has admittedly been the pivotal and, until fairly recently, indeed the exclusive constituting element. However, this is not to say that, in the wider historical perspective, Europe, or the Western law tradition can claim pride of place. As with the presence on earth of man himself, on the chronological table of law systems the coming of age of international legal concepts in the West is a fairly recent phenomenon. Similar concepts in China and notably the Indian subcontinent antedated their maturing in the West by a great lapse of time. It has been established that the legal system in the Indus valley, as well as along the banks of the Nile, were fully developed around 3000 BC. A millennium later the Hindu law and the Chinese system were flourishing. In the next millennium the Jewish system and Buddhism followed suit. By then, African customary law, too, had taken definite shape.

It was only in the following millennium, leading up to the birth of Christianity, that the first glimmerings of Western law were to be observed in the dawn of the Greek era. Soon enough, however, its course was set. Its concepts of legal philosophy were incorporated in the massive codex of the self-imposed legislators of the Western world, the proud Romans: *Tu regere imperio populos, Romane, memento. // Hae tibi erunt artes, pacique imponere morem, // Parcere subjectis et debellare superbos.* (Virgil, *Aeneid* 6.851-53: 'But you, Roman, must remember that you have to guide the nations by your authority, for this is to be your skill, to graft tradition onto peace, to show mercy to the conquered, and to wage war until the haughty are brought low.' – Jackson Knight 1956).

The Mantuan poet served as oracle to Augustus, the architect of the Empire whose legal concepts, by virtue of the idea (how fallacious in itself) of the *translatio imperii* – the transfer of the seat of power with the benefit of succession to all that Rome stood for to Charlemagne and his descendants – would guide the Occident into the modern era. In its Western and Eastern ramifications, Roman praetorian law became the basis for the European Civil Law tradition. Both Justinian's codebook of the 'Second Rome' and the law of the 'Third Rome' – as the 17th century Muscovite State proudly paraded itself – were steeped in this tradition.

In the middle of the next millennium, a second mainstream was to pour its sources into this vast basin. As prelates in Rome engaged in expanding the impressive system of canonical law, in Saxon Britain the stage was set for the Common Law tradition which, again a full millennium later, would along with the Union Jack be planted in all quarters of the globe. Simultaneously though, in the East, another potent and expansive force took form to carry its laws far afield with its banners, to wit Islamic rule. And even here our bird's eye view of major legal systems should not stop. Our parents witnessed the growth and expansion of Socialist law throughout the world.

When considering the patterns of law and the function of lawyers over the full span of space and time, the notions of justice, of equity and of law have differed considerably. As previously stated, merging these varying concepts and principles, customs and feelings into a universal code to the benefit of a multicultural world, will be one of the major challenges of the next millennium. Still, to resume our thesis, for the development of international law as we know it today, the Western traditions of Civil and Common Law have been the paramount and, until the opening of the UN era, virtually unique sources of reference.

If the Western law traditions have been predominant for so long, this was not necessarily by virtue of their intrinsic qualifications. Obviously, it is basically on account of the worldwide political predominance of the European nations in the past few centuries that this legal supremacy was safeguarded. It may be safe to say that it was not so much the superiority of the Western legal concepts as it was the virtual extinction, mostly at gun-point, of the varying non-Western concepts that opposed themselves to it, which facilitated the predominance of European law. Western political supremacy sufficed to assert its values on its spheres of influence. Actually, it was precisely during the first surge of European expansion towards the other continents that modern international law took shape. Indeed, it was this phenomenon which to a great extent provided the backdrop to the genesis of the system of international law. It is only fairly recently that these Western concepts are really being challenged and put to the test in our global society.

Throughout world history, victorious civilizations have shown precious little patience with those they supplanted. Somehow, they always felt entitled – and sometimes felt it to be their vocation – to smother the civilizations they vanquished. The Western world has only rarely cherished different views in that respect, as the Tuscans and Punics – or later the Albigenses and Anabaptists – have experienced. As Horace said of Achilles: 'Laws, he declares, were not for him ordained; By dint of arms he claims all for himself'. 'For those whom Fortune favours might makes right', another classical maxim reads. 'In the state of nature every State disposes of as much right, as much power as it commands', Spinoza observed. 'Nothing is unjust which is expedient', Hobbes would echo Thucydides.

Just as the arrival of man changed the face of the earth, the expansion of the Western powers changed the face of the law. Within a century after Columbus' discovery of the 'Garden of Eden', most of its human species were virtually extinct. 'Any history of pre-Hispanic America ends in sadness. Whatever the ugly aspects of the rich, populous, unevenly sophisticated stone-age society, its obliteration by the Spanish, driven by the zeal of God and gold, is the first and still the most tragic result of the expansion of Europe.' (cf. Lachs, *Teacher* 1987, at p. 32). The Incas vanished, the Aztecs fell silent, the priceless archives of the Maya were burnt. In short, pre-Colombian civilization ceased to exist.

Mutatis mutandis, two centuries later, Africa told a similar tale, although, admittedly, the legal fabric of this vast continent, if only due to its impenetrability and lack of communications, must have been less obvious to Western observers. As was observed in Oxford, fifty years ago: 'Perhaps in the future there will be some African history to teach. But at present there is none; there is only the history of the Europeans in Africa. The rest is darkness and darkness is not a subject of history.' (Lachs, *op. cit.*, at p. 31). But what of the Great Zimbabwe, the once flourishing Hima State of Buganda, the old kingdoms of Ghana and the empires of Mali? They all crumbled before the European invader. In similar vein, the East, long hidden to the West behind the Muslim screen, despite the contacts through the early merchant fleets, remained long cloaked in mystery – and then, to quote Macaulay, '... bowed low before the West, in patient, deep disdain'. India survived on the strength of its magic virtue of absorption, by assimilating British culture- as it had done before with invaders from Greece and Persia.

Niccolò Macchiavelli (1469-1527).

Just as man, in the post-industrial era, is gradually learning to come to terms with the environment the Western world of law, in the post-colonial era, is replacing Eurocentrism with a multicultural approach. A new law is in the making, as much as a new world. However, what were the parameters of the old law, those European precepts which for so long had constituted the mainstream of thought?

The Parameters of European International Law

Firstly, to refer to European international law *tout court*, is not to say that within Europe the rule of law has been virtually undisputed. To maintain this, would be a fallacy. In fact, under the tide of the mainstream of European internationalism runs the sub-current of flat denial of the concept of a rule of law. This sub-current has been a pertinent one throughout. Spinoza insisted on the voluntary action of the State contract; Hobbes regarded society as a *bellum omnium contra omnes* ('war of all against all') and maintained that 'Covenants, without the Sword, are but Words and of no strength to secure a man at all'. These concepts were heralded by Macchiavelli's *Prince*; they were to be repeated in endless variation by such outstanding thinkers as John Austin, who maintained that law was mere positive morality, or Hegel. To the latter, as Lachs observes (*Teacher* 1987, at p. 16) 'the necessities of the historical process which

Title-page of Hobbes' Leviathan *(Amsterdam, 1672), suitably illustrating the temporal and spiritual realms.*

held the secret of wisdom ... led from primitive societies determined by despotism to the State, the acme of free will and hierarchically the highest step on the stairway of social development'. According to Hegel, law was fully subordinated to the abstract notion of the State, the supreme creation which allowed no superior authority. While insisting on the concept of *pacta sunt servanda*, he maintained that war, raised beyond the categories of evil, could be waged in the interest of States, for their aggrandisement as much as their preservation. In his view, there was little room for general international law. In recent times, in Western literature, law has been portrayed as

Friedrich Hegel (1770-1831).

Frontispiece of an early edition of Utopia *(1516) by Thomas More (1478-1535).*

either 'a permanent incitement to hypocrisy' or 'too abstract, too inflexible, too hard to adjust to the demands of the unpredictable and the unexpected'.

Tipping the balance, we find Macchiavelli's counterpoise in Thomas More's *Utopia*, written three years later (1516). Whether to be interpreted as 'the good land' or 'nowhereland' (idealism has often worn the mantle of escapism) and whatever its conception, invariably the ideal world was envisaged by its advocates as far away in space or time. Campanella offered a *Kingdom of the Sun*, Bacon a *New Atlantis*; Fénélon projected his ideal society to Arcady, Bellamy to *The Year 2000*, Mercier to *L'An 2440*, Samuel Butler found it *Erehwon* ('nowhere'). At an earlier stage (Chapter Two), we have discussed the various schemes and projects, courts, leagues and diets to ensure eternal peace that were developed in Europe over six centuries, from 14th century Pierre Dubois to the Hague Peace Conferences.

The Mainstream

Still, for all these side-currents and ramifications, from the early 17th century onwards, the mainstream of Western international law is clearly discernible and has never really been in jeopardy. It found its first persuasive and systematic expression in Grotius' works. In Westphalia this system was first applied to the developing inter-State system. From then on it was the rule of law, if anything, which constituted the common denominator of European society.

Inevitably, the composing elements of this system were manifold and its contributors through the centuries of Western civilization have been numerous. For this reason alone, it would be incorrect to call Grotius either the father or the founder of modern international law. *De jure belli ac pacis* was nothing new. It was 'merely' the systematization of an astoundingly rich legacy. However, it took the unique capacity of Grotius' legal mind and vast learning to seize the reins and bridle the undisciplined team of horses.

In this legacy were accumulated, first, the Roman law tradition from the early days of the *praetor peregrinus* and his *ius fetiale* to its tripartition in *ius civile*, *ius gentium* and *ius naturale*; its incorporation, through Gaius, Ulpian and others, into Justinian's *Corpus*; and finally, its interpretation by the 12th century Bolognese commentators, the so-called *glossatores*, from Irnerius to Accursius.

Encapsulated in it were also the time-honoured ideals of Christianity: Augustine's concept of the transfer of power from a worldly to a spiritual State, the *City of God*, the moral theology of the church fathers and Isidor of Seville's concepts of just war. Also taken into account were the medieval concept of the *civitas maxima*, the casaropapism, Pope Gelasius' 5th century theory of the Two Swords of Christ (the spiritual and the temporal) and the bulk of canonical law as contained in the *Decretum Gratiani* (c. AD 1140).

Prominent, inevitably, was Thomas Aquinas' *Summa Theologica*, that impressive compendium of learning from so many sources, in which Aristotle was mingled with the Arabs: Al-Kindi, Al-Farabi, Averroës, Avicenna and the Paris and Orléans law schools. Nicholas of Cusa was found here, along with the 14th century tracts on reprisals by Bartolus de Saxoferrato and Johannes de Legnano, perhaps the first Western tracts on international law as such.

Yet, acknowledgeably, Grotius' most stimulating sources were his immediate predecessors, the famous Spanish School and the Italians, who were the first to drop the medieval patterns, adjust the law to social circumstances and appreciate the dawn of a new era. In a world of Reformation and Counter-Reformation, with feudalism in retreat and civil militancy on the rise, amidst unprecedented expansion of trade and embassies, Francisco de Vitoria, Domingo de Soto, Balthasar de Ayala, Pierino Belli and Alberico Gentili (it is hard not to play the *Cicerone* as it is called and resist the temptation of attempting an encyclopedic survey of sources) sought new models of law to match the developing *raison d'ètat*, the absolutism of monarchs and the varying State theories of Bodin and Hotman.

It was Alberico Gentili (1552-1608) – an excommunicated exile and convert to Protestantism at the Elizabethan court – who finally dismissed all canonical law, denied the Pope his previous role in international relations, and banned the theologians from the forum of law. He was the first to fully appreciate the contemporary reality of nation-States dealing with each other on equal footing, irrespective of their religious denomination, be this Christian or not – and draw the logical conclusions from it. Henceforth, international law was to be voiced in the will of States, as manifested tacitly, in custom, and explicitly, in treaties. However,

Bartolus de Saxoferrato (1314-1357) lecturing.

this new rule of law was to be conditioned by one paramount principle: good faith.

Following in their footsteps, Grotius shaped a new legal system which redressed the balance in the face of imminent anarchy resulting from the disintegration of the previous medieval system. It is not so much that Grotius' approach to the law was revolutionary, far from it. Neither were his tenets brand new in themselves; in fact most of them are found scattered in the works of predecessors. However, it was his systematic analysis and rubrication, as well as his clear-cut presentation, which made his work the much demanded basic manual for Westphalia and beyond. Legal concepts which had never before been taken into consideration, were now readily available to the world of diplomacy and politics.

The most interesting aspect within our context, in view of later developments, is the way these early internationalists tackled the problem of the relationship between the two major sources of law as they were considered in those days, the *ius naturale* and the *ius positum* (or *positivum*), natural law and positive law or, in other words, the interaction of abstract notions and religious connotations *vis-à-vis* the express will of States. Grotius throughout

'The Law Department'. Fragment from an engraving representing the historical pageant on the occasion of the opening ceremony of Leyden University in 1575.

Among Bartolus' propositions are found the earliest parallels of modern 'equidistance lines'.

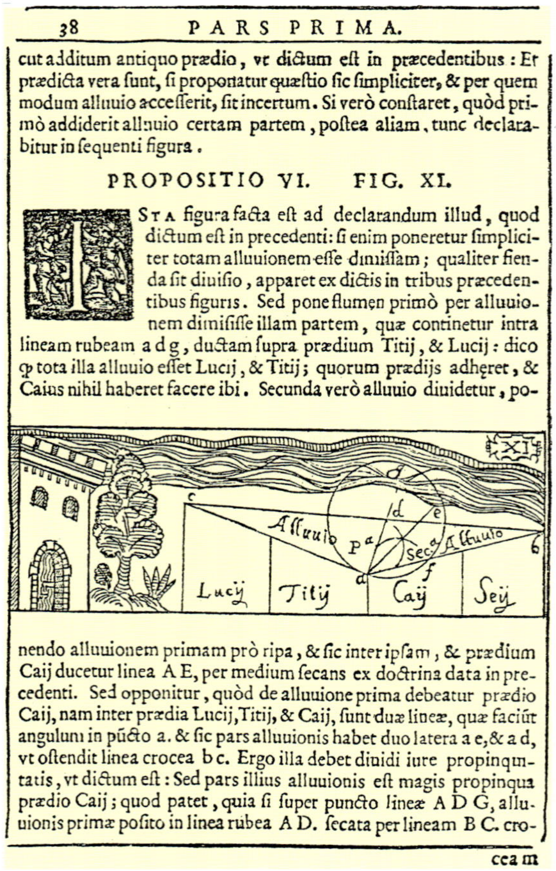

38 PARS PRIMA.

cut additum antiquo prædio, vt dictum eſt in præcedentibus: Et prædicta vera ſunt, ſi proponatur quæſtio ſic ſimpliciter, & per quem modum alluuio acceſſerit, ſit incertum. Si verò conſtaret, quòd primò addiderit alluuio certam partem, poſtea aliam, tunc declarabitur in ſequenti figura.

PROPOSITIO VI. FIG. XI.

ISTA figura facta eſt ad declarandum illud, quod dictum eſt in precedenti: ſi enim poneretur ſimpliciter totam alluuionem eſſe dimiſſam; qualiter fienda ſit diuiſio, apparet ex dictis in tribus præcedentibus figuris. Sed pone flumen primò per alluuionem dimiſiſſe illam partem, quæ continetur intra lineam rubeam a d g, ductam ſupra prædium Titij, & Lucij: dico ꝙ tota illa alluuio eſſet Lucij, & Titij; quorum prædijs adhęret, & Caius nihil haberet facere ibi. Secunda verò alluuio diuidetur, po-

nendo alluuionem primam prò ripa, & ſic inter ipſam, & prædium Caij ducetur linea A E, per medium ſecans ex doctrina data in precedenti. Sed opponitur, quòd de alluuione prima debeatur prædio Caij, nam inter prædia Lucij, Titij, & Caij, ſunt duæ lineæ, quæ faciũt angulum in pũcto a. & ſic pars alluuionis habet duo latera a e, & a d, vt oſtendit linea crocea b c. Ergo illa debet diuidi iure propinquitatis, vt dictum eſt: Sed pars illius alluuionis eſt magis propinqua prædio Caij; quod patet, quia ſi ſuper puncto lineæ A D G, alluuionis primæ poſito in linea rubea A D. ſecata per lineam B C. cro-

ceam

maintained a clear distinction between these two sources of law. To him the principles of nature were paramount and as if a moral code, the ultimate guardian of justice. These principles – and in this his views were new indeed – he held valid irrespective of the Divine Will. Indeed, his famous proposition in *Prolegomenon* 11 (*Etiamsi daremus ...: 'What we have been saying would have a degree of validity even if we should concede that which cannot be conceded without the utmost wickedness, that there is no God, or that the affairs of men are of no concern to Him'*) reads as a milestone along the road towards a secularized law of nature.

The British internationalist Sir Thomas Erskine Holland (1835-1926), Oxford Professor and editor of Alberico Gentili's De jure belli *(1877), was the guest of honour during the commemoration of Gentili's tercentenary in his birthplace in 1908.*

Alongside this postulated *ius naturale*, Grotius argued, another set of rules could progressively be developed, being the expression of the will of States (and preferably of common consent), the positive law of nations or *ius voluntarium*, by which international contacts and ensuing problems were to be regulated. In his view, natural law was as with the modern *ius cogens*, the measuring-rod of positive law, albeit in a rudimentary form. Its cornerstones were good faith and the concept of *pacta sunt servanda*. It left ample space for a very flexible positive law to develop in the day to day practice of nations. The ambit of Grotius' law was the world, irrespective of religious denomination. If anything, Grotius' doctrine was a social one, based on tolerance and a firm belief in the unity of the *societas humani generis*.

Twenty years after the publication of Grotius' *De jure belli ac pacis* (1625), prolonged negotiations at Munster and Osnabruck – the last 'European summit' without Great Britain attending – led to a new legal foundation of the European inter-State system. Here Hapsburg and Papal dominance were buried and French political supremacy was established; here the Dutch Republic was sanctioned and the German patchwork quilt fabricated. From now on States of whatever religious conviction communicated on an equal footing, in mutual respect for each other's independence and territorial integrity. In the event of dispute they had the instruments of diplomacy ready to hand: negotiation, mediation, conciliation and arbitration, and they were bound to the doctrine of just war (*bellum iustum*). In Westphalia it was not just nations, but political philosophy, legal doctrine and State practice that concluded a pact, which could therefore become of great assistance to the rapid development of both diplomacy and trade.

This is not to say that Grotius' theories remained undisputed – far from it. If in retrospect he is considered the founder of international law it is precisely because with him the real debate started. For the next half century, the contentious issue was to become the primacy of either the natural or the positive law element. In England, where Hobbes (1588-1679) in his *Leviathan* bluntly denied the rule of law and Locke

(1632-1704) and later David Hume (1711-1776) empirically examined its values, it was Richard Zouche (1590-1661) who advanced both its claim and its theory. While maintaining Grotius' dichotomy, he upgraded the value of custom and inter-State agreements and at the same time substituted the Dutchman's natural law principles by another governing principle, typical of the period, namely, reason. To him, the *ratio communis humana* was the unifying element of law. Obviously, this meant yet another step away from moral theology. With him, as Lachs observes, positivism had begun in earnest:

> Henceforth the twin streams of positivism and natural law were to flow side by side, though occasionally mingling, throughout the course of international law, with the proponents of each school endeavouring to correct the excesses or remedy the weaknesses of the other. (*Teacher* 1987, at p. 56)

Natural Law and Positivism

Samuel Pufendorf (1632-1694) is the first in line who comes to mind. Leaning towards the primacy of the natural law element, he was keen to harmonize its principles with Cartesian philosophy and build the law upon reason in what was called the 'geometrical method'. In this he was the first representative of the Enlightenment. His ideas ran counter to those of Leibnitz (1646-1716) who was perhaps the last great thinker to cling to the religious overtones of the natural law element.

Pufendorf did adhere to the doctrine of 'just behaviour' underlying international relations. However, the dilemma how best to safeguard the maintenance of the law in practice, that is in the hands of sovereigns endowed with absolute power and no longer bridled by divine rule, was probably first adequately tackled by Cornelis van Bynkershoek (1673-1743). He was, next to Grotius, the 17th century Dutch internationalist of greatest repute, an expert of maritime law and diplomacy, who approached the problem from a very practical viewpoint and with clear-headed rationalism.

Unlike Pufendorf, who ignored customary law, Bynkershoek sought to build society on custom, treaty-law and the consensus of nations. His penetrating studies into the history of the law, notably of the seas, made him point to necessity and self-interest as the commanding

Thomas Hobbes (1588-1679).

John Locke (1632-1704).

The delegates at the Peace Conference of Westphalia (1648). The illustration is found in the Acta Westphalica.

Samuel Pufendorf (1632-1694).

Cornelis van Bynkershoek (1673-1743).

principles governing State conduct. As Grotius had pointed out earlier, he found that State interest was in the end best served by the maintenance of the principle of good faith, that *fundamentum justitiae* as Cicero had called it. To Bynkershoek this was the underlying rationale of all contacts and agreements between States and which in his view replaced divine sanction.

An interesting figure in this context is Christian Friedrich von Wolff, a professor from Halle, Germany, that warbeaten nation still urgently in need and desperately in search of a proper constitution. He was an adherent of – and at some time fell victim to – State absolutism as practised by Frederick the Great. Wolff has been criticized for his quasi-logical systematization of the law on the basis that he resorts to tautology, platitudes and truisms. Still, his identification of natural law with the force of necessity, to be gradually superseded by the positive law created by the will of nations, and his foundation of both upon systematic reason, was another milestone along the road to the internationalism of the middle of the 18th century – an age in which his much better known pupil Emer de Vattel from Neuchatel (1714-1767) would take a place of honour. Before we turn to Vattel and the development of 18th century international law, we must first round off our picture of early internationalism by the discussion of one of its less known constitutive elements, the Hebrew tradition.

The Hebrew Legal Traditions

The Hebrew legal tradition has, if due only to the absence of a State of its own, for almost two millennia, lacked explicit political expression. Still, its concepts have in an important way influenced Western law throughout. In the appreciation of a modern observer: 'More than twenty centuries of scholarly endeavour functioning harmoniously within the ambit of the sacred law, have produced a juristic system of outstanding maturity – deeply responsive to the human urge for justice, and conscious at the same time of the need for that justice to be in accord with the law. Justice-according-to-law, not justice unbridled and at large; law mellowed by reflective interpretation, not law harsh and ill-attuned to social need – these are Hebrew legacies which have fertilised the mainstream of European jurisprudence' (Weeramantry, *An Invitation to the Law*, at p. 24). In fact, as Rosenne observes in a penetrating study on the subject on which we draw heavily throughout, the Jewish element 'is the only non-Roman legal element, and the only non-Christian moral element, which was consciously and deliberately admitted into consideration with any degree of consistency' during the formative period of Western international law.

Generally speaking, there was a readier acceptance of the Hebrew tradition among Protestant authors than among their Catholic counterparts of the 16th to 18th centuries. The former were definitely more steeped in the Old Testament. Grotius, for example, was criticized in his day for the views expounded in Prolegomena 48-49 of his *De jure belli ac pacis*, where he stated:

> I frequently appeal to the authority of the books which men inspired by God have either written or approved, nevertheless with a distinction between the Old Testament and the New. There are some who urge that the Old Testament sets forth the law of nature. Without doubt they are in error, for many of its rules come from the free will of God. And yet this is never in conflict with the true law of nature; and up to this point the Old Testament can be used as a source of the law of nature, provided we carefully distinguish between the law of God, which God sometimes executes through men, and the law of men in their relations with one another.
>
> This error we have, so far as possible, avoided, and also another opposed to it, which supposes that after the coming of the New Testament the Old Testament in this respect was no longer of use. We believe the contrary, partly for the reasons which we have already given, partly because the character of the New Testament is such that in its teachings respecting the moral virtues it enjoins the same as the Old Testament or even enjoins greater precepts. In this way we see that the early Christian writers used the witnesses of the Old Testament. The Hebrew writers, moreover, most of all those who have thoroughly understood the speech and customs of their people, are able to contribute not a little to our understanding of the thought of the books which belong to the Old Testament.

King Solomon sitting in judgment (I Kings 3:16-28). Sculpture by a 17th century Flemish artist in the King's Palace, the former town hall of Amsterdam.

These lines provoked a sharp reaction from his commentator Jean Barbeyrac, who also firmly rejected the rabbinic method of exegesis.

Three further elements constrained the appreciation of the Jewish law tradition: firstly the relatively modest understanding of the Hebrew language even among the best of humanists. Secondly, the difficult access to most post-biblical Jewish law sources in those days. Thirdly, the rather delicate and controversial position of Jews themselves at the time in several parts of Europe. Post-Biblical talmudic literature and the later rabbinic traditions of academies and courts did not find ready entrance. Still, one may say that in as much as the major source of law of the Jewish people, the Bible, to a great extent helped to form European thought and intellectual patterns in general, Western international law is as much the product of the Holy Land as it is of Greece and Rome. The words of Isaiah, engraved upon the UN Headquarters in New York may serve to stress our point: 'And they shall beat their swords into plowshares and their spears into pruninghooks. Nation shall not lift up sword against nation, neither shall they learn war any more.' These lines have provided an intellectual basis for much of the peace ideals in past centuries and embody the perennial striving for peace, not just of the Jewish people but of humanity.

Can we speak of a Jewish tradition of international law properly speaking? Obviously, the history of the *Diaspora* alone forestalls any unqualified answer in the affirmative to this question. Perhaps the best way to approach the problem is first to consider the different sources of Judaic law as they came to be developed in past centuries. In this respect, somewhat surprisingly, much work has still to be done. As Rosenne recalls, traditionally, the Jewish law or *halacha* is regarded as primarily an intimate, domestic matter, which bears a characteristically introspective character.

In one aspect the Jewish law tradition may be called unique within the context of the European world – although, as our survey of law traditions will show, certainly not in comparison to other legal cultures – namely in its interweaving of the spiritual and the secular elements and its virtual identification of law, morality and religion. The first and foremost source of Jewish law is of course the Old Testament in which the history of the Children of Israel and the later Jewish Davidean and Hasmonean Kingdoms is encompassed, their outlook on life guided by the world's most famous short moral code, the Ten Commandments, the divine revelation of *Torah*, and oral law. Generally speaking this covers the period of political independence, although, obviously, well before the destruction of the temple by Titus in AD 70, the Kingdom of Judaea was reduced to a Roman vassal-State.

In following centuries, gradually, due also to the disputations in schools such as the more lenient *Hillel* and more stringent *Shamai*, a written constitution and code of laws was developed in the *Pentateuch*, which was then steadily updated by the accretions of the *Soferim*, the early school of interpreters. Out of these interpretations and accretions, somewhere around the 2nd century AD, in the days of Rabbi Judah, the *Mishna* came into being. This was a code of no less than 523 chapters which, in the course of the following centuries, was again expounded by the *Amoraim* scholars, finally to give rise to the *Talmud*, of which two versions, both running into thousands of pages, were compiled, the Babylonian and Palestinian version. They existed side by side, covering separate geographical areas; it was the Babylonian Talmud which established itself in Europe.

Nothwithstanding the successive persecutions from different sides, the

Moses Maimonides (1135-1204). The illustration was produced in the 19th century.

scholarly tradition was kept alive from Muslim Spain to (notably) Poland, also thanks to the day-to-day guidance of the *rabbi*, whose time-honoured precepts were incorporated in the *Responsa*. Soon enough, this vast material needed new clearing-houses, digests as compiled by Moses Maimonides (1135-1205) in his *Mishneh Torah* (a systematic codification of principles) and the *Shulan 'Aruch*, compiled by Joseph Qaro (1488-1575).

If we turn to the field of international law, in the Bible no distinction whatever is made between laws in the public and private spheres, as little as, for that matter, between law, morals or religion. Its statutory texts, as included in the *Pentateuch*, provide references which are too sparse for us to distill the true notion of international law of the period. In fact, conclusions are for the greater part to be deduced from historical incidents or, *a posteriori*, from later traditions. However, to highlight a few major aspects, in its outlook on the phenomenon of war, as a rule a clear distinction is made between the war waged for a religious duty (*mitzva*) and the so-called voluntary or optional war. It appears that different legal rules and consequences applied to both. The religious war was essentially waged for liberation, survival and self-defence. Its harsher aspects were modified by Mosaic law. Still, it would seem that the more humanizing rules as laid down in *Deuteronomy*, and which for instance allowed for exemption from military service, initially applied to the optional war only. It is only with Maimonides, in the 12th century, that the religious war was assimilated into the optional war.

With regard to the field of diplomacy, the few details preserved do not allow us to draw any firm conclusions, though they do not suggest any very strict rules. It would seem that diplomatic envoys did enjoy a recognized status. According to Josephus, King Herod deemed the murder of ambassadors a justified reason for war. Something resembling the modern concept as of 'safe passage' might be recognized in the negotiations between Moses and the Kings of Moab as recorded in *Numbers* XX. Treaties were invariably reinforced by an oath, adding as it were a religious element to the generally applicable rule of *pacta sunt servanda*. Josephus reports that in Hellenitic times the High Priest in Jerusalem turned down Alexander the Great's overtures on account of his previous oath to the Persian King Darius.

The idea of arbitration too is steeped in Hebrew tradition. Yet, from early on, one of its most striking characteristics is the respect displayed by its legal system for the judge and the judicial process, bound by the twin dictates of the written law and religious duty. In Weeramantry's evaluation: 'These twin dictates produced a resulting tradition wedding justice with law. Neither abstract justice nor strict law by itself was capable of discharging the judicial responsibility. Justice-according-to-law was the epitome of Jewish legal wisdom. That was its richest legacy to all succeeding legal systems' (Weeramantry, *op. cit.*, at p. 26).

The post-biblical period is definitely more amply documented. Legal traditions as contained in the canon of the *Mishna* and amplified in later ages in the *Gemara* up to Maimonides' recapitulation in the 12th century, are found next to the historiographic traditions as exemplified by Flavius Josephus (born AD 37), the Jewish aristocrat and Pharisee priest who chronicled the Jewish revolt (*De bello Judaico*) and composed a history of the Jews from the Creation to AD 66 (*Antiquitates Judaicae*), and Philo Judaeus (30 BC – AD 45), the Alexandrian author in whose works Hellenistic philosophy and Jewish tradition converge. Their works include documents such as arbitral awards and *senatus consulta* which bear ample testimony to the customary laws of the time. The treaty of 160 BC between Judas Maccabaeus and the Roman Senate is reproduced in the form of a Senate decision.

It is interesting that the ideal state of affairs as portrayed by the official legal sources is not always corroborated by State conduct as reported by the historiographers. Worth mentioning too is the relation of power between Kings and Sanhedrin. The *Mishna* laid down that the king could only declare an optional war after a decision of the Great Sanhedrin, which would suggest that this body had a role beyond its purely judicial ambit.

Maimonides, who wrote in a period in which for a long time no Jewish State had existed and therefore from a purely messianic vision of the future, in his Code reflected the basic moral concepts of the Jewish law. His tract on the *Laws of Kings and Their Wars* (which, as Rosenne recalls, antedated King Alfonso of Portugal's famous *Siete Partidas* by a generation) displays a deep moral quality: whatever the King does, should be done for the sake of Heaven and the upliftment of the true religion. The King's complete subjection to the law was symbolized by his duty always to be accompanied with a Scroll of the Law.

Admittedly, ever since the Hasmonean period and the loss of a Jewish State, rabbinical concepts of international law and notions of sovereignty, just war, treaty law and the like were doomed to remain purely theoretical until the mid-20th century. It was only with Herzl and the rise of modern Zionism that these concepts were to be revived, finally to be materialized in the State of Israel.

The Impact of the Hebrew Tradition on Early Western Thinking

So much for Hebrew traditions and Jewish law in their own right. Quite another thing, and our first and foremost concern within our context, is the influence exerted by Jewish law traditions on the development of Western international law. Obviously, as long as law and morality were conceived as part and parcel of theology among Church Fathers, the biblical heritage was preponderant. However, 16th century Spanish scholastics such as De Vitoria and Suarez, who wrote after the expulsion of the Jews from Spain in 1492, display no overt knowledge of biblical texts and, remarkably enough, make no reference whatsoever to post-biblical Hebrew sources, not even Maimonides. To date, it is not yet clear to what extent Hebrew traditions were known in scholastic circles at the Salamanca and Coimbra centres of learning.

The Italian Alberico Gentili who, as will be recalled, wrote in England and was himself a convert to Protestantism, displays intimate familiarity with biblical sources. Indeed, he practised biblical criticism, witness his *Ad I Maccabaeorum disputatio* of 1600. In the opening paragraphs of his *De jure belli* he states: 'The words which are written in the Sacred Books of God will properly be given special weight; since it is evident that they were uttered not merely for the Hebrews, but for all men, for all nations and for all times. For that these words are of a true nature, that is to say, one which is blameless and just, is most certain.' He also quotes extensively from Philo and Josephus, yet does not seem to be familiar with post-biblical original Hebrew literature. Still, it has been argued that in their developing of natural law theories, these early internationalists, for all their heavy leaning on Stoicism, also drew from, or at all events encapsulated, Jewish concepts.

Hugo Grotius is next in line. If in the past he has been hailed by some as the father of international law, by theologians he has no less been hailed as one of the founders of modern biblical criticism. Undoubtedly, some of his best philological work is found in his bulky *Annotata* on the Old and New Testaments, to which he devoted so much of his life. In fact, his basically humanist outlook to biblical exegesis, his stressing of the intertemporal element and his insistance on a truly historical and philological approach make his work a welcome counterpart to the often extremely narrow and religiously biased commentaries of most of his contemporaries. In the Netherlands, Grotius' works in this sphere have been closely studied in recent decades. The picture that emerges is one of a scholar profoundly versed in Jewish antiquities, with a more than rudimentary knowledge of the Hebrew, and a deep interest in rabbinic tradition, though somewhat ambivalent with respect to its value for the Western world. This reservation does not however hold for Maimonides: whatever of his thought was known to Grotius' world, was incorporated in the Dutchman's scholarly work.

It is well-known that around 1615 Grotius was commissioned by the States-General to draft a report on the conditions surrounding Jewish settlement in Holland, the *Remonstrantie nopende de Joden*. Still, Grotius' involvement with Hebrew traditions and biblical studies was evidenced throughout his life, from his early teens and from various angles. His poetical paraphrases of biblical texts, notably the psalms, are rightly famous. The exposition of natural law in his early neo-Latin drama *Adamus Exul* (1601) reveals the legal philosopher and theologist as much as the man of letters. The same holds true for his later dramas *Christus Patiens* (1608) and *Sophompaneas* (1635, on Joseph in Egypt), in which a wealth of biblical and classical sources are majestically entwined in profuse learned references. Again, some-

The coat of arms of Israel.

where at the age of 15, Grotius produced a tract on the Mosaic Law and stated that he had written a now lost comparative study on ancient theologies, called *Philarchaeus*. In a sense, this work must have been the counterpart of that famous tract which has incorrectly been called his first work on international law, the comparison of State policies from the ancient world up to the 17th century, the *Parallelon Rerumpublicarum*.

Much less known, however, is another tract from around 1600, called *De republica emendanda* ('On the Emendation of the Dutch Polity'), which was recovered through a Viennese copy three decades ago. The tract comprises a very practical proposal for a better form of government in the United Provinces, a very topical issue at the time. As with more tracts of young Grotius, notably *De jure praedae* and *De antiquitate*, an essentially political programme is presented as a fundamental, theoretical essay. Encompassing much of the political theory of the time, *De republica emendanda* deals with the projecting of an ideal Dutch State as to be deduced from historical models.

Interestingly enough, it is not the humanists' all-time favorite, the ancient Achaean Confederacy of the Amphictyons that Grotius draws on here, nor the contemporary models of the Swiss Confederacy or Venetian Republic. In the tract it is pointed out that both the similarities and defects of most political constitutions, ancient and modern alike, are to be explained on similar grounds, firstly the imitation of the one by the other, secondly the basic shortcomings of man's political mind. The *ratio humana*, it is stated fifty years before Descartes, must needs be inferior to that other source of knowledge contained in the *revelatio divina*, Divine Revelation. Of all nations, it is the ancient Hebrew polity that uniquely drew from this political philosophy as contained in the Mosaic laws. This suffices to establish the primacy of the ancient Hebrew Republic. In some fifty pages, the author extolls the superb qualities of the Hebrew Constitution. Not surprisingly in view of Grotius' effort to strengthen the authority of the Dutch States-General, it is concluded that the political centre of gravity in the Hebrew constitution rested with the Council of State, identified by Grotius (on the authority of Flavius Josephus) with the Sanhedrin. The work is a counterpoise to the dozens of tracts from the period in the tradition of Bodin's treatise which advocate the monarchy.

It is of interest that Grotius, in defending this thesis, fell in with a well-established Humanist tradition. In the mid-16th century, Sanctus Pagninus of Lucca produced a *Hebraicorum Institutionum Liber*, while in 1574 Bonaventura Bertram of Lausanne published a *De Republica Ebraeorum*, followed in 1585 by a similarly entitled tract by Carolus Sigonius of Modena. In 1617, a close colleague of Grotius, Petrus Cunaeus, would produce the authoritative work in the field, bearing the same title. Young Grotius was well known in circles of Hebraists. One recalls that, freshly enrolled at Leyden, he found lodgings with the irenist Franciscus Junius (François Dujon, 1545-1602) who, apart from being a biblical commentator, was known as the author of a *Grammatica linguæ Hebreæ* (1590) and of a lengthy treatise *De observatione politiæ Moysis* (1593). The rich tradition of Hebrew studies and biblical exegesis at Leyden University, initiated with Raphelengius, Scaliger and Erpenius, was based on the so-called 'Polyglot Bibles' in which the

'The Department of Theology'. Fragment from an engraving representing the historical pageant on the occasion of the opening ceremony of Leyden University in 1575.

Hebrew, Greek and Latin versions were confronted with the Semitic and notably Aramese texts.

The tradition discussed here would alone suffice to indicate the relevance of the Jewish law tradition in the development of early European political theory. Yet, a similar impact of Jewish tradition is found in the work of John Selden (1584-1654), the English author of *Mare Clausum*, the refutation of Grotius' *Mare Liberum* of 1609, which was written in 1618 and first published in 1635. An enthusiastic orientalist and Hebraist, Selden in 1640 published a lengthy treatise on natural law and positive law according to Jewish traditions, *De jure naturali et gentium iuxta disciplinam Ebræorum libri VII*. In this 'quaint work' with 'a certain weird attraction' (Rosenne), Selden drew a distinction between the imperative law of nations as ordained by God and the 'intervenient' law of nations as laid down in Hebrew texts, in fact confusing ancient Jewish polity with natural law.

From then on, the Jewish law tradition could no longer be neglected and authors had to take a position in the debate one way or the other. Pufendorf drew heavily on biblical and rabbinic sources, whereas on the other hand Jean Barbeyrac (1674-1744), Huguenot exile and commentator of Grotius and Pufendorf denigrated any rabbinic contribution to the sphere of international law and actually accused Jewish scholars of corrupting the purity of Mosaic lawgiving. Ironically, the only scholar of repute from Jewish extraction to enter this debate was Baruch Spinoza (1632-1677), a controversial scholar in Jewish circles. He was in many respects an adherent of Hobbes' nihilistic views on the function of law in society, one who saw the state of nature of man as demanding a search for self-interest in the private as well as in the public sphere, where it became the *raison d'état*.

The Eighteenth Century

Vattel's *Le droit des gens* (1758) was perhaps not the best and certainly not the most in-depth study (Bentham found it 'womanish and tautological') but by all means the most popular manual of the 18th century. It exerted considerable influence on the practice of States – and this was precisely what Vattel had in mind. Interestingly, even he could not do without the natural law element, which he considered the expression of both conscience and necessity. Still, positive law, as expressed tacitly in accepted custom and explicitly in covenants and agreed rules, dominates his scene. Typically of the period, he stresses the right of self-defence, diplomatic intercourse and immunities. Vattel was no trained lawyer but an expert diplomat and politician, who knew the pitfalls of every-day diplomacy by own experience.

Less popular, though definitely of greater stature is Georg Friedrich von Martens who, in his famous *Précis du droit des gens modernes de l'Europe* (1789), reduced natural law to the domain of morality and simply distinguished between necessary law, as dictated by reason and usefulness – and voluntary positive law in the way it was understood by Vattel. With Von Martens we definitely enter the rule of positivism. As Lachs observes, he was the first who saw 'that the general and collective interest of nations, which they had identified with natural law, might stand in conflict with the interests of individual States, hence with the positive law flowing therefrom' (*Teacher* 1987, at p. 61). The progress of the theory of the discipline is also attested by the first comprehensive bibliography to appear in those days, Von Ompteda's *Litteratur des gesammten sowohl natürlichen wie positiven Völkerrechts* (1785).

The progress of theory during the late 17th and 18th centuries is, to a great extent, a reflection of a change of attitude in European society. Perhaps the most de-

Baruch Spinoza (1632-1677).

Emmerich de Vattel (1714-1767).

Georg Friedrich von Martens (1756-1821).

cisive element along this path was the progressive process of secularization. Early 17th century warfare, as exemplified by the Thirty-Years War was waged over issues of principle and was waged to the bitter end. Battles were fought by hired armies of professional soldiers. However, with the abating of the religious issue, and certainly once the Peace of Utrecht in 1713 had put an end to the Spanish War of Succession, a distinct urge for a European balance of power became noticeable. No longer were wars started to eliminate adversaries but rather to adjust the system and restore the endangered *status quo*. The codes of war changed too; it was the *Kriegsbrauch* that governed the battlefield. The role of diplomacy increased considerably.

If war, in modern times, has been described as the continuation of negotiations by other means, in the 18th century war primarily served to strengthen one's position at the conference table. Alliances could switch at any given time. Today's enemy, it was now understood, could be tomorrow's ally. It was felt imperative to leave all options open. It has been called an unprincipled approach, but it certainly was a very practical one. Even the Napoleonic crisis did not bring down this system which culminated in Vienna in the hands of Metternich and was taken over by Bismarck in the second part of the 19th century.

Theory closely followed this changing practice. With Ayala, the right of revolt was still denied to the provinces of the Hapsburg Empire. It was left to the Pope exclusively to dethrone the tyrant. Grotius was the first to make law normative to a social contract in a detached analysis of the phenomenon of war as an accepted continuum in the history of mankind. The law was to serve a triple purpose: the prevention of conflict, the curbing of violence and the opening of the way to diplomacy. The military was seen as the instrument and war as the process to restore the fractured legal order. On the basis of Erasmus' pacifist and non-contentious approach, as well as in reliance on Spinoza's realistic views, Grotius, in line with Bodin, deemed the State the *perfectissima societas* which granted a qualified right to revolt. If with him the State, the secularized power, is to dominate the Church, it is to enforce tolerance and to urge co-existence for all denominations, including non-Christians.

Here we observe Grotius both as a product of his age of violence and as a visionary philosopher ahead of his times. To be sure, he did not entrust absolute power to the State: With him the real sovereign is the *interna justitia*, moral justice. As with Bodin, the State is both preconditioned by the legal order and its very expression: *ubi societas, ibi ius* – an interesting observation, one may say, coming from a scholar operating in the context of Richelieu's *Maximes* and *raison d'ètat* and among the nihilist theories of Hobbes, Bossuet or Cardin Le Bret. In his *Prolegomena* to DJBP, Grotius dismissed the exclusive strife for self-interest as narrow-mindedness, not just for the individual but for the State as well. This he maintained not just for practical reasons (in his view, even the State, in the ultimate resort, could not do without allies) but also as a matter of principle. Self-interest ran contrary to the Stoic principle of universalism and the *appetitus socialis* that was prompted by reason. Grotius' legal concepts are neutral in terms of religion, but by no means in terms of morality.

Grotius' theory and his manual were the ideal guidelines for the Munster conference. However, his natural law theory and concept of *bellum iustum* became less relevant once – with the rapid increase of inter-State contacts, diplomacy and commerce – day-to-day practice required very practical answers to very practical problems. Also, the change of the type of conflicts, the so-called 'Cabinet Wars', called for another type of law, the law that is known to us as the *droit de convenance*. It was this law which was to serve what in the Treaty of Utrecht was called the *iustum potentiae equilibrium*, the balance of power. Two publicists were to produce the required guidelines: first Bynkershoek, haphazardly, then Emer de Vattel, systematically. Still, answers on principle to fundamental problems were not offered by these authors. Their manuals were tailor-made for their world and within the prevailing European context. Once this society had collapsed, towards the end of the 19th century, these authors and their manuals inevitably lost their topicality. Inevitably, at that juncture, the new world, in search of laws of universal applicability within a multicultural society, harked back to the 17th century pioneers.

Henry Wheaton (1785-1848).

The Nineteenth Century

The 19th century, here considered to extend from Vienna (1815) to Versailles (1919), is not only the period of industrialization and of nationalism, but also of imperialism, of colonialism and expansion of trade. To parallel this, in fact to put a legal underpinning to this society, it also witnessed the growth of the study of international law on an unprecedented scale. To validate this there was an army of authors and an arsenal of writings. The expansion of positive law was perhaps most impressive in the sphere of treaty law and the increase of international conferences. Legal instruments of all kinds imposed themselves on an ever more complex society. Major diplomatic conferences such as Panama (1826), Paris (1856), St Petersburg (1868) and Berlin (1878 and 1885) went together with Peace Conferences from Brussels to London (1848-1851), Geneva Red Cross conferences (from 1863) and Pan American Conferences (from 1890). Along with the 1868 Mannheim Act to regulate the Rhine traffic, came the funding of the General Post Union in Bern in 1874 and, to mention another major event, the launching of the Oxford Manual on the Laws of War on Land by the *Institut de Droit International* at Oxford in 1880.

Among the theoreticians we find John Austin (1790-1859), whose *Lectures on Jurisprudence* (1861) echo Hobbes, next to Heffter in Germany, whose encyclopaedic mind encompassed the German positivist tradition in a comprehensive study of European Law (*Das Europäische Recht der Gegenwart*, 1844). Perhaps most influential and creative of all was Henry Wheaton (1785-1848), the first Northern American internationalist to enter this arena. His *Elements of International Law* (1836) and *History of the Law of Nations in Europe and America* (1842) are noticeable for their comparative approach. Wheaton maintained that international law was to a great extent conditioned by social circumstance. Thus, he acknowledged a distinct law of Muslim nations. As we will see, his *Elements* was the first introduction to Western law traditions in the Asian world.

In Great Britain, Sir Robert Phillimore (1810-1885) and Sir Thomas Erskine Holland (1874-1910) based their studies, steeped in positivism, on day-to-day practice. In this tradition, the lectures on *International Law* by John Westlake (1828-1913) may perhaps be seen as best representing the period. Pride of place, however, is taken by F. L. Oppenheim (1858-1919), whose *A Treatise on International Law* remains authoritative to this day. The work, a Cambridge classic, was revised first by Alfred McNair, then by Hersch Lauterpacht and recently by Sir Robert Jennings and Sir Arthur Watts, names which figure prominently in these pages on the ICJ.

In France, the leading internationalist of the second part of the century was undisputably Louis Renault (1843-1918), a most inspiring teacher, brilliant orator and stimulating force behind the two Hague Peace Conferences. He was the tutor of the generation of French internationalists who contributed so much to the *Œuvre de la Haye*: Léon Bourgeois, Gilbert Gidel, Paul Fauchille, Henri-Auguste Fromageot, Albert de la Pradelle, Georges Scelle, and André Weiss.

Throughout Europe, these men launched the prominent yearbooks and respectable journals which in the past century have been so vital to the expansion of international law. They were instrumental in the founding of the *Institut de Droit International*, the International Law Association, the Permanent Court of Arbitration, the Hague Academy and so many other time-honoured institutions. We need scarcely recall Bluntschli from Zurich, Pascal Fiore from Turin, the Belgians Rolin-Jaequemyns and Ernest Nys, the Dutch Tobias Asser and Cornelis van Vollenhoven, this gallery is already overcrowded. Still, there is perhaps good reason to add a few lines to a tradition of international law which comes within the European tradition, yet which through the centuries has developed some

The 1856 Paris Peace Conference.

*Sir Robert Yewdall Jennings (*1913), former Judge and President of the ICJ.*

Sir Hersch Lauterpacht (1897-1960), Judge of the ICJ from 1955-1960.

Walther Adrian Schücking (1875-1935), Judge of the PCIJ from 1930-1935.

The First Partition of the Commonwealth of Poland and Lithuania (1773).

André Weiss, Judge of the PCIJ from 1922-1928.

Louis Renault (1843-1918).

Johann Caspar Bluntschli (1808-1881).

Gottfried Wilhelm Leibniz (1646-1716).

characteristics of its own, namely the Eastern European, and notably the Russian tradition of international law.

Its sheer size, its geographical position and its entanglements with both the East and the West engendered within the Moscovite Empire a distinct outlook on the world. From the 16th century onwards Russia's trade expanded from France and Spain to Persia and China. From early on, the British and the Dutch showed a keen interest in trading with the Muscovite State. Early Russian diplomacy, based mainly on custom and treaty law, is documented from the treaty of friendship concluded in Moscow, in 1522, with Suleiman the Magnificent to the treaties of Nerchinsk (1689) and Kiachta (1727) with the Chinese. The intellectual contacts with the West matched the Russian entrance at the political level. In the decades around the Peace of Nystadt (1721) which secured Russia's interests in the European political arena, university centres were developed. The Russian Academy of Sciences was founded in 1725; Leibnitz and Christian Wolff were recruited for Russian service and diplomats charged with the purchase of law books from the West. The works of prominent European internationalists were translated.

Around 1835, international law was introduced as a discipline in its own right. According to Vladimir Grabar (1865-1956) in his *The History of International Law in Russia, 1647-1917* (1958; English translation by W. E. Butler, 1990), all natural law concepts were banned from the law faculties at Moscow and St Petersburg, mostly for reasons of internal policy, and superseded by the fashionable historical and encyclopedical approach.

From 1836 the chair of international law at St Petersburg (until 1863 called all-nations law) was held by Professor Iovanovskii. In 1870 he was succeeded by the man who took such a prominent place among the internationalists gathered at The Hague in 1899, F. F. Martens or de Martens as he is known in the West (1845-1909). His early study on the relations between Russia and the Ottoman Empire had attracted Iovanovskii's attention. Martens was trained at Vienna, Heidelberg and Leipzig but soon called back to become an *ordinarius* in St Petersburg in 1876. His scholarly reputation rests on two fundamental works mainly, his two-volume cours of international law (*Contemporary International Law of Civilized Nations*, 1882-1883), which went through numerous editions and translations, and his fifteen-volume collection of treaties concluded by Russia with foreign nations. This collection on the lines of Dumont was the realization of an idea which Catherine II had cherished in the 18th century; the last volume appeared in 1909. Martens became an active member of the *Institut* as early as 1874 and was instrumental in the drafting of its resolutions on the Suez Canal (1879), the slave trade (1885), and navigation on international rivers (1887). He attended the Red Cross conferences and represented Russia at the 1893-1894 Hague conferences on private international law. He was umpire and member of several arbitration panels, acted twice as arbitrator of the PCA and was on the Supreme Prize Court during the Russo-Japanese War. Still, his main achievement in the diplomatic sphere was at The Hague in 1899. Lapradelle praised the 'skill, courage, and firmness' in the way Martens chaired the Second Commission. In Martens' own estimate, the Second Hague Peace Conference of 1907 was a disillusion.

As Grabar points out (*op. cit.*, at p. 385), Martens was an opponent of the natural law school: 'A change in the conditions of international life must result in a change in law, and therefore only a study of the conditions of international life at a particular time, and of its historical development, can elucidate the true international legal consciousness'. He was convinced of the power of international law: 'Brute force never triumphs finally over law; a pathetic theory of *de facto* events never stifles our feelings of right and justice' (quoted *ibid.*, at p. 387). Martens was succeeded by his pupil M. A. de Taube, a legal historian who wrote a biography of his teacher.

One other name of the period may perhaps be singled out here, if only to show the variety of outlooks. Martens' colleague at the chair of international law at the venerable Moscow University was Leonid Kamarovskii (1846-1912). This prominent Russian scholar was strongly influenced by Bluntschli, whose lectures he heard in his early days in Heidelberg. Kamarovskii took the vacant chair in Moscow in 1874 to hold it until his death in 1912. From 1891 he was a full member of the *Institut*; he became a member of the PCA in 1909. Interestingly, Kamarovskii held religious-ethical views, advocating natural law ideas against the predominant positivism of his time. Although not an original thinker, he did much to disseminate international legal ideas by his lectures and articles in reviews. A tireless worker and the author of over two hundred monographs and articles, notably on non-interference and the idea of an international court, he was an optimist, if not idealist, prominent in the peace movement and a resolute champion of a more stable international order. He devoted many articles to questions of limiting war by law, to the peaceful settlement of disputes, international judicial agencies and projects for a United States of Europe.

In Chapter Three, on the Work of The Hague, we have amply discussed the achievements of 19th century Russian diplomacy and the strength of its peace movement. We have now reviewed some of the attainments of its legal scholarship. All these traditions came to an abrupt end

The Russian Count de Nelidov, President of the Second Hague Peace Conference of 1907.

The 1718 Peace Conference of Posarovice in Poland. The print consists of 11 images representing the stages in the peace process

Paul Henri d'Estournelles de Constant (1852-1924).

in the 1917 October Revolution and the ensuing prominence of socialist philosophy. For a full twenty-five years, Russia was to keep aloof from The Hague. The delegates and Judges that were to resume their seats within the UN Organs and the ICJ after World War II represented a completely different world and were instilled with distinctly different views on the functioning of human society.

The Twentieth Century

In our bird's-eye sketch of the gradual development of international law in the West we have now reached the 20th century. In Chapters Four - Seven, on the various aspects of the successive Courts, we have enlarged on the external history of the Courts, matters of jurisdiction, procedure and elections. In doing so, we have implicitly discussed the parameters of the Western legal traditions. As we have stressed throughout, both the genesis of the Courts in itself, and the constituting of their laws, were to a large extent a European accomplishment, if not the very apex of its joint efforts over the centuries.

In passing we have also referred to the specific contributions made by the major representatives from both the continental and the common law traditions. In extolling their names we trust we have paid due tribute to the French, German, English and American international law traditions in the most general terms. Léon Bourgeois, Louis Renault, Henri Fromageot, the Baron d'Estournelles and Jules Basdevant represent the mainstream of French internationalism of the years leading up to the UN era as much as Lord Pauncefote, Lord Cecil, Cecil Hurst and Viscount Finlay represent the British counterpart. In spite of the traditionally strong current of isolationism in the USA, and its heavy repercussions on the League era, the imposing figures of Elihu Root, Frank Kellogg, James Brown Scott, John Bassett Moore and Manley O. Hudson amply illustrate the US involvement in the Hague Courts.

The coat of arms of Great Britain.

The coat of arms of France.

Before discussing in greater detail the lives and works of their successors on the Bench of the ICJ, as will be attempted in Chapter Nine, it may perhaps be worthwhile to resume our sketch and briefly typify the directions the European international law theory took over the past century. In doing so, we may lend more contours to the intellectual atmosphere that inspired the successive Members of the ICJ.

Classical Legal Concepts in a Changing World

In Chapter One it was argued that, in a sense, international law only fully developed in the past hundred years. In maintaining this we had in mind not so much its theory but rather the ambit of its application and its role in international life. In fact, perhaps the most surprising aspect is that, in the past century, the fundamental issues and problems relating to the effectiveness of the legal system in its understanding with power-politics have lost little of their topicality. Indeed, with ever intensifying global organization they have often become ever more urgent. In many respects the overwhelming changes that have taken place on the international scene have presented new problems which baffle the learned world no less than the practical observer.

Admittedly, treaty law did exist well before 1890; but the sheer number of treaties, the areas they cover and the nations they involve have since expanded beyond comparison. It is true that the notion of the international organization was known before that time, but the role international organizations play in the modern international community helped to change the face of the political world, just as the resolutions passed by their organs increasingly take on a norm-creating status. Obviously, arbitration and adjudication were long familiar concepts. Still, the impact of the rich jurisprudence at the disposal of the modern world of learning, and the steering role played by the case-law of institutional courts in the development of doctrine can hardly be overestimated.

Conversely, familiar long standing concepts have blurred in the past century. The roles multinational corporations play today have in many respects obliterated the traditional bipartition into spheres of public and private law. Similarly, with the increasing intrusion of the supranational into the municipal sphere, the classical distinction between the national and international spheres turns out to be less and less functional.

Most important perhaps, within a relatively short span of time, the circle of participants in international law has expanded considerably. Within the UN Organization, the traditionally dominant agents, the Western 'civilized' nations that were instrumental in creating the institution, are nowadays by far outnumbered by the representatives of distinctly different cultures, ideologies and legal traditions. Familiar homogeneity has given way to puzzling diversity. In short, the transformation has been all-encompassing. Not only did the balance of power shift, the nuclear age transformed the very notion of power. Economical gaps tend to translate themselves with political antagonisms.

In our previous paragraph we discussed the gradual tendency towards a more positivist approach to the law, which may perhaps be seen as a practical means of handling this vastly expanded body of law. Similarly, the central position of the Nation-State in Western Europe quite naturally prompted the emphasizing of the values of sovereignty, immunities, territory and boundary issues. Treaties and rules on responsibilities increasingly regulated inter-State contacts. At face value, this well-established *corpus juris* breathed a deceptive neutrality. It is only with the participation of nations from without the inner circle that its inherent weightage in favour of the developed economies came to be felt – and resented. An example that comes to mind is what happened in the past few decades to what one may call the classical and time-honoured doctrine on the law of the sea.

The concept of the freedom of the seas, long heralded as the expression *par excellence* of a universal principle (be this on the basis of natural law or for reasons of expediency), in recent years proved in urgent need of qualification, if only due to the effects of modern technology. To some less developed nations it became economically almost a matter of life or death to have their fishing areas and subsoils protected from intrusion by the high-tech fleets and industries of their more prosperous neighbours – and therefore to insist on extension of their *national* 'economic zones'. Conversely, the rapidly shrinking natural resources of the earth prompted the creation of a régime of planned sharing to safeguard the 'common heritage of mankind'- and therefore the insistence on *international* monitoring. At the UNCLOS III Conference, the exploitation of sea-bed minerals became a true battlefield of conflicting views between developing nations advocating the New International Economic Order and broad profit sharing, and the individualistic approach of the industrialized world championing the liberal concept of free competition.

Also, in recent decades, some lacunae, which seem incredible in retrospect, were filled. The area of human rights is an example. It is only through the experiences of holocaust, genocide, racial discrimination and apartheid that the world has become more sensitive to the fact that whereas aliens traditionally found adequate protection under the umbrella of international law, stateless persons and refugees did not. It is in order to redress this situation that, in recent decades, instruments such as the Genocide Convention, the Conventions on Human Rights and the Covenants on Civil and Political Rights and on Economic, Social and Cultural Rights came into being.

Doctrinal Developments

Among the law theories developed in this century, socialist doctrine has undoubtedly been one of the most significant ones. In theory, the revolutionary Socialist precepts anticipated future events by championing such concepts as human rights, decolonization and self-determination. However, during its transitory period from capitalism to socialism in the inter-war years, the Russian foreign policy left little latitude for constructive debate between the conflicting powerblocks; antagonism prevailed throughout. Also, a comprehensive Soviet concept of international law was virtually non-existent during these years and the Socialist legal scholarship of the period stood as an accessory to the Soviet foreign policy, playing a frank advocatory role within it.

It was only after the Second World War that a general Soviet theory of international law was to be developed, as in the authoritative 1947 manual of the first Soviet Judge on the Bench, Sergei Krylov and his close colleague, the polymath V. Durdenevsky (1889-1963). From then on, the previous 'nihilism' (as it was viewed by the West) was gradually replaced by a search for co-existence in a politically and

Sergei Krylov and Charles De Visscher, Judges of the ICJ.

ideologically divided world. It was in this atmosphere that Tunkin's concept of the coordination of wills materialized and the idea of a general international law was once more endorsed in Russia. The mid-1980s were to witness a further breakthrough. The acceptance by the USSR of the Court's jurisdiction with respect to major human rights agreements, as announced by Mr Gorbachev in the UN General Assembly of 1988, effectively closed an era and opened new perspectives, also for the ICJ.

Hans Kelsen (1883-1973).

In appreciating the other schools of thought that imposed themselves on the Western World in the past fifty years, we must first mention the philosophy of positivism. Probably most influential within this sphere has been the *Reine Rechtslehre*, the 'pure theory of law' that was developed by Hans Kelsen (1883-1973), the Berkeley professor who was born in Prague and educated in Vienna. In his approach, the law was free of both political and historical influences and as if purified from all relics of ethical, metaphysical and natural law concepts. According to Kelsen, States are not at liberty as to whether or not they comply to the law, but are positively bound to do so by a basic, ultimate norm which is created by customary law to which it is in fact identified and to which treaties and instruments issuing therefrom are subjected.

Benjamin Cardozo (1870-1939).

In this respect, the views Kelsen held are diametrically opposed to the tenets maintained by Lasswell and McDougall, the foremost representatives of the school of 'policy science'. This school does not even consider law as an autonomous entity in its own right; on the contrary, it emphasizes it's social roots and methodologically describes the functioning of the law within a wider political context. In defining the goals of the law, basic values such as the safeguarding of human dignity play a prominent part.

In some respects, these views are shared by the school of so-called 'realists', who appreciate the complexities of the decision-making process in the international sphere and consequently the necessarily fluid character of the law. They stress the fallacy of legalism and emphasize the credulity of the pretention to solve conflict by mere regulation. Instead, they accept realities and take a political foundation as the virtual premise for any sound and effective legal system. In their appreciation, over the centuries, most legal concepts have been consistently manipulated to promote self-interest in the power struggle. Hans Morgenthau (1904-1980), a German-born American political scientist, was a leading analyst of the role of power in international politics. His *Politics among Nations* (1948) presents a modern realist approach to the subject. He defines power as the dominant goal in international politics and interprets national interests in these norms (*In Defense of the National Interest*, 1951). At least in their emphasis on the political element these realists match the socialist approach.

One more name should perhaps be mentioned, that of Benjamin Cardozo (1870-1939). To be sure, Cardozo was not an internationalist. Still, the judicial works and attitudes of this Justice of the US Supreme Court (successor to his idol, the revered Oliver Wendell Holmes), who made such an indelible imprint on his colleagues on the bench during the years of the New Deal, combine a razor-sharp mind and astute legal learning with a due regard to practicalities. For these reasons, the major treatises of this liberal legal realist, such as *The Nature of the Judicial Process* (1921), *The Growth of the Law* (1924) and *The Paradoxes of Legal Science* (1928), have influenced and sharpened the thinking of many a modern judge, both international and domestic.

To date, the role that may be reserved for doctrine in the constitution of the new legal order is widely questioned. According to many interpreters, the gap between rule and State behaviour has only widened in past decades. As Steiner observes (*op. cit.* at p. 308), the high aspirations of doctrine to endow international law with a moral force or vision may well become a major source of growth. At the same time, and this has been pointed out time and again in recent years, so far its aspirations have outweighed its achievements. In fact, the lofty ideals of theory have in recent years often shown a dramatic impotence to settle vital topical issues. New reconciliations will need to be sought of theoretical pronouncements with political realities. Enormous challenges lie ahead and it will be the task of international law to rise and meet these challenges, strengthened by its intellectual inheritance from the past and by the contemporary world's expectations of a just universal order.

The Perspective

In the previous pages we have discussed the various and indeed very different law traditions which, in a process of growth that covers over two millenia, were gradually assimilated, finally to be incorporated in what to the modern scholar appears not just as a conglomerate of laws but, indeed, a solid code of Western international law – a code which in previous centuries did not shrink from presenting itself as a system that could claim universal application. Until the 20th century, whatever the political conflicts were that made demands on the legal order, these were solved within an acknowledged cultural unity and common social traditions. The past hundred years witnessed the worldwide emergence of politically and economically competing forces from completely different social traditions and legal cultures. These conflicts of interest and clashes of doctrine are forging a new international order more adequate to face the many challenges and imminent perils ahead. With the previous internal coherence of the legal fabric in perfect disarray, paradoxically, the urge for collective decision-making has dramatically grown. Some form of agreement has to be reached, shared principles have to be formulated, if only to serve for the time being. A certain readiness for compromise has to prevail until, in the next century, a new dominant teleology may emerge, based on universally acknowledged concepts.

The international law of the future will need to incorporate the wisdom of diverse philosophies. It will have to draw upon the general legal experience of mankind. The injection of all these notions will substantially enrich its concepts even though, in the short term, the process will not facilitate the practical application of the law-in-the-making. In facing these challenges, the reassuring lesson of history is that we are in fact just turning a new page in an ever-ongoing process of adaptation – witness not just the Western law tradition but the history of most of the other time-honoured legal cultures to which we will now turn.

'Never too old to learn'. Judges Hackworth and Read at the English Church in The Hague in April 1946.

Next page:
'Der Mars ist nun im Ars'. A print with rhyming legends illustrating the return of peace in the German countries after the Thirty-Year war. Cologne, 1650.

Hier Reisen frey vnd Wolgemuth, Die Kramer: vnd die Kaufleut Guth.
Frey Sicher ist es in dem Feldt, Was man zu Thun man wolbestelt.
Schmeckt wol Lex Ars vnd ist guth Der wol darein begreiffen Thut
Braucht die Zung zur Sußigkeit, Lex, Ars, ist euch zum dienst berei
Der MARS ist nun im ARS.
Wohlgemeint, vnd boß Verstanden, Machet manche Schrifft zu schanden
Sa, Lex vnd Ars, Die steigen Wieder hoch,
Ihr seydt ist vmb, der Mars hatt nnn ein Loch,
Es hatt genug gedaurt, daß der Mars,
Hatt Ars getrillt, Nun ist der Mars im Ars.
2. Nun halten Lex Vnd Ars, den Mars im Zaum.
Nun Wirdt Vnd ist mir auß dem Mars ein traum,
Im Ars ist Lust, im Lex ist Süßigkeit,
Im Mars gestanck, Von Puluer sturm Vnd streitt
3. Wo Lex vnd Ars, die Oberhandt behelt,
Da scheust der Mars nicht mehr so grob ins feldt
Der Mars ist roth Vnndt Schwartz, Lex aber Weiß,
Vnd Ars Wie Goldt, Lex Ars behelt den preyß.
4. So finster Vnndt so grewlich es im Mars,
So Sonnenklar Vnnd lieblich ist Lex Ars,
Lex Ars sind freundt; vnd halten nichts vom Mars,
Es sey dann Mars ein freundt vom Lex vnd Ars.
5. Wolan O Mars scheuß nur nicht mehr so grob,
Es zörnen sonst Lex vnnd auch Ars darob,
Wan Ars regiert, vnnd Lex die Zunge braucht,
So zittert Mars, scheust er gleich das es raucht
6. Im Mars ist nichts das Vns hertz erfrewt
Lex aber hat viel lust vnndt liebligkeitt
desgleichen Ars, Ars ist so wunder fein
Daß Jedermann im Ars will Burger sein
7. Lex mich im Mars sehr Wenig schützen kan,
Dann Wo der Mars regiert, kombt Lex nicht an,
Nun aber Mars im Ars, Lex mich beschirmt
Vnd hilfft nun nicht daß Mars viel scheust vnstürmt,
8. Küst mir nun Ars vnd Lex vn flücht dem Mars,
Verflucht sey Mars, gekust sey Lex vnndt Ars,
O süsses Lex, o dreymahl schöner Ars
Wir küssen euch, kombt an Verflucht sey Mars
9. Mars scheust vnd stinckt, Ars aber ist sehr mild,
Lex angenehm, der Mars ein greulich bildt,
Ars machet gunst, Lex hat daß lob, was Ars,
Was greulich ist, daß ist furwar im Mars,
10. Weg mit dem Mars, heran mit Lex vnd Ars,
Ars liebt die ruh, Lex auch, krieg aber Mars,
Viel lieber fried als streitt, weil Mars verzehrt,
Was Ars erwirbt, Mars raubt, Lex Ars ernehrt.
Stecke dein nas tieff in Lex Ars Besser als in verstorbenen Mars
Den alle Hochgelehrte Leuth, Schmecken Lex Ars ahnt ugentheit
Mars vnser alter kriegs leuth Gott, Ligt Hier in Armis vnd ist Thot.
Ziehen auff ein ander Orth
Lerm ist gethan wir mussen fort
Hie ligt der Krieg.
Gott erbarme nun Sich.
Odu Thoter Mars Viuat Lex Ars
Mars mit seine waffen Ist Hier entschlaffe

The Asian Component

To ascertain the contribution of the Asian world to contemporary international law and its involvement in the settlement of disputes as attempted in The Hague, it is imperative – in view of historical, religious and cultural differences – to distinguish the Far Eastern, and notably the Chinese and Japanese legal traditions from the South and South East Asian tradition as exemplified by the Indian legal world. Yet another preliminary comment needs to be made. The contribution of the Asian world to contemporary international law cannot be understood or assessed without reference to the teachings and traditions of Hinduism and Buddhism, the two predominant religions in this area, which have to such a large extent determined the way in which the Asian man views the world. Both of these religions originated on the Indian sub-continent, but radiated outwards to influence the civilization and culture of much of Asia.

Admittedly, Asia was subsequently influenced by two other world religions – Islam and Christianity – and in the Far East it developed its own distinctive traditions. Islam reached the Indian sub-continent through trade and conquest and many areas, formerly predominantly Hindu or Buddhist – such as Pakistan, Bangladesh and Kashmir – embraced the Islamic faith. The same applied in regions further afield like Indonesia. The result was that the Indian sub-continent became home to three world religions whose constant interaction enriched its culture and

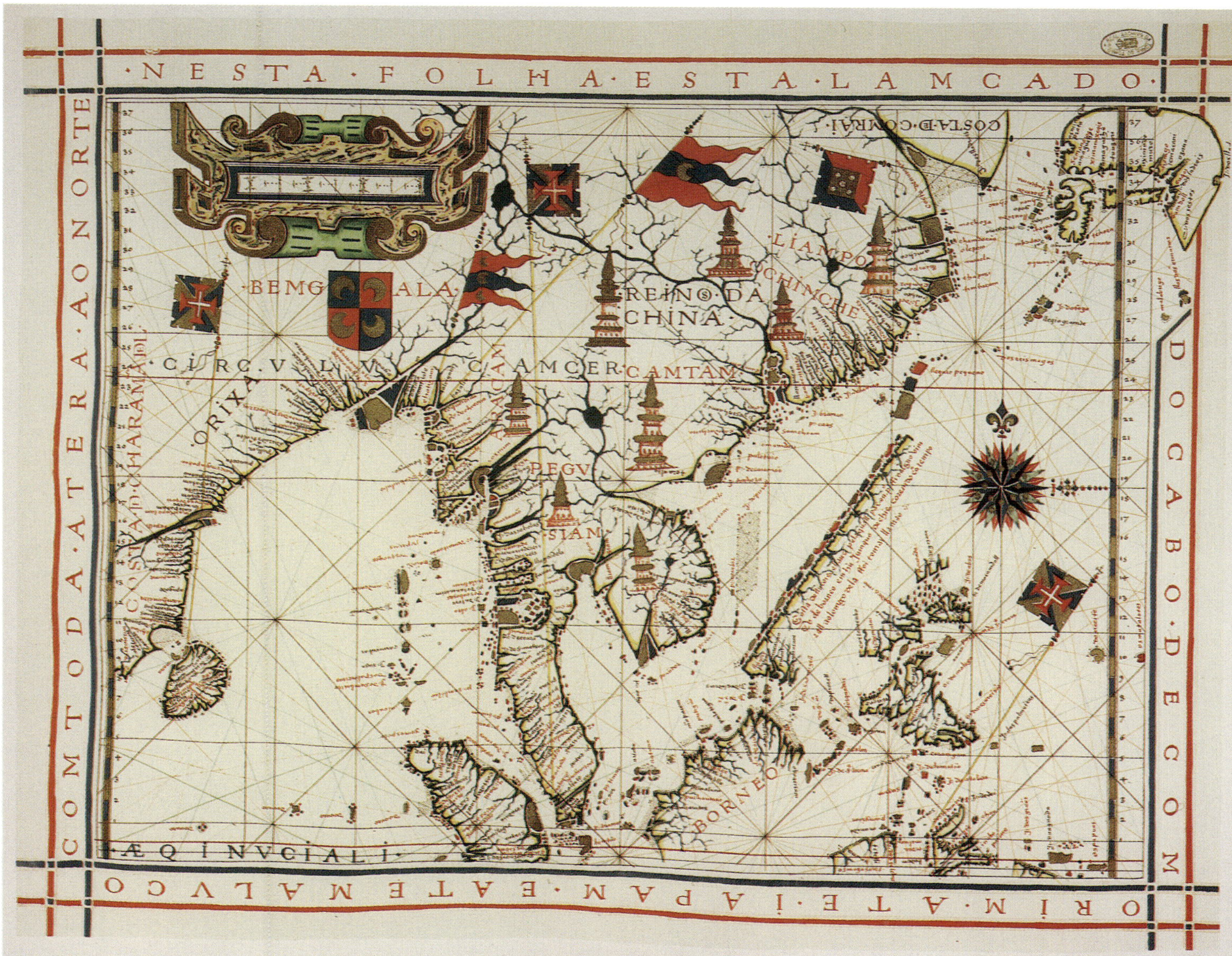

FERNÃO VAZ DOURADO, 1571

Atlas de dezoito folhas – Fol. 3 – Atlas of eighteen sheets

Arquivo Nacional da Torre do Tombo, Lisboa

traditions and through it affected many outlying areas as well.

Similar observations can be made for Christianity. Although communities of Christians were known in South India throughout the Christian era, commencing according to some traditions with Thomas the Apostle, the wider spread of Christianity on the Indian subcontinent came only in modern times with the European expansion into Asia, commencing with Portuguese enclaves in Goa and elsewhere. Under British rule, Christianity gained strength and support. There was also some denigration of classic Hindu beliefs and a lack of respect for its practices, which occasioned a great deal of resentment among the local population. Many Hindus, Gandhi among them, showed profound respect for the ethical teachings of the Gospels, as epitomized in such discourses as the Sermon on the Mount, yet found it impossible to subscribe to their theological superstructure. The relationship of the subcontinent with Christianity was also complicated by the unequal balance of political power and cultural influence.

However, an appreciation of Asian attitudes to law and international relations is impossible without an awareness of the pervasive influence of Hinduism and Buddhism and it is to these two religions that we must primarily turn.

HINDUISM AND THE INTERNATIONAL LAW TRADITION IN SOUTH AND SOUTHEAST ASIA

Unlike Confucianism, Buddhism, Islam or Christianity, Hinduism cannot be linked to a single source – prince, prophet or redeemer – nor can its genesis be fixed at a certain date. The history of Hinduism in India can be traced back to about 1500 BC, when the Brahmanism of the invading tribes of Aryans, the ancestors of the Iranians, blended with the social customs of the indigenous population of the Indian subcontinent, the legendary 'Dravidian' tribes. Hinduism was therefore the outcome of a long process of constant interaction in the religious and social spheres, sometimes referred to as 'Sanskritization'.

During the centuries around the beginning of the Christian era, Hinduism spread all over the Mediterranean world and through vast areas of South-East Asia. Although there is little evidence of its influence on China and Japan – except indirectly, through the intermediary of Buddhism – it reached out as far as Vietnam and Bali in many varying forms, displaying distinctive local features attuned to regional tradition. It did not fail to have some impact on Greek thought either, as witness early Pythagorean concepts or the 3rd century mystical gnosis as represented by Plotinus. Again, frequent contacts along the merchant routes made the Roman world at least marginally aware of Hindu concepts, although it never became familiar with its more recondite aspects. The Middle Ages saw the rise of devotional movements often ascribed to Tamil influence and a sometimes aggressive persecution by Hindu sects of contemporary Buddhism.

With the advent of Islam, royal patronage of Hinduism disappeared in much of the area. Muslim rule varied from a strongly anti-Hindu policy to mild tolerance. Syncretism probably reached its pinnacle in the reign of Akbar (1556-1605), who took a great interest in Hinduism, as he did in Christianity, inviting learned men of all religions to his Court. However, orthodoxy was soon restored. With the advent of British rule, harmonizing tendencies were suppressed. From the 16th century onwards, Portuguese Roman Catholic priests had made converts for Christianity, as Danish Protestant missionaries from the early 19th century, until the British East India Company formally barred any such activities in order to forestall any antagonism. Later on, the Company was to maintain a policy of strict impartiality in matters of religion.

In the opening decades of the 19th century a Hindu reform movement was launched which gained strength all through the century, reaching its zenith in the spiritualism of Ramakrishna and inspiring Western movements such as the New York based Theosophical Society of Helena Blavatsky (1875). Obviously, the revival was closely linked to growing Indian nationalism and, later on, the call for independence. To his followers, Mahatma Gandhi – the leader of the independence movement – was the quintessence of the Hindu tradition. However,

Mohandas Karamchand Gandhi (1869-1948), the leader of the Indian independence and social justice movements and foremost theorist and practitioner of active nonviolence.

increasing nationalism, notably after the partition between India and Pakistan in 1947, also widened the gulf between Hindu and Muslim, culminating in the assassination of Gandhi in 1948. In recent decades, the Hindu world has been applying its time-honoured flexibility to the need to adapt itself to changing global conditions.

The Vedic Law Tradition

The basis of Hindu belief, the Veda ('Knowledge') consists of a collection of sacred scriptures, divine revelations which are regarded as the reflection of eternal Truth. They range from theology to epic stories and to law. As presented in one of its most influential tracts, the 'Song of the Lord' or *Bhagavadgita* (200 BC), three paths to salvation lay open to the Hindu: the disinterested discharge of ritual and social obligations; contemplative training and meditative concentration; and devotion to a personal God.

Again, according to early scholarly writings in the Vedic tradition (the *Vedangas*), society was ritually stratified into four classes, each of which had its own *dharma* (law), or eternal law of conduct. These rules of conduct were contained in legal manuals and elaborate commentaries or *Smritis*. They were known as *dharmasastras*, because they represented scientific and analytical studies of *dharma*, addressing the duties of people at various stages of life, and included the rights and duties of kings. It is here that we find the basis of Hindu law properly speaking. Worth mentioning in this respect is of course the impressive epic *Mahabharata*, which contains a systematic body of political ideas and a comprehensive theory of kingship and government. Entire books, notably the well-known *Bhagavadgita*, are devoted to philosophical and moral discourses. Noteworthy too is the *Arthasastra*, the best known ancient Indian treatise on the principles of law and government, which was rediscovered in 1904, and which around 300 BC enlarged upon the 'duties' of a king towards his subjects rather than his divine 'prerogatives'.

Prominent in this Hindu tradition is the so-called Code of Manu, traditionally ascribed to the legendary first legislator of the Indian world. The Code was conceived around 200 BC, and comprised 18 categories. Mediated by its schools of commentators, this doctrine became the moral code of Hindu society. In other words, in the Hindu tradition, law in the juridical sense remained completely embedded in religious law and practice, which led a recent commentator, Menon, to argue that '[the] early divorce of law from religion furnishes the master key to comprehension of the two great systems, oriental and occidental jurisprudence'.

Hindu law, as we saw, is of Indian extraction. At the same time, as Menon maintains, Hindu law is a personal law:

> Within certain limits it may be said that Hindus take the law with them wherever they go. ... To the Hindu jurist, law is nothing but a collection of human practices or customs based upon principles of morality and natural justice accepted by the general consensus of a society at a particular time. ... To violate a custom is, to a Hindu, nothing short of a sacrilege.

In this perspective, the recent attempt by the Indian Parliament to codify its law and 'lift it out of its archaic grooves' is a task perhaps best compared to the work initiated by Emperor Justinian on behalf of the Roman legal world nearly 15 centuries ago – albeit with one essential difference as, in the Hindu conception, law emanates from a source superior to the king. Admittedly, the sages and philosopher-legislators of the Hindu world had no political authority; they could however lay claim to the profoundest social veneration. Consequently, Menon concludes that 'Hindu

The coat of arms of Sri Lanka.

law is thus primarily the result of social organization, while positive law, as enunciated by western thinkers, is the fruit of political organization'.

Hindu customary law was based on the pillars of social utility and communal necessity, not unlike the Common Law of England. In fact, immemorial customs were the core of Hindu law and the elements of long usage and timeless observance were its very prerequisites. In day to day practice these customs had the force of law – that is, as long as they were not contrary to national policy or prejudicial to the public interest or morality. For, unlike laws in the strict sense, the idea of custom allows of course for regional variants and different practices within a single nation. Customs have their foundation in the collective will or common consent of the people, laws in the will or pleasure of a sovereign or State. In other words, customs, unlike laws, are by definition decentralized.

In modern times, the still prevailing variety of customs within the Hindu world has become increasingly unmanageable, Menon argues:

> Hindu law has suffered from lack of precision and certainty because of its decentralized complexities and scattered character.... Viewed today, the principles of Hindu law constitute an anomaly unparalleled in the history of the world.

Codification, therefore, seems inevitable, as the Indian Parliament has acknowledged. We will now see how the Hindu law tradition has affected the foreign relations of the Indian world.

International Law

In the opening pages of his 1969 monograph *India and International Law*, the former President of the International Court, Nagendra Singh, wrote:

> If the concept of the Law of Nations comprises a body of rules, whether customary or written, which the States in their intercourse with each other consider as binding, it would perhaps not be quite accurate to observe, as Oppenheim has done, that International Law 'is in its origin essentially a product of Christian civilisation, and began gradually to grow from the second half of the middle ages'. Apart from the fact that the Christian civilisation may not have quite enjoyed a monopoly in regard to prescription of rules to govern interstate conduct, it is submitted that the concept of Christianity itself hampered the development of international law on the broad basis on which it exists today. For example, the principle that the rules of civilized conduct among nations applied to States within Christendom alone and nothing of a binding nature could govern the relations of a Christian State with a non-Christian State, did lasting damage to the development of the correct concepts of modern international law which recognizes political entities irrespective of their religious beliefs (*op. cit.* at p. 1-2).

Nagendra Singh from India, Judge (1973-1988) and President (1985-1988) of the ICJ

Alberico Gentili, in his *De jure belli* of 1598, narrates a legendary encounter between Alexander the Great and the Indian king Porus. After having been taken captive by Alexander and upon being asked by his conqueror how he wished to be treated, Porus simply replied: 'Treat me as a King of India'. The incident illustrates one of those typical features of Indian thought in matters of international relations, namely its reliance on humaneness and chivalry.

Universalism and the Code of Manu

Perhaps the most striking of these features and indeed a quite unique characteristic of ancient Indian thinking with respect to international relations was its insistence on universalism. This notion had religious as well as political connotations, as is illustrated by the postulated universality of the individual soul. In political theory this concept was exemplified by a view of world government based on non-violence towards all creation and the indiscriminate equality of mankind. With regard to inter-State conduct, no distinction was recognized between believers and non-believers. Thus, it was expressly enjoined by the sacred laws of *Dharma Sastra* that all belligerents at all times and in all circumstances must adhere to the accepted rules of warfare.

In the early days this idea of universalism found its most meaningful expression in the afore-mentioned Code of Law ascribed to the ancient sage Manu around 200 BC. Particularly noteworthy for our purposes are the chapters of the Code that are devoted to the laws of war and the diplomatic immunity of envoys. The Code of Manu explicitly distinguished between combatants and non-combatants. It provided that no civilian nor any one who had surrendered should ever be killed. Chivalry governed the conduct of administration of enemy occupied territory. After defeat at the hands of king Chandragupta Maurya in 305 BC, the Macedonian king Seleucos was effectively accorded the same treatment as that which King Porus had claimed for himself from Alexander twenty years earlier. This is a consistent strain throughout Indian history. The romantic anecdotes relating to the way Alexander treated the family of the defeated Persian King Darius after Gaugamela are easily paralleled by the stories from the chronicles enlarging upon the contacts between Indian kings and Muslim sultans in the 15th and 16th centuries, as witness for instance the treatment of the family of the defeated Sultan Ibrahim after the battle of Panipat in AD 1526.

The fascination of the Code of Manu – as Nagendra Singh in his various writings on the subject has convincingly demonstrated – is its emphasis on the universal and comprehensive application of its legal concepts, irrespective of caste, creed or religion.

Understandably, this circumstance did much to promote the enforcement of the Code of Manu in the vast and multicultural area that had gradually come under the Indian sphere of influence in the course of previous centuries, and which reached as far as the present Indonesia and Thailand. Conversely, it seems very likely that the pursuit of timeless, absolute values was in itself the outcome of a long evolutionary process, in which the interplay of various ethnic, religious and ideological elements had left its mark on this veritable melting pot of civilizations. One has only to call to mind the prejudiced verdict of the Christian world at the Council of Constance, as late as AD 1418, when it was argued that no rules of a binding nature could govern the relations of Christian States with the non-Christian world, and the similar doctrine of some orthodox Islamic jurists, to appreciate the unique character of this ancient Indian conception of international law.

A drawing presented by the Government of Pakistan, representing 'Peace'.

Territory

The concept of territory in ancient Indian polity comprised both land and water, and included jurisdiction over the coastal sea. Jurisdiction was complete: no king could make use of another king's lands without the latter's previous formal permission. According to the written law, the acquisition of territory was explicitly limited to unconquered and unacquired lands, in other words *terra nullius*. This is to say that the distinction between the occupation of unoccupied land and the appropriation of land previously acquired by others was very clear. In fact, *Smriti* writers advocated the former, while disapproving of the latter. Actual practice was slightly more complex. Acquisition of territory by gift, inheritance or as a result of a treaty was generally accepted, but so was the recovery of land by force from the hands of usurpers or the occupation of another king's lands in order to enforce the right to settle a dispute of a different nature.

Not too much is known of Indian ideas relating to the law of the sea. Coastal states had fishing rights within the adjoining waters and fishermen relinquished parts of their haul as a tax in much the same way as ships calling at harbours had to pay a toll. However, sovereign rights extending over open sea and oceans certainly did not exist.

Diplomatic Relations

Another illustration of the intrinsic universality in Indian thought, irrespective of religion or civilization, can be observed in the field of diplomatic relations. Unlike early Islam or Christendom, ancient India had ambassadors accredited far outside the area of its own civilization. Even if the modern concept of permanent embassies was not known at the time, the institution of *Dutas* and *Rajduts*, that is the sending of envoys for *ad hoc* work or for more permanent sojourns at foreign courts was well established. The Greek historian Strabo records that in the early days of Emperor Augustus ambassadors from India came to visit Rome for commercial purposes. A Sri Lankan diplomatic mission to Rome was recorded by Gibbon as well as, more colourfully, by Milton in his praise of the 'then great and glorious Rome' in *Paradise Regained* (IV. 61-76):

Thence to the gates cast round thine eye, and see
What conflux issuing forth, or entring in ...
Or Embassies from Regions far remote
In various habits on the Appian road ...
From India and the golden Chersoness,
And utmost Indian Isle Taprobane,
Dusk faces with white silken Turbants wreath'd.

Both Christendom and Islam, as a rule, confined official diplomatic intercourse to their own spheres of belief and exchanges of ambassadors beyond their areas of civilization are hardly recorded.

Along with this conduct in matters of diplomatic relations, there was the practice of diplomatic protection and the granting of a right of asylum to persons seeking protection from political persecution. Not surprisingly, from the early days, this right was cherished throughout India as the most noble right exercised by a sovereign independent State and one based on considerations of humanity, even if in practice this often gave rise to complications in inter-State relations, if not to outright war. Inter-State relations, incidentally, were as a rule entrusted to the King himself, as the highest Organ of State, though in practice he could be represented by *Dutas* or *Rajduts*. This practice was well developed and envoys were treated with all due ceremony.

An interesting anecdote from the reign of Harsha (606-647 AD>), the last of the great Emperors of ancient India, illustrates the prevailing code of diplomatic immunity. Having sent envoys to the Emperor of China, he found this gesture reciprocated. However, it so happened that a large Chinese diplomatic mission was staying in India, when Harsha died suddenly. In the ensuing anarchy the usurper of Harsha's throne killed some of the Chinese envoys. At that juncture, the kings of both Eastern India and Tibet came to the rescue and offered the Chinese compensation on behalf of Harsha. In a similar vein, interesting tales circulated with regard to the arrival of Sir Thomas Roe at Surat in September 1615. Roe was the officially accredited envoy of James I to the Moghul Court and entrusted with the negotiation of a commercial treaty and trade agreements. From the many incidents that took place during his mission (the 'barbarous usage' of the search of his luggage on the one hand, his refusal to observe the oriental practice of touching the ground with the forehead on the other) one can gain an idea of the shared intention to respect the time-honoured immunites and privileges of envoys and the widely differing customs in these respects between the Western and Oriental nations.

The coat of arms of India.

The Law of Treaties

The primary purpose of treaties in ancient India was for registering inter-state transactions connected with territorial disputes. These treaties were therefore of a bilateral nature; multilateral conventions or treaties of the law-making type were unknown. A precaution for the due observance of treaties was the taking of hostages. Thus, Alexander once received a thousand hostages and, conversely, the Kushan Emperor Kaniska is recorded to have kept hostages from a Chinese State which had entered into treaty obligations with the Kushan Empire. At the same time 'peace dependent on honesty or oath' was regarded as 'immutable both in this and the next world' and the swearing by fire, water, plough, the shoulder of an elephant or the hip of a horse was common practice. Treaties could be repudiated if conditions and circumstances had radically changed since the time of signing, which may perhaps be seen as a rudimentary form of the *rebus sic stantibus* principle.

The same held true for trade and commercial agreements, as the first British envoys on behalf of the East India Company and King James I, Captain Hawkins and the aforementioned Sir Thomas Roe, were to find out in the opening years of the 17th Century. It was precisely these trading privileges, conferred by imperial decree on the British, which re-introduced Christian civilization to India. Thus, in due course, commercial bonds came to link what religious tenets kept apart. Here, as elsewhere, the dynamic law of State practice came to dictate relations, rather than rigid theory, however divine its origin.

The Islamic attitude to treaties will be described in the section on Islamic law. Its political hegemony, which dominated the sub-continent for some ten centuries, drew to a close with the death of the last great Moghul Emperor Aurangzeb (1707). Hindu ideas regarding treaties, as recorded in the ancient *Srutis* and *Smritis*, were generally respected during the time of Islamic rule. After severe initial clashes, some form of tolerance and co-existence between the rules of Aryan and Islamic law was gradually attained on the basis of reason and reciprocity. Throughout the area, most indigenous Indian States, in their mutual contacts, invariably felt bound by the Hindu Code. The same held true, though to a much lesser degree, in matters of foreign relations, as exemplified in the law of treaties. Islam's relations with non-believers were governed by the word of the Qur'an (IX.7): 'As long as they act uprightly by you, do you act uprightly by them.'; in fact, the principle of *pacta sunt servanda* was a cardinal rule of Islamic law.

With the rapid expansion of Western settlements throughout its territory – be this through diplomatic manoeuvring or at gunpoint – India, during what is called its colonial period (generally taken as being from 1707 to 1947), saw a gradual crystallization of most concepts of modern international law. At times hampered by cultural differences, disturbed by political intrigue, or confused by the ambiguous status of the European settlers *vis-à-vis* their mother countries, general notions such as the immunity of envoys, the right of asylum, and the principle of acquisition of territory by conquest became firmly established.

Similarly, treaty relations between Rajput princes, Muslim sultans and European monarchs expanded enormously from Burma to Jahore. Aitchison's impressive 14 volume compilation of treaties (published 1929-1933) is authoritative in this regard, and also discloses the equality of relations between the contracting parties. Generally speaking, Nagendra Singh concludes that, despite the frequent conflicts and mutual atrocities, the advent of Christianity on the Asian scene only helped to confirm the prevailing legal concepts subscribed to the established political entities representing the Hindu and Muslim world.

Towards Independence

Even the conflicts that marked three centuries of colonization reveal some noteworthy features that are relevant to international relations and peculiar to the Indian tradition. Alongside acts of violence such as the massacres ranging from the slaughter in Dutch-held Amboina in 1605, through the 'Black hole of Calcutta' of 1756 and the 1857 Mutiny, to the Rowlett Act and the 1919 Amritsar slaughter, there is the impressive silent testimony of the 1939 Quit India Movement, Mahatma Gandhi's civil disobedience campaign among the masses and his *Paraupvasa* or fasting unto death. The use of non-violence as a moral

The coat of arms of Thailand.

When visiting the Court in May 1985, His Holinesss Pope John Paul II was welcomed by President Nagendra Singh.

weapon to extract *self-rule* from a militarily superior power, was fully perfected under Mahatma Gandhi.

The India Independence Act of 1947 heralded the unparalleled expansion of international life that was to follow in the whirlwind of decolonization which began to sweep through the East. In its significance for global inter-State relations, this great achievement of the second part of this century is matched only by the impact on human rights of the anti-slavery acts of the previous century.

The Bench of the International Court of Justice reflected the dramatic consequences of the Indian struggle for independence. The internal crises that overwhelmed the multicultural world of the subcontinent are personified in the career of Judge and Court President Zafrulla Khan, who was four times an Indian Minister in the inter-war years and later Pakistani Minister for Foreign Affairs. In the jurisprudence of the Court, these colonial and internal conflicts are reflected in the *Right of Passage over Indian Territory* case (Portugal v. India, 1955-1960), the *Appeal Relating to the Jurisdiction of the ICAO Council* (India v. Pakistan, 1971-1972) and the *Trial of Pakistani Prisoners of War* case (Pakistan v. India, 1973) which will be dealt with in more detail in the appropriate chapter.

As a footnote to this long tale, a truly historic and almost symbolic meeting took place on 13 May 1985, when His Holiness Pope John Paul II, paying a visit to the Court, was welcomed in the Hall of the Peace Palace by H. E. Judge Nagendra Singh, then President of the ICJ.

BUDDHISM AND THE INTERNATIONAL LAW TRADITION OF THE FAR EAST

According to many critics, Buddhism deals with ethics rather than law. Moreover, it has been maintained that the political teachings of Buddhism – although felt throughout Asia in their interplay with Confucian and Hindu belief systems – have only sporadically had any impact on the foreign policy of the Asian nations, and never exterted a sustained influence. On the other hand, as Jayatilleke among others has convincingly demonstrated, Buddhist precepts have undoubtedly had a very direct bearing on the way the Asian peoples look upon notions such as law, justice and equity. Apart from this, as we shall see, Buddhism contains certain elements which in due course have become accepted principles of modern international law.

The Buddha, the 'Enlighted One', flourished in North East India somewhere between 500 and 350 BC. A son of the ruler of a kingdom, he was living in luxury and comfort when, at 29, he decided to renounce his princely life and become a wandering ascetic. In his search for truth and enlightenment, he attained mystical states of elevated consciousness, practising severe austerities and self-mortification. Having accomplished his goal of enlightenment he resolved to teach his fellow men what he had discovered about the nature of reality and the means of transcending the human condition.

The Buddhist religion and philosophy, which spread to Korea, China and Japan, played a prominent role in the spiritual, cultural and social life of much of the Eastern world. Towards the end of the 3rd Century BC its basic doctrine was well-established and formalized in the *Theravada* tradition. In later centuries these texts were supplemented by what is called the *Mahayana* tradition, based on a broader interpretation of the religious texts than was permitted by *Theravada*. *Mahayana* became the predominant form of Buddhism, which had an immeasurable impact on the Chinese, Japanese and Korean civilizations.

Buddhist Legal Concepts

When trying to assess the position of Buddhism with respect to the law, one must bear in mind that Buddhism is not a theistic religion which relates law directly to the divine will – often to find man-made law in conflict with the latter. Contrary to strict legal positivism, which precludes any extra-legal considerations, Buddhist conceptions of law cannot possibly be separated from its moral and social philosophy. In fact, Buddhism looks upon law as meaningful only in so far as it

Two warring tribes lay their weapons at the feet of the Buddha, after hearing a sermon preached to them on the importance of peace and reconciliation. From a drawing by Tissa Ranasinghe.

is implanted in this ethical foundation. As Professor Jayatilleke puts it:

> Buddhism is a religion with a philosophy. It recommends a way of life, which follows from its view of life, which is justified on the basis of the philosophy of Buddhism.

It is this philosophy which puts into motion the 'Supreme Wheel of the Law' or 'The Rule of Righteousness', as the Buddha himself termed it in his first sermon.

One of the basic concepts of Buddhism with respect to the law is that correct, law-abiding behaviour must result from charity, love and understanding, not from the fear of legal sanctions. In similar vein, the *spirit* of the law is considered of higher value than its *letter*. It follows that, in Buddhist thought, not much emphasis is placed on legislation. It is maintained that conformity can be ensured without it, whereas legislation itself contributes to a certain legalistic frame of mind, which is perhaps less welcome in that it tends to invite people to conform to the letter while forgetting the spirit of the law (let alone taking the letter as an excuse for violating the spirit).

Another aspect of legislation in Buddhist eyes is that it tends to promote rigidity and conservatism, whereas Buddhist legal thinking entertains very progressive views, as is illustrated by the well-known parable of the two men who went out in search of treasure and along the road stumbled upon ever new discoveries. The one clung to his first treasure obstinately,

while the other kept on replacing his most recent finds by his latest new discovery. The gist of this parable is that one should gradually discard ideas which have become less relevant in favour of new ideas of higher value, so that, according to the Buddhist way of thinking, legislation serves no more than very pragmatic and utilitarian ends.

International Law

Let us now turn to the international field. Undoubtedly the most prominent Buddhist concept of relevance to the international sphere, is the idea of a common humanity which transcends all national and racial barriers. In short, in Buddhist thought all men are deemed to be equal. In political terms this concept inspired a theory of social contract, in which sovereignty was vested in the people and the State was considered instrumental to the welfare of the people. International relations between the various political entities were regulated by a common philosophy, the *Dhamma*.

Indeed the Buddhist world view goes much further, and in this may have a valuable message for modern jurisprudence. One such aspect of Buddhist thought on rights and duties, the wisdom of which is being increasingly appreciated by modern legal philosophy, is the idea that rights and duties are not limited to human beings. All living inhabitants of the planet – plants and trees not excluded – have a place in Buddhism's universal scheme: the circle of human duties does not end with man. Modern jurisprudence is now beginning to recognize this idea in the context of ecological considerations.

Furthermore, just as the Buddha aimed at the spiritual welfare of mankind, in the same way Buddhism entertains the idea of a world authority based on law, which is expected to ensure the material welfare of the peoples by setting up ideal forms of government and constitutions throughout the world. Once the lessons of history had taught mankind to realize the utter folly of its tireless search for power and it became receptive to these lofty ideas, there would be an authority over the earth 'girdled by the oceans without the rod or the sword through the victory of *Dhamma*', which would result in international peace and prosperity.

Actually, this worldwide authority was identified with the philosophy of the *Dhamma*. Therefore, it was not so much man, as rather the law itself and – even more importantly – the Principle of Righteousness that eventually was to rule the international order. This Principle of Righteousness embodied the Ten Virtues of Buddhism, these being the reflection of its moral code and ethical values. The Principle imposed four very specific requirements on the State. It had to protect the three classes of its citizenry, viz. professionals, religious teachers and the military; it had to prevent crime, to guard against unemployment and poverty and, in determining its policy, to avail it-

ASSOCIATION OF SOUTH-EAST ASIAN NATIONS

Although not the first attempt at regional cooperation in South East Asia, ASEAN has certainly proved to be the most effective and endurable organization in the area. It was founded in 1967 as a natural association of the contiguous States of Indonesia, Malaysia, Thailand, the Philippines and Singapore, which shared economic, socio-political and cultural structures. Established at a time of tension and instability in the region, and faced with both internal and external problems, ASEAN – which in itself therefore was a triumph of diplomacy – initially had to move cautiously.

A first success was the establishment, at the 1976 summit on Bali, of the Treaty of Amity and Cooperation in South-East Asia. Among other things, the Treaty deals with the pacific settlement of disputes under the auspices of a High Council which at the request of parties may provide good offices, mediation and conciliation efforts, without excluding other means of settlement. In the 1976 Declaration, together with economic and commercial objectives in spheres such as commodities and preferential trading arrangements, a study of judicial cooperation was proposed aiming at, amongst other things, an ASEAN extradition treaty.

An agreement was signed, also on Bali, by which a Permanent Secretariat was established at Jakarta, and a full-time Secretary-General appointed to head the 5 Directors-General of the ASEAN National Coordinating Agencies. Later that year, an Expert Group was formed to review economic cooperation. A zone of peace, freedom and neutrality was considered and Committees were formed to explore trade and industrial cooperation with the 'dialogue partners' as they were called, the EEC, Australia and Japan. Though perhaps not as yet so far advanced as other regional groupings in terms of integration and supra-national decision-making, in the economic sphere, at least, the regional organization within ASEAN has proved to be a highly successful initiative.

self of the advice of enlightened philosophers.

It is hard to imagine that this idea of so modern-looking a democratic welfare State was conceived in about the 6th Century BC. For this very reason, it comes as no surprise that the implementation of this philosophy in a multicultural world that was firmly steeped in Hindu doctrine, the Code of Manu and Confucianism proved rather problematic. In fact, in large parts of the Eastern world, the influence of Buddhism on State policies remained at all times peripheral; it did of course contain some dangerous potentialities for absolute rule, but it never replaced the Hindu theory of the State and it never reached out to the masses either, although it did at times exert a decisive influence on enlightened rulers.

Prominent among these rulers was the 'the greatest of kings' as he was called, the Buddhist ruler Asoka (3rd Century BC). This last Indian Emperor of the Mauryan dynasty guaranteed absolute equality for all his subjects in all legal proceedings. In his fourteen 'Rock-Edicts', one of the world's outstanding documents on human rights, a universal message of peace is proclaimed, the use of force is abandoned, and the doctrine of peaceful co-existence is carved on rock pillars for all to read. In his *Edict of Toleration*, in Rock Edict V, we read:

> A man must not do reverence to his own sect or disparage that of another man without reason. Deprecation should be for specific reasons only, because the sects of other people all deserve reverence for one reason or another. By thus acting, a man exalts his own sect, and at the same time does service to the sects of other people. By acting contrariwise, a man hurts his own sect, and does disservice to the sects of other people.

When, in 1954, Prime Minister Nehru put forward his Pañca Sîla principles for peaceful co-existence, he explicitly referred to Asoka.

Still, Asoka's legendary example was not the only one of its kind. In the course of time, all through the Asian world, rulers inspired by Buddhist thought applied its principles of justice, thus improving on the social conditions of their subjects. In Sri Lanka, in the 3rd Century AD, King Tissa reputedly set aside bodily injury as a penalty, while a millennium later another enlightened ruler abolished capital punishment and life imprisonment. As far as the administration of justice was concerned, according to Buddhist concepts, the judge should guard against sinning by being tempted along the 'four avenues of injustice' as they were called, i.e., prejudice, hatred, ignorance and fear.

It would seem that the 12th and 13th Centuries were particularly open to the political application of Buddhist thought. In Thailand, in the 13th Century, impartial justice was attained, as can be seen from inscriptions attesting to an atmosphere of freedom and welfare-state policies. In Tibet, at about the same time, laws were harmonized with the Ten Virtues of Buddhism, while in Burma most Hindu theology was discarded and equality before the law seems to have been realized. Again, in Cambodia, the 12th Century king Jayavarman II ruled in much the same spirit as did Asoka before him.

To be sure, the history of international law in China is an interesting one indeed. From the days the Empire was founded, in 221 BC, until well into the 19th century, Chinese conceptions of inter-State relations closely mirrored the Confucian views on family life, emphasizing the patriarchal wisdom of the *pater familias* on the one hand and the virtue of filial piety of the junior members on the other. As Miyazaki argues (*EPIL* 7, at p. 216), throughout this period, China considered itself the centre of the world, headed by its son of heaven, the universal ruler, and surrounded by barbarian States 'of varying degrees of uncouthness and hairiness'. These latter did best to formally acknowledge themselves as tributaries of the Empire, adopt its calendar and dispatch tribute-bearing missions at regular intervals. In fact, this theory was never seriously questioned until modern times; any deviations were prompted by political necessity. Obviously, this attitude precluded the development of any regular international legal system.

However, prior to the days of the Empire, Chinese historians postulate a period which is usually described in terms paralleling the early Greek commonwealth of city-States. As it is, in the opening centuries of the first millennium BC the Chinese area must have witnessed a conglomerate of independently operating sovereign kingdoms which apparently conducted relations on a perfectly equal footing. Orthodox Confucian belief traditionally referred to this period of the

Tein-Hsi Cheng, Judge of the PCIJ from 1922-1942.

Yorozu Oda, Judge of the PCIJ from 1922-1930.

Harukazu Nagaoka, Judge of the PCIJ from 1935-1942.

The coat of arms of Japan.

Chou dynasty as the Golden Age of the ideal empire. As it is, statehood probably grew only gradually from local and regional units. Still, the existence of some 200 States claiming unlimited sovereignty can be pointed out from 750 BC onwards. Their intensive intercourse invited very definite rules of law and exquisite diplomacy, and produced conferences on such issues as disarmament (in 546 BC), concepts of mediation and asylum, and treaties of alliance, even with non-Chinese tribes. This heyday of internationalism came to a close during the centuries of 'warring states' as the period is commonly called (481-221 BC), when conflicting policies finally tore apart the delicate legal fabric. In this perspective, the rise of the unitarian State in the late 3rd century BC was, in political terms, merely the logical consequence of the previous struggle for power.

Be this as it may, in view of these time-honoured traditions, in China, the introduction of Buddhist concepts proved relatively easy. Most of them, and Asoka's example in particular, were felt to be consonant with the traditional rules of the ancient sages and the ideal of the saintly ruler. This held good for the Buddhist concept of punishment as well. In 65 AD, Emperor Ming decreed that those sentenced to death were to be given an opportunity to redeem themselves.

In Japan, in the 6th Century AD, Prince Regent Shotoku Taishi, one of the first Japanese to understand the moral and philosophical stature of Buddhism, drafted a Constitution in Seventeen Maxims on the basis of social justice. They consist of a set of moral guidelines for the conduct of the state, referring to the *Dhamma* and *Sangha* as the final ideal of all living beings and the ultimate foundation of all nations. In its insistence on impartial justice, tolerance and co-operation among nations, this Constitution, often described as the first Constitution of Japan, combined Confucian and Buddhist concepts:

> [IV] ... the leading principle of the government of the people consists in decorous behaviour....
>
> [V] ... deal impartially with the suits which are submitted to you. ... If the man who is to decide suits at law makes gain his ordinary motive, and hears causes with a view to receiving bribes, then will the suits of the rich man be like a stone flung into water, while the plaints of the poor will resemble water cast upon a stone.
>
> [VI] ... Chastise that which is evil and encourage that which is good. This was the excellent rule of antiquity. ... Flatterers and deceivers are a sharp weapon for the overthrow of the State, and a pointed sword for the destruction of the people. ... From such an origin great civil disturbances arise.

These ideas were echoed in the thirteenth Century by the religious teacher Nichiren, who foresaw a time when righteousness would rule the world.

However, as was observed earlier, despite its being a fountainhead of Asian civilization, Buddhism has only rarely been a dominating factor in its political thought. By vesting sovereignty in the people and restricting the power of government – be this monarch or parliament – by subjecting it to the requirements of the *Dhamma*, it was often destined to remain an ideal rather than become a firm reality. Still, to be sure, Buddhist policy, so akin to Confucian concepts in these respects, is far from being utopian. Admittedly, it does not meet force with force, but attempts to conquer wrath with kindness, greed with charity, falsehood with truth. It argues that wars only result in further wars: 'The victor obtains for himself a vanquisher'. This is not to say, however, that Buddism recommends disbanding armies altogether. It preaches passive resistance and believes in the eventual triumph of this attitude – and modern Asian history has seen ample proof of its strength. Actually, in recommending non-aggression, in its insistence on international co-operation for the common good of mankind, and in its abjuring of isolationist policies – on the ground of expediency as well as of moral obligations – its concepts often read surprisingly much like the basic notions of modern democracy and contemporary international law.

Laws of War

This observation applies in particular to its humanitarian ethics, which through the ages considerably affected the conduct of war, both among the Asian nations and in their contacts with European colonial powers. As recorded in a 9th century Sinhalese work:

An enemy should not be deceived by

unfair means. Nor should he be wounded mortally. – A soldier must not put on armour for fighting a soldier unclad in mail. – One should fight righteously without yielding to wrath or desiring to slay.

As Jayatilleke observes (*RDC* 120, at p. 546ff.) Asoka effectively gave up war as an instrument of policy at the height of his power because he felt remorse at the sufferings caused by war. It has been argued at times that there have been no wars of aggression waged by Buddhists on religious grounds against others or amongst themselves. While this may be something of an oversimplification, Buddhism nonetheless often succeeded to some extent in curbing the desire for conquest. With respect to the problem of war and peace and the nuclear deterrent, Nehru suitably summed up the position of Buddhism on the occasion of the 1955 Bandung Conference:

> We must avoid war and peace should be the decisive factor in the policy of every country. This is not a mere flowery statement, because we can actually bring about a real change in the world and cement the foundations of peace. ... If every country maintained its integrity, it would be thus helping in allaying the possibility of war. The moral strength of Asia and Africa is indeed an important factor which should stand for peace. It has been said that the Pañca Sîla – the five principles upon which Gandhi's policy was based – should prevail. This, in fact, is not new as all great ideas are not new. Coexistence, however, has dominated the minds, because it is more in conformity with modern trends. There is no other way to avoid war.

Diplomacy / Human Rights

Another well-known element of Buddhism is the respect it paid to envoys and embassies. These traditions, again, are attested as far back as the early days of the Roman Empire, as witness Pliny's records. Zurcher refers to the earliest recorded mission to China from Sri Lanka, which took place in 395 AD and in the same vein of mutual respect, he describes it as 'a remarkable happening known from various independent sources and of unquestionable historicity'. One may safely state that Far Eastern States, from the earliest days, entertained diplomatic relations on a footing of equality and in conformity with a civilized code of behaviour.

Its social contract theory of equality made Buddhism quite naturally significant in the sphere of human rights. Buddhist countries readily subscribed to the 1948 Universal Declaration of Human Rights of the United Nations. Among the tenets of Buddhism in this sphere is the one that the law itself should be accessible and that:

> ... a victim of discrimination should be able to seek redress and justice without being hampered by educational and pecuniary disabilities. Good Buddhist kings had a bell outside their palace gates, which anyone with a strong sense of grievance against a judgment given in a lower court, could ring. Legal remedy is reduced to farce if the people cannot understand or afford it through no fault of their own. (*op. cit.*, at p. 559)

International Relations

It was not at The Hague, nor on the occasion of the Hague Peace Conferences that the first contacts between the Far East and Holland in the field of modern international law were made, but rather a full generation earlier when, in 1862, Japan placed a government order for warships with Holland, and a couple of young Japanese academics came to the country to study international law at Leyden University under Professor Simon Vissering. In 1868, one of them, Shusuke Nishi, published a Japanese translation of

Simon Vissering (1818-1888), the Leyden professor of international law.

The Japanese delegate Nishi (back row, second from right) attending the First Hague Peace Conference of 1899.

Henry Wheaton (1785-1848), American jurist, diplomat and historian of international law; the author of Elements of International Law *(1836).*

Vissering's courses, and this became the first introduction to modern international law in the Japanese world. The same Nishi, incidentally, was to attend the First Hague Peace Conference of 1899. As we shall see, the 1860s were indeed momentous years for the development of international law in the Far East.

China

In 1861, China, in the decade of the Japanese Meiji Revolution of 1867, took a truly revolutionary step in forming a first modernizing government. This heralded the opening of a 'foreign learning' College, where an American missionary, Martin, started lecturing on international law. In 1865 he rendered Wheaton's *Elements of International Law* into Chinese. A few years later the work was translated into Japanese, along with the manuals of Martens, Heffter and Bluntschli among others. Ten years later Korean translations appeared. Within two decades the Western international law tradition was available to the Far East.

One can hardly overestimate the historic significance of these events and the impact they had on the Far Eastern world. To appreciate this fully we have to take its history into consideration. In our opening chapter we enlarged on the early stages of the Far Eastern and notably Chinese legal traditions. We spoke of the intensive intercourse among the 200 States of the area and the highly developed rules of international law that prevailed among these nations which dealt with each other on an equal footing. This early Chinese society revealed some characteristics that constitute a remarkable parallel to the Greek City States of about the same period.

However, cicumstances changed dramatically with the creation of the Empire, in 221 BC, when an altogether different theory came to prevail. This saw China, ruled by its Son of Heaven, as the exclusive cultural centre of the world. Its dominant theory of superiority virtually precluded anything remotely resembling intercourse with other nations on terms of equality. In the first centuries of the Christian era, Korea and Japan, as well as the Vietnam and Burma regions, were made into tributaries. In essence, this foreign policy of the Chinese Court was to remain intact until well into the 19th Century – an astonishing phenomenon which serves to typify its rigidly conservative doctrine.

This characteristic of inflexibility was also to determine the Empire's contacts with the West from the time that, in the opening years of the 16th Century, China was confronted by European expansion. In 1517, a first Portuguese diplomatic envoy requested an audience with the Emperor, but this overture was formally rejected. However, the Western mercantile nations were hard to keep at bay. The Portuguese were followed by the Spanish, and a century later by the Dutch and British. Jesuit missionaries like Francis Xavier introduced the Christian creed, while the merchant fleets introduced firearms. China decided not to face the challenge. In fact, the Middle Kingdom tried hard to deny the very existence of anything of relevance beyond its borders and preferred to withdraw into a policy of seclusion.

Admittedly, a few 'concessions' were allowed for foreign trade, as witness the trading posts in Canton and Nagasaki. Furthermore, the Empire did at times condescend to conclude treaties with the 'barbarians', as exemplified by its historic 1689 Treaty of Nerchinsk with Russia, the official Latin text of the treaty being negotiated through the intermediary of Jesuits. However, as late as 1793, the British Ambassador Lord McCartney, in a well known incident, had a flag put in his boat bearing the text 'Tributary Envoy from England'.

The balance shifted with the so-called

'The Mandate of Heaven' and 'The Rectification of Names', calligraphies by Arthur Witteveen.

Opium War, concerning the importation into China of opium from India by the British, which came as a true culture shock. Under the Treaty of Nanking, China ceded Hong Kong to the British. The time-honoured Canton trading system was swept away and replaced by the modern legal order. Still, it was only with the 1860 Treaty of Peking that anything resembling the exchange of diplomatic missions with the Western Nations was established.

Japan and Korea

A similar story unfolded in Japan. However, initially, Japan was not as adamant as China in its rejection of external influences. As early as 1600, that is well before its switch to formal seclusion, it had sent envoys to Europe, even to Rome. Also, throughout the period in which the policy of isolation prevailed, its intense commercial intercourse with the Dutch and with Russia kept it well informed of Western ideas at all times.

Japan's dream of seclusion was brutally disturbed when in 1853 four American warships under Commodore Perry anchored near Tokyo harbour. This necessitated a change of mentality which in due course led to the establishment of the regular contacts for which the West had been asking for centuries. In 1855 an Institute of Western Learning was founded in Tokyo and Western legal advisers made their entrance. It was in the wake of these changes that young scholars like Shusuke Nishi were sent abroad, and Western manuals, on subjects as diverse as anatomy and law, came to be translated and applied in a practical manner. In 1871 a treaty of commerce along Western lines was concluded between China and Japan. That same year the first Japanese permanent diplomatic missions were sent abroad to France and the United States.

The most isolated nation in those days was Korea, the Hermit Kingdom as it was called. As late as 1871, as Japan and China opened up to the West, Korea went to the trouble of erecting stone slabs along its border featuring texts that denied entry to Western representatives. In the long run, it was Japan that opened this region to the outside world through its 1876 Treaty of Amity, which heralded similar treaties to be concluded by Korea with Western nations in the 1880s. In 1887 a first Korean Minister was accredited to Washington.

Medal representing the Japanese Judge and President (1931-1933) of the PCIJ, Minéitciro Adatci (1859-1934).

The Twentieth Century

As in so many cases, the first real test for the application of Western principles of international law amongst these Far Eastern nations was an armed conflict. In 1894 war broke out between China and Japan over their claims to hegemony in Korea. The terms of the peace treaty ceded Taiwan to Japan and China likewise lost control over Korea. Its manifest weakness reduced it to the role of passive spectator in the ensuing 'Scramble for Concessions' among European powers. Germany, France, Britain and Russia all obtained long-term leases on the major Chinese ports. As the century drew to a close, and prompted by these first negative experiences with modern society, anti-

The Korean delegation to the Second Hague Peace Conference of 1907, headed by Prince Yi.

The first Chinese delegate Yang-Yü and his family at the First Hague Peace Conference of 1899.

Western and anti-Japanese movements gathered strength in China. The Empire showed not the least desire to modernize or, in its international contacts, to avail itself of the achievements of Western international law. The parallel with the contemporary vicissitudes of the Ottoman Empire is striking.

Japan, on the other hand, was keen to master Western international law. In 1897 the Japanese Association of International Law was established; its major international journal was launched in 1902. Western legal and diplomatic concepts were closely studied – and succesfully applied, as for instance to compel the revision of the unequal terms of the treaties previously concluded with Western nations. During its successful war with Russia over Korea and Manchuria that ended in the 1905 Portsmouth Peace Treaty, Japan had internationalists monitor the strict observance of the Laws of War by the military.

The Chinese delegation to the Second Hague Peace Conference of 1907, from left to right: Mr Tching-Loh, Mr Sze Chao-Tsang, Colonel W. S. Y. Tinge, His Exc. Lou Tsing-Tsiang, His Exc. Tsien-Sun, Mr Tchang-Tching-Tong, Mr Tchao Hi-Tchiou and Mr Wang-Kuang-Ky.

Japan attended the two Hague Peace Conferences of 1899 and 1907. At the second conference envoys of the Korean Emperor vainly tried to put the issue of its imminent occupation by Japan on the agenda – and in 1914 participated in World War I as a full member of the Allied and Associated Powers. It also gained ample experience of pleading at The Hague. As early as 1905 it was involved in the Permanent Court of Arbitration, in connection with the *Japanese House Tax* case. It was represented on the PCIJ by Judges Oda (1921-1930), Adatci (1931-1934; President of the Court in 1931-1933), and Nagaoka (1935-1942), and was involved in the 1923 *Wimbledon* case and in the 1932 case on the *Interpretation of the Statute of Memel.*

China attended most of the international meetings from the 1899 Hague Peace Conference onwards. However, it did not play a significant role on the international stage during the inter-war years. It was only to emerge on this scene from 1945 onwards. Even then, it looked upon international law, including the ICJ, with traditional suspicion, based on the alleged cultural bias of the Court. China had however been represented on the PCIJ throughout its brief life, during the first period 1922-1931 by Deputy-Judge Wang, and on the Second Bench, from 1931 onwards, firstly by the same Judge Wang, and after his resignation in 1936 by Judge Cheng. It was involved in the case concerning the *Denunciation of the Treaty of 1856*, a treaty it had concluded with Belgium.

In the early post-war years, the Taiwan authorities showed themselves to be resolute supporters of the Court. At San Francisco they proposed that all States should accept its compulsory jurisdiction. The People's Republic has throughout maintained a much more reserved attitude. In common with so many Asian nations, it looked upon the Court's composition, procedure and substantive law as the embodiment of essentially Western thinking. In many respects this attitude has been maintained, and up to 1980 only very few Judges from the Far East had sat on the Bench, i.e., Hsu Mo and

Wellington Koo during 1946-1967 on behalf of the Taiwan authorities, Bengzon from the Philippines and Tanaka from Japan (1961-1970), along with Zafrulla Khan from the South Asian area.

Today, the totality of the Asian world is represented by three seats on the Bench. However adequate this may look at first sight, with the seats of the present-day major powers China and Japan virtually guaranteed, this leaves the remainder of this huge part of the world's population with just a single seat. Quite naturally, this situation is reflected in the unwillingness of Asian nations to submit their disputes to the Court. They have often found it hard to identify themselves with the institution. To date, neither China nor Japan have ever been involved in ICJ cases, and over the full span of fifty years, a mere handful of cases have involved the Asian States. Again, apart from India and Pakistan, only the Philippines, Thailand and Sri Lanka in their treaty-making practice have to any degree availed themselves of the compromissory clause to refer automatically to the Court any disputes arising out of treaties or their interpretation. The People's Republic has long shown itself fiercely opposed to any such provisions.

It has often been maintained that the reluctance among Asian nations to rely on international adjudication is also due to cultural tradition. Admittedly, it is peaceful negotiation, rather than judicial settlement, that represents the most marked and long-standing tradition amongst these nations. China, for these reasons, has long shown a distinct ambivalence in accepting the settlement procedure as a source of law or in recognizing the force of Judgments of the

As Representative of China, V. K. Wellington Koo (1888-1985, Member of the PCA and Judge from 1946-1956) was the first delegate to sign the UN Charter on 24 June 1945.

THE COLOMBO PLAN

In 1950, at a meeting of foreign ministers of the British Commonwealth held in Colombo, in the present Sri Lanka, the initiative was taken to launch a framework for cooperation between the Commonwealth countries in the South and South-East Asian region. Initially for a 6-year period, it was later extended for periods of 5 years, and since 1980 operates for an unlimited period. The original Plan covered 3 regional members (India, Pakistan and Ceylon) and 4 donor members from outside the region (Great Britain, Canada, Australia and New Zealand).

In 1977 the Plan was expanded to non-Commonwealth countries, while Japan and the USA joined as donor members. The Plan was renamed The Colombo Plan for Economic and Social Development in Asia and the Pacific and its objectives slightly changed, putting special emphasis on the provision of technical scholarships and training. The Plan now comprises 26 nations and defines its primary aims as the support of economic and social development in Asia and the Pacific through cooperative efforts.

The interesting, experimental aspect of the Colombo Plan is that, while multilateral in approach insofar as it takes cognizance of the problems of its members and deals with these in a coordinated way, it is bilateral in its operation. Negotiations for assistance are carried out directly between the donor and receiving country, thus essentially promoting self-help.

Structurally, the Plan includes: firstly, a Consultative Committee, which is the principal policy-review body and meets twice annually at ministerial level; secondly, the Council, in which member States are represented at diplomatic level and whose functions include the identification of development issues of current interest; finally, the Bureau, which has its seat at Colombo and serves as a Permanent Secretariat, carrying out research and publishing activities. It participates at meetings in an advisory function and arranges seminars and workshops.

Major initiatives taken in the past decades were the Drug Advisory Programme, launched in 1973, which is carried out in close liaison with the United Nations; and the Staff College for Technical Education, which was established in 1975 at Singapore and transferred to the Philippines in 1987. The College organizes training courses and consultancies for the representatives of member States.

In recent years, the Colombo Plan has paid special attention to its lesser developed Members and the landlocked and geographically disadvantaged States, in providing exchange of resources and facilities from fellow-member States.

Court. Its attitude in these respects can perhaps best be typified as a pragmatic one.

However, in recent years a distinct change has become noticeable in this respect also, and this is perhaps the reflection of a generally greater acceptance of the Court by the developing nations. In 1991 the Representative of the People's Republic on the Sixth (Legal) Committee of the United Nations encouraged States to include a provision for the Court's jurisdiction in treaty clauses and to consider making it possible for the Secretary-General of the United Nations to request Advisory Opinions from the Court.

Original 415×580 mm.

LOPO HOMEM, 1519

Mapa-mundi

Collection de Marcel Destombes, Paris

THE PACIFIC REGION

Geographic and Ethnic Identification

In recent years, the Court's attention has twice been drawn to issues relating to the Pacific Region, firstly in the case concerning *Certain Phosphate Lands* in Nauru (1989-1993), and secondly by virtue of the 1994 General Assembly and WHO requests for an Advisory Opinion in the wake of the French decision to resume its nuclear tests on Mururoa Atoll. The latter issue had come before the ICJ at an earlier stage – it had been brought to the Court by New Zealand in 1973 – but had then been shelved when France announced its intention to desist from further atmospheric testing.

The Pacific Region is not to be interpreted as encompassing all territories washed by the waters of the Pacific Ocean. The Indonesian Archipelago, Japan and the Philippines are commonly regarded as belonging to Asia. However, in recent years, Australia and New Zealand, because of their increasing role in the region, are generally included in the region.

The centre of the region is constituted by the Pacific Islands, which fall into three groups: Micronesia, Melanesia and Polynesia. They broadly represent two ethnic strains: the dark-skinned Melanesians, found in Papua New Guinea, the Solomons, the New Hebrides and New Caledonia, and the comparatively light-skinned Polynesians, who extend across the Pacific to Hawaii in the north, Tahiti in the east and the New Zealand Maoris in the south. The Micronesians, while exhibiting some features of the other two groups, are closely related to the South East Asian mainland.

Legal Concepts of the Area

It is by no means surprising that it has taken the inhabitants of the Pacific Region – or Oceania as the region is often referred to – longer than most areas of the world to establish institutions and mechanisms of regional cooperation, or to attain the notion of a common identity. The area is typified by vast stretches of ocean, interrupted by mostly small, widely scattered islands and tiny atolls, with small populations and few natural resources. The slow pace of political evolution is therefore also due to the sheer isolation of most communities.

Over the centuries, within these small island communities, elaborate systems of customary law – tailor-made for their direct maritime surroundings – developed, in which precise rules regarding the demarcation of fishing grounds and the exploitiation of ocean resources were meticulously observed. However, the inhabitants of these ocean-oriented entities, while sharing most customary laws among themselves, had precious little in common with the customs that came to the fore in the essentially land-based economies of Fiji or Papua New Guinea.

Nonetheless, a few common characteristics may be highlighted here. The predominant one is, perhaps, the group-oriented administration of justice, which contrasts sharply with Western system's preoccupation with the individual. Another special feature is then informality of dispute resolution and the predominant authority of the chief of the tribe in the administration of justice. Understandably, the judicial process within these small communities was not subject to particularly formal procedural rules, but was rather the natural reflection of the day-to-day personal relationship between the parties.

The first breach in a long tradition to be observed in most of these communities, was due to the influx of foreign law concepts from the metropolitan powers that came to administer these territories under the League Mandate system and the

The coat of arms of New Zealand.

A nuclear test.

UN Trusteeship system. This circumstance occasioned yet another differentiation of legal cultures in addition to the one indicated above, as Papua New Guinea inherited English common law concepts, Western Samoa notions of German law and Tahiti the concepts of the French system.

Notwithstanding all local varieties, and in spite of all the changes that were prompted by Western influences, what has remained a persistent characteristic of these cultures to this day is their insistence on informality and their aversion to complex procedures. In this, obviously, time-honoured customary law still holds sway.

Regional Cooperation

Inter-governmental cooperation and organization is a comparatively new phenomenon in the Pacific, owing *inter alia* to the late attainment of full international personality by some entities and the as yet incomplete progress towards independence in the case of several others. To give an idea of the current situation, along with nations that have attained a fully independent status (in chronological order: Samoa, Nauru, Tonga, Fiji, Papua New Guinea, the Solomon Islands, Kiribati, Tuvalu and Vanuatu) there are enities such as the Cook Islands and Niue which are self-governing in free association with New Zealand; the four groups of Pacific islands (Northern Marianas, Micronesia, Palau and the Marshall Islands) which are still a Trust Territory administered by the USA; and finally, the dependent territories, which themselves again fall into two groups, entities with internal self-government and elected legislature (such as New Caledonia and French Polynesia which look to France; the American Samoa and Guam territories; and the Australian Norfolk Island) and entities without these attainments, such as Pitcairn Island (which comes under British rule), Tokelau (New Zealand), Wallis and Futuna Islands (France) and the Coral Sea Islands (Australia).

Prominent among the current Pacific Regional Organizations is the Economic and Social Commission for Asia and the Pacific (ESCAP) which is answerable to ECOSOC. Established in 1947, it includes, since 1973, the Pacific Trust Territories. During its 1975 New Delhi Meeting, ESCAP adopted measures to develop a New International Economic Order in the Asian and Pacific Region.

In 1955, the Asian Development Bank came into being, which regionally covers the same area as ESCAP. Through the Lomé Conventions (1975, 1979), the developing States in the Pacific also enjoy special links with the European Communities with regard to trade cooperation. Not all Pacific States have joined the UN, for various reasons; most of them do, however, subscribe to a number of Special Agencies. Nauru recognizes the Statute of the Court, without being a member State of the UN; in this it occupies a unique position, shared only by Switzerland. All nine fully independent Pacific Island States are members of the British Commonwealth and share in most of its projects.

Also noteworthy is the organization of the South Pacific under the auspices of the South Pacific Commission. This Commission was established in 1947 with the signing of the Canberra Agreement and has its headquarters in Noumea, New Caledonia. Its major purpose is the strengthening of economic and social welfare in the area. Another initiative, taken in 1971 by Fiji, was to provide the region with a venue for discussion of matters of general interest. This initiative resulted in the so-called South Pacific Forum, an essentially non-political debating group. In recent years it has discussed issues such as law of the sea negotiations, trade problems, communications, and nuclear testing and dumping of radioactive wastes in the Pacific. It sponsors the South Pacific Bureau for Economic Cooperation (SPEC) and a Fisheries Agency (FFA). Fishery and shipping services are obviously of paramount importance for this region. In 1974, the South Pacific Conference established a Regional Shipping Council to study the feasibility of a regional shipping line, which materialized a few years later with financial aid from Australia and New Zealand.

Inevitably, nothwithstanding the many potential difficulties, the need for more intense cooperation in the region is a pressing one.

The Islamic Component

Law and Religion

Most modern critics agree that Western international law theory only truly developed when, towards the first half of the 17th Century, its major prerequisite, namely the separation of the secular and the sacred spheres, was gradually being met. No such concept was ever taken into consideration within the Islamic world. Its singular feature, during fourteen centuries of Islam, has been precisely the conditioning of law by religion and its unqualified submission to the Will of God.

Traditionally, Western commentators have interpreted this religious component of Islamic legal doctrine as evidence of an inflexible, static conception of law and of the virtual absence of an Islamic international law theory as such. The issue is debatable: in a sense, the Islamic legal tradition, while being very different from Western legal concepts, reaches both deeper and wider. Much more than just a legal system, the sacred law of Islam is a body of religious duties and a code of social behaviour. It would seem that the Western interpretation is another testimony to the many misconceptions which have all too often undermined the relationship between the two cultures, and to the prejudice that has resulted from long centuries of conflict from Poitiers (AD 732) to Lepanto (AD 1571) and beyond.

It is a tragic fact that this essential difference in outlook has for so many centuries jeopardized the relations between the two major competing ideologies and military powers in the history of the Western world. For whatever may be said of Buddhist, Hindu and Confucian legal cultures, their influence on Western

LOPO HOMEM-REINÉIS

Atlas de 1519

Fol. 2 r.

Bibliothèque Nationale, Paris

political and legal thinking before the 19th Century was peripheral as compared to the direct impact of Islam.

The Worlds of Cross and Crescent

Invariably, commentators on both sides have stressed the many differences between Islam and Christianity, although obviously – in the legal sphere as much as elsewhere – the two cultures have also many elements in common, similarities that would in fact be hard to explain unless by reference to their philosophical roots. This cross-fertilization is amply documented. Through the ages, and side by side with the detrimental effects of political clashes, went the fertilizing impact of cultural exchange. The *Jihad* of early Islam brought Aristotle and the Greek philosophical heritage back to Spain as much as, a few centuries later, the sacking of Constantinople by the Ottomans made Byzantine scholarship take refuge in Italy and stimulate the Renaissance.

Again, the meeting of Saladin and Richard the Lion Heart on the plains of Palestine implied the exchange of silks and satins and notions of chivalry as much as of terms of truce. In the final analysis, the political impact of the military clash of the Crusades was merely ephemeral as compared to the durable benefits gained by the West from the intellectual encounter of the two cultures. At that juncture, the debt of the Western world to the Arabian scholars was impressive. The resurgence of learning in Europe from the 12th Century onwards, be it in astronomy, mathematics, metaphysics or medicine, owed much to the inspiration deriving from the Arab world. Some of the most penetrating tracts and thoughts of ancient Greek culture, that had lain submerged for a full millennium, would probably have been lost forever without the intervention of Arab scholars.

Not surprisingly, Europe came to be greatly indebted to the Islamic world in the legal sphere as well. Law was the pre-eminent province of learning in the Muslim world. Being linked to religion, it was in fact the epitome of Islamic thought, regulating man's duties towards God as much as towards fellow humans. This process is exemplified by the impact on the Western world of learning of the seminal works of Avicenna and Averroes, those stupendous 11th and 12th century Arab interpreters and integrators of Greek and Muslim thought in the triangle of law, religion and philosophy. It was these two scholars who gave the legacy of Plato and Aristotle back to the West, and it was from the blending of their views with Augustinian concepts that the medieval schools of Scholastics gained inspiration and upon which King Alfonso X of Castile drew for his *Las Siete Partidas* of 1263, which contained material anticipatory of modern international law.

The outcome of that exchange between the Muslim, Christian and – not to forget that other consistent component of European civilization – Jewish schools of learning is perhaps best epitomized in the names and works of Thomas Aquinas, Averroes and Maimonides. The foremost Jewish exponent of the period, commentator on the *Mishnah*, Aristotelian scholar and author of the *Guide for the Perplexed* (in Arabic), was Moses Maimo-

The coat of arms of Turkey.

Woodcut representation of a late 15th century battlefield.

nides, who was born in Islamic Córdoba in 1135 (where Averroës was born in 1126). In seeking to reconcile scriptural law with reason, he was instrumental in keeping the Jewish legal tradition in the mainstream of international thought. More than this, through his highly influential philosophical writings, he became a *trait d'union* between the Islamic and Christian cultures of his day.

The same fertilizing exchange of learning can be observed in what is generally considered the classical and constitutive phase of modern international law, in the late 16th and early 17th Centuries. Vitoria, Gentili, Suarez and Grotius, each in their way, were well informed of Islamic legal and cultural traditions. Suarez was born in Granada less than a century after the completion of the *Reconquista* in 1492. If explicit references to Muslim authors are scarce in the works of these authors, one must appreciate the heretical status of the Arab sources. There can be little doubt as to the mutual interests current in both academic worlds – as evidenced by the presence of Averroists at the University of Paris around the time of Aquinas.

To restrict ourselves to the Dutch academic world, from an early stage, at the outset of the 17th Century, Leyden University curators urged embassies and merchant fleets to bring along scholarly works from the Arab world for use in the newly launched department of Oriental Languages at the Leyden Academy. Again, students and scholars, often within the context of their *grand tour* and *perigrinatio studiosa* brought home piles of books, manuscripts and curiosa from the Orient. One of Hugo Grotius' closest friends travelled for some years through Asia Minor, Syria, and Palestine and lived for a while in Istanbul, where he came to be on friendly terms with Meletius Pegas, the Orthodox Patriarch. From the reports of their exchange of views Grotius, then preoccupied with the internal religious strife in the Netherlands, recognized in the patriarch a kindred spirit in his efforts to contribute to religious peace. From these contacts emanated a draft, composed by Grotius in 1611 and suitably entitled *Meletius*, in which the Dutch jurist developed a broad religious concept based on the Stoic concept of consensus. In that text, he enlarged on the idea that right action prevailed over dogma and doctrine, ideas very similar to his later ecumenic (or, to call it by the name of the period 'unionistic') efforts. The tract circulated among friends, but was never published. A copy of the manuscript was rediscovered only in 1984. From its opening paragraphs we take the following statement:

> For not only indifference or rivalry, but also implacable hatred and anger, indeed – something almost unprecedented – wars are started under no other pretext than that of the very religion whose purpose is peace. Yet, if we were willing to consider the people of the Indies, to whom we send our ships so successfully, or the Turks among whom you have lived, or the Jews who are now settling among us, we should be obliged to remember our almost forgotten kinship, even if only by comparing ourselves with them. For are we not strongly united by the very issue that separates us all from them, regardless of whether we consider them as a body or individually? (Hugo Grotius, *Meletius*, par. 2; ed. 1988, at p. 103-104).

Similar reconciliatory thoughts can be picked out over the centuries and in both camps, yet somehow they never entered the mainstream of thinking. As El-Kosheri and Weeramantry have correctly argued in recent years, a great deal of work still

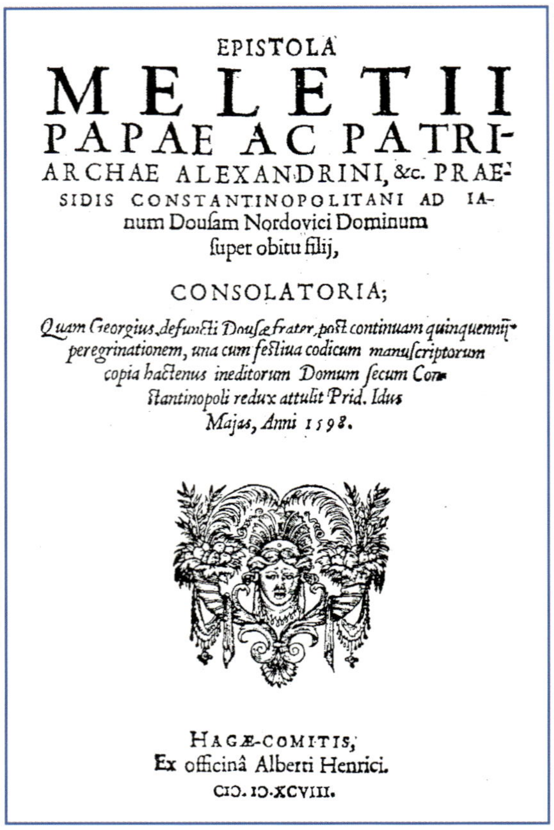
EPISTOLA
MELETII
PAPAE AC PATRIARCHAE ALEXANDRINI, &c. PRAESIDIS CONSTANTINOPOLITANI AD IANUM DOUSAM Nordovici Dominum
super obitu filij,
CONSOLATORIA;
Quam Georgius, defuncti Dousae frater, post continuam quinquennij peregrinationem, una cum festiua codicum manuscriptorum copia hactenus ineditorum Domum secum Constantinopoli redux attulit Prid. Idus Majas, Anni 1598.

HAGÆ-COMITIS,
Ex officinâ Alberti Henrici.
CIↃ. IↃ.XCVIII.

Printed edition of a letter of condolence from Meletius Papas, Patriarch of Alexandria, to Janus Dousa, curator of Leyden University, on the occasion of the decease of the latter's son and namesake (1598).

remains to be done to neutralize the devastating effects of generations of prejudiced writing. An imperative effort, it would seem, is needed today, as extremist writing constitutes a major barrier to harmonious coexistence within a peaceful world order. The very idea, long so common among Western critics, that Islam has no system of international law, no respect for treaties, and no concept of human rights is illustrative of the distortion and misrepresentation of a legal tradition, which can boast a treatise on international law that antedates all the others, i.e., Al Shaybani's eighth century *Introduction to the Law of Nations*.

The Rise of Islam

To be sure, the Arab world cannot boast the oldest legal culture. It was Mohammed who first brought order to the Arab world. 'Might was right, learning was despised, the poor were trodden underfoot' (Weeramantry, *Islamic Jurisprudence*) in the society of merchants into which the Prophet, in the opening years of the 7th Century, introduced the word of God as revealed to him by the Angel Gabriel. Amidst the desert sands, date palms and scattered oases, many savage customs prevailed. No single religion, no superior law was acknowledged by the migrant tribes of the area, nor did they lend a ready ear to Mohammed's teachings, at first. Persecuted and humiliated, the Prophet and his band of followers fled in AD 622 from Mecca to Medina, there to establish the community of Islam – and to return in triumph ten years later. From then on, its message became unstoppable.

Within a century, the *Adhan*, the call of the muezzin from the minaret, re-echoed from Spain to distant China. In unprecedented expansion, the Islam armies wrested Palestine from the Byzantines, overran Egypt, wiped out the Persian Empire, spread to the shores of Africa, besieged Theodosian Constantinople in 716, imperiled the Christian world of Charles Martel at Poitiers in 732 and crushed the Chinese army at Talas in 751. Among the spoils of the latter battlefield they brought back the art of paper-making.

The Caliphate moved its capital from Mecca to Damascus, to Baghdad, then – after a brilliant cultural period of two centuries – fell prey to Mongol invasions and Turkish tribesmen. It nonetheless maintained its inner strength and gradually reconquered its conquerors in the intellectual sphere – as at an earlier stage of history the Greeks had reconquered the Romans and the Romans in turn had reconquered the Goths – to press forward with renewed vitality. Sultanates were set up from Timbuktu to the Niger basin, in Istanbul – and almost in Vienna. The word of the Prophet made a deep impact on the culture of India and crossed the oceans to reach out to Malaysia and the Philippines.

To be sure, Islam did not manage to blend the local customs and legal traditions of the wide diversity of peoples that came to be contained within its boundaries in the same flexible manner as had been achieved by the Roman lawgivers in the previous era. It did, however, have the same unifying effect on its vast Empire as Roman Catholic canonical law (with the help of the Roman legal system) had on the *Respublica Christiana*. Only, with Islam, its stamp was stronger and its social impact went deeper, as its grip upon life was firmer. The word of God, as revealed to the Prophet Mohammed in the 114 *Suras* of the Qur'an, has constituted the unalterable bedrock of law and conduct throughout the vast Muslim world for fourteen centuries.

The Sources of Islamic Law

The overriding importance of the Qur'an as a source of Islamic law is obvious. It constitutes the moral and legal code of the Muslim world, its constant interweaving of spiritual teachings with practical legislation providing a guidance for both the present life and the life hereafter. The non-separation between the religious and the secular elements in Islam is to be interpreted that the social, economic and political behaviour of the individual should be ruled by Islamic morals and ethics, which basically are the same as the ones of Christianity. The Personal Statute is governed by religious rules. Accordingly in interpreting Islamic teachings one should differentiate between those teachings which prescribe detailed rules of conduct and refer to religious rituals and personal statutes and which leave no room for discretion, and those prescripts which announce general principles and whose content has to be adapted to changing circumstances. Thus, in principle, democracy is the preferred form of government in Islam, witness the word of Surat *Al-Shura*:

> Whatever you have been given is only a temporary provision of this life, but that which is with Allah is better and more lasting for those who believe and put their trust in their Lord; ... those who hearken to their Lord, and observe Prayer *and whose affairs are administered by mutual consultation*, and who spend out of whatever We have provided for them. (Surat *Al-Shura*, v. 37-38; italics added)

... but its form is to be decided according to prevailing circumstances.

An essential element in the study of the Qur'an, as Arab scholars realized at a fairly early stage, was its interpretation from a holistic point of view, which stressed the integrated whole and its basic underlying philosophy. In other words, it took the letter of each line as illustrating the spirit of the body of texts.

In cases of doubt and wherever further guidance seemed necessary, a further source – additional to the Qur'an – came into view, namely the sayings and conduct of the Prophet himself (the *hadith*) and the practical rules to be deduced therefrom. The study of these sayings harked back to the early days of Islam, when systematic attempts were made to collect all the details of the Prophet's life and sayings, and all parts of the Islamic world were scoured in a careful attempt to verify the sayings or traditions of the Prophet and establish an authentic tradition. Less than three centuries later, specialized schools of *hadith* inquirers had developed, covering all branches of knowledge.

The naval battle at Zonchio of 1499, featuring the Turkish commander Kemal Ali (Chmali) seizing a Venetian vessel and setting fire to another.

Yet another source of knowledge came to bear on Islamic doctrine, namely the consensus of Muslim scholars in relation to correct conduct, the *ijma*. As Judge Weeramantry explains:

> The authority of *ijma* is based upon distrust of individual opinion. There is assurance of freedom from error in the communal mind. The Prophet had observed: 'My nation will not agree unanimously in error ...'. Viewed from the standpoint of equity, human rights and legal development, *ijma* thus played a most important role, for it provided for the development of the law to meet the needs of changing times rather than freezing into an unyielding and static mould. (*op. cit.*, at pp. 39-40)

In the event that even this source was inadequate to solve problems of a practical nature, final recourse was had by jurists to logical inference and analogy. This painstaking intellectual process aimed at sorting out the general from the incidental and discerning the underlying principle from among all the factual particularities, became known as *qijas*. It resulted in a vast body of jurisprudence until, by the tenth century, the view came to prevail that the actual need for, and consequently the right of further interpretation had disappeared. Doctrine was considered to have reached its perfection. 'The doors of *ijtihad*' were closed – not to be re-opened for ten centuries, as some critics maintain.

If we may venture a few lines to comment on this. It would seem that *ijtihad* has too long been blocked in what basically concerns religious rituals as prescribed by the Qur'an and the Sunna. *Ijtihad* concerning secular matters should have never stopped. The fact that it did in many Islamic societies is probably one of the main causes which deprived Islamic societies of dynamic thinking and social and economic development.

During this whole period, consolidation and highly intelligent but sometimes artificial imitation tended to prevail over independent research. The Egyptian jurist Muhammad Abduh (1849-1905) was probably among the first to put a halt to this process. He strongly advocated innovative thinking and urged the reopening of the doors of *ijtihad* in the light of the vast social changes that had taken place in the world. In recent decades much legal reform has been achieved to adapt Islamic law to the new age of technology and mass communications, as witness the resolutions of the 1962 Cairo Congress of Muslim Learned Men.

International Law of the Muslim World

We may now briefly review the international law element within the Islamic legal tradition. In this we do well to keep to the chronology and consider the four successive periods of Islamic rule. Islam, by insisting on the prevalence of the Qur'an in all legal matters, does not differentiate between the national and the international spheres – just as, obviously, the dualism of natural and positive law noted in Western legal doctrine is not to be

Sultan Suleiman I The Magnificent or The Lawgiver (1494/5-1566).

found in Islamic law. All power, whether applied in the national or international sphere, is seen as emanating from God.

A basic concept of Islamic law which comes to bear on the international relations of the Muslim world and has often been neglected by Western commentators, is its emphasis on the universal brotherhood of mankind. In his Farewell Sermon the Prophet had proclaimed that the Arab was not superior to the non-Arab and *vice versa* and the same applied to the fair-skinned and the dark-skinned. Humans are alike 'as the teeth of a comb'. The whole of humanity is the family of Allah. These notions applied especially to the fields of humanitarian law and human rights.

Accordingly, it is here that its advocates maintain that Islam has contributed most to international law. From early on, mercy was shown to prisoners of war, non-combatant women and children were to be spared and unneccessary cruelties on the battlefield were expressly forbidden. The chronicles of the Crusades bear ample witness to this. As one Western commentator observed: 'The virtues of civilization were all on the side of the Saracens'. For, in the sphere of the law of treaties too, Islamic practice is unequivocal from the 8th Century tracts of Al Shaybani to the 16th Century treaty between Suleiman the Magnificent and Francis I of France. Muslims knew they were specifically obliged by Qur'anic texts to honour treaties, whether with believers or non-believers, and never to break their promises. Diplomatic protection was a well-recognized concept and due respect was paid to envoys and embassies, harking back to the *hadiths* of the Prophet who treated them with honour.

Some illuminating thoughts on these matters can be taken from the Qur'an and more especially the *Al-Anfal Surah*. It may be worthwile here to reproduce a few lines taken from the 1970 English translation which was made by the former President of the International Court of Justice, Muhammad Zafrulla Khan:

On Treaties
Worse than the beasts, in the sight of Allah, are those who have rejected the Signs of Allah and do not believe; those with whom thou makest a covenant, then they break their covenant every time and are not mindful of their obligation to Allah. ... Shouldst thou apprehend treachery from a people who have made a pact with thee, terminate the pact in a manner that should occasion no prejudice to either side. (*Surah Al-Anfal*, v. 56-60)

On Peace
Make ready for them whatever you can of armed strength and of mounted pickets at the frontier, whereby you may daunt the enemy of Allah and your enemy and others beyond them whom you know not, but whom Allah knows. ... Then if they should be inclined to make peace, do thou incline towards it also, and put thy trust in Allah. (*ibid.*, v. 61-64)

On Captives
It behoves not a Prophet to take captives, except in the course of regular fighting. To take captives in the course of skirmishes and small-scale action would mean that you are merely seeking temporal gain, whereas Allah desires for you the Hereafter. ... Enjoy the lawful and good spoils that you win, and be mindful of your duty to Allah. ... O Prophet, say to the captives who are in your hands: If Allah knows of any good in your hearts, He will bestow on you better than that which has been taken from you, and will forgive you. Allah is Most Forgiving, Ever Merciful. If they design treachery against thee, they have already been guilty of treachery towards Allah, yet He gave thee power over them. Allah is All-Knowing, Wise. (*ibid*, v. 68-72)

Islam has an absolute respect for international conventions, considered to be a primary source of international law. As Zafrulla Khan, in his introductory note to the edition of the Qur'an observes: 'Indeed it is most careful in stressing all obligations, even when they are owed to those who are at most serious variance with one in matters of faith'.

The Formative Phase of Islamic Rule

Islamic attitudes towards international law are best understood against the background of the four successive phases of Islamic rule, to which we must now turn. During its first, formative period, covering a century and a half to be reckoned from AD 622 and characterized by rapid expansion and the emergence of the Caliphate, the universal vocation of the new religion imposed a strict and exclusive dominance of Islamic law in the

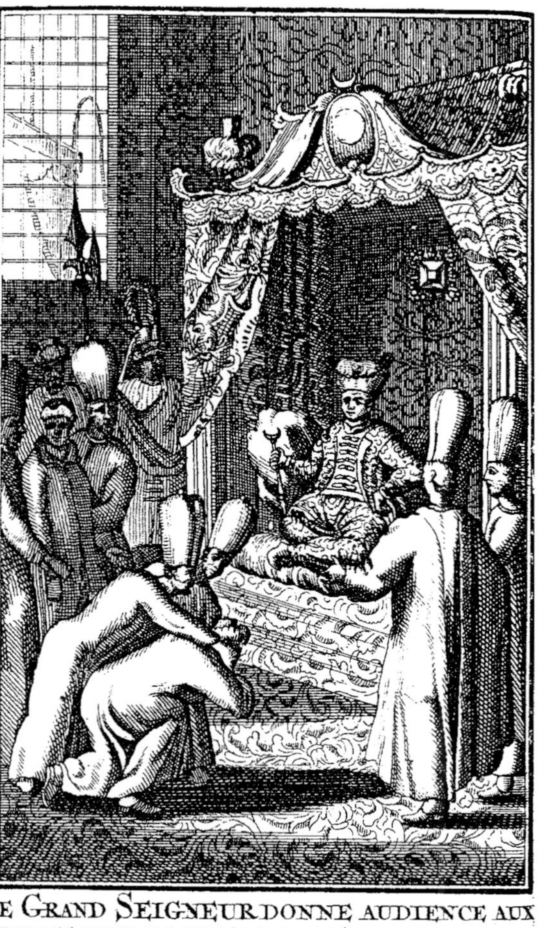
LE GRAND SEIGNEUR DONNE AUDIENCE AUX AMBASSADEURS INTRODUITS DANS LE DIVAN
Tome Troisiéme.

The Sultan giving audience to foreign ambassadors in his Council of State.

international sphere. In fact, the law relating to dealings with non-Islamic States at that stage was expected to be a passing phase, pending the completion of the conversion of the world. Constituting the revealed will of God, the divinely ordained system of the *Shariat-Allah* as expressed in its *fiqh* obviously ran counter to the systematic development of international law concepts.

Even in this formative period of Islam some significant elements pertaining to the laws of war and foreign relations may already be seen. One such element is the granting of protection to the lives and properties of the civilian population in conquered territory. Prophet Mohammed's *Charter of Medina* effectively welcomed Jewish residents within the Empire as an integral part of the community of Islam and on terms which are not dissimilar to the well-known Roman concept of *deditio* (surrender). Neither were war and hostility in themselves considered the natural or inevitable relationship with infidels at that time. Indeed, the Qur'an stipulated that the *Jihad*, the Holy War in self-defence or in support of allies, was the only form of war legally permissible.

The notion of *Jihad* or holy war deserves a few words here, as this concept has probably been the element of Islamic legal doctrine which has occasioned the most confusion, both within and beyond the Muslim world. The proselytising and missionary spirit of the first phase of Islam naturally led to hostilities with the non-responsive non-Islamic world. This even

THE LEAGUE OF ARAB STATES

The call for some form of federalism between the Arab nations, which in the inter-war period had run parallel to their search for independence, prompted the Egyptian government in 1944 to establish a preparatory study group, from whose meetings issued what is now commonly known as the *Protocol of Alexandria*. It is on the principles of this Protocol that, in March 1945, the League of Arab States was founded. Initially, the League consisted of 7 member States. Since then, 15 other States have joined the organization.

The Arab League is a regional organization along the lines of the UN Charter and, by special agreement of 1953, enjoys all the privileges and immunities of an international organization. Its basic objectives are the safeguarding of the independence and sovereignty of its Members, the peaceful settlement of disputes, and cooperation in the political, economic, social and cultural spheres. In line with the UN Charter, the League warrants equal status to its Members, prohibits the use of force to resolve disputes and includes a non-aggression, non-intervention and collective security pact. Membership is open to any independent Arab nation.

In the area of dispute settlement, the League provides two instruments: mediation and arbitration. (Non-binding) mediation is entrusted solely to the Council of the League, which at the request of disputants or other Members may also act as a court of arbitration on all issues except matters of State independence, sovereignty or territorial integrity.

From early on, in 1951, the League – which unlike the United Nations never established a true judicial body – considered the creation of an Arab Court of Justice, to which it thought the adjudication of disputes and the issuing of legal opinions could best be entrusted, actually much along the lines of the ICJ. However, despite detailed studies and frequent discussions, notably during the 1981-1982 Summits, such an institution never materialized. To date, within the League, the Council is still the first and foremost body to resort to in case of dispute or aggression.

The structure of the League, which has its permanent seat at Cairo, provides for three major organs: the Council, the Permanent Committees and the Secretariat-General. The Council is the supreme organ, in which all member States are represented, as a rule at ministerial level. Sessions take place twice annually, mostly in Cairo, once at the ministerial level and once in the form of Summits of the Heads of State. The Council, in which each Member has one vote, appoints the Secretary-General, approves the budget and has the last word in all matters of a general nature and of common interest. For decisions to be binding upon all Members unanimity of votes is required.

The Permanent Committees have a specialized technical nature. They operate in the political, economic, social and cultural spheres. It is at this level that most of the activities of the League are being developed. Over the years, these committees have generated an impressive number of draft resolutions, agreements and specialized reports on behalf of the Council.

The Secretary-General, who is assisted by Assistant-Secretaries and a staff of 450, is appointed by the Council for a 5-year term which is renewable. The League has a number of permanent offices around the world.

In 1950, the Arab League concluded a Treaty of Joint Defence and Economic Cooperation which initiated the creation of 5 institutions which duly reflect the search for cooperation: a Joint Defence Council, a Military Advisory Organization, a Permanent Military Commission, the Arab Unified Command and the Economic Council.

A host of secondary organs, operative in a rich variety of areas, serve to emphasize the in-depth organization of the League, which in the past forty years has grown into the very symbol of Arab Unity. It can boast major achievements in the economic, social and cultural fields, although it has met with only limited success at the political level, the Palestinian problem and the relations with Israel having long been a bone of bitter contention among the member States, and which led to the temporary transfer of the League's Headquarters from Cairo to Tunis (1979-1990). Yet, through its League, the Arab world increasingly presents itself as a regional unity.

led some classical Muslim writers to interpret *Jihad* as an instrument of aggression. However, modern interpreters agree that, in itself, *Jihad* implied a defensive rather than offensive policy. This was more or less recognized within the Muslim world from the opening years of this century. This is not to say that the concept as such is outdated. In its restricted interpretation, as a means towards self-determination and the throwing off of foreign yokes, it can serve as an instrument of modern policy. In fact, according to most modern interpreters, in the original concept of the idea, the *Jihad* is to be undertaken precisely against regimes which oppress free thinking and create obstacles to the promulgation of islamic teachings. In this sense, the *Jihad* is instrumental to peace and the safeguarding of independent thought. This makes it perfectly well reconciliable with the idea of peaceful understanding.

The Second Phase: Traditional Islamic Law Schools

The second phase of Islam, often characterized as a period of military stabilization and legal consolidation (c. AD 750-1050), witnessed conflicting currents.The period was heralded by the fall of Damascus in AD 750 and the passage of power to Baghdad. With the Abassid Caliphs, religious authority was vested in the four orthodox schools of jurists that were then founded. This second phase was, therefore, to become the crucial period in the formation of what is called the 'traditional' Islamic school of international thought. Here we meet the first Islamic internationalists: Al Shaybani, commonly regarded as the founder of Islamic international law and the author of an *Introduction to the Law of Nations*, and Abu Hanifa and Al Shafi'i, the initiators of two prominent schools of thought. All three of them flourished in the 8th Century. Noteworthy among Al Shaybani's theories is the notion of *pacta sunt servanda*, the observance of one's word with respect to treaties.

It is only at this stage, and within the framework of these schools, that Islam was proclaimed to be the universal message to all humanity and the treatment of other systems of belief on equal terms was categorically rejected. From then on, the world was seen as partitioned into a *dar al-Islam* and *dar al-harb*. These concepts of the *Pax Islamica*, so kindred to the Roman ideas of the *ager Romanus* versus the *ager hosticus*, postulated the partition of the known world into two spheres.

However, major contemporary political currents diverged strongly from the concept of central authority as personified in a single Caliph, and from the unitary character of Islamic power. In foreign politics and on the international plane, a tendency towards coexistence was seen as a necessity, prompted also by progressive exposure to foreign concepts. A disintegrating process set in, which was to lead to strife between competing Caliphs. This at times became much more frequent and bitter than were any conflicts with

The statue of Peace about to be overthrown. In the background the Ottoman closely watches the outcome of the internal European rivalry.

foreign powers. At some stages, competing Caliphs did not shrink from entering into alliances with Christian monarchs. This happened to Charlemagne who is reported to have symbolically been presented with the keys of Jerusalem by one Caliph, and then to be offered a lasting peace by a competing Caliph.

The Third Phase: A New Equilibrium

While doctrine and practice thus gradually diverged even at what is considered the zenith of Islamic power, this gap could only widen in subsequent centuries as, responding to internal as well as external pressure, decentralizing forces resulted in the literal fragmentation of the Caliphate into independent political entities. This third phase of Islam, covering no less than seven centuries down to 1800, is typified by the long search for a new equilibrium.

Firstly, centralized power crumbled away into a whole series of virtually independent kingdoms, from Morocco to Anatolia to Persia. Then, hordes of enemies of all kinds overran the Muslim territories, creating yet another unanticipated phenomenon, namely the position of defeated Muslims under Islamic law. Tartars, Crusaders and the Spanish *reconquista* gradually forced the once conquering religion back into a defensive posture. Baghdad itself fell to the Mongols in 1258, Spain was lost in 1492, the Mamelukes lost Cairo to the Ottomans in 1517.

In practice, the Islam world, from then on, accepted the *dar al-sulh*, non-Muslim States susceptible to treaty relations. Examples of (secret) alliances, transactions and *ententes* with non-believers were numerous, as is testified by the chroniclers of the Crusades. Thus, the Frankish Protectorate of Egypt in the 12th Century was more or less solicited by Muslim authorities, mainly to prevent the occupation of the region by the Turks. However, in the long run, the centre of power in the Muslim world passed to the Turkish tribes, the conquerors of Constantinople.

The powerful Ottoman Empire, once established, soon eradicated all internal strife. For a number of centuries it was to add new dimensions to traditional institutions and give a new vitality to Muslim politics. In doing so, it did not, however, hark back to rigid classical doctrine. In 1639 it concluded peace with Persia on terms of mutual recognition. The step can also be interpreted as the adjustment of religious ideals to contemporary political realities and economic forces.

Conversely, a similar phenomenon can be observed in the West at a fairly early stage. Despite Innocent III's firm papal bulls against trading with Muslims, the major outcome of seven bloody crusades was the unprecedented flourishing of commerce between the competing cultures and a marked increase of legal and diplomatic links. In the mid-1100's, Pisa and Genoa concluded commercial treaties with Egypt providing for preferential treatment and permanent emporia. In 1177 the Venetian *Serennissima* concluded a *pax firmissima* with the Egyptian ruler. An Algerian chronicler tells of 3000 Latin Merchants disembarking in 1215 in Alexandria only. Ultimately, the lure of profits prevailed.

These profits also extended to the intellectual sphere. The Qur'an was first translated into Latin in 1143. In order to fully appreciate the opportunities of cultural exchange, one does well to realize that, at this juncture, the Baghdad library contained some 150,000 volumes, and the index at the famous House of Wisdom in Cordoba, where the great Averroes was born during that period, included no less than 500,000 titles – at a time when European libraries still had no more than a few hundred books.

'The famous Crescent divided between the Empire, Poland and Venice'.

In subsequent centuries, Ottoman Sultans and Persian Shahs only encouraged these treaties or 'capitulations', as they came to be known. The pivotal 1535 treaty between Sultan Suleiman I and Francis I of France was soon followed by similar agreements with other sea-going nations, notably the British (1580, 1675). By a treaty of 1774, the Russian Tsar was even granted the protection of Orthodox churches in Istanbul itself. Essential to an understanding of these developments is the fact that, from very early on, the Ottoman rulers openly exercised the prerogative of legislative power, claiming the force of law for their *qanunnama* or canonical acts. In fact, they felt perfectly free to commit themselves both in terms of personal and territorial jurisdiction.

The 'sick man of Europe', as the ageing Ottoman Empire was called in the 19th century

The Fourth Phase: Ageing Structures and New Ideologies

However, from 1800 onwards, at the opening of the fourth and closing phase of Islamic rule, the victorious Ottoman era of four centuries drew to a close. The Empire became increasingly vulnerable to social change and was exposed to the superior military and technological power of the West. The shift in the balance of power and the vulnerability of the ageing Islamic structures were dramatically demonstrated by Napoleon's Egyptian expedition of 1798. It was this cultural shock and the subsequent influx of Western ideas into the Islamic world which forced Muslim statesmen and theoreticians to give thought to the problem of how best to confront the new cultural challenges of the 19th and 20th centuries.

In terms of external policy, the Ottomans, even at that stage, were able to strive off imminent disaster for another full century. They went along with the imperative demands of internationalism in their time and concluded a whole series of short-term defensive alliances with the rival Western nations, as was illustrated during the Napoleonic era. Likewise, three decades later, when the Egyptian *Wali* Mohamad Ali was marching towards Istanbul, the Sublime Porte never hesitated to call in the help of the European powers, finally forcing the *Wali* to come to terms at the 1840 London Convention for the Pacification of the Levant.

Western international law and references had traditionally confined themselves to Christian countries. This pattern was soon to be broken. In 1856 the Sultan proclaimed full equality before the law for all citizens of his Empire, irrespective of race or religion. In the same year, the Sublime Porte was introduced to the Concert of European powers, the intimate circle of 'civilized nations'. The 1856 Paris Peace Treaty which put an end to the Crimean War guaranteed the independence and integrity of the Ottoman Empire, albeit under the protectorate of the major Western Powers. While confirming the status of the Empire, it also painfully revealed its hierarchical subordination within the 'circle'.

Despite all its efforts at administrative innovation and political reorganization, the 'sick man of Europe' – as the labouring Empire came to be called – was not to recover. Little by little, it lost substantial portions of territory until, after World War I and the Treaty of Versailles, it was formally reduced to the secular nation-State of Turkey. Indeed, even during World War I, Muslim Kings and *Sharifs* speculated and negotiated over the post-war distribution of Ottoman territory, in open defiance of the Caliph's call for a last, united *jihad*. In the end, it was internal rebellion that dealt the final blow. In 1924, General Mustafa Kemal, or Ataturk as he was called, officially abolished the institution of the Caliphate.

However, the political end was to become a new ideological beginning. The new credo of 'modernists' and 'realists' advocated the resolute separation of State

The coat of arms of Palestine.

Turkham Pacha in 1899. The official portrait was taken at the 1899 Hague Conference.

and religion. They forced the 'traditionalists', who fervently dismissed any such innovative ideas, into a restatement of classical doctrine and required them to demonstrate its compatibility with modern society and contemporary notions of international law. In doing so, they – interestingly enough – harked back to the first, formative period of Islam and customary rules from earlier periods. They abdicated the doctrine of *dar al-Islam* and *dar al-harb* and claimed that Islamic concepts could indeed be integrated into modern international law. These views in their turn provoked severe criticism from the 'fundamentalists', a third movement which soon became as widespread as the two others. The fundamentalists insisted on the universalism of Islam, on the classic *jihad*, and on the restoration of a true Islamic system. In an attempt to solve this riddle in the legal sphere, scholars have argued in favour of the creation of a legal sub-system for the Islamic world, a regional sphere of law whose role would be to govern internal relations. They looked upon the Organization of the Islamic Conference at Jeddah as an appropriate vehicle to further this concept.

A whole spectrum of attitudes from a world State to co-existence are thus comprised within the long and eventful history of Islam. In retrospect, the spirit of tolerance and humanity, so omnipresent both in the moral precepts of the Qur'an and the teachings of the Prophet, may greatly assist the promotion of justice and the international rule of law.

Islam at the Hague Courts

What impact have the Islamic concepts relating to the rule of law had upon the Hague Courts so far? Initially, their contribution was rather meagre. At the Opening Session of the 1907 Hague Peace Conference, the red fez of Turkham Pacha, the leader of the Ottoman delegation, was conspicuous among the delegates, next to the blue silk national dress of the Siamese representative. Yet no less conspicuously present at The Hague, along with protesting groups of Albanians and Ar-

The gathering of delegates in the Oranjezaal of the Huis ten Bosch during the Hague Peace Conference of 1899: The Turkish delegates in the background.

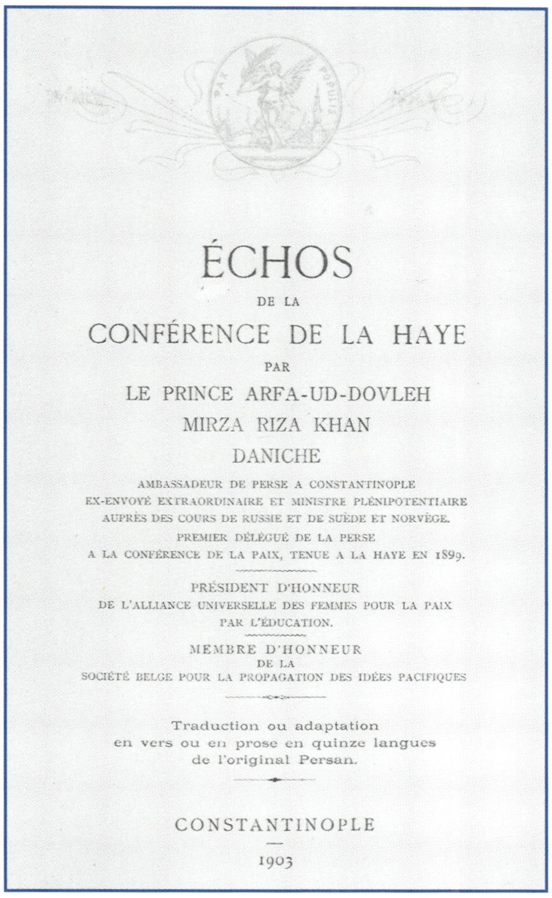
ÉCHOS
DE LA
CONFÉRENCE DE LA HAYE
PAR
LE PRINCE ARFA-UD-DOVLEH
MIRZA RIZA KHAN
DANICHE
AMBASSADEUR DE PERSE A CONSTANTINOPLE
EX-ENVOYÉ EXTRAORDINAIRE ET MINISTRE PLÉNIPOTENTIAIRE
AUPRÈS DES COURS DE RUSSIE ET DE SUÈDE ET NORVÈGE.
PREMIER DÉLÉGUÉ DE LA PERSE
A LA CONFÉRENCE DE LA PAIX, TENUE A LA HAYE EN 1899.
PRÉSIDENT D'HONNEUR
DE L'ALLIANCE UNIVERSELLE DES FEMMES POUR LA PAIX
PAR L'ÉDUCATION.
MEMBRE D'HONNEUR
DE LA
SOCIÉTÉ BELGE POUR LA PROPAGATION DES IDÉES PACIFIQUES
Traduction ou adaptation
en vers ou en prose en quinze langues
de l'original Persan.
CONSTANTINOPLE
1903

menians – seeking support for their demands for independence – were the Young Turks, representatives of the intelligentsia from all quarters of the vast and heterogeneous Ottoman Empire and headed by the eloquent Mr Santo-Semo. He frequently gave speeches at press meetings, advocating an Ottoman Constitution, the formation of a Parliament and decentralized administration. The 'Evolutionaries', as they called themselves, were aiming at reform from within.

In 1912 the Permanent Court of Arbitration was called in by Russia and Turkey in the matter of the *Russian Indemnity* case. No Turkish Judge was ever on the Bench of the PCIJ, although a number of cases were related to Turkish problems, such as the 1925 *Exchange of Greek and Turkish Populations* case, the 1925 *Expulsion of the Oecumenical Patriarch* case, the 1925 *Iraq-Turkey Frontier* case, the 1927 *Lotus* case, the 1928 *Greco-Turkish Agreement* case, and the 1933 *Territorial Waters Between Castellorizo and Anatolia* case.

The first Judge of the ICJ to be recruited from the Muslim world was Judge Badawi of Egypt, who was elected in 1946 and remained in office until 1965, becoming Vice-President under Hackworth from 1955-1958 and presided over the 1955 *Aerial Incident* case. To date, quite a few Judges from the Islamic world have served on the bench of the Court. It is under the Presidency of Judge Bedjaoui from Algeria that the ICJ now celebrates its 50th Anniversary.

To date, the Muslim law tradition is firmly established among the legal components of the ICJ. The biographical sketches devoted to the Judges from the Islamic world highlight some of the perspectives they brought to bear on the jurisprudence of the Court from the specific angle of Islamic traditions. The same holds true for the participation of Muslim States in the Court's activities. In recent years several cases have been submitted to the Court by nations of the Islamic world, more particularly in relation to frontier disputes.

Mr Politis before the PCIJ in the 1934 Lighthouses *case between France and Greece.*

Nº. 101. VENDREDI 11 OCTOBRE 1907

Courrier de la Conférence

DE LA PAIX

Rédigé par WILLIAM T. STEAD

Prix d'abonnement par semaine:
pour la Hollande fl. 0.65
„ l'Etranger fl. 0.75
Prix du numéro:
fl. 0.15.

Collaborateurs:
Mme la Baronne BERTHA VON SUTTNER,
M. ALFRED H. FRIED,
M. FRÉD. PASSY,
M. FELIX MOSCHELES.

Directeurs-Editeurs: MAAS & VAN SUCHTELEN

BUREAUX: Princessegracht 6A, La Haye. — Téléphone No. 287. — Adr. Télégr. MAASSUCHTELEN.

Le Pélerinage de la Paix autour du monde. La Réponse de l'Amérique Latine.

La bienvenue.

Aujourd'hui nous publions la réponse des délégués de l'Amérique Latine à la proposition présentée dans le Courrier de la Conférence du 25 septembre, et portant que la tournée du pélerinage de la Paix commencerait par ce continent. Cette réponse est satisfaisante et encourageante. Du Mexique à l'Argentine il n'y a qu'une réponse unanime: „Soyez les bienvenus!"

L'idée fondamentale du pélerinage est d'en faire une mission, chargée d'expliquer l'importance des principes de la Conférence de La Haye avec toute l'autorité dont jouissent des personnes distinguées constituant un microcosme de la race humaine. On se trouverait en présence d'une Commission internationale non officielle, continuellement en tournée afin de rendre compte de ce qu'on a fait pour donner suite aux conventions et aux voeux de la Conférence de La Haye; de favoriser, dans chaque parlement, l'établissement d'un groupe de l'Union Interparlementaire et d'établir, dans chaque capitale visitée, des centres locaux de l'Union Internationale, composés d'hommes et de femmes, désirant prêter leur concours, sur la base des principes généraux arrêtés à La Haye.

Pour commencer, je propose qu'un groupe de douze représentants, choisis parmi un nombre égal de nationalités, quittent l'Europe au mois de mars prochain, pour entreprendre un pélerinage dans l'Amérique du Sud, en visitant toutes les républiques, qui auront exprimé le désir de recevoir les apôtres internationaux. La tournée devrait durer quatre mois. Mais depuis lors l'Amérique Centrale a émis le désir que nous consacrions également un mois au Mexique et aux républiques voisines.

Comme le pélerinage international ira de capitale en capitale, il répandra partout la lumière brillante de son idéal sublime devant les yeux des nations. Et en même temps il expliquera les devoirs pratiques bien déterminés, arrêtés à La Haye, dont l'accomplissement hâtera la réalisation de cet idéal. La Conférence a voté plusieurs résolutions et elle a rédigé plusieurs articles, en disant „il est utile et désirable", ou „on recommande" etc. Le pélerinage se chargera de propager toutes ces recommandations parmi les peuples et les gouvernements du monde. Il apportera une nouvelle espérance au cœur presque détaillant de l'humanité.

Voici le premier groupe de ceux qui ont déclaré qu'ils sont prêts à nous accompagner dans notre pélerinage, qui sont pénétrés de la grande idée et qui sont à même de parler avec science et autorité des travaux accomplis à La Haye.

Nous espérons réussir à ajouter à ces huit le vétéran, M. Mercadier de l'Agence Havas, qui a déjà visité l'Amérique Latine et qui serait un pélerin qu'on ne saurait assez apprécier. Le colonel Tinge nous a promis un pélerin chinois et nous espérons trouver également un Japonais.

Le Dr. W. Foerster, de l'Université de Berlin, s'efforce de trouver un Allemand parlant l'Espagnol et, en ajoutant un Russe, un Américain du Nord et un Espagnol, le groupe des apôtres sera complet.

Nous espérons publier sous peu un numéro illustré, contenant des communications reçues de délégués qui désirent voir le succès de nos efforts pour faire comprendre au grand public du monde entier la signification de ce qu'on vient de faire à La Haye. Comme nous l'avons toujours dit, c'est la Conférence qui aurait dû se charger de cette tâche. Elle perd la moitié de son influence heureuse par le fait qu'on comprend si peu l'importance de ses travaux. Mais puisqu'une telle action exécutive dépasse le pouvoir de la Conférence, nous espérons sincèrement qu'avant la clôture tous les membres prédominants nous auront fait parvenir quelques mots de conseil et d'encouragement.

Les Prémiers Pélerins de la Paix.

M. Perez Triana *Colombie.* — M. Quesada *Cuba.* — M. Carvajal *Dominicaine.* — M. Matheu *Salvador.* — le Colonel Borel *Suisse.* — Sir T. Barclay *Ecosse.* — Chev. Cortesi *Italie.* — M. W. T. Stead *Angleterre.*

ARGENTINE:

Luis M. Drago

BOLIVIE:

Claudio Pinilla

BRÉSIL:

Ruy Barbosa

CHILI:

Domingo Gana

COLOMBIE:

CUBA:

DOMINICAINE:

EQUATEUR:

GUATÉMALA:

L'Amérique Latine.

HAITI:

MEXIQUE:

G. A. Esteva

NICARAGUA:

PANAMA:

B. Porras

PARAGUAY:

PÉROU:

SAN SALVADOR:

URUGUAY:

VÉNÉZUELA:

The Latin American Component

Vitoria and the Spanish Tradition

Whatever the Latin American concepts of international law prior to the beginning of the period of Spanish and Portuguese colonization in the 16th Century may have been, the complete isolation of the South American continent meant that any such concept had no impact on the Western or for that matter Asian international communities. It may even be argued that, prior to the first decades of the 19th Century and the establishment of the independent Latin-American States, no legal concept typical of the American continent had any real impact on Western thinking.

Paradoxically enough, the discovery of the New World in itself became an extremely important or, indeed, almost a decisive factor in the establishment of modern international law as such. It was, in the most literal sense, the broadening of their horizons which caused European theoreticians to review their thinking and meet practical challenges. The very titles of some major works of the prominent pioneers in the field are sufficient to lead one to this conclusion. The main tracts of the Spanish Dominican Francisco Vitoria (1480-1546) deal with 'The Indians recently discovered' and 'The Law of War Made by the Spanish on the Barbarians'. Along with the idealistic missionary work of Vitoria's fellow-Dominican and kindred spirit Bartholomew de las Casas (1474-1566) – the so-called 'Father of the Indians' – these tracts of Vitoria, which date from about 1540, constitute a welcome counterpart to the ruthless exploitation of the Indians and the ferocious cruelties perpetrated on them by the Western colonial powers.

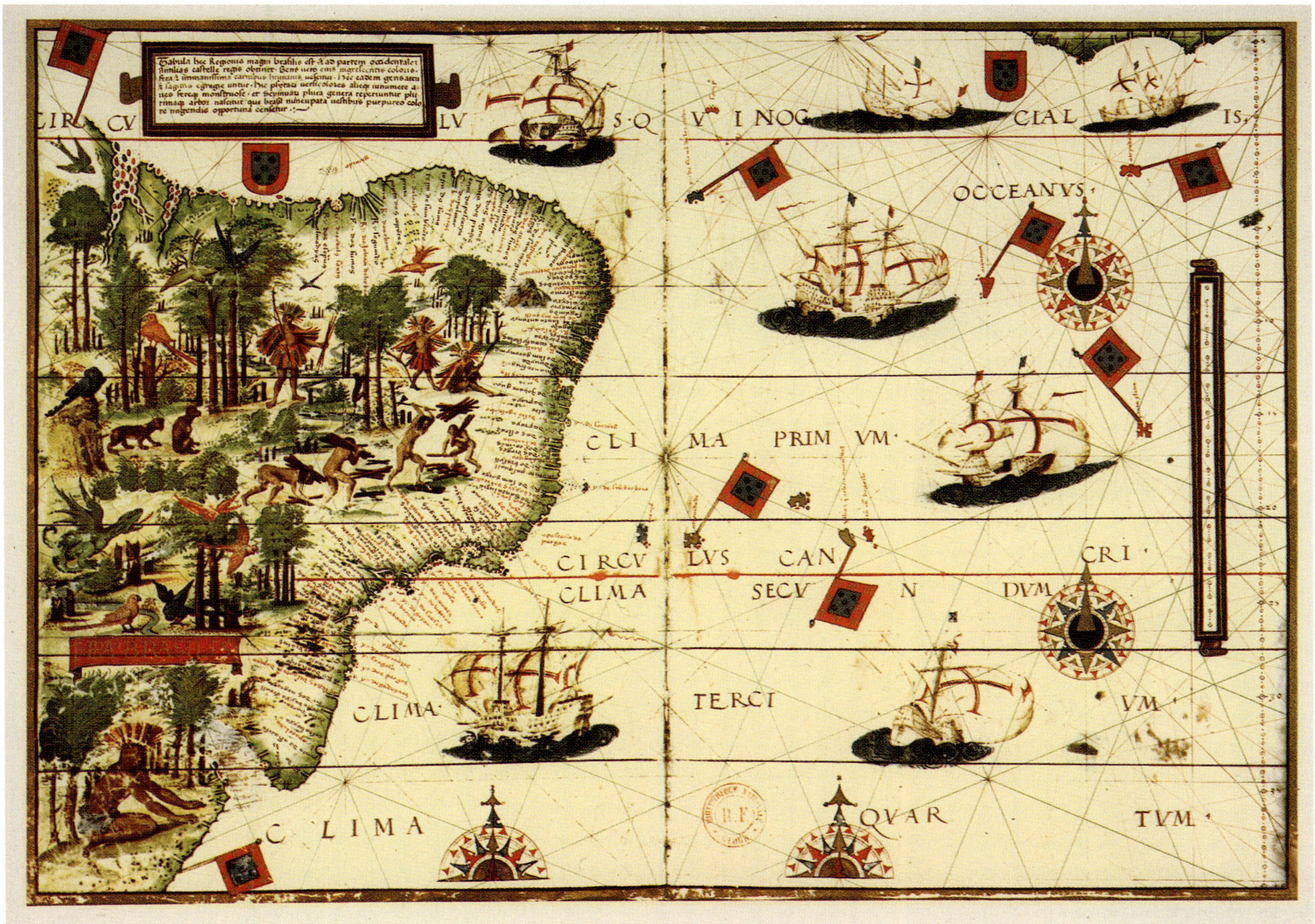

Lopo Homem-Reinéis

Atlas de 1519

Fol. 4 r.

Bibliothèque Nationale, Paris

Francisco de Vitoria (1480-1546), the Spanish Dominican theologian and jurist, professor at Valladolid and Salamanca and author of De Indis et de jure belli relectiones (1532).

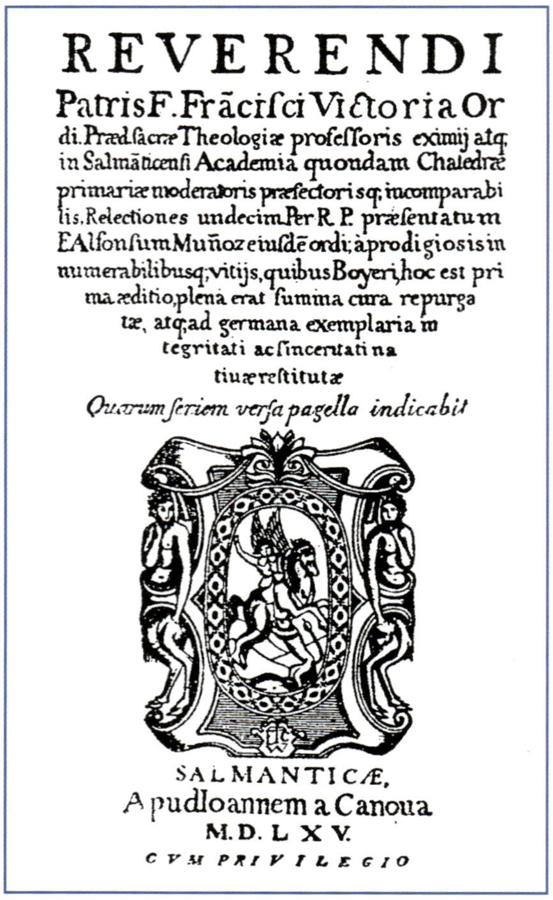
REVERENDI
Patris F. Fracisci Victoria Or
di. Praed. sacrae Theologiae professoris eximij atq;
in Salmaticensi Academia quondam Chaledrae
primariae moderatoris praefectorisq; incomparabi
lis. Relectiones undecim. Per R. P. praesentatum
F. Alfonsum Muñoz eiusdē ordi; a prodigiosis in
numerabilibusq; vitijs, quibus Boyeri, hoc est pri
ma aeditio, plena erat summa cura repurga
tae, atq; ad germana exemplaria in
tegritati ac sinceritati na
tiuae restitutae
Quarum seriem versa pagella indicabit
SALMANTICÆ,
Apud Ioannem a Canoua
M.D.LXV.
CVM PRIVILEGIO

Vitoria's inquiries into the conception of just war, that cornerstone of modern international law, were directed at a critical analysis of the treatment of the native tribes at the hands of the *conquistadores*. Vitoria reviewed these issues in the light of European moral concepts in both the ecclesiastical and secular spheres, and more particularly as comprised in the teachings of Thomas Aquinas. Even though they are steeped in medieval scholasticism, Vitoria's tracts are rare specimens of enlightened humaneness from that early period.

Vitoria was also the first to expound the concepts of freedom of commerce and freedom of the seas, which link him closely to Hugo Grotius' theory of *Mare Liberum* and to 17th Century Dutch colonial expansion. Grotius' views on the indigenous peoples led him, incidentally, to write two rather curious tracts *On the Origin of the American Nations*, which likewise bear witness to the climate of discussion at the time.

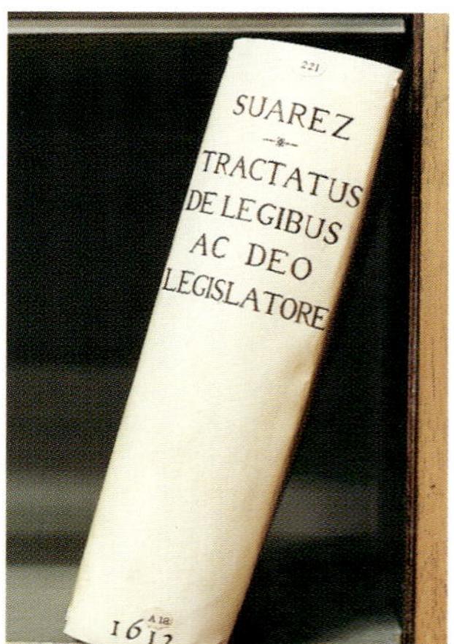

De Legibus ac Deo Legislatore (1621) by Francisco de Suarez (1548-1617), the Spanish Jesuit theologian and natural law philosopher.

The Pre-Colombian Phase

Can one speak of a pre-Colombian tradition of international law? If one maintains that the prerequisite of international law is a 'systematic intercourse among nations on equal terms', Latin America has probably precious little to show. In the area centred on Peru, at least from the 15th Century onwards, the dominance of the Inca Empire and its policy of assimilation through forced migration of populations was of course incompatible with the development of an international order in the true sense of the term. The same holds good, though perhaps less pertinently, for the grim and sombre regime of the Aztecs in the Mexican area during the two centuries prior to the arrival of the colonial powers. The most one can say is that war was subject to customary rules and that the concept of negotiations was widely accepted.

Latin America's first entrance on the international scene was not so much as a subject of international law, but rather as the object of competition among Western nations. In fact, what happened on this continent in the 16th and 17th centuries, was to be repeated in Africa in the late 19th and early 20th centuries. In 1493 the rivalry between the Castilians and Portuguese was settled – as was customary at the time – by a Papal Edict of Pope Alexander VI, the well-known *donatio Alexandrina*, that defined the boundary between the respective spheres of influence of the two rival powers. This partition was adjusted in the Tordesillas and Zaragoza Treaties of 1494 and 1529 respectively.

The Colonial Period

In terms of legal theory, the main issues at stake during this colonial period of over three centuries were, firstly, the legal status of the native inhabitants and secondly, the legality of the seizure of territory. The discussion was initially between, on the one hand, advocates of the traditional Two Swords theory (the doctrine that world hegemony was shared by Pope and Emperor), guided by rather vague Aristotelian notions as to the natural inequality among men and nations and, on the other hand, partisans of the Thomistic theory of natural law, which acknowledged the rights of the native populations, rejected the interference of Pope or Emperor, and insisted on the application of precepts of 'just war' in dealings with these pagan communities.

According to this latter doctrine, the newly discovered regions ought, at the most, to have been turned into temporary protectorates for the purposes of Christianisation and cultural elevation. Juan de Sepulveda (1490-1573) and Francisco de Vitoria may be seen as the major advocates of these views in the early days. In practice, representatives of religious orders, Dominicans like de Montesinos and de Las Casas, Augustinians such as de la Vera Cruz, Franciscans and Jesuits like Vieira in Brazil or Claver in Colombia fought tireless battles on behalf of the natives. The major concerns of these men were in the sphere of human rights, aimed at putting an end to the institution of slavery and the massive imports of African forced labour.

Predictably, the exclusive rights claimed by the Spanish and Portuguese on the newly discovered continent proved untenable in the long run. They were bound to be challenged by the British, Dutch and French, acting on behalf of their newly launched East India Companies. Their arrival on the scene, in about 1600, heralded a period of free buccaneering and the establishment, around the mid-17th Century, of scores of competing petty States in the Caribbean area. The ensuing controversies prompted the further development of theory in relation to the laws of the high seas. They also helped to develop another international concept, namely that of 'effectiveness' (*effectivité*), which took the effective occupation of territory to be the ultimate criterion applicable to any legal claims.

It took Spain some time to come to terms with these new views – as a result of successive treaties with the British (1630, 1670), Dutch (1648) and French (1697). The official renunciation by Spain and Portugal of the controversial demarcation lines of Tordesillas and Zaragoza became effective only in 1750. At about that time, most of Latin America was 'allocated' to the colonial powers and duly incorporated into the European legal system.

National Emancipation

It was around 1800 that the first counter-movement of national emancipation and decolonization took shape. The complex process leading to independence was more or less completed within the astoundingly short period of no more than three decades. In most of the Spanish possessions, this was the outcome of a fierce struggle. However, in Portuguese Brazil the secession took place as early as 1822 and on peaceful terms. Spain gradually recognized the independence of its overseas provinces, starting with Mexico in 1836.

It is to be emphasized here that the North American revolution did much to promote a similar spirit among its Southern neighbours, inasmuch as it helped to develop the concept of brotherhood in this hemisphere and the growing awareness of a distinct culture of its own, extending also to legal aspects. The Monroe doctrine, the isolationist policy proclaimed by USA President Monroe in 1823, which assumed that the nations of the Old and New World were essentially different in both political and economic terms, was wholeheartedly embraced by the Latin American nations.

Latin American Federalism

However, this political climate not only fostered separateness from the mother countries, it also furthered the first fragile attempts at federalism, as exemplified by the Federation of Central America and the 'Great Colombia' movement which, after initial successes, disintegrated in the 1830s. These attempts were essentially inspired by the thinking of Simon Bolivar (1783-1830) who, at the 1826 Panama Congress, launched the idea of an Amphictyonic League along ancient Hellenistic lines. Although this concept failed to gain ground, as did later attempts during the Lima Conferences of 1848 and 1865, the idea of cooperation itself never faded away. In the 1860s, Mexico waged its last fierce struggle against European intervention at the hands of the French.

This is not to say that there were no

Eduardo Jiménez de Aréchaga from Uruguay, Judge (1970-1979) and President (1976-1979) of the ICJ.

José Maria Ruda from Argentina, Judge (1973-1991) and President (1988-1991) of the ICJ.

Mexican law students presenting a portrait of their President to the President of the ICJ, Judge Manfred Lachs.

The coat of arms of Brasil.

internal conflicts among the Latin American nations. On the contrary, controversies abounded. They emanated, in most cases, from practical difficulties arising from attempts to verify the exact boundary-lines of the former Spanish colonial administrative units. Those disputes even led to the genesis of a new concept in international law, the *uti possidetis* rule. According to this rule, nations were entitled to the possessions and boundaries to which they could lay claim at the time of their independence, which for South America was fixed at 1810 and for Central America at 1821. In recent years the rule has been frequently invoked in disputes before the ICJ.

Be this as it may, in the mid 1800s, many bitter and bloody wars were waged within the fraternity of Latin American nations in

THE ORGANIZATION OF AMERICAN STATES

In 1889, the US Government took the initiative in inviting the American nations to an International Conference of American States in Washington, DC. Its purpose was to consider how to prevent wars in the region (arbitration of all disputes being suggested as a possible solution) and how to further communications, commercial and economic relations between the nations of the Western Hemisphere. The Washington Conference marked the beginning of the Organization of American States (OAS), then still called the Union of American Republics, and of what is commonly referred to as the Inter-American System or the Pan-American Movement. The Union was established on 14 April 1890 and ever since that day in April has been celebrated as *Pan-American Day*.

From then on, similar conferences were held periodically in different capitals, along with special conferences which dealt with specific problems. Some noteworthy venues and historic moments within our context were the following.

The Second Conference (Mexico City, 1901) adopted the Protocol of Adherence to the Conventions of the First Hague Peace Conference. The Fifth Conference (Santiago de Chile, 1923), formalized the technique of settlement of disputes in the so-called *Gondra Treaty*, a treaty to avoid or prevent conflicts between the American States. At the Sixth Conference (Havana, 1928), it was the later Judge and President of the ICJ, Guerrero, who introduced a firm resolution on non-intervention.

In 1929, a Special Conference in Washington signed the General Treaty of Inter-American Arbitration and the General Convention of Inter-American Conciliation. The Seventh Conference (Montevideo, 1933) adopted the Convention on the Rights and Duties of States, emphasizing the concepts of equality and non-intervention.

Three years later, at a Special Conference for the Maintenance of Peace in Buenos Aires, a convention highlighted the principle of consultation in cases of controversy. This system of consultation was again broadened in 1945, during a Special Conference in Mexico City which resulted in the *Act of Chapultepec*. This Act, among others, stated that aggression against one American State would henceforward be considered aggression against them all. This meeting also created the Inter-American Economic and Social Council.

It was at the Ninth Conference (Bogota, 1948), that the Charter of the OAS was adopted and the Union renamed the Organization of American States. It was also at this Ninth Conference, that the famous *Pact of Bogota* was approved – as the American Treaty on Pacific Settlement is commonly called – as well as the American Declaration of the Rights and Duties of Man.

Later years saw emphasis placed on Inter-American Cooperation in the economic, social and cultural spheres and the development of further instruments, notably in the sphere of human rights. In 1959 the Inter-American Commission on Human Rights was established, and in 1960 saw the adoption of the *Declaration of San José*, which denounced all types of intervention that could endanger American solidarity. In 1969, under the *Pact of San José*, the Inter-American Convention on Human Rights was adopted, generally along the lines of the 1950 European Convention on Human Rights, and the Inter-American Court of Human Rights was established. In 1971, again at San José, the Charter of the OAS was amended. Two years later, at Washington, DC, a Special Committee was created to upgrade and adjust the Inter-American System to changing hemisphere and world conditions. Among its achievements of recent years are the 1985 *Cartagena Protocol*, which again amended the Charter, and the 1991 Santiago Commitment to Democracy and the Renewal of the Inter-American System, which affirmed the 'inescapable commitment to the defence and promotion of representative democracy and human rights in the region, within the framework of respect for the principles of self-determination and non-intervention'. In 1993, in the *Managua Protocol*, the Inter-American Council for Integral Development was created, in an effort to eradicate extreme poverty from the hemisphere.

The general purposes of the OAS basically come under three categories: firstly, to strengthen security and peace and to ensure pacific settlement of disputes and mutual solidarity in the event of aggression; secondly, to promote, by cooperative action, the economic, social, and cultural development of member States; thirdly, to solve problems of an economic and political nature and notably aspects of human rights.

The Charter of the OAS particularly stresses important principles of international law and the fundamental rights and duties of States; in this, it reflects a time-honoured regional tradition, dating back to the late 19th Century. One such principle is non-intervention, be this by armed force or other means, notably economic aggression. Another principle is the obligation to settle disputes, as emphasized in the essential *Pact of Bogota*, which reaffirmed the basic concept of solidarity among the American nations.

an attempt to resolve such questions. The inconclusiveness of the settlements, often attained with the help of arbitrators, may be understood from the referral of some outstanding issues to the International Court of Justice in the past decade.

However, the idea of a Pan-American Movement was revived towards the end of the century by the newly emerging world power in the area, the United States of America. In 1889, it convened a First International Conference of American States in Washington, which led to the formation of the *Pan-American Union*, itself the cradle of the *Organization of American States* (OAS) that was established in 1948. Over the past hundred years, it was mainly through these institutions that regional organization and cooperation were developed into the elaborate 'Inter-American

The coat of arms of Mexico.

Membership of the OAS is open to all independent American States. Originally, these were the 20 Latin American republics and the USA. Since, 8 newly-independent English-speaking Caribbean States have joined. Also, over the years, some 20 non-American States have attained an observer status and accredited permanent observers.

The structure of the OAS in its present form – this being the outcome of successive amendments and refinements – provides, first, for a General Assembly, which is the supreme organ of the Organization and decides the general action and policy. It convenes its regular sessions annually, and special sessions when convoked by the Permanent Council. A second prominent organ is the Meeting of Consultation of Ministers of Foreign Affairs, which discusses problems of common interest urgent in nature. The amended Charter also provides for three Councils directly responsible to the General Assembly, which meet at least once a year: the Permanent Council, the Economic and Social Council, and the Council for Education, Science and Culture. The Permanent Council keeps vigilance over the maintenance of friendly relations among member States and is composed of representatives at ambassador rank of the member States; its seat is at Washington, DC, as is the seat of the General Secretariat.

This General Secretariat is the oldest, central and permanent organ of the OAS; at present, it has a staff of 700. It is headed by the Secretary-General and the Assistant Secretary-General, whose 5-year terms of office are renewable. They may not be succeeded by a person of the same nationality, in conformity with the general concept of equitable geographical distribution maintained throughout the OAS. The General Secretariat serves as the executive of all decisions taken by the other main organs and has all the features of the modern international secretariat.

Noteworthy, too, is the Inter-American Juridical Committee, composed of persons elected by the General Assembly in their private capacities. This advisory Committee intends to promote the progressive development of international law and its codification. From its outset, in the 1890s, the record of this Committee has been most impressive and numerous treaties and conventions, among which the ones enumerated above, have emanated from it, also in the sphere of private international law.

Among these latter features the famous 1928 *Bustamante Code*, which is still in force for 15 Latin American States. Antonio S. Bustamante y Sirven (1865-1951) was among the Judges of the ICJ who took an active part in the OAS and served on various organs and committees. Also worth mentioning in this respect are Judges Alvarez (who so strongly advocated the regional law traditions), Armand-Ugon, Guerrero (the initiator of the non-intervention treaty) and, in recent years, Judges Jiménez de Aréchaga and, notably in the sphere of human rights, Aguilar-Mawdsley.

In recent years, the OAS has been confronted by a new challenge in the notable reorientation of the traditional policies of the USA and the Latin-American nations *vis-à-vis* each other. This reorientation is marked by a distinct departure from the time-honoured 'special relationship' concept. This change was probably instigated by the 'New Dialogue' proposals generated in the early 1970s by the USA Foreign Office. These proposals put the North-South relations on a new footing, more particularly in the spheres of transnational enterprises and technology transfer.

Also in recent decades, and independently from the OAS, new bodies have been established to govern specific regions or areas in the relationships of the American world. In 1951, subregional cooperation on a limited scale materialized in the establishment of the Organization of Central American States (ODECA) between the five Central American Republics. According to the ambitions formulated in its revised Charter of 1962, the five republics are an economic-political community which aspires to the integration of Central America'.

The Inter-American Development Bank (IDB), constituted in 1959, is in fact the financing agency of the Inter-American System. It shares with the OAS responsibility for development programmes.

Noteworthy, too, are instruments such as the Alliance for Progress, established by the 1961 Charter of Punta del Este; the Special Committee on Latin American Coordination (CECLA) that was founded in 1963; the Latin American Economic System (SELA), that was created in 1975; and, finally, the Latin American Integration Association (LAIA), created in 1980.

At present, Inter-American cooperation and organization are undergoing profound transformation, and these also reflect the universal changes towards global interdependency. Obviously, these are not always easy to harmonize with traditional regional concepts.

Left : Simón Bolívar (1783-1830), the President of Colombia (1821-1830), whose efforts to constitute a Pan-American Union had a continuing ideological impact.

Right: Rui Barbosa (1849-1923), the Brazilian internationalist and Judge of the PCIJ 1922-1923), who was perhaps the most impressive spokesman of the Latin American world at the Second Hague Peace Conference of 1907.

System'as we know it today. The so-called 'Western Hemisphere Idea' and the idea of the 'Special Relationship' between Latin America and the USA have been crucial factors in the effectiveness of this process.

The Hague Peace Conferences

The newly acquired status of the nations of the Western Hemisphere likewise manifested itself on the political stage. This can be suitably illustrated by the prominent role these States played during the two Hague Peace Conferences. In 1899 it was Mexico alone that represented Latin America, but in 1907 all the new nations of the region were represented, with the sole exceptions of Honduras and Costa Rica, which were involved in another struggle at the time. On that occasion, the Latin American nations distinguished themselves in many respects, and this can also be said of some of their delegates, personally. For example, the Brazilian delegation was headed by a former Vice-President, Rui Barbosa, later a Judge of the PCIJ, who strongly advocated the compulsory arbitration of disputes.

The Colombian delegate, Perez Triana, the son of a former President, delivered some splendid speeches in impeccable French. The well-known Argentinian, Luis Maria Drago was reckoned to be among the most charming members of the Conference – although he for his part did not seem too pleased with the attendant social obligations, as one can gather from his comments half-way through the Conference to the effect that he 'could digest Obligatory Arbitration and a Permanent Court, but was since long fed up with the obligatory dinners and permanent salmon'. One may conclude that, from 1907 onwards, the Latin American nations were generally accepted within the concert of so-called 'civilized' nations.

A recent Ten Cruzados banknote of the Banco Central do Brasil, featuring Rui Barbosa and referring to the 1907 Conference.

Responding to this newly acquired status, the Latin American community also contributed some perceptions of its own, which in due course came to bear on the further development of international law. One of the more prominent representatives of the region, the Chilean internationalist and later Judge of the ICJ, Alejandro Alvarez, went so far as to postulate a New International Law which he saw as inherent in the Latin American tradition and complementary to European conceptions in the field; this idea has been abandoned. We will now enlarge on some of these typical regional concepts.

The New International Law

From early on, the very configuration of Latin American nations and their specific problems helped to further the theory of international law and the ready acceptance of a number of basic principles in the sphere of inter-State contacts. Prominent among these, were, apart from the above-mentioned *uti possidetis* rule, were the concepts of recognition, non-intervention and diplomatic asylum, and recourse to arbitration as the most appropriate way of settling disputes.

A number of scholars were instrumental in developing these principles. Among the most important were Andres Bello (1781-1865), who in his *Principios de derecho de gentes* (1832) attempted a synthesis of tenets from natural law and positive law along Grotian lines, the Argentinian Carlos Calvo (1824-1903), a prolific author and confirmed positivist whose historical analyses have remained of some value and, finally, the above-mentioned Chilean, Alejandro Alvarez (1868-1960), who was probably the first to bring certain psychological and sociological concepts to bear on his tenets.

Another typical regional feature is the fact that prominent diplomats helped to formulate distinct doctrines. Calvo formulated the doctrine or 'clause' which provides that aliens having property claims against Latin American governments should seek redress in the municipal courts and renounce diplomatic protection. In 1902 Drago was to rephrase this doctrine, which prompted a convention forbidding nations to use armed force against States that failed to meet their financial obligations, the so-called Drago-Porter Convention of 1907. The Tobar doctrine of the same year rejected the recognition of unconstitutional governments, but by 1930 this doctrine was replaced by the so-called *Estrada* doctrine which ruled out any recognition of governments as such, which it saw as a form of intervention.

The Central American Court of Justice

Possibly the most interesting confederation project in the Latin American context consisted of repeated attempts by the five Central American nations that had succeeded to the former Spanish Captaincy-General of Guatemala to crown their search for cooperation with the establishment of a genuine Central American Court of Justice, which was meant to become a permanent judicial body to deal with disputes. This was indeed a remark-

From top to bottom: caricatures of the Judges Urrutia, Alvarez and Guerrero from the League of Nations period.

Left: Andrés Bello (1781-1865), Chilean poet and scholar, sometimes regarded as the intellectual father of South America and mainly responsible for the model Chilean civil code of 1855. The bust was presented in 1978.

Carlos Calvo (1822-1906), Argentinian internationalist and diplomat, and strong defender of the rights and autonomy of the Latin American States. In his 'Calvo Doctrine' he prohibited armed intervention for the collection of private claims or debts.

Antonio S. de Bustamante y Sirven (1865-1951) from Cuba, Judge of the PCIJ from 1922-1942.

Epitacio da Silva Pessoa (1865-1942) from Brasil, Judge of the PCIJ from 1923-1930.

Francisco J. Urrutia (1870-1950) from Colombia, Judge of the PCIJ from 1931-1942.

able and most welcome initiative, all the more so since, up to that time and despite all efforts to the contrary, the history of those nations had been characterized by a consistent record of revolution and internal discord.

A first, rather artificial attempt, was made in 1902 in Cartagena. A second effort was made in the months following the Second Hague Peace Conference and in the wake of the success of the Washington Peace Conference chaired by Presidents Theodore Roosevelt of the USA and Porfirio Diaz of Mexico. That Conference managed to put an end to the ongoing hostilities between Guatemala, El Salvador and Honduras. The Court functioned from 1908 to 1918, had its seat in Costa Rica (first in Cartago, later in San José) and dealt with ten cases, of which only two resulted in affirmative judgments.

Despite its meagre record and obvious failure – mainly due to the system adopted for the election and payment of Judges, and a consequent lack of independence – the San José Court had all the characteristics of a truly innovative development. Notwithstanding the many shortcomings of the project, by setting high aims it was instrumental in defining the various options for a permanent international tribunal at a crucial stage in the development of international relations.Its typical feature of allowing individuals to bring actions directly against foreign States remains a novelty unparalleled down to the present day.

The Bench of the PCIJ

Six years after the dissolution of the San José Court in 1922, the Brazilian Rui Barbosa and the Cuban Bustamante y Sirven were elected to the first Bench of the PCIJ. The latter was to serve on the second Bench as well. Barbosa died within a year, and was replaced by his compatriot da Silva Pessoa, who in turn was succeeded by the Colombian Urrutia in 1931. The most impressive Latin American Judge of the inter-war period was, however, the Salvadoran Gustavo Guerrero, who was President of the PCIJ from 1936 onwards and later became the first President of the ICJ.

The only case in which Latin American nations were directly involved during the inter-war years was the 1929 *Brazilian Loans* case. Prior to that, however, three Latin American nations had been involved in a number of arbitral procedures before the Permanent Court of Arbitration: Mexico in the *Pious Fund* case (1902), Venezuela in the *Preferential Claims* case (1904) and the *Orinoco Steamship Company* case (1910), and Peru in the *Canevaro case* (1912) and the *Dreyfus* case (1921).

The Bench of the ICJ

In the past fifty years, Latin America has been represented on the Bench of the ICJ by a varied group of fifteen Judges and no fewer than nine nationalities: Argentina, Brazil, Chile, El Salvador, Mexico, Panama, Peru, Uruguay and Venezuela. Latin American nations have been directly involved in ten cases. Those cases, which will be discussed in more detail in the chapter on the caseload of the Court, particularly concerned matters of asylum and aspects of border disputes.

One may say that, over the years, the Latin American contribution to the development of contemporary international law has been considerable. Some of the typical regional legal concepts to which reference has already been made, have considerably influenced the jurisprudence of the ICJ and have by now been incorporated into contemporary practice.

The inauguration of the ICJ on 16 April 1946: H.R.H. Princess Juliana and Prince Bernhard of the Netherlands with President José Gustavo Guerrero of the ICJ.

The African Component

Bordering on the place where Egypt beholds the rays of the rising sun lies the land of Phoenicia, which has made her name in the world through her ambiguous contributions, of which it remains an open question as to whether they have served or rather harmed mankind. Hailed on the one hand is Taautes' invention, the faculty of recording in four times six characters whatever is to be seen at sea, on land or in the movement of the celestial spheres and the upper space which keeps the universe together, or whatever the human mind – itself of no less universal import – is capable of conceiving.

But on the other hand it is this same nation which, as if mankind were not sufficiently stricken by diseases and beasts of prey (in particular that creature which lies in ambush in the waters of the Nile, the crocodile), braved the oceans' high waves in frail boats, thus showing many new ways to die; and which, instead of skirting the shores within sight of land, set sail across the deep oceans, where lands fade away, under the guidance of the southern and northern stars. Not, that is, to carry to or from remote shores man's natural requirements, which are in fact fairly few, but rather to have kings dress up in wools dyed in the ocean's blood, or have the

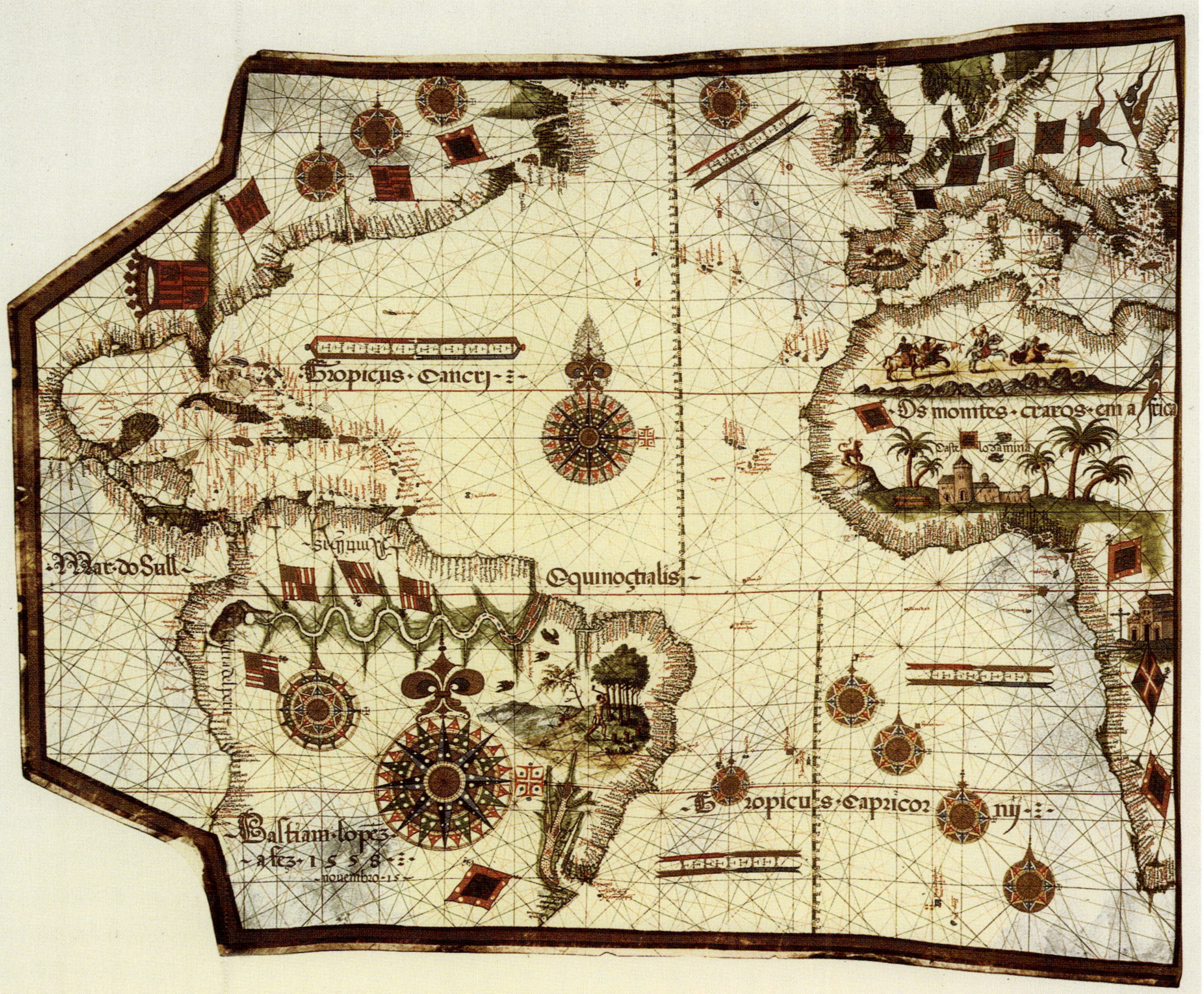

Sebastião Lopes, 1558

British Museum, London

Illustrations taken from Ch. de Matrin-Donos, Les Belges dans l'Afrique Centrale *(3 vols. 1886).*

fingers of the rich adorned with sparkling green gems.

Hence comes this insane thirst for gold. This direful craving, which first taught us to despise the dangers of the heavens and the seas and to commit our lives to a frail piece of timber – to what crimes does it not incite mankind?

Thus, Hugo Grotius, in his neo-Latin drama on the rule of Viceroy Joseph in Egypt depicts the activities of the early Phoenician merchants. The words apply to Africa. It was Phoenician traders who reputedly first skirted its coasts in search of merchandise. According to one legend they even circumnavigated the continent. The Nigerian Yoruba, whose kingdom once extended from Accra to the banks of the Niger, still claim their origins from this 'tribe of Nimrod' and the days of the Meroe Empire.

Soon, the Carthaginians followed suit. Hanno's legendary expedition of the 5th century BC was the first to venture beyond the Pillars of Hercules to discover the wealth of the Senegal River and the Gambian estuary. The expedition penetrated into the Sierra Leone headland, wondered at the 'Chariot of the Gods' as it called the Cameroon Mountain, and founded emporia all along the Gabon River. Whatever had been the expedition's first incentive – exploring, adventure, trade – the lure of gold was enough reason to stay. The Carthaginians were the first to discover the *Hinterland*, from which they enrolled men, like the famous Numidian cavalry of Hannibal's army. They busily exchanged raw products and manufactured goods along the trans-Saharan caravan routes that linked their cities in the north with the Sudan savannah belt. From then on, stories of African treasures never ceased to attract people of all nationalities.

Many centuries later, the gold that was imported into Morocco overland through the Taghaza road, did not fail to lure the Portuguese. Henry the Navigator's seamen thoroughly explored the West coast. On 26 March 1515 King Manuel signed a contract for the trade of Sao Tomé with the Benin chief Fernao Jorge stipulating the annual tribute through the *Carreira da India* of 500 quintals of Maldive cowries – to illustrate the extent of communications entertained in the Guinea region.

Around this time, the kingdom of Benin had attained its apogee, featuring largely urban patterns of settlements and an intricate network of trade in cloth, beads and other luxuries. As with the other African kingdoms, it was the Arab invasion of the Sudan and soon afterwards the arrival of European enterprise and its discovery of new trade routes that gradually broke the back of the long-distance trade and consequently the economy of the time-honoured empires and dynasties. Around 1550 the British stepped in, followed 50 years later by the Dutch. Most of the records from these days which might have attested to these stunning indigenous cultures are lost, which is all the more surprising as they did know the art of writing, using Arabic characters mostly. Still, even the sparse data that remain, reveals the relatively high standards of living in most of the African interior at the time. As early as 1480 AD, a canal was constructed to join Timbuktu with Aiwalatin. Those were the days when the King of the Congo headed an aristocratic hierarchy which impressed even the Portuguese and when alliances for attack and defence were concluded between the Kings of Ghana and Mali and the Moroccan rulers. Around 1600, the Emperor of Bornu negotiated with the Ottoman Sultan at Tripoli on terms of equality.

The reception of a Portuguese delegation by the King of Congo. From an early engraving.

Perhaps the oldest of the African kingdoms was that of Ghana, which flourished during most of the first millennium of the Christian era. The gold of Wangara, the salt of Taghaza and the slave trade with the Maghreb merchants were the bases of its economy which centered around the legendary capital of Kumbi and stretched from the Niger and Senegal Rivers on the east and south to the desert in the north and west. In 1067 Kumbi fell to Islamic expansion and, its inhabitants massacred, was never really to recover.

Sir Henry Morton Stanley (1841-1904), British-American explorer of Central Africa and main agent of King Leopold in the establishment of the Congo Free State (1885).

After a short interval of Susu hegemony, the torch was taken over by the Mali empire which in the 13th century became the dominating force in the whole of the Western Sudan, again on the strength of the Wangara goldfields and the Takodda copper mines. During his pilgrimage to Mecca, the wealth and generosity displayed by Mansa Musa, its early 14th-century ruler, caused a sensation in Cairo and passed into legend for centuries. In the marketplaces of its capital, Timbuktu, the nomads of the desert and the riverine peoples of the Niger exchanged salt and dates for grain, kola nuts and gold dust. Timbuktu was also a centre of culture and scholarship, in close touch with the Egyptian and Arabian worlds of learning, attracting students from far afield. Elias quotes Bovill who commented that Mansa Musa was probably 'the first to penetrate the iron curtain of colour prejudice which shut off the Negro from the civilized world, and to win for the true African a small measure of respect'.

By the beginning of the 15th century, with the decline of Timbuktu, Songhai Goa under Sonni Ali and later Askia the Great, gradually took over. Peopled by fisherfolk and farmers, Goa was divided into a Muslim and pagan quarter. At its apex, the empire overran the Hausa States to extend all the way towards Lake Chad. Askia enjoyed friendly relations throughout the Mediterranean; Western diplomats, doctors and scholars frequented his court.

Around the time the first Portuguese entered the scene, the Niger-based Yoruba, through one of its major offshoots, the Bini of Benin, had taken ascendancy. Portuguese sailors found Great Benin larger than Lisbon, with impressive houses, straight streets, ivory sculpture of high artistic sophistication and a thriving brasswork industry. From here, around 1650, Portuguese, British and Dutch factories rivalled in trading cloth, oil, cowries and ivory for resale along the African coastline.

As Weeramantry maintains (*An Invitation to the Law* 1982, at p.35) all these civilizations, be this the Kingdom of the Congo, the Monomotapa Kingdom in Central Africa or the Zulu Empire in the south east, 'could not, clearly, have existed without correspondingly developed legal systems to support their commercial and administrative needs'. To service these governments, a body of supporting legal concepts and mechanisms must have existed which have yet to be adequately researched. African law was, until the postwar years, a greatly neglected area of legal studies. 'The tendency to dismiss legal systems not consisting of book law as not warranting scholarly study, combined with a vast ignorance of African culture and civilisation, were largely responsible for this neglect'. Also, it would be 'unwise ... to speak of African customary law as though it were one entity capable of adequate survey within the confines of any one study'. A customary law of such antiquity must necessarily be complex. 'The material is vast and bewildering, and while there may be some similarities the differences are considerable. We are indeed looking at a series of legal systems.' African law shows in some respects a surprising maturity and mellowness of principle. An observer from the early 1920s noticed 'almost everywhere an orderly method of procedure before a constitutional tribunal, ... a remarkable taste for juridical casuistry and a keen enjoyment of forensic eloquence'. The Kikuyu of Kenia had their *muthamaki*, a leader in law who was chief spokesman and judge and the settler of disputes by reason of his prestige and legal knowledge. The Tswana of Botswana settled their disputes with the aid of *bagakolodi* or legal experts who were associated with the chiefs in their courts. The machinery developed within the African system of customary law was devoid of formalism. It may afford scholars fresh insights and alternative approaches to the settlement of disputes.

As Weeramantry observes, some of the African legal concepts may well afford inspiration to the legal systems of the future:

> For example, many African peoples view land not as a piece of property exclusively enjoyed by those presently alive, but as the property of the whole community – the deceased, the living and the unborn. The living enjoy it but hold it in trust for the unborn who must enjoy it in their time. Likewise they cannot so use it as to dishonour or desecrate those who were once its owners. An age which in two generations has been consuming a substantial proportion of the earth's resources will derive much benefit from examining more closely such attitudes which emphasise trustee-

ship rather than absolute ownership in regard to the most important of our resources. (*op. cit.*, at p. 36)

One mistake should be avoided in attempting to understand African law:

European law is based largely on individualism whereas the African concept is one of collectivism. African law is aimed at maintaining the equilibrium of society, rather than at dealing with specific infractions. It does not attach importance to written codes, but is an organic growth keeping in tune with the changing needs of society.(*ibid.*, at p. 37)

All these empires and dynasties, whose origins dated back to the early Middle Ages, showed a similar and in fact striking continuity. Eastern Nigeria was ruled by the Kanem-Bornu for over a thousand years, the Songhai lasted 800 years and the same holds true for the Mali kingdom and the Upper Volta area. From 800 BC to AD 300 there flourished the Kush civilization in what is now the Sudan. It was external influences only that unbalanced this society and toppled its dynasties, one after the other. From around 1850 onwards, the European colonizing powers, within a matter of decades, made short shrift of centuries of African culture. First the British 'in a crusade to expiate past sins' (Elias) employed a naval blockade to cut off the supply of African slaves to the trans-Atlantic economy. Then, the opening of the Suez Canal in 1869 and the British occupation of Egypt in 1882 provoked a rivalry among the Western powers that was to have such devastating effects upon the continent. British claims all over Africa were challenged by the French around Zanzibar and Lake Chad, by the Belgians and Portuguese in the Congo basin, the Germans in Dar-es-Salaam and the Italians along the Somali coast. The partition of Africa was about to start.

The Colonial Era

Even as, in the 1890s, the opening scenes were set at The Hague for Tobias Asser's Private International Law Conference (1894-1895) and Martens' First Peace Conference of 1899, the same powers that were talking peace and cooperation in Europe, were engaged in bitter colonial rivalries in Africa. This struggle was the result of yet another European congress – albeit of a very different nature – namely the Berlin West Africa Conference of 1884-85.

By 1870 the expeditions of Stanley, the French Colonel Tilho, and many others, had opened up the time-hallowed seclusion of the forests and plains of Africa to the astonished eyes of the white man. Political and commercial interests grew rapidly. In 1876 Leopold II, the King of the Belgians, initiated the International Congo Association. Likewise, the French launched their *Société française de l'Afrique Equatoriale*. In 1882 the British occupied Egypt. All these military expeditions and commercial undertakings heralded what we have now come to call 'the Scramble for Africa'. In keen competition the 'Civilized World' partitioned, within a matter of decades, some 90 percent of the vast 'Dark Continent'. French, British, Portuguese and German forces zigzagged through the newly accessible regions, claiming sovereignty over wide areas as if they were *terra nullius*, no man's land, and demarcating boundaries irrespective of tribal affiliations.

Only recently, in the 1994 hearings in the Libya-Chad boundary case regarding the Aouzou strip and the Lake Chad area, the ICJ was once more dramatically confronted with this fascinating and tragic era of European imperialism. Within just a few decades, age-old and respected African kingdoms and city States disappeared. Likewise, homogenous ethnic groups were cruelly split up between separate colonial entities. It happened to the Congo, to Togoland, the Cameroons, Somaliland, Katanga and Zambia – to name just a few.

As early as 1878 the danger of clashes among the rival powers became so imminent that the newly founded *Institut de Droit International* saw fit to address the problem and suggest neutralized areas and zones of free trade and navigation. It was in Berlin, in November 1884, that the European Powers finally established the so-called Colonial Régime. Typically enough, and despite the scores of treaties concluded by the Western Powers with the African kings and sovereigns in previous years, not a single African territory was represented or otherwise took part in the Conference.

Admittedly, the Conference did have some positive implications for the African nations: it helped to suppress the slave

Leopold II (1835-1909), King of Belgium (1865-1909), who helped develop the Congo Basin.

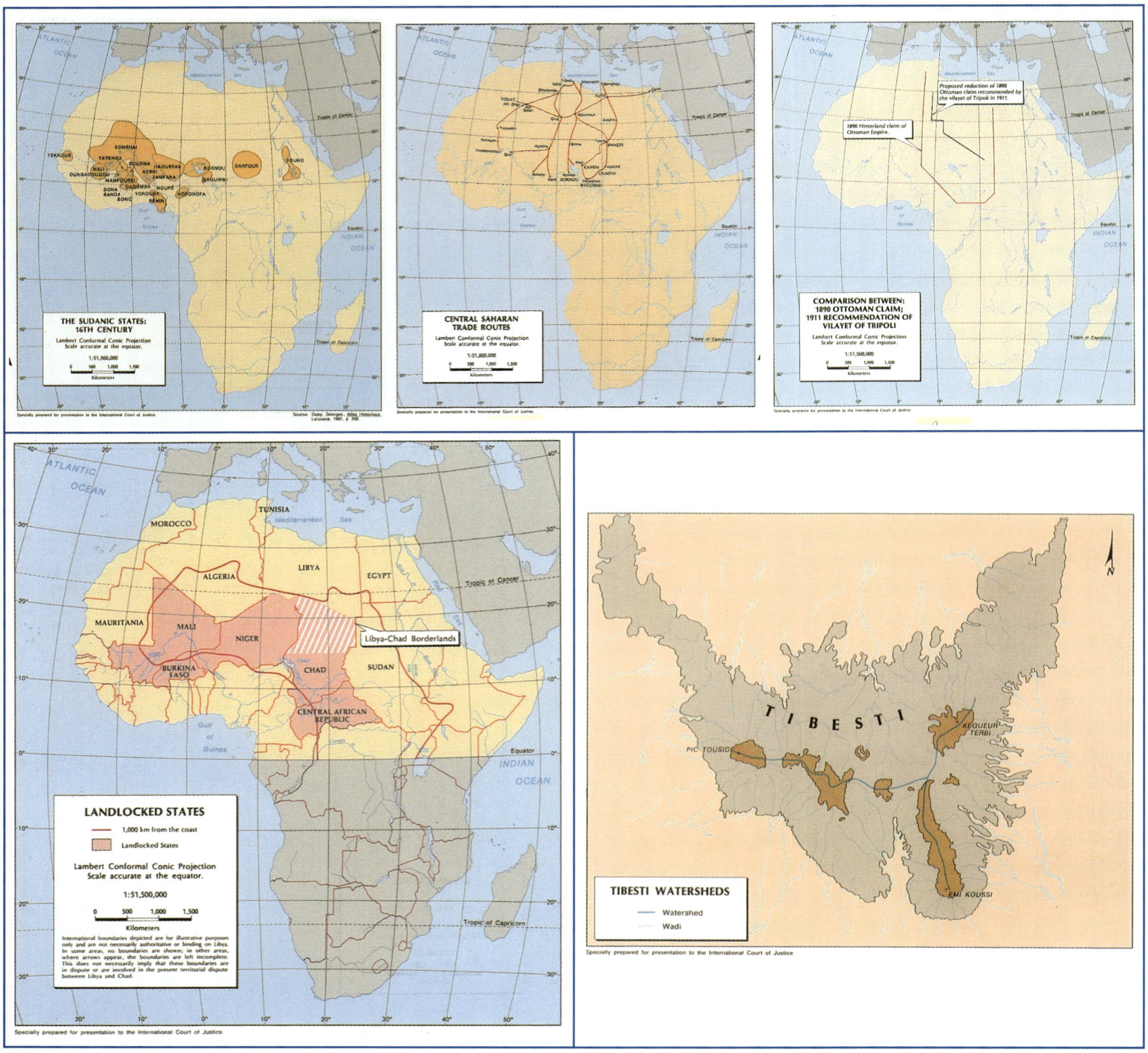

Maps from the 1994 Libya-Chad Boundary *case.*

trade and restrict trade in firearms and liquor; it also fashioned the definition of a new concept in international law, the notion of 'effective occupation', which then became the prerequisite for claims on territory. Still, the Navigation Acts for the Congo Basin, the Niger River Régime and so many other arrangements put together in Berlin – and soon supplanted by later agreements between the English, French and Germans on East Africa (1890), the Congo (1894) and the Nile Basin (1899), effectively introduced the Colonial Era, a period of 60 years during which the African Continent, only just awakening to the challenges of the modern world, came to experience the privilege of being involved in international affairs – though not as a *subject* but merely as the *object* of international law. It was only with the establishment of the United Nations, in 1945, that its status was to change to any substantial extent. From this perspective it is understandable that when, in 1964, the Nine Riparian States established their River Niger Commission, they did not regard themselves as in any way bound by the Berlin Treaty.

The Mandate System

Obviously, the African nations did not attend the Hague Conferences and had no say in the establishment of the League, or for that matter the PCIJ. This is not to say, however, that they were not involved. Matters relating to the Congo, Morocco and Egypt occasioned a number of cases before the Permanent Court. Of these, the 1934 *Oscar Chinn* case on matters of discrimination and expropriation is perhaps the best-known. One issue is, however, worth singling out at this juncture, as it was bound to introduce a new phenomenon into international law in subsequent decades.

In the wake of World War I, defeated Germany was forced to abandon its African colonies. The consequences of this decision were dramatic. (The issue of the Northern Cameroons was to occupy the ICJ as late as 1961). At Versailles, these regions were shared out amongst the Allies as so-called 'mandated territories' consisting of communities, as it was put at the time, 'not yet able to stand by themselves under the strenuous conditions of the modern world'. The Western Powers took it upon themselves to give a helping hand to these populations on their long and difficult path to eventual independence and self-government. Under the Covenant of the League, six African Territories were to be administered by these Mandatory Powers, subject to the League's ultimate responsibility through the Permanent Mandate Commission. The Cameroons and Togo were split up between the British and the French; Rwanda and Burundi went to Belgium, and a mandate for South West Africa was conferred upon the Union of South Africa.

The establishment of this so-called Mandate System was to be of considerable significance to the development of international law in the next half-century – and to the World Court as well. It is here that the roots of the notorious *Namibia* issue, that would preoccupy the ICJ for some twenty years and would, to a large extent, condition the attitude of the developing world to the Court during the 1960-1970s, are to be found.

From Trusteeship to Self-Determination

In the UN Charter of 1945, the concept of mandates was re-styled into what was termed 'trusteeship' and the mandated territories were placed under the auspices of the Trusteeship Council, established for the purpose of promoting their political, economic and social advancement. However, the Union of South Africa refused to place its mandated territory under the UN Trusteeship system, arguing that as a Mandatory Power it was accountable only to the League, to which, in its view, the UN had not succeeded. In 1950, the ICJ found against the Union, which then refused to comply with the Court's Judgment. The case was brought up again in 1962, dramatically reopened in 1966, and finally settled in 1970 (as is described in more detail elsewhere), albeit not without considerable damage to the standing of the Court in the eyes of the developing world.

At the inception of the UN, in 1945, only four African nations were to be found among its 51 Member-States. Today, fifty years later, there are. These figures reveal the relevance of the UN forum to the African continent, and at the same time dramatically illustrate the changes in world organization that have become apparent in recent decades. It was through the UN that Africa attained independence and self-determination between 1945 and 1965, and it is through the UN that Africa, between 1965 and 1985, helped to change the face of the community of nations. It took the young nations of Africa twenty years to get in, and once inside, another twenty years to help fundamentally alter the Organization itself – for, to be sure, the emergence of the new Members has profoundly changed not just the composition, but the very character, orientation and objectives of the United

The official gift from Nigeria, presented to the Court in 1990.

'Law takes precedence over force'. A mosaic that was discovered at Kelibia in Tunisia representing the Myth of Marsyas. It was presented to the ICJ in 1966 by President Bourguiba of Tunisia on the occasion of his visit to the Court.

Nations. On the one hand, existing bodies and organs were enlarged, as was the case with the General Assembly, the Security Council (from 11 members to 15) or ECOSOC (from 18 to 27), while on the other a more equitable geographical distribution was secured. On the one hand, the scope of functions was widened; on the other, new institutions were established.

The young African nations were, moreover, prompted by the example of the United Nations Organization when they reviewed their internal relations and grew into a homogenous group, as exemplified by the OAU, the Organization of African Unity. All these achievements, both internal and external, were obviously dearly won and attained through resistance only. On both levels, unity was the outcome of often bitter combat. On 14 December 1960, when over thirty non-self-governing territories had become independent, the General Assembly in a historic resolution adopted the 'Declaration on the Granting of Independence to Colonial Countries and Peoples', in which it expressed its concern at the slow pace of decolonization which, it felt, militated against the ideal of universal peace for which the UN stood.

On the internal plane, in 1961-1962, the more radical members of the Casablanca Group and the moderate members of the Monrovia Group shook hands at Lagos. In the following year, they came together at Addis Ababa, to proudly toast the Charter of the Organization of African Unity. Similarly, amazing achievements have been effected within the sphere of UNITAR (the UN Institute for Training and Research, launched in 1963 to enhance the effectiveness of the Organization) and UNESCO, and through UNCTAD and the ILC.

THE ORGANIZATION OF AFRICAN UNITY

In April 1958, in Accra, 7 African States (Egypt, Ethiopia, Ghana, Liberia, Morocco, Sudan and Tunisia) met at the Conference of Independent African States, the first meeting of its nature in the African world. It marked a turning point in the history of the Continent. The following year, the ensuing Ghana-Guinea Union, initiated by Liberia's President Tubman, in its *Sanniquellie Declaration* formulated the requirements for the achievement of African Unity and made an appeal to all African nations to sign up to the idea. In 1960, 13 French territories in Africa became independent and joined forces in the so-called Brazzaville Group.

However, the road to unity was to be a problematical one. The Congo crisis spread discord among the young nations, leading to the establishment of new groups of States, the Casablanca and Monrovia Groups. The latter, which included the Brazzaville Group, resulted from the initial, and historic, meeting of all French-speaking and most English-speaking African States.

During its second meeting at Lagos, in 1962, the Monrovia Group broke new ground by approving the Charter of the Organization of Inter-African and Malagasy States. Political disturbances impressed upon the African world the urgent need for reconciliation of the two conflicting groups. This was effected during the 1963 Conference at Addis Ababa, which gave birth to the Organization of African Unity (OAU), with an initial membership of 32 nations.

The OAU Charter was a compromise on Africa's path to freedom from the colonial era and the trauma of subsequent upheaval. It stressed the 'inalienable right of all peoples to control their own destiny', recognized the links between the human and natural resources of the African continent and made a strong appeal to its members to accept the directives of the UN Charter and the Universal Declaration of Human Rights in their future policies. Members pledged to harmonize their policies in all matters of politics and economy.

The OAU intended both to eradicate colonialism and to promote unity and solidarity among the many, inexperienced nations on the basis of sovereignty and territorial integrity. The quality of life in Africa, it maintained, would best be furthered by a coordinated effort to harmonize policies, by the emancipation of all dependent territories and by non-alignment with any external groups. It stressed the concept of non-intervention and excluded from participation any liberation movements and territories still under colonial rule. Cooperation of member States on the basis of equal rights, was the prevailing idea of the Organization which in its Charter borrowed freely from UN constitutive texts. It established four main institutions: the Assembly of Heads of State and Government, the Council of Ministers, the General Secretariat, and the Commission of Mediation, Conciliation and Arbitration – a tested formula.

The Assembly, the supreme Organ, appoints the executive branch, the Administrative Secretary-General and his staff. It adopts resolutions by a two-thirds majority, each member having one vote. The Council, mostly of Foreign Ministers, is responsible to the Assembly. It prepares conferences, implements its decisions and adopts resolutions by simple majority on the basis of a two-thirds quorum.

The Administrative Secretary-General, who is appointed by the Assembly and constitutes the Executive, occupies a prominent position. He is at liberty to impose his own style and approach on the Organization. He is appointed for renewable terms of four years. The Secretariat submits the annual budget to the Council.

Perhaps the most striking feature of the formula adopted for the resolution of possible disputes, is the unvarying reliance on mediation, conciliation and

Africa on the Bench of the ICJ

What impact have these revolutionary developments had upon the body of jurists that constitutes the ICJ? As stated above, in 1966 the ICJ made seats on the Bench available to Africans: it welcomed two at first (Senegalese and Nigerian Judges), but this number was soon enlarged to three. Their inclusion was not achieved by enlarging the Bench, but through an internal, that is regional redistribution of seats. It is no secret that this change was made under external pressure after the controversial 1966 *Namibia* Judgment and that, in itself, the re-distribution did not do much to enhance the image of the Court in the Developing World. Around 1965, the idea of an inner circle of civilized nations and the application by the Court of traditional European custom was still widely believed in.

The Council for Mali during the hearings in the Burkina Faso/Mali Frontier Dispute case (1983-1986).

arbitration, as duly reflected in the name of the special Commission. It is perhaps noteworthy, too, that even within these three specified categories – which therefore exclude adjudication by the ICJ among others -, the most frequently invoked method is the more informal mediation procedure. We may well find here a reflection of customary law and time-honoured traditions.

To date, Member States have shown little interest in the much more complex conciliation procedure, which calls *inter alia* for the appointment of a Board of Conciliators. The same can be said of the arbitral procedure, which provides for the designation of one arbitrator by each party and of a third member, to serve as Chairman, by these two arbitrators or, in case of disagreement, by the Bureau.

The Charter also provides for the establishment of Specialized Commissions or Agencies to deal with matters of a socio-economic or cultural nature, and various areas such as national defence and health care.

Over the past thirty years, the OAU has experienced a number of dramatic events which have, at times, all but torn apart its still fragile fabric. War, famine and intrigue have shattered the continent; tribal strife, refugees issues, disputes in areas with undefined boundaries, as well as matters of apartheid and decolonization, have posed scores of insurmountable problems for the OAU. The refugee problem in particular, self-assuredly tackled by the 1967 Addis Ababa Conference, by the special Bureau that was then established and by the 1969 Refugee Convention, which governed the OAU approach to the problem for the next two decades, has still baffled all efforts. Still, it bravely faced the challenges, and documents such as the 1969 *Lusaka Manifesto*, which called for peaceful negotiation and compromise, or the draft African Charter of Human Rights, negotiated at Monrovia in 1979, constitute landmarks in the chequered struggle to achieve unity and liberty for all. It has overcome serious threats such as, in 1982, the issues of the admission of the Saharan Arab Democratic Republic and the representation of Chad which kept its members sharply divided, and quite a number of civil uprisings such as the Nigerian and Angolan civil wars, the Guinea/Senegal dispute and the Somalian/Ethiopian border dispute.

It now has, working at its Headquarters and regional offices, a staff of 600, from over 40 independent African countries, including some 150 in the professional category.

In 1964 a Committee of Fifteen on Refugees was set up to supervise this problem. Again. in 1988, during a joint Conference with the UN in Oslo, the OAU launched the *Oslo Plan for Action*, seeking international humanitarian aid and calling for research for lasting solutions to the refugee problem.

In 1981 the African Charter of Human and Peoples' Rights was signed. Again, in 1986, the African Commission on Human and Peoples' Rights was set up. During its 1993 Summit in Cairo, the OAU established the Mechanism for Conflict Prevention, Management and Resolution.

An economic committee studies the steady deterioration of terms of trade and export of African nations which, at present, still harbours two-thirds of the least developed countries of the world. Accordingly, the African continent is very eager and concerned over the global efforts to achieve an equitable distribution of the world's resources through the establishment of a New International Economic Order, as exemplified by the 1980 Lagos Plan of Action and Africa's Priority Programme for Economic Recovery launched in 1985 and the establishment of a Common Relief Fund in 1991. That same year African leaders signed the Treaty establishing the African Economic Community.

Simultaneously, blueprints for a rational continental telecommunications network have been prepared, air strips are being developed, and highways, railways and bridges built all over the continent.

The African Cultural Charter, adopted in 1976 on Mauritius, is designed to affirm the cultural identity of the peoples of Africa and guarantee free access to culture for all.

There can be little doubt that the conservatism displayed by one side was often challenged by the other. There is perhaps no issue that the African Judges have stressed more insistently (as for that matter have the Asian and Latin-American) than the need for a new, *contemporary* international law and the replacement of the static views of the past by a recognition of the principle of progressive *development* of international law. The International Law Commission, another body which grew from 15 to 25 Members in 1961, has been particularly instrumental in these respects in recent decades. Major stepping-stones towards recognition were, furthermore, the appointment of a Secretary-General and Under-Secretaries-General from the developing world, and the increasing recruitment of Secretariat Staff from developing world countries. The election of Judge Elias to the Presidency of the Court in 1982 was a truly historic moment for the whole of Africa.

In an attempt to explain the initially somewhat negative attitude of the newly independent nations towards the Court, it has often been maintained that the African world is, by its very tradition, opposed to the idea of adjudication itself, and to compulsory jurisdiction in particular, and that it much prefers extra-legal procedures of dispute settlement, such as mediation, conciliation, political negotiation, or, for that matter, arbitration. There is little to show that this is in fact the case, except that in principle African nations are naturally disposed to begin by seeking for a compromise in a spirit of brotherhood, which holds true especially in the politically sensitive area of boundary disputes.

An altogether different matter, however, is the way in which these young States often questioned the objectivity, universality and the effectiveness of international law as they found it when first entering upon the international stage. As has already been pointed out, the reference in the essential Article 38(1) of the Statute of the Court to 'international custom' and 'civilized nations' gave them some grounds for misgivings. Customary international law was, in their eyes, the creation, the practice, and in fact nothing more than the reflection of power structures within the European *côterie*, and more often than not ran contrary to non-European interests. What they demanded was at least a critical re-evaluation of these rules in the light of the traditions, practice and topical needs of a *global* community. Likewise, the bias implicit in the phrasing 'civilized nations' needs no further comment. As maintained by a representative of Burundi in a General Assembly Meeting in 1970: '... no State or group of States ha[s] a monopoly of civilization in the modern world'.

Another point was that – and certainly at the outset – the young nations had not yet familiarized themselves with the intricacies of the procedure of the ICJ. Their lawyers lacked the required expertise and some of those nations could not afford, financially, to embark on time-consuming pleadings in The Hague. All these problems have been solved over time and by dint of strenuous efforts on both sides. However, the most important single factor which affected the attitudes of the African States was undoubtedly the 1966 judgment on Namibia, of which a Ghanaian representative once commented:

> The decision of the ICJ ... must constitute a serious affront to the legal conscience of the world community and shake the very basis of decency in international life. It is the unspeakable irony of our time that an institution of the order of the International Court of Justice, forged out of contemporary norms and principles, should be used to frustrate and stultify the implementation and furtherance of these ideals.

One must conclude that for a number of years the reluctance of African nations to refer cases to the Court, was fostered by the fear of a judgmental process which might thus be weighted against them.

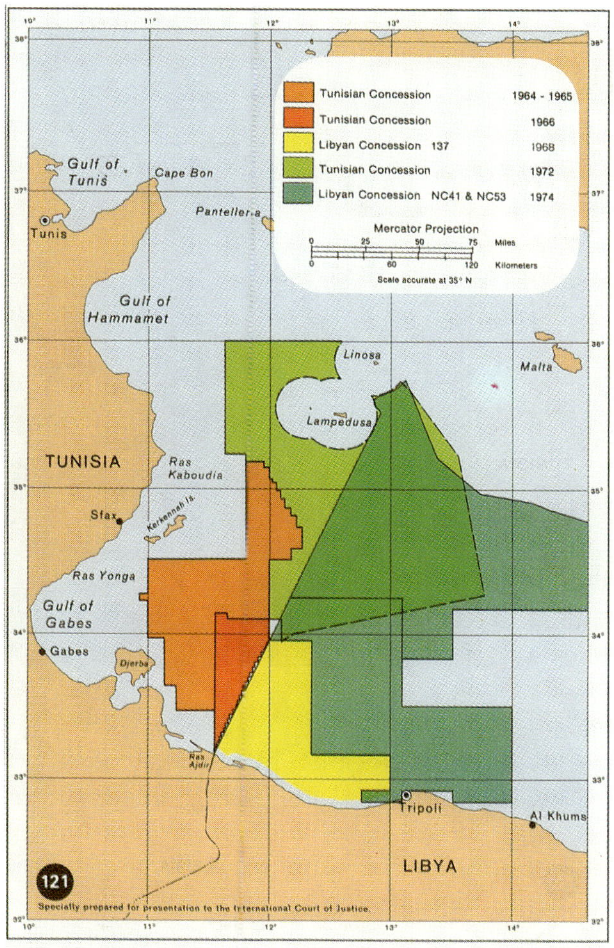

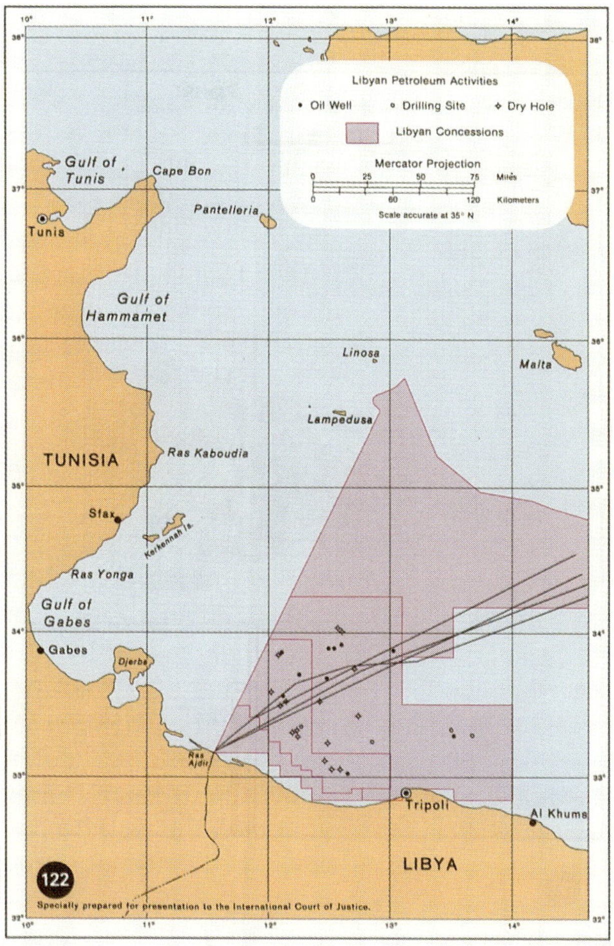

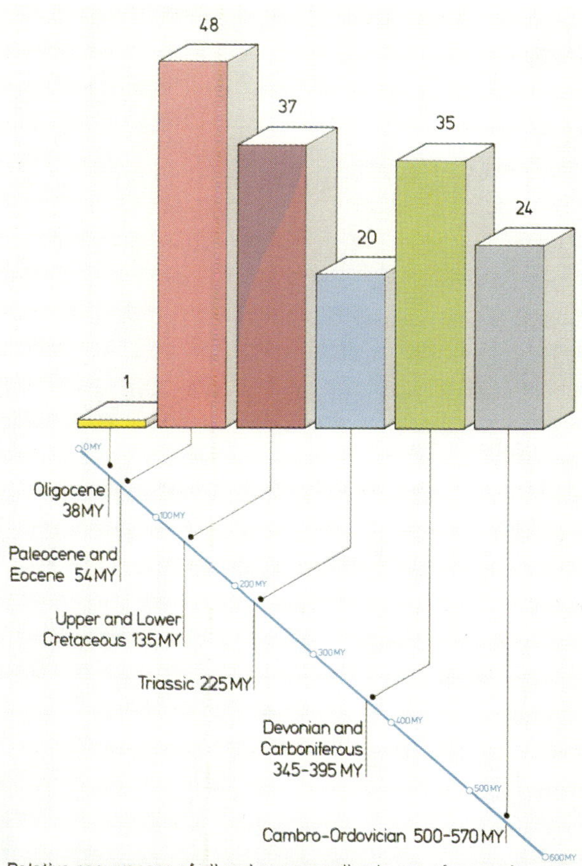

Relative occurrences of oil and gas according to age of reservoir — on-shore and off-shore Libya, Tunisia and Algeria.

109

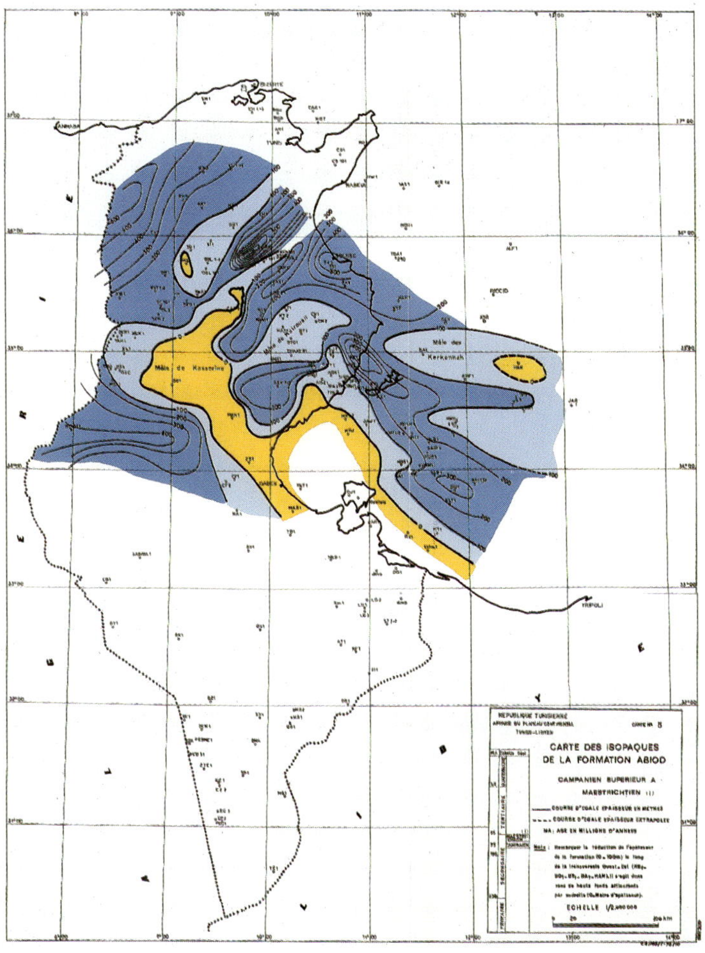

Aspects of the Continental Shelf *case between Tunisia and Libya.*

Taslim Olawale Elias from Nigeria, Judge (1976-1991) and first African President of the Court (1982-1985).

Decolonisation

In what ways have the African Judges on the Bench in the past thirty years distinguished themselves, what have been their major concerns and in what ways have they been able to leave their mark on the jurisprudence of the Court? In a sense, and certainly during the earliest years of their presence, their approach was extremely pragmatic. They came to disseminate their views in such province of the law as they considered to be amenable to the promotion of developing world interests. Foremost in their minds, no doubt, was the process of decolonisation. It naturally followed that a major concern of theirs was the concept of State sovereignty and, in particular, the recognition of the right of peoples to self-determination. Consequently, they fought against the concept of *terra nullius*, advocated the independence of non-self-governing territories and sometimes even endorsed the right to revolt if intended to resist an illegitimate annexation.

The Law of the Sea

The law of the sea, an extremely topical issue throughout the 1960-1970's, was another area in which they distinguished themselves – if only from sheer necessity. Confronted with the exploitation of their fishing grounds and natural resources by industrially more advanced and technologically better equipped nations, they insisted on the expansion of the territorial sea and the protection of the exclusive economic zone; in this they often asserted historic rights. This is not to say, incidentally, that all African Judges – or for that matter Asian Judges with similar backgrounds – necessarily agreed upon every detail. With respect to the actual implementation of a given concept they often notably disagreed, such as, for instance, in the recurrent issue before the Court regarding the extension of the EEZ, the Exclusive Economic Zone, towards a 12-mile-limit: some deemed this to be a bare minimum, while others thought that it represented an absolute maximum. However, they would invariably stress the relevance of global solidarity in the ecological and economic spheres, and were likewise extremely keen on issues such as the continental shelf or equidistance lines. In our sketches of Judges Ammoun, Bengzon, Bustamante and Tanaka we have inserted some pertinent references and quotations in respect of these issues.

The coat of arms of Nigeria.

Economic Independence

Generally speaking, the first generation of African Judges championed rights and ideals in the political sphere. However, in due course, economic aspects became preponderant. It was feared that the attainment of political independence, which had become a reality in most cases towards the mid-sixties, could only too easily be replaced by economic dependency or, as was all too common, virtually nullified at the hands of foreign private investors. Thus, African Judges – often passionately, yet understandably – militated against the intervention by major financial conglomerates and multinationals in the economy of their nations, which significantly deprived them of the fruits of their political victories.

Human right have obviously become a major issue in recent decades. Several African and Asian Judges played a key part in the ramification of primary and secondary human (social and cultural) rights. In recent years we observe the same tendency, predictably, in the environmental sphere.

Views on the Judicial Function

Hearing in the interim measures phase of the Land and Maritime Boundary *case between Cameroon and Nigeria in March 1996.*

In the strictly judicial sphere, several Judges from the new nations have distinguished themselves by their tendency to develop new methods of interpretation, often aimed at the extension of the judicial function itself. It has long been disputed by students of the ICJ whether the Court acts as a legislator in the creation of international law or whether it has to restrict itself to interpreting existing principles. In the mid-seventies the French Judge Gros pointed to the risks of attributing to the Court a 'law-creating role', notably with regard to political issues. Among developing world representatives, Judges Forster of Senegal and Padilla Nervo of Mexico were especially concerned with such issues.

Developing World Judges have been more assertive, as a rule, and less divided in matters of international custom and the so-called general principles of international law to be applied by the Court. Generally speaking one may say that they were strongly opposed to the traditional application of custom as the reflection of unilateral European concepts and have insisted on the codification, preferably through the ILC, of customary norms on a new footing, by seeking norms of truly universal application, through the incorporation of concepts from all areas of the world.

Among the sources of international law which the Court has to take into account, they put a relatively high value on unilateral acts of State and resolutions of international organisations, notably the General Assembly and the Security Council of the United Nations. Here lies another well-known and longstanding point of difference among Judges, as exemplified by a few citations and references in the biographical sketches of Judges which follow. Judges Onyeama and Ammoun have particularly stressed the binding force of such resolutions, which has often been challenged by Socialist Judges on account of their political connotations.

A final, very noteworthy aspect is the treatment by African Judges of the notion of equity, that time-honoured, yet ambiguous concept which mitigates the harshness of strict law. It is fair to say that the idea of equity itself has a long tradition in all cultures but, even so, the extent of its application by the Bench has often aroused controversy. In the tradition of Roman law, its being ancillary to justice is adequately expressed in the Latin definition *ius est ars boni et aequi*, whereas the strained relation of law to justice may be neatly summarized in two other maxims from the same sphere, i.e., on the one hand its rejection in *dura lex, sed lex*, and on the other, the desperate plea implied in *summum ius, summa iniuria*. In this connection it is recalled that the Court is authorized by its Statute, at the specific request of Parties, to consider a case *ex aequo et bono*.

Be this as it may, it is of distinct interest to observe that it is precisely in this sphere that the influence of African – and developing world Judges in general – has manifested itself. Traditionally – and one may perhaps say in spite of the 1945 Truman Declaration – the majority of the Court has rarely found in favour of the application of the concept of equity which Judges Tanaka or Koretsky maintained was not even a legal one. From 1969 onwards we notice a distinct switch. Judge Ammoun was among the first to emphasize, with explicit reference to the Qur'an (*Surah* IV. 61: *If you judge, be just and equitable*) its long tradition in Muslim, Hindu and Chinese law. Judge Elias similarly stressed its relevance for the African nations. In recent years it is notably Judge Weeramantry of Sri Lanka who has advocated its application, as will be seen from his biography.

LÁZARO LUÍS, 1563

Atlas de dez folhas
Atlas of ten sheets
Fol. 3 v.

Academia das Ciências de Lisboa

Original 432×613 mm.

CHAPTER NINE

The Judges

1907-1995

Judge:	1979-1995
Contentious Cases:	24
Advisory Requests:	6
Declarations:	1
Sep. Opinions:	6
Dis. Opinions:	2

Roberto Ago

A towering figure of legal thought has disappeared. ... An institution, not just a man is leaving us.

With these words Judge Bedjaoui, President of the ICJ, paid tribute, early in 1995, to the memory of one of the most gifted internationalists of the present era. Endowed with a refined mind, crystal-clear at all times, Judge Ago combined his theoretical insights with the keen sense of measure which made him an advocate of rare cogency and persuasiveness in any forum. To this he added the innate *joie de vivre* of the true Mediterranean.

Born in Vigevano (Milan), Roberto Ago held a doctorate of law and political sciences from Naples. He began in private law, but held chairs of public international law for almost 50 years (1934-1982), at four university centres in succession: first briefly in Catania and Genoa; from 1938 in Milan; and from 1956 in Rome. Throughout, his keen scholarly appetite found its outlet in a true avalanche of monographs and review articles covering both the public and private spheres.

From his early thirties, his Government eagerly availed itself of his genius in the diplomatic and judicial areas as well. Thus, for more than 30 years he was Italy's first representative at the ILO Conferences, to which he was particularly attached. He helped negotiate the revision of the Lateran Concordat on Italy's behalf and attended most UN Conferences of the period: on the Law of the Sea (1958, 1960), Diplomatic Relations (1961) and the Law of Treaties (1968-1969), which Conference he chaired. He was a Member (1956) and from 1991 President of the *Institut de Droit International*. As a Member and at one time Chairman of the International Law Commission, one of his major achievements was eight reports on State Responsibility (1969-1979), an area on which he had focussed from his early days. This found expression in a set of articles 'as fine as lace'. When he turned 80, Judge Ago was fittingly honoured by his colleagues on so many committees, boards and benches with a Festschrift, appropriately entitled *International Law at the Time of Its Codification*, to do justice to this meticulous codifier and legislator.

No less impressive is his record in the sphere of dispute settlement. Having only just turned 30, he distinguished himself before the PCIJ in the *Phosphates in Morocco* case. Even then, he had already built himself a reputation at The Hague as the youngest scholar ever to have lectured at its Academy. (He would return to the Academy regularly and ended his career as President of its Curatorium.) Until his last day he was to remain involved in a range of ongoing matters of conciliation, arbitration and adjudication, in diverse capacities, before a variety of tribunals, and at the request of a number of nations. As a Member of the PCA, he presided over tribunals such as the Franco-German Saar Tribunal, and those on the Franco-American *Interpretation of the Air Transport Agreement* (1963) and the *Grands Moulins de Dakar* dispute (1972).

Having at an earlier stage served as Judge *ad hoc* in the *1906 Arbitral Award* case, Judge Ago was elected to the bench of the ICJ in 1979 and re-elected in 1988. He rendered 6 Separate and 2 Dissenting Opinions. Perhaps his major achievement was his Presidency of the Chamber in the *Gulf of Maine* case (1981-1984), which called upon all of his tact, insight into human nature and keen sense of reality. His last Opinion on the 1992 *Nauru* case attests to the strains of the judicial office:

> I deeply regret being unable to associate myself with the Judges who have voted in favour of the present Judgment. I regret it all the more since I am certainly no less sensitive than my colleagues to the frustration felt by the Nauruans when they gaze upon the present state of their small island's territory. I also hope with all my heart that it will be possible for this people once again to find in its country of origin conditions of life favourable to its development. But these perfectly justified emotional reactions should not blind us to the fact that the questions we have to consider in this preliminary phase are very specific questions of law and that it is by reference to the law, and only to the law, that they have to be answered. (*ICJ Reports* 1992, at p. 326)

Andrés Aguilar-Mawdsley

1924-1995

Judge:	1991-1995
Contentious Cases:	15
Advisory Requests:	1
Declarations:	3 (1 Joint)
Sep. Opinions:	–
Dis. Opinions:	1 Joint

By some whim of fate the nation of Andrés Bello, that pioneer of international law in Latin-America and founder of the South-American equivalent of the *Code Napoléon*, had never, since the days of the famous *Preferential Claims* and *Orinoco* cases before the Permanent Court of Arbitration in 1903 and 1910 had any real connection with the Hague Courts; nor had Venezuela ever had any Member on the Bench. It became a party to the Hague Convention of 1899 in 1907. Perhaps the last contribution on record by a Venezuelan jurist regarding the ICJ is the sensible objection by Dr Gómez-Ruiz, who was on the 1945 San Francisco Committee of Jurists that prepared the Statute of the ICJ, to opening the Court to disputes between International Organizations and States. This situation came to an end when, in February 1991, Judge Aguilar-Mawdsley of Caracas was sworn in as a Member of the ICJ.

Judge Aguilar obtained his Doctorate in Political and Social Sciences from Caracas Central University. Subsequently, he took a Master's degree in Civil Law from McGill University in Montreal. From 1948-1958 he lectured in civil law at the Central and Andrés Bello Universities in Venezuela, concurrently with legal adviserships to commercial firms. At the age of 34, however, he was appointed Minister of Justice (1958-1962). From then on his life would revolve around diplomacy and international affairs in a wide variety of functions. In 1963 he became Permanent Representative to the UN Office in Geneva, and the next year he was President of the International Labour Conference. Meanwhile he developed activities in the sphere of human rights, which became one of his major fields of interest. He was a Member and several times President of the Inter-American Commission on Human Rights and participated in a number of examinations on the spot in several countries of the region. From 1968 to 1972 he was a Member of the UN Commission on Human Rights. He was Co-Chairman of the Committee appointed by the Secretary-General on the question of US diplomats taken hostage in Iran (1980).

From 1969 to 1972 and again from 1986 to 1991 he was Permanent Representative in New York and Acting Head of the Delegation to the General Assembly, which saw him in 1971 as one of its Vice-Presidents. In the previous year he had chaired the First Committee. From 1972 to 1974 he was Ambassador to the USA. He headed the Venezuelan Delegation to UNCLOS III (1973-1982) and chaired its 2nd Committee. From 1986-1992 he was President of the International Commission of Jurists. In 1986 he also represented his nation in the Security Council, over which he presided in 1987. The next year he was President of ECOSOC, and for the following two years he chaired the Unitar Research Institute.

Judge Aguilar-Mawdsley was a Member of the ASIL, of the *Institut de Droit International* and of the *Société Française*. He has written extensively on human rights and law of the sea issues. During his term on the Bench, which was cut short by his untimely death in October 1995, he was very much in favour of consensus and has been part of the majority in all but one of the decisions. He delivered 3 Declarations (1 Joint) and 1 Joint Dissenting Opinion with Judge Ranjeva, in the 1991 Judgment on the *1989 Arbitral Award* case (Guinea-Bissau v. Senegal).

In their Opinion the Judges rendered a very severe judgment on the arbitral panel that had handled the maritime delimitation dispute concerned, and seriously questioned the validity of the Award on various grounds:

> The case is of a particular significance because of the problems of judicial and arbitral method that it raises. ... In our preliminary observations, we mentioned that the Court has criticized the Award. Moreover, the arbitral proceedings were punctuated by various regrettable facts. We refer, in particular, to the method and excessive lengthy duration of the arbitral proceedings, the Tribunal's technique of work, the unjustified absence of one arbitrator, the declaration made by the President of the Tribunal, and the incomplete character of the delimitation after the Tribunal had done its work. Taken separately, these criticisms may not suffice to justify, in strict law, a finding of nullity. However, if considered cumulatively.... (*ICJ Reports* 1991, at pp. 120 and 122)

*1934

Judge:	1991-1994
Contentious Cases:	14
Advisory Requests:	–
Declarations:	–
Sep. Opinions:	4
Dis. Opinions:	2

Prince Bola Adesumbo Ajibola

> Again, I ask myself what is justice in a case of this nature. ... To me, the fundamental focus and obligation as judges of the Court must be to do justice in accordance with the spirit of Article 1 of the Charter: to maintain international peace and security; to take effective measures to prevent and remove all threats to peace; to suppress all threats of aggression or any form of breaches of peace in any part of the world within the spirit of the Charter and in accordance with international law. To me, justice requires prompt action to prevent deterioration of peaceful co-existence among nations of the world. No one goes to sleep when the house is burning. (*ICJ Reports* 1992, at p. 93)

The Court has counted distinguished names and many a man from noble family. Among its Members, it has seen Knights, and it recently welcomed a Dame. Still, Judge Bola Ajibola, who in 1991 came to replace the 'institution' that Judge and former President Elias had become in the previous fifteen years, was the first Judge on the Bench to be born into a Royal Family, viz. that of Gbdaela II, in Ogun State, Nigeria.

He was called to the Bar at Lincoln's Inn in 1962 as Barrister-at-Law and was a legal practitioner in Lagos and other parts of Nigeria for 23 years, having law firms of his own, with a special bias for Commercial Law and International Arbitration. He then turned to the political field, to become Attorney-General and Minister of Justice of the Federal Republic of Nigeria from 1985-1991. In 1990 he headed the Task Force for the Revision of the Laws of the Nigerian Federation. He represented Nigeria at international, ECOWAS and Commonwealth conferences, in matters of criminal law, drugs and narcotics, and at the World Peace Through Law Conferences. In 1986 he was Member of his nation's Delegation to the UN General Assembly and its Representative to the Sixth Committee. In 1990 he was Temporary President of the General Assembly at its special session on narcotic drugs.

Judge Bola Ajibola was a Member of the ILC from 1986-1991, is a Member of the PCA and the Paris-based ICC Court of Arbitration and International Maritime Arbitration Commission, as well as the London-based Court of International Arbitration. He was President of the World Association of Judges and President of the Nigerian Bar Association. He is editor of *Nigeria's Treaties in Force 1970-1990*, and the *All Nigeria Law Reports*, and the author of several monographs, notably on Nigerian Law (administration of justice, 1987, 1988; criminal law, 1989; narcotics, 1989; banking frauds, 1989; women and children, 1990; human rights under military rule, 1991) and a treatise on *The Integration of the African Continent Through Law* (1988) along with works on international (commercial) arbitration: *Principles of Arbitration* (1980); *New Concepts in the Resolution of Disputes in International Construction Contracts* (1981); *Arbitration and State Enterprises* (1983), and *The Law and Settlement of Commercial Disputes* (1984). He is a Knight of the Order of the British Empire.

Prince Bola Ajibola served on the Court from December 1991 to February 1994. Since then, he has been Judge *ad hoc* in the *Land and Maritime Boundary* case between Cameroon and Nigeria. At present he is a judge of the Constitutional Court of Bosnia and Herzegovina; a judge of the World Bank Administrative Tribunal and one of the Commissioners empanelled by the United Nations Compensation Commission to decide on the Compensation Claims filed by Kuwait against Iraq as a result of the Gulf War.

During his term of office Judge Bola Ajibola rendered 2 Separate Opinions and dissented in the *Application of the 1971 Montreal Convention* cases following the Lockerbie Incident.

We opened the page with a quote from this Dissenting Opinion, and will now close it with another:

> Each case must be decided on its own merits. Situations are always changing. The world is in a state of flux economically and politically. International law has been enriched by its dynamic development from this Court. ... The world is constantly faced with new situations from day to day, and it is imperative that the Court must always rise to the occasion and meet the new demands and challenges of our time as they surface. (*ICJ Reports* 1992, at p. 92)

Ricardo Joaquin Alfaro

1882-1971

Judge:	1959-1964
Vice-President:	1961-1964
Contentious Cases:	10
Advisory Requests:	2
Declarations:	1
Sep. Opinions:	1
Dis. Opinions:	–

In the long and often chequered history of dispute settlement the 1826 Panama Treaty, negotiated by Simon Bolivar among others, still constitutes a landmark. Through actually never ratified, the treaties that were signed on this occasion were among the very first to include the so-called Compromissory Clause of arbitration. The conference initiated two decades of Latin American treaty-making, covering virtually the whole of the Western Hemisphere and, in the latter part of the century, similar procedure was adopted in dealings with the European Powers. It is recalled here that, in September 1880, Colombia and Chile concluded a 'General, Permanent and Absolute Arbitration Treaty', which predated by far any undertaking of the sort in the Western World. In short, the settlement of international disputes by arbitration was built into the Constitutions of some of the young Latin American Republics.

It is in this tradition that the Panamanian Judge Ricardo Alfaro was educated and came to distinguish himself in the course of his career. A life-long supporter of arbitration and other formulas for the pacific settlement of disputes, he earned himself an early reputation with his learned comments and painstaking diplomacy concerning a national issue of his day, namely the Panama Canal. He was a member of the US-Panamanian mixed arbitration commission which settled the claims resulting from the expropriation of the Canal and, in 1912, he was called in to help solve the Costa Rica-Panama boundary dispute. A leading figure in the Pan American movement, he was pivotal to its 1929 Conference on Conciliation and Arbitration, which success earned him - at the age of 47 - membership of the PCA. During the war years the gentle and humane Alfaro, known for his polite diplomacy and his natural inclination to further humanitarian causes, developed into an outspoken and indeed most eloquent supporter of the Allied cause.

The next two decades saw him deeply engaged in national politics. He successively served as an Under-Secretary of Foreign Affairs, Secretary of Justice, First Vice-President and finally as President (1931-1932). In later years he helped draft the Panamanian Constitution (1944). He was Minister of Foreign Affairs from 1945 to 1947, then withdrew from active politics to combine a State Counsellorship with a chair of international law at Panama University.

After the war he laboured to further the cause of the United Nations, attending the San Francisco Conference, supervising the Spanish drafting of the Charter and chairing the Judicial Committee of the Assembly in 1948. For many years he served on the International Law Commission, of which he was President in 1953. He looked upon the idea of collective security as the best guarantee for world order. His successful Presidency of the *Ambatielos* arbitration between Greece and Great Britain in 1956 was among the factors which earned him his election to the Court.

Thus, when, in 1959, he was elected to the ICJ, to fill the vacancy caused by the death of Judge Guerrero, Judge Alfaro was already a celebrated arbitrator and statesman in his own right. His years on the Court were indeed the closing years of a most distinguished career. He was elected Vice-President in 1961 and resigned after this three-year term. During his 5 years on the Bench Judge Alfaro rendered 1 Declaration and 1 Separate Opinion, in the 1962 Judgment on the Merits in the *Temple of Preah Vihear* case, in which he enlarges on the principle that:

> ...a State party to an international litigation is bound by its previous acts or attitude when they are in contradiction with its claims in the litigation. ... The principle, not infrequently called a doctrine, has been referred to by the terms of 'estoppel', 'preclusion', 'foreclusion', 'acquiescence'. I abstain from adopting any of these particular designations, as I do not believe that any of them fits exactly to the principle or doctrine as applied in international cases. (*ICJ Reports* 1962, at p. 39)

1868-1960

Judge:	1946-1955
Contentious Cases:	15
Advisory Requests:	8
Declarations:	2
Sep. Opinions:	2
Dis. Opinions:	7

Alejandro Alvarez

More changes have taken place in international life since the last great social cataclysm than would normally occur in a century. Moreover, this life is evolving at a vertiginous speed: inter-State relations are becoming more and more various and complex. The fundamental principles of international law are passing through a serious crisis, and this necessitates its reconstruction. A new international law is developing, which embodies not only this reconstruction, but also some entirely new elements. (ICJ Reports 1947-1948, at p. 67*)*

The name of the Chilean scholar and diplomat Alejandro Alvarez will probably be linked if anything to his highly intriguing set of ideas concerning what he himself called 'Regional Particularism' in international law and his visionary views regarding what is now commonly referred to as the New International Economic Order. Judge Alvarez was a man of outspoken tenets. He championed the idea of a distinct American school of international law, retracing its tradition to the works of the 16th-17th century Spanish school of Vitoria and Suarez. In attaining a felicitous synthesis of the Anglo-Saxon legal system and the Roman outlook of the Latin-American world, Alvarez maintained, the nations of the Western Hemisphere had developed distinct views through the years. Their views had come to form a valuable counterpoint to the then prevailing European legal tradition that was the outcome of centuries of power politics. Concepts such as arbitral procedure, domestic jurisdiction and the rights and duties of States he looked upon as typical products of this American outlook.

The wide acclaim his views received from the developing world, perhaps also due to these nations' dislike of traditional Eurocentrism, led him to expand his tenets into the philosophy of a 'new international law'. What he meant by this was a flexible set of legal values - keeping pace with social change - that reflected the recognition of global interdependence and put a check on absolute State sovereignty. During his term on the Bench his ideas provoked interesting debate with the 'universalists' among his colleagues. In the end, as Judge Lachs observes (*Teacher* 1987, at p. 88):

> ...his views of a separate and independent international law for Latin America (as indeed for any continent or any group of States) could not be accepted. What became a reality was the emergence of certain practices specific to that continent, such as the Calvo clause.

Alvarez was a doctor of law from Paris and maintained the best of contacts with French internationalists. He was Vice-President of the *Institut*, co-founder with De Lapradelle and Fauchille of the *Institut des Hautes Études Internationales*, and at the same time, with Brown Scott, of the *American Institute of International Law*. He represented Chile at League Assemblies and notably at the 1930 Hague Codification Conference. A Member of the PCA from 1907-1920 he was on the panel of the *Hungarian-Czech Mixed Arbitral Tribunal*. Yet the most familiar podium to him was provided by the 4th-7th Pan-American Conferences, from which his ideas were transferred to the world at large. Judge Alvarez was a prolific author on American diplomatic history and the psychology of the peoples of the New World:

> We have before us a case which involves the interpretation of the UN Charter; it refers therefore to a new question of international law. This case must be decided in accordance with the new international law, which is now emerging. What is this law to-day? Since the recent upheaval which opened the greatest period in the history of humanity, profound changes have suddenly appeared in almost all spheres of activity, particularly in the international field. The psychology of peoples has undergone a great change; a new universal international conscience is emerging, which calls for reforms in the life of peoples. This circumstance, in conjunction with the crisis which classic international law has been traversing for some time past, has opened the way to a new international law. (*ICJ Reports* 1950, at p. 12)

Fouad Ammoun

1899-1977

Judge:	1965-1976
Vice-President:	1970-1976
Contentious Cases:	8
Advisory Requests:	3
Declarations:	2
Sep. Opinions:	4
Dis. Opinions:	1

For if there is a principle recognized by the municipal law of the community of nations which demands adoption by analogy into international law as a general principle of law, at least as much as so many others which it has already borrowed, it is clearly the principle which nominates equity as the basis of law and as the objective of its implementation. (*ICJ Reports* 1969, at p. 136)

On 16 November 1965 Judge Ammoun of the Lebanon was elected to fill the vacancy created by the premature death of Judge Badawi who had served on the Court for twenty years. Judge Ammoun was re-elected in 1967 and was to serve as Vice-President from 1970 to 1976. He wrote 4 Separate Opinions and 1 Dissenting Opinion, and shared in 2 Joint Declarations. Interestingly enough, Judge Ammoun, who had followed a career in the judiciary and the diplomatic service and till then had only produced a few articles in scholarly reviews, delivered three rather lengthy opinions, which reveal a philosophical bent and a tendency to expound on the general principles applicable to the specific issues of the case at hand.

After his legal studies Judge Ammoun became President of the Lebanese Court of Appeal and Cassation at the age of 36 and later its Procuror-General. He helped draft the 1949 Lebanese criminal code and was a legal adviser to his Foreign Ministry, where he served as Secretary-General for many years and chaired the Lebanese Unesco Commission (1945-1956 and 1960-1963). In the intervening years he combined advocacy at the Court of Appeal with a professorship at the Lebanese Academy. In later years he was Minister for Planning and National Economy and Minister for Foreign Affairs and Lebanese Overseas. In these capacities he chaired Lebanese Delegations to conferences of the Arab Heads of State - where he helped draft the Covenant of the Arab League and its Joint Defence Treaty - and of the Non-Aligned Countries. For a number of years he also chaired his nation's delegation to the UN General Assembly and Security Council, and to UN Conferences, such as those on Trade and Development.

It was these political and diplomatic experiences, no doubt, that added a special practical flavour to his Opinions when considered within the strictly judicial setting of the Court. Judge Ammoun liked to elaborate on the social and moral connotations of a case and to stress the various non-legal constituents of a judgment.

A few citations may serve to illustrate this:

> The radical transformations which have occurred in economic affairs in the last half-century ... and the new problems to which these changes have given rise, call for a corresponding development of juridical structures. The law, a rigid conservative kind of law, cannot adapt the emerging reality to sacrosanct rules rooted in the remote past. It must, on the contrary, adapt itself to the imperious needs of an international society which is moving towards universalism; it must adapt itself thereto in order to avoid confrontation between peoples, and lest it lose its footing in the upward march of progress towards better justice and the common aspiration towards the ideals of prosperity and peace. (*ICJ Reports* 1970, at pp. 287-288)

In his Separate Opinion on the 1969 *Continental Shelf* case Judge Ammoun offers a panorama of the concept of equity in all cultural traditions (*ICJ Reports* 1969, at pp. 139-140), in which broader context he also observes:

> Morality, it has been said, hovers around the law; and one may add, with N. Politis and following Ulpian and Cicero, that it should have dominion over it. In turning away from it, international law condemns itself to sterility in face of a society bubbling over with life. The normative school and its pure theory of law, in rejecting the moral, social and political elements, described as metajuridical, become isolated from international realities and their progressive institutions: *ubi societas, ibi jus'*. (*ICJ Reports* 1969, at p. 137)

1893-1984

Judge:	1952-1961
Contentious Cases:	25
Advisory Requests:	5
Declarations:	–
Sep. Opinions:	1
Dis. Opinions:	4 (1 Joint)

Enrique C. Armand-Ugon

Never before 1950 had Uruguay had any dealings with any of the Hague Courts. It never had a Judge on the Bench and no case had ever had any direct bearing on it. Then came Judge Armand-Ugon. Although he had actually attended a few Sessions of the League of Nations Assembly and of its post-war successor, Judge Armand-Ugon, who was elected in December 1951 to fill the vacancy caused by the death of Judge Azevedo of Brazil, was on his arrival virtually a *tabula rasa* to his colleagues-to-be, that is to say those from outside the Latin-American world. He brought to the Court a rich judicial experience gathered in a variety of positions in Uruguayan courts. Also, he had from early on taken an active part in the Inter-American movement.

Born at Colonia Voldense, he became a Bachelor in Arts in 1912, a Doctor in Law and Provincial Attorney in 1918, and a Judge of the Court of First Instance in 1920, at the age of 27. In 1933 he served on the National Commissions for the Drafting of the Codes of Procedure and Commerce. In 1938 he was Judge in the Court of Appeal, in 1945 Judge in the High Court, and in 1949 he was elected Court President. He was representative to the Second Inter-American Conference of Lawyers in 1943 and to the First Meeting of the Inter-American Council of Jurists in 1950. In 1931 he attended a Session of the League in Geneva and after the war headed the Uruguayan Delegation to the Third and Fifth Sessions of the General Assembly. His years at the Court (1951-1960) produced 1 Separate and 4 Dissenting Opinions (1 Joint). His Separate Opinion in the 1959 *Aerial Incident* case is an indication of his judicial reasoning:

> It is not permissible to indulge in extensive interpretation where there is nothing to require such an interpretation. The clear and precise consequences of a text are none other than those intended by that text; to seek to attribute other consequences to it presupposes an unjustified modification of the text. This argument was not discussed in the oral proceedings; there is, however, nothing to prevent the argument being upheld, in accordance with the well-known principle applied by international courts in procedural matters, that the Court may *proprio motu* seek and select the legal basis for its decision on the final submissions of the Parties, *iura novit curia*. (*ICJ Reports* 1959, at p. 155)

Earlier that year, in the *Interhandel* case, Judge Armand-Ugon had tackled another issue of endless debate, the thorny distinction between the decision on the admissibility of a case and the decision on the Court's jurisdiction. This time, the matter arose within the context of an American objection based on the so-called *local remedies rule*, which demands that before seeking international adjudication the Parties must be satisfied that all possible avenues of dispute settlement before *national* courts have been exhausted:

> The Third Objection is founded upon the rule of the exhaustion of local remedies ... it is invoked as a general principle of international law. The plea is an objection to the admissibility of the Application; it contests that admissibility only and is not directed against the Court's jurisdiction. The rule of the exhaustion of local remedies does not affect the jurisdiction of the Court, which may be competent, even if internal remedies have not been exhausted. Accordingly, the question of the admissibility of the Application lies outside the field of jurisdiction. ... Therefore the Court cannot adjudicate on the admissibility of the Application until it has established its jurisdiction. (*ICJ Reports* 1959, at p. 85)

As with some others among his colleagues from the developing world, Judge Armand-Ugon was strongly opposed to the importance accorded to *custom* in international law, for the reason that he viewed custom as in fact constituting *European* customary law. More often than not, he felt this was alien to his experience and caused concern to him as it tended to work to the disadvantage of the new nations. Both on principle and in terms of content, therefore, it provoked his protest. Established practice, he observed, needs to be accompanied by a *conscience commune* in order to create a right. Neither frequency of use nor habit can on their own create such a right.

José Philadelpho de Barros e Azevedo

1894-1951

Judge:	1946-1951
Contentious Cases:	7
Advisory Requests:	6
Declarations:	–
Sep. Opinions:	3
Dis. Opinions:	4

Literal interpretation will not prevail, even through the sinister adage fiat justitia pereat mundus. *The aims of the United Nations must be served so that mankind may flourish. Even long practice, usually a good guide to interpretation, cannot frustrate a pressing teleological requirement. (ICJ Reports* 1950, at p. 24*)*

Brazil had built itself an early reputation in circles of internationalists at The Hague. During the 1907 Hague Peace Conference, its main Representative, Professor Rui Barbosa, had made an indelible impression. 'Mr Verbosa' as he was called at the time, had proven himself a born fighter and a cool debater: 'le cœur si chaud et la main tellement froide', someone had once observed. A brilliant internationalist, he had greatly distinguished himself in campaigning for the equality of all States before the law and for the compulsory arbitration of conflicts. Later, he had become Judge at the PCIJ, from 1921 until his death in March, 1923. His successor was Dr E. da Silva Pessõa.

At San Francisco, Brazil stood alone with France and Great Britain in preferring the maintenance of the Permanent Court to its replacement by a new Court. In 1946, its candidate, Judge Azevedo, was allotted a term of nine years. However, his untimely death in 1951, at the age of 57, prevented him from completing his allotted term.

Judge Azevedo was yet another example of the men of varied experience who came to sit on the Court. Trained in law both at Rio de Janeiro and at the Paris School of Political Science, he had at some stage been barrister, professor, dean and vice-rector at the University of Brazil, president of the Brazil Institute of advocates, *procureur général* at the Court of Appeal, Justice at the Supreme Court - and mayor of Rio de Janeiro. He had helped to revise the Brazil Civil Code, advised the Foreign Ministry, represented his nation at diplomatic conferences and published widely on such diverse topics as real property, authors' rights and treaty law. In his opinion, treaties - and notably the UN Charter - should be interpreted as designed strictly to fulfill fundamental, objective rights and not serve parochial political issues.

Judge Azevedo's *cursus honorum* had not only given him a wide experience and competence, it had also left a definite mark on his legal views, as can be distilled from his outspoken individual, Separate and Dissenting Opinions, notably in the cases on the *Conditions of Admission of a State to Membership in the UN* (1948), *Competence of the General Assembly for the Admission of a State to the UN* (1950) and *Interpretation of Peace Treaties* (1950).

For one thing, he set great store by the strict separation of the juridical and political elements within the United Nations, as represented by the Court and the Security Council respectively. In his opinion, the Court should be very careful never to get entangled in any political issues.

Again, Judge Azevedo liked to interpret the UN Charter as a real *contrat social* and as an expression of universal values of a higher legal order, just as he looked upon the United Nations itself from a teleological perspective, always bearing in mind the loftiest ideals of world organization that are its objectives. He shared Judge Alvarez' views as to the specific value of the Latin-American component in the fabric of international law:

> ... the interpretation of the San Francisco instruments will always have to present a teleological character if they are to meet the requirements of world peace, co-operation between men, individual freedom and social progress. The Charter is a means and not an end. To comply with its aims one must seek the methods of interpretation most likely to serve the natural evolution of the needs of mankind. (*ICJ Reports* 1950, at p. 23)

Judge Azevedo is also known for his disapproval of the appointment of Judges *ad hoc* in Advisory Proceedings and his extensive interpretation of the legal effects to be accorded to such an Opinion.

1887-1965

Judge:	1946-1965
Vice-President:	1955-1958
Contentious Cases:	36
Advisory Requests:	12
Declarations:	3
Sep. Opinions:	3 (1 Joint)
Dis. Opinions:	10 (1 Joint)

Abdal-Hamid Badawi

Despite an early career at university centres and a number of scholarly publications, notably a monograph *On the impact of foreign capitulatory rights on the Egyptian judiciary and legislation* (1914), Judge Badawi of Egypt was first and foremost the practitioner of law, who felt at home both in the private and public spheres. From the Ministry of Justice he rose to the position of chief legal adviser of the Egyptian Government (1926-1940) before entering the cabinet himself, first as Minister of Finance (1941), and later as Minister for Foreign Affairs (1945-1946), in which latter capacity he spoke eloquently for Egypt's independence from British rule. His regular functioning as a delegate to conferences and his accomplished diplomacy brought him into the international sphere. At the 1945 San Francisco Conference he persuasively advocated the idea of a strong General Assembly, indeed with veto power over the Security Council. Subsequently, he took part in the Washington Conference which formulated the Statute of the ICJ. On 6 February 1946, he was elected Judge; he was re-elected in 1949 and again in 1958. He was Vice-President of the Court from 1955 to 1958.

During his term of nearly twenty years Judge Badawi on several occasions delivered Separate or Dissenting Opinions. Perhaps the most pronounced expression of his views and a good example also of his juridical reasoning was his Opinion in the 1957 *Norwegian Loans* case concerning the interrelationship of municipal and international law which apparently lay close to his heart:

> In its Judgment ... the Court did not think it necessary to undertake an examination of the municipal character of the dispute. ... I consider that the dispute does possess that character. ... It was asserted, however, that the case falls within the domain of international law because the French Government has adopted the cause of its nationals and is exercising diplomatic protection on their behalf, thereby conferring an international character on the case. It is hardly necessary to point out that this begs the question, since the contention put forward in this Objection is, in fact, that there were no grounds for the exercise of this protection. ... It would be very strange, and even paradoxical, to consider that the denial of the international character of a question of municipal law and the discussion entered into in that connection confer on that very question an international character. (*ICJ Reports* 1957, at pp. 29, 32, 33)

An intriguing suggestion regarding the jurisdiction of the Court was made by Judge Badawi, representing Egypt, at the stage of the drafting of its Statute. As Rosenne records (*Law and Practice* 1985, at p. 365), during the Washington redrafting of the Statute in 1945 various nations intimated to the Committee their wish to see the compulsory jurisdiction of the Court affirmed by a clause in the Statute 'so that, as the latter was to become an integral part of the Charter, the compulsory jurisdiction of the Court would be an element of the international organization'. However, the Washington Conference had noted that 'in spite of this predominant sentiment, it did not seem certain, nor even probable, that all the nations whose participation ... appears to be necessary, were now in a position to accept the rule of compulsory jurisdiction...'. As is known, it was notably the great Powers that did not accept that position. 'A suggestion was then made', Rosenne continues, 'by the Egyptian delegation, to seek a provisional solution in a system which, while adopting compulsory jurisdiction as a general rule, would permit each State to escape it by a reservation, i.e, to substitute for the existing system of *contracting-in* a new system of *contracting-out*'. Eventually, the suggestion did not meet with a favourable response from the Committee.

Jules Basdevant

1877-1968

Judge:	1946-1964
Vice-President:	1946-1949
President:	1949-1952
Contentious Cases:	36
Advisory Requests:	12
Declarations:	2 (1 Joint)
Sep. Opinions:	3 (1 Joint)
Dis. Opinions:	7 (2 Joint)

Dans les discussions au sein de la Cour, il écoutait en silence, très attentif à chacun, saisissant chaque point de vue - en puis enfin il levait son crayon, en un geste inimitable, et en quelques phrases lapidaires et judicieuses, semait de l'ordre partout. Pour lui, la forme, le style, la méthode complétaient et enrichissaient la substance. Ce n'était nullement du formalisme, c'était de la bonne forme. Incontestablement, à mon avis, ... il était un des grands juges à la Cour. (Fitzmaurice, in *AIDI* 1969/II, at pp. 38-39)

The 1870s brought France quite a few internationalists whose names have a familiar ring even today - Albert de la Pradelle, Georges Scelle and Gilbert Gidel, to name only three. As a colleague of these men stands Jules Basdevant - and yet one is inclined rather to link his name to that other formidable figure in the best French legal tradition, Louis Renault, who, a native of the same area in Saône-et-Loire, was Basdevant's inspiring teacher and whose career shows the same rare combination of the professor, state counsel and international magistrate.

Jules Basdevant's record at the ICJ is impressive. Having been his country's agent in a number of cases before the PCIJ from 1932 to 1938, he was called to the new bench in 1946 and elected Vice-President, becoming its President three years later (1949-1952). He then served for a further fifteen years. Throughout this period he was highly influential, thanks also to his steadfast character. For all his courtesy, Jules Basdevant was a man of firm principles and deep conviction. Having distinguished himself quite early (1900-1904) with historical theses on the relation of church and state and on the law of war, he started off on an academic career with chairs in Rennes and Grenoble (1903-1910). But then, in 1914, he was enlisted to defend the nation. The Jules Basdevant that emerged from *la grande guerre* was no longer a mere scholar, but a decorated officer with lifelong diplomatic and international interests. In 1918, he was to become professor in Paris and Member of the Preparatory Commission of the League of Nations.

Also from these years date his famous *Recueils* of French and international treaties and Italian and British jurisprudence (1914-1927), initiated by Renault and Descamps. Thus, two parallel careers gradually emerged: the academic one, exemplified by brilliant courses at the Hague Academy, and the diplomatic one, exemplified by his attendance at the League of Nations or at the Hague Codification Conference (1930), and the London Naval Conference (1930), which he combined with frequent pleadings before the Permanent Court. In all these undertakings, Basdevant distinguished himself through his extreme clarity of thought and expression, his unequivocal integrity and his ardent national pride.

The latter was put to the test in a dramatic way on 29 May 1941, when as legal adviser to the Vichy regime he handed his personal letter of resignation to Maréchal Pétain. It stands as a unique testimony to the high moral standards of a man who had already lost two sons in the war: 'la conception que j'ai de l'honneur ne me permet pas de me placer dans mes conseils sur le terrain adopté par votre gouvernement'. He was suspended from his university chair, helped organize the *Résistance* and from 1945 resumed all his former functions with the same buoyant energy!

In 1946 he was called to the membership of the new Court which he had so eagerly helped to shape at Washington and San Francisco, after having done the same for the League of Nations twenty-six years earlier. For twenty years the Court would profit from his vast learning and rare insight. His 1960 *Dictionnaire de la terminologie du droit international*, 'une nomenclature vraiment scientifique des mots' will remain a classic. Judge Basdevant remained active until his final days. At ninety, the man who had lost sons full of promise in the World War had the pleasure of witnessing the Nice session of his beloved *Institut de Droit International*, of which he had once been the Vice-President, proceed under the direction of his daughter Mme Paul Bastid (1906-1995), who was to become the first female Judge *ad hoc* on the ICJ in 1978.

1921-1980

Judge:	1979-1980
Contentious Cases:	2
Advisory Requests:	–
Declarations:	–
Sep. Opinions:	–
Dis. Opinions:	–

Richard R. Baxter

> *The very word 'custom' has a ring of antiquity about it, but antiquity is not necessarily a relevant criterion in determining the existence of a rule of customary law. ... What is important is the existence of 'extensive and virtually uniform' State practice. ... The new customary rule will be established as soon as it acquires the necessary degree of acceptance. (RDC* 1970/1, vol. 129, at p. 67*)*

The election of Richard R. Baxter to the Court, in February 1979, raised the highest expectations among his colleagues-to-be. A former President of the American Society of International Law, but better known as the long-time Editor-in-Chief of its journal, the *American Journal of International Law* (1970-1978), there were few authors in the field who had not been in touch with him and come to appreciate his painstaking care and searching criticism as an editor (a 'labor of love' to him) or the personal involvement of this deeply humane man. An Associate of the Institute of International Law, his name had recently come to the fore as the authoritative Chief Reporter of the 1978 *New Restatement of the Foreign Relations Law of the United States*.

It was not to be. The untimely death of this lean, spartan yet ebullient man of military bearing, after a protracted illness, on 26 September 1980 - that is within 18 months of his election - came as a deep shock. It was only in the deliberations of the *Case concerning United States Diplomatic and Consular Staff in Tehran* that the Court had been given the opportunity to watch his analytical mind at work. Thus the career of a man expected to become a leading Judge of the Court was painfully cut short. Judge Lachs had a vivid recollection of his former colleague:

> He was an excellent companion in both serious and light conversations, with a most attractive sense of humour; erudite, but very modest about his learning. His lectures attracted crowds. He had a pragmatic and very realistic approach to the law. (*Teacher* 1987, at p. 148)

Though a graduate of Brown University, from which he was on his election to the Court to receive an honorary degree, as well as Harvard Law School, Judge Baxter was every inch the Harvard man. Having joined its Law Faculty in 1954, he became the first holder of the Manley Hudson Chair of International Law (1976). He proved an inspiring teacher who wore his learning lightly, because of the wit and eloquence that were the signs of his innate high spirits. His broad interests led him well beyond the borders of the legal field, to encompass many of the humanities. This may also account for his sympathy to different outlooks and his gentle approach to people.

Through the years, due to his sound reasoning, practical sense and analytical mind, he became a prized consultant both to the US Departments of State and Defense, notably in matters of the law of the sea, and to various UN organs, in particular UNITAR. In carrying out these tasks, he showed boundless energy and total commitment, never shrinking from what he called the 'donkey work'. His office lights at Harvard Law School usually burned the latest.

Judge Baxter's numerous publications reflected the breadth of his interests. A wartime soldier, later, after the war, a career officer in the Judge Advocate General's Corps, he ultimately became a reserve colonel in the US Army.

His interest in the field of international law was consolidated by Sir Hersch Lauterpacht during Baxter's stay in Cambridge in 1950-1951 - where he developed great expertise in humanitarian law. He drafted the monumental *Draft Convention on Responsibility of States for Injuries to Aliens* together with Louis Sohn. Later he wrote extensively on the relation of treaty and customary law and co-authored a treatise on the Panama Canal, which proved the stepping stone to the monograph that was closest to his heart, *The Law of International Waterways* (1964). Less well-known, but typical of Judge Baxter were his seminal contributions to the founding of *International Legal Materials* and the student moot court competition nowadays known as the *Jessup Competition*.

Mohammed Bedjaoui

*1929

Judge:	1982-present
President:	1994-present
Contentious Cases:	21
Advisory Requests:	5
Declarations:	–
Sep. Opinions:	2 (1 Joint)
Dis. Opinions:	2

Jadis l'Occident projetait sur le monde son droit et son pouvoir. Il avait écrit l'histoire du monde par ses soldats, ses marchands, ses missionnaires et ses légistes. Il a dominé la planète au nom de son droit. La puissance économique était son fait. Il détenait entre ses mains puissance et droit. Le tiers-monde était quasi inexistant jusqu'en 1960. Tout laisse croire que nous assistons au crépuscule d'une époque qui achève sa fonction historique et que nous vivons une veillée d'armes dans l'attente d'une grande révolution structurelle dans tous les domaines...

When, in the opening years of the 17th Century, Hugo Grotius was contracted by the Dutch authorities to plead their historic rights as an independent legal entity *vis-à-vis* the Spanish Empire, it was generally felt to be not 'just' his legal genius which qualified him for this task, but likewise his superior elegance of style. For a nation to really prove its autonomy, the marks of its cultural identity and literary accomplishments were deemed of no lesser import perhaps than the case it advocated in its own right. At the opening of our new era of international law, the developing countries could hardly have wished themselves a better advocate to plead its case than Mohammed Bedjaoui. Like the silver rays of Grotius' Tacitean Latin, President Bedjaoui's sparkling way with words never fails to scintillate his audience. One wonders: if a Party is not supposed to allure a Judge, is a Judge entitled thus to spellbind his public?

Mohammed Bedjaoui was born at Sidi-Bel-Abbes in Algeria and in 1956 became a Doctor of Law with a thesis entitled *Fonction publique internationale et influences nationales*. He was Research Assistant at the *Centre national de la recherche scientifique* in France, then became Legal Adviser to the Provisional Government of the Republic of Algeria (1958-1961) and expert adviser in its independence negotiations. He was Executive Secretary to the President of the National Constituent Assembly and Secretary-General of the Government (1962-1964). He was then appointed Minister of Justice and Keeper of the Seals (1964-1970). During the next decade he served as Ambassador to France and Permanent Delegate to Unesco, while heading Algerian Delegations to the UN Conferences on Succession of States in Respect of Treaties (1977) and UNCLOS III (1976-1980). Similarly, he attended conferences of the OAU and the Non-Aligned Countries. From 1979-1982 he was Permanent Representative of Algeria to the UN in New York, and served as Vice-President of the UN Council for Namibia, Co-President of the UN Commission of Enquiry to Iran, and Chairman of the Committee on the Drafting of the Mercenaries Convention. From 1981-1982 he was Chairman of the Group of 77.

A tireless worker, Judge Bedjaoui served many years on the ILC (1965-1982) and drafted numerous reports on Succession of States (see *Yearbooks ILC*, 1968-1977). He has been a member of the *Institut de Droit International* since 1985 (Associate 1977-1985). He was member or president of several panels for international commercial arbitration and is a prolific author. Apart from an early monograph on *La révolution algérienne et le droit* (1961), he wrote articles in the *Annuaire français de droit international* on 'excès de pouvoir' (1956), 'fonctionnaires internationaux' (1957) and 'règlement pacifique des différends africains' (1972), and more than 160 articles in various other legal publications. His main works however date from recent years: *Towards a New International Economic Order* (1979), and *The New World Order and the Security Council: Testing the Legality of its Acts* (1994). He is the General Editor of the impressive Unesco manual *International Law: Achievements and Prospects* (1991), a truly multicultural publication and perhaps the first manual of collective authorship to cover systematically the entire range of international law. He has lectured extensively at various universities and has given two courses at the Hague Academy of International Law (in 1970 and 1976 respectively).

Mohammed Bedjaoui became a Member of the ICJ in March 1982 and chaired the Chamber in the Burkina Faso/Mali *Frontier Dispute* (1983-1987) He was elected President of the Court in February 1994. During his term Judge Bedjaoui also served on the Guinea/Guinea-Bissau (1983-1985) and Guinea-Bissau/Senegal (1985-1989) Arbitration Tribunals.

1896-1992

Judge:	1967-1976
Contentious Cases:	8
Advisory Requests:	3
Declarations:	1
Sep. Opinions:	2
Dis. Opinions:	2 Joint

Cesar Bengzon

Judge Cesar Bengzon was elected to the Court in February 1967 to succeed the Chinese Judge Wellington Koo. As other Permanent Members of the Security Council, China in practice is accorded a permanent place on the Bench at The Hague. However, in 1967 the Republic of China (Taiwan) no longer pressed its claims, notably in view of the changing attitude within the UN on the issue of Chinese representation. The issue was finally settled in 1971, when the General Assembly recognized the People's Republic as the only representative of China in the Organization. Even so, the People's Republic did not nominate a candidate to a seat on the Court until 1984.

During the interval of 15 years, the vacant position on the Bench passed to another member of the regional group. In the first of the two intervening terms (1967-1976) the seat was occupied by the candidate from the Philippines, Judge Bengzon. The Philippines, incidentally, were among the very few States in the post-war period not to append the 'exclusion clause' to its acceptance of the jurisdiction of the Court, this being the usual means used to limit a nation's acceptance of the Court's jurisdiction to disputes arising subsequent to the date of its independence.

Cesar Bengzon was a graduate, later law professor, of the University of Manila. From the position of Assistant Attorney he rose to become first Solicitor-General, then Under-Secretary of Justice, and finally Chief Justice of the Supreme Court of his country. His chairmanship of national delegations at such meetings as the International Commission of Jurists, the Bandung Conference and the Asian Judicial Conference in the early 1960s brought him into the international sphere. In 1966 he was a Member of the Philippines delegation to the UN General Assembly.

Despite his advanced age, Judge Bengzon served on the Court for a full span of nine years and left a personal mark on the case-law of the Court through a number of Declarations and Dissenting Opinions. Thus, in the 1967 *Continental Shelf* case he declared himself unable to concur with the majority of his colleagues, insisting on 'the equidistance principle as the rule for delimitation which may even be derived from the general principles of law'.

Again, in 1972, in the *Fisheries Jurisdiction* case, along with Judge Jiménez de Aréchaga, Judge Bengzon objected on principle to the decision of the Court to order Parties to restrict their Memorials and Counter-Memorials to the question of jurisdiction only, where no formal preliminary objections had been raised by either Party and matters of jurisdiction and merits were clearly interrelated:

> There are, in our view, even stronger considerations of convenience and of the due protection of the interests of both Parties which made it advisable in this case to request the Parties to submit a proper and complete Memorial and Counter-Memorial. ... It is only in the light of such a complete Memorial that (1) the respondent must take a final decision as to whether it shall appear to defend its case or not, and (2) the Court must, in case of default, base its final pronouncement as to whether it will 'decide in favour of [the applicant's] claim'. For such a purpose the Court must determine 'that the claim is well founded in fact and in law'. How will this be done if the Memorial is defective in respect of the facts or the law concerning the merits of the claim? (*ICJ Reports* 1972, at p. 185)

He was also among the Judges who added a strong Joint Declaration to the 1974 Judgment in the *Nuclear Tests* case. In this he spoke in defence of the Court's policy regarding the unprecedented incident concerning the Court's Order of 22 June 1973, when prior to the public reading of the Order press reports appeared 'which exceeded what is legally admissable in relation to a case *sub judice*' as President Lachs put it at the time. 'Good administration of justice and respect for the Court require that the outcome of its deliberations be kept in strict secrecy and nothing of its decision be published until it is officially rendered', it was stated. The incident provoked much criticism and resulted in an official though fruitless enquiry on the part of the Court that included the formal questioning of an Agent.

Judge Bengzon retired in 1976, at the age of 80.

José Luis Bustamante y Rivero

1894-1989

Judge:	1961-1970
President:	1967-1970
Contentious Cases:	5
Advisory Requests:	1
Declarations:	–
Sep. Opinions:	4
Dis. Opinions:	2

In February 1961 the Peruvian Judge Bustamante y Rivero came to replace Judge Armand-Ugon from Uruguay. The last three years of his term Judge Bustamante served as President, being the first Latin-American after Judge Guerrero to be called to this office. Judge Bustamante was a versatile scholar, politician and diplomat. He had studied law and politics, philosophy, history and letters at the universities of Arequipa and Cuczo. At some stage he taught archaeology, and held a professorship of modern philosophy. He spent fifteen years in legal practice at the bar and in the judiciary before steering his course into political waters. A member of the Arequipa City Council, in 1930 he was appointed Minister of Justice and Education, after which he entered the Foreign Service. He was Minister to Bolivia (1934-1938), then Ambassador to Uruguay (1939-1942) and Bolivia (1942-1945). Meanwhile, he attended the 8th Inter-American Conference at Lima (1938) and the 2nd South American Congress at Montevideo (1939-1940). From 1945 to 1948 he was President of Peru.

Judge Bustamante was a Member of numerous Academies and learned societies. He was Associate Member of the *Institut* and Honorary Member of the Inter-American Bar Association. Besides this, he was a prolific author on legal, political, historical and literary issues. Noteworthy are his studies on the Pan-American System.

During his years at the Court Judge Bustamante delivered 2 Dissenting and 4 Separate Opinions, most of them of considerable length. In these he expanded on the subjects of discontinuance, the essential characteristics of Advisory Opinions *vis-à-vis* contentious cases and, in the 1963 *Northern Cameroons* case, on the relationship between the ICJ and the Political Organs of the United Nations, notably the so-called 'duplication' theory according to which the two means, administrative and judicial, can be utilized to settle issues raised in the United Nations:

> According to that country [Great Britain], if the Application of Cameroon is, nothwithstanding resolution 1608 (XV) of the General Assembly, to be submitted to the Court, this would in fact amount to establishing a sort of superior Court, and to a veritable revision of the decisions of the United Nations by the Court, which would destroy all the authority of the organs of the International Organization. This kind of dependence or subordination of these organs in relation to the Court would not be in conformity with the spirit of the Charter. ... To sum up in a couple of words: although the concept of law is not foreign to the administrative activities of official institutions - including the organs of the United Nations - resolutions of this kind are primarily of a political nature and do not always reflect a scrupulous adaptation of the rules of law to political requirements. ... In the Charter of the United Nations there is not to be found, with regard to the resolutions of the General Assembly, any provision excluding all judicial jurisdiction. On the contrary, the general purport of the Charter seems to me to reveal a certain parallelism and a clear compatibility of the two institutions. (*ICJ Reports* 1963, at pp. 176, 177-178)

Another cause of dissent on his part concerned the concept of the Continental Shelf as formulated during the 1958 Geneva Conference. Judge Bustamante maintained (as did his successor Judge Jiménez de Aréchaga, for slightly different reasons), that the method applied in measuring the Shelf, namely by commencing from beyond the outer limit of the territorial sea, was to the detriment of equity and was:

> artificial and highly debatable because it contradicts the idea of adjacency and upsets the geological concept of the land territory of which the continental shelf is but the physical prolongation under the territorial sea and even beyond it. Geology admits neither a break nor an intermediate space... It seems to me that the truth is otherwise: that the territorial sea is superjacent to that part of the shelf which is closest to the coast. (*ICJ Reports* 1969, at pp. 59-60)

It is interesting that as late as 1982 Libya, in its dispute with Tunisia before the Court, would refer to his views.

1882-1971

Judge:	1951-1955
Contentious Cases:	8
Advisory Requests:	2
Declarations:	–
Sep. Opinions:	2
Dis. Opinions:	4 (1 Joint)

Levi Fernandes Carneiro

The system of the United Nations as a whole is of more importance than the literal meaning of a few words taken from the Statute and the Regulations. (ICJ Reports 1954, at p. 92*)*

On 7 May 1951 the Brazilian Judge Azevedo suddenly died. On 6 December a supplementary election was held in the General Assembly and Security Council to fill the vacancy for the remaining five years of Judge Azevedo's term. On 15 May 1952, at the first public sitting of the Court in its new composition after the regular elections of February 1951, Judge Carneiro made the solemn declaration as prescribed by the Statute.

Judge Carneiro was educated at the Faculty of Law and Social Sciences at Rio de Janeiro University. He first distinguished himself as secretary to the Brazilian Delegation at the 1912 International Conference of Jurisconsults. From 1930 to 1932 he was Legal Adviser to his Government, in 1933-1934 he was Member of the National Assembly and in 1935-1937 Member of Parliament. In 1938-1940 he was Professor at the Law Faculty of the University of Brazil.

For many years Judge Carneiro served his nation on a number of international committees and conferences. Thus, he was member of the Joint Brazilian-United States Conciliation Committee and chairman of the Brazilian Unesco Committee. In 1938 he was his nation's representative at the 8th Pan-American Conference at Lima and in 1947 at the Conference for the Maintenance of Peace and Security in the Continent. In the next few years he was Legal Adviser to the Ministry of Foreign Affairs and also became a Member of the Permanent Court of Arbitration.

Judge Carneiro had a strong interest in literary and historical studies. He served for a term as President of the Brazilian Academy of Letters and was on the board or a member of quite a number of historical societies in Brazil and Portugal. His publications are diverse and, though not numerous, appropriately reflect his many interests. He wrote short tracts, mostly on such various subjects as federal justice, constitution and federalism, neutrality, the territorial sea, human rights, diplomatic immunity and commercial obligations, along with some biographical tracts on great predecessors in the field such as Ruy Barbosa and Joaquim Nabuco. His major work is entitled *O direito internacional e a democracia* (1945).

During his four years at the Court (1951-1955), Judge Carneiro participated in 10 cases, which resulted in 6 Separate and Dissenting Opinions on his part, in the *Ambatielos* case, the *Anglo-Iranian Oil Co.* case, the *Minquiers and Ecrehos* case, the *Monetary Gold* case, *the US Nationals in Morocco* case, and the Advisory Opinion on the *Effect of Awards of Compensation made by the UNAT*. In addition to their meticulous reasoning these reveal a careful style and a distinct historical interest. An interesting observation is made in his *Minquiers* Opinion on the evidence of maps:

> At any rate, maps do not constitute a sufficiently important contribution to enable a decision to be based on them. I shall not take the evidence of maps into consideration. (*ICJ Reports* 1953, at p. 105)

In the *Effect of Awards of Compensation made by the UNAT* he makes the following observation on principle:

> Having, to my regret, given an answer different from that of the Court to the questions submitted to it, I must set out very briefly the grounds for my opinion. In order to resolve these questions, it seems to me that the system of the United Nations regarded as a whole is of more importance than the literal meaning of a few words taken from the Statute and the Regulations. Indeed, even with regard to literal interpretation, this Court has already affirmed a principle laid down by the Permanent Court of International Justice: '...words must be interpreted in the sense which they would normally have in their context, unless such interpretation would lead to something unreasonable or absurd'. (*ICJ Reports* 1954, at p. 92)

Federico de Castro y Bravo

1903-1983

Judge:	1970-1979
Contentious Cases:	8
Advisory Requests:	3
Declarations:	–
Sep. Opinions:	6
Dis. Opinions:	3

> In litigation, the parties are masters of the evidence: the court has a passive role. In the words of the traditional axiom of procedure, the court says to the party: *da mihi factum, dabo tibi jus*. (*ICJ Reports* 1975, at p. 138)

Judge Federico de Castro served on the Court for one full term (1970-1979). At least initially, he may well have considered himself a relative outsider amongst his colleagues, for Judge de Castro's initial interests were in civil law rather than public international law. A prolific author, his numerous works which span four decades represent his wide interests: they comprehensively cover the fields of private international and municipal law. Apart from his major trilogy on Spanish civil law, *Introducción* (2 volumes, 1952-1955), a later *Compendio* (1966) and finally his *Temas* (1972), he wrote extensively on matters of nationality, personal and family law, the law of obligations, commercial law and the unification of the laws on sales. Yet his publications nowhere so much as touch upon the field of public international law. Therefore, one would rather expect to find Judge de Castro connected with that other illustrious gathering of legal minds in The Hague, namely the *Hague Conference on Private International Law*, the brainchild of the Dutch Professor Tobias Asser; in fact, de Castro did attend its conferences.

Judge de Castro was a doctor of laws and also of literature and philosophy at Madrid, and held chairs at La Laguna, Salamanca, Sevilla and Madrid. He was supervising editor of the *Anuario de Derecho Civil*, and editor of the *Revista española de derecho internacional*. As a Legal Adviser to his Foreign Ministry, he was Chief Delegate to the Conference on the Law of Treaties (1968-1969). In 1969 he was elected to the ICJ. His first contacts with the Court went back to 1959-1961, when he had been Judge *ad hoc* in that most complex case from the early years of the Court, the *Barcelona Traction* case. During his term on the bench Judge de Castro wrote 6 Separate and 3 Dissenting Opinions, some quite elaborate (such as in the *Namibia* and *Western Sahara* cases). Of particular interest is his legal reasoning in the *Aegean Sea* case, in which his interpretation of a one-time reservation made by Greece restricting jurisdiction of the Court to 'disputes relating to the territorial status of Greece' led him to question whether this would cover disputes over the continental shelf. This resulted in an observation of general application on what has proved to be a recurrent theme in the jurisdiction of the Court, the *intertemporal* aspect:

> The meaning of words may change with time. In order to interpret any statement to ascertain its real meaning, we must first of all concentrate on the meaning which it could have had at the time when it was made. Words have no intrinsic value in themselves. They are, or represent, sounds (*phonema*), but their semantic value depends on the time and the circumstances in which they were uttered. (*ICJ Reports* 1978, at p. 63)

Another interesting observation on his part is the following:

> Dissenting and Separate Opinions are criticized, especially in countries which follow the Latin system, because they weaken the authority of judgments: it is not the Court, it is said, but only a tiny minority which takes the decision; furthermore, in Separate Opinions, some of the arguments on which the judgment rests are called into question by members of the majority. On the other hand, such Opinions are evidence of the life and of the evolution of legal doctrine. Some Dissenting Opinions are the law of the future; others are the expression of the resistance of old ideas. Personally, I think Separate Opinions have their uses: they give judges an opportunity to explain the reasons for their votes. The drafting of a judgment is a very delicate task, for it must, with great prudence, reflect the 'consensus' of the majority and it must do so clearly, simply and unambiguously. In these circumstances, if the arguments which a judge regards as conclusive do not find expression in the judgment, a Separate Opinion makes it possible for them to be stated. Separate Opinions provide a means for making known the reasons for the votes of members of the majority and this may be useful for the purpose of critical studies by commentators. (*ICJ Reports* 1972, at p. 116)

1899-1967

Judge:	1955-1964
Contentious Cases:	21
Advisory Requests:	4
Declarations:	–
Sep. Opinions:	1
Dis. Opinions:	1

Roberto Córdova

Judge Roberto Córdova was a Mexican lawyer who came to the Court in 1955 from a predominantly diplomatic background. He was born in Mexico City and held a law degree from the National University of Mexico. Already in 1928, in his late twenties, he was secretary of the Mexican delegation to the Sixth International Conference of American States in Havana, and he was to become the chief representative of that delegation 20 years later. He served as Attorney of the Mexican Agency to the US-Mexican General Claims Commission from 1928-1933 and was Mexican Agent to the same Commission from 1937-1940.

During most of the 1940s Judge Córdova served his nation as a diplomat. In 1942 he was Ambassador in Costa Rica. He also took an active part in the Inter-American movement. In 1940 he was member of the Inter-American Neutrality Committee. In 1941 he became Legal Adviser to the Mexican Foreign Service and from 1942 onwards to his Government, covering, *inter alia*, the 1945 Chapultepec Inter-American Conference on Problems of War and Peace. From 1947-1951 he was Ambassador Extraordinary and Plenipotentiary and Adviser to the Ministry for Foreign Affairs. In these capacities he was Delegate to the 1947 Inter-American Conference for the Maintenance of Peace and Security in the Continent at Rio de Janeiro, and the 1948 Ninth International Conference of American States at Bogota.

Also in 1945 Judge Córdova was appointed a Member of the Committee of Jurists to draft the Statute of the ICJ. He attended the 1945 San Francisco Conference as well as the 1946 Paris International Labour Conference. In 1948 he was elected Member of the ILC and in 1951 he became its Special Rapporteur on the issue of *Nationality including Statelessness*; he came to be a true specialist on the subject. In 1952 he attended the UN General Assembly session.

During his nine-year term (1955-1964) on the Bench Judge Córdova participated in 25 cases and produced one Dissenting and one Separate Opinion. The former, on the 1958 Judgment in the *Convention of 1902* case, concerned the interpretation of treaties. In the latter, in the 1959 *Interhandel* case, he insisted on the application of the principle of exhaustion of local remedies:

> The principle ... is based and justified on grounds perhaps more important than the mere possible avoidance of conflicting procedures and decisions. The main reason for its existence lies in the indispensable necessity to harmonize the international and the national jurisdiction... (*ICJ Reports* 1959, at p. 45)

Perhaps the best perception of Judge Córdova's keen sense of realism can be gained from an article he wrote on the development and codification of international law in the collection of essays entitled *The United Nations Ten Years' Legal Progress* (1956). Here he states, referring to the so-called *optional clause*:

> The reluctance of the great Powers to accept the compulsory jurisdiction of the Court is largely based on the absence of a definite, concise, and precise body of legal rules binding States and freely elaborated and accepted by them. All nations share this feeling, to a greater or lesser degree, thus making it almost impossible for a judicial organ with compulsory jurisdiction to exist and function in a way similar to the highest judicial bodies of the States themselves.

And again:

> With the natural reluctance of States to give up the slightest portion of their sovereignty - an attitude on which unfortunately the smaller countries seem to be even more keen than the larger ones - the work of development and codification of international law will not be made any easier, in spite of the fact that for the smaller States this new source of international law, in which they share alike with the big Powers, constitutes the best means of protecting their legitimate interests against encroachments by the powerful nations.

Another outspoken statement reads:

> None of the Articles of the Charter subordinates the use of force to the law; reference is made to 'peace-loving nations' but never to 'law-abiding nations'. ... The Charter is merely a renewed attempt to establish an international political regime based upon the balance of power, without any foundation upon the supreme authority of law.

Hardy Cross Dillard

1902-1982

Judge:	1970-1979
Contentious Cases:	8
Advisory Requests:	3
Declarations:	3 Joint
Sep. Opinions:	5
Dis. Opinions:	2

> The notion that a legal question is simply one that invites an answer 'based on law' appears to be question-begging and it derives no added authority by virtue of being frequently repeated. (*ICJ Reports* 1975, at p. 117)

Judge Dillard, who came to the Court in February 1970 to serve one full term, was a University of Virginia lawyer and a Virginia gentleman. It was in Virginia that he graduated, lectured and held numerous management functions, along with an occasional practice at the bar, until the outbreak of war. In the Armed Forces he rose from major to colonel, was awarded a number of honours and from 1946 onwards held staff and command assignments in the USA, Europe and the Far East, all concerned with military administration. At one stage he was Director of Studies at the National War College and was attached to the Office of the High Commissioner in West Germany. Quite naturally, many of his early writings deal with issues related to military administration.

In 1957 Judge Dillard lectured at the Hague Academy on aspects of law and diplomacy. That same year he became Vice-President of the American Society of International Law and in 1962-1963 eloquently served as its President. Concurrently, he served on the Editorial Board of the *American Journal of International Law*. From 1966 to 1970 he was a Permanent Advisory Counsel to the Air Force Academy and in 1968 was on the Commission to Revise the Constitution of Virginia. He served as Dean of the University of Virginia Law School, and lectured widely and wittily. He appeared as an appellate counsel in cases at the Virginia Supreme Court. After his election to the ICJ, Judge Dillard was appointed Member of the Arbitral Tribunal in the *Beagle Channel* case between Argentina and Chile (1971-1977).

Perhaps typical of Judge Dillard's views are the concluding remarks of his Separate Opinion in the 1971 Advisory Opinion on Namibia (*Legal Consequences...*):

> The legal issues involved in this proceeding were not simple or easily resolved. Indeed they were resolved only after hearings and deliberations extending over a period of many months. It should be added that the great learning and consummate skill brought to bear on the issues by the representatives of South Africa were in the highest tradition of the legal profession. It may be hoped and expected that South Africa, as a great nation, will respect the judicial pronouncement of this Court and the almost unanimously held view in the United Nations that its administration of Namibia must come to an end. It may be hoped, also, that in the delicate and difficult era that lies ahead, especially in the period of transition, a spirit of mutual good will may, in time, displace one based on mutual misunderstanding. (*ICJ Reports* 1971, at pp. 168-169)

'At the risk of appearing textbookish', as Judge Dillard once put it himself (but by way of illustrating the common sense that guided the judgment of this broadly-cultured man), the following statements he made in the course of his nine years on the bench in The Hague may suffice:

> On principle therefore it seems to me clear that the allegedly clear-cut, but questionable, distinction between procedural and substantive issues does not for purposes of grounding an appeal embrace a plea to the jurisdiction. (*ICJ Reports* 1972, at p. 93)

> It seemed hardly necessary to make more explicit the cardinal restraint which the legal right of self-determination imposes. That restraint may be captured in a single sentence. It is for the people to determine the destiny of the territory and not the territory the destiny of the people. (*ICJ Reports* 1975, at p. 122)

In his obituary in the *American Journal* (1982, at p. 595), Oscar Schachter wrote of Judge Dillard:

> Judge Dillard brought to his judicial role the wide learning and humanistic concerns that graced his writing and teaching. The individual opinions he wrote on the Court are evidence of his sensitivity to the fundamental dilemmas faced by international law generally. Perhaps more than any other judge in recent times, Judge Dillard looked beyond the field of international law for understanding of the issues presented to the Court.

1920-1981

Judge:	1979-1981
Contentious Cases:	2
Advisory Requests:	1
Declarations:	–
Sep. Opinions:	1
Dis. Opinions:	–

Abdullah El-Erian

Earlier in this survey of Judges we mentioned the premature and much regretted death, in September 1980, of the newly sworn in Judge Baxter. The elections of 1979 proved ill-omened. In October 1980 Judge Tarazi met with a tragic accident. On 15 August 1981, the President of the Court, Sir Humphrey Waldock, passed away while still in office. In mid-December 1981, the Court was startled by a fourth sudden loss: that of the warm personality of a lawyer of high promise, the newly appointed Egyptian Judge Abdullah El-Erian. To this loss there was an additional cause for grief, witness Judge Lachs:

> The youthful looks and stately bearing of Abdullah El-Erian ... were somewhat belied by his deep, sad eyes. ... His diplomatic career frequently prevented him from pursuing what he loved most: teaching and practising international law. ... Finally he was elected to a post which gave him full satisfaction: the bench of the ICJ. But this career was cut short by his sudden death. (*Teacher* 1987, at p. 149)

Abdullah El-Erian was an alumnus of Cairo University, who subsequently studied at Harvard and obtained a Ph.D. in international law at Columbia University. He lectured in Cairo, until he was requested by his Government to assume diplomatic functions abroad. From 1968 to 1979 he was Deputy Permanent Representative to the UN in New York and Permanent Representative in Geneva. Meanwhile he was ambassador first to France (1971-1973), then to Switzerland (1975-1979). For many years (1953-1970) Judge El-Erian represented Egypt in the Sixth (Legal) Committee of the General Assembly, which he chaired in 1965. Similarly, he was on the International Law Commission almost without interruption for twenty years (1957-1978) and was its Chairman in 1976. He was Expert Consultant at the Conference on the Representation of States in their Relations with International Organizations (1975) and is well-known for the eight reports he produced in his capacity of Special Rapporteur on this issue (1963-1978). He was a Member of the *Institut de Droit International* from 1977-1981.

On behalf of his nation he attended most UN Conferences of the period, such as those on the Law of the Sea (1958-1960), Diplomatic Relations (1961) and the Law of Treaties (1968) and sessions of the Security Council, ECOSOC and the Trusteeship Council. At the same time, he played a part in the regional organisation of the developing world, at the Asian-African Bandung Conference (1955), the OAU Conference at Addis Ababa (1963), the summits of the Non-Aligned at Cairo (1964) and of the Arab States at Alexandria (1964). Among other publications Judge El-Erian wrote some fine monographs, including *Condominium* (1951) and his *Principles of International Law - A Treatise* (co-authorship, 1953).

That Judge El-Erian's premature death deprived the Court of an expert internationalist can be easily seen in the single Separate Opinion he left in the 1980 request for an Advisory Opinion on the *Interpretation of the 1951 Agreement between the WHO and Egypt*. The lucid, clear-cut style of the opinion, in which he elaborated on the inevitable intertwining of the political and legal elements in requests such as the one at issue, and his acute and compelling reasoning are particularly noteworthy:

> A distinction should, therefore, be made between the political character of the problem which gives rise to a request for Advisory Opinion and the legal character of the question which constitutes the subject-matter of the requested Opinion. The criterion is the intrinsic nature of the question rather than the various extrinsic factors. ...
>
> It is imperative for international organizations to base their actions on valid and solid legal grounds and take their decisions in full awareness of their legal implications and guided by an authoritative interpretation of their constitutions. ...
>
> The common interest of the member States of the organization can be adequately assured not through the excessive influence of political considerations which are of a transient character but on the basis of respect for legal safeguards and constraints. (*ICJ Reports* 1980, at pp. 164-165)

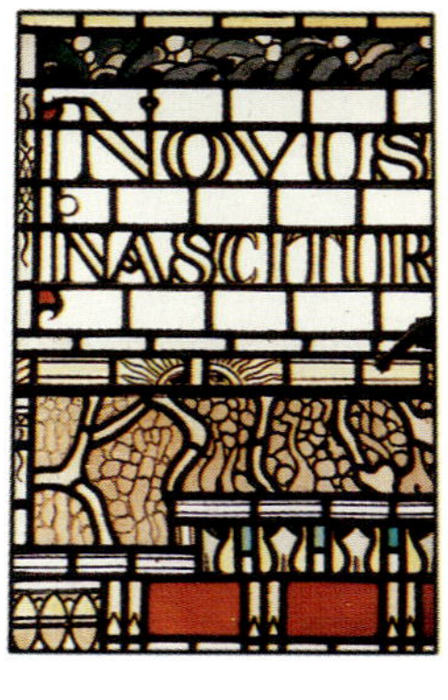

Taslim Olawale Elias

1914-1991

Judge:	1976-1991
Vice-President:	1979-1982
President:	1982-1985
Contentious Cases:	13
Advisory Requests:	5
Declarations:	1
Sep. Opinions:	2
Dis. Opinions:	1

Since the enlargement of its membership began in 1955, the UN has never been the same. It has influenced and in turn been influenced by the Organization's programme of work. The New States, no less than the old ones, have gained from it all. The UN has in this exhilirating adventure been acquiring, through its organs, old and new, as well as its increasing intergovernmental and administrative activities, the wherewithals of a world body capable of tremendous possibilities for the future of the international community. (Africa and the Development of International Law, 1988, at p. 61*)*

In February 1981, after 35 years, the International Court of Justice welcomed its first elected African President. From 1981 to 1984 Taslim Olawale Elias from Nigeria, the man who was once characterized as 'the first legal luminary of exceptional quality in the African world', would steer the Court with determination through a most interesting period.

His term was to be marked *not* by the issues that had so long dominated the Court's caseload, namely matters of decolonization and self-determination, but by three cases that were typical of the years immediately following the UNCLOS Conference (1973-1982) and the Montego Bay Convention: the *Gulf of Maine* case and the *Tunisia-Libya* and *Libya-Malta* delimitation cases - in short: maritime boundary issues and matters of continental shelf demarcation. It was marked even more by the first phases of *Military and Paramilitary Activities in and against Nicaragua*.

Judge Elias was a man of dignity, vitality and learning and was endowed with a great memory. A native of Lagos, he was educated at Cambridge and London Universities and was on intimate terms with English literature, as shown in his many writings. He was called to the Bar at the Inner Temple (1947) and for many years served as a legal counsel concurrently with Research Fellowships at Manchester and Oxford Universities. He became a Queen's Counsel in 1961. Back in Nigeria, his academic career included a professorship (1966-1972) and Life Chancellorship at Lagos University. In 1960 he was appointed Attorney-General of Nigeria and that same year became Minister of Justice. Subsequently, from 1967 to 1972, he was Commissioner for Justice and for the next three years served as Chief Justice of the Nigerian Supreme Court.

Ever since the early 1960s Judge Elias was involved in matters of international law and African unity. In 1961 he was a Member of the UN Expert Committee which drafted the Constitution of the Congo, and in 1963 of the Committee that drafted the Charter of the Organization of African Unity (OAU). He became President of the Nigerian Society of International Law (1968), the Asian-African Legal Consultative Committee (1972) and the African Society of International and Comparative Law (1986).

In 1961 Judge Elias became a Member, in 1965 a General Rapporteur and in 1970 Chairman of the International Law Commission. Again, in 1963 he helped negotiate the Draft Convention on the Settlement of Investment Disputes; in 1968-1969 he played a major part at the Vienna Conference on the Law of Treaties; in 1980-1981 he was Vice-President of the World Bank Administrative Tribunal.

To many Taslim Elias was the standard bearer of African scholarship. His career is marked by a virtually endless list of awards and honorary doctorates. Inevitably, Judge Elias was on the Board of a number of scholarly journals. He was himself a prolific author on such diverse matters as Nigerian and African customary law, British Colonial law, the Law of Treaties and various aspects of the judicial process. Major titles from his later years are *New Horizons in International Law* (1979), *Africa before the World Court* (1981) and *The ICJ and Some Contemporary Problems* (1983).

Judge Elias had been involved in the proceedings in the *Legal Conseqences* case concerning Namibia before, in 1976, he was elected Judge. His second term was cut short by his death in August 1991.

*1925

Judge:	1981-1985
Contentious Cases:	3
Advisory Requests:	2
Declarations:	1
Sep. Opinions:	–
Dis. Opinions:	2

Abdallah Fikri El-Khani

In January 1981, Judge El-Khani came to replace his compatriot Judge Tarazi (who in mid-term had met with a tragic tram accident) and fulfilled the latter's term till February 1985. He was therefore the second Syrian lawyer to be elected to the Court. Educated in law at the Syrian University in Damascus and the Université St Joseph at Beirut, and in political sciences and philosophy at the American University of Beirut, Judge El-Khani began his career as a lawyer (1947-1949), Secretary-General of the Presidency of the Republic (1949-1959) and lecturer at the School of Law of the Syrian University (1954-1958). In the 1960s he was Minister-Counsellor, then Minister-Plenipotentiary in Madrid, Brussels, Ankara, London and Paris. In 1966 he was appointed Syria's Permanent Representative to Unesco and in 1970 headed the Syrian delegation to the UN General Assembly and Security Council. He then entered national politics.

From 1969 to 1972 Judge El-Khani was Secretary-General at the Ministry of Foreign Affairs, where he served as a Deputy-Minister in 1976. From 1972-1976 he was Minister for Tourism. He was Ambassador to India, accredited to Bangladesh, Burma, Nepal and Sri Lanka, and Ambassador designate to Afghanistan (1978-1981). He served concurrently on the United Nations Sub-Commission on Prevention of Discrimination and Protection of Minorities (1978-1981) and was Chairman of its 33rd session.

In the very months he was elected to the International Court of Justice, Judge El-Khani attended the Islamic Summit Conference of 1981, where among other things he helped prepare the draft Statute of an International Islamic Court of Justice. This 'Arab Court of Justice' was to be modelled along the lines of the ICJ and to adjudicate disputes between Arab States and issue legal opinions. The idea harked back to the early days of the Arab League. It was first considered in 1951 and had been a recurrent item during successive conferences of the Arab world; to date the Court has not materialized.

Judge El-Khani's 2 Dissenting Opinions and 1 Declaration reveal his definite views on the status and functioning of the Court. In the opening lines and concluding paragraph of his Dissenting Opinion in the 1982 *Application for Review of Judgment No. 273 of UNAT* he stated the following:

> To my great regret I find myself obliged to dissociate myself from the Advisory Opinion which the Court has seen fit to give in the present case, because I consider that, for reasons of principle bound up with the very nature of the Court's jurisdiction, and having regard to the procedural irregularities committed by the body which referred the case to it, the Court, in this instance, ought to have refused to comply with the request for an Advisory Opinion. ... the Court, whose primary role is to deal with cases between States, should not be led into giving Opinions which finally result in diverting it from its principal sphere of jurisdiction and reducing it to being a court of appeal from judgements of the United Nations Administrative Tribunal in cases between officials and the Secretary-General. (*ICJ Reports* 1982, at pp. 446 and 453)

Perhaps even more rooted in principle is the other Dissenting Opinion in the 1982 *Gulf of Maine* case, when the Court had been pressed by the Parties both with regard to the time-limit for the constitution of the Chamber (the first ever) and to its actual composition and the possible replacement of Judges:

> I find that the imposition of an unduly close time-limit for the Chamber's formation and of a particular composition renders the Court no longer master of its own acts, deprives it of its freedom of choice and is an obstacle to the proper administration of justice. Furthermore it diminishes the prestige of the Court and is harmful to its dignity as the principal judicial organ of the United Nations. It results in its regionalization by depriving it of its basic and essential characteristic of universality and produces the indirect result of there being more than one judge of the same nationality acting in the name of the Court, one in the Chamber and the other in the Court, which does not correspond to the Statute. On these grounds I find that this ought not to constitute a precedent, as it would be a dangerous course to follow in the future. (*ICJ Reports* 1982, at p. 12)

Jens Evensen

The integrity of a person's family and family life is a basic human right protected by prevailing principles of international law which derive not only from conventional international law or customary international law but from 'general principles of law recognized by civilized nations'. (ICJ Reports 1989, at pp. 210-211)

*1917

Judge:	1985-1994
Contentious Cases:	17
Advisory Requests:	3
Declarations:	2 Joint
Sep. Opinions:	2
Dis. Opinions:	1

Jens Evensen's contacts with the ICJ, in various capacities, span no less than 45 years. He served a full term as Judge from 1985 till 1994, but first entered the Great Hall of Justice as Legal Counsel for Norway as early as 1949, on the occasion of the *Fisheries* case between his country and Great Britain. He returned five years later in the same capacity in the case of the *Norwegian Loans*, a dispute with France, and appeared again in 1961 as Counsel in the advisory procedure concerning *Certain Expenses of the UN*. Through the years, incidentally, Judge Evensen represented his nation in similar capacities before the European Court of Human Rights and on a number of other Tribunals. In 1978 he was appointed Judge *ad hoc* at the ICJ in the case concerning the *Continental Shelf* between Tunisia and Libya, which kept him at The Hague till 1982. Less than three years later he was elected to the bench.

Judge Evensen held a law degree from Oslo University and was further trained at the Minnesota, Columbia and Harvard Law Schools, obtaining a Doctorate from the latter. During the war he took an active part in the Norwegian resistance movement. He started his career as a public prosecutor in the *High Treason* cases immediately after the war, then became an advocate at the Supreme Court. He held a Lecturership for a while, but soon turned away from the academic sphere to become Director-General of the Legal Department of the Foreign Ministry (1961-1973).

In this capacity he negotiated the 1972 trade agreement with the European Communities. In subsequent years he was Minister of Commerce and Shipping (1973-1974) and Minister for the Law of the Sea (1974-1978). This made him a natural choice of Norway as chairman of its delegation to the Third UNCLOS Conference (1973-1982), where he acted as one of its Vice-Presidents. Similarly, he sat on the Preparatory Commission for the International Tribunal for the Law of the Sea (1983-1985).

Judge Evensen also represented his nation on the Sixth Committee of the General Assembly. He became Member of the *Institut de Droit International* in 1971 (Associate) and of the Permanent Court of Arbitration in 1978, and was a Member of the International Law Commission from 1979 to 1985. During this time he acted as its Special Rapporteur on the Law of the Non-Navigational Uses of International Watercourses. His expertise on the law of the sea quite naturally made Judge Evensen (who was an enthusiastic marine yachtsman himself!) the clear choice of his nation to be its representative on the Conciliation Commission in the Jan Mayen Continental Shelf dispute with Iceland.

Judge Evensen published extensively on matters of the law of the sea, but also on radio communications and interrelated matters such as pirate broadcasting stations operating from ships. His other major field of interest comprised space law, nuclear energy and atomic weapons. During his years with the ICJ Judge Evensen delivered 2 short Separate and 1 lengthy Dissenting Opinion (in the advisory request on the *Application for Review of Judgment No. 333 of UNAT* concerning the rights of UN staff members) and shared in 2 Joint Declarations. Illustrative here perhaps is his opinion in an altogether different matter, *viz.* the ECOSOC Advisory Request concerning the *Applicability of Art. VI, Sect. 22 of the Convention on the Privileges and Immunities of the UN*, the so-called Mazilu case, in which he held that:

> The integrity of a person's family and family life is a basic human right protected by prevailing principles of international law which derive not only from conventional international law or customary international law but from 'general principles of law recognized by civilized nations'. (*ICJ Reports* 1989, at p. 210)

Isidro Fabela Alfaro

1882-1964

Judge:	1946-1952
Contentious Cases:	11
Advisory Requests:	6
Declarations:	–
Sep. Opinions:	–
Dis. Opinions:	–

Isidro Fabela was the first Mexican Judge on the Court. He was elected in 1946, during the first elections held by the Security Council and General Assembly (then still sitting in London), and was among the judges who were - chosen by lot drawn by the Secretary-General - appointed for a term of six years. Fabela was a prominent lawyer at the time, in the 1930s, when his nation launched its famous *Estrada* doctrine that helped to overcome an obstacle to the development of the theory of recognition by divorcing diplomatic practice from the question of the legitimacy of régimes. Mexico, incidentally, was the only Latin American nation to be represented during the First Hague Peace Conference. As Mr Gonzalo A. Esteva, its First Delegate at the Second, 1907 Conference proudly stated when interviewed by William Stead, the editor of the *Courrier de la Conférence*:

> En 1899 le Mexique fut la seule Puissance de l'Amérique latine invitée à cette Conférence et qui prit part à ses délibérations. Le Mexique fut en outre le premier pays du monde parmi ceux qui furent invités à donner des preuves positives de son acceptation de l'arbitrage international et de sa confiance dans le Tribunal de Justice International établi à La Haye. Le premier cas présenté à La Haye fut la question des réclamations pécuniaires entre le Mexique et son puissant voisin et ami. (*Courrier*, 11 October 1907, at p. 3)

The reference is to the 1902 *Pious Fund* case between Mexico and the USA, the first case to be dealt with by the Permanent Court of Arbitration. The case concerned claims made against Mexico by the Roman Catholic Bishops of California on the basis of a 1868 Convention. The dispute was referred to a panel of five arbitrators who rendered a unanimous award with which Mexico readily complied. Mexico's relations with the Hague Courts remained fairly limited: it had no Judge on the bench of the PCIJ and no case had any direct effect on it.

Unfortunately, there is little record of Judge Alfaro's work at the Court. No Opinions were left by him and in none of his numerous works can references to the Court be found. This is all the more surprising because from his days as a Mexican judge in the Mexican-Italian Claims Commission (1929-1933) he left an extensive personal file, later published in his *Votos Internacionales*. He had wide experience in a variety of functions in the public, judicial and academic spheres at the time he was elected to the Court in 1946.

Judge Alfaro obtained his Doctorate in 1908 at the National School of Jurisprudence. In 1913 he entered the field of diplomacy as Acting Secretary of State for Foreign Affairs in Carranza's provisional Constitutionalist government after the overthrow of President Huerta. In subsequent years he held diplomatic posts both in Europe and Latin-America and at the Third Conference of Caribbean States. He was then appointed to the abovementioned Claims Commission.

Judge Alfaro's versatility is indicated by the fact that he concurrently held chairs of international law at the University of Mexico (since 1921) and of history and literature at the *Instituto Cientifico* of Chihuahua. He was a Member of the Court of Arbitration from 1936 until his death. In 1938 he served as President of the first Permanent Agricultural Conference in Geneva. Finally, he held the position of Governor in Mexico in the years 1942-1945.

Judge Alfaro published extensively on a wide range of subjects: neutrality; intervention; Mexico's rights on Belize; Mexican diplomatic history; the above-mentioned *Votos Internacionales*, and treatises issued for private circulation on the Drago and Carranza doctrines; essays on international law and politics; a history of the Claims Commissions; on the relations of Mexico and the American Continent with the League and on the position of Cuba in international law.

In the years leading up to the Second World War he was Founder and Director of the legal and diplomatic review *Mundo Libre*. Judge Fabela served on the Court until 1952.

Luigi Ferrari Bravo

*1933

Judge:	1995-present
Contentious Cases:	1
Advisory Requests:	1
Declarations:	–
Sep. Opinions:	–
Dis. Opinions:	–

To the inner circle in The Hague, for two decades, Italian international law was virtually synonymous with Roberto Ago. Luigi Ferrari Bravo, who succeeded to Judge Ago last year, can point to three undeniable facts among his credentials: he too graduated from Naples; he too held chairs for 35 years at prominent Italian university centres; he too held the chair in Rome for 20 years - and in Rome, as in The Hague, he replaced Judge Ago. Admittedly, times have changed - and the two men differ. But then, history, when it repeats itself, never does so in the same manner.

Judge Ferrari Bravo was born in Naples, where he graduated in Law. He embarked upon an academic career which brought him Full Professorships in Bari, Naples and Rome, first at the High School of Public Administration, then in the Faculties of Political Science and Law at the University. All in all, he taught International Law in Naples, Bari and Rome between 1956-1974 and 1982-1991; the Law of International Organization from 1961-1965 in Bari and from 1974-1979 in Naples; and European Community Law from 1965 till 1995 in Rome. He lectured twice at the Hague Academy (1975, 1985) on private international law and international customary law.

Judge Ferrari Bravo holds a number of functions in the international legal field: he is Secretary-General of the Italian Society for International Organization, Member of the *Institut de Droit International*, Member of the ILA and ASIL and of the *Société française*, and he is also on the Executive Council of the European Science Foundation, the national UNESCO Committee and the Italian Olympic Committee. He is currently President of 'Unidroit'. Again, he is on the editorial board of the series of EEC/ECSC Treaty Commentaries and of prominent reviews such as the *Cahiers de droit européen*, the *Rivista di diritto internazionale* and the *German Yearbook*. He is currently Editor-in-Chief of *La Comunità Internazionale* and General Editor of the *Italian Yearbook*. Judge Ferrari Bravo has authored works on evidence in international procedure (1958), international and municipal law in the treaty-making process (1964), the law of torts and the conflict of laws (1973) and *Lezioni* in international law (1973, 1986).

In his capacity of Legal Adviser and, since 1985, as Head of the Legal Service of the Foreign Ministry, Judge Ferrari Bravo joined and often chaired Italian Delegations, as for instance to the Tehran Human Rights Conference (1968), the Geneva Humanitarian Conference (1975-1977), the Vienna Codification Conference on Treaties (1986) and the 1991 Valletta European Security Meeting. Similarly, he advised the Italian Permanent Missions in New York and Geneva from 1981-1985, was on the UN Special Committee on Aggression (1973-1974) and on the Charter Committee (1975-1983), and was a Member of the *ad hoc* Committees on Hostages (1979) and Mercenaries (1982-1983). He attended the Meetings of the Sixth Committee of the General Assembly from 1976-1983 and chaired this Committee in 1978. In past years, he has gained wide experience in the international judicial sphere as Agent of Italy before the Court of Justice of the EC, the European Commission and the ECHR. He appeared before the ICJ as Agent of Italy in the ELSI case. In his 1985 Academy Course on international custom in State practice, he said of the ICJ:

> La sensibilité de la Cour Internationale de Justice aux nouvelles tendances du droit international se manifeste aussi par rapport aux formes diverses que prend la pratique contemporaine des États ... Si les prises de position de la Cour ... témoignent de l'attention de la plus haute juridiction internationale à la phénoménologie contemporaine de la pratique des États, elles témoignent aussi du désir de la Cour de se tenir le plus proche possible des particularités de l'affaire concrète qui est soumise à son jugement. Cela non seulement dans le but de rechercher une solution juste en droit et aussi équitable (but qui pourtant nous semble de plus en plus préoccuper la Cour), mais aussi pour faire ressortir le plus clairement possible que la solution à laquelle la Cour arrive dans sa décision est aussi une solution que les parties auraient trouvée par consentement mutuel si elles avaient mené jusqu'au bout des négociations entre elles. (*RDC* 192 (1985-III), at pp. 313-314)

1901-1982

Judge:	1960-1973
Contentious Cases:	8
Advisory Requests:	3
Declarations:	2 Joint
Sep. Opinions:	6
Dis. Opinions:	2 (1 Joint)

Gerald Gray Fitzmaurice

It is a fact, wrote Lord Buchan, that the greatest judges have usually been men of wide general culture. Sir Gerald Fitzmaurice was such a man. He was dedicated to international law; he also took a keen interest in mathematics, painting, poetry (notably Keats) and the theatre. He looked reserved to many at first sight. But then, first appearances can be deceptive. Judge Lachs knew him for 36 years; his apparent reserve, he tells us, was modesty if anything:

> Far from inaccessible, Sir Gerald was helpful and kind, generous in counsel, and an excellent colleague.

He was educated at Gonville and Caius College, Cambridge, a pupil of Arnold McNair. Judge Fitzmaurice was fond of paradox and there were paradoxes in his life. Though by nature every inch the scholar, he never had a full-time academic appointment. Again, a first rank author and an elegant stylist, he did not produce a monograph upon a legal subject:

> One could say that Gerald's style had a Roman cadence and Corinthian ornamentation. In this, Gerald Fitzmaurice was a master of classical English, one who seemed incapable of committing jargon or officialese, or penning any sentence which failed to bear the stamp of his personality.

International law was his exclusive province from the very beginning:

> For nearly forty years, the person of Gerald Fitzmaurice formed an eminence in the international legal landscape, a feature without which, that is to say, the scene would have looked significantly different. ... Of all the motley garb he must needs have put on to play those parts, the sober gown and jabot of The Hague Court fitted him best I believe. (Lachs, in *NILR* 1983)

Sir Gerald's *credo* as comprehensively summed up by Sir Robert Jennings:

> ...expresses something central to Fitzmaurice's constant belief that juristic problems are intellectual problems and that only a law that satisfies reason will carry authority; and, moreover, that the preservation of the intellectual integrity of the system is, therefore, a *sine qua non* for the establishment of the rule of law in international affairs ... which is at the heart of all his work in international law. (Jennings, in *BYBIL* 1984)

Judge Fitzmaurice was called to the Bar at Gray's Inn in 1925 and practised in London until entering the Foreign Service for what was to be a long spell as a Legal Adviser. From 1939-1943 he served in the Ministry of Economic Warfare. Back at the Foreign Office in 1945, he became the Legal Adviser in 1953 and Queen's Counsel in 1957. He served at the 1944 Chicago Aviation Conference, was Secretary to the Inter-Allied Committee of Jurists, helped draft the UN Charter at San Francisco, and attended the Paris and Japanese Peace Conferences. He was a Member of the Sixth Committee, and took part in the 1954 Berlin and Manila conferences, and the 1958-1960 Law of the Sea Conferences. Sir Gerald was Member of the ILC from 1955-1962, its Chairman in 1959 and General Rapporteur from 1957-1960. He wrote 5 Reports for the Commission on the Law of Treaties. He was member of the *Institut* from 1954 and its President in 1967-1969. He lectured three times at the Academy. Having published extensively in the *British Year Book* in the 1930s, from 1950-1959 he published an extraordinary collection on *The Law and Procedure of the ICJ* (collected in 1986), including 3 articles on *Hersch Lauterpacht - The Scholar as Judge*. Sir Gerald was British Counsel before the ICJ in 6 cases between 1948-1954, before becoming a Member of the Court (1960-1973). He was Acting President for periods in 1967 and 1970. His Opinions were deemed real pearls of law, wisdom and culture:

> From the day he mounted the bench, his words and his views became the property of the Court. From that very day he was and remained unsurpassed in the esteem and prestige he enjoyed as a man and as a judge. ... He had a prodigious memory; no-one equalled him in the knowledge of precedents; he was always the first to find the right formula and word. (Lachs)

His retirement in 1973 was not the end of his career. In 1971 he chaired the *Beagle Channel* arbitration panel. From 1974-1980 he was Judge on the ECHR. Even then he remained active, 'the vein of wisdom showing no sign of exhaustion yet' (Lachs).

Carl-August Fleischhauer

*1930

Judge:	1994-present
Contentious Cases:	2
Advisory Requests:	1
Declarations:	–
Sep. Opinions:	–
Dis. Opinions:	–

Fifty-nine years after the much regretted death, in mid-term, of Judge Walther Schücking, in 1935, and nine years after Judge Hermann Mosler had left The Hague, a third German Judge made his entrance. Judge Fleischhauer brought exceptional credentials. He became the first Judge on the ICJ to have been recruited, if one may say so, 'from within', that is from the United Nations Secretariat, and therefore the International Civil Service. After a distinguished career in the diplomatic Service of the Federal Republic of Germany, Judge Fleischhauer served for 11 years (1983-1994) as Under-Secretary-General for Legal Affairs, the Legal Counsel of the UN It is because of these circumstances that, before becoming a Judge in his own right, he had been involved in cases before the Court in two other capacities: twice on the side of the Federal Republic: in the 1967-1969 proceedings in the *North Sea Continental Shelf* case and in the 1972-1974 proceedings in the *Fisheries Jurisdiction* case; three times on behalf of the UN: in the 1984-1987 proceedings on the Advisory Request on the *Application for Review of Judgment No. 333 of UNAT*, again in 1988 on the *Applicability to Arbitrate under the 1947 HQ Agreement* and lastly on the *Applicability of the Convention on Privileges and Immunities of the UN*, in 1989.

Carl-August Fleischhauer was born in Düsseldorf and studied in Heidelberg, Grenoble and Paris. He was a Fulbright Scholar at the University of Chicago Law School in 1954-1955, before becoming a Junior Barrister in Düsseldorf and Heidelberg (1955-1959). In 1960 he attended the Hague Academy. He was a Research Fellow at the Max Planck Institute in Heidelberg, whose director at the time was Hermann Mosler. He was to join the Curatorium of that Institute in 1975. Under the supervision of Hermann Mosler he wrote a Dissertation on the limits of the material competence of the Federal Constitutional Court in the control of the legislative power, the executive branch and the political parties (in German).

In 1962 he entered the diplomatic service. He was assigned to Tehran (1962-1963) and Montevideo (1969-1971) and held various posts in the Legal Department of the Federal Foreign Office. From 1976 to 1983 he was the Legal Advisor to the Federal Foreign Office and the Director General of its Legal Department. His multilateral assignments included the Committee of Experts on Human Rights of the Council of Europe in Strasbourg (1964-1967) and, in various capacities, attendance of the General Assembly and its Sixth Committee (1968, 69, 73-82). He, *inter alia*, helped draw up the Hostages Convention.

Judge Fleischhauer was a Member of the Delegations of his country to the Vienna Conference on the Law of Treaties (1968-1969), the Third UNCLOS Conference (1974-1982), the CSCE Conference at Geneva and Helsinki (1974-1975) and the Diplomatic Conference on Humanitarian Law in Geneva (1974-1977). He headed the FRG Delegation to the Conference on State Succession in Relation to Treaties in Vienna (1977-1978). He was awarded the German Cross of Merit, First Class and foreign decorations (all before 1983).

Judge Fleischhauer has written on various issues of international law. In an article on the Development and Codification of International Law, in which he discusses the progress that has been made in recent years, notably through the International Law Commission and UNCITRAL, the experienced negotiator Fleischhauer observes:

> Very careful consideration must be given to the appropriate balance, in a given field, between making substantial progress and achieving wide acceptance. If the latter is to be accomplished, it is necessary to negotiate a consensus at whatever the highest common denominator of agreement may be - which may be very low - but then insist that no deviations from the standard are permissible. Alternatively, if more substantial progress is to be achieved and yet wide participation is desired, it may be necessary to permit extensive reservations or the choice between a number of options. Other relevant variables may be the minimum number and importance of the States required for bringing a treaty into force. *(Indian JIL* 1985, at p. 7)

1903-1984

Judge:	1964-1982
Contentious Cases:	11
Advisory Requests:	5
Declarations:	2 Joint
Sep. Opinions:	5
Dis. Opinions:	3

Isaac Forster

Judge Forster was born in Dakar and educated at the Lycée Hoche in Versailles. A *Licencié en droit* of the Paris Law Faculty, he made his career in the Judiciary. He became a Deputy Judge in 1933 and Deputy to the Procureur at Conakry in 1933. He then served as Judge in St Denis, Réunion and Madagascar. In 1942 he was appointed *Procureur de la République* at Lomé; in 1945 Judge of the Appeal Court in Guadeloupe, and in 1947 Judge at the Appeal Court of French West Africa. He was a Member of the Private Office of Presidents Auriol (1952) and Coty (1956).

In 1958 Judge Forster became Secretary-General of his Government, in 1959 *Procureur Général* at Dakar, and later First President of the Supreme Court of Senegal. He gained his international experience, up to his election to the Court, notably from his work on Commissions of Experts and Inquiry of the ILO, and more particularly in a complaint by Ghana against the observance by Portugal of the *Abolition of Forced Labour Convention* (1957-1962). He was a Member of the *Institut de Droit International*.

Isaac Forster became a Member of the Court in February 1964 and was re-elected in 1973. After having completed his second term, he continued to sit in the *Continental Shelf* case between Tunisia and Libya. During his 19 years at the Court he produced 2 Dissenting and 5 Separate Opinions, and 2 Joint Declarations, which allow us a glimpse of his views. Among others, they show him as a protagonist of the extension of the 12-mile zone. His stand in the *Nuclear Tests* case is particularly noteworthy. He dissented on grounds of procedure and merits alike. Firstly, he reserved to France, as not having adhered to any Convention to the contrary, the sovereign rights of territorial intangibility and freedom of decision:

> France is absent from these proceedings; but I conceive that the right which it has and which is to be protected is that of every State, namely the right to undertake in full sovereignty on its own territory any action appropriate for ensuring its immediate or future national security and national defence. Of course, in the exercise of this right each State remains responsible for any consequent injury to third parties. (*ICJ Reports* 1973, at p. 114)

Secondly, he observed:

> An additional consideration leads me to differ from the majority of my colleagues. The interim measures requested by Australia are so close to the actual subject-matter of the case that they are practically indistinguishable therefrom. Ultimately the only alternatives are the continuance or the cessation of the French nuclear tests in the Pacific. This is the substance of the case, upon which, in my opinion, it was not proper to pass by means of a provisional Order, but only by a final judgment. ... This, it seems to me, is what the Applicant was counting on ... the intention of the Applicant is to obtain, by means of a request for the indication of interim measures of protection, an actual judgment on the legality, or rather the illegality, of further nuclear tests. I cannot lend myself to this, which is not what interim measures were intended for. (*ibid.*, at p. 113)

Thirdly, another matter of principle disconcerted him:

> Even when it considers that circumstances require the indication of provisional measures, the Court, before proceeding to indicate them, must satisfy itself that it has jurisdiction. Neither the provisional character of the measures nor the urgency of the requirement that they be indicated can dispense the judge from the necessity of ascertaining his jurisdiction *in limine litis*; especially when it is seriously and categorically contested by the State proceeded against, which is the case at present. I am aware of the existence of certain past decisions ... But ... however illustrious their reputations, our predecessors on the Bench cannot now take our place, nor can their decisions take the place of the one we have to render in an exceptionally difficult affair... (*ibid.*, at p. 111)

Sergei Alexandrovich Golunsky

1895-1962

Judge:	1952-1953
Contentious Cases:	–
Advisory Requests:	–
Declarations:	–
Sep. Opinions:	–
Dis. Opinions:	–

Judge Golunsky is unique among the Judges in that though elected to the Court, he never functioned on the bench. He was elected on 6 December 1951 to replace Judge Krylov whose allotted term of six years at the Court was then expiring but proved unable to travel to The Hague. His arrival was first postponed; in 1953, when there was no noticeable improvement in his condition, he submitted his letter of resignation. In November Judge Kojevnikov was elected to hold office for the remainder of Judge Golunsky's term.

Sergei Golunsky was born in Moscow. He graduated from the faculty of law at Moscow University in 1917. He first worked as a prosecutor, then became a lecturer and later Professor of Criminal Law and Process. From 1943-1952 he worked at the Ministry of Foreign Affairs, from 1945 as the Head of the Legal Questions and Treaties Department. Concurrently, he was Professor of International Law in the Moscow Academy of Social Sciences. From 1952-1962 he was teacher in a number of Moscow institutes and from 1958-1962 Editor-in-Chief of the journal *Soviet State and Law*. He was a prolific author, mainly in the spheres of criminal law and process, the theory and history of law, and international law. He was the author of one of the first Soviet text-books on the theory of state and law (published in 1940, in collaboration with M. S. Strogovich) and of text-books on the detection of crimes and the criminal process. He was editor of the Russian translation of Oppenheim's *International Law*.

Through 1944-1945 Judge Golunsky took part in several of the great international conferences that helped shape the post-war era, such as Dumbarton Oaks, San Francisco, Yalta and Potsdam. At San Francisco he was assisted by Judge Krylov, his predecessor on the ICJ, in a Delegation that was chaired by Mr Molotov and Mr Gromyko, then Ambassador to the USA. In the Closing Plenary Session, on 26 June 1945, Acting-Chairman Gromyko addressed the Conference in the following terms:

> Today we sum up the results of the historic Conference of the United Nations, gathered to work out the Charter of the Organization on the maintenance of peace and security. The foundation ... was laid at the Moscow Conference ... at the Dumbarton Oaks Conference and at the historic Crimea Conference. ... In this connection it is neccessary to point out specially the significance of those provisions of the Charter which refer to peaceful settlement of disputes and conflicts. Under the Charter, members of the International Organization obligate themselves to achieve peaceful settlements of the disputes. Let us hope that this aim will be fully realized. (*UNCIO Documents*, Vol. 1, General, at pp. 694, 696)

Judge Golunsky was on the *Advisory Committee of Jurists* chaired by Hackworth and comprising the illustrious names of Sir William Malkin, Jules Basdevant, Hsu Mo and Alfonso García Robles. (Interestingly enough, the Russian, the American, the French and the Chinese delegates were to become Judges at the ICJ). During their second meeting, in the Opera House, the Committee discussed *inter alia* the signing of the Statute of the ICJ. The records read:

> The question was raised as to whether the Statute of the ICJ should be signed separately at the time of signing the Charter. Mr Golunsky commented that this was related to another very important question: the manner in which later members would be admitted into the Organization. Mr Hackworth stated that such members would not sign the original Charter. Mr Hsu Mo expressed the view that they would deposit separate instruments of ratification. So far as the Court is concerned, the Committee felt that the question is governed by the terms of Article 60, which refers to 'the annexed Statute which forms an integral part of this Charter'. It was therefore agreed that the Court Statute would not be signed separately, but would be annexed and bound together with the Charter under the title: 'Statute of the International Court of Justice'. (*UNCIO Documents*, Vol. 17, Part 1, at p. 398)

It can be seen from these lines that Judge Golunsky took an active part in the decision-making at a crucial moment in the constitutional history of the Court. After these Conferences, he was appointed Assistant Prosecutor before the International Military Tribunal in the Far East.

*1908

Judge:	1964-1984
Contentious Cases:	13
Advisory Requests:	5
Declarations:	7 (1 Joint)
Sep. Opinions:	4
Dis. Opinions:	9

André Gros

La recherche du consensus tend à faire de la Cour une sorte de conciliateur amiable dont les actes juridictionnels ne seraient plus que des recueils de conseils; ce rôle peut être exercé par d'autres mais le juge dit le droit et rien que le droit.

André Gros, definitely one of the major figures in the Court's history, was born in Douai and obtained a Doctorate of Law from Lyons and Paris Universities. Initially he entered upon an academic career. In 1930 he became Lecturer in Paris, in 1934 in Nancy and in 1937 in Toulouse. During the war years he advised the National Committee in London and from then on was put forward by his Government as a seasoned veteran of diplomacy. From 1943 to 1948 he was on the UN War Crimes Commission; in 1944 he joined the Committee that discussed the future of the PCIJ, in 1945 he was on the Allied Reparation Commission, and in 1946 at the Peace Conference. Like so many Judges, he then turned his attention from the purely academic to the public and international spheres, in his case to the Legal Department of the Foreign Ministry (1947-1963). In 1954 he became Counsellor of State and represented France at numerous conferences on such varying issues as Trade (1946), the E.E.C. (1948), the Schumann Plan (1950), Indo-China (1954), Suez (1956), the Law of the Sea (1958, 1960), the Antarctic (1959) and Laos (1961). Prominent, too, are his activities on the Rhine, Danube and Moselle Commissions. From 1961-1963 he was Vice-Chairman of the International Law Commission; in 1979 he was President of the session of the *Institut de Droit International*.

During the 1950s Judge Gros also gained much experience on arbitration panels. He sat on the Permanent Commission of Arbitration between Denmark and Greece (1949), Denmark and Turkey (1953) and was Agent before the Franco-Swiss, Franco-Italian, and Franco-Thai Conciliation Commissions (1954-1956). In 1951 he was Agent in the *Monetory Gold* case, he was Counsel in the Franco-Spanish *Lake Lanoux* case (1957), he sat on the Commission of Inquiry in the British-Danish *Red Crusader* dispute (1962) and, having been a Member of the PCA from 1950 onwards, served in the *Beagle Channel* case between Argentina and Chile (1971-1977) and the French-British dispute on the *Delimitation of the Continental Shelf* (1975-1978). Similarly, he served as Agent for France in six cases before the ICJ. By 1964, his election to the Court seemed quite natural. Judge Gros was re-elected in 1973 and continued to sit after 1982 in the Tunisia/Libya *Continental Shelf* case and in the Chamber of the *Gulf of Maine* dispute.

In 1959 Judge Gros lectured at the Hague Academy on *La convention sur la pêche* and with Paul Reuter he published a volume of *Traités et documents diplomatiques* (1960). Several of his 20 articles in journals are pertinent to the ICJ: *Le problème du recours juridictionnel contre les décisions d'organismes internationaux* (1950), *Observations sur le mode de déliberation de la CIJ* (1975) and *La recherche du consensus dans les décisions de la CIJ* (1983). On the latter problem, namely, whether the search for consensus is actually favourable to the functioning of the Court, his conclusions read:

> Alors que la pratique du consensus n'a en rien amélioré l'efficacité du rôle judiciaire de la Cour, il faut en voir tous les effets dommageables pour l'avenir du contentieux international. Lorsqu'une affaire est complexe ... il n'est pas bon de prendre comme méthode de travail judiciaire l'effacement systématique des difficultés, la transformation des questions posées, l'accord sur le plus facile et le silence sur le reste. Lorsqu'il s'agit du seul organe juridictionnel permanent dans les relations internationales contemporaines il convient de demander à un tribunal de traiter les problèmes qu'on lui pose, de les régler par une majorité, quelle qu'en soit l'ampleur, la minorité exprimant ses vues. Ce sont deux philosophies qui s'opposent, non seulement de la justice, mais de la vie internationale et le débat n'est pas nouveau. La recherche du consensus tend à faire de la Cour une sorte de conciliateur amiable dont les actes juridictionnels ne seraient plus que des recueils de conseils; ce rôle peut être exercé par d'autres mais le juge dit le droit et rien que le droit. (*Festschrift Mosler* 1983, at pp. 357-358)

José Gustavo Guerrero

1876-1958

Judge:	1946-1958
President:	1946-1949
Vice-President:	1949-1955
Contentious Cases:	27
Advisory Requests:	10
Declarations:	1
Sep. Opinions:	–
Dis. Opinions:	1

Among his colleagues, Judge Guerrero of San Salvador may claim a distinct place of honour. He had the unique distinction of serving both the PCIJ and the ICJ and of being President and Vice-President of both benches. To be sure, this was not just a matter of coincidence. From the very beginning Judge Guerrero had shown himself a zealous advocate of the League of Nations, just as he was a warm supporter of the Pan-American movement and, later on, of the Federation of Central American States. Judge Guerrero was therefore every inch the internationalist. Throughout his life he strongly argued for the use of customary law and the decisions of international tribunals as primary sources for an international code. He was totally committed to the ideal of pacific settlement by any possible means, be this arbitration, conciliation or adjudication.

In the opening years of the century, José Guerrero, a young doctor of law from the Salvador and Guatemala universities with a somewhat conservative thesis on the international responsibility of States, rose rapidly from the diplomatic ranks in the embassies in France, Italy and Spain, to become Minister of Public Instruction, Justice and Foreign Affairs - three areas which suitably reflected his lifelong interests.

Then, for a full decade (1920-1930) he was his country's delegate to the League Assembly, where he earned a name for himself as a champion of arms control. He presided over its 1929 session. In this capacity his tact, courtesy and natural authority impressed all critics.

In 1928, at the 6th Pan-American Conference in Havana, Judge Guerrero introduced a firm resolution on non-intervention. From then on his international career gained tremendous momentum. He was a Member of the Committee of Experts for the progressive codification of international law, analysed its 1930 Hague Conference in a masterful study, *La codification du droit international* (1930) and was elected Judge to the Permanent Court in September 1930 to become its Vice-President only three months later, on January 1, 1931. He became its President in 1937. At the same time, he chaired arbitral tribunals in cases concerning railway concessions arising out of the eclipse of the Hapsburg Empire (1928-1929, 1933-1934, 1937-1938).

Upon the invasion of The Netherlands in May 1940, the Permanent Court moved to Geneva (its Vice-President, the Dutchman Van Eysinga, keeping vigil in the Peace Palace) and kept up records and correspondence throughout the war years. After the dissolution of the League and the installation of the ICJ in February 1946, President Guerrero, who had quite naturally helped shape the contours of the new world organization at the Lake Success Conference, was re-elected to the Court and served as its first President. He was to round off this second *cursus honorum* with another Vice-Presidency from 1949-1952. In 1954 he was re-elected and remained uninterruptedly in office until, in 1958, his strength ran out. He had been on the bench for 28 years and had chaired it for almost half this period.

At 82 his life drew to a close. Judge Guerrero had always shown a genial disposition, exquisite diplomacy, eminent learning, *une plume éléganté* and, remarkably enough, a progressive development from an initially rather traditional approach towards a very independent one. His Dissenting Opinion in the *Norwegian Loans* case (1957) stands out as a true philippic against the undermining of the *optional clause* by States who preferred to keep issues of national interest from submission to the Court:

> It has rightly been said already that it is not possible to establish a system of law if each State reserves to itself the power to decide itself what the law is. ... The problem to be solved is, however, a simple one. It is, in fact, the problem whether the unilateral will of one State or the common will of the Parties before the Court can have priority over the collective will expressed in an instrument as important as the Statute of the Court. (*ICJ Reports* 1957, at p. 69)

*1930

Judge:	1987–present
Contentious Cases:	16
Advisory Requests:	3
Declarations:	2 Joint
Sep. Opinions:	–
Dis. Opinions:	–

Gilbert Guillaume

An international court, like any court of law, traditionally plays a double rôle: it settles the disputes referred to it and contributes to the development of the law. These two functions complement each other, as the court must give its reasons for the solution that it adopts and it is that very statement of reasoning that causes the rule of law to progress.

In September 1987, Gilbert Guillaume became the fourth French Judge of the International Court of Justice, after Jules Basdevant, André Gros and Guy Ladreit de Lacharrière. His election to the Bench followed on from a national and international career that had been divided between the functions of judge, counsel and teacher.

Gilbert Guillaume was born at Bois-Colombes, near Paris. He holds a Bachelor's Degree in Law and a Diploma in Economics from the University of Paris, as well as a Diploma from the Paris Institute of Political Studies. An alumnus of the Ecole Nationale d'Administration, he was placed at the head of the list for his year and was appointed Auditeur at the Conseil d'État. He was promoted Maître des Requêtes in 1963, becoming Conseiller d'État in 1981. He spent a great many years serving in that capacity, and worked for nine years as Commissaire du Gouvernement before carrying out the same duties at the Tribunal des Conflits.

Having been Legal Adviser to the State Secretariat for Civil Aviation from 1969 to 1979, he served on that account as French Representative on the Legal Committee of ICAO of which he was Chairman from 1971 to 1975. He likewise represented France at different conferences on air law and was President of the Diplomatic Conference on the Liability of the Air Carrier that was held in Montreal in 1975. He is Honorary Chairman of the French Society for Air and Space Law and Chairman of the Board of Directors of the *Revue française de droit aérien et spatial*. He likewise acts as Chairman of the Arbitration Committee of Intelsat and the Appeals Board of Eutelsat. He was Chairman of the Conciliation Committee of the OECD from 1973 to 1979, and subsequently headed the Legal Service of that Organization. In addition he was, during that period, Chairman of the Appeals Board of NATO and served on of the Appeals Board of the European Space Agency.

Lastly, from 1979 until his election to the Court in 1987, Judge Guillaume served as Director of Legal Affairs at the Quai d'Orsay. In that capacity, he participated in the meetings of the Sixth Committee and was head of the French Delegation to the Third United Nations Conference on the Law of the Sea (1982), to the Vienna Conference on Succession of States (1983) and the Vienna Conference on the Law of Treaties between States and International Organizations (1986). He represented France on the Rhine Commission of which he acted as Chairman in 1981-1982. He was Counsel for France in the 1978 Arbitration in relation to the Franco-American Air Transport Agreement, and was his country's Agent in the 1986 Arbitration on the Franco-Canadian Fisheries Agreement. He was Agent for France in numerous cases before the Court of Justice of the European Communities and the European Court of Human Rights. Judge Guillaume has been a member of the Permanent Court of Arbitration since 1980 and is included on the lists of arbitrators of ICAO, the ICC, the ICSID and the OSCE.

Judge Guillaume taught International Law for ten years at the Paris Institute of Political Studies, and has also taught at the Ecole Nationale d'Administration and a great many other establishments. He is currently President of the French Branch of the International Law Association and Vice-President of the French Society for International Law. In 1995, he was elected to associate membership of the *Institut*. Among his numerous publications, we would mention his course on 'Terrorism and International Law' at the Hague Academy of International Law in 1989, his 1992 monograph on *Les formations restreintes des juridictions internationales* and, more recently, his book on *Les grandes crises internationales et le droit* (1994).

A Member of the ICJ since September 1987, Judge Guillaume has, ever since, invariably voted with the majority, never filed a Separate or Dissenting Opinion.

Green H. Hackworth

1883-1973

Judge:	1946-1961
President:	1955-1958
Contentious Cases:	34
Advisory Requests:	11
Declarations:	2
Sep. Opinions:	1
Dis. Opinions:	5

In a way it was Green Hackworth who, more than anyone, can be said to have stood at the cradle of the International Court in its present form. It was he who chaired the historic Committee of Jurists that first convened in April 1945 in Washington to prepare the initial draft of the ICJ Statute. Later that year, at the San Francisco Conference, he served again on the Fourth Committee that finalized the constitutional text. Subsequently, in 1946, and on the express recommendation of three former American Secretaries of State, he was succesfully put forward as a candidate for the Court. For this there were reasons in abundance. Not only was Judge Hackworth a highly competent and extremely experienced lawyer, a man of energy and amazing memory, used to making practical decisions; more than this, during the inter-war period, from his office at the State Department overlooking the White House, he had for more than twenty years (the longest tenure in history) served five successive Secretaries of State (Hughes, Kellogg and Stimson among them) as Legal Adviser. During the war years, Secretary of State Hull and President Roosevelt himself had been the prime beneficiaries of his wise counsel:

> Courageous in his recommendations, he was soft-spoken in their presentation ... He was perforce in the center of things involving the USA and its foreign relations from the period of US neutrality prior to US entry into World War I through World War II. (Marjorie M. Whiteman in *AJIL* 1974, at p. 92)

Judge Hackworth was born at Prestonsburg, Kentucky and educated at the Valparaiso, Georgetown and George Washington Universities, and was to become a Doctor of Laws at the University of Kentucky. He was Member of the Bar of the District of Columbia and of the Supreme Court. Attorney (1916), Solicitor (1918) and Legal Adviser to the Department of State for an unparalleled period (1925-1946), he served as Representative of the US Government before the International Joint Commission under the Canadian-American 1909 Boundary Water Treaty. He was its delegate to (among others) the 1930 Hague Conference on the Codification of International Law, the 1938 Lima Conference of American States and the 1940 Inter-American Maritime Conference. In 1943 he attended the Moscow Conference, and the next year saw him at Dumbarton Oaks. In 1945 he advised the US Government at San Francisco on the drafting of the UN Charter, then, in 1946, attended the first part of the First Session of the General Assembly of the UN in London.

Among his publications by far the most prominent is his *Digest of International Law* (8 volumes, 1944), a development of the earlier collections compiled by Wharton and John Bassett Moore and covering the years 1906-1944 in a wealth of sources. As stated in its Preface:

> ... the documents and files accumulated in the Department of State since 1906 ... are more voluminous than those of the entire period prior to that year. ... The importance of a proper understanding of the facts of a situation in an evaluation of opinions and pronouncements relating to it, has been recognized by the attention given to the historical and factual settings of the material presented.

It was deemed by Jules Basdevant, Hackworth's French counterpart at the *Quai d'Orsay* and later his colleague on the Bench, to be the most important contribution to international law during the war years. The work was complemented by Hackworth's close collaborator in the State Department, Marjorie M. Whiteman (*Digest*, 15 volumes, 1963-1973).

In 1946 Judge Hackworth published an essay on the ICJ and the codification of international law. On his election to the ICJ in February 1946, he was allotted a term of six years. In 1952 he was re-elected and in 1955 elected President. A tireless worker, he retired reluctantly in 1961 and lived to reach the age of 91.

During his 15 years on the Bench Green Hackworth served in 17 cases and helped render 11 Opinions. He often complained of the light case-load of the Court. He delivered 2 Declarations, 1 Separate and 5 Dissenting Opinions. At the State Department Green Hackworth was known for his clear, cogent memoranda. At the ICJ his Opinions were likewise considered exemplary. His influence on the Bench was considerable.

Géza Herczegh

*1928

Judge:	1993-present
Contentious Cases:	5
Advisory Requests:	1
Declarations:	–
Sep. Opinions:	–
Dis. Opinions:	–

For almost half a century the seat on the Court that in principle is reserved for the regional group to which Hungary belongs, seemed virtually the exclusive domain of Poland. Two Polish Judges, Winiarski (1946-1967) and Lachs (1967-1993) together shared an unparalleled period in the history of the ICJ. Nor had any Hungarian Judge ever sat on the Permanent Court. In fact, the relations of Hungary with the ICJ had been confined to two incidents in which its role had been a passive one: the 1950 Advisory Opinion on the *Interpretation of the Peace Treaties* with Bulgaria, Hungary and Romania in matters of human rights, and the 1954 dispute on the aerial incident and the *Treatment in Hungary of Aircraft and Crew of the USA*. The latter case was soon removed from the Court's list due to the unwillingness of the Respondent States (Hungary and the USSR) to submit to the jurisdiction of the Court.

By a twist of fate, it would seem, within two months after the installation of the first Hungarian Judge, in May 1993, Hungary and the Slovak Republic submitted to the Court by Special Agreement their difference concerning the *Gabčíkovo-Nagymaros Project* in the Danube River. Thus, at a crucial juncture, another rich cultural and legal tradition so far virtually unknown to the Court was added to those already interlinked on the Bench - this one actually represented by an internationalist who, among other things, has authoritatively recorded his nation's diplomatic history.

Judge Herczegh was born in Nagykapos and educated at a French Grammar School. He is a Bachelor of Law from the University of Szeged (1951) and a Member of the Hungarian Academy of Sciences since 1985. Judge Herczegh has combined an academic with a professional career. He was Research Fellow in International Law at the Institute of Political Sciences in Budapest from 1951-1967, then became Professor of Law and Head of the International Law Department at the University of Pécs (1981-1987). In the intervening period he was a Senior Fellow in the West, notably at Paris (1966) and Salzburg (1970), and lectured frequently on international humanitarian law at research centres in Bayreuth, Cambridge, Marburg, Moscow, and Vienna. In recent years he was Lecturer at Warsaw (1985) and Vegimont (1989). From 1990-1993 he was Judge and Vice-President of the Constitutional Court of the Republic of Hungary.

Judge Herczegh's major expertise is humanitarian law, on which he wrote a monograph *Development of International Humanitarian Law* (1984). He was National Representative at the 1971-1972 Geneva Humanitarian Conferences and represented the Hungarian Red Cross at its 1971-1973 Hague, Vienna and Tehran meetings and again in Monaco in 1984. He was on the Hungarian Delegation at the 1974-1977 Geneva Diplomatic Conference on the protection of victims of armed conflicts (in 1977 he served as Vice-President of the Conference) and at the 1977 UNESCO Conference in Sofia. He was Rapporteur during the Third Conference of the Council of Europe on Parliamentary Democracy in Strasbourg (1991) and Member of the expert working group preparing the Draft Convention on pacific settlement within the framework of the CSCE (Paris, 1992).

Judge Herczegh has published extensively on various topics. He wrote a monograph on *The Colonial Question and International Law* (1962), and essays in Hungarian on the International Trusteeship System (1953) and the Right to Self-Determination (1956); a *History of Diplomatic Relations, 1914-1945* (1964-1965) and a work on the *Foreign Policy of Hungary, 896-1919* (1987); also treatises on international law: *General Principles* (1969) and a *Manual* (1976, 1989). His many articles touch on minorities and human rights; totalitarian regimes; the 1948 Danube Convention; international rivers; general principles of law and the ICJ Statute; the use of force, war reprisals, and bacteriological weapons. Judge Herczegh has served on the Court from May 1993 when he was elected to fill the short remainder of the term of Judge Lachs, and was re-elected in his own right in February 1994.

Rosalyn Higgins

*1937

Judge:	1995-present
Contentious Cases:	1
Advisory Requests:	1
Declarations:	–
Sep. Opinions:	–
Dis. Opinions:	–

In 1984, the Court was gratified to be informed that Tunisia, in the phase of interpretation of the Court's Judgment in its *Continental Shelf* dispute with Libya, had chosen Suzanne Basdevant, Mme Paul Bastid, as Judge *ad hoc*. In the very year Mme Bastid died, and after almost 75 years of adjudication at The Hague, the Court in 1995 saw its first woman Member sworn in on the Bench. As with Mme Bastid, Judge Higgins needed no introduction to her colleagues-to-be. They had heard her argue in Court and appreciated her through her books and lecturing. Still, a notable precedent had been set.

Judge Higgins was educated at Girton College, Cambridge, where she was Bryce-Tebbs scholar. In 1958 she was an interne at the Office of Legal Affairs of the UN and from 1959-1961 was a Graduate Fellow at Yale Law School and at the Brookings Institution, Washington. She then became Junior Fellow in international studies at the London School of Economics (1961-1963), where she was to become a Visiting Fellow from 1974-1978. In the intervening years she was Staff Specialist at the Royal Institute of International Affairs. In 1978 she was appointed Professor of International Law at the University of Kent at Canterbury and from 1981 held a similar chair at the University of London. Judge Higgins is a prolific author. She wrote monographs on *The Development of International Law Through the Political Organs of the UN* (1963); *Conflict of Interests: International Law in a Divided World* (1965); *The Administration of the British Foreign Policy through the UN* (1966); *UN Peacekeeping: Documents and Commentary* (4 volumes, 1969-1981); she co-authored *Liberté de circulation des personnes en droit international* (1988, with M. Flory). She has lectured twice at The Hague Academy. In 1983 she lectured on *The Taking of Property by States* and in 1991 she gave a General Course, as the first British international lawyer to be so invited in twenty years, on *Avoidance, Containment and Resolution of Disputes* which she redrafted into the monograph *Problems & Process, International Law and How We Use it.* (1994) Judge Higgins has written numerous articles in the fields of international legal theory, United Nations law, the use of force, state and diplomatic immunities, human rights, and international petroleum law. She was a member of the board of editors of the *American Journal of International Law* (1975-1985), and an editor of the *British Year Book* and the *Journal of Energy and Natural Resources Law.*

Judge Higgins is Queen's Counsel and a Bencher of the Inner Temple, and has practised public international law and petroleum law. From 1984 until her election to the ICJ she served as a member of the Human Rights Committee monitoring the Covenant on Civil and Political Rights. She was counsel for the International Tin Council in the British courts and was President of the ICSID Tribunal in *Amco v. Indonesia* (1989). Before being sworn in on the ICJ in September 1995, to succeed Sir Robert Jennings, who resigned mid-term, she had pleaded in the Great Court Hall as counsel in the Libya/Chad *Territorial Dispute*, the *East Timor* case, the Lockerbie case on the *1971 Montreal Convention*, and, had she not been elected to the Court, would have pleaded in the *Gabčíkovo-Nagymaros Project* case. On several occasions Judge Higgins has demonstrated her critical approach to traditional concepts and values in the study of international law. To this, her recent, stimulating monograph is no exception:

> International law is not rules. It is a normative system. ... The role of law is to provide an operational system for securing values that we all desire - security, freedom, the provision of sufficient material goods. It is not, as is commonly supposed, only about resolving disputes. If a legal system works well, then disputes are in large part avoided. (*Problems and Process*, 1994 at p. 1)

> It is not enough to be familiar with the current 'buzz-words' of international law. There is a contemporary trend of mindless invocation of the fashionable concepts - self-determination, rights *erga omnes, uti possidetis*, etc. But these are not *mantras*, the mere chanting of which is sufficient in itself. We have to see, rigorously, what exactly these legal concepts mean, and when they are appropriately applicable. (*ibid.* at p. 262)

1893-1956

Judge:	1946-1956
Contentious Cases:	21
Advisory Requests:	10
Declarations:	1
Sep. Opinions:	1
Dis. Opinions:	2 Joint

Hsu Mo

It is thus clear that this Court, as the substitute for the Permanent Court of International Justice, cannot exercise jurisdiction conferred upon it by Article 29 of the Treaty of 1926, in a dispute relative to the interpretation or application of the Declaration of 1926.

Judge Hsu Mo can perhaps be seen as a typical representative of the generation of Chinese jurists eager to extricate itself from the discomforting memories of the nation's recent past and from humiliations suffered at the hands of foreign powers; the young intelligentsia that went in search of a new identity by adapting time-honoured traditions to modern exigencies and sought to gradually restore national pride by having China play a prominent role within the rapidly developing new international community.

Trained at home in Peiyang and abroad at Washington and Melbourne Universities, Hsu Mo entered the diplomatic service in Beijing in 1919 and from 1922 held a chair of International Law and International Relations at Nankai. He published extensively on Chinese diplomatic history and contibuted to leading reviews on various topical issues.

In 1926 Judge Hsu Mo was appointed Judge, then Presiding Judge of the Criminal Chamber of the Shanghai District Court and finally became Court President. He later joined the Foreign Office, first as a Counsellor, in 1928, then as head of the European and American Affairs Department from 1931 to 1940 as Vice-Minister. Subsequently, he was Minister Plenipotentiary to Australia (1941-1944) and Ambassador to Turkey (1945-196).

In the international sphere he first earned himself a reputation in Washington, in 1945, through his membership of the Committee of Jurists that prepared the Draft Statute of what was to become the ICJ. He drafted the section of the UN Charter on disputes. He was deeply convinced of the need for China to regain international esteem through International Organizations, and was an adviser to his Government at the 1945 San Francisco Conference. The next year he was elected unanimously to the bench of the ICJ, where he was among the Judges to be elected for a three year term only. However, he was re-elected in 1949, the very year the rival People's Republic of China was proclaimed and the Kuomintang forces were driven from the mainland to Taiwan. However, the authorities in Taiwan remained for many years the sole China representative at the UN Judge Hsu Mo served on the Court until his death.

During his ten years at the Court, the reputedly stern and commanding Hsu Mo delivered 2 (Joint) Dissenting Opinions, 1 Declaration of Dissent and 1 Separate Opinion. In the 1951 *Fisheries* case he expounded on the principle governing the demarcation of the territorial sea which he held should be measured from the coast line at low tide. As for the historic title claimed by Norway in this case he stated:

> In support of her historic title, Norway has relied on habitual fishing by the local people and prohibition of fishing by foreigners. As far as the fishing activities of the coastal inhabitants are concerned, I need only point out that individuals, by undertaking enterprises on their own initiative, for their own benefit and without any delegation of authority by their Government, cannot confer sovereignty on the State, and this despite the passage of time and the absence of molestation by the people of other countries. (*ICJ Reports* 1951, at p. 157)

The next year, in the *Ambatielos* case, Judge Hsu Mo dissented from the majority by denying the Court's jurisdiction in regard to a *Declaration* disputed by the Parties (Greece v. Great Britain), on the basis of a 1926 Treaty of more general scope conferring jurisdiction on the PCIJ (in Art. 29). Judge Hsu Mo argued against jurisdiction on the basis that:

> It is a well-recognized principle of interpretation that a specific provision prevails over a general provision. Therefore, even if the Declaration had actually been written into the Treaty as an additional article, it must, nevertheless, in the absence of any indication to the contrary, form an exception to the applicability of Article 29. (*ICJ Reports* 1952, at p. 88)

Louis Ignacio-Pinto

1903-1984

Judge:	1970-1979
Contentious Cases:	8
Advisory Requests:	3
Declarations:	7
Sep. Opinions:	2
Dis. Opinions:	2

Judge Ignacio-Pinto was born at Porto-Novo in Benin and educated in Dahomey (Nigeria) and Bordeaux. He was *Licencié ès lettres* as well as in law and held *diplômes* in law and economy. He became an Advocate at the Paris Court of Appeal and later Advocate-Defence Counsel at Conakry (alongside Judge Forster) and at Cotonou. From 1946 to 1956 he was Senator of the French Republic for Dahomey. In 1957 he was Minister of Economy and the following year Minister of Justice in the First Dahomey Government. He then entered upon a diplomatic career, initially as Counsellor at the French Embassy to the Holy See, soon to be followed by Ambassadorships of Dahomey to the USA and the UN (1960-1967), Canada, Brazil and Haiti. In 1967-1968 he was President of the Special Criminal Court and later of the Supreme Court of Dahomey, and President of its Constitutional Committee.

By then a seasoned public official, diplomat and Judge, Louis Ignacio-Pinto embarked upon an international career. Again like Judge Forster, he served on various ILO Commissions (1950-1957) and in 1959 was Chairman of the *Commision Africaine du travail*. In 1961 he chaired the First Committee of the General Assembly and was a Member of the UN Sub-Committees on Angola and on Narcotic Drugs.

The following years he served on the UN Administrative Tribunal and as Rapporteur of the Commission on Human Rights. Concurrently he chaired the Dahomey Delegation at the First UNCTAD Conference in Geneva and at ECOSOC Sessions. In 1965 he became a Member of the International Law Commission. Before being elected to the Court, in 1970, he co-chaired the UN Committee on the Reorganization of the Secretariat.

Judge Ignacio-Pinto's work at the ICJ, which spanned the years 1970-1979, included 2 Dissenting and 2 Separate Opinions as well as 7 Declarations. His Opinions were often quite outspoken, as in the 1974 *Fisheries Jurisdiction* case:

> The Court has deliberately evaded the question which was placed squarely before it in this case, namely whether Iceland's claims are in accordance with the rules of international law. Having put this question on one side, it constructs a whole system of reasoning in order ultimately to declare that the Regulations issued by Iceland .... are not opposable to ... Germany. In my view the whole problem turns on this, since this claim is based upon facts which, at least under present-day law and in the practice of the majority of States, are flagrant violations of existing international conventions.
>
> In taking this viewpoint I am not unaware of the risk that I may be accused of not being in tune with the modern trend for the Court to arrogate a creative power which does not pertain to it under either the UN Charter or its Statute. Perhaps some might even say that the classic conception of international law to which I declare allegiance is out-dated; but for myself, I do not fear to continue to respect the classic norms of that law. Perhaps from the Third UNCLOS some positive principles accepted by all States will emerge. I hope that this will be so, and shall be the first to applaud - and furthermore I shall be pleased to see the good use to which they can be put, in particular for the benefit of the developing countries. But since I am above all faithful to judicial practice, I continue fervently to urge the need for the Court to confine itself to its obligation to state the law as it is at present in relation to the facts of the case brought before it. (*ICJ Reports* 1974, at pp. 209; 210-211)

Noteworthy, too, is his stand in the *Nuclear Tests* case where he defended the sovereign rights of France along similar lines to Judge Forster:

> Of course, Australia can invoke its sovereignty over its territory and its right to prevent pollution caused by another State. But when the French Government also claims to exercise its right of territorial sovereignty, by proceeding to carry out tests in its territory, is it possible legally to deprive it of that right, on account of the mere expression of the will of Australia? (*ICJ Reports* 1973, at p. 131)

*1913

Judge:	1982-1995
President:	1991-1994
Contentious Cases:	22
Advisory Requests:	4
Declarations:	–
Sep. Opinions:	3 (2 Joint)
Dis. Opinions:	4

Robert Yewdall Jennings

In a society of States much divided by ideologies, by religion, by poverty and wealth, by power and weakness, by size, by history, and by geography, it is well never to lose sight of the fact that the one vocabulary of ideas that they have in common is public international law. (BYBIL *1984, at p. 61)*

'What ease!', one was tempted to observe, watching Sir Robert at work. Sir Robert definitely amazed people. Admittedly, the Court has seen many brilliant scholars, and many a wise man among them. Yet, during those 50 years, few Judges carried their knowledge and wisdom, that rich harvest of a lifetime, so lightly, and with such comfort and ease... *Simplex veri sigillum* reads the proverb. Sir Robert's intellect served the world, yet in his heart he remained the Yorkshire lad: simple, forthright, modest - and witty. Perhaps even more than admiration, he seemed to inspire warmth in colleagues and students alike. In the midst of strenuous labour on complex issues and cases of the utmost urgency or political topicality he seemed perfectly at ease, reserving time for each and everyone. Sir Robert believed in international law and was devoted to it. In fact, he was on such intimate terms with the subject that he could speak of it in an almost detached manner, and in the plainest of words. 'What is international law and how do we tell it if we see it?' reads a typical title.

Sir Robert Jennings was born at Idle, Yorkshire and educated at Belle Vue Grammar School, Bradford, and Downing College, Cambridge. He was a Choate Fellow at Harvard University in 1937, then started out as Assistant Lecturer at the London School of Economics (1938-1939). During the War he served with the British Army, then went to Cambridge, where he was Lecturer before succeeding his mentor, Judge Lauterpacht, to the Whewell Professorship of International Law (1955-1982), one of the oldest and most distinguished chairs of international law in the world. He was Fellow (1939), Senior Tutor (1949) and Acting President of Jesus College. Sir Robert was called to the Bar at Lincoln's Inn in 1943, where he became Honorary Bencher in 1970, and Queen's Counsel in 1969.

During the many years he held the Whewell Chair, Sir Robert was Editor-in-chief of the *British Year Book of International Law*, the first 15 years with Sir Humphrey Waldock. As another testimony to his standing, he was Associate (1957), Member (1967), Vice-President (1979) and President (1981) of the *Institut de Droit International*, where he has been an Honorary Member since 1985. Likewise he is Honorary Member of the American and Indian Societies of International Law. In recent years he succeeded Judge Lauterpacht as editor, together with Sir Arthur Watts, of *Oppenheim's International Law* (9th edition). Apart from two Hague courses on air law (1949) and general principles (1967) and numerous review articles, Sir Robert produced two classic monographs on *The Progress of International Law* (1960) and *The Acquisition of Territory in International Law* (1963), and a famous tract on 'Nullity and Effectiveness' in the *Cambridge Essays in Honour of Lord McNair* (1965).

Sir Robert was legal adviser to various Governments and counsel in a number of arbitrations, such as the *Rio Encuentro*, the *Beagle Channel*, the Franco-British *Continental Shelf Delimitation* and the Dubai-Sharjah *Frontier Delimitation* dispute. In 1982 he served as Judge *ad hoc* on the European Court of Human Rights. His first appearance before the ICJ was in 1978 as Counsel in the Tunisia/Libya *Continental Shelf* case. In February 1982 he succeeded Sir Humphrey Waldock, the then President of the Court, who had died on 15 August 1981. During his term on the Bench he was Member of the Chamber in the El Salvador/Honduras *Frontier Dispute*, and in the *ELSI* case. Sir Robert was re-elected in 1991 and served as President of the Court from 1991-1994. In these thirteen years he rendered 4 Dissenting and 3 Separate Opinions (2 Jointly). In 1995, at the age of 81, Sir Robert took the rare step of resigning mid-term of his own accord.

Philip C. Jessup

1897-1986

Judge:	1961-1970
Contentious Cases:	4
Advisory Requests:	1
Declarations:	2
Sep. Opinions:	3
Dis. Opinions:	1

All I wish to know is to understand in common, simple words the problems that face us in the world of today.

Of Philip Jessup it is said, as of Judges Basdevant and De Visscher, that it was the traumatic experience in the trenches in France during World War I, where he fought, a light machine gun in his hand, in some decisive battles with the American Expeditionary Forces, that made him turn towards international law as a path toward the *pacific* settlement of disputes. It certainly moulded his character. Philip Jessup, Judge Lachs once remarked, was:

> ... marked by a curious combination of knowledge, industry, deep humanity and an exceptional sense of humor ... He spoke well, convincingly, never trying to impose his will, but trying rather to convey his thoughts in a way that others would understand. A perfect partner for a dialogue. A man of great wisdom and tolerance, of great modesty and humility, a friend upon whom one could rely.

Or, as Judge Schwebel once put it:

> ... he conveyed to all who knew him, or even encountered him, a warmth and sympathy that was exceptional. No man in the world of international law aroused more universal admiration and affection than did Philip Jessup. ... A man whose superb intellect, legal imagination and liberal ethic were matched by a character and grace no less outstanding.

Philip Jessup sensed the imperative need for change in the law to reflect a changing world. He would speak of *transnational* law, rather than *international*, wishing to avoid the dogmas and fictions associated with traditional international law. He was deeply committed to what he called 'parliamentary diplomacy', to improve the condition of man through multilateral negotiations in UN bodies. In this respect he would speak of 'the rocky road to international justice' and 'the price to be paid for peace'. *The Enlighted Crusader*, Lachs characterized him.

Philip C. Jessup was born in New York and educated at Hamilton College (A.B., 1919; LL.D., 1937), Columbia (M.A., 1924; Ph.D., 1927) and Yale (LL.B., 1924). He was admitted to the District of Columbia Bar in 1925 and to the New York Bar in 1927, where he was member of a law firm until 1943. In 1924 he became Assistant Solicitor at the State Department. Concurrently, he began teaching at Columbia and was Hamilton Fish Professor of International Law from 1946-1961. He was Visiting Professor at Harvard, Storrs Lecturer at Yale, and Cooley Lecturer at Michigan. From the very first days he was involved in the shaping of the post-war world. He attended Bretton Woods and San Francisco, and in 1947 played a seminal role in the creation of the ILC. He had been assistant to Elihu Root at the 1929 Conference of Jurists on the PCIJ. In fact, as Judge Schwebel observes, the humane liberal Jessup would come to mean to the founding of the ILC what the conservative Root had been to the creation of the PCIJ. He was Delegate at the UN from 1948-1953. An Ambassador-at-Large, he played a leading diplomatic role, particularly in the contacts that led to the lifting of the Berlin blockade.

Judge Jessup was President of the ASIL from 1954-1955, President of the *Institut* in 1960-1961, and a Member of the Curatorium of the Hague Academy, where he lectured on parliamentary democracy (1956). He was on the Board of the *American Journal*, and Reporter of the *Harvard Research Project*. Among his publications were *A Modern Law of Nations* (1948) and *Transnational Law* (1956) and a treatise on *Outer Space and Antarctica* (1959). Noteworthy in our context are his biography of *Elihu Root* (1938) and the tract *The United States and the World Court* (1929).

Before he was elected to the Bench in 1961, Jessup had been counsel for Nicaragua in 1958-1960, in the 1906 *Arbitral Award* case. Philip Jessup served one term, in what was not the busiest period of the Court. He made the best of it, initiating the Revision of the Rules and trying to get the ICJ back into the mainstream of events. He revived the ideas of *ad hoc* chambers and of empowering Supreme Courts of States to request Advisory Opinions. He delivered a strong and famous Dissenting Opinion, in the 1966 *South West Africa* case, a Judgment he took as a personal defeat that hurt him to the bone.

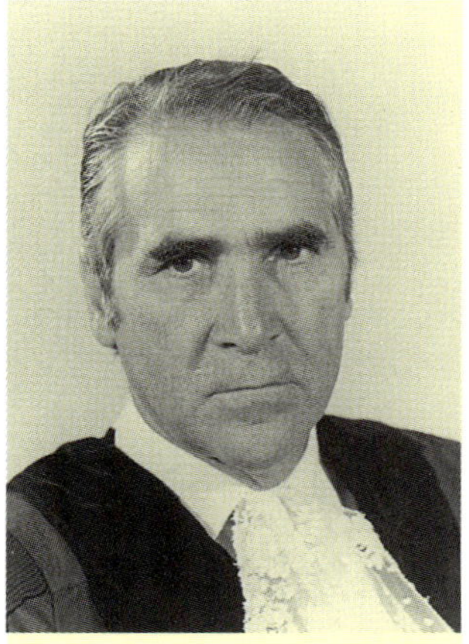

1918-1994

Judge:	1970-1979
President:	1976-1979
Contentious Cases:	8
Advisory Requests:	3
Declarations:	7 (3 Joint)
Sep. Opinions:	5 (2 Joint)
Dis. Opinions:	4 (3 Joint)

Eduardo Jiménez de Aréchaga

To many, not just at The Hague, Judge Eduardo Jiménez de Aréchaga will forever remain the epitome of the Latin lawyer: courteous, distinguished, good looking, charming and at ease in many languages. By his colleagues on the bench he was acknowledged as the most prominent Latin-American internationalist of his generation, a widely read scholar and a most accomplished international official.

Judge Jiménez de Aréchaga was born in Montevideo and became a Doctor of Law at the University of Uruguay in 1942. Concurrently with a Professorship at Montevideo Law School and an active role in the Inter-American movement, he had an impressive career as a public official. At a fairly young age he served as Under-Secretary of State for Foreign Affairs (1950-1952) and Secretary of the National Council of Government (1952-1955), and was to become Minister of the Interior in 1968.

Likewise, his contacts with the UN matured early. In 1947 he joined the Uruguayan delegation to the General Assembly and was for some years on the Staff of the UN Secretariat, at the Department of Security Council Affairs. A monograph on *Voting and Handling of Disputes in the Security Council* (1951) and his first (1954) Course at the Hague Academy on related matters reflect this experience. (His frequent lectures at the Academy resulted in a membership of its Curatorium.) In 1961 Judge Jiménez joined the International Law Commission which he chaired in 1963. He was a founding member, and for ten years President of the World Bank Administrative Tribunal and played a prominent role in the Conference on the Law of Treaties in Vienna in 1968-1969 as Rapporteur of the Committee of the Whole.

His first contacts with the ICJ date back to 1966 when he was appointed Counsel for Spain in the *Barcelona Traction* case (1966-1969). In February 1970 he was sworn in as Judge, and was elected to the Presidency of the Court in 1976. Few cases came his way during his Presidency, but the term is marked by the 1976 Revision of the *Rules of Court* in which he took an active part and which, by establishing the Chamber procedure, did much to open up new horizons for the Court. His years at The Hague were darkened by a tragic accident of a daughter that made him withdraw from the Bench at the closure of his first term. Still, he would return regularly, be it as Counsel or Judge *ad hoc*, as in the Tunisia/Libya and Libya/Malta *Continental Shelf* cases. Concurrently, he chaired various arbitral tribunals, the Canada-France *St Pierre and Miquelon* dispute to mention just one, and published extensively. Over the years he commented on such diverse matters as recognition, arbitration, responsibility and compensation, treaty stipulations, international watercourses, UN Law, the Charter and UN relations to the Organization of American States. His major works were his 2 volume *Curso* on international law (1959, 61), his *Derecho Internacional Contemporáneo* (1980) and, within the present context, 'The Participation of International Organizations in Advisory Proceedings before the ICJ' (in *Studi Morelli*, 1978).

During his years on the Bench Judge Jiménez delivered 7 Declarations (Joint), 5 (Joint) Separate and 4 (Joint) Dissenting Opinions, most of them brief and extremely pointed. His only lengthy Opinion is the Separate Opinion as a Judge *ad hoc* in the Tunisia/Libya *Continental Shelf* case on matters of delimitation and historic rights, which is a true gem. Yet no less noteworthy are his comments on the relationship of provisional measures and jurisdiction to the merits in the 1973 *Nuclear Tests* and 1976 *Aegean Sea* cases:

> The essential object of provisional measures is to ensure that the execution of a future judgment on the merits shall not be frustrated by the actions of one party pendente lite. In cases in which there is no reasonable possibility, prima facie ascertained by the Court, of jurisdiction on the merits, it would be devoid of sense to indicate provisional measures to ensure the execution of a judgment the Court will never render. (*ICJ Reports* 1976)

Another tragic and untimely accident ended Judge Jiménez's life in the very months that his numerous friends all over the world were putting together a well-deserved Festschrift to celebrate his 75th birthday.

1885-1965

Judge:	1946-1961
President:	1958-1961
Contentious Cases:	34
Advisory Requests:	11
Declarations:	2
Sep. Opinions:	3
Dis. Opinions:	5 (1 Joint)

Helge Klaestad

Judge Klaestad of Norway was elected to the Court in 1946 and allotted a term of 6 years. In 1952 he was re-elected and in 1958 succeeded Judge Hackworth as President. He retired after the expiration of his second term in 1961. Apart from this record of 15 years with the ICJ, Judge Klaestad also earned himself a reputation by virtue of his many activities in the sphere of arbitration. A Member of the Permanent Court of Arbitration since 1929, he was frequently called upon during the inter-war period to help to settle disputes.

Born in Oslo, Judge Klaestad was a *doctor juris* of the University of his native town. Somewhat surprisingly, his judicial career began not at home but abroad. For a full decade he was very much involved in problems raised by the Peace Treaties in the wake of World War I. Perhaps his first recorded public office was his Legal Advisorship to the Reparation Commission in Vienna during the years 1920-1921. Four years later he was in London presiding over the Anglo-German Mixed Arbitral Tribunal.

In the following year he was appointed Sole Arbitrator between Germany and the British Empire in matters relating to the Treaty of Versailles (1926-1929); in 1927 he was Sole Arbitrator between Austria and the British Empire (Treaty of Saint-Germain; 1927-1931). In 1929 he occupied a similar position in matters relating to the Treaty of Trianon, between Hungary and the British Empire (1929-1931). In 1930 he joined the Permanent Commission of Conciliation and Arbitration between Norway and Poland, and, a year later, became a member of a very similar Commission in an arbitration between Germany and Luxemburg, while at the same time acting as Joint Commissioner of the Permanent Commission of Conciliation between the United States of America and Italy.

At this juncture, in 1931, his career took a turn with his appointment as a Judge in the Supreme Court of Norway. He had no dealings whatever with the PCIJ at any stage. It was with his election to the ICJ in 1946 that his name once again came to the fore in the international field. Although he was the author of a number of books and review articles, the fact of their being in Norwegian probably served to impede their wider reception abroad.

During his years with the Court, Judge Klaestad produced 3 Separate and 5 Dissenting Opinions (1 Joint) and 2 Declarations. They reveal the meticulous lawyer and conscientious Judge. There was little in them to indicate a tendency to philosophical or theoretical speculation. A matter he dealt with in some detail concerned requests for reviews of decisions of Administrative Tribunals, the implicit equality between parties in cases and the thorny relationship between the ICJ and other Organs of the UN with regard to these issues. This was illustrated in the following manner in relation to the 1956 Advisory Opinion on the *ILO Administrative Tribunal*:

> Though the decisions of the Administrative Tribunal are rendered in disputes between the international organization and individuals, only the organization is accorded the right to challenge the validity of the decisions in this manner. The other parties to the disputes, the individuals, have no corresponding right. ... The provisions of Article XII have thus established a manifest inequality between the parties. ... The Article has introduced a review procedure which fails to observe fundamental principles of equality of justice and impartiality of procedure. (*ICJ Reports* 1956, at p. 111)

Being desirous to co-operate, as far as possible, with another organ of the United Nations in the discharge of international duties, the Court has departed from its usual procedure by dispensing with oral hearings and by receiving from the individuals concerned, who have no access to the Court, written statements transferred to the Court by the Organization. Whatever may be thought of such a departure from a normal judicial procedure, the Court cannot in any case disregard or compromise with the fundamental principle of the equality of parties - equality in law as well as in fact - a principle which is expressly confirmed by Article 35, paragraph 2, of the Statute of the Court. (*ICJ Reports* 1956, at p. 112)

*1903

Judge:	1953-1961
Contentious Cases:	24
Advisory Requests:	5
Declarations:	8
Sep. Opinions:	–
Dis. Opinions:	–

Feodor Ivanovich Kojevnikov

Judge Kojevnikov was born in Smolensk and studied law at Moscow University, from which he graduated in 1927 and where he held a professorship and was twice Dean of his Faculty. Concurrently he was a People's Juryman of the Supreme Court of the Soviet Union, President of the Legal Section of the Society for Cultural Relations of the USSR with Foreign Countries, and Member of the Committee of Experts in Legal Science at the Ministry of Culture of the USSR. From 1952-1953 he was a Member of the International Law Commission. He took part in international conferences on culture and jurisprudence and published extensively on international law: *Russian State and International Law*, vol. I (up to the Twentieth Century; 1947); *Soviet State and International Law, 1917-1947* (in collaboration; 1948); *International Court of Justice; Aims and Practice* (1971). Besides, he was editor and co-author of a number of textbooks on international law. He was a Member of the Editorial Committee of the journal *The Soviet State and Law*, a publication of the Institute of State and Law at the Soviet Academy of Sciences.

Judge Kojevnikov was elected to the ICJ in November 1953 to replace Judge Golunsky, the successor to Judge Krylov who, having been elected in February 1952, was forced by ill-health to resign on 25 July 1953. Judge Kojevnikov was to hold office until the end of Judge Golunsky's term (1952-1961). On 8 occasions during these years he found reason to append a short Declaration to a decision of the Court, which texts however do not reveal much of his personal views.

This is not to say that Judge Kojevnikov did not maintain strong points of views on topical issues of the time. His views are reflected in many articles, notably on the law of treaties, dispute settlement and the law of the United Nations, subject-matter that played an important role in post-war Soviet doctrine of international law, and on which Judge Kojevnikov found ample occasion to expand during his years on the International Law Commission. In his *Soviet Public International Law, Doctrines and Diplomatic Practice* (1970), Grzybowski shows us an example of this within the broader context of Soviet doctrine:

> One basic principle upon which the socialist judges continually insisted was that national sovereignty, as a legal and a political principle, continued to be the keystone of relationships between independent states within the international community. Accordingly therefore the creation of the United Nations had produced essentially no basic changes in the legal position of member states. (*op. cit.*, at p. 459)

Membership in the United Nations organization did not vitally affect the sovereign rights of member nations. In the same vein:

> Soviet diplomatic practice tends toward the view that the right to interpret treaties is, in the first place, vested in the states which are parties to the treaties. Pronouncements by the socialist judges seem to indicate that states have the right to rely upon their own understanding of the meaning of treaties even when their views are not shared by the other parties to the treaty. ... While Soviet legal scholars admit the possibility of a legal question including the interpretation of the UN Charter being submitted to the Court, they are of the opinion that the International Court of Justice should not interpret the Charter without such a request. (*op. cit.*, at p. 464)

As early as the 1946 Peace Conference in Paris, the Soviet delegates objected to the referral of a future dispute as to the interpretation of the Peace Treaties to the ICJ. Consequently, no sure method for the resolution of such disputes could be agreed upon. 'This was convincingly demonstrated by the case of the human rights guarantees involving the interpretation of the same Peace Treaties', which was brought before the Court in 1949-1950 (*Interpretation of Peace Treaties with Bulgaria, Hungary and Romania*). The three respondent states refused to cooperate, contending that the issues raised by their opponents were not disputes within the meaning of the Peace Treaties. On that occasion their point of view was endorsed by Judge Kojevnikov, then Soviet member of the International Law Commission, who 'was convinced that the parties alone had the right to interpret the compromise submitting the dispute to an arbitral tribunal' (*op. cit.*, at p. 465).

Vladimir M. Koretsky

1890-1984

Judge:	1961-1970
Vice–President:	1967-1970
Contentious Cases:	5
Advisory Requests:	1
Declarations:	2
Sep. Opinions:	–
Dis. Opinions:	3

Judge Koretsky, 'an *institution* in his native Kiev, the Ukraine and well beyond' (Lachs), came to the Court in 1961, being the fourth Soviet Judge of the ICJ after Judge Krylov, Judge Golunsky and Judge Kojevnikov, and the first Soviet Judge to be elected Vice-President (1967-1970). He was born in Dniepropetrovsk and was educated at the universities of Moscow and Kharkov. At Kharkov he held a chair for thirty years (1920-1949) with a short interruption. He was a Member of the Ukrainian Academy of Sciences at Kiev and became Vice-President of the Soviet International Law Association.

In the late 1940s Judge Koretsky served as Legal Adviser to the Soviet Delegation to the UN, and attended the 1946 Paris Peace Conference. He was Soviet Representative on both the Committee on the Progressive Development of International Law and the Human Rights Commission. He was a Member of the ILC during the period 1949-1951, Associate Member of the *Institut* from 1965 and attended a number of UN Conferences such as the Conference on the Abolition of Slavery in 1956, the 1957 Unesco Meeting on Peaceful Co-operation and the Geneva Conferences on the Law of the Sea in 1958 and 1960. A Member of the PCA since 1957, he joined the Polish-Norwegian Permanent Conciliation Commission in 1959. He published extensively at the Ukrainian Special Institute of State and Law. Several of his works, which were written in Russian and Ukrainian, were subsequently rendered into Chinese, Romanian and German. His *General Principles of Law in International Law* (1957, in Russian) constitutes a landmark. Koretsky had a penchant for history, and wrote on the peace project of Georg of Podiebrad (1946) and feudal law in Europe (1961). Judge Lachs wrote appreciatively that:

> One always found Koretsky ready to engage in a lengthy conversation not only on law but on literature or philosophy; he took a lively interest in all facets of life. An avid reader, he impressed those who did not know him, by his illuminating and encyclopaedic culture which was never advertised but had to be elicited. He never insisted, was never self-righteous, but simply strove through dialogue to explore the subject and have his own views understood. On leaving the Peace Palace after office hours one would find him waiting for 'his' bus. While his colleagues owned luxurious cars, he did not even use one. And despite his considerable achievements, he was no less the acme of modesty in his work. (*Teacher* 1987, at pp. 141-142)

Judge Koretsky had a philosophical nature. Thus, in the *Northern Cameroons* case, he observed that:

> One cannot regard rules of procedure as being simply technical. They determine not only a way of proceeding but procedural rights of parties as well. Their strict observance in the International Court of Justice, one might say, is even more important that in national courts. The Court may not change them *en passant* in deciding a given case. A revision of the Rules of Court should be effected (if necessary) in an orderly manner and, in any case, the changed rules should be known to parties beforehand. (*ICJ Reports* 1963, at p. 40)

In the controversial 1966 *South West Africa* case he dissented on the grounds that:

> The Court has said in the operative part of its Judgment that 'the Applicants cannot be considered to have established any legal right or interest appertaining to them in the subject-matter of the present claims...' But the question of the Applicants' 'legal right or interest' ... was decided already in 1962 in the first phase (the jurisdictional phase) of these cases. ... The question of an applicant's 'interest' (as a question of a *qualité)* even in national law systems is considered as a jurisdictional question. For example, *le défaut d'intérêt* of an applicant is considered in the French law system as a ground for *fin de non-recevoir de procédure*. (*ICJ Reports* 1966, at p. 237)

In the 1969 *North Sea Continental Shelf Cases* he made the observation that:

> By and large, customary international law turns its face to the past while general international law keeps abreast of the times. (*ICJ Reports* 1969, at p. 156)

At the age of 80, Koretsky returned to his beloved Kiev, his Institute, and his students.

*1943

Judge:	1994-present
Contentious Cases:	2
Advisory Requests:	1
Declarations:	1
Sep. Opinions:	–
Dis. Opinions:	1

Abdul G. Koroma

> The reading of the Judgment, which is preferred by the majority of the Members of the Court, while respectable, is not unassailable or free from doubt. Any such doubts in the reading of that Judgment, given the nature and gravity of the Request, should have been resolved in favour of the State alleging that the basis of the Judgment had been affected. (*ICJ Reports*, 1995)

In these words Judge Koroma took a stand on principle against the Order made in September 1995 in the wake of the French decision to resume nuclear tests. The case, or rather New Zealand's attempt to reopen the case it had brought to the Court in 1973 but which had then been shelved when France had announced its intention to desist from atmospheric testing, exercised the minds of the Judges as it had done 20 years previously. *Prima facie* evidence, the restrictive or more liberal interpretation of jurisdiction..., all came back again. As Judge Koroma observed '...this is the second time that New Zealand has brought a case on the issue of nuclear tests in the Pacific region; ... on both occasions the Court has declined to consider the merits of its case'.

Judge Koroma of Sierra Leone was educated at King's College, London and Kiev State University. He is Barrister-at-Law at Lincoln's Inn. In 1964 he joined the Government Service in Sierra Leone and in 1969 its Foreign Ministry. He was called to the Bar at Lincoln's Inn, London and became Barrrister and Legal Practitioner at the High Court, before being appointed State Counsel and Special Adviser to the Attorney-General and Minister of Justice. He was Legal Adviser to the Sierra Leonese Permanent Mission to the UN, and served on the Sixth (Legal) Committee for 16 years, as well as serving on the Committee to Review the United Nations Charter, UNCITRAL and the Outer Space Committee; he participated in various UN conferences and was signatory to the Conference on Succession of States in Respect of Property and to UNCLOS, where he chaired the African Group. Between 1981 and 1985 he was his country's Ambassador to the UN. From 1985-1988 he was Ambassador to the European Communities and UNESCO, France and the Benelux; from 1988-1992 he was accredited to the OAU, and Ethiopia, Kenya, Tanzania and Zambia. As a Member of the ILC he contributed to the elaboration of the Draft Code of Crimes against Peace and Security of Mankind.

Throughout those years Judge Koroma wrote and lectured on issues of self-determination, human rights, humanitarian law, the law of the sea, Antarctica and the settlement of disputes. The thesis that he wrote for the University of London concerned the *Settlement of Territorial and Boundary Disputes in Africa*. Judge Koroma is Vice-President of the African Association of International Law, a Member of the ASIL and currently an expert advising the Geneva Red Cross Committee. He was elected to the Court in 1994. In the context of the 1995 *Request for an Examination of the Situation ... in the Nuclear Tests case*, from which we quoted above, he brought up the issue of *prima facie* evidence:

> ... In recent years a settled case-law has emerged in the Court which allows issues relating to incidental jurisdiction to be decided if title to jurisdiction can be adduced and is not manifestly invalid, and if the circumstances so require. The Court has taken the position that the mere fact that a State has challenged the basis of its jurisdiction does not suffice to prevent it from indicating interim measures of protection; nor need it come to the conclusion that where it has jurisdiction to deal with the merits of a case it must decide whether to grant interim provisional measures of protection. Given the seriousness of the matter New Zealand has raised in its Request, and the weight of the evidence presented both in terms of facts and the law, it is my considered opinion that it has clearly shown both that its Request has a legal basis, and that it falls within the provisions of paragraph 63. Had the Court applied the appropriate standard of proof, it would have come to the conclusion that New Zealand had established a prima facie case for the Court not only to have granted its request for the indication of provisional measures of protection, but to have assumed jurisdiction to consider the merits of the Request. (*ICJ Reports* 1995)

Sergei Borisovitch Krylov

1888-1958

Judge:	1946-1952
Contentious Cases:	11
Advisory Requests:	6
Declarations:	2
Sep. Opinions:	1 Joint
Dis. Opinions:	5

It was a worthy representative of the Russian tradition of international law who served as the first of the series of Soviet Judges of the Court. Judge Krylov was not only a highly competent scholar and the prolific author of numerous publications in both the public and private fields. His publications also reveal his pride in and awareness of the Russian tradition of international law later to be found in Grabar. In his 1947 Course at the Hague Academy on the Soviet doctrine he attested to the time-honoured relations of Kiev in the days of the Rurik Dynasty and later of the Principality of Moscow with both Europe and Asia. Issues such as the freedom of the seas were amply discussed by the envoys of Boris Godounov long before Grotius; other examples are constituted by the Act of Armed Neutrality of 1780, the Declaration of St Petersburg of 1868 and the initiative taken by the Empire to launch the Hague Peace Conferences. In recent years, he argued, authors like F. F. Martens and N. M. Korkounov had enriched the academic world with new landmarks in the same tradition. Noteworthy are Judge Krylov's acknowledgments at the outset of his *Course,* of his colleagues Golunsky, Kojevnikov at Moscow and Koretzky at Kharkov, the very men who were to succeed him on the bench of the ICJ - in that very order.

Judge Krylov was an enthusiastic teacher. Generations of internationalists, including Judges Lachs and Vereshchetin, cherish the best of memories of his learned and witty lectures and the excellent training they received from him:

> ... the seriousness with which he approached even the minutest details of law, in his friendliness and helpfulness to students and openness ...

A student of Martens and a close friend of Durdenevsky, with whom he prepared a well-known *Manual* published in 1947, Judge Krylov held a doctorate in law from Leningrad University, where he occupied the chair of comparative constitutional and international law for some thirty years. In the 1930s he was Dean of the Institute at Leningrad University. Apart from being a competent international lawyer, Sergei Krylov was a seasoned soldier who was gravely wounded during the 1916 offensive of General Brussiloff and again, 25 years later, took part in the heroic defence of Leningrad. From 1942 he was Legal Adviser to the Commissariat of Foreign Affairs and concurrently Professor of International Law at the Moscow Institute of International Relations and at the Higher Diplomatic School. He was Deputy to the Municipal Soviet of Leningrad. Many of his early publications, notably in the private sphere, reflected the concerns of his public office, such as *The Foundations of Budget Law in the Soviet Federal System* (1928). He defended a thesis on radio communication. Among his major works in later years were manuals on private (1930 and 1939) and public (1947) international law and a treatise on air law (1933).

His international contacts dated from the years 1944-1945 when he attended Dumbarton Oaks and San Francisco (where he signed the Charter). Later he served on the International Law Commission. He was Counsellor to the Committee of Jurists at Washington and to the Executive Committee of the UN and attended the First Session of the General Assembly in London. It was then that he was elected to the new Court, being among the Judges to whom a term of six years was allotted.

In his view treaties and customs were the major sources of international law. He took a firm stand against colonialism. No less noteworthy is his comment on the controversial General Assembly Request for an Advisory Opinion of 1948 on the *Conditions of Admission of A State to Membership in the UN*, in which he expressed resentment of its political aspects:

> Appearances are deceptive: though framed in a legal form, it is a question put with a definitely political purpose; it is political in conception; though abstract in form, it is a concrete question which expressly refers in one of its paragraphs to the 'exchange of views which has taken place in the Security Council at its 204th, 205th and 206th Meetings'; though impersonal in form, it is a question designed to censure the reasons given by a permanent member of the Security Council. (*ICJ Reports* 1947-1948, at p. 107)

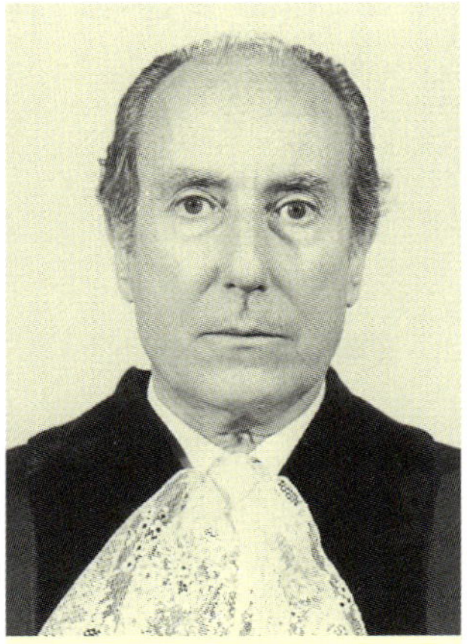

1919-1987

Judge:	1982-1987
Vice–President:	1985-1987
Contentious Cases:	5
Advisory Requests:	2
Declarations:	–
Sep. Opinions:	1
Dis. Opinions:	–

Guy Ladreit de Lacharrière

And indeed, during these five memorable years of his distinguished sojourn in The Hague, he gave the best of himself to our institution. Who among us can forget his sober and trenchant interventions, his swift manner of seizing the heart of a problem, his crystalline prose, the elegant logic of his thinking and the clarity of his fertile mind? For all who worked alongside him, he was a man whose sheer lucidity disclosed to his hearers what is often least obvious yet always most arresting, by which I mean simply the inescapable truth.

It was with this *éloge funèbre* that the then Judge Bedjaoui - now President of the Court - flanked by his colleagues on the Bench bade a last farewell to a good friend and a very remarkable French jurist, a highly intelligent man, a linguistic genius and a man who, according to his successive superiors at the *Quai d'Orsay*, Michel Debré and Maurice Schumann, was a civil servant and *conseiller* on whose sound and balanced judgment they were able to rely at all times.

Guy Ladreit de Lacharrière was born in Marseille in 1919. He studied law, political science and oriental languages in Paris. He was holder of the diploma of the *Institut de Droit Comparé* in Paris for Russian legal terminology and translation. In 1946 he entered the diplomatic service as attaché at the French Embassy in Moscow. In 1948 he became Head of the Office of International Organizations at the Ministry of Foreign Affairs. Concurrently he was Permanent Delegate to UNESCO and Secretary-General of the French delegation to its General Conference. From 1952 to 1957 he was Assistant Director of the Department of Social Sciences of UNESCO.

For the next twenty years he worked at the Ministry of Foreign Affairs and held such functions as Director of the Department of the UN and International Organizations (1964-1969) and Director of Legal Affairs (1969-1979). He was chairman of the governing body of the *Institut français des Relations Internationales*, while continuing to be a Lecturer at the *Institut d'Études Politiques* (1954-1981), at the *École Nationale d'Administration* and the *Institut des Hautes Études Internationales* in Paris. From these years date monographs such as *L'Idée fédérale en Russie* (thesis, 1945), *Commerce extérieur et sous-développement* (1964), *La nouvelle division internationale de travail* (1969) and *La stratégie commerciale du développement* (1973).

In his successive capacities Judge de Lacharrière served France in various organs of the UN, notably in the Sixth Committee. He headed the French Delegation at the 1973-1982 UNCLOS Conference. From 1975 to 1981 he was a Member of the PCA and actually dealt with various disputes. For example, he was Agent of France in its arbitrations with Great Britain concerning the *Delimitation of the Continental Shelf* (1975-1978) and with the United States in matters relating to the Franco-American *Air Services Agreement* (1978).

He also worked on cases before the Court of Justice of the European Communities. Judge de Lacharrière was elected to the Court in 1982 and became its Vice-President in 1985. He died in early 1987, in mid-term. To quote once again the tribute paid by Judge Bedjaoui:

> Since he and the Court joined forces, all who have closely followed our work will have noted that he never appended to the Court's decisions any Declaration or Separate or Dissenting Opinion, however brief. Constrained as I am by the secrecy of the deliberations, I must leave it to you to divine the reason for this. But your answer will be the right one if it points you to the full measure of the Vice-President's direct contribution in elaborating the Court's jurisprudence. The part which he has always played in the Court's labours will remain for us the fated consummation rather than the fateful close of his career.

The 1989 *Hommage* in its title rightly encapsulates the services rendered by this man to his nation: *Guy Ladreit de Lacharrière et la politique juridique extérieure de la France.*

Manfred Lachs

1914-1993

Judge:	1967-1993
President:	1973-1976
Contentious Cases:	29
Advisory Requests:	8
Declarations:	9
Sep. Opinions:	8
Dis. Opinions:	2

Judge Manfred Lachs still holds two records among the Members of the Court: he was at the time of his election the youngest elected Judge and President and was on the bench for the longest span of time, i.e. 26 years. Manfred Lachs was born in the polyglot region of Galicia in Poland, as was Sir Hersch Lauterpacht. He studied in Vienna and Nancy before enrolling at the London School of Economics. He happened to be in Cambridge at the outbreak of World War II, which saved him from the tragic fate suffered by his family at home. His prolonged stay in England was to leave an indelible impression on him. He was fond of quoting English Law Lords and developed a love for English literature. It was in England too that he commenced his career as an internationalist: he was a Polish delegate to the UN War Crimes Commission (1944-1946) and took part in the Nuremberg prosecution, which inspired his *War Crimes: An Attempt to Define the Issues* (1945).

After the war years he returned to Poland. His country's delegate to the UN General Assembly for twenty years (1946-1966) and three times president of its Legal Committee, he did much to elaborate the UN legal system, notably with respect to the Genocide Convention (1961) and the law of treaties, which led to his monograph *Multilateral Treaties* (1958). His many contacts in the West, his fluency in half a dozen languages and his innate tact and urbanity made him welcome in the international sphere where he could help to bridge the ideological gap. He also had a keen interest in the impact of science and technology on the law, notably air and space law, and published extensively on the subject (*The Law of Outer Space*, 1972).

A natural conciliator, Judge Lachs had already gained esteem in the field of arbitration before being elected to the Court. He had been a Member of the PCA since 1956 and would later Chair the *Guinea/Guinea-Bissau* arbitral tribunal (1983-1985). On 6 February 1967, Judge Lachs filled the vacancy left by Judge Winiarski. In his first case, the *North Sea Continental Shelf*, he distinguished himself with a lucid Dissenting Opinion regarding the equidistance rule He was to dissent only once more in his career on the bench.

For 25 years the Court was virtually his life. Colleagues have justly called him a 'missionary' and a 'tireless crusader' for adjudication. He had outspoken ideas on the functioning of the Court:

> I always considered the Advisory Opinions being much more important for the development and interpretation of international law than the settlement of disputes.

He was the visionary type of jurist, always brimming with creative ideas and averse to narrow conceptions:

> The jurist cannot be parochial or myopic; he must be imaginative and critical.

To him law was a vehicle for change:

> If you consolidate the past and call it law, you may find yourself outlawing the future.

Judge Lachs was elected to the Court shortly after the controversial *South West Africa* Judgment of 1966. He helped the Court to overcome it, through Judgments such as in the *Barcelona Traction* case when, in a famous *obiter dictum*, the notion of *obligationes erga omnes* was advanced. Here, as in the Judgment on self-determination in the *Namibia* case, the influence of Judge Lachs was pivotal. Quite recently, in the *Aerial Incident at Lockerbie* case, he once more spoke up against the blurring of two elements, believing it imperative that the provinces of the International Court and the Security Council be kept strictly separate.

Undeniably, he left a personal stamp on his Presidency (1973-1976): 'he served with a flair and panache that was unusual' (Schwebel). His Presidency was marked too by warm relations established with the legal and administrative communities in The Netherlands. Judge Lachs was on terms of personal friendship with Members of the Royal House, government officials and university dons alike. Manfred Lachs was a born teacher with a fine, resonant bass voice and a mischievous twinkle in his eye. He was eloquent, witty, brightening his speeches with anecdotes, fond of the paradox. The harvest of this long career was a dozen monographs, 150 articles, honorary degrees from 18 universities in 13 countries and a veritable avalanche of awards.

1897–1960

Judge:	1955–1960
Contentious Cases:	18
Advisory Requests:	4
Declarations:	–
Sep. Opinions:	3
Dis. Opinions:	2

Hersch Lauterpacht

In his lifetime, Professor Lauterpacht was widely regarded as the world's leading international legal scholar; certainly his distinction in the English-speaking world (in which he principally wrote) was unmatched. As a teacher, his painstakingly prepared and vigorously delivered lectures packed Cambridge University halls; a legion of devoted students included Joseph Gold, Nagendra Singh, Richard R. Baxter, Stephen M. Schwebel, Derek Bowett, D. P. O'Connell and Arthur Watts.

As a scholar, his bold and progressive writings combined erudition, idealism, realism, and trenchancy in extraordinary measure. After his death, another titan of international law, Wilfred Jenks, wrote an appreciation of Lauterpacht entitled 'The Scholar as Prophet', which encapsulated his achievements in these terms:

> Five major monographs each of which is in effect a treatise on its special subject which has marked an epoch in the development of contemporary thought on the matter, namely, *Private Law Sources and [Public] Analogies of International Law* (1927), *The Function of Law in the International Community* (1933), *Recognition in International Law* (1947), *International Law and Human Rights* (1950) and *The Development of International Law by the International Court* (1958); a succession of editions of Oppenheim's *International Law* which have transformed the original work so completely as almost to constitute a new comprehensive treatise on the contemporary law; an unusually voluminous body of shorter writings of exceptional range, depth and originality; a particularly memorable editorship of the *British Year Book of International Law*; the *Annual Digest of Public International Law Cases*, gradually developed into *International Law Reports*, covering a period of almost forty years; a notable series of individual opinions as a Judge of the International Court; these are indeed a titanic intellectual monument. But there is a fundamental unity in all of Lauterpacht's work which greatly lightens the burden of attempting to state its general effect. It is inspired by an all-persuasive moral earnestness, by a belief in right and justice and the contribution of government under law to the pursuit of right and justice, by the conviction that moral and legal principles apply to the conduct of States in the same manner and measure as to the conduct of individuals, and by a sense of urgency arising from the gravity of the problems confronting human society in the twentieth century.

Judge Lauterpacht was born in Zolkiew, Poland, educated at Lwów, and graduated in Vienna as Doctor of Laws (1922) and Political Science (1923) under the great jurisprudentialist, Hans Kelsen. In the mid-1920s, he migrated to Great Britain to study in London with Arnold McNair. Under the tutorship and patronage of McNair, and by the force of his extraordinary intellect and industry, Lauterpacht made his way rapidly in the British academic world. In 1927, he became Lecturer at the London School of Economics, in 1934 Reader at the University of London and, in 1937, he succeeded McNair as the Whewell Professor of International Law at Cambridge University. He became a member and Bencher of Gray's Inn, and King's Counsel.

In 1945-1946, he was a member of the British War Crimes Executive and was extensively consulted by Justice Jackson in the preparations for the Nuremberg Trials. In 1948, as consultant to the United Nations, he prepared a searching survey of the possibilities of the codification of international law which played a fundamental part in setting the agenda of the ILC for decades. Upon his election to the Commission, he was one of a succession of distinguished British members who served as Special Rapporteur on the law of treaties, being succeeded on his election to the Court by the future Judge Fitzmaurice.

Sir Hersch Lauterpacht came to the Court in 1955. His tenure, which gave rise to the highest expectations, was cut short by his premature death in May 1960. His 3 Separate and 2 Dissenting Opinions display the creativity and discipline that was characteristic of his life's work. His analysis of self-judging reservations to the Court's compulsory jurisdiction under the Optional Clause demonstrated the intellectual integrity and boldness of thought so typical of him.

Kéba Mbaye

*1924

Judge:	1982-1991
Vice–President:	1988-1991
Contentious Cases:	12
Advisory Requests:	4
Declarations:	1
Sep. Opinions:	2
Dis. Opinions:	–

Judge Mbaye, a native of Kaolack in Senegal and pupil of the William Ponty *école normale*, was trained as a private lawyer at the Paris Law Faculty and holds a certificate from the *Ecole nationale de la France d'outre-mer*. He was a lecturer at the Law Faculty of Dakar University and at the Senegal National School of Administration (1967-1978), but then turned to the Judiciary to become the First President of the Supreme Court of Senegal from 1964 to 1982. In his writings he commented extensively on the (sub-Saharan) African and Senegalese legal and judicial systems.

Judge Mbaye has a long-standing record of international activities, as a former Chairman of the International Commission of Jurists and Honorary President of the World Federation of UN Associations. His main activities are in the human rights sphere. Among the bodies he has served on - and these are numerous indeed - is the Commission of Human Rights and the Commission for the Settlement of Disputes between Parties of the Convention against Discrimination in Education, both of which he chaired.

Judge Mbaye was on the Special Committee to investigate the treatment of the Palestinians and the Working Group on human rights violations in Southern Africa. He is a standing member of the ILO Committee of Experts. He is on the Board of the International Institute of Human Rights of the René Cassin Foundation, Honorary Member of the International Institute of Humanitarian Law, and former President of the International Academy of Human Rights. He was General Rapporteur at the OAU when it adopted the African Charter on Human and Peoples' Rights.

These interests of Judge Mbaye are amply reflected in his writings which include articles on personal and family law and the right to (economic) development. Concurrently, Judge Mbaye is a Member of the International Academy of Comparative Law, of the Curatorium of the Hague Academy and of the *Institut de Droit International*. He was for many years on the Board of the International Olympic Committee.

Before he was elected to the ICJ, in 1982, Judge Mbaye had gained a great deal of experience and a distinguished reputation in the sphere of dispute settlement and international tribunals. He was Vice-Chairman of the ICC International Court of Arbitration, Chairman of the International Tribunal of Sport and is a Judge *ad hoc* in the *Land and Maritime Boundary* dispute between Cameroon and Nigeria. Judge Mbaye served one full term on the Court (1982-1991) and was its Vice-President from 1988 to 1991. Thereafter he served as Judge *ad hoc* in the dispute between Guinea Bissau and Senegal over the *1989 Arbitral Award*.

His views are reflected in 2 Separate Opinions and 2 Declarations. Likewise of note is his intriguing 1988 Academy Lecture on the *Intérêt pour agir*; an exhaustive study on the interest to sue and the *ius standi* before the Court:

> Les tribunaux, qu'ils soient nationaux ou internationaux, ne sont ouverts aux plaideurs que sous certaines conditions. Les règles qui énoncent ces conditions se groupent sous les vocables 'compétence' et 'recevabilité'. Alors que celles du premier groupe relèvent de la question de savoir si une cour puise dans la nature et dans l'objet de la contestation portée devant elle le pouvoir d'en connaître, celles du second groupes servent à vérifier si les conditions auxquelles est subordonné l'exercise de ce pouvoir se trouvent réunies dans une espèce donnée.
>
> On distingue les conditions de recevabilité matérielle, qui sont du côté de l'action en justice, des conditions de recevabilité matérielles, il y en a une qui est généralement considérée comme essentielle. C'est l'existence d'un intérêt pouvant justifier l'action du plaideur. Il est convenu de l'appeler l'intérêt pour agir et de la considérer comme une règle de procédure. Pour agir devant une juridiction il faut en conséquence pouvoir justifier d'un intérêt. (*RDC* 1988/2, vol. 209, at p. 231)

1885-1975

Judge:	1946-1955
President:	1952-1955
Contentious Cases:	15
Advisory Requests:	8
Declarations:	1 Joint
Sep. Opinions:	2
Dis. Opinions:	5 (1 Joint)

Arnold Duncan McNair

Sir Arnold McNair was an unusually versatile lawyer. Though very much an English common lawyer - he was Master of the Bench at Gray's Inn - he had a special fondness for civil law studies, inspired perhaps by the Romanist Buckland, with whom he participated in the well-known comparative study *Roman Law and Common Law* (1937). The freedom with which he quoted Latin legal maxims is not surprising.

Lord McNair - as he was to become upon his retirement from the Court - looked upon the function of law in society as, by necessity, a limited one. A practical man, preferably guided by a concrete case of interest, he insisted on clearly defined rules, strict codification and what he termed hard law', on the solid base of treaty provisions, precedent, established State practice or *communis opinio juris*. Perhaps his best-known work was his *International Law Opinions* (3 vols., 1956).

Along the same positivist lines (generally preponderant on the Bench during those years) he saw the role of tribunals as being inevitably restricted to defining rights and duties rather than creating obligations of their own accord. Over the years he became less optimistic about the chances of a universally imposed rule of law, although in the sphere of human rights he insisted on the harmonizing value of the European Convention. This great administrator and remarkably gifted scholar served as President of the ICJ in The Hague, of the European Court of Human Rights in Strasbourg and of the *Institut* in Geneva:

> ... he was the 'natural' president of any institution or entity he belonged to, by reason of the confidence he inspired. This was due to his qualities of authority, wisdom, integrity and objectivity, combined with the more human virtues of kindliness, understanding and accessibility (Fitzmaurice).

However, in terms of career planning, Arnold McNair seemed to take a long time to find his true vocation. Born in London, he graduated from Gonville and Caius College, Cambridge, where from 1912 he lectured in law whilst practising as a solicitor in London, specializing in contracts, which was, indeed, his life-long special interest. On the international plane this interest led him to write his masterly *Law of Treaties* (1938, 1961). From 1917 he served as Secretary to the Coal Industry Commission, until the misery of World War I awakened his international interests and prompted his authoritative study on *The Legal Effects of War* (1920), which ran through various editions. Subsequently, he joined the League of Nations Codification Commission and served on the ILO Commission of Experts on Labour Conventions. In 1926 he became a Reader of Public International Law in the University of London (where his most prized student was Hersch Lauterpacht, later to succeed him as Whewell Professor at Cambridge). He edited *Oppenheim's International Law* (4th ed., 1928), wrote two monographs on topical issues, *The Law of the Air* (1932) and *Collective Security* (1936), and seemed dedicated to a strictly academic career when, in 1935, he was called to the prestigious Whewell Chair in Cambridge. However, within 3 years his life took another turn when, for 8 years, he was a successful and devoted Vice-Chancellor and administrator of the University of Liverpool. In 1945 he returned to Cambridge, to teach Comparative Law and draft his *Dr Johnson and the Law* (1948). Within a year he was elected to the ICJ. It was only at this stage that he seemed to turn to international law exclusively. Sir Arnold served one term on the Bench, crowned by his Presidency from 1952-1955. Only rarely did he append an Opinion to a decision:

> ... it was evidently McNair's policy to encourage the Court to act as a cohesive unit as much as possible without undue recourse to individual views. ... Of McNair therefore it can truly be said that his main contribution to the work of the Court is to be found in the corporate body of that work itself - a fact that can only enhance the value of his comparatively rare statements of separate or dissenting view. (Fitzmaurice).

After his departure in 1955, at the age of 75, Sir Arnold still found the energy to engage in arbitral counselling, preside over the Argentine-Chilean *Andes* Arbitration, and to serve as President in Strasbourg from 1959 to 1965 before retiring - and live on for another decade.

Gaetano Morelli

1900-1989

Judge:	1961-1970
Contentious Cases:	5
Advisory Requests:	1
Declarations:	1
Sep. Opinions:	5
Dis. Opinions:	3

Born in Crotone in Calabria, Judge Morelli became a Doctor of Law in Rome in 1921 under the stimulating guidance of Dionisio Anzilotti. For forty years, until his election as a Member of the Court in 1961, he taught law at various university centres: the first ten years he was a lecturer in Urbino; subsequently he was a full Professor, first for two years in Modena and for three years in Padua, then for fifteen years in Naples; finally, from 1951, in Rome; initially, for five years, at the Faculty of Political Sciences, then for five years at the Law Faculty, where he succeeded Tomaso Perassi. During his term in Rome, he was a Member of the Higher Council of Public Education, a befitting post for this born teacher and educator.

From the late 1930s, Judge Morelli served Italy with his expertise at many international conferences, for example in 1937 at Montreux (on the capitulations in Egypt), in 1951 at the Hague Conference on Private International Law, and from 1956 to 1961 on the national Unesco Commission. He was a long-standing Member of the Council for Contentious Diplomatic Questions, and of the Permanent Conciliation Commission between Luxemburg and Switzerland. From 1955 Judge Morelli was a Member of the PCA and from 1959 a titular Member of the *Institut de Droit International* over which he presided during its centenary session. He lectured twice at the Hague Academy (1937, 1956).

Yet, more than anything, he was - and for no less than thirty years - the stimulating yet meticulous (and at times exacting) editor of his beloved *Rivista di diritto internazionale*, known for his dislike of long titles and until his last days, when he became hampered by an eye disease, commenting severely (with his typical green fountain pen) on the slightest flaws in the manuscripts laid before him. All his life he had a keen eye for the smallest detail.

Another favourite of Judge Morelli was the *Trattato di diritto internazionale*, in which series he produced a volume on procedural law (1954). Procedural law was indeed his specific field of expertise and the Festschrift that was presented to him in 1975 was quite rightly entitled *Il processo internazionale*. It was here, too, notably in his *Studi* (1963) and *Nuovi Studi* (1972), into which all his experience with the Court was condensed, that his two prominent characteristics - next to his innate gentleness - came to the fore: a truly systematic mind and an extremely refined style. His other publications include the *Nozioni* and *Lezioni* of international law, and *Elementi* of private international law; all three ran through numerous editions.

Judge Morelli first came to the Court as a Judge *ad hoc* in the *Monetary Gold* case (1954) and returned as Counsel for Nicaragua in 1958 in the *Arbitral Award made in 1906* case. He was elected in 1961 and during his one term delivered 1 Declaration, 5 Separate and 3 Dissenting Opinions. The most typical of these was perhaps his systematic analysis of the disputed legal rights of Ethiopia and Liberia in the 1962 *South West Africa* case:

> It must be pointed out that, although, as will be seen hereafter, a dispute cannot exist without a certain attitude of the will of one, at least, of the parties, a dispute is a fact capable of being objectively found. A dispute is one thing; the opinion of one or other of the parties as to the existence of a dispute is something different. In its opinion, ... the Court said: 'The mere denial of the existence of a dispute does not prove its non-existence'. ... But it might equally be said: the mere assertion of the existence of a dispute by one of the parties does not prove that such a dispute really exists. If no dispute exists it is not possible to set the machinery of the Court in motion. ... it is possible to refer to the Court a question of international law or a question concerning the existence of a fact. It is, however, beyond doubt that the existence of a question, although the subject of controversy, on a point of law or fact is not sufficient to enable that question to be referred to the Court. For that to be possible, it is necessary that the question should be in a certain relationship with a dispute, in the sense that the settlement of the dispute must depend upon the answer to be given to that question of law or fact. (*ICJ Reports* 1962, at pp. 565, 567-568)

1898-1979

Judge:	1955-1964
Contentious Cases:	21
Advisory Requests:	5
Declarations:	2
Sep. Opinions:	1
Dis. Opinions:	5

Lucio Manuel Moreno Quintana

Judge Moreno Quintana, the descendant of a family of diplomats and a grandson of President Moreno of Argentina (1904-06), was born at the Argentine Legation in Paris. In 1920 he became a Doctor of Law at Buenos Aires. For 25 years he was a university professor (in various fields such as history, law and political economy) and a prolific author who represented his nation abroad on many missions. A number of his memberships of learned societies reveal his historic leanings, as he was a member of the Institute of Hispanic Culture, of the Francisco de Vitoria Institute, of the Hispano-Luso-American Institute and of the Presidium of the Grotian Foundation for the Propagation of International Law - at the Peace Palace, where he lectured in 1927. He was a Member of the PCA from 1945 to 1955.

Judge Moreno's main occupations at the time of his election to the Court were a professorship and, concurrently, a directorship of the International Law Institute in Buenos Aires. Previously he had taught at the Naval War College and had had a career in public life; he was twice Under-Secretary for Foreign Affairs and had led the Argentine Delegation to the First General Assembly of the United Nations. He published prolifically, notably a three-volume *Treatise on International Law* (1963) and monographs on the American International System, Immigration, Asylum, Treaties of Commerce, and diplomatic issues. He lectured all over the world and was awarded numerous honours and distinctions.

Judge Moreno was elected to the Court in 1955 and served a full term. He expressed himself with great feeling in his Opinions, as in the *1902 Convention* case:

> The chief consideration in my mind is that a question of principle has to be settled ... Side by side with its function of deciding 'in accordance with international law such disputes as are submitted to it'... the ICJ has also ... a doctrinal function of the greatest importance. The Court can and must discharge this function in the present case with a view to the progressive development of international law on the question submitted for its consideration concerning the principle of the relationship between *ordre public* and an international Convention. ... the Statute moreover enjoins the Court to apply 'the teachings of the most highly qualified publicists of the various nations, as subsidiary means for the determination of rules of law'. (*ICJ Reports* 1958, at p. 102)

In the 1960 phase of the *Right of Passage over Indian Territory* case Judge Moreno Quintana that:

> The Court must first of all, and indeed exclusively, ascertain whether a right of passage existed in Portugal's favour ... The existence of a right in international relations is a fact which, when contested, must be proved by the party which invokes it. That is an elementary principle of procedure. However the Court's task is not so simple as that, owing to the frequent changes made by the applicant in its submissions and to the uncertainty it has betrayed at different stages in the case concerning the foundation of its right. At one time, as in its Application, it asks for full recognition of a right, at another, in the Memorial, it reduces the claim, and again, in its Reply, limits the exercise of that right. (*ICJ Reports* 1960, at p. 89)

In the 1962 *Temple of Preah Vihear* case he considered the value of evidence provided by maps, a recurrent issue in the case law of both the PCIJ and the ICJ:

> Now, territorial sovereignty is not a matter to be treated lightly, especially when the legitimacy of its exercise is sought to be proved by means of an unauthenticated map. As was said by Max Huber in his Arbitral Award in the *Island of Palmas* case: 'only with the greatest caution can account be taken of maps in deciding a question of sovereignty ... If the Arbitrator is satisfied as to the existence of legally relevant facts which contradict the statements of cartographers whose sources of information are not known, he can attach no weight to the maps, however numerous and generally appreciated they may be ... a map affords only an indication - and that a very indirect one - and, except, when annexed to a legal instrument, has not the value of such an instrument, involving recognition or abandonment of rights'. (*ICJ Reports* 1962, at p. 70)

Platon Dmitrievich Morozov

1906-1986

Judge:	1970-1985
Contentious Cases:	12
Advisory Requests:	6
Declarations:	1
Sep. Opinions:	3
Dis. Opinions:	7

Judge Morozov was born in Leningrad and graduated from the Legal Institute of that city. For some twenty years he worked in the courts of law as a practising barrister and as State Judicial Counsellor in the office of the Procurator General of the Soviet Union. Like his early predecessor at the Court, Judge Golunsky, he was a Member of the Soviet Delegation at the 1946 Tokyo War Tribunal. He then held posts as Ambassador Extraordinary and Plenipotentiary. From 1951 to 1968 he was the USSR Representative at the United Nations Commission on Human Rights, attended a number of General Assembly Sessions and participated in the work of the Special Political Committee and the Third, Fourth and Sixth Committees. Concurrently he was Deputy Director of the Legal Questions and Treaties Department of his country's Ministry of Foreign Affairs. From 1960-1968 he was the USSR Deputy Representative to the Security Council and Deputy Permanent Representative at UN Headquarters.

A Lecturer at the Moscow State Institute of International Relations, Judge Morozov represented his nation in various capacities on UN Committees, during negotiations and at Conferences such as those on the Preparation of the 1948 Genocide Convention, the 1949 Geneva Conventions for the Protection of War Victims, and the 1967 Outer Space Treaty. These activities were cut short when he was elected to the Court in 1969. He was to serve for fifteen years and, in August 1985, resigned for health reasons.

The numerous cases in which Judge Morozov took part, led him to write 7 Dissenting and 3 Separate Opinions and 1 Declaration. Of these, 3 Dissenting Opinions relate to an issue which was close to his heart, i.e. the functioning of the ICJ as a Court of Appeal against Judgments of Administrative Tribunals. Judge Morozov's major objection, which was indeed a matter of principle, concerned the fact that of necessity these cases made private persons parties in cases before the Court, which in his opinion was contrary to the text of the ICJ Statute. In the 1972 *Appeal Relating to the Jurisdiction of the ICAO Council* he stated:

> I consider that the Judgment now delivered by the ICJ, acting for the first time in its history as a court of appeal, creates a misleading and regrettable precedent for the future activity of the Court in this field. ... the Court, by delivering its present Judgment, *has in effect acted as if it was the ICAO Council itself*, and touched on a number of problems related to the merits which were closely connected with the question of jurisdiction of the Council. (*ICJ Reports* 1972, at pp. 157-158)

In the 1973 Application for Review of Judgment No. 158 of UNAT he pointed out that:

> Nothing can cover up the fact that, albeit by means of so-called advisory procedure, private persons become parties to the proceedings before the Court. These persons can *initiate* the procedure of appeal ... and have a right to make an oral statement.

This procedure, as he stated earlier, was:

> ... contrary to the provisions of Article 34 of the Court's Statute, which lays down that 'only States may be parties in cases before the Court'. ... Now it is necessary to recall that the question of the competence of the ICJ was settled by the UNCIO in very clear terms... It is well known that one of the delegations suggested at that time that Article 34 of the Statute be redrafted to include provision that not only States but also private persons could be permitted to be parties before the Court in cases of review ... That suggestion was rejected by the Conference. (*ICJ Reports* 1973, at pp. 296-297)

Again, in the 1982 Application for Review of Judgment No. 273 of UNAT he emphasized, with reference to the controversial 1955 Resolution of the General Assembly that had authorized the Court to review UNAT decisions:

> During the discussions on this resolution many of the Members of the UN strongly objected to the procedure suggested ... Some of them stressed that such a procedure undermined the cornerstone of the Court's Statute, which provided that only States could be parties before the Court, but not private individuals. (*ICJ Reports* 1982, at p. 435)

*1912

Judge:	1976–1985
Contentious Cases:	7
Advisory Requests:	3
Declarations:	–
Sep. Opinions:	6 (2 Joint)
Dis. Opinions:	1

Hermann Mosler

Most Judges are ready to admit that their work at the ICJ has been the acme of their career. To a few, who have served a little longer, it may have seemed like their life's work. For many, it will be by their work at the Court that they will primarily be remembered. None of this holds true for Judge Hermann Mosler. However competently he served the Court, however significant his election was in political terms - as he was the first German Judge after Walter Schücking (1931-1935) elected shortly after Germany had entered the UN family - his name is inseparably linked to two other institutions in the field: first and foremost to one of the finest research centres of international law in Europe, the Heidelberg Max Planck Institute for Comparative Public Law and Public International Law; and secondly, to the Court at Strasbourg (the European Court of Human Rights), rather than to the one that has its seat in The Hague. Judge Mosler served the ICJ for nine years, while the ECHR and the Max Planck Institute occupied the better part of his working life.

Judge Hermann Mosler was born at Hennef near Bonn. In 1937 he became a Doctor of Law at Bonn and research fellow at the Kaiser Wilhelm Institute in Berlin, under politically complicated circumstances. After the War he was first a barrister-at-law and *Privatdozent* in Bonn, then became a Professor in Frankfurt (1949). In 1951 he became Head of the Legal Department of the Foreign Ministry of the Federal Republic, in 1954 a Member of the PCA, and in 1957 an Associate Member of the *Institut de Droit International*. In 1954 he became a Professor at Heidelberg and concurrently Director of the aforesaid Max Planck Institute, which under his stimulating guidance developed into a true paradise for internationalists. The combining of all those functions was, incidentally, typical of the man who was equally well suited to the *vita contemplativa* and the *vita activa*.

During the second part of his life Judge Mosler served on various international tribunals. For more than 20 years (1959-1981) he was Judge and from 1974 Vice-President of the Court in Strasbourg, while at the same time he served as Co-Chairman of the Austro-German Compensation Tribunal (1969-1972). In those years he also served on the Advisory Council to the Foreign Ministry (1972-1976). In 1976, upon his election to the ICJ, Judge Mosler joined the Curatorium of the Hague Academy. In 1981, at the age of 68, when work at Strasbourg became ever more demanding, Judge Mosler decided to concentrate on the ICJ and resigned.

Judge Mosler's first contacts with the ICJ dated from 1967-1969, when he served as a Judge *ad hoc* in the *North Sea Continental Shelf* cases. He became a Member of the Court in 1976 and served one term. He then remained on the Bench for the duration of the proceedings in the Libya/Malta *Continental Shelf* case. During his term Judge Mosler dissented just once, in the Libya/Malta case, and had occasion to render 6 Separate Opinions, two of which were written jointly with other colleagues.

For nearly 20 years Hermann Mosler was Director of the *Zeitschrift für Ausländisches öffentliches Recht und Völkerrecht* and of the publications of his Institute, notably the invaluable series of the *Beiträge* and the *Fontes Iuris Gentium*.

The Festschrift that was presented to him in 1982 bears the title: *Völkerrecht als Rechtsordnung, Internationale Gerichtsbarkeit, Menschenrechte*. It duly encompasses the three areas in which Judge Mosler felt so much at ease.

Among his writings we should mention *The International Society as a Legal Community* (Hague Academy General Course, 1974, Rev. ed. 1980), *Der Internationale Gerichtshof* (in: Kommentar zur Charter der Vereinten Nationen, 1991, English ed. 1995), *L'Application du droit international public par les tribunaux nationaux* (1957, Hague Academy Course), and the 1972 Heidelberg Symposium on *Judicial Settlement of International Disputes*.

Nagendra Singh

1914–1988

Judge:	1973–1988
Vice–President:	1976–1979
President:	1985–1988
Contentious Cases:	15
Advisory Requests:	6
Declarations:	6
Sep. Opinions:	10
Dis. Opinions:	–

The Hague is all too obviously a redbrick tower institution, which all hard-headed thinkers will see as a guarantee of a similarly clear vision of reality.

'A Legal Luminary from the Orient' was how Judge Nagendra Singh was characterized in 1988 by Judge Ni Zhengyu. The poetic language is fully justified, as Judge Singh had the gift of the spoken word. Plain truth, with him, would find expression in the most elegant of terms, as when he addressed the 1985 General Assembly and, quoting Shelley, said:

> [The Court's] members are not, like poets, the unacknowledged legislators of mankind. At most they may declare which litigant speaks the more authentic legal prose.

In Judge Singh personal charm and professional ability were happily combined. A born diplomat and a man of innate culture and deep religious feeling, he was also a man of keen intellect, who, perhaps more than anyone, helped open the eyes of Western scholars to the time-honoured Eastern sources of international law. A realistic humanist, who during his 16 years with the Court insisted on its universalist vocation, he spoke with true conviction when he said that:

> And so the law of international relations grows in strength and scope by a symbiosis of diplomacy and adjudication which nobody can properly appreciate if he or she remains mesmerized by the simplistic notion of politics and law as antipoles.

As Judge Weeramantry concluded in his obituary:

> In Nagendra Singh's life, work and judgments, old-world charm and clear-headed realism blended in a mix that few could match.

Judge Nagendra Singh, born of a noble family at Dungarpur, Rajasthan, was educated at Agra University and St John's, Cambridge where he became a Doctor of Law. He toured academic centres abroad before entering the Indian Civil Service in 1937. He became a Barrister-at Law in 1942, and in 1947-1948 served on the Constituent Assembly of India. He was Joint Secretary at the Defence Ministry from 1946 to 1956, then Director-General of Shipping and subsequently Secretary to the Government. Through the years 1966-1972 he was Secretary to the President of India, and represented India at the Sixth Committee, at UNCTAD and three times at the General Assembly. He presided over the Inter-Governmental Maritime Consultative Organization and the Load-Line Committee in London and chaired the 1970 maritime session of the ILO. A leading specialist in this field, he produced a monumental *International Maritime Law* (4 vols, 1983). In 1969 he was Vice-Chairman of the ILC, and a delegate to the 1960 UNCLOS Conference and became a Member of the *Institut* and the ILA. He was a Member of 'Unidroit' and of the PCA, lectured at university centres throughout the world and throughout his life was awarded doctorates, honours and prizes. He published on the environment, human rights and (historical) aspects of Indian law. Noteworthy within our context are his *Termination of Membership of International Organizations* (1958), his pivotal work on the illegality of nuclear arms: *Nuclear Weapons and International Law* (1959) and *The Defense Mechanism of the Modern State* (1963).

Judge Nagendra Singh gained experience in the judiciary as a Supreme Appellate Authority at the Prize Court of India, and served as a Judge *ad hoc* of the ICJ in the 1972 *ICAO Council Appeal* case. He was elected to the Court in 1973, re-elected in 1982, was Vice-President from 1976 to 1979 and President, 1985-1988. In this capacity he received His Holiness Pope John Paul II, who visited the Court in 1985. Judge Nagendra Singh died at The Hague in mid-term in December 1988.

The year 1989 witnessed the posthumous publication of his monograph on the *Role and Record of the ICJ*, in which he made interesting suggestions for enhancing the use of the Court: firstly, by opening its advisory procedure to inter-State disputes, secondly, by using its contentious jurisdiction for declaratory judgments, thirdly, by having recourse to Chamber procedure. The third suggestion has been successfully applied in recent years.

*1906

Judge:	1985–1994
Contentious Cases:	17
Advisory Requests:	3
Declarations:	2
Sep. Opinions:	2
Dis. Opinions:	–

Ni Zhengyu

After a period of almost twenty years since the days of Judges Hsu Mo (1946-1956) and Wellington Koo (1957-1967), Judge Ni Zhengyu in 1985 became the third Chinese Judge, and the first from the People's Republic, to serve as a Member of the Court. The People's Republic of China, since taking up China's seat at the United Nations in 1971, had for some years remained aloof from the World Court. The election of a Chinese Judge in December 1984 accordingly ushered in a new era. The quiet, sympathetic Judge Ni Zhengyu, who was a distinguished scholar and Legal Adviser of ample experience, served for one term.

Judge Ni was born in Jiangsu, was educated at the Chitz, Soochow and Dongwu Universities in Shanghai and obtained a Doctorate of Law at Stanford University Law School (USA). A Member of the Chinese Bar Association from 1931 he lectured at various Chinese research centres, mostly in Shanghai. In 1946 he was appointed Prosecutor at the International Military Tribunal for the Far East (in which Judges Golunsky and Morozov were also involved). He was a Member of the National Committee of the Chinese People's Consultative Council during the period 1959-1984.

However, during this period he primarily served as Legal Counsel attached to the Ministry of Foreign Affairs of the People's Republic of China and in those capacities quite naturally attended many international conferences. For example, in the 1970s, he attended various General Assembly Sessions, was on the UN Seabed Committee and participated in numerous sessions of the Third UNCLOS Conference. A Member of the Board of Directors of the Chinese Society of International Law since 1980, Judge Ni served the International Law Commission during the period 1982-1984 and in 1991 was elected a Member of the *Institut de Droit International*.

Judge Ni published extensively in the fields of international and comparative law, and it is here that his keen interest in and in-depth knowledge of the judiciary come to the fore. Among his major publications are *The question of Judicial Jurisdiction in International Law*, *The Judicial Systems in the USA and UK*, and *The Theory and Practice Concerning Jurisdictional Immunities of States*.

The cases in which Judge Ni participated during his term - with notable conscientiousness and incisiveness - resulted in 2 Separate Opinions and 2 Declarations; he never dissented. In his Opinion appended to the 1986 Judgment in the *Nicaragua* case, Judge Ni made some pertinent remarks on the Law of Treaties:

> It is to be pointed out that claims based on a treaty do not only owe their creation and existence to the treaty. They are also to be regulated by the treaty in question. It can hardly be imagined that claims are based on a treaty but not regulated by it. It is owing to the peculiarity of affecting a third party or parties by the application of multilateral treaty law, that the Court is asked to refrain from exercising jurisdiction in a case such as the present. Therefore, where the Court refrains from exercising jurisdiction because of the multilateral treaty reservation, it will be precluded from applying multilateral treaty law. Conversely, if the Court does exercise jurisdiction nothwithstanding the multilateral treaty reservation, it logically follows that the multilateral treaty law, which regulates the mutual rights and obligations of the parties, will be applied for the settlement of the dispute before the Court. The multilateral treaty reservation of the United States, though procedurally linked to jurisdiction, is in substance related to the regulation of the rights and obligations of the Parties. The United States cannot claim that the multilateral treaty reservation concerns only the jurisdiction of the Court and is without relation to the question of the applicable law. These two aspects are intimately related and cannot contradict each other, if the reservation is to have any meaning at all. (*ICJ Reports* 1986, at pp. 198-199)

Shigeru Oda

*1924

Judge:	1976–present
Vice–President:	1991–1994
Contentious Cases:	25
Advisory Requests:	6
Declarations:	8
Sep. Opinions:	16
Dis. Opinions:	8

Shigeru Oda was trained in law at the University of Tokyo, where he was a Research Fellow during the period 1947-1949. It was Kisaburo Yokota, the pioneer of modern Japanese international law, and a confirmed adherent of Kelsen, Verdross and the Vienna School of the *Reine Rechtslehre*, who instilled in him the then predominant doctrine of historical positivism. Professor Yokota put forward his pupil for a Rockefeller Fellowship which allowed the young Oda to spend three years at Yale University (only interrupted by a summer course at the Hague Academy in 1951). It was at Yale that Oda first met that imposing figure of such an altogether different kind who would come to mean so much to him, the charismatic Myres McDougal, whose 'Policy Science' was the revolutionary counterpart to the 'classic' doctrine taught at Yale by Edwin Borchard. Back in Japan, in 1953, Judge Oda served as Associate, and then Full Professor (1959-1976) of International Law at Tôhoku University in Sendai City.

It was in response to a suggestion made by McDougal that the young Oda turned to the field of the Law of the Sea, at that time still an uncharted area. His thesis on *The Riches of the Sea* was probably the first of its kind. It was in this field, too, that he gained worldwide fame as a leading expert. This he owed, basically, to his felicitous combination of scientific knowledge and practical experience, the mixture of the academic and the professional elements.

For nearly twenty years he was, in one capacity or another, involved in all the topical issues of the time. He was a Delegate to all three UNCLOS Conferences (1958-1975), and a Member of the UN Experts Group on Marine Science and Technology (1967-1968) and of the Oceanographic Commission (1969). He was on the UN Committee on the Sea-bed and Ocean Floor (1968-1973), and Legal Consultant to ESCAP on Mineral Resources (1969-1975). He served with Rousseau and Riphagen on panels of the Atomic Energy Agency in matters of Radio-active Waste and Peaceful Nuclear Explosions.

At the same time he made his expertise available to the Japanese Government, but also maintained his lines in the academic world. After earlier publications in Japanese, he published in the Netherlands *The International Law of the Ocean Development* (4 volumes, 1971-1979), followed by *The Law of the Sea in Our Time* (2 volumes, 1977), and *International Law of the Resources of the Sea* (1979, a revision of his 1969 Hague Academy lecture), recently supplemented by *International Control of Sea Resources* (1989). Not surprisingly, he is now General Editor of a prestigious series 'Publications on Ocean Development'. He is a Member of the *Institut de Droit International*; an Honorary Member of the American and Indian Societies, and is on the Hague and Thessaloniki Curatoria. In 1993, Judge Oda lectured a second time at the Hague Academy, on *The International Court of Justice Viewed from the Bench*.

Judge Oda has an impressive record of achievements. His first appearance in Court (after two earlier cases in which he was counsel for Japan had been amicably settled) was as Counsel for the Federal Republic of Germany in the 1969 *North Sea Continental Shelf* cases. Judge Oda is fluent in German and was a regular visitor at Hermann Mosler's Max Planck Institute. He became a Member of the Court in 1976, his candidature being greatly furthered at the time by his intimacy with Western thinking, his fluency in English and his Law of the Sea expertise. He has since been re-elected on two occasions (1985, 1994). He served on two Chambers, was Vice-President of the Court from 1991-1994 and Acting President when the Court considered the two *Lockerbie* cases.

Judge Oda has assembled his impressions of service on the Bench in *The International Court of Justice* (1987). From 1976 to 1995 he rendered 8 Declarations and 24 Opinions - often lengthy, but invariably well-documented; never easy reading, but always worthwhile. They have been analysed by Prof McWhinney in *Judge Shigeru Oda and the Progressive Development of International Law* (1993). During the various stages of its debates in past years on technicalities of equidistance, natural prolongation, baselines, ridges and low-water marks the Court must at times have felt only too happy to have the comprehensive expertise of Judge Oda close to hand.

*1917

Judge:	1967–1976
Contentious Cases:	8
Advisory Requests:	3
Declarations:	7
Sep. Opinions:	3
Dis. Opinions:	4

Charles D. Onyeama

Judge Onyeama was born at Eke near Enugu in Nigeria and educated at the Catholic Mission at Eke and Umuahia College, before going to King's College in Lagos (1931-1935) and Achimota College, Gold Coast. In 1940 he obtained a Bachelor of Laws degree at University College, London, and then proceeded to Brasenose College, Oxford (1941). He was a Barrister-at-Law of Lincoln's Inn. Returning to his homeland he became a Member of the Legislative Council and the House of Assembly (1946-1951). He was on the Constitutional Drafting Committee (1948-1950) and was Chief Magistrate (1952-1956). From 1957 to 1964 he was High Court Judge at Lagos, and was then appointed Justice of the Supreme Court of Nigeria (1964). He was elected to the ICJ in 1967. During his term he served on the arbitration panel in the *Beagle Channel* case between Argentina and Chile (1971-1976).

Judge Onyeama was of a very independent cast of mind. At times his views were at variance with those held by his developing world colleagues on the bench, notably in respect of the restricted competence he was prepared to allow to the Court. He made decisions which were contrary to the policy of his country, as in matters of the extension of the 12-mile maritime zone. His line of thinking was that State practice was not uniform and often contradictory, that attempts towards extension had not met with general acceptance and that, for these reasons, the concept was not yet incorporated into customary law and consequently ran counter to international law. In the meantime Nigeria (in 1971) had extended its jurisdiction to the 30-mile limit.

In other respects he was somewhat on the conservative side. Thus, in the 1970 Advisory Opinion on the *Legal Consequences* of the situation in Namibia he was not in favour of a general boycott, confining himself to observing that all States 'are obliged to do nothing to aid the continuance of the unlawful presence of South Africa or its administration in the Territory of Namibia'. Neither did he follow the Court majority in its categorical decision not to recognize the administration in Namibia, but reserved certain rights for this *de facto* government and, on the grounds of *effectivity* of the regime, rejected the obligation *erga omnes* as asserted by his colleagues in condemnation of its illegal presence. His point of view, Sicart-Bozec concludes (*op. cit.*, at p. 62), was perhaps more moderate than that of most developing world Judges but also more in line with the demands of international society and commercial intercourse. When, in the 1974 *Nuclear Tests* case, France had announced its intention to stop the tests, the Court decided that the intervention by Fiji no longer served any purpose and dismissed further proceedings, upon which Judge Onyeama observed:

> The implication is that if the claim had had an object and the Court had been called upon to give a decision thereon, there would have been a possibility of intervention in this case. Fiji was not, at any time material to these proceedings, a party to the General Act of 1928 nor to the optional clause of the Statute of the Court on which the applicant State sought to base the Court's jurisdiction, nor has she invoked any basis of jurisdiction *vis-à-vis* France in her request to intervene. The Court ... should, in my view, have rejected it on the ground that the condition of reciprocity of an obligation to accept the Court's jurisdiction was wholly absent between Fiji and France. (*ICJ Reports* 1974, at pp. 536-537)

In the 1974 *Fisheries Jurisdiction* case he dissented for the following reasons:

> In the forefront of the submissions of the United Kingdom ... was a request for a decision by the Court that there is no foundation in international law for the claim by Iceland to be entitled to extend its fisheries jurisdiction ... This, it seems to me, was the gravamen of the dispute, but the Court now declines to decide it. The decision appears to approach the dispute, not from the point of view of the conflict of the extension with any conventions or with customary international law, but from the point of view that the extension was an exercise of preferential rights which did not give due regard to established rights. This was not the dispute between the Parties and it forms no part of the claim made by Iceland. (*ICJ Reports* 1974, at p. 171)

Luis Padilla Nervo

1898-1985

Judge:	1964-1973
Contentious Cases:	5
Advisory Requests:	2
Declarations:	–
Sep. Opinions:	3
Dis. Opinions:	5

Luis Padilla Nervo was born in Zamora, Michoacán and graduated from the Faculty of Law at the University of Mexico and from the George Washington University Law School. Subsequently, he took courses at Buenos Aires and at the London School of Economics and then entered upon an impressive diplomatic career. He served as Embassy Secretary in Washington, London and Madrid and became Minister Plenipotentiary in the USA and in several Latin-American nations, but was also posted in the Netherlands, Denmark and Cuba. From 1952 to 1958 he was Secretary of State for Foreign Affairs. His experience with International Organizations started in the late 1930s when he was Delegate to ILO Conferences and to the League of Nations in Geneva, and at a later stage he was sent to FAO and Inter-American Conferences. His contacts with the United Nations dated back to its earliest days, and they were intense. Indeed, there were but few major conferences relating to the UN and its Agencies that Judge Padilla Nervo did not attend. He was at the 1945 San Francisco Conference, on the United Nations Preparatory Commission in London, at the first UNESCO, ECOSOC and IAEA Meetings, and was Permanent Representative at United Nations Headquarters (1946-1952, 1958). In 1949 he was Vice-President of the Trusteeship Council and in 1951 he presided over the Sixth Session of the General Assembly. He was elected Member of the ILC in 1955 and twice served as its Chairman. From 1959 to 1964 he was President of the United Nations Disarmament Commission. It was at this juncture that he was called to the Court.

Judge Padillo Nerva served one term (1964-1973) and rendered 3 Separate and 5 Dissenting Opinions. In his Separate Opinion in the 1970 *Barcelona Traction* case he emphasized what he saw as the urgent need for international law to help protect economically weaker entities, such as developing world countries, against the ever more powerful multinational companies.This was just one sign of a more general re-orientation of attitudes towards matters of international law that occurred in some quarters during these years. Whereas twenty years earlier the concentration was on the struggle for political independence and effective liberation from colonialism, the emphasis had shifted more to the economic implications of principles of international law, as in the sphere of the Law of the Sea. The young nations, which had not been represented at the 1957-1958 Geneva Conferences, felt that their interests, and notably their maritime resources, were threatened. In the 1972 *Fisheries* case Judge Padilla Nervo voiced their apprehension about the 'harmful effects of the ever greater threat of highly developed fishing effort' by the use of ultra-modern equipment by the leading seafaring nations, which made it imperative for the developing world to protect 'the resources on which its economic development and the livelihood of its people depends'. (*ICJ Reports* 1972, at pp. 42 and 44) and have its sovereignty over its natural and mineral resources established.

Another interesting debate in which Judge Padilla Nervo was very much involved concerned the fate of Namibia, and notably the presence of both political and legal elements in the request for an Advisory Opinion:

> The question put to the Court by the Security Council can be said to be intertwined with certain political elements, but the actual wording of such question, asking the Court what are the *legal* consequences for States of the continued presence of South Africa in Namibia, indicates that the position is in fact a legal one even if it may have a political aspect. In the nature of things it could not be otherwise. The line between political and legal questions is often vague. Examining the close interrelation between the political and legal factors in the development of international law, Dr Rosenne makes the following comments: 'That interrelation explains the keenness with which elections of members of the Court are conducted'. (*ICJ Reports* 1971, at p. 103)

*1928

Judge:	As of 1996
Contentious Cases:	1
Advisory Requests:	-
Declarations:	-
Sep. Opinions:	-
Dis. Opinions:	-

Gonzalo Parra-Aranguren

Very shortly before the Court's Golden Jubilee, on 28 February 1996, the eighty-second Judge of the ICJ was elected. Judge Parra-Aranguren of Venezuela succeeded his compatriot Andrés Aguilar-Mawdsley, who died in October 1995. To be sure, Judge Parra-Aranguren's name was well known in The Hague. Over the last twenty years, Judge Parra-Aranguren – in various capacities – attended all Sessions of the *Conférence de la Haye de droit international privé*, the 'Hague Conference'; he has lectured twice at the Hague Academy, first in 1979 on the conflict of laws conventions in Latin America and again in 1988, when he held one of the prestigious general courses. This is indeed the sphere of law to which Judge Parra-Aranguren has given most of his attention in past years and in which he has earned an outstanding reputation. He is an acknowledged authority on matters of nationality, codification and civil procedural law and was on the legislative committees that drafted the section on nationality of the 1961 Venezuelan Constitution and the Code of Commerce in its 1965 revision. His specific expertise may add a distinct new flavour to the already rich blend on the Bench.

Judge Parra-Aranguren was born in Caracas and trained at the Law School of the Central University of Venezuela, where he obtained a degree in political science. He followed postgraduate courses at the Inter-American Law Institute of New York University to obtain a masters degree in comparative law and jurisprudence in 1951-1952. He then obtained a doctorate of law at the Ludwig-Maximilian University in Munich, defending a thesis on *Die Regel 'Locus Regit Actum' und die Formen des Testaments* (1955). From the mid-1950s he was a Titular Professor of private international law at the Central University and the Catholic University Andrés Bello in Caracas, where his predecessor, Judge Aguilar-Mawdsley taught civil law at the time. From 1958-1971 Judge Parra-Aranguren was Mercantil Judge of First Instance in Caracas, then to become a practising lawyer. From 1987 he was Co-Judge of the Civil Chamber of the Supreme Court of Justice and in 1992 he was elected Alternate Judge.

Also, he acted as arbitrator both in Venezuela and abroad. In 1990 he became a member of the Legal Advisory Council of the National Congress. From 1993-1995 he presided over the Academy of Political and Social Sciences of Caracas. He thus has a combination of forensic, academic and judicial experience.

From the mid-1970s onwards Judge Parra-Aranguren also worked on the international plane. He represented Venezuela at the UNCLOS Conference, during meetings of the Spanish-Venezuelan Mixed Commission and during the five successive Inter-American Specialized Conferences on private international law (CIDIP I-V: 1975, 1979, 1984, 1989, 1993), where he chaired Committees. In 1979 he was elected member of the *Institut de Droit International*, and in 1984 joined the legal advisory committee of the Venezuelan Ministry of Foreign Affairs. In 1985 he was on the Commission of Inquiry appointed by the ILO to consider the implementation by the Federal Republic of Germany of its Discrimination Convention. That same year he was elected Member of the Venezuelan National Group at the PCA. From 1982-1993 he was a member of the Governing Council of UNIDROIT. As mentioned above, he was delegate to the Thirteenth to Seventeenth (1976, 1980, 1984, 1988, 1993) and the 1985 Extraordinary Session of the Hague Conference on Private International Law. In pursuance of his being Rapporteur to its 1993 Session, he was on the Special Commissions which studied the application of its Convention to minors who are refugees and on the protection of minors and incompetent adults.

Among Judge Parra-Aranguren's major publications are *La Nationalidad Venezolana Originaria* (2 vols., 1964) and *La Nacionalidad Venezolano* (2 vols., 1983), *La Constitutión de 1830 y los Venezolanos por Naturalizacion* (1969), Codificación del Derecho Internacional Privado en América (1982), *Monografías Selectas de Derecho Internacional Privado* (1984), and *Ensayos de Derecho Procesal Civil Internacional* (1986).

Raghunandan Swarup Pathak

*1924

Judge:	1989–1991
Contentious Cases:	5
Advisory Requests:	1
Declarations:	–
Sep. Opinions:	–
Dis. Opinions:	–

The newly emergent States of Africa and Asia constitute a group of underdeveloped and developing nations.They value their independence and look with wariness at rules of international law which limit their independence. ... It is natural that they should question some of the basic postulates shaped by the jurisprudence of the European colonial powers. ... In their effort to modernise international law they recognise that earlier concepts will die hard, but they ... will dedicate themselves to the removal of political, economic and social inequalities. ... It is time that the developed nations convinced themselves that an economic equation must be established with the developing States. It is true to say that international peace in indivisible, it is an equal truth that international prosperity is indivisible. (*Indian JIL* 1984, at pp. 15-16)

These and similar observations by Judge Pathak in successive issues of the *Indian Journal* properly illustrate the interests and tenets that he brought to the Court when he was elected in 1989 to replace Judge Nagendra Singh who had died in mid-term. Judge Pathak only served for the remaining three years of the late Judge's term of office, and the cases in which he sat did not lead him to render any Declarations or Opinions. However, his overall views on the present-day international system can be discerned from the *Editorial Note* to *International Law in Transition*, the 1992 essays in memory of his predecessor which he co-edited:

> International law stands today on the threshold of unprecedented changes as mankind moves towards a new world order. ... More and more, the United Nations is becoming involved in the resolution of problems *within* national societies, rather than settling conflicts *between* nations. ... The United Nations is also becoming vulnerable to the movements of change, and a groundswell of opinion is gathering strength for a revision of the Charter. There is little doubt that the circumstances in which the Charter was fashioned do not exist any longer. They have suffered considerable modification with radical changes in the composition of the international community. ... The principal jural postulates and the imperatives of the New International Law are indicative of the major global issues of our times: 'The peace imperative .....the imperative of decolonization and self-determination of the people ... the imperative of human rights ... the imperative of economic sovereignty ... the imperative of one world and global eco-order ... the imperative of a new information and communication order'. These imperatives and jural postulates of contemporary international law indeed reflect the values of the global family.

Judge Pathak was born at Bareilly, the son of a Vice-President of India, and educated in law and political science at Allahabad University. He enrolled as advocate in the Supreme Court of India in 1957 and served as Judge in the Allahabad High Court from 1963 to 1972. From 1972 to 1978 he was Chief Justice of the Himachal Pradesh High Court, before being elected Judge of the Supreme Court of India (1978-1986). From 1986, until his election to the ICJ, he was Chief Justice of India.

In these successive capacities he attended numerous international conferences. An Honorary Bencher of Gray's Inn and Honorary President of the World Peace Through Law Center in Washington, Judge Pathak was President of the Indian Law Institute and the Indian Society of International Law and Editor-in-Chief of the *Indian Journal of International Law*. He lectured on such varied topics as law and medicine, human rights and environmental law, and published papers on the sources, development and codification of international law, the work of the ILC, the law of the sea, State responsibility, and science and international law. During the 1980s he participated in Russian-Indian and German-Indian international law colloquia and attended the 1989 Environmental Law Conference in Rome. He was a member of the Advisory Board of the 1984 UN University Project on the Common Patrimony and Intergenerational Equity.

1908-1976

Judge:	1967-1976
Contentious Cases:	8
Advisory Requests:	3
Declarations:	4 (2 Joint)
Sep. Opinions:	5
Dis. Opinions:	7

Sture Petrén

Judge Sture Petrén, the first and only Swedish Judge at The Hague since Åke Hammarskjøld served from October 1936 to July 1937, was born in Stockholm and held degrees in Swedish law (1930) and humanities (1932) from Lund University. Both areas would remain of lifelong interest to him. He was a Member of the Royal Swedish Academy of History and Literature and was on the Chapter of the Diocese of Stockholm. He also chaired the Committee for Cultural Co-operation in Europe and served on the Boards of Museums, at one time presiding over the Swedish Tourist Club. He was often able to combine both the legal and cultural elements, in his work as legal historian or while attending the Conference on the Revision of the Berne Literary Convention (1948) or the Universal Copyright Convention (1952) in his capacity of Legal Adviser to the Foreign Ministry.

The first ten years of Judge Petrén's career were taken up with service in various law courts, until he became an Associate Judge at the Stockholm Court of Appeals in 1943. In 1947 he became Assistant Professor at the Stockholm School of Economics and in 1949 was appointed Director of the Legal Department of the Foreign Ministry where he would serve until 1963. During those years, he attended the 1948-1961 Sessions of the General Assembly and conferences of a widely differing nature, including that on the Status of Refugees (1951) and the 1958 and 1960 Law of the Sea Conferences. This he combined with a Vice-Presidency of the Swedish Labour Court (1951-1963) and membership of the United Nations Administrative Tribunal (1952-1966). Concurrently he was Member (1954) and President (1962-1967) of the European Commission on Human Rights. He also presided over the Royal Svea Court of Appeal.

Judge Petrén became a Member of the PCA in 1955 and served on various arbitration tribunals: he chaired the 1958 *Lake Lanoux* case. From 1971-1976 he was on the panel in the *Beagle Channel* case (in both tribunals he served along with André Gros).

His activities are reflected in a number of learned articles, notably on aspects of human rights and the law of the sea, and in a 1963 Hague Academy Course on the confiscation of goods. He wrote two intriguing articles on the international judiciary: 'La CIJ comme juridiction de recours' (in the 1975 *Studi Morelli*) and 'Forms of Expression of Judicial Activity' in *The Future of the ICJ* (1976). In the latter article he (a noted horseman) enlarges on the freedom available to a Judge to develop his own train of reasoning:

> In any event, the individual judge who would find it difficult to breathe inside... could always saddle his own horse, named Separate Opinion, and gallop away from the paddock prepared by the drafting committee into the fields of his own legal thinking.

He became a Member of the Court in 1967. His years at The Hague resulted in no less than 4 Declarations (2 Joint), 5 Separate and 7 Dissenting Opinions. Judge Petrén was notably in disagreement with the majority during most stages of the 1972-1974 proceedings in the *Fisheries Jurisdiction* cases.

In the 1971 *Namibia* Advisory Opinion Judge Petrén made an observation on judges *ad hoc*:

> There are of course divergent opinions as to the value of the institution of Judges *ad hoc*, but so long as it remains in the Court's Statute it will represent a safeguard of a procedural kind which is offered to a State which is a party in a contentious case when there is no judge of its nationality among the regular Members of the Court. Advisory proceedings are also part of the Court's judicial function, and Article 68 of the Statute lays down the principle that they should as far as possible be assimilated to contentious proceedings. The departure from the principle laid down in Article 68 of the Statute which the Court evinced in rejecting South Africa's request for a Judge *ad hoc* is accentuated by another majority decision of the Court. (*ICJ Reports* 1971, at p. 130)

Raymond Ranjeva

*1942

Judge:	1991-present
Contentious Cases:	15
Advisory Requests:	1
Declarations:	2
Sep. Opinions:	1
Dis. Opinions:	2

In common with some other Judges who have been appointed to the Court in recent years from countries of the developing world, as for example Judge Weeramantry, Judge Ranjeva brings to the Court a strong academic background. He was born at Antananarivo, Madagascar and there obtained degrees in law and administration before becoming a trainee in the Judicial Division of the *Conseil d'État* in Paris (1965-1966). In the next two years he obtained *diplômes* in political science and public law in Paris and Madagascar respectively. He then obtained his Doctorate of Law at Paris II on *La succession d'organisations internationales en Afrique* and in 1972 passed the *Agrégation des Facultés de Droit* to obtain the title of Professor of Law. Having served as a Civil Administrator from 1966, he became Lecturer (1972) and Professor (1981) at Madagascar University, where he was Dean of the Faculty of Law, Economics, Management and Sociology. In 1988, he was appointed first Rector of the University of Antananarivo. Since 1970 Judge Ranjeva has been on the list of Conciliators at the World Bank's ICSID. In 1973 he was Consultant for Madagascar on the transfer to the State of the *Eau-Electricité de Madagascar* and *Electricité de France*.

Fairly early in his career Judge Ranjeva gained experience at the international level. From 1979-1990 he was on the Malagasy Delegation to the General Assembly. He attended the UNCLOS Conference and the 1979 Conference of Non-Aligned Countries, headed his nation's Delegation to the UN Conference on the Succession of States in Respect of Treaties (1976-1977), helped revise the co-operation agreements with France and was on the Preparatory Commission for the International Seabed Authority and the Law of the Sea Tribunal. From 1987-1991, he was Vice-President at the Conference of French-speaking Faculties of Law and Political Science.

Judge Ranjeva, who is a Member of the African, the French and the Quebec Societies of International Law, and a Founding Member of the Malagasy Human Rights Committee, has published extensively. He belongs inter alia to the Malagasy Academy as an Honorary Vice-President, to the *Académie des Sciences d'Outre-Mer*, to the *Institut de Droit International* and the ICC Court of Arbitration and the Arbitral Tribunal of Sports. In 1983-1986 he was Counsel for the Republic of Mali in its *Frontier Dispute* with Burkina Faso. He returned to The Hague in 1987 as Director of the research seminar at the Hague Academy. In 1991, at the age of 48, he was one of the youngest Judges ever to be elected to the Court. To date Judge Ranjeva has dissented twice: in the *Arbitral Award 1989* case and in the 1971 *Montreal Convention* cases, concerning the Lockerbie bombing, and recently delivered a Separate Opinion in the 1995 *Case Concerning East Timor*. In this context he observed:

> Realism in ... a tricky case [must] led the Court to offer the Parties involved an appropriate legal framework for holding in check the undesirable effects of a legal act or a situation ... a difficult exercise ... [b]ut in dealing with these difficulties, the Court is laying down the framework for the development of international law and performing one of its principal functions... (*ICJ Reports* 1995, at p. 133)

In his 1991 Dissenting Opinion in the *Arbitral Award 1989* case, Judge Ranjeva enlarged on the concept of *res judicata*:

> The concept of *res judicata* which underlies the very authority of any judicial decision, goes beyond the framework of the axiomatic bases of the law. It is a consequence of a whole set of phenomena (acts, rules, conduct, attendant circumstances...) which have to be taken into consideration, as they contribute to the reinforcement of the *convictio juris*. ... [A] tribunal, while adopting a specific form of procedure, to use, in order to develop its reasoning, a number of different techniques of argument so as to support and validate its own method and conclusions ... [relies] at once upon what is likely, what is plausible, and what is probable. (*ICJ Reports* 1991, at p. 122)

Judge Ranjeva's views with respect to the judicial function of the Court can be taken from his Dissenting Opinion in the *1971 Montreal Convention* cases:

> The new dimension [of collective security in the case] did not permit the Court to limit itself to a passive approach to its judicial function. (*ICJ Reports* 1992, at p. 76)

1887–1953

Judge:	1952–1953
Contentious Cases:	2
Advisory Requests:	–
Declarations:	–
Sep. Opinions:	–
Dis. Opinions:	1 Joint

Benegal Narsing Rau

'A promise unfulfilled'. This phrase, or words of similar import, must have echoed in the Great Hall of Justice a number of times at funeral speeches during the past fifty years. They certainly applied to Sir Benegal Rau. Judge Rau was the first Indian Judge ever to sit on the Bench of the ICJ. He was elected in December 1951 and, having been Prime Minister of Kashmir, brought with him both a high reputation in public life and a rich experience of administration. He made his solemn declaration in February 1952, along with (amongst others) the Soviet Judge Golunsky. The elections proved ill-fated: Judge Golunsky soon fell ill and hardly attended any sessions of the Court, and Judge Rau did not serve for long either. His health started to fail early in 1953 and his participation in the work of the Court was greatly restricted throughout that year. After a prolonged illness he passed away on 30 November 1953, and was replaced by Judge Zafrulla Khan of Pakistan. During his short term Sir Benegal Rau did not, however, fail to impress his colleagues, as President Sir Arnold McNair testified in his public funeral oration on 10 May 1954:

> Apart from his great legal and political experience, his outstanding qualities were his learning and his sympathetic understanding, his patience and his firmness. He inspired not only confidence but affection. His services to his country and his contributions to the work of the UN in New York and Geneva lie in the past and are on record. For us his untimely death means disappointment and a great promise unfulfilled.; for it is rare to find a man whose moral and intellectual qualities combined with his experience and temperament fit him so admirably to hold judicial office. Those of us who were privileged to work with him are not likely to forget the example of this great public servant.

Sir Benegal Rau was born at Karkal, India, and graduated from the universities of Madras and Cambridge. In 1910 he entered upon a career with the Indian Civil Service. He was Secretary to the Assam Legislative Department and its Legislative Council and served the Government of Assam in various functions, notably as its Legal Adviser from 1925 to 1933. He then joined the Legislative Department of the Government of India and advised it on legal matters. From 1935-1937 he revised the entire Indian Statute Book and in the following year served as Reforms Commissioner. From 1939-1944 he was Judge of the High Court of Judicature of Bengal. Concurrently he chaired the commission that adjudicated the inter-State dispute regarding the waters of the Indus River System and the committee that codified Hindu Law; on these activities he reported extensively. In 1945 he became Prime Minister of Kashmir and from 1946-1949 was Constitutional Adviser to the Constituent Assembly of India. He also helped formulate the 1947 Constitution of Burma.

In 1949 Sir Benegal Rau became Permanent Representative of India to the United Nations, and in this capacity attended the Fourth, Fifth and Sixth Sessions of the General Assembly as well as the meetings of the Security Council in 1950-1951. In 1949 he was elected Vice-Chairman of the International Law Commission. Sir Benegal Rau was a Member of the International Institute of Political and Constitutional History of the Sorbonne in Paris. This membership, as well as his publications, notably a monograph on *Constitutional Precedents*, duly reflect his interests, which were mainly focused on matters of legislation and constitution.

Elected in 1952, Sir Benegal Rau served on 3 cases and signed 1 Joint Dissenting Opinion, together with Judges Hackworth, Badawi, and Levi Carneiro, which was appended to the 1952 Judgment on the *Case Concerning Rights of Nationals of the USA in Morocco*.

John E. Read

1888-1973

Judge:	1946-1958
Contentious Cases:	27
Advisory Requests:	10
Declarations:	–
Sep. Opinions:	3
Dis. Opinions:	9 (1Joint)

Why is it that our world has strained at the Geneva gnat, while the seventeenth-century world swallowed, with gusto, the Grotian camel? (*The Rule of Law*, at p.6)

Judge Read, so far the only Canadian Judge of the Court, was born in Halifax and educated at Dalhousie and Columbia Universities and at University College, Oxford. He was admitted to the Bar of Nova Scotia in 1913 and was engaged in general practice until 1920 becoming a K.C. in 1925. He served in the Canadian Army during World War I and was appointed Professor of Law and later of Constitutional and International Law at Dalhousie University. He served on the Canadian Conference of Commissioners on Uniformity of Legislation and advised the Department of External Affairs from 1929-1946. He was his nation's Agent and Counsel before the well-known *I'm Alone* and *Trail Smelter* arbitral tribunals and represented it in litigation before the Canadian and US Supreme Courts, the Judicial Committee of the Privy Council and US Federal Courts. In April 1945 he was Canadian Representative to the UN Committee of Jurists preparing the Draft Statute for the new Court and in 1946 represented his country during parts of the First Session of the General Assembly. Judge Read was elected to the ICJ in 1946 and allotted a term of three years. In 1949 he was re-elected and served another full term, until 1958. His dissent in the *Peace Treaties* case was especially noteworthy.

Judge Read was not a prolific writer, but he has left a most charming little book, *The Rule of Law on the International Plane*, which is the record of his 1960 W. M. Martin Lectures at the University of Saskatchewan. In it, he points to the unifying moral elements of Christendom, to the universal Latin language, to the reaction against the horrors of the Thirty Years War - and to the respect for jurists at that time. With the expansion of the family of nations and the crumbling of Western civilization all this has gone. Thus:

> Today, one of the greatest obstacles to international agreement is the lack of a common tongue. Genuine discussion - whether at summit, on commission or committee - is impossible. Translation, even if simultaneous, is an effective barrier to interchange of ideas. (*The Rule of Law*, at p. 7)

This is not to say that he was a pessimist. In a historical survey, which also covers the traditional Canadian attitude towards the Court and with reference to the *I'm Alone* and *Trail Smelter* arbitrations, the *Gulf of Maine* Boundary, the *Oregon* dispute, and the *Alaskan Panhandle*, he enlarges upon what is needed to make progress towards the rule of law:

> The first is the approach to the problem of jurisdiction. All international jurisdiction is based on consent ... Legal opinion is divided, as regards the basic approach to problems of jurisdiction, into two schools of jurists, a majority and a minority ... The jurists of the majority school approach the problem of interpretation rightly feeling that jurisdiction must not be imposed on a respondent State without its consent. They consider that the exercise of jurisdiction would be a limitation on the respondent's sovereignty. ... The minority jurists have a different approach. They ... consider that the applicant and respondent share with our civilized States a paramount interest that right should be done and that there should be no denial of justice. (*op. cit.*, at p. 39.)

Apart from practical improvements in the functioning of the Court and the election of Judges, it is, if anything, the general acceptance of the so-called Optional Clause, providing for the compulsory jurisdiction of the Court, that he felt constituted the best instrument and the virtual prerequisite to the establishment of the rule of law. To attain these ends:

> There is need for a revolution in our thinking and in our policy ... there is a need to abandon clichés as substitutes for reason and to open the mind to facts. ... After all, few prices are too great to pay for peace. There is need to abandon the new diplomacy, which now, in all too many countries, consists of vituperation, tantrums, and impassioned speeches aimed at the voter at home... (*op. cit.*, at p. 56)

1924-1994

Judge:	1973-1991
President:	1988-1991
Contentious Cases:	20
Advisory Requests:	7
Declarations:	–
Sep. Opinions:	10
Dis. Opinions:	1

José Maria Ruda

Despite all his impressive learning, and all his dignity, it is for his boyish enthusiasm that Judge Ruda will live on in the memories of his colleagues at the Court. Ebullience, warmth and vitality were his most striking features. He represented the type of man - so prominent among the Judges - who from his early years combines all sorts of posts and functions and never seems to need a break. When his life came to an abrupt end at the age of 70, in July 1994, he was still in the midst of everything, appearing full of boundless energy.

For most of his active life Judge Ruda was a scholar, a diplomat and a judge or arbitrator (interstate *and* commercial) at the same time. With his demise, the Court had lost two eminent Latin-American internationalists within a period of but three months, as Ruda's close friend Eduardo Jiménez de Aréchaga had preceded him in the spring.

Judge Ruda was born in Buenos Aires where he became a Doctor of Law in 1949. The winning of a contest, made him, one might say, stumble into an international career and serve the Office of Legal Affairs at the UN Secretariat for five years. In 1955 he obtained a Master in international law from New York University and then embarked upon a diplomatic career. He served his country as Counsellor at the Embassy in Bolivia (1957-1959) and at the Ministry of Foreign Affairs (1959-1965), notably as Legal Counsel. Concurrently, he was Rapporteur of the Sixth Committee of the General Assembly in 1962 and chaired the Committee in 1963. That year he also headed his nation's delegation to the Mixed Argentine-Bolivian Commission and attended the Vienna Conference on Consular Relations where he joined the Drafting Committee that prepared the Convention. During the next year he served on the Commission on River Traffic with Paraguay and the Mixed Argentine-Uruguayan Commission on the River Plate.

In 1964 he also became a Member of the International Law Commission, which he chaired in 1968. He was Agent for Argentina in the 1965-1968 *Rio Encuentro* arbitration, and was its Permanent Representative to the UN and Security Council from 1965-1970. In this capacity he attended the 1968 Vienna Conference on Treaties and was on various UN Seabed Committees (1968-1970). After returning home, he was Under-Secretary for Foreign Affairs from 1970-1973. Despite these other commitments, he held the chair of international law at Buenos Aires from 1960-1973.

A Member of the *Institut de Droit International*, the ILA, the PCA and the Hague Curatorium, Judge Ruda was elected Judge of the ICJ in 1973; an election which was remarkable for two reasons: firstly because of his age (at the time he was only 49) and secondly because he was not the candidate supported by his regional group or even by Argentina, so that it was his reputation alone that won him the day. He served two full terms, the last three years (1988-1991) as President of the Court.

Although he himself had a highly independent mind, as can be seen from his stand in the Honduras/El Salvador and Nicaragua cases, he attached great value to unanimity on the Bench. He was a Member of the Chamber in the 1983-1987 Burkina Faso/Mali *Frontier Dispute* and chaired the Chamber in the 1987-1989 *Elsi* case.

During his almost twenty years with the Court Judge Ruda presented 10 Separate Opinions and dissented just once, in the 1975 *Western Sahara* Advisory Opinion. After his retirement from the ICJ he served as Judge *ad hoc* for Qatar in its *Maritime Delimitation* dispute with Bahrain. Concurrently, he was President of the Iran-USA Claims Tribunal (1991-1993) – further evidence of his undisputed standing – and of the ILO Administrative Tribunal. He was on the list of Conciliators at the ICSID and the panel of Arbitrators at the Yugoslavia Conference. He was a productive writer, notably on Latin America and the UN and on UN Law, and with Prof. Podesta Costa co-authored a manual on international law (1979).

Stephen M. Schwebel

*1929

Judge:	1981–present
Vice–President:	1994–present
Contentious Cases:	23
Advisory Requests:	5
Declarations:	1
Sep. Opinions:	10
Dis. Opinions:	11

'There is need for realism, for sobriety, for a critical spirit - and for a constructive spirit', Judge Schwebel writes in one of his collected papers. Perhaps this is precisely the gist of what his considerable contribution to the Bench has been in the past fifteen years. 'The Court is a body of high achievement and unused potential. But it is not a body of uniformly high achievement or unlimited potential' reads another line of his. Few Judges over the past decades have brought a more practical mind and more common sense to the Court. Judge Schwebel's experience in the practice of law, law teaching, in the US Department of State, as well as in international commercial arbitration, have made him a judge of the ultimate cause of dispute: human nature. Still in the same article from 1985 (included in: *Justice in International Law*, 1994, at p.13) he argues:

> Human institutions rarely grow and prosper in an unbroken pattern of progress. It is not surprising that so frail an institution as international adjudication not only has congenital weaknesses but that it may have caught some of the diseases of its environment. We live in a world in which international law and international institutions, while enormously valuable, are nevertheless dangerously far from being as effective as they should be and need to be if this is to be a less troubled and precarious world.

Stephen M. Schwebel was born in New York City and educated at Harvard College, Cambridge University, and Yale (LL.B., 1954). His days at Cambridge coincided with those of Richard Baxter; both became the favorite students of Hersch Lauterpacht. He was admitted to the Bar in 1955 and practised in New York as an attorney until 1959 when he became Assistant Professor of Law at Harvard. In 1961 he turned to the Department of State, initially as Assistant Legal Adviser for United Nations Affairs (1961-1966) and finally (1974-1981) as Deputy Legal Adviser. He attended the Sixth Committee from 1961-1965 and chaired US Delegations to other UN Committees, including those on Friendly Relations (1964) and on the Question of Defining Aggression (1971). He was a Member of the ILC from 1977-1981, chaired its Drafting Committee and was Special Rapporteur on International Watercourses. From 1967 to 1981, Judge Schwebel was Edward B. Burling Professor of International Law at The Johns Hopkins University (Washington). He lectured at Cambridge (1957, 1983) and the Australian National University (1959), was on the Editorial and Advisory Boards of the *American Journal of International Law* and *International Legal Materials* and was Executive Director of the American Society of International Law (1967-1973). He became Honorary President of the Society in 1996. He is a member of the *Institut* and since 1994 has been President of the IMF Administrative Tribunal.

Judge Schwebel is a productive author. He was research and drafting assistant to Secretary-General Trygve Lie in the writing of Lie's memoirs, *In the Cause of Peace* (1954), prepared Reports for the ILC on the Use of Watercourses, wrote some hundred articles in law reviews and the press, lectured at the Hague Academy on *Aggression, Intervention and Self-Defence* (1972), edited *The Effectiveness of International Decisions* (1971), and published monographs on *The Secretary-General of the United Nations: His Political Powers and Practice* (1952) and *International Arbitration: Three Salient Problems* (1987); recently he produced *Justice in International Law* (1994), a selection of published articles, including some on topical matters of the Court. Judge Schwebel served as Representative, Counsel and Deputy-Agent on behalf of the USA before the ICJ. He was elected to the Court in 1981 to succeed Judge Baxter who had died in September 1980, and was re-elected in 1988. He was a Member of the *Gulf of Maine* and *ELSI* Chambers, and is currently Vice-President of the Court. He has played a major part in the administration as well as juridical work of the Court. His Dissenting Opinion in *Military and Paramilitary Activities in and against Nicaragua* attracted particular attention. Judge Schwebel has voted against positions of the State of his nationality six times, a record of judicial independence which, in the words of the late Court President Nagendra Singh, is 'unsurpassed in the history of the Court'.

*1920

Judge:	1979-1992
Vice–President:	1982-1985
Contentious Cases:	17
Advisory Requests:	5
Declarations:	–
Sep. Opinions:	3
Dis. Opinions:	2

José Sette-Camara

Judge Sette-Camara was born in Alfenas, in Minas Gerais, Brazil. He became a Master of Laws at McGill University in Montreal and at the age of 25 entered the diplomatic service. In 1958 he was Secretary of the Presidency of the Republic, in 1959 he was Governor of the State of Guanabara (Rio de Janeiro) and the following year was Mayor of Brasilia. He served as Permanent Representative in Geneva (1960-1961), Ambassador to Canada (1961) and Switzerland (1963-1964) and Permanent Representative to the United Nations in New York (1964-1968). In 1964 he was Head of the Delegation of Brazil to Paris for Negotiating and Rescheduling of the Foreign Debt. During these latter years he was Representative to the Security Council and from 1970 to 1978 was Delegate to the Sixth Committee of the UN General Assembly, concurrently serving as Ambassador to Czechoslovakia (1972-1979).

A Member of the *Institut*, the PCA and the Brazilian Society of International Law, Judge Sette-Camara was in 1970 elected as a Member of the ILC to complete the mandate of Gilberto Amado (in 1987 he delivered a lecture *Gilberto Amado - A Hundred Years of Plenitude*) and was then elected on two more occasions from 1971 to 1982. He acted as General Rapporteur, Vice-Chairman and Chairman. In 1975 he presided the UN Conference on the Representation of States in their Relations with International Organizations. He headed the Brazilian Delegation to the UN Conference on the Succession of States in Respect of Treaties. A recent landmark was his Presidency of the ILO Commission of Enquiry on the Application of the Labour Conventions in Nicaragua, in 1990.

Judge Sette-Camara has written extensively. Of particular note (apart from articles in the *Boletim* of the Brazilian Society) are a monograph on *The Ratification of International Treaties* (1949), a contribution on the Vienna Convention on the Representation of States in *UN Law/ Fundamental Rights*, ed. Cassese 1979; a Hague Academy Course on *Pollution of International Rivers* (1984); 'The International Law Commission, Discourse on Method', in *Festschrift Ago 1987*, and a chapter on 'Methods of Obligatory Settlement of Disputes', in *International Law, Achievements and Prospects*, ed. Bedjaoui, 1991.

Judge Sette-Camara was elected to the ICJ in 1979 to replace Judge Jiménez de Aréchaga and served one term on the Bench, until 1988. He then continued to sit as President of the Chamber dealing with the El Salvador/Honduras *Frontier Dispute* until 1992. Again, in 1993-1994 he served as Judge *ad hoc* for Libya in its *Territorial Dispute* with Chad. Judge Sette-Camara was Vice-President of the Court from 1982-1985. He dissented twice, in the Libya-Chad case and as Vice-President in the 1984 Libya/Malta *Continental Shelf* Judgment, on intervention. To him this was a matter of principle:

> When the founding fathers of the Statute of the Old Court decided to find a place in the draft prepared by the Hague Advisory Committee of Jurists for the institution of intervention, they were not innovating in any way. They did nothing but introduce in the basic document of the Court a procedural remedy known and recognized by all the legal systems of the world as a legitimate means by which third parties, extraneous to a legal dispute, have the right to come into the proceedings to defend their legal rights or interests which might be impaired or threatened by the course of the contentious proceedings. In most systems of law - through different models - principal or accessory intervention, assistance or 'aggressive' intervention, the legal basis is always the same: the existence of a right or of an interest of a legal nature of a third party that may be affected by the course of the proceedings. The proof of the existence of this legal interest is by necessity not definitive and beyond dispute. Already in Roman law the simple appearance of its existence was enough to justify intervention. ... Those who insist on the need of the jurisdictional link do not see the difference of treatment given by the Statute to normal and principal cases and to cases of incidental jurisdiction. Intervention is one of the latter, together with the interim measures of protection, interpretation and revision of judgments. (*ICJ Reports* 1984, at p. 71 and 87)

Mohamed Shahabuddeen

*1931

Judge:	1988–present
Contentious Cases:	16
Advisory Requests:	3
Declarations:	1
Sep. Opinions:	16
Dis. Opinions:	2

...isn't it here that you take half a step wrong and wake up a thousand miles astray?

Judge Shahabuddeen of Guyana came to the ICJ in February 1988. During the past eight years he has dissented twice, but he has rendered no less than 16 Separate Opinions. The number attests, not only to the increased caseload, but also to Judge Shahabuddeen's conscientious and meticulous approach. By now, students of the Court's judgments have come to appreciate his analytical mind.

Mohamed Shahabuddeen passed his Bar Finals at the London Inns of Court in 1952 and is a Ph.D. and an LL.D. of London University. He was called to the Bar at the Middle Temple in 1954. He became Queen's Counsel in 1966. After some years of private practice in Guyana he turned to the public legal service, becoming in due course Solicitor General (1962-1973) and Attorney General (1973-1987) successively.

He was Minister of Justice of Guyana from 1978-1987 and, at times, Acting Foreign Minister. From the early sixties Judge Shahabuddeen represented Guyana on diplomatic missions and from 1972 attended meetings of international and regional organizations. For example, he attended the 1972 General Assembly Session and the 1977 Vienna Conference on the Succession of States in respect of Treaties. He was a Delegate to Meetings of the Commonwealth Heads of Government from Lusaka (1979) to Vancouver (1987), and to its Law Ministers Meetings from Lagos (1975) to Harare (1986). He attended the 1981 General Assembly of the OAS, and the meetings of the Non-Aligned Countries in Georgetown (1972), Algiers (1981) and New Delhi (1983). Judge Shahabuddeen is Associate Member of the *Institut de Droit International* and Headquarters Member of the ILA. He is an Honorary Member of the Middle Temple, and is on the Advisory Board of the *European Journal of International Law*.

A writer on various aspects of Guyanese society: its legal system (1973), its constitutional development (1978), the nationalisation of its bauxite (1981) and its sugar industry (1983), Judge Shahabuddeen after coming to The Hague turned his attention to the ICJ. This led to a string of intriguing papers (as 'Kleine Schriften'): *The ICJ: First Impressions* (1991); *The ICJ: An End to Underemployment* (1991); *The ICJ: The Integrity of an Idea* (1992); *The ICJ: The Road to Universality* (1992); *The ICJ: The View from the West Indies* (1992); *The ICJ: Image, Mission, Mandate* (1994); *The ICJ: Towards the 21st Century* (1994).

In 'The Integrity of an Idea', he wonders whether undue emphasis on jurisdictional voluntarism can prejudice the judicial character of the Court. In other words, is the ICJ a real Court of Justice:

> The ICJ is, of course, a very special court. It is not a replica of any national court, and hasty analogies from municipal law are to be distrusted. ... The ICJ can fairly be seen as a Court of Justice, but ... as was observed by Professor Sauser-Hall ... what is exaggerated does not exist, a remark which applies equally to differences and to similarities. It is submitted that it is important to avoid any exaggeration of the differences between the ICJ and a national court which could upset a reasonable balance between the rights of the parties to avail themselves of the voluntary nature of the jurisdiction of the Court, on the one hand, and the duty of the Court to preserve its paramount judicial identity, on the other. ... Through no fault of its own, the World Court has not realized the more ambitious of the aspirations of some of its well-wishers. But it was and remains a real court. And it was and is a great idea. Its establishment marked the realization of the dreams of men who, while familiar with arbitration, had laboured long and hard for the establishment of something substantially different. They did not achieve all that they wanted; but what they achieved they valued, both in itself and as the basis for judicial developments that might yet come. And it is here that the traveller confronts the troubling image presented by Confucius - the image of Yang Chu weeping at the crossroads and saying, 'isn't it here that you take half a step wrong and wake up a thousand miles astray?' (in *International Law in Transition* 1992, at pp. 359-361)

*1926

Judge:	1994–present
Contentious Cases:	1
Advisory Requests:	1
Declarations:	1 Joint
Sep. Opinions:	–
Dis. Opinions:	–6

Shi Jiuyong

Was China a birthplace of international law – as Korovin and Abi-Saab have argued, among others - or was there no international law at all in China before the 1860s, as Nussbaum maintained in his *Concise History*? How should one interpret the international connotations ascribed to these legendary periods of *Spring and Summer* and the *Warring States* (722-221 BC) in the heydays of the Zhou Dynasty? In his penetrating 1990 Hague Academy Course the Nestor of Chinese internationalists, Wang Tieya, observed that at least some of the concrete problems faced by the People's Republic of China in its often frustrating relations with the West over the past 45 years may well have very definite historical and cultural undertones - for instance, in the spheres of the concept of sovereignty and the law of treaties, notably with respect to the doctrines of *pacta sunt servanda* and *rebus sic stantibus*.

In seeking to apply international law more effectively to present-day multicultural society, one cannot afford *not* to take into account *any* extant, operative legal tradition, including their typical biases and sensitivities. In this perspective one cannot neglect, let alone deny - although a different question altogether may be how to globally implement - such intriguing phenomena as the 1954 *Five Principles* doctrine of the People's Republic of China, upon whose acceptance, it is maintained, all peaceful co-existence between nations should be based, the principles in question being respect for territorial integrity and sovereignty; non-aggression; non-interference in internal affairs; equality and mutual benefit; and, finally, the very intention of peaceful co-existence.

In his impressive career both as a scholar and a civil servant the present Chinese Judge on the Bench, Shi Jiuyong, had ample occasion to watch internationalists from all quarters of the globe at work - and clashing at times. Judge Shi Jiuyong was born in Zhejiang and was educated in political science and law at St John's University, Shanghai and Columbia University, N.Y, where he studied international law from 1951-1954. He was Associate Professor of International Law at the Foreign Affairs College in Beijing (1958-1964), then Research Fellow at the Institutes of International Law and International Studies in Beijing (1964-1973; 1973-1980), before returning to the Foreign Affairs College as a full Professor (1984). Concurrently he taught law at the Ministry of Justice of the People's Republic. He is a Council Member of the Chinese Society of International Law.

From 1980-1993 Judge Shi was Legal Adviser to the Ministry of Foreign Affairs and to the Sino-British Joint Liaison Group in matters regarding Hong Kong. In the former capacity he attended the 1980 Meeting of the Board of Governors of the IMO and the International Bank for Reconstruction and Development, as well as the 1980-1983 Sessions of the General Assembly. On those occasions he was China's Alternative Representative (later Delegate) to the Sixth Committee.

Judge Shi was delegate and legal adviser to various sessions of the Asian-African Legal Consultative Committee, at the talks on China's Membership in the Asian Development Bank and during his country's bilateral negotiations with the USA in matters of the Mutual Promotion and Protection of Investment Agreement. He also took active part in the drafting and negotiating of the 1974 Sino-British Joint Declaration on the Question of Hongkong. He lent his expertise to the UN Montevideo Environmental Programme at Geneva and Nairobi and to the 1991 Disarmament Conference relating to chemical weapons.

Perhaps even more pertinent within our context: Judge Shi was a Member of the Steering Committee of the PCA on the question of revision of the 1907 Convention on Dispute Settlement, and a Member (1987-1993), Rapporteur (1988) and Chairman (1990) of the International Law Commission. He is a productive author and has lectured frequently including lectures given at the 1987 Beijing Regional Programme of the Hague Academy and at Geneva. He came to the Court in February 1994 as successor to Judge Ni Zhengyu.

Percy C. Spender

1897-1985

Judge:	1958-1967
President:	1964-1967
Contentious Cases:	16
Advisory Requests:	2
Declarations:	2
Sep. Opinions:	6
Dis. Opinions:	4 (2 Joint)

In the nature of things different minds approach problems in different ways. The approach to a legal problem is no exception. What is to be solved will be solved according to the manner of him who solves it. (*ICJ Reports* 1962, at p. 101)

Born in Sydney, Sir Percy Spender studied law and political science. In 1915 he entered public service. He was called to the Bar in 1923, was appointed King's Counsel in 1935 and was created a KBE in 1952 and KCVO in 1957. He became a Member of the House of Representatives in 1937 and served on various Parliamentary Committees before becoming Member of the Menzies Ministry and the Federal Executive Council in 1939. During the war years he was successively Minister without Portfolio, Treasurer, Minister of State for the Army and Member of the War Cabinet and the Advisory War Council.

In 1949 Judge Spender became Minister for External Affairs and in 1951 was appointed Ambassador to the USA (1951-1958). Being concurrently Chairman of the Australian Delegation to the UN, in 1951 he was elected Vice-President of the UN General Assembly. For a number of years he was (Alternate) Governor of the International Monetary Fund and the International Bank (1951-1956). He chaired a number of British Commonwealth Conferences, attended the Second Suez Conference in London in 1956 and helped negotiate the Draft Statute for the International Atomic Energy Agency in Washington. He was indeed a well-versed negotiator and seasoned diplomat when he was elected to the ICJ.

Sir Percy Spender was on the Bench from 1958 to 1967 and its President from 1964-1967. In a charming booklet, entitled *Ambassador's Wife* (1968), from which we have quoted extensively in this book, Sir Percy's wife, Jean Spender, has enlarged on the professional and social aspects of their life at The Hague. Sir Percy's Opinions reveal the trained, conscientious jurist. Apart from his Opinion on the evidence of maps in the 1962 *Temple of Preah Vihear* case, his Declaration on the status of Dissenting Opinions is particularly noteworthy:

I would not wish to say anything which would unreasonably restrict the right accorded to a judge by Article 57. It is an important right which must be safeguarded. Can it be, however, that there are no limits to the scope and extent of the exercise of this right by any individual judge? I cannot think so. There must, it seems to me, be some limits, to proceed beyond which could not be claimed to be a proper exercise of the right the Statute confers. ... The right of a Judge to express a Dissenting Opinion in whole or in part was not easily won. In the Hague Convention of 1899 a right of dissent from arbitral decisions was recognized; it was adopted without discussion. At the Hague Conference of 1907 the question of dissent or no dissent was discussed at considerable length. In the result the right of dissent was suppressed. The Committee of Jurists ... reached the conclusion that a judge should be allowed to publish his dissent, but not his reasons. This however failed to receive the approval of the Council of the League ... There was then introduced into the text the right of a judge who did not concur in all or part of the judgment to deliver a Separate Opinion. (*ICJ Reports* 1966, at pp. 52-53)

During his presidency, Sir Percy introduced several innovations which he had felt for some time were much needed. Simultaneous translation was the first and perhaps the most important among these changes which did much to 'bring the Court into the 20th Century', as it was held at the time.

The name of Sir Percy Spender, will remain indissolubly linked to the dramatic Judgment pronounced by the Court on 18 July 1966 in the *South West Africa* cases (Second Phase), which for so many years produced such strong repercussions on the Court in the world at large. On that day, the votes being equally divided (7-7), it was the delicate duty of the Court's President (performed with characteristic courage) to decide.

Thus, it was the casting vote of Sir Percy that caused the claims of the Applicants, the Governments of Ethiopia and Liberia, to be deemed inadmissible on the ground of their not having established legal right or interest in the subject matter.

1896-1972

Judge:	1958-1967
Contentious Cases:	16
Advisory Requests:	2
Declarations:	5
Sep. Opinions:	–
Dis. Opinions:	1

Jean Spiropoulos

Judge Spiropoulos was born in Greece but educated abroad, notably in Zurich and Leipzig where he became a Doctor of Law in 1922. Lachs states (*Teacher* 1987, at p. 116) that in his views he was close to the German and Viennese Schools, yet called orthodox positivism a 'stillborn child', and emphasized the value of general principles of international law as next in importance to treaty and customary law. These were to be inferred from State practice and constituted virtually 'norms of natural law'. He lectured in Kiel before becoming Professor of International Law at Salonika in 1928. However, he soon turned his attention to Athens, to become concurrently Director of the Legal Department of the Ministry of Foreign Affairs. He then entered upon an international career. Successively, he was President of the Greek Association of International Law, Chairman of the ILC, Member of the PCA, President of a Commission on Conciliation between Sweden and Colombia and Member of the *Ambatielos* Arbitral Commission. He served as Judge *ad hoc* in the *Ambatielos* case (upon which he commented in a learned article in the *Festschrift Herbert Kraus*, 1954), represented Greece at the Codification Conference (1930) and the four Balkan Conferences (1930-1933), was on the Washington Committee of Jurists to draft the Statute of the ICJ, attended the 1945 San Francisco and the 1946 Paris Peace Conferences and was delegate to all UN General Assembly Sessions from 1946-1957. He was Rapporteur to the Sixth Committee and to the ILC on the Nuremberg principles, the Draft Code on Crimes against Mankind and the Definition of Aggression.

Judge Spiropoulos published extensively, notably five treatises dealing with the theory of public and private international law (1927-1940), and on *de facto* government (*Die de facto-Regierung im Völkerrecht*, 1926). He lectured at the Hague Academy on the individual in international law (1932). He was elected in 1958 to succeed Judge Zoričíč and served one term. He wrote 5 brief Declarations and 1 Dissenting Opinion, in the 1959 *Interhandel* case, on the interrelation between preliminary objections and adjudication on the merits. Noteworthy are his comments (in the 1956 *Festschrift Hans Wehberg*, at p. 374-384) on the amendments to the Statute of the Court, as proposed in 1954 (at the suggestion of Judge Guerrero) by the *Institut de Droit International* and intended to forestall negative political influences with regard to the election of Judges. Its first suggestion concerned the two criteria of election as formulated in Articles 2 and 9. Here the *Institut* wished to revise the text so as to emphasize the *personal qualities* of a Judge, at the cost of the second criterion, i.e. that of the *regional representation*. Judge Spiropoulos commented:

> Le point de vue de l'Institut d'après lequel les juges à la Cour doives être élus avant tout en fonction de leur qualité individuelle est, certes, à approuver. ... Cependant, il serait une erreur de croire que pareille précision aurait le moindre effet sur la pratique actuelle dans l'élection des juges. L'Assemblée générale et le Conseil de Sécurité sont des corps politiques où les aspects politiques prévalent. La rédaction actuelle ... aurai[en]t permis aux deux Organes ... , si tel était leur désir, de donner la primauté aux qualités scientifiques des personnes à élire. Si cette idée, cependant, n'a pas toujours prévalu dans l'élection des juges, c'est que le jeu des combinaisons politiques a, aux Nations Unies, le pas sur toute autre considération. Aussi il nous semblerait chimérique de penser que par un simple modification du texte des articles 2 et 9 du Statut de la Cour, on écarterait les combinaisons politiques de l'élection des juges.

He made similar comments regarding the position of the Judge *ad hoc* and the competence of the Court or the proposal to increase the number of Judges:

> Personne ne saurait nier que l'augmentation du nombre des juges ne contribuera pas à faciliter les délibérations de la Cour. On pourrait même considérer le nombre de 15 juges comme exagéré. Le nombre de 9 juges aurait, peut-être, suffi.

He was in favour of fixing one term of 15 years for Judges, suppressing re-election ('car ceux-ci étant nommés pour une période déterminée, il est humain qu'ils ne soient pas indifférents à leur réélection'), and setting the age limit at 75.

Kotaro Tanaka

1890-1974

Judge:	1961-1970
Contentious Cases:	5
Declarations:	2 Joint
Advisory Requests:	1
Sep. Opinions:	2
Dis. Opinions:	2

Kotaro Tanaka was born at Kagoshima and in 1915 graduated in law from Tokyo Imperial University. He was a post-graduate student of commercial law both in the USA and Europe before in 1922 returning to his university, where he held a chair until 1946. Concurrently he was on the Jury of State Examination for judges, lawyers and administrative officials. In terms of publications, commercial law and legal philosophy were his provinces, although 'Natural law in the works of Savigny', and 'Law and World Peace' were also among his titles.

Judge Tanaka had the best of contacts with numerous academic centres abroad and lectured extensively all over the world. He was awarded many honorary doctorates and prestigious titles such as honorary membership of the Council of Vatican City. His most distinguished function was, however, his tutorship of the Crown Prince and Princess from 1951-1960. Judge Tanaka became a Member of the House of Peers in 1946 and was Minister of Education from 1946-1947. Subsequently, he was Chief Justice of the Supreme Court from 1950 to 1960. He became an Associate Member of the *Institut* in 1948.

Judge Tanaka came to the Court in 1961 and served one full term on the bench. Noteworthy are his 2 Dissenting Opinions, of which the first was in the 1966 *South West Africa* case, in which he enlarged at great length (some 75 printed pages) on the various aspects of 'legal interest'. For this there was every reason, he stated, because:

> ... the Applicants' claims are declared to be rejected on the ground of the lack of any legal right or interest appertaining to them in the subject-matter of the present claims and that the 1962 Judgment is substantively overruled concerning its decision on the third preliminary objection. Although we do not deny the power of the Court to re-examine jurisdictional and other preliminary matters at any stage of proceedings *proprio motu*, we consider that there are not sufficient reasons to overrule on this point the 1962 Judgment. (*ICJ Reports* 1966, at p. 248)

His second Dissenting Opinion was submitted in the 1969 *North Sea Continental Shelf Cases* and focused on the concepts of continental shelf and equidistance. It is intriguing to see Judge Tanaka - in the opening years of a debate that would so often occupy the ICJ in the ensuing two decades - expound on issues that were later to become the province *par excellence* of Judge Shigeru Oda:

> An originally geological and geographical concept, i.e., that of the continental shelf, by reason of its intrinsic economic interests (natural resources, particularly minerals such as oil, gas from the subsoil of the seabed) which have become susceptible of exploration and exploitation as the result of recent technological development, has been vested with legal interests and presents itself as a subject-matter of rights and duties subject to the rule of law and constituting an institution belonging to international law.
>
> First, the Court recognizes that delimitation by the application of the equidistance principle would produce in the present cases an unjust and inequitable effect detrimental to the Federal Republic of Germany. .... Secondly, on this hypothesis, the Court admits in favour of the Federal Republic an appeal to higher ideas of law such as justice, equity or equitableness, and reasonableness, which are self-evident but which, owing to their general and abstract character, are unable to furnish any concrete criteria for delimitation in the present cases. Thirdly, ... it appears extremely doubtful whether the negotiations could be expected to achieve a successful result, and more likely that they would engender new complications and chaos. .... The important matter in connection with the present cases is that the Parties should have a guarantee of being able to terminate the possibly endless repetition of detailed negotiations by the final application of the equidistance principle. Another important matter should be that the Court by according the equidistance principle the status of a world law would make a contribution to the progressive development of international law. (*ICJ Reports* 1969, at p.172 and pp. 195-196)

Nikolai Konstantinovitch Tarassov

1923-1994

Judge:	1985-1994
Contentious Cases:	16
Advisory Requests:	3
Declarations:	4
Sep. Opinions:	–
Dis. Opinions:	2

The year 1985 will long be seen as a landmark in history. President Gorbachev's policy of *Glasnost* and *Perestroika* radically put an end to 40 years of Cold War. The election to the Court of Nikolai Tarassov in December 1985 coincided with these dramatic changes in the Soviet foreign policy, which did not take long to have their impact on its views regarding the role of the ICJ as well. On 7 December 1988, in a personal address to the United Nations, Mr Gorbachev suggested that all States should accept the compulsory jurisdiction of the ICJ with respect to the interpretation and application of human rights agreements. On the following 10 February, the Supreme Presidium of the Soviet adopted a Decree providing for that acceptance. In the covering letter informing Mr Pérez de Cuéllar of this Decree, Foreign Affairs Minister Shevardnadze stated:

> In taking that decision the Soviet Union has been guided by the interests of strengthening the international legal order ensuring the primacy of law in politics. ... Naturally such an approach presupposes a comprehensive use of all means for peaceful settlement of disputes, including the active use of the potential of the ICJ.

After 40 years of dissonance at the United Nations, during which the USSR resisted the least infringement of its sovereign rights, it had now dropped its shield. It now became conceivable that the USSR might one day be a respondent before the Court.

Judge Tarassov was born in Moscow and graduated from the Law Faculty of Moscow University. He was Consultant to the Legal Department of the Presidium of the Supreme Soviet (1949-1953) before becoming Head of the Secretariat for the Secretary of the Presidium. From 1956 to 1961 he was Counsellor at the USSR Embassy in Iran. He then moved back to the Ministry of Foreign Affairs and in 1968 became Deputy Permanent Representative to the UN replacing Judge Morozov whom he succeeded as Judge on the ICJ 15 years later. In 1972 he was appointed Ambassador to Mexico. From 1976 up to his election to the Court he was back in Moscow as Principal Counsellor for Foreign Policy Planning at the Ministry of Foreign Affairs.

During his time in New York, Judge Tarassov represented his country on numerous UN bodies, including the Commission on Human Rights. He attended several Sessions of the UN General Assembly, including special sessions dealing with the Namibian and Arab-Israeli conflicts. He was the head of the USSR Delegation to the 1976-1981 Vienna talks on armaments reductions in Central Europe. In his personal capacity he was member of the Committee for the Elimination of Racial Discrimination and of the International Civil Service Advisory Board (1970-1972).

Judge Tarassov was not destined to complete his term. In September 1994 he passed away in The Hague. During his eight years with the Court he dissented twice, and wrote 4 Declarations. His most outspoken comment on the functioning of the Court is to be found in his 1993 Dissenting Opinion in the *Case Concerning Application of the Convention on the Prevention and Punishment of the Crime of Genocide*, on the conflict in the former Yugoslavia. His deep concern for issues of human rights, apparent throughout his career, inspired the following peroratio:

> The immense sufferings of all the ethnic and religious segments of the population in Bosnia and Herzegovina - Muslims, Serbs, Croats and others ... in my view, provided the Court with every reason to assert its moral authority - as was done recently by the Security Council ... Unfortunately ... the Court, on the most vital issue for all sections of the population of Bosnia and Herzegovina, who might possibly become victims of the crime of genocide - cessation of hostilities and reaching a just and comprehensive political settlement - has preferred to remain silent. (*ICJ Reports* 1993, at p. 452)

Salah El Dine Tarazi

1917-1980

Judge:	1976-1980
Contentious Cases:	3
Advisory Requests:	1
Declarations:	–
Sep. Opinions:	2
Dis. Opinions:	1

Judge Tarazi had been with the Court for four and a half years when he met with a tram accident in The Hague. Thus, in a tragic and untimely way, the life of a strong personality and competent internationalist was cut short. Born in Damascus, Judge Tarazi became a Licentiate of the French school in Beirut in 1939. There he also obtained diplomas in public and private law, and gained a doctorate in 1945. From 1940 onwards he was a practising lawyer and associate professor in Damascus. In 1945 he was appointed Director of the Legal Department of the Syrian Ministry of Finance. In 1949 he switched to the Ministry of Foreign Affairs to become, firstly, Director of Political Affairs, then Secretary-General. He entered the diplomatic service as *Chargé d'affaires* in Belgium (1951), and subsequently became the ambassador of Syria to the USSR (1957-1958; 1965-1970), Turkey (1970-1974) and Ambassador of the UAR to Czechoslovakia (1958-1959) and China (1960-1961). At the same time he was Deputy Permanent Representative (1953-1956) and later Permanent Representative (1962-1964) of Syria to the United Nations. He attended some ten Sessions of the General Assembly and took part in the work of various commissions. In 1949 he attended the Syro-Israeli Armistice Conference, in 1951 he was on the Committee for the Creation of an International Criminal Court, in 1952 he attended the Congress of the Universal Postal Union and in 1953 he was Rapporteur of the Special Committee Defining Aggression. He worked on behalf of the Trusteeship Council, helped to revise the UN Staff Rules and represented Syria at the 1968 Vienna Conference on the Law of Treaties. In 1975 he chaired the Committee that amended the Pact of the League of Arab States. Judge Tarazi was the author of monographs on the Syrian public service, the organization of the judiciary in the new French Constitution and the 'statut personnel' in Arab and African countries.

Judge Tarazi produced 1 Separate and 2 Dissenting Opinions. In the 1980 *Case Concerning the US Diplomatic and Consular Staff in Tehran* he commented:

> I was pleased to note that the Judgment took particular account of the traditions of Islam, which contributed along with others to the elaboration of the rules of contemporary public international law on diplomatic and consular inviolability and immunity. (*ICJ Reports* 1980, at p. 58)

He then quoted from a 1937 Hague Academy lecture by Ahmed Rechid:

> In Arabia, the person of the ambassador had always been regarded as sacred. Muhammad consecrated this inviolability. Never were ambassadors to Muhammad or to his successors molested. One day, the envoy of a foreign nation, at an audience granted to him by the Prophet, was so bold as to use insulting language. Muhammad said to him: 'If you were not an envoy I would have you put to death'. The author of the Siyer, which relates this incident draws from it the conclusion that there is an obligation to respect the person of ambassadors. (*ICJ Reports* 1980, at pp. 58-59)

In the 1976 *Aegean Sea Continental Shelf Case* Judge Tarazi enlarged on the power and role of the Court in the UN System:

> At the same time as it requested the Court to indicate interim measures, Greece turned to the Security Council to request it to examine the situation. ... Now, while the oral proceedings were taking place before the Court, the Security Council ... recommended the parties to continue their negotiations and address themselves, if appropriate, to the Court. There can be no doubt that this .... created a new element... For if it is true and certain that the Court is an independent and judicial organ, and that neither the General Assembly nor the Security Council are able, without the consent of the interested parties, to withdraw from it any case which has been referred to it, it is no less true that it is an integral part of the United Nations ... Such was not the case with the Court's predecessor. The Covenant of the League of Nations did not provide that the PCIJ should be one of its organs. The Court itself had been set up independently of the elaboration and adoption of the Covenant. That being so, the present Court, while maintaining its independence, should not fail to take into consideration this basic truth, namely that it is an integral part of the United Nations. (*ICJ Reports* 1976, at p. 33)

Vladlen Stepanovich Vereshchetin

*1932

Judge:	1994-present
Contentious Cases:	2
Advisory Requests:	1
Declarations:	1 Joint
Sep. Opinions:	1
Dis. Opinions:	–

At about the same time as Judge Vereshchetin was making his solemn declaration as a Member of the ICJ, internationalists were gathering in Moscow to celebrate the 150th birthday of one of the pioneers of the *Œuvre de La Haye*, and the concept of arbitration in general: the St Petersburg scholar F. F. Martens (1845-1909). There could hardly be a more appropriate testimony to illustrate the change of atmosphere in Russian thinking on international law in the past decade. A new biographical study, critical essays, and the reprint of Martens' major treatise, the classic *Contemporary International Law of Civilized Nations* (1882) paid due homage, through him, to the long-standing tradition of international law in pre-revolutionary Russia.

If Martens' Eurocentric ('civilized nations') approach, so typical of the period, may now seem outdated, nonetheless it reminds one of Russia's time-honoured links with Western thought. More than this, Martens' re-evaluation in modern Russia marks the end of what was termed by Western, 'bourgeois' scholars of the inter-war and Cold War periods, the monolithic doctrine of socialist dogma, and of a class-oriented approach to international law.

In the opening up of these new horizons to condition fertile dialogue, Judge Vereshchetin among other Russian scholars, has played a critical role, as can be seen from his contributions to monographs such as *Perestroika and International Law* (1990) and *From Co-existence to Co-operation. International Law and Organization in the Post-Cold War Era* (1991). When one considers the works and career of Judge Vereshchetin, one is reminded of another Russian scholar, i.e. the visionary E. Korovin (1892-1964), who was perhaps the first internationalist to perceive the legal implications of developments in outer space technology. It is precisely to space law that Judge Vereshchetin has devoted most of his energy, at the Moscow Institute of State and Law (that impressive think-tank of its Academy where he worked for the better part of his career) in circles of *Intercosmos*, and in international organizations.

Starting out with a thesis on the law of the sea and his first monograph on freedom of navigation, Judge Vereshchetin soon turned to the atmosphere and outer space. It is only in recent years, and also prompted by circumstance, that he has applied his ample experience in the international sphere to legal issues of a more general import, guided by his inspiring teacher, the polymath and polyglot V. Durdenevsky (1889-1963).

Judge Vereshchetin was born in Briansk and took a higher degree in international law at the Moscow Institute of International Relations. For most of his career he was linked to the Academy of Sciences, notably its Moscow Institute of State and Law, where he defended his dissertation on international space law (1976) and became Deputy Director and Head of the International Law Department in 1981. He became Professor of International Law in 1982, and Vice-President of the Russian International Law Association since 1985.

During the 1960-1980s Judge Vereshchetin was much involved in all topical subjects of space law: he legally advised the Americo-Russian co-operation in the Apollo-Sojuz project, and helped negotiate major intergovernmental agreements on space co-operation. For a long time he was Vice-President of the International Institute of Space Law. During the period 1979-1990 he took part in the work of the UN Committee on the Peaceful Uses of Outer Space and its Legal Sub-Committee. Judge Vereshchetin's publications reflect the successive legal issues at stake, i.e. co-operation in space (1977), the prevention of outer space arms race (1986), and manned space flights (1986). Recently he co-authored and co-edited the new Russian *Course of International Law* (7 volumes, 1989-1993). He has been a Member of the PCA from 1984, a Member of the International Law Commission from 1992, and its Chairman from 1994-1995, when the Commission adopted the draft Statute for an International Criminal Court. He was elected to the ICJ in January 1995.

Charles De Visscher

1884-1973

Judge:	1946-1952
Contentious Cases:	7
Advisory Requests:	6
Declarations:	–
Sep. Opinions:	1
Dis. Opinions:	1 Joint

If one considers the personal life of Charles De Visscher the resemblance with Jules Basdevant is striking: the same setbacks and hardships, yet a similar determination and will to overcome all deprivation. Both men's careers were if anything directed by the successive World Wars, both lost their promising eldest son (a jurist) in the first days of World War II, both then decided to help organise the national resistance movement - and thus almost automatically entered the political sphere. Judge De Visscher even served for six months as a Minister without Portfolio in the first Belgian post-war cabinet.

Charles De Visscher, who was orphaned at an early age, matriculated at Ghent where he graduated and was appointed Professor of Private International Law in 1911. Albéric de Rolin was among his teachers and Henri Rolin was among his first students. Labour contracts were his initial field of research (*Le contrat collectif de travail*, 1911). However, as an evacuee in Oxford during the First World War, his resentment of the German legal justification for its violation of the Belgian neutrality inspired his monograph *Belgium's Case. A Juridical Inquiry* (1916) and made him enter the international sphere. It would dictate the main theme of his work for the rest of his life, the interplay of theory and practice in international relations. His *chef d'œuvre* remains his often reprinted and translated *Théories et réalités* (1953).

During the 1920s De Visscher distinguished himself as a legal counsel, as the young director of the *Revue de droit international et de législation comparée* and of the *Institut de Droit International*. In 1931 he moved from Ghent to Louvain, where he was to teach public international law until his death. The 1920s also saw him gravitate to The Hague, first as a frequent lecturer at the Academy (1923, 1925, 1929, 1935), and later as counsel for the Romanian, Polish and Danish governments in cases before the PCIJ: the *Commissions for the Danube and Oder Rivers*, *Polish Rights in Danzig* and notably the *Eastern Greenland* case. A Member of the PCA from 1923, a delegate to the Rhine Commission, a Member of the 1923 Committee of Jurists and of the Commission for Progressive Codification, his election to the PCIJ in 1937 came as no surprise to associates in the field.

June 1945 saw him at San Francisco, helping to draft the UN Charter and shape the Draft Statute for the ICJ, to which he was then very properly elected for a term of six years in 1946. Charles De Visscher was highly respected: 'l'un des grands juristes du siècle, vénéré et respecté de tous de la vieille génération comme de la jeunesse.' Sadly enough, as it was generally felt, political factors prevented his re-election. As Rosenne puts it (*Law and Practice* 1985, at p. 186):

> ... the undoubted efforts of the Security Council to maintain the balance between the criteria of the Statute in the membership of the Court have not been able to influence the general trend of voting in the General Assembly. These reflections are prompted particularly by the non-election of Judge De Visscher in 1951, for the non-election of a judge of considerable experience and proved competence, after he had received the required absolute majority in the Security Council, is a serious matter.

However, it was precisely the subsequent two decades of leisure that would prove the most creative and productive period of his life. To these years we owe five volumes of diplomatic documents and several monographs. Apart from his *Théories et réalités*, one must mention a Hague Academy Course on the *Principles of International Law* (1954), the well-known *Problèmes d'interprétation judiciaire* (1963), *Les aspects récents du droit procédural de la CIJ* (1966) and tracts on *effectivités* (1959, 1967) and equity in dispute settlement (1972). Concurrently, Charles De Visscher presided over arbitration tribunals (*Buraimi Oasis*, 1958; *Détournement de l'avion des chefs nationalistes algériens*, 1962; *Red Crusader*, 1962) and helped to launch the *Revue belge*. Life had taught Charles De Visscher to be realistic about the function of law in society. Without being a devotee of natural law or an excessive voluntary positivist, he stressed the need for morality in international relations.

1904-1981

Judge:	1973-1981
President:	1979-1981
Contentious Cases:	8
Advisory Requests:	3
Declarations:	5
Sep. Opinions:	2
Dis. Opinions:	2

Humphrey Waldock

Virtually all Judges, of any period in the history of the Court, can show an impressive record of service. Yet no one else can boast, as could Sir Humphrey at the close of his life, of having presided over the Court at The Hague, the Court at Strasbourg, the European Commission of Human Rights and the International Law Commission. How can one typify such a man? He was a man of strong character, yet not a man of monolithic views. As a scholar, he sought for balance between the old and the new, and was susceptible to the need for flexibility in situations of apparent social change. On the bench he strove to promote a collegiate policy, and broadly-based and therefore authoritative decisions, though not at any price. Inflexible he was in just one respect: in his insistence on strict impartiality in any case he was involved with - to the point of not wishing to speak to British counsel.

Claude Humphrey Meredith Waldock was born in what was then Ceylon and educated at Uppingham School and Brasenose College, Oxford. He was called to the Bar at Gray's Inn in 1928, joined the Midland Circuit and practised for a time; he took silk in 1951. Except for his war years at the Admiralty, he remained a tutor at Brasenose until 1947. His prime interests at the time were equity, real property and the law of mortgages. In 1947 he was elected to the Chichele Chair at Oxford, which brought him into the international sphere, and at times he carried out missions for the British Government. In 1953, Secretary-General Dag Hammarskjøld took him to the People's Republic of China on a delicate mission concerning the detention of airmen from the UN forces in Korea.

Judge Waldock was elected to the European Commission of Human Rights in 1954 and was its President from 1955-1961. He became Editor of the *British Year Book* (1955-1973) - for which he wrote a famous article on 'The Decline of the Optional Clause' - , and Vice President of the *Institut* from 1963-1965. In 1963 he edited Brierly's *Law of Nations*. In 1967 he chaired the ILC; from 1961-1966 he was its Special Rapporteur on the Law of Treaties (6 Reports), and from 1968-1972 on Succession of States in Respect of Treaties (4 Reports). These reports were perhaps his most impressive publications. In 1966 he was elected Judge of the European Court of Human Rights, was Vice-President in 1968 and became President in 1971. A Member of the PCA, he was Counsel for Great Britain before the ICJ in three cases. Later he acted as Counsel for India, Spain, Denmark and the Netherlands.

He was elected Judge in 1973 and became President of the Court in 1979. His term was cut short by his sudden death at The Hague on 15 August 1981. In the *Nuclear Tests* cases 'he participated in a densely reasoned Joint Dissenting Opinion which showed a willingness to grasp nettles not always evident in the policies of the majority in those cases'. As President in *US Diplomatic and Consular Staff in Tehran*, he led the Court in its rapid and decisive issuance of provisional measures and its adoption of a judgment widely viewed as exemplary. As Ian Brownlie, whom we quote here, argues in his evaluation of Waldock's life (*BYBIL* 1982), his years at The Hague were a difficult period for the Court. Too often it was confronted with respondent States that failed to appear. Sir Humphrey's search for cohesion and effectiveness was beyond complaint. As Judge Elias wrote:

> All ... admired his enormous industry, his direct grasp of the issues in a case, and his gift of lucid exposition and drafting. ... no reader of Sir Humphrey's vigorous Separate or Dissenting Opinions will doubt the extent of his contribution ... Behind the orderly process of discussion and debate which he was the first to safeguard and promote, one could always detect from the look, the posture - and occasionally a sigh - a chafing eagerness to press on.

Brownlie, in his final analysis, states:

> Waldock always expounded his views with great clarity and careful ordering of the material. ... He was a keen observer of the behaviour of States and was well aware of the underlying issues of policy ... His wavelength was a good balance of optimism and scepticism, and he did not badger students with any special brand of idealism or with fashionable ideas borrowed from that most vacuous of spheres, political science. (*op.cit.*, at p. 63)

Christopher Gregory Weeramantry

*1926

Judge:	1991–present
Contentious Cases:	14
Advisory Requests:	1
Declarations:	1 Joint
Sep. Opinions:	2
Dis. Opinions:	4

Throughout his forensic, judicial and academic career Judge Weeramantry has shown himself a man of broad interests. He has lectured in every continent and is a prolific author. Yet, at the root of a myriad of activities and publications, two elements are distinguishable: a deep social conscience and a truly philosophical bent of mind, inspired by Eastern and Western sources of law, letters and wisdom alike. He draws from Plato, Stone or Cardozo as readily as from Hindu or Buddhist sources.

Typical of his universalist approach is the monograph *The Law in Crisis: Bridges of Understanding* (1975), of which Lord Denning wrote in his Foreword that it was 'Not for the lawyers only. But for all who would look beyond today into the unknown tomorrow'. In it Judge Weeramantry contends that the present insistence of the legal profession on functioning in terms of formalistic procedures and concepts may in the end result in an overall indifference towards the legal system itself.

Judge Weeramantry was born in Colombo, Sri Lanka and was awarded the LL.D. of London University for his two-volume treatise on the Roman Dutch law, English law and Customary Law of Contract, as practised in Sri Lanka, described by *The Law Quarterly Review* as comparable, in its field, only with the 'magisterial treatise' of Wessels. The first part of his career (1948-1965) was spent as an Advocate of the Supreme Court of Sri Lanka and as a lecturer at the Ceylon Law College. He assumed judicial office in 1965 as Commissioner of Assize and became a Justice of the Supreme Court in 1967, the youngest in its nearly 200 year history. As Justice Weeramantry, his judgments on the Roman Dutch law and on Islamic law received recognition beyond Sri Lanka, being referred to in other jurisdictions.

From 1972 until his election in 1990 to the Court, he was Sir Hayden Starke Professor of Law at Monash University in Melbourne. At the World Congress on Equality and Freedom, held in 1976 at St Louis, Missouri to mark the US Bicentennial, three speeches analysed equality and freedom from the standpoint of the Western, the Communist and the developing world. Professor Weeramantry, as he then was, was invited to make the presentation for the developing world. This was the basis of his later work *Equality and Freedom: Some Third World Perspectives*.

Judge Weeramantry has also written monographs on *Human Rights in Japan* (1979), *Apartheid: The Closing Phases?* (1980), *Nuclear Weapons and Scientific Responsibility* (1987), *Islamic Jurisprudence: An International Perspective* (1988), and *Nauru: Environmental Damage under International Trusteeship* (1992). *An Invitation to the Law* (1980) is a jurisprudential and comparativist approach to law. *The Slumbering Sentinels: Law and Human Rights in the Wake of Technology* (1983) and *Law: The Threatened Peripheries* (1984) warn of impending dangers to legal order, particularly from technology. He has also edited two volumes for the United Nations University - a theoretical study (1990) and a set of global case-studies (1993) on the impact of technology on human rights. Judge Weeramantry was Chairman of the Nauru Commission, which inquired into international responsibility for phosphate mining of that island. The 10-volume Report of this Commission led to the institution of Nauru's case against Australia in the ICJ and Judge Weeramantry excused himself from participation in this case. He has, at the time of writing, rendered 4 Dissenting and 2 Separate Opinions. Noteworthy are his searching dissent to the Court's recent Order rejecting New Zealand's request to re-open the *Nuclear Tests* judgment and his 70-page Opinion in the 1993 Judgment on the *Jan Mayen* case, devoted to the concept of equity. In stressing the value of equity for international law, he characteristically draws upon such cross-cultural sources as Sophocles' *Antigone*, the notion of *dharma* in *The Bhagavad Gita*, Buddhist legal conceptions, Judaic philosophy, Matthew, and Qur'an Surah 5: 'If thou judge, judge in equity between them, for God loveth those who judge in equity', to conclude:

> Of equity, perhaps more than of any other department of legal thought, it could truly be said that, 'Under the surface eddies created by the decisions of individual cases, there surges a mighty tide of the fundamental principles of justice'. (*ICJ Reports* 1993, at pp. 278-279)

1888-1985

Judge:	1957-1967
Vice–President:	1964-1967
Contentious Cases:	17
Advisory Requests:	2
Declarations:	2
Sep. Opinions:	5
Dis. Opinions:	3 (1 Joint)

V.K. Wellington Koo

Judge Wellington Koo died at the age of 97, so that the years he spent at the Court, his seventies, were not exactly the last years of his life. Still, when one is dealing with a man who was Prime Minister of China at the age of 37 and had been in the forefront of political debate throughout the inter-war period one may perhaps call that period the 'sunset years'. Indeed, Judge Wellington Koo's impressive career reached its pinnacle during the days of the League and the earliest years of its successor, the United Nations. Dumbarton Oaks, San Francisco and the UN Preparatory Commissions were the fora that availed themselves of his mature genius and his long years of experience of international issues.

Judge Wellington Koo had a western legal training at Columbia, where he obtained a Doctorate with a thesis on *The Status of the Alien in China*. From 1912 to 1915 he was a government official, and helped to draft the Constitution for the young Republic. A Minister to Mexico, Cuba and the USA from 1915 to 1920, he headed the Chinese Delegation to the 1919 Versailles Conference. A First Delegate to the League Assembly and Chinese Representative on its Council, he was Plenipotentiary at the 1921-1922 Washington talks on arms reduction. From 1922-1924 he was Foreign Minister, in the following two years Finance Minister and from 1926-1927 both Prime Minister and Foreign Minister. In 1932, not long after the Mukden Incident, he assisted the League Commission on the Manchurian question, and compiled the *Memorandum to the Lytton Commission*. He then became Ambassador to France until well into World War II (1932-1941). During the remaining war years (1941-1946) he was Ambassador to Great Britain.

During the 1930s Judge Wellington Koo was Representative of China at the League, the Armaments Reduction Conference (1933) and the Far East Conference (1937). In 1934 he became a Member of the PCA. He attended San Francisco and helped to constitute the United Nations. During the decade prior to his election to the Court (1946-1956) he was Ambassador to the USA. He participated in the War Crimes Commission and attended the 1946-1949 Sessions of the General Assembly.

In 1956 Judge Wellington Koo was asked by his Government to complete the remaining year of the term of Judge Hsu Mo who had died. In April he sailed on the *Nieuw Amsterdam*, and a year later he was re-elected. The cases in which he participated occasioned 2 Declarations, 5 Separate and 3 Dissenting Opinions. During his Vice-Presidency he dissented in the *South West Africa* case. As recorded elsewhere, in 1967 his Government no longer proposed a candidate, in view of the changing attitude within the UN on the Chinese representation issue. The seat on the Court was passed to the candidate from the Philippines. Judge Wellington Koo retired to his Park Avenue apartment to compile his *Reminiscences*.

In his monograph on *The Prospects of International Adjudication*, Wilfred Jenks refers to Judge Wellington Koo's Dissenting Opinion in the *Temple of Preah Vihear* case, where the Judge observes that the legal significance of the conduct of a State may vary by reason of conditions in a given part of the world at a particular period. Judge Wellington Koo considered that whether given facts created a presumption of acquiescence in the absence of protest, must be determined in the light of customary ways of Oriental courtesy and prevailing conditions in Asia at the time (Jenks, *op. cit.*, at p. 279).

In his Separate Opinion in the 1964 *Barcelona Traction* case Judge Wellington Koo states the following:

> International law, being primarily based upon the general principles of law and justice, is unfettered by technicalities and formalistic considerations which are often given importance in municipal law. As has already been stated above, the fundamental right of diplomatic intervention of a State to protect its nationals against another State and to seek redress for them for any wrongful act on its part aims generally to protect the genuine interests of its nationals. It is the reality which counts more than the appearance. It is the equitable interest which matters rather than the legal interest. In other words it is the substance which carries weight on the international plane rather than the form. (*ICJ Reports* 1964, at pp. 62-63)

Bohdan Stefan Winiarski

1884-1969

Judge:	1946-1967
President:	1961-1964
Contentious Cases:	36
Advisory Requests:	12
Declarations:	2
Sep. Opinions:	3
Dis. Opinions:	9

On connait le rôle que les grands cours d'eau jouèrent dans l'histoire de toutes les civilisations. Reclus à écrit quelque part que les fleuves roulent dans leurs flots l'histoire et la vie des nations. ... Le droit fluvial international suivra son cours aussi sûrement invariablement que les fleuves eux-mêmes suivent le leur. (*RDC* 45 (1933-III), at pp. 84 and 212)

The ICJ has known two Polish Judges: Judge Winiarski and Judge Lachs. Both were very gifted personalities and both led dramatically eventful lives. They both served international organizations for no less than half a century and between them they almost span the full 50 years of the history of the Court. While on the Bench, they both masterfully steered their course amid Cold War tensions and, in acknowledgement of their merits, were elected President of the Court.

Judge Winiarski studied law at Warsaw, Cracow, Heidelberg and Paris. He was lecturing on constitutional law at Cracow when, in 1915, he was enlisted in the Russian Army. In 1917 he joined the Polish National Committee in Paris and served as Legal Adviser to the Paris Peace Conference (1919-1920). He then returned to teach international law in Poznan. Gifted with the talent to link theory with practice he served on diplomatic missions to the 1921 Barcelona Conference and to the League of Nations. From 1925 to 1946 he was President of the League Committee on River Law. In this capacity he also served as Assessor to the PCIJ in matters of Communication and, not surprisingly, he was the Agent of Poland in the 1929 *River Oder* case. He returned in 1933 to lecture at the Hague Academy.

Judge Winiarski was a prolific author on such diverse subjects as air law, Polish political institutions, security, arbitration, disarmament, self-defence, and communications. He translated Vattel's *Droit des gens* into Polish. His speciality, though, was international river law.

> Winiarski was a realist; he tried to approach all situations with a careful and sound analysis. Committed to the rule of law, he seemed as both a scholar and a practitioner to have been ever watchful lest it remain helpless through disregard of the circumstances in which it was to be applied. (Lachs, *Teacher* 1987, at p. 135)

During the inter-war period, Winiarski was an active politician. He was Commissioner for the liquidation of German property (1924-1927) and Deputy in the Polish Diet (1928-1935) where he opposed the Pilsudski regime. In September 1939 he was arrested and deported with his family while his property was confiscated. He was able to join the Polish Government-in-exile in London, took up the Presidency of the London-based Bank of Poland and taught international law at Oxford. In 1944 he joined Malkin's Committee on the Future of the PCIJ. In 1946 he was elected Judge and allotted three years. In 1949 he was re-elected and again in 1957. In 1961 he became President. His time in office has only been surpassed by his successor Judge Lachs.

Judge Winiarski rendered no less than 9 Dissenting Opinions. This is not to say that he dissented more vehemently than most of his colleagues. As with the other East European Judges, one must keep in mind that they represented an outspoken social philosophy which, by definition, constituted a minority on a Bench whose views are determined by a majority. As the final draft of a Judgment of the ICJ (in which so many social spheres and legal traditions are represented) is in itself almost inevitably a negotiated compromise, the Socialist Judges, if only to have their views made known to the world at large, often resorted to Separate Opinions. Incidentally, this is a perfectly legitimate way of expressing one's divergent views and the use made of it by the East European Judges only serves to emphasize the value of the instrument. To take an example: Judge Winiarski's personal ideas were in line with Soviet doctrine in his rigid opposition to any decision being taken *ex aequo et bono*. In his 1962 Opinion appended to the *South West Africa* Judgment he commented severely on this issue. His outstanding judicial independence was however demonstrated in his *South West Africa* vote of 1966.

1893-1985

Judge: 1954–1961 / 1964-1973	
Vice–President:	1958-1961
President:	1970-1973
Contentious Cases:	21 + 5
Advisory Requests:	4 + 2
Declarations:	8
Sep. Opinions:	1
Dis. Opinions:	–

Muhammad Zafrulla Khan

In 1970 Judge Zafrulla Khan, 'The Silent Judge' as he was once called, had the honour of being elected the first Asian President of the Court. A former member of the Supreme Court of India (1941-1947) and a former President of the General Assembly of the United Nations, Zafrulla Khan was a deeply religious man who has to his credit monographs such as *Islam. Its meaning for modern man* (1962) and *Pilgrimage to the House of Allah* (1970).

Four times an Indian Minister between 1932 and 1939, with the portfolios of Education; Railways; Commerce and War Supply successively, Judge Zafrulla Khan was to serve as first Minister for Foreign Affairs of the newly created Republic of Pakistan from 1947 to 1954. Having been head of the Indian Delegation to the League of Nations in 1939, he became Permanent Representative of Pakistan to the United Nations from 1961 to 1964.

Even his service on the Bench of the Court was interrupted in an unprecedented manner as he served from 1954 to 1961, was not re-elected, but returned three years later, from 1964 to 1973. He was Vice-President towards the end of his first term, and President in the closing years of his second term. Judge Zafrulla Khan, who also served as Judge *ad hoc* in the case of the *Trial of Pakistani Prisoners of War* in 1973, left a lasting impression on his colleagues. Reciprocally, in a 'personal narrative' (*Servant of God*, 1983) he on his part devoted some 25 most lively and interesting pages to his personal experiences with the Court, the Judges, the Registry and the Dutch social entourage.

Sir Muhammad Zafrulla Khan was a Bachelor of Arts from Punjab University (1911) and a Bachelor of Laws from King's College, London (1914), where he became an Honorary Fellow in 1937. He held Honorary Doctorates from Cambridge and several American universities. He became a Barrister-at-Law of Lincoln's Inn in 1914 and an Honorary Bencher in 1945. From 1914 to 1935 he practised as Advocate at the Lahore High Court. He was a Member of the Punjab Legislative Assembly in 1927-1935 and Delegate to the Round Table Conferences on Indian Reforms in 1930-1932. As stated above, during the 1930s he held several Ministerial portfolios. In 1947 he served as Constitutional Adviser to His Highness the Ruler of Bhopal. In 1962-1963 he presided over the UN General Assembly. His first election to the ICJ in 1954, to fill the vacancy occasioned by the death of the Indian Judge Sir Benegal Rau, was a bitter contest with the Indian candidate. Sir Zafrulla Khan has written interestingly about this in his memoirs, already referred to, in which he he looks back on the period, giving a wealth of detail, also of private affairs:

> There was an Ahmadiyyah mosque at The Hague and thus he had available a spiritual asylum, which for a short while became his home also. ... Eventually he purchased a small apartment in Scheveningen, not far from the beach. His early morning walk to the Peace Palace was a source of delight in all weathers. (in *Servant of God*)

In 1961 Judge Zafrulla Khan was not re-elected:

> One morning, the Deputy Registrar, a very good friend, came in, a little flustered, and said: 'I bring you bad news. None of the outgoing Judges have been re-elected'. There is nothing bad in this news. If such is God's design, I am content. He obviously desires that I should serve in some other capacity, His will be done. (*op.cit.*, p. 231)

When he left in 1961 the then President Basdevant wrote him a letter of farewell:

> When you were elected to the Court, having known of your activities in the United Nations, I was apprehensive that you might bring to bear on your work on the Court a political rather than a judicial outlook. But during the exchange of views on cases coming before the Court, my apprehension was soon dispelled. I found you an experienced jurist and judge. You studied every case carefully and possessed the faculty of separating the relevant and the important from the irrelevant and unimportant. Often your views helped me to clarify my own. In the exchange of views, I waited eagerly for the expression of your view.' Coming from President Basdevant this was high praise indeed, perhaps not altogether deserved, but an accolade just the same.

Milovan Zoričić

1884-1971

Judge:	1946-1958
Contentious Cases:	27
Advisory Requests:	10
Declarations:	3
Sep. Opinions:	1
Dis. Opinions:	3

Now, it is a fundamental rule of international law that no State can be compelled to submit its disputes with other States to any procedure, judicial or otherwise, without its consent. That legal rule is founded on the principle of the sovereign equality of States, a principle which is the corollary of independence and which is expressly recognized by the Charter of the United Nations. (ICJ Reports 1950, at pp. 99-100)

Judge Zoričić obtained his Doctorate of Law degree at Zagreb. He travelled extensively through Europe before embarking upon a judicial career at the Zagreb District Court. In 1910 he was attached to the Attorney-General's office at Zagreb as Legal Agent for the Treasury and Adviser to the Government of Croatia and Slavonia.

In 1918, after the political upheaval, he helped to organize the new Yugoslav Administration. He was Head of the Political Department of the Croatian-Slavonic Administration and in 1929 President of the Administrative Court.

His international career started in 1932 when he was invited by the Council of the League of Nations to join the Governing Commission of the Saar Territory. He was its Vice-President when in 1935 he was appointed a Member of the PCA. In 1936 he was chosen as a Judge *ad hoc* of the PCIJ in the *Pajs-Csáky-Esterházy* and *Losinger* cases.

After the occupation of Yugoslavia in 1941 he was dismissed from office and arrested. In 1945 he attended the First Session of the UN General Assembly before being elected to serve as Judge at the Zagreb Supreme Court of Justice. In 1946 he was elected to the ICJ for three years. He was re-elected in 1949 and served a full term. He wrote 3 Declarations of Dissent, 1 Separate and 3 Dissenting Opinions, twice in Advisory procedures.

The 1948 request from the General Assembly concerning the *Conditions of Admission of a State to Membership of the United Nations* provoked severe comments from Judge Zoričić (as well as from Judges Krylov and Winiarski; the East European Judges being unanimous and adamant on this occasion):

> The Court is thus drawn on to the slippery ground of politics, and its reply may well become an instrument in political disputes between States. This may do considerable harm to the Court's prestige and to the confidence that the Court should inspire in all nations if it is to fulfill its important duties as guardian of the law and principal judicial organ of the United Nations. (*ICJ Reports* 1947-1948, at p. 95)

The same situation arose once more in 1950, and with respect to the same Judges, in the matter of the Advisory Opinion regarding problems that had arisen with respect to the *Interpretation of Peace Treaties* concluded in 1947 by the Allied Powers with Bulgaria, Hungary and Romania. Here, the East European Judges insisted that the Court lacked jurisdiction to deal with the request for an opinion. The issue, they maintained, could not be submitted to the Court when the three nations involved were vehemently protesting against such procedure.

Judge Zoričić argued that the present request was nothing more than a round-about way of circumventing procedural problems that would have confronted the Court in a contentious procedure. It therefore amounted to an improper use of the advisory facilities made available by the Court and could serve as a psychological means of pressure on the Governments of the States involved (*ICJ Reports* 1950, at p. 102).

Moreover, the Socialist Judges argued, the proceedings in question ran counter to the principle of independence of States and were tantamount to an interference in the internal affairs of the States concerned - particularly in matters of human rights (for these were the issues at stake) - an area which, in the Eastern European view, was generally reserved for the competence of the internal administration and judiciary. It is against this historical background that the step taken in 1988 by the Gorbachev Administration to drop its reservations on Human Rights Conventions is to be seen.

CHAPTER TEN BY ARTHUR WITTEVEEN

A Review of the Court's Case-Law

Since it came into being in 1946 the Court has dealt with a total of 96 cases, 74 of which have been contentious cases between States, while the remaining 22 have related to requests for advisory opinions by international organizations. In those cases the Court has handed down 60 judgments and 21 advisory opinions.

It is hoped that the short review of the Court's case-law given below will present the reader with a relatively complete overview of the ways in which the Court has contributed to the achievement of the purposes and principles set forth in the UN Charter, especially in relation to the attainment of peace and justice and the development and primacy of international law.

At the outset it should however be clear that the aim of this review is to give a general impression of the nature of the Court's work rather than an exhaustive enumeration of the cases it has dealt with. This has implied a grouping of those cases under common headings, according to a classification which reflects the particular views of the author. Taking the first case brought before the Court, the *Corfu Channel* case, as an example, the reader will find that case under the heading 'disputes concerning the law of the sea', while one might equally argue that the questions of territorial sovereignty and of State responsibility raised by the case should lead to a different classification.

One other proviso should be made before entering upon the task at hand; namely that in a considerable number of cases brought unilaterally before the Court by one State (the Applicant State), the competence of the Court was contested by the Respondent State. The grounds on which such contestation is based have to do either with the Court's jurisdiction in general (questions of jurisdiction) or with the 'nature' or circumstances of the particular case (questions of admissibility). If the Court's jurisdiction or the admissibility of the Application have been contested, the Court will first decide those questions, in a full Judgment, before entering upon the merits of the dispute. Thus, in the description that follows, reference is sometimes made to a judgment of the Court on questions of jurisdiction or admissibility even if the fact that jurisdiction was contested, or the arguments on which this was based, are not mentioned.

The Temple of Preah Vihear.

Territorial and Boundary Disputes

A considerable number of cases have concerned territorial disputes. In 1953 the Court had before it a case between France and the United Kingdom concerning certain islets in the English Channel which the Court decided were under British sovereignty. In 1959 the Court found in favour of a claim put forward by Belgium against the Netherlands with regard to some enclaves near the Belgian-Dutch frontier. In a 1960 decision the Court found that Portugal had, in 1954, a right of passage over Indian territory between its enclaves situated therein, but only in respect of private persons, civil officials and goods in general, not of armed forces, armed police and arms and ammunition; and that India had not acted contrary to the obligations imposed on it by the existence of that right. And in the 1959-1962 case concerning the Temple of Preah Vihear, located in the border area between Cambodia and Thailand, the Court decided that that temple was actually on Cambodian territory, and that consequently Thailand had to withdraw.

In 1985 fighting broke out between Burkina Faso and Mali while those two West African States were involved in proceedings before a Chamber of the Court in relation to a frontier dispute. Notwithstanding these difficulties, which made it necessary for the Chamber to indicate provisional measures in order to prevent an aggravation of the dispute, the frontier line as determined by the Chamber in its final decision of December 1986 was fully accepted by the two countries, whose two Presidents sent appreciative letters to the President of the Chamber of the Court.

Disputed territory .... a patch of desert is at the centre of a land wrangle between Chad and Libya

PHOTOGRAPH: JOHN ISAAC

Justice sans frontières

For decades the International Court was out of favour – now nations are lining up to settle their disputes

pear. In 1973 France refused to accept jurisdiction after New Zealand and Australia asked the court to ban French nuclear tests. In 1966, the court refused to deal with a complaint from Ethiopia and Liberia on South Africa's rule of South-West

court's bark is far worse than its bite. "I believe that the court has re-established its reputation as an international tribunal. But if a country refuses to comply with a ruling, what can you do about it? You don't have a police force at your

The Guardian, 5 October 1993.

Another territorial dispute, also dealt with by a Chamber of the Court, was between El Salvador and Honduras in Central America. The dispute related to six sectors of the land boundary, the legal status of certain islands in the Gulf of Fonseca, and the legal status of the waters both inside and outside that Gulf. It had evolved over the years, from the time the two States had gained their independence from Spain in the first half of the 19th century and had become members of the subsequently created Federal Republic of Central America.

Some of the questions concerning the status of the Gulf of Fonseca had been the subject of a decision by the Central American Court of Justice in 1917. Further, unsuccessful, negotiations had continued over several decades when, in 1969, the so-called 'football war' broke out between the two countries. The occasion was a football match between them in the World Championship; the cause was the underlying tensions of the long-standing frontier dispute. That short but intense period of fighting, which the Organization of American States succeeded in stopping only after several thousand lives had been lost, led to renewed negotiations resulting in the conclusion of a Peace Treaty in 1980 in which the Parties provided for the referral of their dispute to the Court. The Chamber's delimitation of the frontier, which followed a period of five years during which the Parties presented their arguments, was again fully accepted by those parties, thus finally settling a 90-year old dispute.

The most recent territorial dispute to be decided by the Court was between Libya and Chad. Those two States had, since the time of their independence, been involved in a dispute over their borderlands, notably the so-called Aouzou Strip, situated in the Sahara desert, near the Tibesti Mountains. Serious hostilities broke out between the two countries, during which Libya occupied the whole of the Aouzou Strip. Mediation by the Organization of African Unity brought about the conclusion of a treaty in which the two countries undertook to continue negotiating for one more year and, in the event of the negotiations not proving successful, to lay their dispute before the Court. This is in fact what happened.

In February 1994 the Court delivered its Judgment, in which it found that the boundary between the two countries was defined by a 1955 treaty between France (Chad at that time being under French colonial administration) and the Kingdom of Libya. On that basis the Aouzou Strip effectively belonged to Chad. The two Parties concluded an agreement on the implementation of the Court's Judgment which, in the beginning of May 1994, led to the establishment by the Security Council of the UN Aouzou Strip Observer Group to supervise the withdrawal of all Libyan troops from that territory. By the end of May all those troops had in fact been withdrawn.

Pending before the Court is a dispute which Cameroon brought against Nigeria in March 1994. Cameroon, referring to 'an aggression by the Federal Republic of

HMS Mauritius and HMS Saumarez in the Corfu Channel.

Nigeria, whose troops are occupying several Cameroonian localities on the Bakassi Peninsula' and to skirmishes in the Lake Chad area, requested the Court to decide on the whole of 'the frontier between Cameroon and Nigeria from Lake Chad to the sea'.

Disputes Concerning the Law of the Sea

In the very first case referred to it, concerning damage suffered by British warships passing through Albanian waters in the Corfu Channel, the Court found, in 1949, that the mines which had caused the damage could not have been laid without the knowledge of Albania and that consequently that State was obliged to give warning to vessels passing through the strait; Albania therefore had to pay compensation. The Court also found that a right of innocent passage existed for warships through international straits in time of peace and that consequently the United Kingdom had not violated Albanian sovereignty by the passage of its warships. It had however done so by its subsequent minesweeping operation in the strait, which had been undertaken without the consent of Albania.

The rules on innocent passage and on the obligations of coastal states which the Court had found to exist were later incorporated into the 1958 Convention on the Territorial Sea and the Contiguous Zone as well as into the subsequent 1982 UN Convention on the Law of the Sea. In May 1992, the United Kingdom and Albania reached an understanding which provided for the payment by the latter State of compensation and for the return by the United Kingdom of Albanian gold which had been kept in the vaults of the Bank of England since the Second World War.

In a fisheries dispute between the United Kingdom and Norway, in which it gave judgment in 1951, the Court decided that the use of straight lines connecting the outermost points and islands off the coast, following the general direction of that coast, as the baselines for the measurement of the breadth of the territorial sea - as had been Norway's practice - was not contrary to international law.

In 1974, in two parallel cases brought by the United Kingdom and Germany against Iceland concerning a dispute which had led to the so-called 'Cod War', the Court found that Iceland could not, as it had purported to do by its legislation of 1972, unilaterally extend from 12 to 50 nautical miles its exclusive fishing rights and exclude British and German fishing vessels from areas which lay beyond the limits which had been agreed between the three States in 1961.

In this group there is a further cluster of cases which concern the existence and the delimitation of the continental shelf, the exclusive economic zone or fisheries zones. In two cases brought in 1969 by Germany and Denmark and Germany and the Netherlands respectively, the Court considered that the continental shelf constituted a 'natural prolongation of [a State's] land territory into and under the sea' and that its delimitation was to be effected 'by agreement in accordance with equitable principles and taking account of all the relevant circumstances'. This jurisprudence of the Court influenced the drafting of Article 76 of the 1982 Convention on the Law of the Sea which defines the continental shelf, as well as of Articles 74 and 83 which prescribe the method of delimitation for the exclusive economic zone and the continental shelf.

Another continental shelf delimitation case was brought to the Court by Greece in August 1976. Great tension had arisen at that time because of the exploratory actions of a Turkish vessel in what Greece alleged was its continental shelf in the Aegean Sea. The dispute had also been brought before the Security Council. The Court, after declining to indicate interim measures of protection, found in its 1978 Judgment that, although a legal dispute existed between the two countries, it had no jurisdiction to entertain the Application by Greece.

A subsequent delimitation case, concerning the continental shelf between Tunisia and Libya, was laid before the Court by the two States Parties upon the basis of a Special Agreement. In that case, Malta made a request for permission to intervene because it considered that its legal interests in the continental shelf might be affected by the Court's decision. After the Court declined to grant permission, and rendered judgment between Tunisia and Libya, Libya and Malta concluded an agreement to bring their dispute before the Court. Although Italy requested permission to intervene in the second case as Malta had done in the first, and the Court likewise rejected that request, this did not result in a third case.

The case between Libya and Tunisia was one of delimitation between adjacent States, although because of the concavity of the Tunisian coast, the continental shelves were partly lying opposite each other. The second case (Libya/Malta) was a matter of delimitation between States whose coasts were wholly opposite. In both cases the Court once more invoked equitable principles and relevant circumstances, and referred in that connection *inter alia* to the configuration of the coasts and the principle of proportionality between the extent of the continental shelf and the length of the coastline.

In 1981 Canada and the USA asked the Court to form the first *ad hoc* Chamber to decide upon their delimitation dispute in the Gulf of Maine area. The Chamber was requested to draw a single maritime boundary for both the continental shelf and the 200-mile exclusive fisheries zone. In doing so the Chamber, in its 1984 Judgment, presented a catalogue of equitable principles as follows:

> There has been no systematic definition of the equitable criteria that may be taken into consideration for an international maritime delimitation, and this would in any event be difficult *a priori*, because of their highly variable adaptability to different concrete situations. Codification efforts have left this field untouched. Such criteria have however been mentioned in the arguments advanced by the parties in cases concerning the determination of continental shelf boundaries, and in the arbitral decisions in those cases. There is, for example, the criterion expressed by the classic formula that the land dominates the sea; the criterion advocating, in cases where no special circumstances required correction thereof, the equal division of the areas of overlap of the maritime and submarine zones appertaining to the respective coasts of neighbouring States; the criterion that, whenever possible, the seaward extension of a State's coast should not encroach upon areas that are too close to the coast of another State; the criterion of preventing, as far as possible, any cut-off of the seaward projection of the coast or of part of the coast of either of the States concerned; and the criterion whereby, in certain circumstances, the appropriate consequences may be drawn

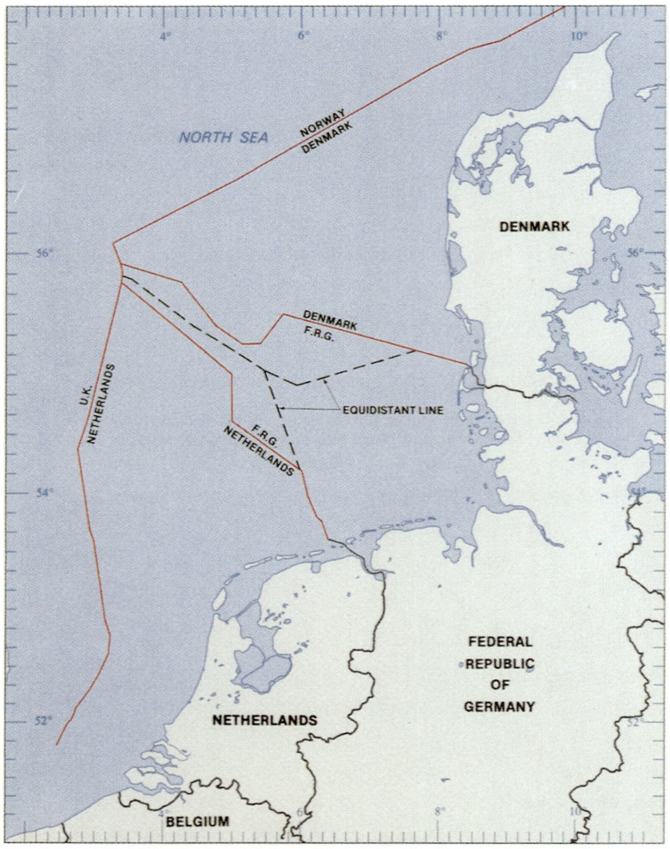

AGREED NORTH SEA CONTINENTAL SHELF BOUNDARIES AS COMPARED TO EQUIDISTANT LINES

The red lines represent the continental shelf boundaries established by agreements between the States concerned. The black, dashed lines represent the equidistant lines that had been proposed as boundaries by Denmark and the Netherlands.

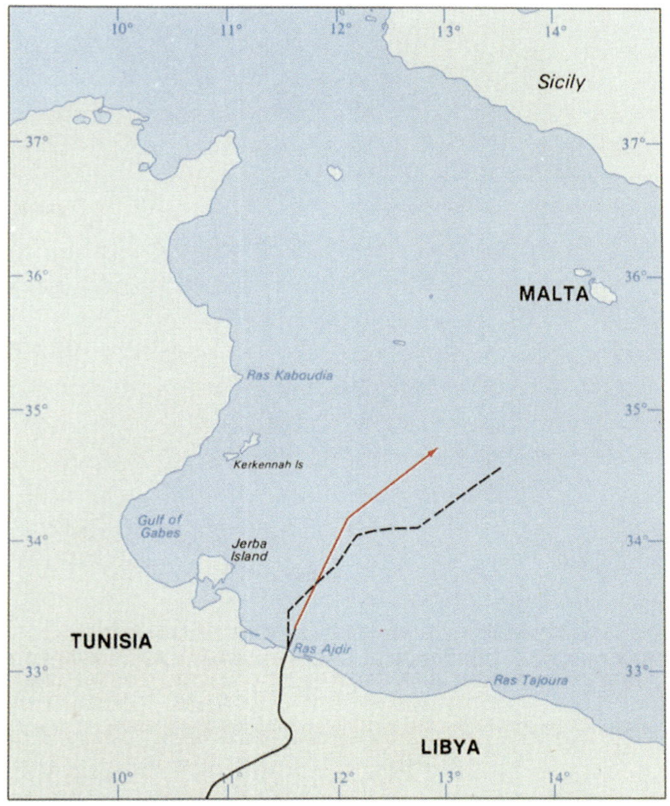

TUNISIA/LIBYA CONTINENTAL SHELF BOUNDARY AS COMPARED TO THE EQUIDISTANT LINE

The red line represents the continental shelf boundary as described in *I.C.J. Reports 1982*, p. 90, map No. 3. The black, dashed line is the equidistant line.

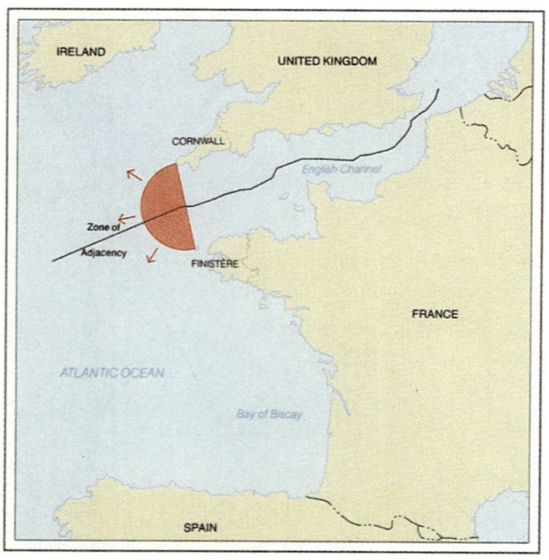

Figure 7

The Opposite or Adjacent Relationship of the Coasts Relative to the Atlantic Region in the Anglo-French Continental Shelf Arbitration

Line determined by the Court of Arbitration in the 1977 Anglo-French Continental Shelf Award

Zone of Oppositeness

The application of the mathematical analysis of the opposite or adjacent relationship of coasts relative to the area to be delimited demonstrates that the relationship of the coasts of Cornwall and Finistère vis-à-vis the greater part of the area delimited by the Court in the Atlantic Region is predominantly adjacent.

Projection – Mercator
Scale – 1:10 000 000 at 48°N

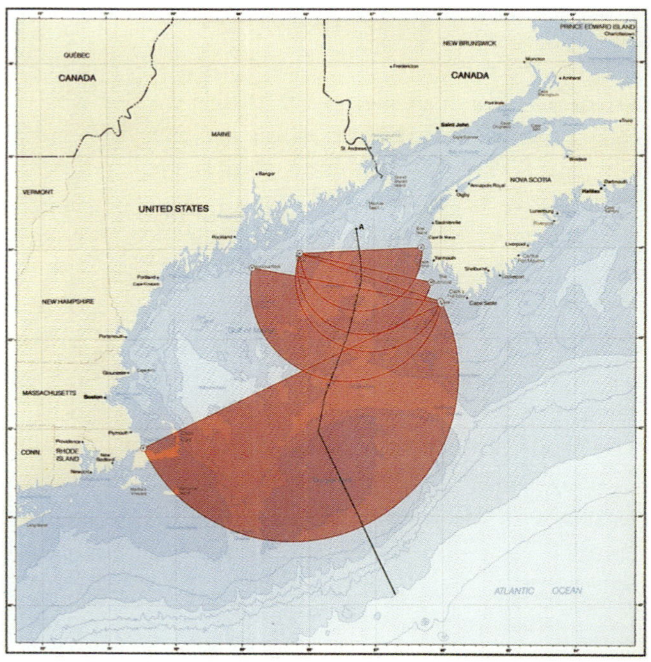

Figure 8

Mathematical Analysis of the Opposite or Adjacent Relationship of the Coasts Relative to the Area to be Delimited, as Applied to the Basepoints Used in the Construction of the Canadian Line

Basepoints used in the construction of the Canadian line

Zones of oppositeness

Depths in Metres
Projection – Mercator

Maps showing examples of the application of several delimitation techniques and criteria to different coastal configurations: the equidistance principle, the opposite/adjacent relationship, the proximity test, and the relevance of fisheries coasts.

Figure 37

The Proximity Test

A
Coastal fronts used in testing the relative proximity of Nova Scotia and the state of Maine to Georges Bank

B
Area of Nova Scotia that lies closer to the farthest point claimed by Canada on Georges Bank than does the coastal front of the state of Maine

C
Area of Nova Scotia that lies closer to the central part of the disputed area on Georges Bank than does the coastal front of the state of Maine

D
Area of Nova Scotia that lies closer to the northeast peak of Georges Bank than does the coastal front of the state of Maine

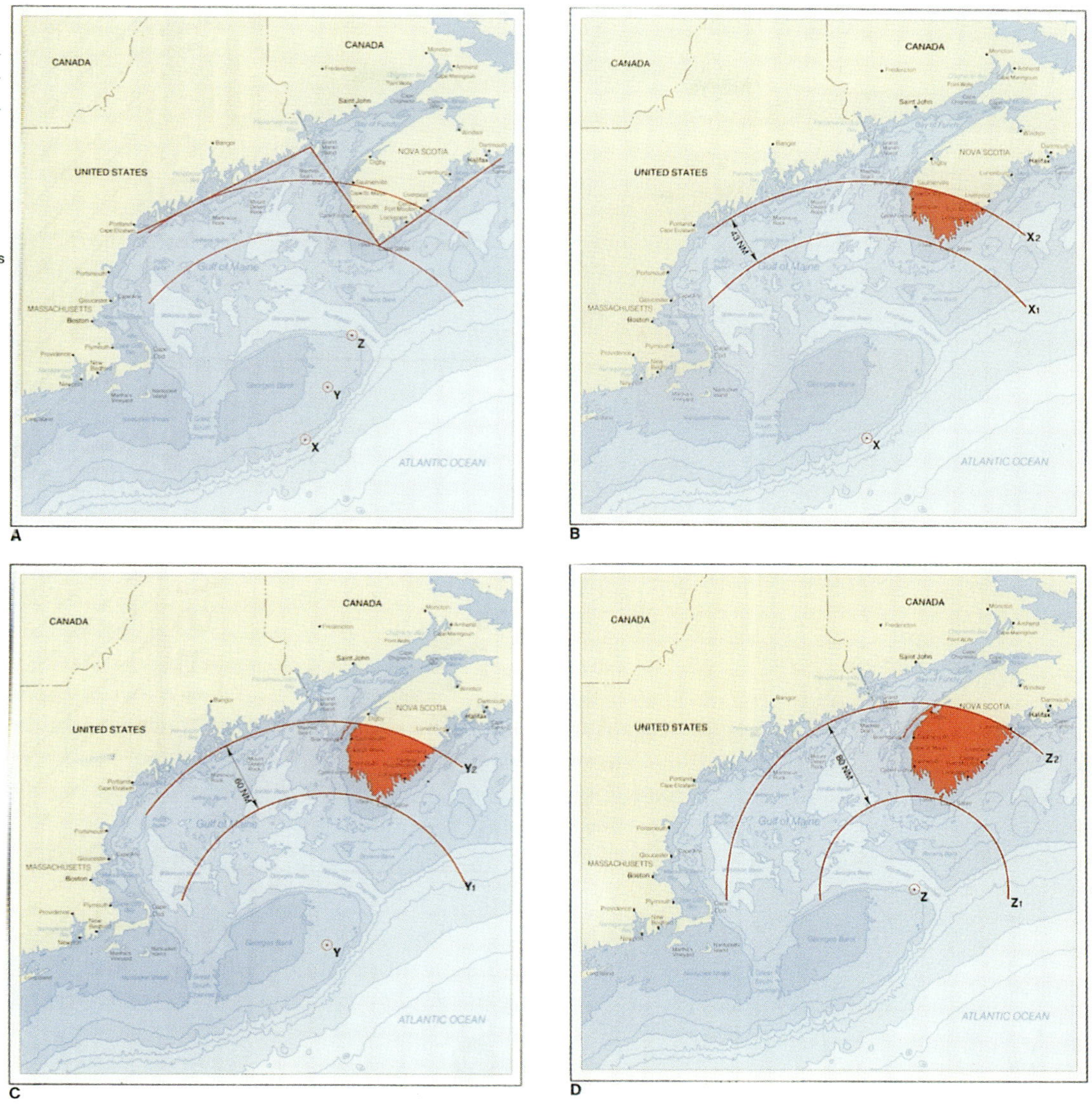

Depths in Metres
Projection–Mercator
Scale–1:7 300 000 at 41°N

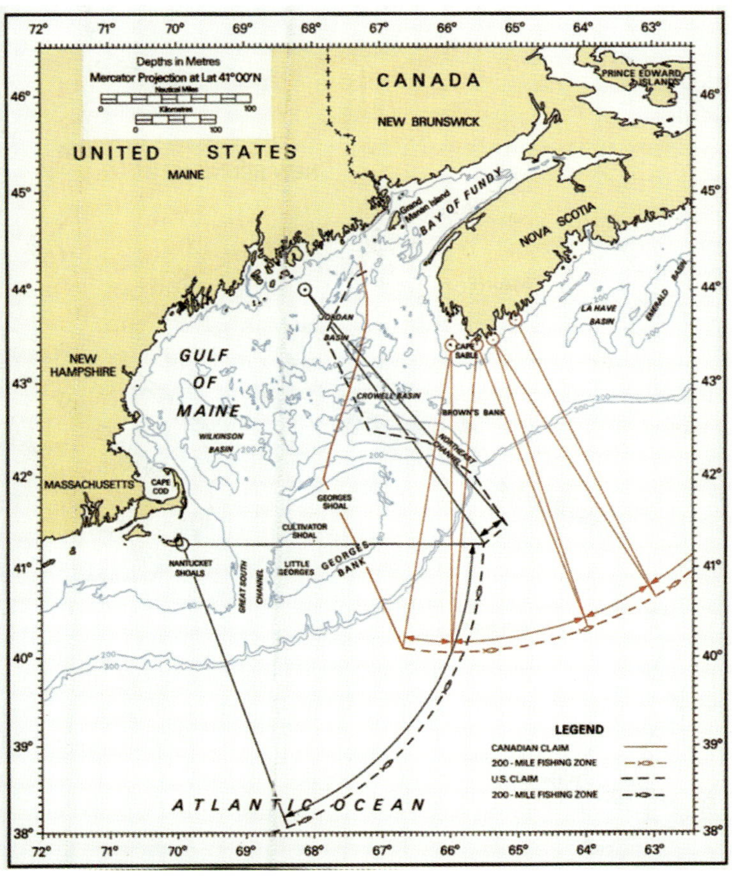

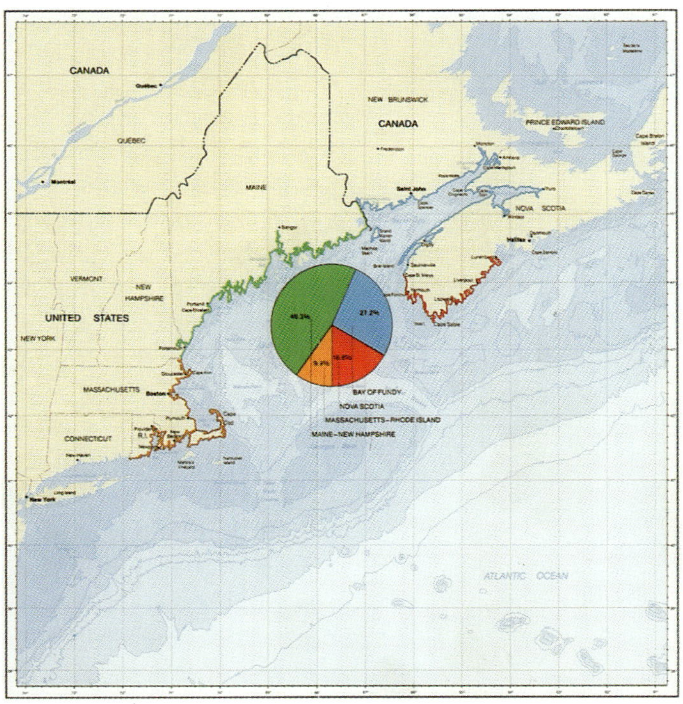

Figure 11

The Relevant Fishing Coasts: The Inner Area

- Nova Scotia coastal wing ports
- Bay of Fundy ports
- Maine-New Hampshire ports
- Massachusetts-Rhode Island coastal wing ports

Note: The percentages of total catch from the inner area by area of landing illustrated in the pie chart relate to the period 1969-1978. Values have been calculated by using 1978 Canadian offshore prices at Lunenburg. These data reflect the established fishing links between the relevant coasts and the inner area. The inner area has been defined by reference to NAFO subdivisions 5Yb, 5Yc, 5Yd, 5Ye, 5Yf, 4Xs, 4Xr and 4Xq. Catch data are taken from official statistics of Canada and the United States.

Depths in Metres
Projection–Mercator
Scale–1:4 700 000 at 41°N

Construction of the bridge over the Great Belt by Denmark.

from any inequalities in the extent of the coasts of two States into the same area of delimitation.

It then observed that:

> With regard to these and other possible criteria, the Chamber does not think it would be useful to undertake a more or less complete enumeration in the abstract of the criteria that are theoretically conceivable, or an evaluation, also in the abstract, of their greater or lesser degree of equitableness. As the Chamber has emphasized a number of times, their equitableness or otherwise can only be assessed in relation to the circumstances of each case, and for one and the same criterion it is quite possible to arrive at different, or even opposite, conclusions in different cases. The essential fact to bear in mind is, as the Chamber has stressed, that the criteria in question are not themselves rules of law and therefore mandatory in the different situations, but 'equitable', or even 'reasonable', criteria, and that what international law requires is that recourse be had in each case to the criterion, or the balance of different criteria, appearing to be most appropriate to the concrete situation. (*ICJ Reports* 1984, pp. 312-313)

Another delimitation of both the continental shelf and fisheries zones, likewise on the basis of equitable criteria leading to an equitable result, is to be found in the Court's 1993 Judgment in the case concerning *Maritime Delimitation in the Area between Greenland and Jan Mayen*, brought by Denmark against Norway.

No judgment was rendered by the Court in a case in which Finland instituted proceedings against Denmark in a dispute concerning the consequences which the construction of a bridge over the Great Belt would have for the passage of ships (notably drill ships and oil rigs) through that international strait. Following an Order in which the Court declined to indicate provisional measures, but pointed out the desirability of a direct and friendly settlement and urged further negotiations, the Parties reached an agreement and the case was withdrawn.

Two more maritime delimitation cases have recently been brought before the Court, one between Guinea-Bissau and Senegal, the other between Qatar and Bahrain. In 1991 the Court gave judgment on the validity of an arbitral award purporting to settle aspects of a long-standing maritime delimitation dispute between Guinea-Bissau and Senegal. The Court found that Award to be valid. While that case was being considered Guinea-Bissau brought a second case, the subject of which was partly dependent upon the outcome of the first. The two Parties finally concluded an agreement to discontinue the second case, which was then removed from the Court's list.

In the case between Qatar and Bahrain, which besides maritime delimitation concerned certain territorial questions, the Court, in its Judgment of July 1994, afforded the Parties 'the opportunity to submit to the Court the whole of the dispute'. Subsequently, in its February 1995 Judgment, the Court decided that it was competent to deal with the dispute.

Finally, a case was brought by Spain against Canada in March 1995. After the *Estai*, a fishing boat sailing under the Spanish flag, had been boarded on the high seas by Canadian coast-guards and then confined to a Canadian harbour, Spain applied to the Court, arguing that Canada had violated rules of international law concerning the freedom of the high seas and the rights of Spain as the flag State. In bringing its case Spain indicated that the dispute referred to the Court did not specifically relate to fisheries under the North Atlantic Fisheries Organization arrangements, but was a dispute over the 'the title invoked to justify the Canadian measures and their acts of enforcement, a piece of legislation which, going a great deal further than the mere management and conservation of fishery resources, is in itself an internationally wrongful act of Canada'. The first phase of the proceedings before the Court will address the question of the Court's jurisdiction to entertain the dispute.

Questions of State Jurisdiction (Territorial and Personal), Diplomatic and Consular Law

The first case of this nature, on the *Protection of French Nationals and Protected Persons in Egypt* (France v. Egypt) was brought in 1949 but withdrawn in 1950, because the Egyptian Government did not pursue its policy of measures against the property of French nationals and protected persons as originally indicated.

The year 1949 also saw the beginning of several cases between Colombia and Peru concerning the right of asylum. Mr Victor Raúl Haya de la Torre, a Peruvian statesman accused of having plotted a military coup d'état against his Government, had been granted asylum in the Colombian Embassy in Lima in January 1949. The Court, rejecting Colombia's arguments, decided that it was not for Colombia to qualify the offence as a political act nor was Peru obliged to provide a safe-conduct for Mr Haya de la Torre to leave the country. The Court further found in favour of a Peruvian counter-claim that the asylum had been irregularly granted. A Colombian request for an interpretation of that decision, made in the same year, was declared inadmissible by the Court.

In a follow-up case (*Haya de la Torre*), brought by Colombia in December 1950, and in which Cuba intervened, the Court concluded that Colombia was not obliged to surrender Mr Haya de la Torre to Peru, but that nevertheless the asylum should have ceased immediately after the Court's earlier Judgment. The Court could draw these two seemingly contradictory conclusions because it had first declared that there were different ways of bringing the asylum to an end, to be decided upon by the Parties, not by the Court.

Other cases in the 1950s concerned the rights of US nationals and related questions of US consular jurisdiction in Morocco (*Rights of Nationals of the USA in Morocco* (France v. USA), and a question of nationality and diplomatic protection (*Nottebohm*, Liechtenstein v. Guatemala). In the latter case the Court found that Liechtenstein's claim for restitution and compensation, based on Guatemala's

Peru Lets Haya Leave Country After 5 Years in Embassy Refuge

By SAM POPE BREWER
Special to THE NEW YORK TIMES.

CARACAS, Venezuela, March 23—Victor Raul Haya de la Torre, Peruvian radical leader, who has been living under protection of the Colombian Embassy in Lima for the last five years, will be allowed to leave Peru under safe conduct.

Señor Haya de la Torre was traveling by air tonight from Lima to Montevideo, it was reported on good authority, though nothing was said officially.

The declaration that he was free to leave Peru was made tonight by Evaresto Sourdis, Foreign Minister of Colombia, to the Tenth Inter-American Conference plenary session here. It was the most emotional moment attained by this gathering. When political issues arose, there was keen interest at the conference, but nothing like the tension caused by the settlement.

The whole question of the right of asylum for political refugees is one that arouses strong emotion in Latin America and the Haya case has remained very much in the public mind for five years.

This particular agreement ends one of the thorniest diplomatic problems of recent years in Latin America and one that has seriously disturbed relations between Colombia and Peru.

The conference deserves no small share of credit for the settlement. Peru was determined the question should not be brought up here and Colombia's efforts to do so caused a notable change in Peru's formerly reluctant attitude toward bilateral negotiations.

Two Peruvian representatives

Continued on Page 10, Column 4

Continued From Page 1

had been negotiating in Bogota with two Colombians since just before the opening of this conference. After several false alarms, when an agreement that was apparently almost concluded ran into new snags, they finally reached the settlement.

In his statement Senor Sourdis said:

"I come here to carry out the welcome duty of announcing to Tenth Inter-American Conference the happy culmination of direct negotiations between Colombia and Peru to carry out the decisions of the National Court [at The Hague] on the disputed question of asylum between those two countries.

"The agreement solves satisfactorily the problem and puts an end to any difference that might have disturbed during this long drawn out case the friendship of the two nations that are committed to act unitedly in defense of democracy and of American solidarity."

Victor Belaunde, Peruvian delegate, replied to Señor Sourdis, saying he felt "profound satisfaction" in announcing on behalf of his Government the agreement reached in Bogotá and that "as an example of friendly settlement the agreement signed in Bogotá takes into consideration the dignity of both countries and is equally satisfactory for both."

The operative part of The Hague tribunal's findings was the suggestion that Peru and Colombia settle the matter between themselves. After stating that Colombia was not justified in the circumstances in giving asylum to Señor Haya de la Torre, the court said Colombia still was not obliged to hand him over to the Peruvians.

It then added the remark—when asked for clarification—that there were other solutions that could be reached by the two countries through direct negotiation and that is what finally happened.

It is recognized by many Peruvians that the long dispute and the elaborate police guard over the Colombian Embassy—seriously complicating the life of Colombian diplomats—have done more harm to Peru in world opinion than Senor Haya de la Torre would be likely to do if allowed to go abroad.

Associated Press
Victor Raul Haya de la Torre

Senor Haya de la Torre, chief of Apra (People's American Revolutionary Alliance) took refuge in the Colombian Embassy in January, 1949. The Peruvian authorities wanted to prosecute him as the instigator of an unsuccessful but bloody revolt in El Callao, seaport of Lima, in October, 1948.

There is ample evidence that his party indulged in terrorist activities, but, in the view of the Colombian Embassy he was being sought as a political leader and not (as Peruvian authorities asserted) as a common criminal. Even on charges of military rebellion—the only ones actually brought against him—he would not be considered a "common criminal," as laws of asylum generally are applied in South America.

Colombia sought to bring the question before this conference for settlement, but Peru strenuously opposed the idea. Peru takes the stand that the case was settled by the Hague Court, but that the tribunal's decision actually was so ambiguous that it settled nothing.

New York Times, 24 March 1953.

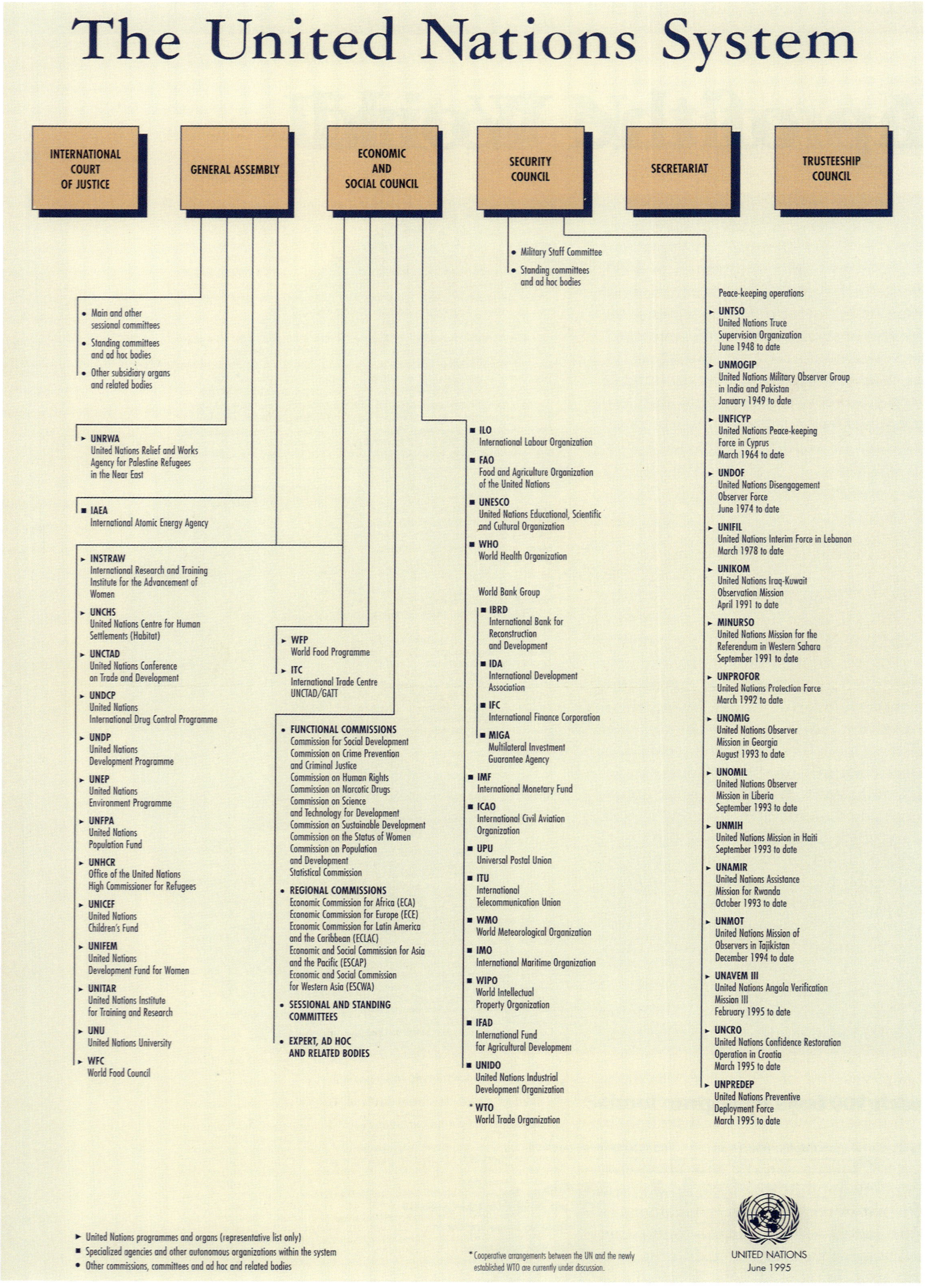
The United Nations System
INTERNATIONAL COURT OF JUSTICE
GENERAL ASSEMBLY
ECONOMIC AND SOCIAL COUNCIL
SECURITY COUNCIL
SECRETARIAT
TRUSTEESHIP COUNCIL
• Military Staff Committee
• Standing committees and ad hoc bodies
• Main and other sessional committees
• Standing committees and ad hoc bodies
• Other subsidiary organs and related bodies
▸ UNRWA United Nations Relief and Works Agency for Palestine Refugees in the Near East
■ IAEA International Atomic Energy Agency
▸ INSTRAW International Research and Training Institute for the Advancement of Women
▸ UNCHS United Nations Centre for Human Settlements (Habitat)
▸ UNCTAD United Nations Conference on Trade and Development
▸ UNDCP United Nations International Drug Control Programme
▸ UNDP United Nations Development Programme
▸ UNEP United Nations Environment Programme
▸ UNFPA United Nations Population Fund
▸ UNHCR Office of the United Nations High Commissioner for Refugees
▸ UNICEF United Nations Children's Fund
▸ UNIFEM United Nations Development Fund for Women
▸ UNITAR United Nations Institute for Training and Research
▸ UNU United Nations University
▸ WFC World Food Council
▸ WFP World Food Programme
▸ ITC International Trade Centre UNCTAD/GATT
• FUNCTIONAL COMMISSIONS
Commission for Social Development
Commission on Crime Prevention and Criminal Justice
Commission on Human Rights
Commission on Narcotic Drugs
Commission on Science and Technology for Development
Commission on Sustainable Development
Commission on the Status of Women
Commission on Population and Development
Statistical Commission
• REGIONAL COMMISSIONS
Economic Commission for Africa (ECA)
Economic Commission for Europe (ECE)
Economic Commission for Latin America and the Caribbean (ECLAC)
Economic and Social Commission for Asia and the Pacific (ESCAP)
Economic and Social Commission for Western Asia (ESCWA)
• SESSIONAL AND STANDING COMMITTEES
• EXPERT, AD HOC AND RELATED BODIES
■ ILO International Labour Organization
■ FAO Food and Agriculture Organization of the United Nations
■ UNESCO United Nations Educational, Scientific and Cultural Organization
■ WHO World Health Organization
World Bank Group
■ IBRD International Bank for Reconstruction and Development
■ IDA International Development Association
■ IFC International Finance Corporation
■ MIGA Multilateral Investment Guarantee Agency
■ IMF International Monetary Fund
■ ICAO International Civil Aviation Organization
■ UPU Universal Postal Union
■ ITU International Telecommunication Union
■ WMO World Meteorological Organization
■ IMO International Maritime Organization
■ WIPO World Intellectual Property Organization
■ IFAD International Fund for Agricultural Development
■ UNIDO United Nations Industrial Development Organization
* WTO World Trade Organization
Peace-keeping operations
▸ UNTSO United Nations Truce Supervision Organization June 1948 to date
▸ UNMOGIP United Nations Military Observer Group in India and Pakistan January 1949 to date
▸ UNFICYP United Nations Peace-keeping Force in Cyprus March 1964 to date
▸ UNDOF United Nations Disengagement Observer Force June 1974 to date
▸ UNIFIL United Nations Interim Force in Lebanon March 1978 to date
▸ UNIKOM United Nations Iraq-Kuwait Observation Mission April 1991 to date
▸ MINURSO United Nations Mission for the Referendum in Western Sahara September 1991 to date
▸ UNPROFOR United Nations Protection Force March 1992 to date
▸ UNOMIG United Nations Observer Mission in Georgia August 1993 to date
▸ UNOMIL United Nations Observer Mission in Liberia September 1993 to date
▸ UNMIH United Nations Mission in Haiti September 1993 to date
▸ UNAMIR United Nations Assistance Mission for Rwanda October 1993 to date
▸ UNMOT United Nations Mission of Observers in Tajikistan December 1994 to date
▸ UNAVEM III United Nations Angola Verification Mission III February 1995 to date
▸ UNCRO United Nations Confidence Restoration Operation in Croatia March 1995 to date
▸ UNPREDEP United Nations Preventive Deployment Force March 1995 to date
▸ United Nations programmes and organs (representative list only)
■ Specialized agencies and other autonomous organizations within the system
• Other commissions, committees and ad hoc and related bodies
* Cooperative arrangements between the UN and the newly established WTO are currently under discussion.
UNITED NATIONS
June 1995

General view of the 48th Session of the General Assembly, UN Headquarters New York, 27 September 1993.

actions towards Mr Nottebohm (a national of Liechtenstein) was inadmissible, because that nationality was not based on any genuine prior link between Mr Nottebohm and Liechtenstein. Only a bond of nationality which constitutes the juridical expression of a close connection between an individual and a State entitles that State to espouse international claims on the individual's behalf.

In 1979, when the régime of the Shah of Iran had been overthrown and the Ayatollah Khomeini had become that country's leader, the USA applied to the Court in a case concerning the seizure of its Embassy in Teheran and the detention of its diplomatic and consular staff. In its Order indicating provisional measures of December 1979 and its Judgment rendered in May of the following year, the Court ruled that Iran was obliged to release the hostages, enabling them to leave the country, to hand back the US Embassy premises, property, archives and documents and to make reparation. If the Parties failed to agree on the form and amount of such reparation, the Court was to settle those questions. Before that stage was reached, however, the Parties concluded the 1981 Algiers Accords concerning the settlement of their dispute and the case was removed from the Court's list.

In another case between Iran and the USA, pending since 1989, Iran requested the Court to find that the USA, by shooting down an Iranian civil aircraft flying over Iranian territorial waters - an incident in which all the passengers on board were killed - had violated international law and should consequently pay damages to Iran and, through that State, to the families of the victims. The hearings on questions of jurisdiction and admissibility in that case, scheduled for September 1994, were, however, postponed *sine die* at the request of the two Parties. Following the conclusion of an agreement the case was withdrawn in early 1996.

Emblem of the International Maritime Organization.

The jurisdiction of the Court and the admissibility of the Application instituting proceedings were also contested in another pending dispute brought by Iran against the USA, in 1992, concerning the bombardment and destruction of several Iranian oil platforms by American warships in 1987 and 1988.

The Law of International Organizations

The power of veto, as used from the inception of the United Nations on certain occasions to block a recommendation of the Security Council for the admission to membership of certain States, led to the first request for an advisory opinion by the General Assembly in 1947. The Court declared that the conditions laid down in Article 4 of the Charter for the admission of States were exhaustive and that if, consequently, a State fulfilled all of those conditions the Security Council ought to give a favourable recommendation for admission to the General Assembly. Another advisory opinion followed, again upon the General Assembly's request, stating that the absence of a recommendation by the Security Council could not be interpreted as an unfavourable recommendation, so that the General Assembly in such a case, acting contrary to that indication, could still admit a State. The underlying problem was solved only in 1955 by a package deal effecting the admission 'en bloc' of all applicant States.

The importance of the third advisory opinion to be mentioned here can hardly be over-estimated. The case concerning *Reparation for Injuries Suffered in the Service of the United Nations* was brought before the Court after the assassination, in September 1948 in Jerusalem, of the Swedish Count Bernadotte, who was the UN Mediator in Palestine. The General Assembly requested an advisory opinion on whether the United Nations could claim reparation for injuries suffered in its service. The Court found that the Organization indeed had the capacity to bring such an international claim, in view of the rights and obligations incumbent upon it - which were different from those of its Member States - and the consequently broad scope of its international personality.

In 1962 the Court, responding to another request from the General Assembly, found that the expenditures authorized by the Assembly in relation to the UN peacekeeping operations in the Congo and in the Middle East - which several States had strongly opposed and were consequently refusing to pay for - were 'expenses of the Organization' within the meaning of Article 17, § 2 of the Charter. The consequence of that Opinion was that those expenditures had to be borne by the Member States as apportioned by the General Assembly. In the controversy over assessments for peacekeeping, a majority of Member States had voted in favour of the draft resolution requesting the advisory opinion, with a view to subsequent action against the delinquent States, possibly the suspension of voting rights in the General Assembly as provided by Article 19 of the Charter. However, in the event the General Assembly did not apply Article 19 to the peacekeeping expenses at issue.

In 1988 a dispute arose between the UN Secretary-General and the USA, when that State adopted the Anti-Terrorism Act which *inter alia* declared the establishment or maintenance of an office of the Palestine Liberation Organization within the jurisdiction of the USA to be illegal. Under those provisions the New York office of the Observer Mission of Palestine to the United Nations would have had to close down. The question put to the Court by the General Assembly was whether under the provisions of the Headquarters Agreement the USA was under an obligation to enter into arbitration to resolve the dispute between itself and the United Nations. In view of the entry into force of the legislation concerned, the request for an advisory opinion was made on a basis of urgency. The Court delivered its Opinion within two months, finding that a dispute concerning the interpretation and the application of the Headquarters Agreement did indeed exist and that the USA was obliged to resort to arbitration. There was, however, no need for the Secretary-General to take action in that respect, as shortly afterwards a USA District Court decided that:

> The Anti-Terrorism Act does not require the closure of the PLO Permanent Observer Mission to the United Nations nor do the act's provisions impair the continued exercise of its appropriate functions as a Permanent Observer at the United Nations as an invitee of the

United Nations under the Headquarters Agreement and its status is protected by that agreement. The Headquarters Agreement remains a valid and outstanding treaty obligation of the USA. It has not been superseded by the Anti-Terrorism Act, which is a valid enactment of general application.

After the State Department's announcement that the USA would not appeal the decision of the District Court, the Secretary-General, in his report to the General Assembly, concluded that 'The dispute between the United Nations and its host country concerning the PLO Observer Mission has thus come to an end'.

The most recent advisory opinion, handed down by the Court in 1989 in response to the first request made to it by the Economic and Social Council, concerned the status of a UN rapporteur on human rights questions. Such rapporteurs, who often do not possess the status of UN officials but who have been entrusted with a mission by the Organization are, the Court found, entitled to enjoy the privileges and immunities provided for in the relevant section of the Convention on the Privileges and Immunities of the United Nations. That is the case even with regard to the State of their nationality or residence. This advisory opinion provided another example of a finding of the Court on a rule of international law, which would be applicable to future State practice even if the opinion itself was not acted upon: Mr Dimitri Mazilu, the Romanian rapporteur who had been prevented by his own Government from travelling to Geneva to submit his report, and in relation to whom the opinion was requested, became his country's Vice-President upon the fall of the Ceaucescu régime, two weeks after the Court rendered its Advisory Opinion.

In 1960 the Court responded in the negative to a request by the Assembly of the Intergovernmental Maritime Consultative Organization on the constitutionality of the Maritime Safety Committee, as recently composed. In 1972 India appealed against a decision of the Council of the International Civil Aviation Organization to deal with a complaint by Pakistan against the suspension by India of flights over its territory by Pakistani civil aircraft. Pakistan objected to the Court's jurisdiction. The Court decided that it was competent to entertain the appeal but rejected the Indian claim, finding that the ICAO Council indeed had jurisdiction to deal with the dispute Pakistan had laid before it.

Subsequently in 1980, responding to a request from the World Health Organization, the Court interpreted the Regional Headquarters Agreement between the WHO and Egypt and set forth the legal principles and rules concerning consultation, negotiation and notice that would apply as between the WHO and Egypt if the Regional Office of the WHO for the Eastern Mediterranean, in Alexandria, were to be transferred from Egyptian territory.

Five advisory opinions have related to the status and powers of administrative tribunals within the United Nations Organization. The first declared the judgments of the UN Administrative Tribunal - which the Court said was 'an independent and truly judicial body pronouncing final judgments without appeal within the limited field of its functions' - to be binding and found that the General Assembly did not therefore have 'the right on any grounds to refuse to give effect to an award of compensation by that Tribunal'. In the second such advisory opinion the Court found that the International Labour Organisation Administrative Tribunal, whose jurisdiction had been accepted by Unesco for certain staff matters, had been competent to hear the complaints referred to it by certain staff members of Unesco, as the rights claimed by those staff members were the subject of an administrative memorandum of a general nature which might reasonably be regarded as binding on the Organization.

In 1955 the General Assembly set up the Committee on Applications for Review of Administrative Tribunal Judgments, which it authorized to request advisory opinions from the ICJ. That could be done if a Member State, the Secretary-General or the staff member concerned objected to a judgment of the Administrative Tribunal 'on the ground that the Tribunal has exceeded its jurisdiction or competence or that the Tribunal has failed to exercise jurisdiction vested in it, or has erred on a question of law relating to the provision of the UN Charter, or has committed a fundamental error in procedure which has occasioned a failure of justice ...'. Three requests for an advisory opinion concerned judgments of the UN Admin-

Emblem of the World Health Organization.

The Island of Nauru.

istrative Tribunal and were made on one or more of these grounds (cases concerning the review of Judgments Nos. 158, 273 and 333 of UNAT). In all three cases the Court found, however, that the Administrative Tribunal had not committed any such error.

Issues of Decolonization

The question of the decolonization of Namibia - previously South West Africa - has been the subject of several, mostly advisory, cases before the Court. In 1949 it was asked to deal with the question of whether South Africa could unilaterally change the status of the Territory of South West Africa, integrating it into the Union, notwithstanding the fact that under a League of Nations Mandate South Africa was only to administer the territory on behalf of the League, for the promotion of the well-being and development of the inhabitants. In its Opinion rendered in July 1950, the Court considered that South West Africa was indeed a territory under mandate, that South Africa had to continue supervising the territory and reporting on it, *in casu* to the United Nations, that the system for transformation of South West Africa into a Trust Territory was to be found in Chapter XII of the Charter, but that South Africa was not legally bound to place the territory under trusteeship. South Africa was, however, precluded from modifying the status of the territory without the consent of the United Nations. Two subsequent requests concerned the procedures to be followed by the General Assembly and by the Committee on South West Africa in dealing further with questions relating to reports and petitions concerning the Territory.

The mined phosphate lands in Nauru.

In 1960 Ethiopia and Liberia brought cases against South Africa regarding the continued existence of the mandate and the duties and performance of South Africa as the Mandatory Power. After joining the proceedings in the two cases the Court found, in 1962, that it had jurisdiction to deal with the case. However, delivering a Judgment in 1966, the Court, being equally divided, found by a casting vote of the President that the Applicant States had not established any legal right or interest in the subject-matter of their claims, and rejected those claims. The strong political views of a large part of the international community with respect to the subject matter at hand, led to strenuous criticism of the latter decision by members of that community, and especially by developing countries.

Five years later, in 1971, the Court rendered its first and only advisory opinion upon a request by the Security Council, which may be said to have laid the legal foundation for the creation of the Council for Namibia and contributed to the subsequent independence of that country. In that Opinion, the Court declared that the continued presence of South Africa in Namibia was illegal and must be terminated as soon as possible, that the Member States of the United Nations should refrain from any acts implying recognition of the legality of South Africa's presence in the territory, and that such an obligation extended to States not Members of the United Nations.

In 1975 the Court rendered an Advisory Opinion on certain questions concerning the Western Sahara, a non-self-governing territory, which, in the wake of its decolonization by Spain, had been claimed by Morocco to the north as well as by Mauritania to the south. The Court found that at the time of the Spanish colonization, beginning in 1884, the Western Sahara was not *terra nullius* (a territory belonging to no one), and that while legal ties existed between that territory and Morocco as well as Mauritania, they did not establish any bond of territorial sovereignty 'of such a nature as might affect the application of General Assembly resolution 1514 (XV) in the decolonization of Western Sahara and, in particular, of the principle of self-determination through the free and genuine expression of the will of the peoples of the Territory'.

In 1989, Nauru brought Australia before the Court alleging that Australia, by mining phosphates on the island during the years of the trusteeship, had in the process destroyed the habitat of the Nauruan people and had thereby violated its obligations under the Trusteeship Agreement. After the Court, rejecting Australia's arguments, had found that it had jurisdiction, the two Parties reached an agreement whereby Australia was to pay compensation to Nauru and the case was discontinued.

In the recent contentious case brought by Portugal against Australia concerning a treaty of December 1989 between Australia and Indonesia on the exploitation of the continental shelf of the so-called 'Timor Gap', the Court found that it could not deal with the dispute as laid before it because to do so would entail its adjudging acts of a State (Indonesia) not party to the proceedings. In its reasoning, the Court pointed out 'that for the two Parties, the Territory of East Timor remains a non-self-governing territory and its people has the right to self-determination'.

International Peace and Security, the Use of Force and Intervention

The fact that the Court's jurisdiction is based upon the consent of the parties is illustrated particularly clearly by the group of cases brought during the 1950s that concerned certain aerial incidents involving the shooting down of aircraft over Eastern European territory as well as the treatment of their crews. In five cases, the USA, when applying to the Court, declared that it submitted to the Court's jurisdiction for the purpose of those cases and indicated that the Respondent State might do the same. In each of those cases the Court found that its jurisdiction had not been accepted, as suggested, by the Respondent and that no further action could be taken, and removed the case from the list.

In the case brought by Israel against Bulgaria - in which the facts and issues sharply differed from the cases brought by

Rear part of fuselage showing broken off empennage. Bulgarian group in background.

the USA referred to above - the Court found that Bulgaria's declaration of acceptance of the jurisdiction of the Permanent Court of International Justice, made in 1921, was not a valid basis for the jurisdiction of the present Court, as had been claimed by Israel. Following the Court's Judgment, the United Kingdom and the USA, which had brought cases based upon the same incident, withdrew them.

Another case withdrawn before any written pleadings had been filed, although a request for provisional measures had been made, was the case concerning certain Pakistani prisoners of war whom India proposed to hand over to Bangladesh, *Trial of Pakistani Prisoners of War* (Pakistan v. India). In this case, however - in which India stayed the transfer in view of a request from the President of the Court - negotiations between the Parties were successful.

In 1973-1974, when the Court was considering the Applications of Australia and New Zealand against France in the *Nuclear Tests* cases, it indicated provisional measures stating, in particular, that the French Government should avoid nuclear tests causing the deposit of radioactive fallout on the territory of the Applicant States. In the Judgments rendered in December 1974, the Court however declared that, in view of France's undertaking to conduct no further nuclear tests in the atmosphere in the South Pacific, the dispute had ceased to exist, the claims no longer had any object, and there was nothing on which to give judgment.

In August 1995 there was a sequel to one of those cases when New Zealand filed in the Court a Request for an Examination of the Situation arising out of the planned series of eight nuclear weapons tests in the South Pacific announced by France which would, if carried out, 'affect the basis of the Judgment rendered by the Court on 20 December 1974 in the *Nuclear Tests Case* (New Zealand v. France)'. In its Order of 22 September 1995, the Court found, however, that New Zealand's request did not fall within the provisions of paragraph 63 of the 1974 Judgment, which would have empowered that State to make such a request, and had consequently to be dismissed.

The unstable situation in Central America in the early 1980's led Nicaragua to institute proceedings before the Court, against the USA in 1984 (*Military and Paramilitary Activities in and against Nicaragua*) and against both Costa Rica and Honduras, in 1986 (*Border and Transborder Armed Actions*). In the first case the USA refused to recognize the jurisdiction of the Court. After the Court had found, in a 1984 Judgment, that it had jurisdiction, it determined, in June 1986, that the USA, by supporting the contras in Nicaragua and by laying mines outside that country's ports - acts that the Court held the USA could not justify on the basis of collective self-defence - had violated its international legal obligations not to intervene in the affairs of another State and not to use force against another State. The USA was therefore to make reparation to Nicaragua 'the form and amount of [which] ..., failing agreement between the Parties, will be settled by the Court ...'. In 1987 Nicaragua asked the Court to determine that question. However, after elections in that country which led to a change of government, negotiations between the Parties resulted, in September 1991, in a discontinuance of the proceedings and the removal of the case from the Court's General List.

Following the 'Esquipulas II' Agreement, entitled *Procedimiento para establecer una paz firme y duradera en Centro América* signed in Guatemala City on 7 August 1987, Nicaragua withdrew its case against Costa Rica during that same month. In May 1992, after the Court had upheld its jurisdiction, the case against Honduras was withdrawn.

In that same year Libya instituted proceedings against the United Kingdom and the USA respectively in two cases concerning the destruction of a PanAm flight over Lockerbie, Scotland, on 21 December 1988. Libya referred to the indictment, in the United Kingdom and the USA, of two Libyan nationals alleged to have 'caused a bomb to be placed aboard [that flight] ... which bomb had exploded causing the aeroplane to crash' and to the fact that those States were threatening various actions against Libya in order to compel it to surrender its two accused nationals. It claimed that the 1971 Montreal Convention for the Suppression of Unlawful Acts Against the Safety of Civil Aviation was the only appropriate convention with regard to those matters and that, while Libya had fully complied with its obligations under that convention, the United Kingdom and the USA had breached their obligations, and were obliged to cease doing so and to stop the use of force and any violations of the sovereignty, territorial integrity and political independence of Libya. The competence of the Court to deal with these cases has been contested by the two Respondent Parties and time-limits for the filing of written pleadings on that subject have been fixed.

In the pending case concerning the *Application of the Convention on the Prevention and Punishment of the Crime of Genocide* (Bosnia and Herzegovina v. Yugoslavia, i.e. Serbia and Montenegro), brought before it in 1993, the Court twice indicated provisional measures. The first Order of the Court called upon the Parties immediately to stop any practice of genocide and not to further aggravate the dispute between them. The second Order, rather than indicating any new measures of that kind, reaffirmed those indicated previously and called upon the Parties to implement them 'immediately and effectively'. In this case, as in the abovementioned *Lockerbie* cases, the jurisdiction of the Court has been contested.

Protection of Private Interests

Several disputes have come before the Court in which the Applicant State put forward a claim on behalf of one of its nationals or national companies concerning their private, often economic, interests. The first such case (*Ambatielos*, Greece v. United Kingdom) concerned the question of whether the United Kingdom was obliged to submit to arbitration with regard to claims made by Mr Ambatielos, a shipowner of Greek nationality. The

Court found, in a 1952 Judgment, that it had jurisdiction to deal with the case and in the subsequent 1953 Judgment on the merits it determined that the United Kingdom was indeed under such an obligation. In the next two cases of this kind (*Certain Norwegian Loans*, France v. Norway, and *Interhandel*, Switzerland v. USA) the Court found that it lacked jurisdiction.

Then, in 1958 in the first instance (in which the Court declared itself competent, but the Application inadmissible), and in 1962 by a second application, Belgium brought a claim against Spain in exercise of diplomatic protection of Belgian shareholders in a Canadian company (Barcelona Traction) with regard to certain measures taken against that company in Spain. After proceedings which were probably the longest and the most voluminous in the Court's history, the Court, in its Judgment on the merits of 1970, found that Belgium lacked *jus standi* to exercise diplomatic protection.

In another case of diplomatic protection the USA brought a claim against Italy for certain actions of the Italian authorities in relation to the requisition and bankruptcy of Elettronica Sicula S.p.A. (ELSI), an Italian company wholly owned by two US Corporations. The two States Parties agreed that the case be dealt with by a Chamber of the Court. The Chamber found that Italy had not violated the Treaty of Friendship, Commerce and Navigation with the USA which had been signed in Rome on 2 February 1948.

Before concluding this chapter it would seem useful to revert for a moment to the remarks on classification made at its beginning. There are two notable fields of international law which at the present time command great attention but which have not been represented in the classification adopted: environmental law and the law of human rights.

With regard to the latter, although no cases have been dealt with by the Court which solely or mainly concerned questions of human rights, many cases have nevertheless raised such questions and required decisions of the Court thereon; it was Vice-President Schwebel who concluded, after a survey of the case law of the present Court as well as of its predecessor, the Permanent Court of International Justice, 'that the influence of the Court on the evolution of international human rights law has been considerable and constructive'.

Some cases which have been dealt with by the Court presented important aspects of an environmental nature. The *Nuclear Tests* cases, brought against France by Australia and New Zealand, with their sequel of the 1995 proceedings brought by the latter State (see above) as well as the case concerning *Certain Phosphate Lands in Nauru* (Nauru v. Australia) could well have been treated under a heading of environmental law.

The same is true for the pending case concerning the *Gabčíkovo-Nagymaros Project* (Hungary/Slovakia) which one of the parties claims presents environmental aspects, in addition to questions of treaty law. This case, the second one to be brought before the Court by two formerly Socialist States of Eastern Europe, concerns a project for a hydroelectric dam built to harness the waters of the River Danube. The exploitation of the dam is alleged by Hungary to have grave consequences for the environment.

The growing attention paid to questions of this kind led the Court to signal, in July 1993, its preparedness in this field by establishing a seven-member Chamber for Environmental Matters 'in view of the developments in the field of environmental law and protection which have taken place in the last few years and considering that it [the Court] should be prepared to the fullest possible extent to deal with any environmental case falling within its jurisdiction'.

CHAPTER ELEVEN BY ARTHUR WITTEVEEN

The Role of the Court

The Advisory Function

The review of the cases in Chapter 10 seems to warrant some reflection on the way the Court has functioned and the role it has played, within the United Nations Organization as well as in international relations in general. Some comments may appropriately be made with regard to both the advisory and the contentious function.

According to Article 96 of the Charter, the General Assembly and the Security Council may request an advisory opinion of the Court 'on any legal question'. The second paragraph of that Article provides that the General Assembly may also authorize other organs of the United Nations and Specialized Agencies to request advisory opinions, but only 'on legal questions arising within the scope of their activities'.

Out of 22 requests for advisory opinion, 13 have been made by the General Assembly, and one by the Security Council. This number certainly falls far short both of the number of requests submitted to the Permanent Court of International Justice by the Council of the League of Nations alone, not counting the Assembly, as well as of expectations at the time of the creation of the present Court.

The part of Article 14 of the Covenant providing for the advisory competence of the PCIJ was worded as follows: 'The Court shall be competent to hear and determine any dispute of an international character which the parties thereto submit to it. The Court may also give an advisory opinion upon any dispute or question referred to it by the Council or by the Assembly'. The Permanent Court, in its subsequent practice, exercised the advisory function in a manner which encompassed dispute settlement as well as a purely advisory role.

When, after the Second World War, the International Court of Justice was integrated into the United Nations Organization as one of its principal organs, a clear distinction was drawn between its two future functions: the dispute settlement function which would be open to States only, and the advisory function which would be available to a select number of international organizations. There exists a small number of dispute settlement clauses contained in subsequently concluded treaties between States and international organizations and in the Statutes of the ILO and UN Administrative Tribunals, which provide for an advisory opinion which will be 'binding'. In its Opinion of 23 October 1956, on an appeal from certain judgments of the ILO Administrative Tribunal by the Executive Board of UNESCO, the Court made the following observations, which it has echoed in several other cases of a similar nature:

Under Article XII of the Statute of the

1994
General List
No. 95

I. THE SECRETARY-GENERAL OF THE UNITED NATIONS TO THE PRESIDENT OF THE INTERNATIONAL COURT OF JUSTICE

19 December 1994.

I have the honour to inform you that at its 90th meeting held on 15 December 1994, under its agenda item 62 entitled "General and Complete Disarmament: Report of the First Committee" (A/49/699), the General Assembly adopted resolution 49/75 K, "Request for an Advisory Opinion from the International Court of Justice on the Legality of the Threat or Use of Nuclear Weapons". The text of the resolution is attached.

In this resolution, the General Assembly decided, pursuant to Article 96, paragraph 1, of the Charter of the United Nations:

> "to request the International Court of Justice urgently to render its advisory opinion on the following question: 'Is the threat or use of nuclear weapons in any circumstance permitted under international law?'"

Pursuant to Article 65, paragraph 2, of the Statute of the International Court of Justice, the Secretariat is now in the process of preparing a dossier containing "all documents likely to throw light upon the question", which will be transmitted to the Court as soon as possible.

(Signed) Boutros Boutros-Ghali.

> Administrative Tribunal, the Opinion thus requested will be 'binding'. Such effect of the Opinion goes beyond the scope attributed by the Charter and by the Statute of the Court to an Advisory Opinion. However, the provision in question is nothing but a rule of conduct for the Executive Board, a rule determining the action to be taken by it on the Opinion of the Court. It in no wise affects the way in which the Court functions; that continues to be determined by its Statute and its Rules. Nor does it affect the reasoning by which the Court forms its Opinion or the content of the Opinion itself.

In the Court's interpretation its competence to give an advisory opinion is confined to questions of a legal nature, usually couched in general terms; and it certainly does not extend to disputes that are exclusively disputes between States. The Court has confirmed on several occasions that the principle of consent by the States parties to contentious cases should not be circumvented by bringing a dispute in through the back door in the guise of a request for an advisory opinion. At the same time, the Court will give a requested opinion in the absence of compelling reasons to the contrary. The fact that in quite a number of advisory cases the questions put to the Court have seriously divided the requesting body into opposing political camps - with the result that in some cases the Court's opinion was ultimately not applied - may explain to some extent the relatively low number of requests the Court has received.

In recent years, successive Presidents of the Court have, in their annual addresses to the General Assembly, drawn attention to this situation. Certainly in furtherance of the concept of preventive diplomacy, as proposed by Secretary-General Boutros Boutros-Ghali in his 1992 'Agenda for Peace', a greater use of the Court by the political organs might be expected. It has been asserted in this connection that the procedure before the Court is too cumbersome and time-consuming, but this criticism was shown to be unfounded in one of the most recent requests to the Court, concerning the status of the observer mission to the United Nations of the Palestine Liberation Organization in New York. The whole of the proceedings, including the submission of the case file by the Secretary-General, the holding of hearings and the preparation of the Court's opinion, took no more than two months.

One proposal which, if adopted, would be likely to generate a number of requests for advisory opinions is that the Secretary-General should be authorized to request advisory opinions. The Secretary-General himself has so proposed, but as yet the General Assembly has not endorsed this. Another proposal, which attracted support in the US Congress, is to set up a procedure by which the supreme courts of States could seek the advisory opinion of the International Court of Justice on questions of international law arising in those courts.

In all, the relatively small number of requests for advisory opinion has not prevented the Court from contributing considerably to the development of international law by the exercise of its advisory function. Advisory opinions rendered by the Court may have a distinct influence upon subsequent State practice. For instance, its treatment of reservations to treaties in the *Genocide Reservations* case had a decisive influence on the drafting of relevant parts of the Vienna Convention on the Law of Treaties.

Although the Court was not established as a constitutional court, with a power of judicial review of the activities of the other principal organs, it has from the outset been called upon several times by the General Assembly to interpret Charter provisions in order to determine the respective competence of that organ and of the Security Council (e.g., questions concerning the admission of new members to the United Nations). Moreover, the Security Council, in its only request for an advisory opinion, asked if not for a test of constitutionality, then at least for a decision about the legal consequences for States of its own actions.

The Contentious Practice of the Court

This question of the relationship between the Court and, more particularly, the Security Council has also arisen in contentious cases in the last two decades. In the 1970s, in the *Aegean Sea Continental Shelf* case, Greece brought its dispute with Turkey over the continental shelf in the Aegean Sea virtually simultaneously to the Security Council and to the Court. In

The Security Council authorizes use of 'all necessary means' to establish secure environment for humanitarian relief operations in Somalia, 3 December 1992.

the *Hostages* case also, both the Council and the Court were involved at the same time and, in a late stage of that dispute, reference was made by the Court to Security Council decisions and *vice versa*. In these and other cases, in which the Court had occasion to observe that the fact that a dispute was already being dealt with by the Security Council was not an impediment to the Court's treatment of the legal aspects of such a dispute, the two organs pursued more or less complementary courses of action. They exemplify the comment made by President Bedjaoui of the Court in his 1994 address to the General Assembly:

> As such, the Court is clearly an essential part, not just of the machinery set up by the Charter for the peaceful settlement of disputes, but also of the general system for the maintenance of international peace and security that it introduced.

In the first phase of the proceedings in two cases which are still pending before the Court, however, the Applicant has sought to obtain from the Court a decision which would have affected the implementation of certain resolutions adopted by the Security Council.

Libya, when it brought the *Lockerbie* cases before the Court, requested the indication of provisional measures, a procedure which is intended to protect the rights of the parties while the case is pending and no final decision on those rights has yet been reached. The USA and the United Kingdom had, before Libya came to the Court, referred their dispute over responsibility for the Lockerbie incident to the Security Council, and the Council had adopted a resolution demanding Libya to respond, urgently and effectively, to requests by the United Kingdom and the USA for the surrender of two Libyan nationals who had allegedly been involved in placing the bomb on board the plane which exploded over Lockerbie, Scotland.

Libya, in its request for the indication of provisional measures, asked the Court *inter alia* to enjoin the two States 'from taking against Libya measures calculated to exert coercion on it or compel it to surrender the accused individuals to any jurisdiction outside of Libya'. Three days after the close of the hearings before the Court on the Libyan request, the Security Council adopted a second resolution under Chapter VII of the Charter in which

Meeting of Mr Boutros Boutros Ghali, Secretary-General of the UN, with the ICJ in 1993.

it declared an air traffic embargo against Libya on account of its 'failure ... to demonstrate by concrete actions its renunciation of terrorism and in particular its continued failure to respond fully and effectively' to the requests made earlier.

In its Order on the Libyan request made shortly thereafter, the Court indicated that, in accordance with Article 25 of the Charter, the Parties before the Court were obliged to accept and carry out the decision contained in the second resolution of the Security Council and that, in accordance with Article 103 of the Charter, their obligations in that respect prevailed over their obligations under any other international agreement, including the Montreal Convention. For those reasons, the Court declined to indicate provisional measures.

In the case concerning the Genocide Convention brought by Bosnia and Herzegovina against Yugoslavia (i.e., Serbia and Montenegro), Bosnia and Herzegovina made two consecutive requests for the indication of provisional measures. In that case Bosnia alleged that Yugoslavia was responsible for certain acts of genocide, violating not only the Genocide Convention, but also other international agreements, such as the UN Charter, the four Geneva Conventions of 1949 and the Universal Declaration of Human Rights. Bosnia and Herzegovina further argued that Yugoslavia was also using force and the threat of force against Bosnia and Herzegovina, violating the latter's sovereignty and intervening in its internal affairs.

As a consequence, Bosnia and Herzegovina had a right to self-defence and could invoke the right of collective self-defence recognized by Article 51 of the Charter in order to request assistance from other States, who for their part had the right to provide such assistance. In the view of Bosnia and Herzegovina, this meant that it had the right to request other States to provide it with arms and those States could legally do so, notwithstanding the Security Council resolution declaring a weapons embargo for the whole of the territory of the former Yugoslavia.

However, at the opening of the hearings on the requests by Bosnia and Herzegovina, the President of the Court reminded the Parties that the jurisdiction of the Court to deal with the case had been founded by the Applicant State on the Genocide Convention and indicated that the pleadings should, for that reason, be restricted to questions of genocide. Since all questions other than the alleged violation of the Genocide Convention were thus put aside, the Court did not confront the thrust of the cited resolution of the Security Council.

While it is clear that at the San Francisco Conference the Court was not given powers of judicial review with regard to the activities of the other principal organs, it has still to be determined to what extent - if at all - the legality of the decisions of those organs may be subject to consideration by the Court.

The aforementioned developments with regard to the question of the relationship between the principal organs are however of a recent nature. Much more consistent in their effect on the Court's contentious practice are the attitude of prospective States parties with regard to the composition of the Court and the acceptance by those States of its compulsory jurisdiction.

Chambers

While for much of the 1960s and 1970s its caseload was small, the Court embarked on a review of its functioning and formed a Committee to revise the Rules of Court. One of the revisions proposed by that Committee was the insertion of a number of articles on the operation of the Court's Chambers. The Statute, in Article 29, provides that the Court shall form annually a five-member Chamber of summary procedure; it also provides, in Article 26, for the possibility of the Court forming a chamber to deal with a particular category of cases or with one particular case.

The provisions of Article 26 had, however, remained a dead letter, and the proposals for amendment made by the Rules Committee were, in consequence, not based upon any existing practice with regard to such Chambers; they were rather intended to draw the attention of States to the possibility of their requesting the constitution of an *ad hoc* Chamber to deal with cases they might submit to the Court.

And indeed, after the amendments to the Rules in 1972 and 1978, the Court received its first request for a Chamber to deal with a case in 1981. This was followed by three more requests in 1983, 1986 and 1987 respectively. Although the intention behind the amendments was thus given effect, the first case immediately revealed the problems involved in the composition of an *ad hoc* Chamber. The Parties in the *Gulf of Maine* case had expressed their views on that composition, not only in terms of the number of Judges to be involved, but also in terms of who those Judges were to be. In its Order on the composition of the Chamber formed to deal with the case, the Court made it clear that it was its prerogative to decide the membership of the Chamber; but in exercising that prerogative it followed the views on composition that had been expressed by the Parties.

In the other three cases referred to a Chamber of the Court, the views of the Parties on its composition were equally influential. Although in the beginning some fears were expressed to the effect that 'regional' Chambers might develop - which might have been inconsistent with the provision of the Statute on the representation on the Court of the main civilizations and principal legal systems of the world - then that fear has certainly not been justified. Although the presidents of the Chambers in the Burkina Faso/Mali and the El Salvador/Honduras frontier disputes did come from the regions concerned, the general composition of those Chambers was certainly not a regional one, nor did the judgments of those Chambers manifest a parochial approach.

The horrors of war.

The four disputes dealt with by Chambers of the Court might well not have been referred to the Court at all had not attention been drawn to this particular procedure by the amendments to the Rules of Court. Although, for that reason, those amendments constituted a step forward in the Court's practice, some problems have become apparent. One of them concerns the consistency of the jurisprudence of the Court. Unlike the Court of Justice of the European Communities, the International Court has no provision in its Statute for review by the full Court of Chamber decisions; the Chamber is the Court. In the European Court, the Chambers are bound to refer to the full Court when a principle of jurisprudence is involved. The decision, taken by the Chamber in the El Salvador/Honduras case, to allow a third State to intervene in that case, even if not as a party, drew attention to the fact that no such provision exists in the ICJ.

The functioning of the Chambers has further given rise to practical problems in relation to the organization of the work of the Court. The members of a Chamber likewise participate in the work on the cases which are before the full Court. This has created some difficulties regarding a manageable workload especially when, as has been the case, members of a Chamber subsequently became the President or Vice-President of the Court. Although no Chamber cases are currently pending, this practical difficulty may require consideration.

The Court has also provided for the possibility of the use by parties of a standing environmental Chamber (as distinct from an *ad hoc* Chamber formed for a particular dispute). As indicated above, the Court formed the Chamber for Environmental Matters, consisting of seven members, in July 1993. It is the first example of a Chamber created under Article 26, paragraph 1 of the Statute to deal with a certain category of cases. Although no case has as yet been referred to it, its creation shows that the Court is alive to changes in international relations and the developing concerns of the international community.

Trust Fund

While the Court itself has thus tried to be more responsive to the preoccupations of potential parties, the UN Secretary-General, for his part, made a valuable contribution by the creation of the 'Secretary-General's Trust Fund to Assist States in the Settlement of Disputes through the International Court of Justice'. In his announcement to the General Assembly on the creation of the Fund in November 1989, the Secretary-General referred to the judgments of the Court as 'the world's most authoritative pronouncement[s] on international law' and to his own special responsibility to promote the judicial settlement of disputes by the Court. Referring to the lack of legal expertise or of adequate funds that might constitute a problem for certain States parties to a dispute, he indicated that the purpose of the Fund was to provide financial assistance to developing States for expenses incurred in connection with a dispute submitted to the Court by way of a Special Agreement, or with the execution of a judgment of the Court resulting from such a Special Agreement, but not in connection with cases which were submitted to the Court by one State unilaterally.

Those restrictions mean that in cases brought before the Court upon the basis of a dispute settlement clause in a treaty or of the reciprocal effect of unilateral declarations of acceptance of the Court's compulsory jurisdiction, financial assistance cannot as yet be requested from the Fund. That approach was taken in order that the Fund not be used to finance cases in which the Respondent State contested the jurisdiction of the Court but at the same time, through its participation in the Fund, was contributing to the financing of that case.

Session of a Chamber of the Court.

Over 50 States have made significant contributions to the Fund, while others have indicated that they would be prepared to do so in response to specific applications. This recalls the beginnings of the Fund when Switzerland declared that it was willing to provide the funds needed for the implementation of the decision which a Chamber of the Court had rendered in 1986 in the frontier dispute between the two West African States of Burkina Faso and Mali. The cost of that implementation - delimitation of the frontier in the desert with the aid of a geostationary satellite - was prohibitive for the two States concerned. Only with the considerable financial help of Switzerland was the delimitation finally effected.

Another State which has applied for and has been granted assistance from the Fund is Chad, in its dispute with Libya.

The Court's Jurisdiction

The importance of the question of the Court's jurisdiction has already been touched upon on several occasions, as in the case of the Trust Fund. Let us therefore examine some aspects of that question.

There has been a tendency to regard the number of declarations made under the so-called 'Optional Clause', by which States accept, on a basis of reciprocity, the Court's jurisdiction as compulsory with regard to legal disputes, as constituting a statistical indication of the extent of that jurisdiction. However, something more needs to be said on this point than may seem warranted at first sight.

At the time of the creation of the Permanent Court of International Justice, the proposal of the drafters of its Statute was to create a court to which any State in any legal dispute with any other State could have recourse at any time. When this progressive project turned out to be unacceptable to some of the States - notably, the Great Powers on the League Council - which had to decide on this proposal with all that it implied for their sovereign prerogatives, the present provision of Article 36, paragraph 2, of the Statute was substituted. If it had proved impossible to compel all States to submit to the Court's jurisdiction, why not at least offer that possibility to those States that were willing to do so? In the League Assembly which finally adopted the Court's Statute, this 'Optional Clause' was proposed by Brazil and accepted.

Possibly as a consequence of the fact that during the period of the League most States then independent shared the same fundamental conception concerning the role to be played in international relations by the existing body of legal principles, the number of declarations of acceptance of the compulsory jurisdiction of the Permanent Court was much greater in terms of percentage that it has ever been for the present Court under the United Nations.

Moreover, taking into account the additional consideration that the reservations which have been made by States under the present system are generally greater in number and of much wider scope than those made at the time of the League, there is no escape from the conclusion that the resulting compulsory jurisdiction of the Court has considerably diminished - at any rate, relatively, since the 1930's. Some comfort may be derived from the fact that, in the last few years, the number of declarations under the Optional Clause has started to rise again, largely as a result of the change of attitude of the former Socialist States with regard to the Court's jurisdiction, while an increase in the number of declarations made by African States can also be noted. Even though in percentage-terms the growing number of declarations only equals the growth in the membership of the United

BOTSWANA

16 III 70.

I, Sir Seretse Khama, President of the Republic of Botswana, have the honour to declare on behalf of the Government of the Republic of Botswana, that it recognizes as compulsory *ipso facto* and without special agreement, on condition of reciprocity, the jurisdiction of the International Court of Justice, in accordance with paragraph 2 of Article 36 of the Statute of the Court.

This Declaration does not extend:

(a) to disputes in respect of which the parties have agreed or shall agree to have recourse to another means of peaceful settlement; or

(b) to disputes relating to matters which, by international law, are essentially within the domestic jurisdiction of the Republic of Botswana.

The Government of the Republic of Botswana also reserves the right at any time, by means of a notification addressed to the Secretary-General of the United Nations, and with effect as from the moment of such notification, either to add to, amend or withdraw any of the foregoing reservations, or any that may hereafter be added.

Done at Gaborone this 14th day of January in the year of our Lord one thousand nine hundred and seventy.

(Signed) Seretse M. KHAMA,
President.

Nations, the 'decline of the optional clause' - as the title of a 1956 article written by a former President of the Court, Sir Humphrey Waldock, significantly reads - seems to have been halted.

The declarations of acceptance of the compulsory jurisdiction of the Court do not form the only basis upon which States lay their disputes before it. As already pointed out, a *Compromis* has been the basis for several very successful and effective decisions by the Court in land boundary cases and other cases. It is also the basis of the pending case between Hungary and Slovakia on the Gabčikovo-Nagymaros hydroelectric dam project in the Danube River.

That case is a further sign of the new willingness of the former Socialist States to submit to the Court's jurisdiction - a development that was triggered by the address that Mr Gorbachev gave to the General Assembly of the United Nations on 7 December 1988, in which he said:

> We believe that the jurisdiction of the International Court of Justice at The Hague as regards the interpretation and implementation of agreements on human rights should be binding on all States.

A few months later the Soviet Union withdrew its reservations with regard to the Court's jurisdiction under six major treaties on human rights. Many States of Eastern Europe followed suit and withdrew their reservations in a similar way for a great number of treaties, and not only human rights treaties.

In any event, whatever the variations in the Court's compulsory jurisdiction, the simple fact that the Court has at present more cases pending before it than ever before in its history (as many as fourteen in 1995), shows that the three traditional bases of jurisdiction - a *Compromis*, a dispute settlement clause in a treaty, and declarations of acceptance of the Court's compulsory jurisdiction - are sufficiently effective, provided that there is a basic political will of States to come to the Court.

It is sometimes suggested that States in recent years have 'abused' the Court by bringing cases for political and publicity purposes. However, the decision of a State to come to the Court of its own free will is always to a certain extent a political one; and the views expressed by the States parties before the Court on the interpretation of the law which, in their view, the Court should apply, often involve political aspects. Secondly, the interest of States in the public nature of the hearings before the Court and of the decision rendered by it is a perfectly legitimate one. And, finally, a dispute referred to the Court, being an international dispute, virtually always unfolds in a context that has its political elements. However, the Court's reasoning will be of a legal nature and will lead to a legal decision, whatever the motives of the parties.

The international press is nowadays more than ever interested in the Cases brought to the Court.

One cannot leave the question of the Court's jurisdiction without having addressed - at so significant a point in history as its 50th anniversary - so important a topic as the restriction of the Court's jurisdiction to cases between States only. It was precisely during those past fifty years that States, which were the bearers *par excellence* of rights and duties under international law, saw new subjects of international law come into being, i.e., intergovernmental and non-governmental international organizations, multinational companies and, last but not least, individuals. Following the changes in the content of the law which those developments have brought about the time may be approaching to consider changes in the Statute to grant access to the Court to such categories of litigants other than States. But the difficulties of so doing should not be underestimated.

Conclusion

In view of all that has been said one would seem justified in concluding that the Court in its fifty-year existence has fulfilled the tasks incumbent upon it. It has been instrumental in the peaceful settlement of many a dispute between States, on occasion contributing to a lessening of tension in the wider region concerned. Moreover, in the process, it has greatly contributed to the elucidation and development of international law, not only with regard to more specialized subjects such as the law of treaties, the law of the sea and diplomatic protection, but also on questions of international peace and security.

Another fundamental contribution has been the confirmation of the principle of the stability of borders. The law of international organizations, of self-determination and of territorial sovereignty, as well as questions of human rights, have been clarified and expanded by the Court in its advisory function.

In these ways, within the limits imposed upon it by the provisions of the Charter and of the Statute, the Court's role in the unfolding history of international relations has been considerable.

Looking to the future, to the next fifty years, one might however wonder whether some fundamental changes might not be called for. Suggestions to extend the Court's contentious jurisdiction (to international organizations or individuals) as well as its advisory jurisdiction (to the Secretary-General or national courts), the idea of a constitutional role for the Court and, in the context of the creation of specialized international tribunals, such as the Law of the Sea Tribunal and, potentially, an international criminal court, the suggestion that the International Court might be given the additional function of serving as a Court of Appeals, all deserve study.

Their implementation - were such radical developments to be considered desirable and feasible - would have far-reaching effects upon and require fundamental changes to the practice and procedures that have been followed by the Court, from the beginning of the Permanent Court of International Justice in the 1920s down to the present time.

Statistics

A FEW FIGURES CONCERNING THE FUNCTIONING OF THE ICJ IN THE PAST FIFTY YEARS

Number of Cases:	96
Advisory:	22
Contentious:	74
by Unilateral Application:	62
by Special Agreement:	12
Number of Judges:	82
Nationalities represented:	44
Number of Judges *ad hoc*:	59
Nationalities represented:	36
Nations represented:	47
Number of Cases:	41
Number of Judgments:	60
on Jurisdiction:	8
on Preliminary Objections:	11
on Intervention:	3
on Merits:	7
on Compensation:	1
Number of Advisory Opinions:	22
by General Assembly:	14
by Security Council:	1
by ECO SOC:	1
by IMO:	1
by UNESCO:	1
by WHO:	2
by Committee Review UNAT:	3

Number of Cases Withdrawn, Removed or Discontinued:	22
Number of Orders:	290
on Time-Limits:	152
on the Extension of Time-Limits:	71
on Time-Limits for Choosing a Judge *ad hoc*:	1
on the Appointment of a Judge *ad hoc*:	2
on the Composition of the Court:	4
on the Constitution of a Chamber:	6
on Interim Measures of Protection:	20
on Intervention:	9
on the Appointment of Experts:	4
on the Joining of Cases:	2
on the Joining of Preliminary Objections to the Merits:	1
on the Withdrawal of Preliminary Objections:	1
on the Inspection *in loco*:	1
on the Removal of a Case:	23
Number of Declarations:	155
Number of Separate Opinions:	244
Number of Dissenting Opinions:	245

JUDGES OF THE INTERNATIONAL COURT OF JUSTICE 1946-1996

Name	Nationality	Judge	President	Vice-President	Contentious Cases	Advisory Opinions	Declarations	Separate Opinions	Dissenting Opinions
Ago	Italy	1979-1995			24	6	1	6	2
Aguilar	Venezuela	1991-1995			15	1	3 (1 Joint)	–	1 Joint
Ajibola	Nigeria	1991-1994			14	–	–	4	2
Alfaro	Panama	1959-1964		1961-1964	10	2	1	1	–
Alvarez	Chile	1946-1955			15	8	2	2	7
Ammoun	Lebanon	1965-1976		1970-1976	8	3	2	4	1
Armand-Ugon	Uruguay	1952-1961			25	5	–	1	4 (1 Joint)
Azevedo	Brazil	1946-1951			7	6	–	3	4
Badawi	Egypt	1946-1965		1955-1958	36	12	3	3 (1 Joint)	10 (1 Joint)
Basdevant	France	1946-1964	1949-1952	1946-1949	36	12	2 (1 Joint)	3 (1 Joint)	7 (2 Joint)
Baxter	USA	1979-1980			2	–	–	–	–
Bedjaoui	Algeria	1982-	1994-		21	5	–	2 (1 Joint)	2
Bengzon	Philippines	1967-1976			8	3	1	2	2 Joint
Bustamante	Peru	1961-1970	1967-1970		5	1	–	4	2
Carneiro	Brazil	1951-1955			8	2	–	2	4
Castro	Spain	1970-1979			8	3	–	6	3
Córdova	Mexico	1955-1964			21	4	–	1	1
Dillard	USA	1970-1979			8	3	3 (Joint)	5	2
El-Erian	Egypt	1979-1981			2	1	–	1	–
Elias	Nigeria	1976-1991	1982-1985	1979-1982	13	5	1	2	1
El-Khani	Syria	1981-1985			3	2	1	–	2
Evensen	Norway	1985-1994			17	3	2 (1 Joint)	2	1
Fabela Alfaro	Mexico	1946-1952			11	6	–	–	–
Ferrari Bravo	Italy	1995-			1	1	–	–	–
Fitzmaurice	UK	1960-1973			8	3	2 Joint	6	2 (1 Joint)
Fleischhauer	Germany	1994-			2	1	–	–	–
Forster	Senegal	1964-1982			11	5	2 Joint	5	2
Golunsky	USSR	1952-1953			–	–	–	–	–
Gros	France	1964-1984			13	5	7 (1 Joint)	4	9
Guerrero	El Salvador	1946-1958	1946-1949	1949-1955	27	10	1	–	1
Guillaume	France	1987-			16	3	2 Joint	–	–
Hackworth	USA	1946-1961	1955-1958		34	11	2	1	5
Herczegh	Hungary	1993-			5	1	–	–	–
Higgins	UK	1995-			1	1	–	–	–
Hsu Mo	China	1946-1956			21	10	1	1	2 Joint
Ignacio-Pinto	Benin	1970-1979			8	3	7	2	2
Jennings	UK	1982-1995	1991-1994		22	4	–	3 (2 Joint)	4
Jessup	USA	1961-1970			4	1	2	3	1
Jiménez de A.	Uruguay	1970-1979		1976-1979	8	3	7 (3 Joint)	5 (2 Joint)	4 (3 Joint)
Klaestad	Norway	1946-1961	1958-1961		34	11	2	3	5 (1 Joint)
Kojevnikov	USSR	1953-1961			24	5	8	–	–
Koretsky	USSR	1961-1970		1967-1970	5	1	2	–	3

JUDGES OF THE INTERNATIONAL COURT OF JUSTICE 1946-1996 (continued)

Name	Nationality	Judge	President	Vice-President	Contentious Cases	Advisory Opinions	Declarations	Separate Opinions	Dissenting Opinions
Koroma	Sierra Leone	1994-			2	1	1	–	1
Krylov	USSR	1946-1952			11	6	2	1 Joint	5
Lacharrière	France	1982-1987		1985-1987	5	2	–	1	–
Lachs	Poland	1967-1993	1973-1976		29	8	9	8	2
Lauterpacht	UK	1955-1960			18	4	–	3	2
McNair	UK	1946-1955	1952-1955		15	8	1 Joint	2	5 (1 Joint)
Mbaye	Senegal	1982-1991		1988-1991	12	4	2	2	–
Morelli	Italy	1961-1970			5	1	1	5	3
Moreno-Quintana	Argentina	1955-1964			21	5	2	1	5
Morozov	USSR	1970-1985			12	6	1	3	7
Mosler	FR Germany	1976-1985			7	3	–	6 (2 Joint)	1
Nagendra Singh	India	1973-1988	1985-1988	1976-1979	15	6	6	10	–
Ni Zhengyu	China	1985-1994			17	3	2	2	–
Oda	Japan	1976-		1991-1994	25	6	8	16	9
Onyeama	Nigeria	1967-1976			8	3	7	3	4
Padilla Nervo	Mexico	1964-1973			5	2	–	3	5
Parra	Venezuela	1996-			1	1	–	–	–
Pathak	India	1989-1991			5	1	–	–	–
Petrén	Sweden	1967-1976			8	3	4 (2 Joint)	5	7
Ranjeva	Madagascar	1991-			15	1	2	1	2
Rau	India	1952-1953			2	–	–	–	1 Joint
Read	Canada	1946-1958			27	10	–	3	9 (1 Joint)
Ruda	Argentina	1973-1991	1988-1991		20	7	–	10	1
Schwebel	USA	1981-	1994-		23	5	1	10	11
Sette-Camara	Brazil	1979-1992		1982-1985	17	5	–	3	1
Shahabuddeen	Guyana	1988-			16	3	1	16	2
Shi Jiuyong	China	1994			1	1	1 Joint	–	–
Spender	Australia	1958-1967	1964-1967		16	2	2	6	4 (2 Joint)
Spiropoulos	Greece	1958-1967			16	2	5	–	1
Tanaka	Japan	1961-1970			5	1	2 Joint	2	2
Tarassov	Russia	1985-1994			16	3	4	–	2
Tarazi	Syria	1976-1980			3	1	–	2	1
Vereshchetin	Russia	1994-			2	1	1 Joint	1	–
De Visscher	Belgium	1946-1952			7	6	–	1	1 Joint
Waldock	UK	1973-1981	1979-1981		8	3	5	2	2
Weeramantry	Sri Lanka	1991-			14	1	1 Joint	2	4
Wellington Koo	China	1957-1967		1964-1967	17	2	2	5	3 (1 Joint)
Winiarski	Poland	1946-1967	1961-1964		36	12	2	3	9
Zafrulla Khan	Pakistan	1954-1961		1958-1961	21	5	3	1	–
		1964-1973	1970-1973		4	2	–	–	–
Zoričić	Yugoslavia	1946-1958			27	10	3	1	3

JUDGES *AD HOC* AT THE INTERNATIONAL COURT OF JUSTICE 1946-1996

Name	Nationality	Judge	Country	Case
Abi-Saab, G.	Egypt	1983	Mali	Frontier Dispute
	Egypt	1990-	Chad	Territorial Dispute
Aghahosseini, M.	Iran	1989-	Iran	Aerial Incident 1988
Ago, R.	Italy	1960	Honduras	Arbitral Award 1906
Ajibola, Prince B. A.	Nigeria	1994-	Nigeria	Land and Maritime Boundary
Alayza y Paz Soldán	Peru	1950-51	Peru	Asylum
				Interpretation Judgment Asylum Case
				Haya de la Torre
Armand-Ugon, E. C.	Uruguay	1969-70	Uruguay	Barcelona Traction (New Phase)
Arruda Ferrer-Correia, A. de	Portugal	1991-	Portugal	East Timor
Barwick, Sir Garfield	Australia	1973-74	New Zealand	Nuclear Tests
Bastid, Mrs S.	France	1984-85	Tunisia	Revision 1982 Continental Shelf
Beb a Don, P.	Cameroon	1963	Cameroon	Northern Cameroons
Boni, A.	Ivory Coast	1975	Morocco	Western Sahara (Advisory Opinion)
Broms, B.	Finland	1991-92	Finland	Passage Great Belt
Caicedo Castilla, J. J.	Colombia	1950-51	Colombia	Asylum
				Interpretation Judgment Asylum Case
				Haya de la Torre
Carry, P.	Switzerland	1957-59	Switzerland	Interhandel
Castañeda, J.	Mexico	1982-84	Malta	Continental Shelf (Libya/Malta)
Castro, F. de	Spain	1959-61	Spain	Barcelona Traction
Chagla, M. A. C.	India	1957-60	India	Right of Passage
Cohen, M.	Canada	1981-84	Canada	Gulf of Maine
Colliard, C.-A.	France	1984-86	Nicaragua	Military/Paramilitary Activities
Daxner, I.	Czechoslovakia	1948	Albania	Corfu Channel
Ečer, B.	Czechoslovakia	1948-49	Albania	Corfu Channel
El-Kosheri, A. S.	Egypt	1992-	Libya	Aerial Incident Lockerbie
Evensen, J.	Norway	1978-82	Tunisia	Continental Shelf (Tunisia/Libya)
Fernandes, M.	Portugal	1957-60	Portugal	Right of Passage
Fischer, P. H.	Denmark	1988-93	Denmark	Maritime Delimitation Jan Mayen
		1991-92	Denmark	Passage Great Belt
Ganshof v.d. Meersch, W. J.	Belgium	1959-61	Belgium	Barcelona Traction
		1962	Belgium	Barcelona Traction (New Phase)
García Bauer, C.	Guatemala	1955	Guatemala	Nottebohm
Goitein, D.	Israel	1959	Israel	Aerial Incident 1955
Guggenheim, P.	Switzerland	1955	Liechtenstein	Nottebohm
Jiménez de Aréchaga, E.	Uruguay	1978-82	Libya	Continental Shelf (Tunisia/Libya)
		1982-85	Libya	Continental Shelf (Libya/Malta)
		1984-85	Libya	Revision 1982 Continental Shelf

JUDGES *AD HOC* AT THE INTERNATIONAL COURT OF JUSTICE 1946-1996 (continued)

Name	Nationality	Judge	Country	Case
Kreca, M.	Yugoslavia	1993-	Yugoslavia	Application Genocide Convention
Lauterpacht, E.	UK	1993-	Bosnia/Herzegovina	Application Genocide Convention
Luchaire, F.	France	1983	Burkina Faso	Frontier Dispute
Mbanefo, Sir Louis	Nigeria	1962	Ethiopia/Liberia	South West Africa
		1965-66	Ethiopia/Liberia	South West Africa
Mbaye, K.	Senegal	1991	Senegal	Arbitral Award 1989
		1994-	Cameroon	Land and Maritime Boundary
Morelli, G.	Italy	1954	Italy	Monetary Gold
Mosler, H.	F.R. Germany	1968-69	F.R. Germany	North Sea Continental Shelf
Nagendra Singh	India	1972	India	Appeal ICAO Council
Offerhaus, J.	Netherlands	1958	Netherlands	Application 1902 Convention
Rigaux, F.	Belgium	1992-	Iran	Oil Platforms
Riphagen, W.	Netherlands	1969-70	Belgium	Barcelona Traction (New Phase)
Ruda, J. M.	Argentina	1991-	Qatar	Maritime Delimitation Qatar-Bahrain
Sandjabi, K.	Iran	1952	Iran	Anglo-Iranian
Skubiszewski, M.	Poland	1995	Portugal	East Timor
		1995-	Slovakia	Gabčíkovo-Nagymaros Project
Sette-Camara, J.	Brazil	1990-	Libya	Territorial Dispute
Sørensen, M.	Denmark	1968-69	Denmark/Netherlands	North Sea Continental Shelf
Spiropoulos, J.	Greece	1952-53	Greece	Ambatielos
Stassinopoulos, M.	Greece	1976-78	Greece	Aegean Sea Continental Shelf
Stephen, Sir Ninian	Australia	1991-95	Australia	East Timor
Sterzel, F. J. C.	Sweden	1958	Sweden	Application 1902 Convention
Thierry, H.	France	1989-91	Guinea-Bissau	Arbitral Award 1989
Torres Bernárdez, S.	Spain	1991-92	Honduras	Land, Island and Maritime Frontier
		1995-	Spain	Fisheries Jurisdiction
Urrutia Holguín, F.	Colombia	1960	Nicaragua	Arbitral Award 1906
Valticos, N.	Greece	1984-85	Malta	Continental Shelf (Libya/Malta)
		1987-91	El Salvador	Land, Island and Maritime Frontier
		1991-	Bahrain	Maritime Delimitation Qatar-Bahrain
Virally, M.	France	1987-88	Honduras	Land, Island and Maritime Frontier
Wyk, J. T. van	South Africa	1962	South Africa	South West Africa
		1965-66	South Africa	South West Africa
Yaqub Ali Khan, M.	Pakistan	1973	Pakistan	Trial Pakistani Prisoners
Zafrulla Khan, M.	Pakistan	1973	Pakistan	Trial Pakistani Prisoners
Zourek, J.	Czechoslovakia	1959	Bulgaria	Aerial Incident 1955

LIST OF CASES OF THE INTERNATIONAL COURT OF JUSTICE 1946-1996

No.	Case	Parties	Status	Opinion/ Judgment/ Order	Aspect	Voting	Declaration	Sep. Opinion	Dis. Opinion
1	Corfu Channel	UK v. Albania	Contentious	Judgment					
1a				25.03.48	Prelim. Obj.	15-1		7	1
				9.04.49	Merits	Vary	2	1	5
				Order					
				31.07.47	Time-limits				
				10.12.47	Time-limits				
				26.03.48	Time-limits				
				17.12.48	Experts				
				9.04.49	Time-limits				
				24.06.49	Extension				
				19.11.49	Experts				
2	Corfu Channel		Contentious	Judgment	Compensation				
				15.12.49		12-2			2
3	Conditions of Admission of a State to Membership in the UN (Art. 4 Charter)		Advisory	Opinion					
				28.05.48		9-6		2	6
				Order					
				12.12.47	Time-limits				
4	Reparation for Injuries Suffered in the Service of the UN		Advisory	Opinion					
				11.04.49		Vary		2	4
				Order					
				11.12.48	Time-limits				
5	Fisheries	UK v. Norway	Contentious	Judgment					
				18.12.51		Vary	1	2	2
				Order					
				9.11.49	Time-limits				
				29.03.50	Extension				
				4.10.50	Extension				
				10.01.51	Extension				
6	Protection of French Nationals and Protected Persons in Egypt	France v. Egypt	Contentious	Order					
				29.03.50	Removal				
7	Asylum	Colombia/Peru	Contentious	Judgment					
				20.11.50		Vary			5
				Order					
				20.10.49	Time-limits				
				17.12.49	Extension				
				9.05.50	Extension				
8	Interpretation of Peace Treaties	Bulgaria, Hungary, Romania	Advisory	Opinion					
				30.03.50		11-3		1	3
				18.07.50		11-2	1		2
				Order					
				7.11.49	Time-limits				
				5.05.50	Time-limits				
9	Competence of the General Assembly for the Admission of a State to the UN		Advisory	Opinion					
				3.03.50		12-2			2
				Order					
				2.12.49	Time-limits				
10	International Status of South West Africa		Advisory	Opinion					
				11.07.50		Vary	3	2	3
				Order					
				30.12.49	Time-limits				

LIST OF CASES OF THE INTERNATIONAL COURT OF JUSTICE 1946-1996 (continued)

No.	Case	Parties	Status	Opinion/ Judgment/ Order	Aspect	Voting	Declaration	Sep. Opinion	Dis. Opinion
11	Rights of Nationals of USA in Morocco	France v. USA	Contentious	Judgment					
				27.08.52		Vary	1		4
				Order					
				22.11.50	Time-limits				
				25.06.51	Time-limits				
				31.10.51	Withdrawal				
				31.03.52	Extension				
12	Reservations to the Convention on the Prevention and Punishment of the Crimes of Genocide		Advisory	Opinion					
				28.05.51		7-5			5
				Order					
				1.12.50	Time-limits				
13	Request for Interpretation of the Judgment of 20 November 1950 in the Asylum Case	Colombia v. Peru	Contentious	Judgment					
				27.11.50		12-1			1
14	Haya de la Torre	Colombia v. Peru	Contentious	Judgment					
				13.06.51		Vary			1
				Order					
				3.01.51	Time-limits				
15	Ambatielos	Greece v. UK	Contentious	Judgment					
				1.07.52	Prelim. Obj.	Vary	1	2	5
				19.05.53	Merits	10-4			4
				Order					
				18.05.51	Time-limits				
				30.07.51	Extension				
				9.11.51	Extension				
				16.01.52	Extension				
				14.02.52	Time-limits				
				18.07.52	Time-limits				
16	Anglo-Iranian Oil Company	UK v. Iran	Contentious	Judgment	Prelim. Obj.				
				22.07.52		9-5		1	4
				Order					
				5.07.51	Interim Measures				
				5.07.51	Time-limits				
				22.08.51	Extension				
				20.12.51	Extension				
				11.02.52	Time-limits				
17	Minquiers and Ecrehos	France/UK	Contentious	Judgment					
				17.11.53		12-0	1	2	
				Order					
				15.01.52	Time-limits				
				26.06.52	Time-limits				
				27.08.52	Extension				
				29.01.53	Extension				
18	Nottebohm	Liechtenstein v. Guatemala	Contentious	Judgment					
				18.11.53	Prelim. Obj.	12-0	1		
				6.04.55		11-3			3
				Order					
				26.01.52	Time-limits				
				7.03.52	Extension				
				21.03.53	Time-limits				
				15.01.54	Extension				
				8.05.54	Time-limits				
				13.09.54	Extension				

LIST OF CASES OF THE INTERNATIONAL COURT OF JUSTICE 1946-1996 (continued)

No.	Case	Parties	Status	Opinion/ Judgment/ Order	Aspect	Voting	Declaration	Sep. Opinion	Dis. Opinion
19	Monetary Gold Removed from Rome in 1943	Italy v. France, UK and USA	Contentious	Judgment 15.06.54		Vary	1	1	1
				Order 1.07.53	Time-limits				
				3.11.53	Time-limits				
				26.01.54	Extension				
20	Electricité de Beyrouth Company	France v. Lebanon	Contentious	Order 20.10.53	Time-limits				
				8.04.54	Extension				
				29.07.54	Removal				
21	Effect of Awards of Compensation made by the UNAT		Advisory	Opinion 13.07.54		9-3		1	3
				Order 14.01.54	Time-limits				
22	Treatment in Hungary of Aircraft and Crew of USA	USA v. Hungary	Contentious	Order 12.07.54	Removal				
23	Treatment in Hungary of Aircraft and Crew of USA	USA v. USSR	Contentious	Order 12.07.54	Removal				
24	Voting Procedure Concerning the Territory of South West Africa		Advisory	Opinion 7.06.55		15-0	1	3	
				Order 14.12.54	Time-limits				
25	Aerial Incident of 10 March 1953	USA. v. Czechoslovakia	Contentious	Order 14.03.56	Removal				
26	Antarctica	UK v. Argentina	Contentious	Order 16.03.56	Removal				
27	Antarctica	UK v. Chile	Contentious	Order 16.03.56	Removal				
28	Aerial Incident of 7 October 1952	USA v. USSR	Contentious	Order 14.03.56	Removal				
29	Certain Norwegian Loans	France v. Norway	Contentious	Judgment 6.07.57		12-3	1	2	3
				Order 19.09.55	Time-limits				
				24.04.56	Time-limits				
				29.05.56	Extension				
				28.09.56	Joining Merits				
30	Judgements of Administrative Tribunal of ILO upon Complaints Made against UNESCO		Advisory	Opinion 23.10.56		Vary	1	3	4
				Order 5.12.55	Time-limits				
31	Admissibility of Hearings of Petitioners by the Committee on South West Africa		Advisory	Opinion 1.06.56		8-5	4	1	5
				Order 22.12.55	Time-limits				

LIST OF CASES OF THE INTERNATIONAL COURT OF JUSTICE 1946-1996 (continued)

No.	Case	Parties	Status	Opinion/ Judgment/ Order	Aspect	Voting	Declaration	Sep. Opinion	Dis. Opinion
32	Right of Passage over Indian Territory	Portugal v. India	Contentious	Judgment					
				26.11.57	Prelim. Obj.	Vary	2		3
				12.04.60	Merits	Vary	5	1	7
				Order					
				13.03.56	Extension				
				27.11.56	Extension				
				16.04.57	Extension				
				18.05.57	Extension				
				10.02.58	Extension				
				28.08.58	Extension				
				6.11.58	Extension				
				17.01.59	Extension				
33	Application of the Convention of 1902 Governing the Guardianship of Infants	Netherlands v. Sweden	Contentious	Judgment					
				28.11.58		11-4	2	6	3
				Order					
				19.08.57	Time-limits				
				17.04.58	Time-limits				
34	Interhandel	Switzerland v. USA	Contentious	Judgment					
				21.03.59	Prelim. Obj.				
				Order					
				24.10.57	Interim Measures		4	2	
				24.10.57	Time-limits				
				15.01.58	Extension				
				26.06.58	Time-limits				
35	Aerial Incident of 27 July 1955	Israel v. Bulgaria	Contentious	Judgment					
				26.05.59	Prelim. Obj.	12-4	1	2	4
				Order					
				26.11.57	Time-limits				
				27.01.58	Time-limits				
				17.12.58	Time-limits				
36	Aerial Incident of 27 July 1955	USA v. Bulgaria	Contentious	Order					
				26.11.57	Time-limits				
				27.01.58	Time-limits				
				19.05.58	Extension				
				12.08.58	Extension				
				8.10.58	Extension				
				9.09.59	Time-limits				
				23.10.59	Extension				
				30.05.60	Removal				
37	Aerial Incident of 27 July 1955	UK v. Bulgaria	Contentious	Order					
				26.11.57	Time-limits				
				27.01.58	Time-limits				
				19.05.58	Extension				
				27.05.59	Extension				
				3.08.59	Removal				
38	Sovereignty over Certain Frontier Land	Belgium/ Netherlands	Contentious	Judgment					
				20.06.59		10-4	2		2
				Order					
				12.12.57	Time-limits				
				27.05.58	Extension				
				1.07.58	Time-limits				

LIST OF CASES OF THE INTERNATIONAL COURT OF JUSTICE 1946-1996 (continued)

No.	Case	Parties	Status	Opinion/ Judgment/ Order	Aspect	Voting	Declaration	Sep. Opinion	Dis. Opinion
39	Arbitral Award Made by the King of Spain on 23 December 1906	Honduras v. Nicaragua	Contentious	Judgment 18.11.60 Order 3.09.58 7.10.59	 Time-limits Extension	 14-1	 1	 1	 1
40	Aerial Incident of 4 September 1954	USA v. USSR	Contentious	Order 9.12.58	 Removal				
41	Barcelona Traction, Light and Power Company, Ltd.	Belgium v. Spain	Contentious	Order 18.10.58 5.12.59 20.06.60 11.11.60 10.04.61	 Time-limits Extension Time-limits Extension Removal				
42	Compagnie du Port, des Quais et des Entrepôts de Beyrouths	France v. Lebanon	Contentious	Order 18.06.59 15.10.59 6.01.60 31.08.60	 Time-limits Extension Time-limits Removal				
43	Constitution of the Maritime Safety Comittee of the IGMCO		Advisory	Opinion 8.06.60 Order 5.08.59	 Time-limits	 9-5			 2
44	Aerial Incident of 7 November 1954	USA v. USSR	Contentious	Order 7.10.59	 Removal				
45	Temple of Preah Vihear	Cambodia v. Thailand	Contentious	Judgment 26.05.61 15.06.62 Order 5.12.59 10.06.60 26.05.61	 Prelim. Obj. Merits Time-limits Time-limits Time-limits	 12-0 Vary	 4 2	 2 2	 3
46/ 47	South West Africa	Ethiopia v. South Africa; Liberia v. South Africa	Contentious	Judgment 21.12.62 18.07.66 Order 13.01.61 13.01.61 20.05.61 5.12.61 5.02.63 18.09.63 20.01.64 20.10.64 18.03.65 29.11.65	 Prelim. Obj. Time-limits Time-limits Joining Cases Appointment Judge *ad hoc* Time-limits Time-limits Extension Time-limits Extension Composition Court Inspection *in loco*	 8-7 8-7	 1 1	 3 2	 6 7

LIST OF CASES OF THE INTERNATIONAL COURT OF JUSTICE 1946-1996 (continued)

No.	Case	Parties	Status	Opinion/ Judgment/ Order	Aspect	Voting	Declaration	Sep. Opinion	Dis. Opinion
48	Northern Cameroons	Cameroon v. UK	Contentious	Judgment					
				2.12.63	Prelim. Obj.	10-5	3	4	3
				Order					
				6.07.61	Time-limits				
				2.11.61	Extension				
				25.04.62	Extension				
				10.07.62	Extension				
				3.09.62	Time-limits				
				27.11.62	Extension				
				11.01.63	Extension				
49	Certain Expenses of United Nations (Art. 17 §2 Charter)		Advisory	Opinion					
				20.07.62		9-5	1	3	5
				Order					
				27.12.61	Time-limits				
50	Barcelona Traction, Light and Power Company Ltd. (New Application: 1962)	Belgium v. Spain	Contentious	Judgment					
				24.07.64	Prelim. Obj.	Vary	4	3	2
				5.02.70		15-1	3	8	1
				Order					
				7.08.62	Time-limits				
				16.03.63	Time-limits				
				28.07.64	Time-limits				
				11.06.65	Extension				
				12.01.66	Time-limits				
				23.11.66	Extension				
				12.04.67	Extension				
				15.09.67	Extension				
				24.05.68	Extension				
51/ 52	North Sea Continental Shelf	FR Germany/ Denmark FR Germany/ Netherlands	Contentious	Judgment					
				20.02.69		11-6	2	4	5
				Order					
				8.03.67	Time-limits				
				8.03.67	Time-limits				
				1.03.68	Time-limits				
				1.03.68	Time-limits				
				26.04.68	Joining of Two Cases				
53	Legal Consequences for States of the Continued Presence of South Africa in Namibia		Advisory	Opinion					
				21.06.71		Vary	1	6	2
				Order					
				5.08.70	Time-limits				
				28.08.70	Extension				
				26.01.71	Composition (1)				
				26.01.71	Composition (2)				
				26.01.71	Composition (3)				
				29.01.71	Appointment Judge *ad hoc*	10-5			5
54	Appeal Relating to the Jurisdiction of the ICAO Council	India v. Pakistan	Contentious	Judgment					
				18.08.72		Vary	2	5	2
				Order					
				16.09.71	Time-limits				
				3.12.71	Extension				
				19.01.72	Time-limits				
				20.03.72	Extension				

LIST OF CASES OF THE INTERNATIONAL COURT OF JUSTICE 1946-1996 (continued)

No.	Case	Parties	Status	Opinion/ Judgment/ Order	Aspect	Voting	Declaration	Sep. Opinion	Dis. Opinion
55	Fisheries Jurisdiction	UK v. Iceland	Contentious	Judgment					
				2.02.73	Jurisdiction	14-1	1	1	1
				25.07.74	Merits	10-4	3	8	3
				Order					
				17.08.72	Interim Measures	14-1	3		1
				18.08.72	Time-limits	9-6			2
				15.02.73	Time-limits				
				12.07.73	Interim Measures				
56	Fisheries Jurisdiction	Germany v. Iceland	Contentious	Judgment					
				2.02.73	Jurisdiction	14-1	1	1	1
				25.07.74	Merits	10-4	3	8	3
				Order					
				17.08.72	Interim Measures	14-1	3		1
				18.08.72	Time-limits	9-6			2
				15.02.73	Time-limits				
				12.07.73	Interim Measures				
57	Application for Review of Judgement No. 158 of the UNAT		Advisory	Opinion					
				12.07.73		Vary	3	3	4
				Order					
				14.07.72	Time-limits				
58	Nuclear Tests	Australia v. France	Contentious	Judgment					
				20.12.74		9-6	6	4	6
				Order					
				22.06.73	Interim Measures	8-6	4		4
				12.07.73	Intervention Fiji	8-5	4		
				28.08.73	Extension				
				20.12.74	Intervention				
59	Nuclear Tests	New Zealand v. France	Contentious	Judgment					
				20.12.74		9-6	6	4	6
				Order					
				22.06.73	Interim Measures	8-6	4		4
				12.07.73	Intervention Fiji	8-5	4		
				28.08.73	Extension				
				20.12.74	Intervention				
60	Trial of Pakistani Prisoners of War	Pakistan v. India	Contentious	Order					
				13.07.73	Time-limits	8-4		1	1
				29.09.73	Extension				
				15.12.73	Removal				
61	Western Sahara		Advisory	Opinion					
				16.10.75		Vary	3	6	1
				Order					
				3.01.75	Time-limits				
				22.05.75	Judge *ad hoc*	Vary	1		1

LIST OF CASES OF THE INTERNATIONAL COURT OF JUSTICE 1946-1996 (continued)

No.	Case	Parties	Status	Opinion/ Judgment/ Order	Aspect	Voting	Declaration	Sep. Opinion	Dis. Opinion
62	Aegean Sea Continental Shelf	Greece v. Turkey	Contentious	Judgment					
				19.12.78	Jurisdiction	12-2	2	3	2
				Order					
				11.09.76	Interim Measures	12-1		8	1
				14.10.76	Time-limits				
				18.04.77	Extension				
63	Continental Shelf	Tunisia/Libyan Arab Jamahiriya	Contentious	Judgment					
				14.04.81	Intervention	16-0		3	
				24.02.82	Malt	10-4		3	3
				Order					
				20.02.79	Time-limits				
				3.06.80	Time-limits				
				16.04.81	Time-limits				
64	United States Diplomatic and Consular Staff in Tehran	USA v. Iran	Contentious	Judgment					
				24.05.80		Vary		1	2
				Order					
				15.12.79	Interim Measures				
				24.12.79	Time-limits				
				12.05.81	Removal				
65	Interpretation of Agreement of 25 March 1951	WHO and Egypt	Advisory	Opinion					
				20.12.80		Vary		8	1
				Order					
				6.06.80	Time-limits				
66	Application for Review of Judgement No. 273 of the UNAT		Advisory	Opinion					
				20.07.82		Vary		4	4
				Order					
				6.08.81	Time-limits				
				8.10.81	Extension				
67	Delimitation of the Maritime Boundary in the Gulf of Maine Area	Canada/USA	Contentious	Judgment					
				12.10.84		4-1		1	1
				Order					
				20.01.82	Const. Chamber				
				1.02.82	Time-limits				
				28.07.82	Extension				
				5.11.82	Time-limits				
				27.07.83	Time-limits				
				30.03.84	Tech. Expert				
68	Continental Shelf	Libyan Arab Jamahiriya/Malta	Contentious	Judgment					
				21.03.84	Intervention	11-5		4	5
				3.06.85	Italy	14-3	1	6	3
				Order					
				27.07.82	Time-limits				
				26.04.83	Time-limits				
				21.03.84	Time-limits				
69	Frontier Dispute	Burkina Faso/ Republic of Mali	Contentious	Judgment					
				22.12.86		5-0		2	
				Order					
				3.04.85	Chamber				
				12.04.85	Time-limits				
				3.10.85	Time-limits				
				10.01.86	Interim Measures				
				9.04.87	Nomination of Experts				

LIST OF CASES OF THE INTERNATIONAL COURT OF JUSTICE 1946-1996 (continued)

No.	Case	Parties	Status	Opinion/ Judgment/ Order	Aspect	Voting	Declaration	Sep. Opinion	Dis. Opinion
70	Military and Paramilitary Activities in and against Nicaragua	Nicaragua v. USA	Contentious	Judgment					
				26.11.84	Jurisdiction	Vary		6	1
				27.06.86	Merits	Vary		7	3
				Order					
				10.05.84	Interim Measures	Vary		2	1
				14.05.84	Time-limits				
				04.10.84	Intervention	Vary		8	1
				22.01.85	Time-limits				
				18.11.87	Time-limits				
				26.09.91	Removal				
71	Application for Revision and Interpretation of the Judgment of 24 February 1982	Tunisia v. Libyan Arab Jamahiriya	Contentious	Judgment					
				10.12.85		14-0		4	
72	Application for Review of Judgement No. 333 of the UNAT		Advisory	Opinion					
				27.05.87		Vary	1	3	3
				Order					
				13.09.84	Time-limits				
				30.11.84	Extension				
73	Border and Transborder Armed Actions	Nicaragua v. Costa Rica	Contentious	Order					
				21.10.86	Time-limits				
				21.07.87	Extension				
				19.08.87	Removal				
74	Border and Transborder Armed Actions	Nicaragua v. Honduras	Contentious	Judgment					
				20.12.88	Jurisdiction	14-0	1	3	
				Order					
				22.10.86	Time-limits				
				31.03.88	Interim Measures				
				21.04.89	Time-limits				
				31.08.89	Extension				
				14.12.89	Extension				
				27.05.92	Removal				
75	Land, Island and Maritime Frontier Dispute	El Salvador/ Honduras	Contentious	Judgment					
				13.09.90	Intervention	5-0		1	
				11.09.92		4-1	1	2	1
				Order					
				8.05.87	Chamber		1		
				27.05.87	Time-limits				
				29.05.87	Time-limits				
				12.01.89	Extension				
				13.12.89	Extension				
				13.12.89	Chamber	13-0		1	
				28.02.90	Intervention	12-3	1		3
				14.09.90	Time-limits				
76	Elettronica Sicula S.p.A (ELSI)	USA v. Italy	Contentious	Judgment					
				20.07.89		Vary		1	1
				Order					
				02.03.87	Time-limits/ Chamber				
				17.11.87	Time-limits				
				20.12.88	Chamber				

LIST OF CASES OF THE INTERNATIONAL COURT OF JUSTICE 1946-1996 (continued)

No.	Case	Parties	Status	Opinion/ Judgment/ Order	Aspect	Voting	Declaration	Sep. Opinion	Dis. Opinion
77	Applicability of the Obligation to Arbitrate under section 21 of the UN Headquarters Agreement of 26 June 1947		Advisory	Opinion					
				26.04.88		15-0	1	3	
				Order					
				9.03.88	Time-limits				
78	Maritime Delimitation in the Area between Greenland and Jan Mayen	Denmark v. Norway	Contentious	Judgment					
				14.06.93		14-1	4	5	1
				Order					
				14.10.88	Time-limits				
				21.06.90	Time-limits				
79	Aerial Incident of 3 July 1988	Islamic Republic of Iran v. USA	Contentious	Order					
				13.12.89	Time-limits	14-0	1	2	
				12.06.90	Extension				
				09.04.91	Time-limits				
				18.12.91	Extension				
				5.06.92	Extension				
				22.02.96	Removal				
80	Certain Phosphate Lands in Nauru	Nauru v. Australia	Contentious	Judgment					
				26.06.92		Vary		1	4
				Order					
				18.07.89	Time-limits				
				8.02.91	Time-limits				
				29.06.92	Time-limits				
				25.06.93	Time-limits				
				13.09.93	Removal				
81	Applicability of Article VI, Section 22, of the Convention on the Priveleges and Immunities of the UN		Advisoy	Opinion					
				15.12.89		14-0		3	
				Order					
				14.06.89	Time-limits				
82	Arbitral Award of 31 July 1989	Guinea-Bissau v. Senegal	Contentious	Judgment					
				12.11.91			2	4	4
				Order					
				1.11.89	Time limits				
				2.03.90	Interim Measures	14-1		2	1
83	Territorial Dispute	Libyan Arab Jamahiriya/Chad	Contentious	Judgment					
				3.02.94		16.1	1	2	1
				Order					
				26.10.90	Time-limits				
				26.08.91	Time-limits				
				14.04.92	Time-limits				
84	East Timor	Portugal v. Australia	Contentious	Judgment					
				30.06.95		14-2		4	2
				Order					
				3.05.91	Time-limits				
				19.06.92	Time-limits				
85	Maritime Delimitation between Guinea-Bissau and Senegal	Guinea-Bissau v. Senegal	Contentious	Order					
				8.11.95	Removal				
86	Passage Through The Great Belt	Finland v. Denmark	Contentious	Order					
				29.07.91	Interim Measures	16-0	1	3	
				29.07.91	Time-limits				
				10.09.92	Removal				

LIST OF CASES OF THE INTERNATIONAL COURT OF JUSTICE 1946-1996 (continued)

No.	Case	Parties	Status	Opinion/ Judgment/ Order	Aspect	Voting	Declaration	Sep. Opinion	Dis. Opinion
87	Maritime Delimitation and Territorial Questions between Qatar and Bahrain	Qatar v. Bahrain	Contentious	Judgment					
				01.07.94		15-1	1	2	1
				15.02.95		10-5			5
				Order					
				11.10.91	Time-limits				
				26.06.92	Time-limits				
				28.04.95	Time-limits				
				1.02.96	Extension				
88	Questions of Interpretation and Application of the 1971 Montreal Convention arising from the Aerial Incident at Lockerbie	Libyan Arab Jamahiriya v. UK	Contentious	Order					
				14.04.92	Interim Measures	11-5	6	2	5
				19.06.92	Time-limits				
				22.09.95	Time-limits				
89	Questions of Interpretation and Application of the 1971 Montreal Convention arising from the Aerial Incident at Lockerbie	Libyan Arab Jamahiriya v. USA	Contentious	Order					
				14.04.92	Interim Measures	11-5	6	2	5
				19.06.92	Time-limits				
				22.09.95	Time-limits				
90	Oil Platforms	Islamic Republic of Iran v. USA	Contentious	Order					
				4.12.92	Time-limits				
				3.06.93	Time-limits				
				18.01.94	Time-limits				
91	Application of the Convention on the Prevention and Punishment of the Crime of Genocide	Bosnia and Herzegovina v. Yugoslavia (Serbia and Montenegro)	Contentious	Order					
				8.04.93	Interim Measures				
				16.04.93	Time-limits				
				13.09.93	Interim Measures	Vary	1	4	2
				07.10.93	Time-limits				
				21.03.95	Time-limits				
				14.07.95	Time-limits				
92	The Gabčíkovo-Nagymaros Project	Hungary/ Slovakia	Contentious	Order					
				14.07.93	Time-limits				
				20.12.94	Time-limits				
93	Legality of The Use by the State of Nuclear Weapons in Armed Conflict		Advisory	Order					
				13.09.93	Time-limits				
				20.06.94	Time-limits				
94	Land and Maritime Boundary between Cameroon and Nigeria	Cameroon v. Nigeria	Contentious	Order					
				16.06.94	Time-limits				
				10.01.96	Time-limits				
				15.03.96	Interim Measures	Vary	8	1	
95	Legality of the Threat or Use of Nuclear Weapons		Advisory	Order					
				1.02.95	Time-limits				
96	Fisheries Jurisdiction	Spain v. Canada	Contentious	Order					
				2.05.95	Time-limits				

A FEW FIGURES CONCERNING THE FUNCTIONING OF THE PCIJ

Number of Cases:	66
Advisory:	27
Contentious:	36
Number of Cases Withdrawn, Removed or Discontinued:	10
Number of Judges:	31
Nationalities represented:	20
Number of Deputy-Judges:	8
Nationalities represented:	8
Number of Judges *ad hoc*:	23
Number of Cases involved:	33
Number of Nations involved:	11
Number of Judgments:	32
on Jurisdiction:	7
on Merits:	25
in Chamber Summary Procedure:	2
Number of Advisory Opinions:	27

Number of Orders:	137
Number of Orders Printed:	28
on the Extension of Time-Limits:	1
on Interim Measures of Protection:	8
on the Appointment of Experts:	2
on the Joining of Preliminary Objections to the Merits:	4
on the Withdrawal of Preliminary Objections:	5
on the Discontinuance of a Case:	2
Number of Declarations:	1
Number of Observations:	2
Number of Separate Opinions:	25
Number of Dissenting Opinions:	42
Number of Statements of Dissent:	5

JUDGES OF THE PERMANENT COURT OF INTERNATIONAL JUSTICE 1922-1942

Name	Dates	Nationality	Judge	President	Declaration	Observation	Separate Opinion	Dissenting Opinion	Statement Dissent
Adatci, Minéitciro	1869-1934	Japanese	1931-1934	1931-1933				1	2
Altamira y Crevea, Rafael	1866-1946<	Spanish	1922-1942				1	3	
Anzilotti, Dionisio	1876-1960	Italian	1922-1942	1928-1930			6	5	
Barbosa, Rui	1849-1923	Brazilian	1922-1923						
Bustamante y Sirven, Ant. S. de	1865-1951	Cuban	1922-1942					1	
Cheng, Tein-Hsi	1884-1970	Chinese	1936-1942				1		
Erich, Rafael Waldemar	1879-1946	Finnish	1938-1942				1	1	
Eysinga, Willem J. M. van	1878-1961	Dutch	1931-1942				3	7	2
Finlay, Viscount	1842-1929	British	1922-1929						
Fromageot, Henri	1864-1949	French	1929-1942					1	
Guerrero, J. Gustavo	1876-1958	Salvadoran	1931-1942	1936-1942				1	
Hammarskjøld, Åke	1905-1961	Swedish	1936-1937				1		
Huber, Hans Max	1874-1960	Swiss	1922-1930	1925-1927					
Hudson, Manley O.	1886-1960	American	1936-1942				4	2	
Hughes, Charles E.	1862-1948	American	1928-1930						
Hurst, Cecil J. B.	1870-1963	British	1929-1942	1934-1936			2	5	
Kellogg, Frank B.	1856-1937	American	1930-1935					1	
Loder, Bernard C.J.	1849-1935	Dutch	1922-1930	1922-1924					
Moore, John B.	1860-1947	American	1922-1928						
Nagaoka, Harukazu	1877-1949	Japanese	1935-1942				2		
Negulescu, Dumitru	1875-1950	Romanian	1931-1942					2	
Nyholm, Didrik G. G.	1858-1931	Danish	1922-1930						
Oda,Yorozu	1878-1945	Japanese	1922-1930						
Pessôa, Epitacio da Silva	1865-1942	Brazilian	1923-1930						
Rolin-Jaequemyns, Edouard	1863-1936	Belgian	1931-1936					2	
Rostworowski, Michel J. C.	1864-1940	Polish	1931-1940		1		1	4	
Schücking, Walther	1875-1935	German	1931-1935			1	1	3	
Urrutia, Francisco J.	1870-1950	Colombian	1931-1942					2	
Visscher, Charles De	1884-1973	Belgian	1937-1942				2		1
Wang, Ch'ung-hui	1881-1958	Chinese	1931-1936			1		1	
Weiss, Charles A.	1858-1928	French	1922-1928						

DEPUTY-JUDGES
OF THE PCIJ 1922-1936

Name	Nationality	Years
Beichmann, Frederik V. N.	Norwegian	1922-1930
Erich, Rafael W.	Finnish	1931-1936
Matta, José C. Da	Portugese	1931-1936
Negulesco, Dimitru	Romanian	1922-1930
Novacovitch, Mileta	Yugoslav	1931-1936
Redlich, Josef	Austrian	1931-1936
Wang-Ch'ung-hui	Chinese	1922-1930
Yovanovitch, Michailo	Serb-Croat-Slovene	1922-1930

NATIONAL JUDGES/JUDGES *AD HOC*
OF THE PCIJ 1922-1942

Name	Year	Case
Bruns, V.	1931	A/B 43
	1931	A/B 44
Calloyanni, M.A.	1924	A 2
	1925	A 5
	1927	A 11
	1930	B 17
	1932	A/B 45
Dreyfus, E.	1929	A 22
	1930	A 24
	1932	A/B 46
Ehrlich, L.	1927	A 9
	1927	A 13
	1928	A 17
Feïzi Daïm Bey	1927	A 10
Fromageot, H.	1929	A 20/21
Hermann Otavsky, M.	1933	A/B 61
Huber, M.	1935	A/B/ 67
Novacovitch, M.	1929	A 20/21
Pappazoff, T.	1930	B 17
	1932	A/B 45
	1939	A/B 77
Rabel, E.	1925	A 6
	1925	A 7
	1927	A 9
	1927	A 13
	1928	A 17
Römer'is, M.	1932	A/B 47
	1932	A/B 49
	1938	A/B 75
	1939	A/B 76
Rostworowski, M.	1925	A6
	1925	A7
	1929	A 23
Seferiades, S.P.	1934	A/B 62
	1937	A/B 71
Shücking, W.	1923	A 1
Stasinskas, M.	1931	A/B 42
Strandman, M.	1938	A/B 75
	1939	A/B 76
Tenekides, C.G.	1939	A/B 78
De Tomcsanyi	1933	A/B 61
	1935	A/B 68
Vogt, B.	1932	A/B 48
	1933	A/B 53
Yovanovitch, M.	1930	B 18
Zahle, H.	1932	A/B 48
	1933	A/B 53
Zoričíč, M.	1935	A/B 67
	1935	A/B 68

LIST OF CASES OF THE PERMANENT COURT OF INTERNATIONAL JUSTICE 1922-1940

No.	Series	Case	Parties	Status	Opinion/ Judgment/ Order	Aspect	Voting	Declaration	Sep. Opinion	Dis. Opinion
1	B1	Designation of the Workers' Delegate for the Netherlands at ILC		Advisory	Opinion 31.07.22					
2	B2-3	Competence of the International Labour Organisation		Advisory	Opinion 12.08.22					
3	B4	Nationality Decrees issued in Tunis and Morocco on 8 November 1921		Advisory	Opinion 7.02.23					
4	B5	Status of Eastern Carelia		Advisory	Opinion 23.07.23					4
5	A1	The S. S. Wimbledon	UK, France, Italy, Japan v. Germany	Contentious	Judgment 28.06.23	Intervention				3
6	B6	Questions Relating to Settlers of German Origin in Poland	Germany, Poland	Advisory	Opinion 10.09.23					
7	B7	Questions Concerning the Acquisition of Polish Nationality	Finland	Advisory	Opinion 15.09.23					
8	B8	Delimitation of the Polish-Czechoslovakian Frontier	Czechoslovakia, Poland	Advisory	Opinion 6.12.23					
9	A2	The Mavrommatis Palestine Concessions	Greece v. UK	Contentious	Judgment 30.08.24	Jurisdiction				5
10	B9	The Monastery of Saint-Naoum	Albania, Yugoslavia	Advisory	Opinion 4.09.24					
11	A3	Treaty of Neuilly, Article 179, Annex, Paragraph 4	Bulgaria v. Greece	Contentious	Judgment 12.09.24	Chamber for Summary Procedure				
12	B10	Exchange of Greek and Turkish Populations	Greece, Turkey	Advisory	Opinion 21.02.25					
13	A4	Interpretation of Judgment No. 3	Greece v. Bulgaria	Contentious	Judgment 26.03.25					
14	A5	The Mavrommatis Jerusalem Concessions	Greece v. UK	Contentious	Judgment 26.03.25	Merits				1
15	B11	Polish Postal Service in Danzig	Danzig, Poland	Advisory	Opinion 16.05.25					
16	A6	Case Concerning Certain German Interests in Polish Upper Silesia	Germany v. Poland	Contentious	Judgment 25.08.25	Jurisdiction				1
17	B12	Interpretation of Article 3, Paragraph 2, of the Treaty of Lausanne	UK, Turkey	Advisory	Opinion 21.11.25					
18	A7	Case concerning Certain German Interests in Polish Upper Silesia	Germany v. Poland	Contentious	Decision concerning 5.02.26 Judgment 25.08.26	Joinder Merits				1

LIST OF CASES OF THE PERMANENT COURT OF INTERNATIONAL JUSTICE 1922-1940 (continued)

No.	Series	Case	Parties	Status	Opinion/ Judgment/ Order	Aspect	Voting	Declaration	Sep. Opinion	Dis. Opinion
19	B13	Competence of the International Labour Organisation		Advisory	Opinion 23.07.26					
20	A8	Denunciation of the Treaty of 2 November 1865 Between China and Belgium	Belgium v. China	Contentious	Order 8.01.27 15.02.27 18.06.27	Interim Measures Interim Measures Interim Measures				
21	A9	Case Concerning the Factory at Chorzów	Germany v. Poland	Contentious	Judgment 26.07.27	Jurisdiction	10-3			1
22	A10	The Lotus Case	France v. Turkey	Contentious	Judgment 7.09.27	Composition				6
23	A11	Case of the Readaptation of the Mavrommatis Jerusalem Concessions	Greece v. UK	Contentious	Judgment 10.10.27	Jurisdiction Preliminary Objections	7-4			4
24	A12	Case Concerning the Factory at Chorzów	Germany v. Poland	Contentious	Order 21.11.27	Interim Measures				
25	B14	Jurisdiction of the European Commission of the Danube between Galatz and Braila	UK, France, Italy, Romania	Advisory	Opinion 8.12.27					1
26	A13	Interpretations of Judgments Nos. 7 and 8	Germany v. Poland	Contentious	Judgment 16.12.27					1
27	A14	Denunciation of the Treaty of 2 November 1865 Between China and Belgium	China v. Belgium	Contentious	Order 21.02.28					
28	B15	Jurisdiction of the Courts of Danzig	Danzig, Poland	Advisory	Opinion 3.03.28		12-0			
29	A15	Rights of Minorities in Upper Silesia	Germany v. Poland	Contentious	Judgment 26.04.28		8-4			
30	A16	Denunciation of the Treaty of 2 November 1865 Between China and Belgium	China v. Belgium	Contentious	Order 13.08.28					
31	B16	Interpretation of the Greco-Turkish Agreement of 1 December 1926	Greece-Turkey	Advisory	Opinion 28.08.28					
32	A17	The Factory at Chorzów	Germany v. Poland	Contentious	Judgment 13.09.28 Order 13.09.28	Merits Expert Enquiry	9-3			2
33	A18-19	Denunciation of the Treaty of 2 November 1865 Between China and Belgium	China v. Belgium	Contentious	Order 25.05.29 Order 25.05.29	Withdrawal Expert Enquiry				
34a	A20	Case Concerning the Payment of Various Serbian Loans	France v. Yugoslavia	Contentious	Judgment 12.07.29		9-3			3

LIST OF CASES OF THE PERMANENT COURT OF INTERNATIONAL JUSTICE 1922-1940 (continued)

No.	Series	Case	Parties	Status	Opinion/ Judgment/ Order	Aspect	Voting	Declaration	Sep. Opinion	Dis. Opinion
34b	A 21	Case Concerning the Payment in Gold of Brazilian Loans Issued in France	Brazil v. France	Contentious	Judgment 12.07.29					2
35	A22	Case of the Free Zones of Upper Savoy and the District of Gex	France v. Switzerland	Contentious	Order 19.08.29	First Phase			3	
36	A23	Case Relating to the Territorial Jurisdiction of the International Commission of the River Oder	UK, Czecho-slovakia, Denmark, France, Germany, Sweden; Poland	Contentious	Judgment 10.09.29		9-3			
37	B17	The Greco- Bulgarian 'Communities'	Bulgaria, Greece	Advisory	Opinion 31.07.30					
38	B18	City of Danzig and International Labour Organisation		Advisory	Opinion 26.08.30		6-4		2	
39	A24	Case of the Free Zones of Upper Savoy and the District of Gex	France v. Switzerland	Contentious	Order 6.12.30	Second Phase				6
40	A/B 40	Access to German Minorities Schools in Upper Silesia	Germany, Poland	Advisory	Opinion 15.05.31					1
41	A/B 41	Customs Régime between Germany and Austria	Austria, Czecho-slovakia, France, Germany, Italy	Advisory	Opinion 5.09.31				1	7
42	A/B 42	Railway traffic between Lithuania and Poland	Lithuania, Poland	Advisory	Opinion 15.10.31					
43	A/B 43	Access to, or Anchorage in, the Port of Danzig, of Polish War Vessels	Danzig, Poland	Advisory	Opinion 11.12.31					1
44	A/B 44	Treatment of Polish Nationals and other Persons of Polish Origin or Speech in the Danzig Territory	Danzig, Poland	Advisory	Opinion 4.02.32				1	4
45	A/B 45	Interpretation of The Greco-Bulgarian Agreement of 9 December 1927	Bulgaria, Greece	Advisory	Opinion 8.03.32					
46	A/B 46	Case of the Free Zones of Upper Savoy and the District of Gex	France v. Switzerland	Contentious	Judgment 7.06.32	Third Phase				3
47	A/B 47	Interpretation of the Statute of the Memel Territory	UK, France, Italy, Japan v. Lithuania	Contentious	Judgment 24.06.32	Jurisdiction				
48	A/B 48	Legal Status of the South-Eastern Territory of Greenland	Norway v. Denmark Denmark v. Norway	Contentious	Order 2.08.32 3.08.32	Joinder of Suits Interim Measures				

LIST OF CASES OF THE PERMANENT COURT OF INTERNATIONAL JUSTICE 1922-1940 (continued)

No.	Series	Case	Parties	Status	Opinion/ Judgment/ Order	Aspect	Voting	Declaration	Sep. Opinion	Dis. Opinion
49	A/B 49	Interpretation of the Statute of the Memel Territory	UK, France, Italy, Japan v. Lithuania	Contentious	Judgment 11.08.32	Merits				5
50	A/B 50	Interpretation of the Convention of 1919 Concerning Employment of Women during the Night		Advisory	Opinion 15.11.32					1
51	A/B 51	Case concerning the Delimitation of the Territorial Waters Between the Island of Castellorizo and the Coast of Anatolia	Italy v. Turkey	Contentious	Order 26.01.33	Withdrawal				
52	A/B 52	Prince Von Pless Administration	Germany v. Poland	Contentious	Order 4.02.33	Joining Merits and Preliminary Objections				
53	A/B 53	Legal Status of Eastern Greenland	Denmark v. Norway	Contentious	Judgment 5.04.33					2
54	A/B 54	Prince Von Pless Administration	Germany v. Poland	Contentious	Order 11.05.33	Interim Measures				
55	A/B 55	Legal Status of South-Eastern Territory Greenland	Norway v. Denmark	Contentious	Order 11.05.33	Withdrawal				
56	A/B 56	Appeals from certain Judgments of the Hungaro-Czecho-slovak Mixed Arbitral Tribunal	Czechoslovakia v. Hungary	Contentious	Order 12.05.33	Withdrawal				
57	A/B 57	Prince Von Pless Administration	Germany v. Poland	Contentious	Order 4.07.33	Prorogation				
58	A/B 58	Case concerning the Polish Agrarian Reform and the German Minority	Germany v. Poland	Contentious	Order 29.07.33	Interim Measures				3
59	A/B 59	Prince Von Pless Administration	Germany v. Poland	Contentious	Order 2.12.33	Withdrawal				
60	A/B 60	Case concerning the Polish Agrarian Reform and the German Minority	Germany v. Poland	Contentious	Order 2.12.33	Withdrawal				
61	A/B 61	Appeal from a Judgment of the Hungaro-Czechoslovak Mixed Arbitral Tribunal	Czechoslovakia v. Hungary	Contentious	Judgment 15.12.33					1
62	A/B 62	Lighthouse case between France and Greece	France v. Greece	Contentious	Judgment 17.03.34				2	
63	A/B 63	The Oscar Chinn Case	Belgium v. UK	Contentious	Judgment 12.12.34				3	2

LIST OF CASES OF THE PERMANENT COURT OF INTERNATIONAL JUSTICE 1922-1940 (continued)

No.	Series	Case	Parties	Status	Opinion/ Judgment/ Order	Aspect	Voting	Declaration	Sep. Opinion	Dis. Opinion
64	A/B 64	Minority Schools in Albania	Albania, Greece	Advisory	Opinion 6.04.35					3
65	A/B 65	Consistency of Certain Danzig Legislative Decrees with the Constitution of the Free City	Danzig	Advisory	Opinion 4.12.35			1	2	
66	A/B 66	The Pajzs, Csáky, Esterházy Case	Hungary v. Yugoslavia	Contentious	Order 23.05.36	Joining Merits to Prelim. Objections				
67	A/B 67	The Losinger & Co. Case	Switzerland v. Yugoslavia	Contentious	Order 27.06.36	Joining Merits to Prelim. Objections				2
68	A/B 68	The Pajzs, Csáky, Esterházy Case	Hungary v. Yugoslavia	Contentious	Judgment 16.12.36	Merits			5	1
69	A/B 69	The Losinger & Co. Case	Switzerland v. Yugoslavia	Contentious	Order 14.12.36	Discontinuance				
70	A/B 70	Diversion of Water from the Meuse	Netherlands v. Belgium	Contentious	Judgment 28.06.37				3	3
71	A/B 71	Lighthouses in Crete and Samos	France v. Greece	Contentious	Judgment 8.10.37				4	
72	A/B 72	The Borchgrave Case	Belgium v. Spain	Contentious	Judgment 6.11.37	Jurisdiction				1
73	A/B 73	The Borchgrave Case	Belgium v. Spain	Contentious	Order 30.04.38	Discontinuance				
74	A/B 74	The Phosphates in Morocco Case	Italy v. France	Contentious	Judgment 14.06.38	Jurisdiction			1	1
75	A/B 75	The Railway Line Panevezys-Saldutiskis	Estonia v. Lithuania	Contentious	Order 30.06.38	Joining Merits to Preliminary Objections				
76	A/B 76	The Railway Line Panevezys-Saldutiskis	Estonia v. Lithuania	Contentious	Judgment 30.06.38				2	2
77	A/B 77	The Electricity Company of Sofia and Bulgaria	Belgium v. Bulgaria	Contentious	Judgment 4.04.39				3	4
78	A/B 78	The 'Société Commerciale De Belgique'	Belgium v. Greece	Contentious	Judgment 15.06.39				1	1
79	A/B 79	The Electricity Company of Sofia and Bulgaria	Belgium v. Bulgaria	Contentious	Order 5.12.39	Interim Measures				
80	A/B 80	The Electricity Company of Sofia and Bulgaria	Belgium v. Bulgaria	Contentious	Order 26.02.40					

Bibliography

This bibliography covers publications referred to in this book, publications that have been consulted and publications suggested for further reading on specific topics dealt with. In its presentation the listing approximately follows the successive chapters of the book.

Publications on the International Court of Justice over the past fifty years are numerous, a comprehensive listing of which can be found in the annual *Bibliography* produced by the Court's Registry. The present bibliography aims to represent the major publications on the Court produced by the academic world over the past fifty years. Titles have in some cases been abbreviated. For example, the International Court of Justice is referred to as the ICJ. Names of periodicals have also been abbreviated, a listing of which follows.

ABBREVIATIONS

ABAJ	American Bar Association Journal
AFDI	Annuaire français de droit international
AHLADI	Anuario hispano-luso-americano de derecho internacional
AIDI	Annuaire de l'Institut de Droit International
AJICL	African Journal of International and Comparative Law
ASIL	American Society of International Law
AV	Archiv des Völkerrechts
AYBIL	Asian Yearbook of International Law
BJIL	Brooklyn Journal of International Law
BUILJ	Boston University International Law Journal
BYBIL	British Year Book of International Law
CBR	Canadian Bar Review
CIJ	Cour internationale de Justice
CJTL	Columbia Journal of Transnational Law
CLB	Commonwealth Law Bulletin
CLJ	Cambridge Law Journal
CLR	California Law Review
CPJI	Cour Permanente de Justice Internationale
CWILJ	California Western International Law Journal
CWRJIL	Case Western Reserve Journal of International Law
DI	Diritto internazionale
DJIL	Dickinson Journal of International Law
DJILP	Denver Journal of International Law and Policy
EJIDR	Emory Journal of International Dispute Resolution
EJIL	European Journal of International Law
EPIL	Encyclopedia of Public International Law
GJICL	Georgia Journal of International and Comparative Law
GLJ	Georgetown Law Journal
GYBIL	German Yearbook of International Law
HAIL	Hague Academy of International Law
HICLR	Hastings International and Comparative Law Review
HLR	Hokkaido Law Review
HRIR	Hellenic Review of International Relations
HYBIL	Hague Yearbook of International Law
ICJ	International Court of Justice
ICLQ	International and Comparative Law Quarterly
IJIL	Indian Journal of International Law

ILA	International Law Association
ILC	International Law Commission
IowaLR	Iowa Law Review
ILR	Israel Law Review
IR	International Relations
IYBIL	Italian Yearbook of International Law
JAIL	Japanese Annual of International Law
LAICLJ	Loyola of Los Angeles International and Comparative Law Journal
LJIL	Leiden Journal of International Law
MJILT	Maryland Journal of International Law and Trade
MJIL	Michigan Journal of International Law
MLR	Modern Law Review
MULR	Melbourne University Law Review
MYBILS	Michigan Yearbook of International Legal Studies
NDL	Notre Dame Lawyer
NILR	Netherlands International Law Review
NJW	Neue Juristische Wochenschrift
NTIR	Nederlands Tijdschrift voor Internationaal Recht
NTIRJG	Nordisk Tidsskrift for International Ret og Jus Gentium
NYLSJICL	New York Law School Journal of International and Comparative Law
NYUJILP	New York University Journal of International Law and Politics
OAS	Organization of American States
OAU	Organization of African Unity
OSLJ	Ohio State Law Journal
ÖZöRV	Österreichische Zeitschrift für öffentliches Recht und Völkerrecht
PBAQ	Pennsylvania Bar Association Quarterly
PCA	Permanent Court of Arbitration
PaceYBIL	Pace Yearbook of International Law
PCIJ	Permanent Court of International Justice
PrASIL	Proceedings American Society of International Law
PYBIL	Polish Yearbook of International Law
RBEP	Revista brasileira de estudios políticos
RDC	Recueil des Cours / Collected Courses Hague Academy of International Law
RDI	Rivista di diritto internazionale
RDILC	Revue de droit international et de législation comparée
REgDI	Revue égyptienne de droit international
REsDI	Revista española de derecho internacional
RGDIP	Revue générale de droit international public
RHDI	Revue hellénique de droit international
SJIL	Stanford Journal of International Law
SJILC	Syracuse Journal of International Law and Commerce
SJIR	Schweizerisches Jahrbuch für Internationales Recht
STLJ	Suffolk Transnational Law Journal
TILR	Texas International Law Journal
TLCP	Transnational Law & Contemporary Problems
UDLR	University of Dayton Law Review
VJIL	Virginia Journal of International Law
VJTL	Vanderbilt Journal of Transnational Law
WLR	Washington Law Review
YBILC	Yearbook of the International Law Commission
YBWA	Yearbook World Affairs
ZaöRV	Zeitschrift für ausländisches öffentliches Recht und Völkerrecht

THE HISTORY OF INTERNATIONAL LAW

Aitchison, C.: A collection of treaties, 14 vols., 1929-1933. Reprint 1973.
Al-Ghunaimi, M. T.: The Muslim conception of international law and the Western approach, 1968.
Alexandrowicz, C. H.: The Afro-Asian world and the Law of Nations. RDC 123 (1968/1) 117-214.
Alexandrowicz, C. H.: An introduction to the history of the Law of Nations in the East Indies (16th, 17th and 18th centuries), 1967.
Alexandrowicz, C. H.: Treaty and diplomatic relations between European and South Asian powers in the 17th and 18th centuries. RDC 100 (1960/2) 203-321.
Alvarez, A.: La codification du droit international, 1912.
Alvarez, A.: Le droit international américain, son fondement, sa nature, 1910.
Alvarez, A.: The Monroe Doctrine, 1924.
Austin, J.: Lectures on jurisprudence or the philosophy of positive law, 1885.
Bacon, F.: The advancement of learning, ed. G. W. Kitchen, 1950.
Barberis, J. A.: Les règles spécifiques du droit international en Amérique latine. RDC 235 (1992/4) 81-230.
Beach, D.: The Shona and Zimbabwa 900-1850, 1981.
Becker, C. L.: The heavenly city of the eighteenth-century philosophers, 1932.
Bello, A.: Principios de derecho de gentes, 1832.
Bergh, G. C. J. J. van den: Themis en de muzen. De functie van de gebonden vormen in het recht, 1964.
Bluntschli, J. C.: Das moderne Völkerrecht der civilisierten Staten als Rechtsbuch dargestellt, 1878.
Bonfils, H.: Manuel de droit international public. Paris, 1898.
Bovill, E. W.: The golden trade of the Moors, 1958.
Brasslof, S.: Der römische Staat und seine internationale Beziehungen, 1928.
Bynkershoek, C. van: De dominio maris dissertatio, 1702. Reprint Washington, 1923 (ed. Carnegie Endowement).
Bynkershoek, C. van: De foro legatorum, 1721.
Bynkershoek, C. van: Quaestionum juris publici libri II, 1737.
Calvo, C.: Le droit international théorique et pratique, 1896.
Calvo, C.: Derecho internacional teórico y práctico de Europa y América, 2 vols., 1868.
Castañon, C. G. F.: Les problèmes coloniaux et les classiques espagnols du droit des gens. RDC 86 (1954/2) 557-700.
Catalano, P.: Linee del sistema sovranazionale romano, 1965.
Catton, B.: The centennial history of the Civil War, 3 vols., 1966.
Chacko, C. J.: India's contribution to the field of international law concepts. RDC 93 (1958/1) 117-221.
Chatterjee, H.: International law and inter-state relations in Ancient India, 1958.
Claude, I. S., Jr.: Swords into plowshares. The problems and progress of international organisation, 1971.
Contamine, Ph.: La guerre au moyen âge, 1986.
Coulson, N. J.: A history of Islamic law, 1964.
Crowe, S. E.: The Berlin West Africa Conference (1884-1885), 1942.
Compendium volkenrechtsgeschiedenis, ed. A. C. G. M. Eyffinger, 1991 (contr. C. H. Bezemer, C. G. Roelofsen, G. J. Tanja, J. C. M. Willems, L. C. Winkel)
Depping, G. B.: Histoire du commerce entre le Levant et l'Europe, 2 vols., 1830.
Dickmann, F.: Der Westfälische Frieden, 1972.
Dione, A.: L'exposé du droit international public de l'Imam al-Shaybani, 3 vols., 1975.
Drouet, J.: L'Abbé Saint-Pierre, 1912.
El-Kosheri, A.: History of the Law of Nations. Regional developments: Islam. EPIL 7 (1984) 222-230.
Elias, T. O.: The nature of African customary law, 1956.
Elias, T. O.: Africa and the development of international law, 1972.
Escarra, J.: La Chine et le droit international, 1936.
Gabrieli, F.: Chroniques arabes des croisades, 1977.
Gardot, A.: Jean Bodin, sa place parmi les fondateurs du droit international. RDC 50 (1934/4) 549-747.
Grabar, Vl.: The history of international law in Russia (1647-1917), 1958; English edn, ed. W. E. Butler, 1990.
Grewe, W. G.: Epochen der Völkerrechtsgeschichte, 1984.
Grotius, H.: Sophompaneas tragoedia (1635), ed. A. Eyffinger, 1992.
Grotius, H.: Meletius, ed. G. H. M. Posthumus Meyjer, 1988.
Grotius, H.: De jure belli ac pacis (1625), ed. B. J. A. de Kanter-van Hettinga Tromp, 1939; annotated reprint, ed. R. Feenstra, C.E. Persenaire, 1993.
Grotius, H.: De jure praedae, ed. H. G. Hamaker, 1848.
Hugo Grotius and international relations, ed. H. Bull, B. Kingsbury, A. Roberts, 1990.
Gruen, E. S.: The Hellenistic world and the coming of Rome, 2 vols., 1984.
Guani, A.: La solidarité internationale dans l'Amérique latine. RDC 8 (1925) 207-337.
Guggenheim, P.: Der Völkerbund in seiner politischen-rechtlichen Wirklichkeit, 1932.
Gutierrez, C. J.: La Corte de Justicia Centro-Americana, 1978.
Hackworth, G. H.: Digest of international law, 8 vols., 1940-1944.
Haggenmacher, P.: Grotius et la doctrine de la guerre juste, 1983.
Haggenmacher, P.: Grotius and Gentili: A reassessment of Thomas E. Holland's Inaugural Lecture. In: Hugo Grotius and international relations, ed. H. Bull et al., 1990, 133-176.
Hall, W. E.: A treatise on international law, 1880.
Hazard, P.: La crise de la conscience européenne (1680-1715), 3 vols., 1935.
Heffter, A. W.: Das Europäische Völkerrecht der Gegenwart, 1844.
Hemleben, S.: Plans for world peace through six centuries, 1943.
Hertslett, E.: The map of Africa by treaty, 3 vols., 1967.
Hobbes, Th: Leviathan, 1650.
Irye, K.: The principles of international law in the light of Confucian doctrine. RDC 120 (1967/1) 1-59.
Jayatillike, K. N.: The principles of international law in Buddhist doctrine. RDC 120 (1967/1) 441-567.
Janssen, W.: Die Anfänge des modernen Völkerrechts und der neuzeitlichen Diplomatie, 1965.
Kaminski, G.: Chinesische Positionen zum Völkerrecht, 1973.
Kant, I.: Zum ewigen Frieden, 1795.
Karnes, T. L.: The failure of a union: Central America, 1824-1960; 1961.
Keen, M. H.: The laws of war in the late Middle Ages, 1965.
Klose, P.: Die völkerrechtliche Ordnung des hellenistischen Staatenwelt in der Zeit von 280 bis 168 v. Chr., 1972.
Knight, W. S. M.: The life and works of Hugo Grotius, 1925.
Lange, Chr. L.: Histoire de l'internationalisme, 3 vols., 1919.

Larsen, A. O.: Greek Federal States, 1968.
Leibnitz, G. W.: Codex juris gentium diplomaticus, 2 vols., 1693-1700.
Lombard, M.: L'Islam dans sa première grandeur (VIIIe-XIe siècle), 1971.
Maalouf, A.: Les croisades vues par les Arabes, 1983.
Mahmassani, S.: The principles of international law in the light of Islamic doctrine. RDC 117 (1966/1) 205-323.
Martens, F. F.: International law of civilized nations, 2 vols., 1882.
Martens, F. F.: Recueil des traités et conventions conclus par la Russie avec les puissances étrangères, 15 vols., 1874-1909.
Martens, G. F. von: Précis du droit des gens moderne de l'Europe, 1788.
Martin, V.: La vie internationale dans la Grèce des cités, 1940.
Martin, W. A. P.: Les vestiges d'un droit international dans l'Ancienne Chine. RDILC 14 (1882) 227-242.
Mattingly, G.: Renaissance diplomacy, 1955.
Medlicott, W. N.: Bismarck, Gladstone and the concert of Europe, 1956.
Menzel, A.: Kallikles. Eine Studie zur Geschichte der Lehre vom Rechte des Stärkeren, 1922.
Meulen, J. ter: Der Gedanke der internationalen Organisation in seiner Entwicklung, 3 vols., 1917-1940.
Michelis, F. de: Le origini storichi e culturali del pensiero di Ugo Grozio, 1967.
Miquel, A.: L'Islam et sa civilisation (VIIe-XXe siècle), 1977.
Miyazaki, S.: History of the Law of Nations. Regional developments: Far East. EPIL 7 (1984) 215-222.
Molen, G. H. J. van der: Alberico Gentili and the development of international law, 1968.
Moore, J. B.: A digest of international law, 8 vols., 1906.
Moore, J. B.: American diplomacy, 1905.
Morse, H. B.: The international relations of the Chinese Empire, 3 vols., 1910-1918. Reprint 1964.
Muir, W.: The Caliphate. Its rise, decline and fall, 1963.
Munro, D. G.: The five Republics of Central America, 1918. Reprint 1967.
Nawaz, M. K.: The doctrine of 'Jihad' in Islamic legal doctrine. IJIL 8 (1959) 32-48.
Nussbaum, A.: A concise history of the Law of Nations, 1958.
Nys, E.: Les origines du droit international, 1894.
Nys, E.: Le droit international, 3 vols., 1904-1906.
Nys, E.: Le droit de la guerre et les précurseurs de Grotius, 1882.
Ompteda, D. H. L. von: Literatur der gesammten sowohl natürlichen wie positiven Völkerrechts, 2 vols., 1785.
Paradisi, B.: Civitas maxima. Studi di storia del diritto internazionale I, 1974.
Parry, J. H.: Trade and dominion. The European Oversea Empires in the eighteenth century, 1971.
Pauw, F. de: Grotius and the Law of the Sea, 1965.
Penn, W.: An sssay towards the present and future peace of Europe, 1693.
Phillimore, R.: Commentaries upon international law, 4 vols., 1854-1861.
Phillimore, R.: International law, 3 vols., 1864-1873.
Phillimore, W. G. F.: Three centuries of treaties of peace, 1918. Reprint 1973.
Preiser, W.: History of the Law of Nations. Basic questions and principles. EPIL 7 (1984) 126-132.
Preiser, W.: History of the Law of Nations. Ancient times to 1648. EPIL 7 (1984) 132-160.
Preiser, W.: Frühe völkerrechtliche Ordnungen der aussereuropäischen Welt, 1976.
Pufendorf, S.: De jure naturae et gentium libri octo, 1672.
Queller, D. E.: The office of ambassador in the Middle Ages, 1967.
Quintana, J. J.: The Latin American contribution to international adjudication. NILR 39 (1992) 127.
Rechid, A.: L'Islam et le droit des gens. RDC 60 (1937/2) 375-504.
Reibstein, Völkerrecht, Eine Geschichte seiner Ideen in Lehre und Praxis, 1958.
Rifaat, A. M.: International aggression. A study of the legal concept: its development and definition in international law, 1979.
Roelofsen, C. G.: Grotius and the international politics of the seventeenth century. In: Hugo Grotius and international relations, ed. H. Bull et al., 1990, 95-131.
La República Argentina en la segunda conferencia internacional de la paz (Haya 1907), 1908.
Rosenthal, E. I. J.: Political thought in medieval Islam, 1962.
Russel, F.: The just war in the Middle Ages, 1975.
Ryder, A. F. C.: Benin and the Europeans (1485-1897), 1969.
Saletore, B. A.: Ancient Indian political thought and institutions, 1963.
Sastri, K. A. N.: Inter-state relations in Asia. IJIA 2 (1953) 133-153.
Sastry, K. R. R.: Hinduism and international law. RDC 117 (1966/1) 503-615.
Schacht, J.: The origins of Muhammadan jurisprudence, 1953.
Schindler, D., J. Toman (eds.): The laws of armed conflict: A collection of conventions, resolutions and other documents, 1988.
Scott, G.: The rise and fall of the League of Nations, 1973.
Scott, J. B.: The Spanish origin of international law. Francisco de Vitoria and his Law of Nations, 1934.
Singh, N.: India and international law, 1969.
Smith, R. S.: The Kingdom of the Yoruba, 1969.
Soder, J.: Francisco Suárez und das Völkerrecht, 1973.
Southern, R. W.: Western views of Islam in the Middle Ages, 1978.
Spinoza, B.: Ethica ordine geometrico demonstrata, 1677.
Spinoza, B.: Tractatus theologico-politicus, 1670.
Die Staatsverträge des Altertums, ed. H. Bengtson, vols. 2-3, 1969, 1975.
Staunton, Sir George: An authentic account of an Embassy from the King of Great Britain to the Emperor of China, 1799.
Thomas, J. A.: History and international law in Asia: A time for review? In: Essays Wang Tieya, ed. R. St. John Macdonald, 1994, 813-857.
Triepel, H.: Völkerrecht und Landesrecht, 1899.
Truyol y Serra, A.: History of the Law of Nations. Regional developments: Latin America. EPIL 7 (1984) 231-237.
Tuck, R.: Natural rights theories: Their origins and development, 1979.
Umozurike, U. O.: International law and colonialism in Africa, 1979.
Urrutia, F. J.: El ideal internacional de Bolívar, 1911.
Urrutia, F. J.: Le continent américain et le droit international, 1928.
Vattel, E.: Le droit des gens ou principes de la loi naturelle appliquées à la conduite et aux affaires des nations et des souverains, 1758.
Verdross, A.: Die Quellen des universellen Völkerrechts. Eine Einführung, 1973.

Verosta, S.: History of the Law of Nations: 1648-1815. EPIL 7 (1984) 160-179.
Verosta, S.: Die Geschichte des Völkerrechts, in: A. Verdross: Völkerrecht, 1964, 31-94.
Verzijl, J. H. W.: International law in historical perspective, 12 vols., 1969-1992.
Vinogradoff, P.: Historical types of international law I, 1913.
Vollenhoven, C. van: The three stages in the evolution of the Law of Nations, 1919.
Walker, R. L.: The multi-state system of Ancient China, 1953.
Walters, F. P.: A history of the League of Nations, 1952.
Wang Tieya: International law in China: Historical and contemporary perspectives. RDC 221 (1990/2) 195-370.
Westbrook, D. A.: Islamic international law and public international law: Separate expression of world order. VJIL 33 (1993) 819-897.
Ward, R.: An enquiry into the foundations of history of the Law of Nations in Europe from the times of the Greeks and Romans to the age of Grotius, 2 vols., 1795.
Weeramantry, C. G.: An invitation to the law, 1982.
Weeramantry, C. G.: Islamic jurisprudence, 1988.
Weeramantry, C. G.: The law in crisis: Bridges of understanding, 1975.
Wehberg, H.: Die Satzung des Volkenbundes, 1931.
Westlake, J.: International law, 2 vols., 1904-1907.
Wheaton, H.: Elements of international law, 1836.
Wheaton, H.: History of the Law of Nations in Europe and the Americas, 1845.
Wolf, D.: Die Irenik des Hugo Grotius, 1972.
Wolff, C.: Jus gentium methodo scientifica pertractum, 1749.
Wolff, C.: Jus naturae, 8 vols., 1740-1748.
The world of Hugo Grotius. Proceedings of the 1983 colloquium Royal Netherlands Academy, ed. R. Feenstra, 1984.
Wright, Q.: Mandates under the League of Nations, 1930.
Yepes, J. M.: Del congreso de Panamá a la conferencia de Caracas, 1826-1954, 2 vols., 1955.
Yepes, J. M.: La contribution de l'Amérique latine au développement du droit international public et privé. RDC 32 (1930/2) 697-795.
Zavala, S.: Las instituciones jurídicas en la conquista de América, 1971.
Ziegler, K.-H.: Die Beziehungen zwischen Rom und dem Partherreich, 1964.
Zorn, P.: Die Zukunft des Völkerrechts, 1918.
Zorn, P.: Grundzüge des Völkerrechts, 1901.
Zorn, P.: Deutschland und die beiden Haager Friedenskonferenzen, 1920.
Zouche, R.: Juris et judicii fecialis, sive juris inter gentes, et quaestionum de eodem explicatio, 1650.

PEACE STUDIES

Angell, N.: The great illusion, 1911. Reprint 1972.
Bentham, J.: Plan for an universal and perpetual peace, 1939. Reprint 1974.
Bloch, J. de: The future of war in its technical, economic, and political relations: Is war now impossible? 1899. Reprint 1971.
Cobden, R.: The political writings of Richard Cobden, 2 vols., 1903. Reprint 1973.
Cruce, E.: The new Cineas, 1623. Reprint 1972.
Erasmus, D.: The complaint of peace, 1517.
Fried, A. H.: Handbuch der Friedensbewegung, vol. 1, 1911. Reprint 1972.
Kant, I.: Zum ewigen Frieden, 1795. Reprint 1972.
Ladd, W.: An essay on a Congress of Nations, 1840. Reprint 1971.
Levi, L.: War and its consequences: With proposals for establishing a Court, 1881.
McNamara, H. T. J.: Peace, permanent and universal: Its practicability, value and consistency with divine revelation, 1841.
Passy, F.: Pour la Paix, 1909. Reprint 1972.
World encyclopedia of peace, 4 vols., ed. L. Pauling, 1986.
Podebrad, J. Z.: The universal peace organization of King George of Bohemia: A fifteenth century plan for world peace. Reprint 1972.
Saint-Pierre, C. (Abbé de): Mémoires pour rendre la paix perpétuelle en Europe (1713). Reprint 1974.
Schlochauer, H. J.: Die Idee des ewigen Friedens, 1935.
Stead, W. T: The United States of Europe on the eve of the parliament of peace, 1899. Reprint 1971.
Sully, M. de: Grand design of Henry IV (Le grand dessein, 1638). English Reprint 1972.
Suttner, B. von: Lay down your arms, 1894 (Die Waffen Nieder, 1889). English Reprint 1972.
Whitney, E. L.: The American Peace Society: A centennial history, 1928.
Wright, Q.: A study of war, 1965.

THE HAGUE PEACE CONFERENCES / THE PEACE PALACE

Die Abkommen der Haager Friedenskonferenzen, der Londoner Seekriegskonferenz nebst Genfer Konvention, 1910.
Académie de droit international de La Haye / The Hague Academy of International Law. Livre jubilaire / Jubilee Book, 1923-1973, ed. R. J. Dupuy, 1973.
Adler, A.: Die Haager Friedenskonferenz des Jahres 1907 und die Fortbildung des Völkerrechts, 1909.
Arnaud, E.: La troisième conférence de la paix, 1913.
Asser, T. M. C.: De tweede vredes-conferentie: een terugblik, 1908.
Barbosa, R.: Actes et discours, 1907.
Bederman, D. J.: The Hague Peace Conferences of 1899 and 1907. In: International courts for the twenty-first century, ed. M. W. Janis, 1992, 9-11.
La Belgique et l'arbitrage obligatoire à la deuxième conférence de la paix, 1908.
Blankert, A.: Ferdinand Bol (1616-1680), 1976.
Bustamante y Sirvén, A. S. de: La segunda conferencia de la Paz reunida en El Haya en 1907; 1908.
Choate, J. H.: Horace Porter and James Brown Scott: American addresses at the Second Hague Peace Conference, 1910.
Choate, J. H.: The two Hague conferences, 1913.

Les conventions et déclarations de La Haye de 1899 et 1907, accompagnées de tableaux des signatures, ratifications, et adhésions et des textes des réserves, 1918.
Darby, W. E.: The peace conference at The Hague: Its history, work, and results, 1900.
Davis, C. D.: The USA and the Second Hague Peace Conference. American diplomacy and international organization (1899-1944), 1975.
Davis, C. D: The USA and the First Hague Peace Conference, 1962.
Les deux conférences de la paix, 1899 et 1907. Recueil des textes arrêtés par ces conférences et de différents documents complémentaires, 1909.
Deuxième conférence internationale de la paix: La Haye 1907; actes et documents, 1907.
Dunant, H.: La proposition de Sa Majesté l'Empereur Nicolas II, 1898.
Dungen, P. van der: Jean de Bloch and the First Hague Peace Conference, 1983.
Ernst, A.: L'œuvre de la deuxième conférence de la paix. Exposé juridique et texte des conventions, 1908.
Eyffinger, A.: The Peace Palace: Residence for justice, domicile of learning, 1988.
Fried, A. H.: Die Haager Konferenz: Ihre Bedeutung und ihre Ergebnisse, 1900.
Fried, A. H.: Die zweite Haager Konferenz: Ihre Arbeiten, ihre Ergebnisse und ihre Bedeutung, 1907.
Gobat, A.: Le développement des conventions de la Haye du 29 juillet 1899; 1907.
Hay, J., E. Root: Instructions to the American delegation to the Hague conferences of 1899 and 1907; 1913.
Higgins, A. P.: The Hague peace conferences and other international conferences concerning the laws and usages of war, 1909.
Holls, F. W.: The peace conference at The Hague and its bearings on international law and policy, 1914.
Hull, W. I.: The two Hague conferences and their contributions to international law, 1908.
Informes y notas de la delegación de Colombia en la 2ª Conferencia de la paz de La Haya (reunida en 1907), 1908.
Kemény, F.: Entwurf einer internationalen Gesammt-Academie: Weltacademie, 1901.
Kok, J. J.: Het Vredespaleis, 1909.
LaFontaine, H.: La conférence de la paix, 1908.
Lange, Chr. L.: Développement de l'œuvre de La Haye. Organisation de la Conférence de la Paix, 1917.
Lawrence, T. J.: International problems and Hague conferences, 1908.
Léger, A. N.: La doctrine Drago et la deuxième conférence de la paix, 1915.
Lysen, A.: History of the Carnegie Foundation and of the Peace Palace at The Hague, 1934.
Martens, F. de: La conférence de la paix à La Haye: étude d'histoire contemporaine, 1900.
Melville, Edgar de [= Henri Ch. G. J. van der Mandere]: L'œuvre de La Haye (1871-1921). Exposé du travail des conférences de La Haye et de la Cour permanente d'Arbitrage, 1924.
Meurer, Chr.: Die Haager Friedenskonferenz, 2 vols., 1905-1907.
Nippold, O.: Die zweite Haager Friedenskonferenz, 2 vols., 1908-1911.
The peace crusade: A record of the peace conference at The Hague, May 18 to July 29, 1899; 1899.
Pédoya, J. M. G.: Les conférences de La Haye: Arbitrage-désarmement, 1907.
Perris, G. H.: A history of the peace conference at The Hague, 1899.
The proceedings of the Hague peace conferences. Translation of the official texts under the supervision of James Brown Scott, 1920.
Renault, L.: L'Œuvre de La Haye en 1899 et en 1907; 1908.
Rozenburg 1883-1917: Geschiedenis van een Haagse fabriek, ed. M. Boot, 1983.
Scherpenhuyzen, J.: Het Vredespaleis, 1945.
Schücking, W.: The international union of The Hague conferences, 1918.
Schücking, W.: Der Staatenverband der Haager Konferenzen, 1912.
Scott, J. B.: The Hague Peace Conferences of 1899 and 1907. Lectures Johns Hopkins University 1908, 2 vols., 1909.
Stead, W. T.: La chronique de la conférence de la Haye 1899; 1901.
Stead, W. T.: The parliament of peace and its members, 1899.
Stead, W. T.: Courier de la conférence de la paix, 1907.
Steur, J. A. G. van der: Het Vredespaleis, 1920.
Suttner, B. von: Die Haager Friedenskonferenz: Tagebuchblätter, 1901.
Timmers, J. J. M.: G. Lairesse als plafond- en kamerschilder. Bulletin Rijksmuseum 18 (1970).
The Tzar's rescript: A series of papers issued and circulated widely by the Peace society, 1899.
Wehberg, H.: Die Abkommen der Haager Friedenskonferenzen, der Londoner Seekriegskonferenz nebst Genfer Konvention, 1910.
Wehberg, H.: La contribution des conférences de la paix de La Haye au progrès du droit international, 1932.
Zorn, Ph.: Deutschland und die beiden Haager Friedenskonferenzen, 1920.

THE PEACEFUL SETTLEMENT OF DISPUTES

General Studies

Allsebrook, M.: Prototypes of peacemaking: The first forty years of the United Nations, 1986.
Bilder, R. B.: International dispute settlement and the role of adjudication, 1986.
Bilder, R. B.: An overview of international dispute settlement. EJIDR 1 (1986) 1-32.
Bos, M.: The interpretation of international judicial decisions. REDI 33 (1981) 11-50.
Bosco, G.: La soluzione delle controversie giuridiche internazionali nel quadro delle Nazioni Unite, 1989.
Bowett, D.: Contemporary developments in legal techniques in the settlement of disputes. RDC 180 (1983/2) 169-236.
Bowett, D.: The impact of Security Council decisions on dispute settlement procedures. EJIL 5 (1994) 89-101.
Broms, B.: The declaration on the peaceful settlement of international disputes (Manila). In: Essays Manfred Lachs, 1984, 339-353.
Broms, B.: The role of the UN in the peaceful settlement of

disputes. In: The UN and the maintenance of international peace and security, 1987, 73-98.
Cerna, Chr. M.: The Inter-American Court of Human Rights. In: International courts for the twenty-first century, ed. M. W. Janis, 1992, 117-158.
Charney, J. I.: Third State remedies in international law. MJIL 10 (1989) 57-101.
Chauhan, B. R.: Peaceful change: The concept and the mechanism for peaceful settlement of international disputes within the structure of UN. In: UN for a better world, ed. J. N. Saxena, a.o., 1986, 58-82.
Chinkin, C. M.: The peaceful settlement of disputes: New grounds for optimism? In: Essays Wang Tieya., ed. R. St. John Macdonald, 1994, 165-179.
Coussirat-Coustère, V.: Le règlement des différends dans l'œuvre de la CDI 1: Vers une codification progressive? In: Perspectives du droit international et européen. Recueil d'études Gilbert Apollis, 1992, 29-46.
Current developments concerning the settlement of disputes involving States by arbitration and the World Court. Proceedings ASIL 83 (1989) 568-589.
Delbez, L.: L'évolution des idées en matière de règlement pacifique des conflits. RGDIP 55 (1951) 5-22.
Dispute settlement in public international law: Texts and materials, ed. K. Oellers-Frahm, N. Wühler, 1984.
Elaboration du projet de manuel sur le règlement pacifique des différends entre Etats. Rapport du Secrétaire général sur l'état d'avancement des travaux (Nations Unies A/AC.182/L.68, 1990).
Giardina, A.: La mise en œuvre au niveau national des arrêts et des décisions internationaux. RDC 165 (1979/4) 233-352.
Handbook on the peaceful settlement of disputes between States, ed. United Nations, 1992.
Higgins, R.: International law and the avoidance, containment and resolution of disputes. RDC 230 (1991/5) 9-342.
Infante Caffi, M. T.: El pacto de Bogotá, vigencia y propuestas de reforma. AHLDI 10 (1993) 229-254.
International disputes: The legal aspects. David Davies Memorial Institute of International Studies, 1982.
Jennings, R. Y.: The judicial function and the rule of law in international relations. In: International law at the time of its codification. Essays Roberto Ago, vol. 3 (1987) 139-151.
Jiménez de Aréchaga, E.: La solucion pacifica de controversias en la Carta de las Naciones Unidas. Dans: Liber amicorum Antonio Rodriguez Sastre, 1985, 229-234.
Judicial settlement of international disputes. An international symposium, 1974.
Kleckner, S.-M.: Peaceful settlement of disputes in international law: International Law Bibliography, 1985.
Lachs, M.: United Nations and the ICJ. In: The UN and the maintenance of international peace and security, 1987, 147-159.
Lauterpacht, E.: Aspects of the administration of international justice, 1991.
Lowenfeld, A. F.: International litigation and arbitration, 1993.
Maluwa, T.: The peaceful settlement of disputes among African States, 1963-1983: Some conceptual issues and practical trends. CLB 15 (1989) 1505-1520.
Manila Declaration on the peaceful settlement of international disputes. Resolution No. 37/10 of 15 November 1982. Official Records of the General Assembly of the United Nations (A/37/51).
Manuel sur le règlement pacifique des différends entre Etats, ed. Nations Unies, 1992.
Merrills, J. G.: International dispute settlement, 1984.
Merrills, J. G.: The principle of peaceful settlement of disputes. In: The UN and the principles of international law: Essays Michael Akehurst, ed. V. Lowe, C. Warbrick, 1994, 49-65.
Sahovic, M.: La Déclaration de Manille sur le règlement pacifique des différends internationaux. In: Essays Manfred Lachs, 1984, 449-458.
Sohn, L. B.: The future of dispute settlement. In: The structure and process of international law, 1983, 1121-1146.
Trindade, A. A.-C.: O direito internacional e a soluçao pacifica das controvérsias internacionais, 1988.

Negotiation / Conciliation / Inquiry / Good Offices / Mediation / Fact Finding / Inquiry

Bar-Yaakov, N.: The handling of international disputes by means of inquiry, 1974.
Bensalah, T.: L'enquête internationale dans le règlement des conflits, 1976.
Cot, J.-P.: La conciliation internationale, 1968.
Dimitriou, E.: International negotiations under the Charter of the UN. In: Thesaurus acroasium 18 (1991) 503-509.
Fombad, Ch. M.: Consultation and negotiation in the pacific settlement of international disputes. AJICL 1 (1989) 707-724.
Geamanu, G.: Les négotiations: moyen principal du règlement pacifique des différends internationaux. In: Essays Manfred Lachs, 1984, 375-387.
Ghozali, N.-E.: La négociation diplomatique dans la jurisprudence internationale. 25 RBDI (1992) 323-350.
Iklé, P.: How nations negotiate, 1985.
Kerameus, K. D.: The use of conciliation for dispute settlement. RHDI 32 (1979) 41-53.
Lachs, M.: International law, mediation and negotiation. In: Multilateral negotiation and mediation. Instruments and methods, 1985, 183-195.
Lall, A. S.: Multilateral negotiation and mediation. Instruments and methods, 1985.
Leurdijk, J. H.: Fact-finding: Its place in international law and international politics. NTIR 14 (1967) 141-161.
Liñan Nogueras, D. J.: Algunas consideraciones sobre la evolución de la conciliación. In: Hacia un nuevo orden internacional y europeo. Estudios Manuel Díez de Velasco, 1993, 439-455.
New approaches to international mediation, ed. C. R. Mitchell, K. Webb, 1988.
Patchen, M.: Resolving disputes between nations: Coercion or conciliation, 1988.
Pechota, V.: The quiet approach. A study of the good offices exercised by the UN Secretary-General in the cause of peace. A Unitar Study, 1972.
Probst, R. R.: Good offices in the light of Swiss international practice and experience, 1989.
Processes of international negotiations, ed. F. Mautner-Markhof, 1989.
Rolin, H. (et al.): La conciliation internationale, in: AIDI 48/1 (1959) 501-530; 49/2 (1961) 193-271.
Ruegger, P.: Nouvelles réflexions sur le rôle des procdures internationales d'enquête dans la solution des conflits internationaux. In: Etudes Roberto Ago, vol. 3 (1987) 327-361.
Schücking, W.: Das völkerrechtliche Institut der Vermittlung, 1923.

Shore, W. I.: Fact-finding in the maintenance of international peace, 1970.
Touval, S., W. Zartman: International mediation in theory and practice, 1985.
Villani, U.: La conciliazione nelle controversie internazionali, 1989.

Arbitration / The Permanent Court of Arbitration

Bemis, S. F.: Jay's Treaty. A study in commerce and diplomacy, 1962.
Benia, M.: L'exécution de la sentence arbitrale. Thesaurus acroasium 18 (1991) 511-516.
Butler, W. E.: The Hague Permanent Court of Arbitration. In: International courts for the twenty-first century, ed. M. W. Janis, 1992, 43-53.
Cory, H. M.: Compulsory arbitration of international disputes, 1932.
Eisenbach, W.: Internationale Schiedssprechung in Amerika, 1932.
El-Enani, I. M.: L'arbitrage international. REDI 35 (1979) 99-148.
Finlay, R. B.: International arbitration, 1904.
The flame rekindled: New hopes for international arbitration, ed. S. Muller, W. Mijs, 1994.
Foster, J. W.: Arbitration and the Hague Court, 1904.
Fox, H.: States and the undertaking to arbitrate. ICLQ 37 (1988) 1-29.
François, J. P. A.: La Cour Permanente d'Arbitrage. RDC 87 (1955/1) 460-551.
Gray, Chr, B. Kingsbury: Developments in dispute settlement: Inter-state arbitration since 1945. BYIL 63 (1992) 7-134.
Hudson, M. O.: The Permanent Court of Arbitration. AJIL 27 (1933) 440-460.
International arbitration: Past and prospects. Symposium J. H. W. Verzijl (1888-1987), ed. A. H. A. Soons, 1990.
LaPradelle, A. de, N. Politis: Recueil des arbitrages internationaux, 3 vols., 1905-1954.
Lingens, K.-H.: Internationale Schiedsgerichtsbarkeit und Jus Publicum Europaeum 1648-1794, 1988.
Lowenfeld, A. F.: International litigation and arbitration, 1993.
Malauzat, A.: La Cour de Justice Arbitrale, 1914.
Menthon, F. de: Le rôle de l'arbitrage dans l'évolution judiciaire, 1926.
Mérignhac, A.: Traité théorique et pratique de l'arbitrage internationale, 1895.
Moore, J. B.: American diplomacy, 1905.
Moore, J. B.: History and digest of the international arbitrations to which the United States has been a Party, 6 vols., 1898.
Newcomb, J. T.: New light on Jay's Treaty. AJIL 28 (1934) 685-692.
The prospects of international arbitration, ed. M. A. Chaudri, 1966.
Ralston, J. H.: International arbitration from Athens to Locarno, 1929.
Richards, H. E.: Progress of international law and arbitration, 1911.
Roelofsen, C. G.: The Jay Treaty and all that. In: International arbitration: past and prospects, ed. A. H. A. Soons, 1989.
Rosenne, S.: The ICJ and international arbitration. In: The flame rekindled: New hopes for international arbitration, ed. S. Muller, W. Mijs, 1994, 99-124.
Sax, B.: Histoire de l'arbitrage international permanent, 1903.
Schindler, D.: Die Schiedsgerichtsbarkeit seit 1914; 1938.
Schwarzenberger, G.: Present-day relevance of the Jay Treaty arbitration. NDL 53 (1978) 715-733.
Simpson, J. L., H. Fox: International arbitration. Law and practice, 1959.
Stuyt, A. M.: Survey of international arbitration (1794-1970), 1990.
Taube, M. de: Les origines de l'arbitrage international, Antiquité et Moyen Âge. RDC 42 (1932/4) 5-114.
Tod, M. N.: International arbitration in the Greek world, 1932.
Urrutia, F. J.: La evolución del principio de arbitraje en América, 1920.
Wetter, J. G.: The international arbitral process, public and private, 5 vols., 1979.

THE PERMANENT COURT OF INTERNATIONAL JUSTICE (PCIJ/CPJI)

Baker, P. J.: The obligatory jurisdiction of the Permanent Court of International Justice. BYBIL 6 (1925) 68-102.
Beckett, W. E.: Decisions of the Permanent Court of International Justice on points of law and procedure. BYBIL 11 (1930) 1-54.
Beckett, W. E.: Les questions d'intérêt général au point de vue juridique dans la jurisprudence de la Cour permanente de Justice internationale. RDC 50 (1934/4) 193-310.
Borchard, E. M.: The Permanent Court of International Justice, 1923
Bruns, V.: La Cour permanente de Justice internationale, son organisation et sa compétence. RDC 62 (1937/4) 551-671.
Douma J.: Bibliography on the International Court including the Permanent Court (1918-1964), 1966. [Vol. 4C of E. Hambro, The Case Law of the International Court, 1952 -]
Dunne, M.: The United States and the World Court, 1920-1935; 1988.
Fachiri, A. P.: The Permanent Court of International Justice. Its constitution, procedure and work, 1932. Reprint 1980.
Fontes Juris Gentium. Handbuch Entscheidungen StIGH/ Répertoire Décisions CPJI/ Digest Decisions PCIJ, 4 vols., 1931-1964.
Genet, R.: Précis de jurisprudence de la CPJI, 1939.
Geocze, B. von: Die Zuständigkeit der Internationalen Gerichtshöfe, 1933.
Glichitch, S.: La juridiction obligatoire de la CPJI, 1940.
Guggenheim, P.: Répertoire des décisions et des document de la CPIJ 1922-1945, 3 vols., 1961-1973.
Hammarskjøld, Å.: Extension de l'arbitrage obligatoire et compétence obligatoire de la CPJI. RDI 55 (1928) 83-99
Hammarskjøld, Å.: Quelques aspects de la fonction consultative de la CPJI. In: Festgabe Max Huber, 1934, 146-181.
Hudson, M. O.: Handbook of the World Court, 1938.
Hudson, M. O.: Obligatory jurisdiction under Article 36 of the Statute of the PCIJ. IowaLR 19 (1933-1934) 190-217.
Hudson, M. O.: The Permanent Court of International Justice 1920-1942. A treatise, 1943. Reprint, ed. L. B. Sohn, 1972.
Hudson, M. O.: World Court reports, 4 vols., 1934-1943.
Jacoby, S. B.: Some aspects of the jurisdiction of the PCIJ. AJIL 30 (1936) 233-255.

Magary, G. de: La juridiction de la CPJI, 1931.
Pomerance, M.: The United States and the advisory function of the Permanent Court of International Justice. In: International law at a time of perplexity. Essays Shabtai Rosenne, ed. Y. Dinstein, 1989, 567-592.
Remlinger, E.: Les avis consultatifs de la CPIJ, 1938
Ruda, J. M.: The opinions of Judge Dionisio Anzilotti at the PCIJ. EJIL 3 (1992) 100-122.
Rundstein, S.: La Cour permanente de Justice internationale comme instance de recours. RDC 43 (1933/1) 5-112.
Salvioli, G. : La jurisprudence de la CPJI. RDC 12 (1926/2) 5-113.
Schenk Graf von Stauffenberg, B.: Statut et règlement de la CPJI, 1934.
Schlochauer, H.-J.: The Permanent Court of International Justice. EPIL 1 (1981) 163-179.
Scott, J. B.: The project of a PCIJ and resolutions of the Advisory Committee of Jurists, 1920.
Sörensen, M.: Les sources du droit international. Etude sur la jurisprudence de la CPJI, 1946.
Strupp, K.: Le droit du juge international de statuer selon l'équité. RDC 33 (1930/3) 357-478.
Verzijl, J. H. W.: International law in historical perspective, Part 8: Inter-state disputes and their settlement, 1976.
Verzijl, J. H. W.: The jurisprudence of the World Court. A case by case commentary, I: The PCIJ (1922-1940); 1965.
Visscher, C. de: Les avis consultatifs de la CPJI. RDC 26 (1929/1) 5-73.
Wehberg, H.: Das Problem eines internationalen Staatengerichtshofes, 1912.

THE INTERNATIONAL COURT OF JUSTICE (ICJ/CIJ)

General Studies

Abi-Saab, G.: De l'évolution de la CIJ: réflexions sur quelques tendances récentes. RGDIP 96 (1992) 273-298.
Anand, R. P.: The World Court on trial. In: International law in transition: Essays Nagendra Singh, ed. R. S. Pathak, R. P. Dhokalia, 1992, 245-265.
Bedjaoui, M.: L'avenir de la CIJ. Hommage François Rigaux. Annales de Droit de Louvain, 1994, 503-514.
Bierzanek, R.: Some remarks on the function of international Courts in the contemporary world. PYBIL 7 (1975) 121-150.
Chehab, M.: Le rôle de la CIJ dans l'interprétation et la création des règles du droit international, 1963.
Condorelli, L.: La CIJ: 50 ans et (pour l'heure) pas une ride. EJIL 6 (1995) 388-400.
Donner, R.: International adjudication: Using the International Court of Justice. With special reference to Finland, 1988.
Dubisson, M.: La Cour internationale de Justice, 1964.
El-Erian, A.: The ICJ and the concept of universality. CJTL 19 (1981) 197-211.
Elian, G.: The International Court of Justice, 1971.
Elias, T. O.: Africa before the World Court. Gandhi Memorial Lectures, 1981.
Elias, T. O.: The International Court of Justice and some contemporary problems. Essays on international law, 1983.
Fifty Years of the International Court of Justice. Essays in honour of Sir Robert Jennings, ed. V. Lowe, M. Fitzmaurice, 1996.
Fitzmaurice, G.: The law and procedure of the International Court of Justice, 2 vols., 1986.
Forty years International Court of Justice: Jurisdiction, equity and equality, ed. A. Bloed, P. van Dijk, 1988.
Franck, Th. M.: Judging the World Court, 1986.
The future of the ICJ, ed. L. Gross, 2 vols., 1976.
The future of the World Court. Judges' Conference. NYU Center for International Studies, 1970.
Gros, A.: La CIJ 1946-1986: Les reflexions d'un juge. In: International law at a time of perplexity. Essays Shabtai Rosenne, ed. Y. Dinstein, 1989, 289-306.
Gross, L.: Essays on international law and organization, 2 vols., 1984; notably vol. 2, 677-704; 845-930; 931-1003.
Guillaume, G.: Les formations restreintes des juridictions internationales, 1992.
Guillaume, G.: The future of international judicial institutions. ICLQ 44 (1995) 848-862.
Highet, K.: Winning and losing: The commitment of the USA to the ICJ. What was it, what is it, and where has it gone? TLCP 1 (1991) 157-200.
Hubbard, H. K.: Separation of powers within the UN: A revised role for the ICJ. SLR 38 (1985-86)) 165-194.
The International Court of Justice at a crossroads, ed. L. F. Damrosch, 1987.
International Court of Justice [Interviews with Nagendra Singh, Guy de Lacharrière, Manfred Lachs, Stephen Schwebel, Ni Zhengyu, Nikolai Tarassov and Christopher Weeramantry]. In: Sturgess, Garry and Philip Chubb: Judging the world: Law and politics in the World's Leading Courts, 1988.
International law at a time of perplexity. Essays Shabtai Rosenne, ed. Y. Dinstein, 1989.
Janis, M. W.: The International Court. In: International Courts for the twenty-first century, ed. M. W. Janis, 1992, 13-41.
Jaenicke, G.: The role of the ICJ in the UN peace-keeping system. Aussenpolitik 36 (1985) 345-353.
Jenks, C. W.: The prospects of international adjudication, 1964.
Jenks, C. W.: The status of international organisations in relation to the ICJ. Transactions Grotius Society, 32 (1947) 1-49.
Jessup, P. C.: The International Court of Justice revisited. VJIL 11 (1971) 299-309.
Judicial settlement of international disputes: ICJ; Other courts and tribunals; Arbitration and conciliation. An International Symposium, 1974.
La juridiction internationale permanente. Colloque de Lyon de la Société française de droit international, 1987.
Kelly, J. P.: The changing process of international law and the role of the World Court. MJIL 11 (1989-90) 129-166.
Kerno, I. S.: L'Organisation des NU et la CIJ. RDC 78 (1951/1) 511-574.
Klein, E.: Paralleles Tätigwerden von Sicherheitsrat und IGH bei friedensbedrohenden Streitigkeiten. In: Völkerrecht als Rechtsordnung. Festschrift Hermann Mosler, 1983, 467-491.
Lachs, M.: La CIJ et le règlement de différends récents. In: Guy Ladreit de Lacharrière et la politique juridique extérieure de la France, 1989, 290-298.
Lauterpacht, E.: Aspects of the administration of international justice, 1991

Lauterpacht, H.: The development of international law by the International Court, 1958.
Lissitzyn, O. J.: The ICJ. Its role in the maintenance of international peace and security, 1951.
Lutz, R. E.: The World Court in a changing world: An agenda for expanding the Court's role from a US perspective. Stanford JIL 27 (1991) 265-343.
MacPherson, B. F.: World Court enhancements to advance the rule of law, 1994.
McWhinney, E.: The International Court of Justice and the Western tradition of international law, 1987.
McWhinney, E.: Judicial settlement of international disputes: Jurisdiction, justiciability and judicial law-making on the contemporary International Court, 1991.
McWhinney, E.: The World Court and the contemporary international law-making process, 1979.
Mangoldt, H. von: Die Schiedsgerichtsbarkeit als Mittel internationaler Streitschlichtung, 1974.
Marion, L. C.: La saisine de la CIJ par voie de compromis. RGDIP 100 (1995) 257-301.
Merrills, J. G.: International dispute settlement, 1991.
Mosler, H.: The ICJ at its present stage of development. Dalhousie LJ 5 (1979) 545-567.
Mosquera Irurita, T.: La Corte internacional de Justicia, 1988.
Oda, Shigeru: The International Court of Justice Viewed from the Bench (1976-1993). RDC 244 (1993/7) 9-90.
Oliver, C. T.: The World Court and world order: Today and what of tomorrow. In: Public international law and the future world order. Liber Amicorum A. J. Thomas, Jr., ed. J. J. Norton, 1987, 10/1-10/10.
Pellet, A. Le glaive et la balance: remarques sur le rôle de la CIJ en matière de maintien de la paix et de la sécurité internationales. In: International law at a time of perplexity. Essays Shabtai Rosenne, ed. Y. Dinstein, 1989, 539-566.
Prott, L. V.: Consensus and opinion analysis at the ICJ. NILR 14 (1983) 69-85.
Prott, L. V.: Die internationale Richter im Spannungsfeld der Rechtskulturen, 1975.
The role of Courts in society, ed. S. Shetreet, 1988.
Role of the ICJ. Possible wider use of the Court by agreement of States Parties. Study Asian-African Legal Consultative Committee. Annex to GA Document A/40/682.
Rosenne, S.: The law and practice of the International Court of Justice, 1987.
Rosenne, S.: The World Court: What it is and how it works, 5th rev. edn., 1995.
Rosenne, S.: The changing role of the International Court. ILR 20 (1985) 182-205.
Ruda, J. M.: Presente y futuro del Tribunal internacional de Justicia, 1990.
Schlochauer, H.-J.: International Court of Justice. EPIL 1 (1981) 72-92.
Schwebel, S. M.: Reflections on the role of the International Court of Justice. WLR 61 (1986) 1061-1071.
Shahabuddeen, M.: The International Court of Justice: The integrity of an idea. CLB 19 (1993) 738-753.
Singh, N.: The role and record of the International Court of Justice, 1989.
Steinberger, H.: Judicial settlement of international disputes. EPIL 1 (1981) 120-133.
Taha, M. M. A.: International law and the ICJ, 1985.
Thirlway, H.: The law and procedure of the International Court of Justice 1960-1989: I-V. BYBIL 60 (1989) 1-157; 61 (1990) 1-133; 62 (1991)1-75; 63 (1992) 1-96. [To be continued]
Virally, M.: Le champ opératoire du règlement judiciaire international. RGDIP 87 (1983) 281-314.
Weeramantry, C.: Expanding the potential of the World Court. In: Perspectives on international law, 1990, 309-346.
Wehberg, H., H.W. Goldschmidt: Der IGH, Entstehungsgeschichte, Analyse, Dokumentation, 1973.
Wehberg, H.: Der Internationale Gerichtshof, 1948.
The World Court. Proceedings of the 80th annual meeting of the ASIL, 1987.

Elections / Composition / Members of the Court

Brownlie, I.: The calling of the international lawyer: Sir Humphrey Waldock and his work. BYBIL 54 (1983) 7-74.
Conforti, B.: The activities of national judges and the international relations of their state / L'activité du juge interne et les relations internationales de l'Etat. AIDI 65/1 (1993) 327-357.
Dupuy, P.-M.: Dionisio Anzilotti and the law of international responsibility of States. EJIL 3 (1992) 139-148.
El-Erian, M. A.: El Erian and the passage of time. Part 1: Abdullah El-Erian, Judge of the ICJ: Personal account of his life (1920-1981), 1989. [In Arabic]
Fitzmaurice, G.: Hersch Lauterpacht and his attitude to the judicial function. BYBIL 50 (1979) 1-12.
Gaja, G.: Necrologio Gaetano Morelli. RDI 73 (1990) 114-126.
Gaja, G.: Positivism and dualism in Dionisio Anzilotti. EJIL 3 (1992) 23-138.
Higgins, R.: Judge Dillard and the right to self determination. VJIL 23 (1982-1983) 387-394.
Hussain, I.: Sir Zafrulla Khan - The silent judge. AV 23 (1985) 478-492.
Kwiatkowska, B.: Judge Shigeru Oda's Opinions in Law-of-the-Sea Cases: Equitable maritime boundary delimitation. GYBIL 36 (1993) 225-294.
Lachs, M.: A Few thoughts on the independence of Judges of the ICJ. CJTL 25 (1987) 593-600.
Lachs, M.: Some reflections on the nationality of Judges of the ICJ. Pace YBIL 4 (1992) 49-68.
McWhinney, E.: 'Internationalizing' the International Court: The quest for ethno-cultural and legal-systemic representativeness. In: Essays Taslim Olawale Elias, vol. 1: Contemporary international law and human rights, ed. E. G. Bello, B. A. Ajibola, 1992, 277-289.
McWhinney, E.: Judge Manfred Lachs and judicial law-making: Opinions on the ICJ, 1967-1993; 1995.
McWhinney, E.: Judge Shigeru Oda and the progressive development of international law: Opinions (Declarations, Separate Opinions, Dissents) on the ICJ, 1976-1992; 1993.
McWhinney, E.: Law, politics and 'Regionalism' in the nomination and election of World Court Judges. SJILC 13 (1986-1987) 1-28.
Millan Moro, L.: El juez *ad hoc* en la Corte internacional de Justicia. Cursos de derecho internacional Vitoria-Gasteiz, 1990, 211-258.
Ni Zengyu: A legal luminary from the Orient: Judge Nagendra Singh's concept of human rights, peace and development. IJIL 28 (1988) 337-347.
Prott, L. V.: The role of the judge of the ICJ. RBDI 10 (1974) 473-507.
Schachter, O.: Philip Jessup's life and ideas. AJIL 80 (1986) 878-895.
Schwarzenberger, G.: The judicial corps of the ICJ. YBWA (1982) 241-267.

Sicart-Bozec, M.: Les juges du Tiers Monde à la CIJ, 1986.
Torres Bernárdez, S.: Resignations at the World Court. In: International law at a time of perplexity. Essays in honour of Shabtai Rosenne, ed. Y. Dinstein, 1989, 953-975.
Valencia-Ospina, Ed.: Le droit et son interprète. In: Guy Ladreit de Lacharrière et la politique juridique extérieure de la France (1989) 381-393.
Zafrulla Khan, M.: Servant of God. A personal narrative, 1983.

Chambers

Bedjaoui, M.: Remarques sur la création de chambres *ad hoc* au sein de la CIJ. In: La juridiction internationale permanente. Colloque de Lyon, 1987, 73-78. [See also 79-100]
Bedjaoui, M.: Universalisme et régionalisme au sein de la CIJ: la constitution de chambres *ad hoc*. In: Liber amicorum José Pérez Montero, vol. 1, 1988, 155-171.
Escobar Hernández, C.: Las Salas *ad hoc* del Tribunal Internacional de Justicia. In: Hacia un nuevo orden internacional y europeo. Estudios Manuel Díez de Velasco (1993) 291-317.
Guilds, J. C.: 'If it quacks like a duck': Comparing the ICJ Chambers to international arbitration for a mechanism of enforcement. MJILT 16 (1992) 43-82.
Jennings, R.: Chambers of the ICJ and Courts of arbitration. In: Humanité et droit international. Mélanges René-Jean Dupuy, 1991, 197-201.
Lachs, M.: Some comments on *ad hoc* Chambers of the ICJ. In: Humanité et droit international. Mélanges René-Jean Dupuy, 1991, 203-210.
McAuliffe, C.: La chambre environnementale au sein de la CIJ. Il foro italiano, 1994, 184-192.
Meyer, L. H.: The *ad hoc* Chambers: Perspectives of the Parties and the Court. AV 27 (1989) 413-441.
Moore, A. F.: *Ad hoc* Chambers of the International Court and the question of intervention. CWRJIL 24 (1992) 666-698.
Mosler, H.: The *ad hoc* Chambers of the ICJ: Evaluation after five years of experience. In: International law at a time of perplexity. Essays Shabtai Rosenne, ed. Y. Dinstein, 1989, 449-460.
Oda, S.: Further thoughts on the Chambers procedure of the ICJ.AJIL 82 (1988) 556-562.
Ostrihansky, R.: Chambers of the ICJ. ICLQ 37 (1988) 30-52.
Pillepich, A.: Les Chambres. In: La juridiction internationale permanente. Colloque de Lyon, 1987, 45-72. [See also 79-100]
Poulantzas, N. M.: The Chambers of the ICJ and the judicial settlement of disputes: The delimitation of the maritime boundaries in the Gulf of Maine Area Case. RDI 63 (1985) 323-328.
Rosenne, S.: Article 27 of the Statute of the ICJ. VJIL 32 (1991-1992) 213-231.
Saavedra y Muguelar, A. de: La creación y el funcionamiento de las Salas *ad hoc* del Tribunal internacional de Justicia. Dans: Liber amicorum: Colección de estudios José Pérez Montero, vol. 2, 1988, 1285-1299.
Schwebel, S. M.: Chambers of the ICJ formed for particular Cases. In: International law at a time of perplexity. Essays Shabtai Rosenne, ed. Y. Dinstein, 1989, 739-770.
Zimmerman, A.: *Ad hoc* Chambers of the ICJ. DJIL 8 (1989-1990) 1-32.

Jurisdiction of the Court in Contentious Cases

Andrassy, J.: Betrachtungen über die Zuständigkeit des Internationalen Gerichtshofes. Festgabe Alexander Makarov. ZaoRV 19 (1958) 1-23.
Bernardini, A.: Trasferimento alla Corte internazionale di Giustizia della giurisdizione convenzionale della Corte permanente. RDI 44 (1961) 220-262.
Bramson, A.: Problèmes de compétence dans le Statut et la jurisprudence de la CIJ. Annales Univ. Mariae Curie-Sklodowska, Lublin, sectio G, VIII (1961) 101-148.
Bretton, Ph.: L'URSS et la compétence de la CIJ en matière de protection des droits de l'homme. AFDI 35 (1989) 261-275.
Briggs, H. W.: Nicaragua v. United States: Jurisdiction and admissibility. AJIL 79 (1985) 373-378.
Casado Raigón, R.: La jurisdicción contenciosa de la Corte internacional de Justicia: Estudio de las reglas de su competencia, 1987.
Castberg, F.: La compétence des tribunaux internationaux. RDILC 52 (1925) 155-172, 310-348.
Cavaré, L.: Les recours en interprétation et en appréciation de la légalité devant les tribunaux internationaux. ZaöRV 15 (1953-1954) 482-520.
Charney, J. I.: Compromissory clauses and the jurisdiction of the ICJ. AJIL 81 (1987) 855-887.
Ciobanu, D.: Preliminary objections related to the jurisdiction of the United Nations political organs, 1975.
Colette, J.: Les principes de droit des gens dans la jurisprudence de la Cour permanente de Justice internationale, 1932.
Debbasch, C.: La compétence 'ratione temporis' de la CIJ. RGDIP 64 (1960) 230-259.
Elias, T. O.: The ICJ in relation to the United Nations Administrative Tribunal. Thesaurus acroasium 18 (1991) 271-345.
Elsen, Th. J. H.: Litispendence between the ICJ and the Security Council, 1986.
Fitzmaurice, G: The law and procedure of the ICJ, 1951-4: Questions of jurisdiction, competence and procedure. BYBIL 34 (1958) 1-161.
Furukawa, T.: La CIJ et la discrétion de décliner de statuer. Kokusaiho gaiko zassi 87 (1988-1989) 113-159. [In Japanese, French résumé 257-258]
Gerber, F.: Le consentement de l'Etat à la juridiction de la CIJ. Thèse Université d'Orléans, 1980.
Góralczyk, W.: Changing attitudes of Central and Eastern European States towards the judicial settlement of international disputes. In: The peaceful settlement of international disputes in Europe: Future prospects, ed. D. Bardonnet, 1991, 477-495.
Gray, Chr. D.: Judicial remedies in international law, 1987.
Guillaume, G.: Les formations restreintes des juridictions internationales, 1992.
Hambro, E: The jurisdiction of the ICJ. RDC 76 (1950/1) 125-215.
Highet, K.: Evidence, the Court, and the Nicaragua Case. AJIL 81 (1987) 1-56.
Howard, M. B.: Military and paramilitary activities in and against Nicaragua (Nicaragua v. USA): The ICJ's jurisdictional dilemma. LAICLJ 7 (1984) 379-408.
Iaccarino, U.: Della c.d. competenza sulla competenza dei tribunali internazionali. DI 14 (1960) 357-425.
Johnson, D. H. N.: The Case of the Monetary Gold Removed from Rome in 1943.ICLQ 4 (1955) 93-115.

Lizzi, M.: Delimiting the World Court's jurisdiction: Realism in the interest of progress. NYLSJICL 12 (1991) 203-235.
Matscher, F.: Standing before International Courts and Tribunals. EPIL 1 (1981) 191-196
Mbaye, K.: L'intérêt pour agir devant la CIJ. RDC 209 (1988/2) 223-345.
McWhinney, E.: Acceptance, and withdrawal or denial, of World Court jurisdiction: Some recent trends as to jurisdiction. ILR 20 (1985) 148-166.
Morelli, G.: La théorie générale du procès international. RDC 61 (1937/3) 253-373.
Mosler, H.: The area of justiciability: Some cases of agreed delimitation in the submission of disputes to the ICJ. In: Essays Manfred Lachs, 1984, 409-421.
Rasmussen, H.: Le juge international en évitant de statuer obéit-il à un devoir judiciaire fondamental? In: La juridiction internationale permanente. Colloque de Lyon, 1987, 383-407. [See also 409-427]
Rosenne, S.: The Qatar/Bahrain Case – What is a treaty? A framework agreement and the seising of the Court. LJIL 8 (1995) 161-182.
Rousseau, Ch.: L'aménagement des compétences en droit international. RGDIP 37 (1930) 420-460.
Sabourin, Ph.: La contestation de la compétence de la CIJ dans les affaires contentieuses récentes. 1984-1985.
Salvioli, G.: La compétence de la Cour permanente de Justice internationale dans les controverses de fait. RDILC 59 (1932) 71-88.
Salvioli, G.: Les rapports entre le jugement sur la compétence et celui sur le fond dans la jurisprudence internationale. RGDIP 36 (1929) 108-115.
Salvioli, G.: Sul potere dell'arbitro a pronunciarsi sulla sua competenza. DI 13 (1959) 119-122.
Scheffer, D. J.: Non-judicial State remedies and the jurisdiction of the ICJ. SJIL 27 (1990-1991) 83-154.
Schwebel, S. M.: Preliminary rulings by the ICJ at the instance of national courts. VJIL 28 (1988) 495.
Shihata, I. F. I: The power of the ICJ to determine its own jurisdiction. Compétence de la compétence, 1965.
Siorat, L.: L'article 37 du Statut de la CIJ. AFDI 8 (1962) 285-330.
Smith, C.: The relation between proceedings and premises: A study in international law. NTIRJG 32 (1962) 5-138.
Stanczyc, J.: Application for interpretation of a judgment delivered by the ICJ. PYBIL 17 (1988) 193-210.
Stanczyk, J.: The ICJ on the competence and function of the Security Council, related to the cases brought before it. PYBIL 15 (1986) 193-216.
Suy, E.: Les actes juridiques unilatéraux en droit international public, 1962.
Teson, F. R.: Appraisals of the ICJ's decision: Nicaragua v. United States (Merits). AJIL 81 (1987) 77-183.
Torres Bernárdez, S.: Spain and the jurisdiction of the ICJ: From past to present. AV 32 (1994) 235-270.
Turner, R. F.: Peace and the World Court: A comment on the paramilitary activities case. VJTL 20 (1987) 53-79.
Verdross, A.: L'excès de pouvoir du juge arbitral dans le droit international public. RDILC 55 (1928) 225-242.
Virally, M.: Le champ opératoire du règlement judiciaire international. RGDIP 87 (1983) 281-314.
Visscher, C. de: Problèmes d'interprétation judiciaire en droit international public, 1963.
Wagner, M. L.: Jurisdiction by Estoppel in the ICJ. CLR 74 (1986) 1777-1804.
Witenberg, J. C.: La recevabilité des réclamations devant les juridictions internationales. RDC 41 (1932/3) 1-136.
Zeler, K.: Das Problem der völkerrechtlichen Verankerung des Südtirol-Pakets und die Zuständigkeit des internationalen Gerichtshofs, 1989.

Acceptance of the Compulsory Jurisdiction of the Court

Alexandrov, S. A.: Reservations in unilateral declarations accepting the compulsory jurisdiction of the ICJ, 1995.
Anand, R. P.: Compulsory jurisdiction of the ICJ, 1961.
Briggs, H. W.: Reservations to the acceptance of compulsory jurisdiction of the ICJ. RDC 93 (1958/1) 223-367.
Buigues, J. L. I.: Les déclarations d'acceptation de la juridiction obligatoire de la CIJ: Leur nature et leur interprétation. ÖZöRV 23 (1972) 255-288.
Carty, A.: The UK, the compulsory jurisdiction of the ICJ and the peaceful settlement of disputes. In: Perestroika and international law, ed. A. Carty, G. Danilenko, 1990, 129-146.
Casado Raigón, R.: El enfoque jurisprudencial de los articulos 36, paragrafo 5.°, y 37 del Estatuto de la Corte internacional de Justicia. RespDI 39 (1987) 23-44.
Charney, J. I.: Compromissory clauses and the jurisdiction of the ICJ. AJIL 81 (1987) 855-887.
Cocatre-Zilgien, A.: Justice internationale facultative et justice internationale obligatoire. RGDIP 80 (1976) 689-737.
The compulsory jurisdiction of the ICJ: A turning point? Proceedings of the Roundtable, in honour of Louis B. Sohn, ed. N. Sybesma-Knol, 1990.
Cottereau, G.: Positions de la France à l'égard de juridiction internationale. Thèse Paris-V, 1980.
Crawford, J.: The legal effect of automatic reservations to the jurisdiction of the International Court. BYBIL 50 (1979) 63-86.
D'Amato, A.: Modifying US acceptance of the compulsory jurisdiction of the World Court. AJIL 79 (1985) 385-405.
D'Amato, A.: The United States should accept, by a new declaration, the general compulsory jurisdiction of the World Court. AJIL 80 (1986) 331-336.
Debbasch, Ch.: La compétence ratione temporis de la CIJ dans le système de la clause facultative de juridiction obligatoire. RGDIP 64 (1960) 230-259.
L'Elaboration d'une clause modèle de compétence obligatoire de la CIJ. Délibérations de l'IDI. AIDI 44/1(1952) 458-468; 45/1 (1954) 310-406; 46 (1956) 178-264, 360-364.
Délibérations de l'Institut et le texte de la résolution. AIDI 48/2 (1959) 55-177, 358-363.
Dolzer, R.: Connally reservation. EPIL 1 (1981) 55-56.
Elkind, J. B.: Normative surrender. MYBILS 9 (1988) 263-289.
Engel, S.: The compulsory jurisdiction of the ICJ. GLJ 40 (1951) 41-66.
Fachiri, A. P.: Repudiation of the optional clause. BYBIL 20 (1939) 52-57.
Farmanfarma, A. N.: The declarations of the States accepting the compulsory jurisdiction of the ICJ. Interpretation of Art. 36, para. 2 of the Statute, 1952.
Franckx, E.: The changing attitude of the USSR. In: The compulsory jurisdiction of the ICJ: A turning point? Proceedings Roundtable Louis B. Sohn, ed. N. Sybesma-Knol, 1990, 33-50.
Gardner, R. N.: US termination of the compulsory jurisdiction of the ICJ. CJTL 24 (1985-1986) 421-427.
Glennon, M. J.: Nicaragua v United States: Constitutionality of US modification of ICJ jurisdiction. AJIL 79 (1985) 682-689.

Gross, L.: Bulgaria invokes the Connally Amendment. In: Essays on international law and organization, vol. 2., 1984, 727-751.

Hambro, E.: Some observations on the compulsory jurisdiction of the ICJ. BYBIL 25, 1948, 133-157.

Hassan, F.: A legal analysis of the US' attempted withdrawal from the jurisdiction of the World Court in the proceedings initiated by Nicaragua. UDLR 10 (1985), 295-318.

Hohmann, H., P. J. I. M. de Waart: Compulsory jurisdiction and the use of force as a legal issue: The epoch-making judgment of the ICJ in Nicaragua v. USA. NILR 34 (1987) 162-191.

Ioannou, K. M.: Reservations to the acceptance of compulsory jurisdiction of the ICJ: A tabular analysis of their procedural treatment. (HRIR 1 (1980) 415-437.

Janis, M. W.: Somber reflections on the compulsory jurisdiction of the International Court. AJIL 81 (1987) 144-146.

Jenks, C. W.: Compétence obligatoire des instances judiciaires et arbitrales internationales.

Jennings, R. Y.: Recent cases on 'automatic' reservations to the optional clause. ICLQ 7 (1958) 349-366.

Jiménez de Aréchaga, E.: The compulsory jurisdiction of the ICJ under the Pact of Bogotá and the optional clause. In: International law at a time of perplexity. Essays Shabtai Rosenne, ed. Y. Dinstein, 1989, 355-360.

Jones, G. F.: Termination of declarations under the optional clause: Military and paramilitary activities in and against Nicaragua. TILJ 20 (1985) 557-581.

Kelsen, H.: Compulsory adjuducation of international disputes. AJIL 37 (1943) 397-406.

Kooijmans, P. H.: Who tolled the death-bell for compulsory jurisdiction? In: Realism in law-making. Essays Willem Riphagen, ed. A. Bos, H. Siblesz, 1986, 71-87.

Kopal, Vl.: Evolution of the position of Czechoslovakia in relation to the obligatory jurisdiction of the World Court. In: The peaceful settlement of international disputes in Europe: Future prospects, ed. D. Bardonnet, 1991, 497-508.

Lamm, V.: Kötelező Nemzetközi Bíráskodás az Allandó Nemzetközi Bíróság idején. Allam és Jogtudomány 30 (1987-1988) 75-121.

Lamm, V.: A Connally-fenntartás és a nemzetközi bíróság kötelező joghatósági rendszere. Allam és Jogtudomány 30 (1987-1988) 403-473.

Lauterpacht, H.: The absence of an international legislature and the compulsory jurisdiction of international tribunals. BYBIL 11 (1930) 134-157.

Lawson, R. C.: The problem of the compulsory jurisdiction of the World Court. AJIL 46 (1952) 219-238.

Lloyd, L.: 'A springboard for the future': A historical examination of Britain's role in shaping the optional clause of the PCIJ. AJIL 79 (1985) 28-51.

Maus, B.: Les réserves dans les déclarations d'acceptation de la juridiction obligatoire de la CIJ, 1959.

Merrills, J. G.: The optional clause today. BYBIL 50 (1979) 87-116.

Merrills, J. G.: The optional clause revisited. BYBIL 64 (1993) 197-244.

Morelli, G.: Accettazione incondizionata della giurisdizione della Corte internazionale di Giustizia. RDI 66 (1983) 94-101.

Morrison, F. L.: Reconsidering US acceptance of the compulsory jurisdiction of the ICJ. World Affairs 148 (1985) 63-70.

Morrison, F. L.: Potential revisions to the acceptance of compulsory jurisdiction of the ICJ by the USA. In: The USA and the compulsory jurisdiction of the ICJ, ed. A. C. Arend, 1986, 29-69. [Discussion, 107-185]

Münch, F.: Das Institut de Droit International und die obligatorische Gerichtsbarkeit. Justitia et pace. Festschrift IDI, ed. W. Wengler, 1974, 101-132.

Münch, F.: Zum Stand der internationalen obligatorischen Gerichtsbarkeit. ZaöRV 21 (1961) 221-248.

Niedermeier, W.: Der Beitritt der Bundesrepublik zum Statut des IGHs unter besonderer Berücksichtigung des obligatorischen Gerichtsbarkeit, 1975.

Nuñez y Bandera. J. H.: La cláusula facultatíva de competencia obligatoria en el Estatuto de la Corte internacional de Justicia, 1973.

Oda, S.: Reservations in the declarations of acceptance of the optional clause and the period of validity of those declarations: The effect of the Schultz Letter. BYBIL 59 (1988) 1-30.

Oellers-Frahm, K.: Die 'obligatorische' Gerichtsbarkeit des IGH: Anmerkungen anlässlich der Zuständigkeitsentscheidung im Fall 'Nicaragua' gegen USA. ZaöRV 47 (1987) 243-264.

Oellers-Frahm, K.: Probleme und Grenzen der obligatorischen internationalen Gerichtsbarkeit. AV 27 (1989) 442-454.

Orihuela Calatayud, E.: España y la jurisdicción obligatoria del Tribunal internacional de Justicia. REspDI 41 (1989) 69-98.

Quintana, J. J.: The Hague declaration and the acceptance of the compulsory jurisdiction of the ICJ: A missed opportunity? LJIL 3 (1990) 43-49.

Reisman, W. M.: The other shoe falls: The future of Article 36 (1); jurisdiction in the light of 'Nicaragua'. AJIL 81 (1987) 166-173.

Reisman, W. M.: Termination of the US declaration under Article 36 (2) of the Statute of the ICJ. In: The USA and the compulsory jurisdiction of the ICJ, ed. A. C Arend, 1986, 71-103. [Discussion, 107-185]

Rosenne, S.: The time factor in the jurisdiction of the ICJ, 1960.

Rotter, M.: Art 36 Abs. 2 des Statuts des IGH. Bestandsaufnahme und Versuch einer öffentlichrechtlichen Deutung. In: Ius Humanitatis. Festschrift Alfred Verdross, 1980, 631-651.

Sauveplanne, J. G.: Les limitations ratione temporis dans l'application de la clause facultative. NILR 3 (1956) 342-354.

Schweissfurth, Th.: The acceptance by the Soviet Union of the compulsory jurisdiction of the ICJ for six human rights conventions. EJIL 2 (1991) 110-117.

Scott, G. L., K. D. Csajko: Compulsory jurisdiction and defiance in the World Court: A comparison of the PCIJ and the ICJ. DJILP 16 (1988) 377-392.

Scott, G.L., C.L. Carr: The ICJ and compulsory jurisdiction: The case for closing the clause. AJIL 81 (1987) 57-76.

Sohn, L. B.: American acceptance of the jurisdiction of the ICJ: Experiences and prospects. GJICL 19 (1989) 489-502.

Sohn, L. B.: Compulsory jurisdiction of the World Court and the US position: The need to improve the US declaration. In: The US and the compulsory jurisdiction of the ICJ, ed. C. A. Arend, 1986, 3-28. [Discussion, 107-185]

Sohn, L. B.: Suggestions for the limited acceptance of compulsory jurisdiction of the ICJ by the United States. GJICL 18 (1988) 1-18.

Soubeyrol, J.: Validité dans le temps de la déclaration

d'acceptation de la juridiction obligatoire. AFDI 5 (1959) 232-257.

Szafarz, R.: Changing state attitudes towards the ICJ In: Forty years ICJ: Jurisdiction, equity and equality, ed. A. Bloed, P. van Dijk, 1988, 1-26.

Szafarz, R.: The compulsory jurisdiction of the ICJ, 1993.

Szafarz, R.: Poland accepts the optional clause of the ICJ Statute. AJIL 85 (1991) 374-375.

Thirlway, H. W. A.: Reciprocity in the jurisdiction of the International Court. NYBIL 15 (1984) 97-138.

Torres Bernardez, S.: Reciprocity in the system of compulsory jurisdiction and in other modalities of contentious jurisdiction exercised by the ICJ. In: Essays Taslim Olawale Elias, Vol. 1: Contemporary international law and human rights, ed. E. G. Bello, B. A. Ajibola, 1992, 291-329.

Torres Bernardez, S.: La 'reciprocidad' en el 'sistema de jurisdicción obligatoria' establecido en el artí. 36, párrafo 2, del Estatuto de la CIJ. In: Cursos de derecho internacional de Vitoria-Gasteiz, 1988, 317-438.

Trindade, A. A. C.: Nicarágua versus Estados Unidos (1984-1985): Os limites da jurisdiçao 'obrigatória' da CIJ e as perspectivas da soluçao judicial de Controvérsias int. RBEP 63-64 (1987) 139-170.

Verzijl, J. H. W.: La clause d'acceptation bilatérale ou multilatérale de la juridiction obligatoire de la CIJ. Mélanges Gilbert Gidel, 1961, 585-600.

Verzijl, J. H. W.: The system of the optional clause. IR 1 (1959) 585-610.

Vulxan, C.: La clause facultative. Acta Scandinavica Iuris Gentium, 1947-1948, 30-35.

Waldock, C. H. M.: Decline of the optional clause. BYBIL 32 (1955-1956) 244-287.

Williams, J. F.: The optional clause. The British signature and reservations. BYBIL 11 (1930) 63-84.

Wolfrum, R.: IGH: Vereinigte Staaten künftig nicht mehr der obligatorischen Jurisdiktion unterworfen - Klage Nicaraguas als Hintergrund. Vereinte Nationen 34 (1986) 79.

Xaashi Jaamac, I.: The compulsory jurisdiction of the ICJ. Declarations under the 'optional clause' of the Statute of the ICJ. Majaladda Xeerka 5 (1977) 37-50.

Advisory Jurisdiction of the Court

Ago, R.: Les avis consultatifs 'obligatoires' de la CIJ: problèmes d'hier et d'aujourd'hui. In: Le droit international au service de la paix, de la justice et du développement. Mélanges Michel Virally, 1991, 9-24.

Ago, R.: I pareri consultativi 'vincolanti' della Corte internazionale di Giustizia: problemi di ieri e di oggi. RDI 73 (1990) 5-23.

Alcázar, J. R.: Advisory opinions of the ICJ: The possibility of the Secretary-General of the UN to ask for an advisory opinion, 1991.

Anand, R. P.: Compulsory jurisdiction of the ICJ, 1961. [Advisory Opinions, 264-282]

Audéoud, O.: La CIJ et le règlement des différents au sein dees organisations internationales. RGDIP 81 (1977) 945-1006.

Bacot, G.: Réflexions sur les clauses qui rendent obligatoires les avis consultatifs de la CPJI et de la CIJ. RGDIP 84 (1980) 1027-1067.

Benvenuti, P.: L'accertamento del diritto mediante i pareri consultivi della Corte internazionale di Giustizia, 1985.

Calling for the establishment of a Special Committee on Advisory Opinions from the ICJ. Hearing before the Subcommittee on Human Rights and International Organizations of the Committee on Foreign Affairs, 1981

Chacko, C. J.: The possible expansion of the advisory jurisdiction of the ICJ. In: Essays Krishna Rao, 1976, 214-240.

Charney, J. I.: Compromissory clauses and the jurisdiction of the ICJ. AJIL 81 (1987) 855-887.

Choi, W.: Judicial review of international Administrative Tribunal judgments. In: Contemporary issues in international law. Essays Louis B. Sohn, 1984, 347-370.

Contemporary international law and human rights, ed. E. G. Bello, B. A. Ajibola, 1992, 291-329.

Ciobanu, D.: Litispendence between the ICJ and the political organs of the United Nations. In: The future of the ICJ, ed. L. Gross, vol. 1, 209-275.

Elias, T. 0.: How the ICJ deals with requests for advisory opinions. In: Essays Manfred Lachs, 1984, 355-374.

Elias, T. O.: UN Charter and the World Court, 1989. [Advisory opinions, 80-97]

Gomula, J.: The ICJ and Administrative Tribunals of international organizations. MJIL 13 (1991-1992) 83-121.

Grabowska, G. M.: Les avis consultatifs de la CIJ. PYBIL 18 (1989-1990) 17-29.

Greig, D. W.: The advisory jurisdiction of the ICJ and the settlement of disputes between States. ICLQ 15 (1966) 325-368.

Gros Espiell, H.: El recurso ante la CIJ contra las sentencias de los tribunales administrativos internacionales. Bol. Fac. de Direito, Univ. de Coimbra, 1986. Número especial: Estudos A. Ferrer-Correia, 3-67.

Guyomar, G.: Commentaire du règlement de la CIJ, adopté le 14 avril 1978: Interprétation et pratique, 1983.

Hambro, E.: The authority of the advisory opinions of the ICJ. ICLQ 3 (1954) 2-22.

Keith, K. J.: The extent of the advisory jurisdiction of the ICJ, 1971.

Kelly, J. P.: The changing process of international law and the role of the World Court. MJIL 11 (1989-1990) 129-166.

McLaughlin, W. T.: Allowing federal Courts access to ICJ advisory opinions: Critique and proposal. HICLR 6 (1983) 745-772.

Olivares, G.: Les avis consultatifs de la Cour de La Haye: Évolution et aspects récents. Analyse doctrinale et jurisprudentielle, 1992.

Ostrihansky, R.: Advisory opinions of the ICJ as reviews of judgments of international Administrative Tribunals. PYBIL 17 (1988) 101-121.

Pomerance, M.: The advisory function of the International Court in the League and U.N. Eras, 1973.

Pomerance, M.: The admission of Judges *ad hoc* in advisory proceedings: Some reflections in the light of the Namibia Case. AJIL 67 (1973) 446-464.

Pratap, D.: The advisory jurisdiction of the International Court, 1972.

Puentre Egido, J.: Consideraciones sobre la naturaleza y efectos de las opiniones consultativas. ZaöRV 31 (1971) 730-809.

Schwebel, S. M.: Was the capacity to request an advisory opinion wider in the Permanent Court of International Justice than it is in the ICJ? BYBIL 62 (1991) 77-118.

Schwebel, S. M.: Authorizing the Secretary-General of the United Nations to request advisory opinions of the ICJ. AJIL 78 (1984) 867-878.

Sugihara, T.: The advisory function of the ICJ. JAIL 18 (1974) 23-50.

Szasz, P. C.: Enhancing the advisory competence of the World Court. In: The future of the ICJ, ed. L. Gross, vol. 2, 1976, 499-549.

Thirlway, H. W. A.: Advisory opinions of international courts. EPIL 1 (1981) 4-9.

Vanda, L.: Kötelező Nemzetközi Bíráskodás az Allandó Nemzetközi Bíróság idején. Allam és Jogtudomány (Budapest), 30 (1987-1988) 75-121.

Waldock, H.: Aspects of the advisory jurisdiction of the ICJ, 1976.

Contentious and Advisory Procedure in General

Aguilar Mawdsley, A.: Evidence before the ICJ. In: Essays Wang Tieya, ed. R. St. John Macdonald, 1994, 533-550.

Alvarez, J. E.: Burdens of proof [Book review of: Fact-finding before international Tribunals, ed. R. B. Lillich, 1992]. MJIL 14 (1992-1993) 399-427.

Bedjaoui, M.: La 'fabrication' des arrêts de la CIJ In: Le droit international au service de la paix, de la justice et du développement. Mélanges Michel Virally, 1991, 87-107.

Bos, M.: Les conditions du procès en droit international public, 1957.

Brower, Ch. N.: Evidence before international Tribunals: The need for some standard rules. International Lawyer 28 (1994) 47-58.

Cassese, A.: The concept of 'legal dispute' in the jurisprudence of the ICJ. In: Il processo internazionale. Studi Gaetano Morelli, 1975, 173-200.

Coussirat-Coustère, V., P-M. Eisemann: La procédure devant les juridictions internationales permanentes. Dans: La juridiction internationale permanente. Colloque de Lyon, 1987, 103-165.

Fact-finding before international Tribunals, ed. R. B. Lillich. 1992

Gill, T. D.: Litigation strategy at the International Court: A case study of the Nicaragua v. United States dispute, 1989.

Grisel, E.: 'Res judicata': L'autorité de la chose jugée en droit international. In: Mélanges Georges Perrin, 1984, 139-160.

Gros, A.: La recherche du consensus dans les décisions de la CIJ. In: Völkerrecht als Rechtsordnung. Festschrift Hermann Mosler, 1983, 351-358.

Gross, L.: Participation of individuals in advisory proceedings before the ICJ: Questions of equality between the Parties. In: L. Gross: Essays on international law and organization, vol. 2, 1984, 705-726.

Gross, L.: The time element in the contentious proceedings in the ICJ. In: L. Gross: Essays on international law and organization, vol. 2, 1984, 831-843.

Guillaume, G.: Preuves et mesures d'instruction. In: La juridiction internationale permanente. Colloque de Lyon, 1987, 191-218.

Guyomar, G.: Commentaire du Règlement de la CIJ, adopté le 14 avril 1978: Interprétation et pratique, 1983. Publications RGDIP 40.

Günther, M.: Sondervoten sowjetischer Richter am IGH, 1966.

Hamacher, P.: Die Maxime audiatur et altera pars im Völkerrecht. Ein Beitrag zum internationalen Verfahrensrecht unter besonderer Berücksichtigung der Rechtsgutachten des IGH, 1986.

Hussain, I.: Dissenting and separate opinions at the World Court, 1984.

Jennings, R.: The internal judicial practice of the ICJ. BYBIL 59 (1988) 31-47.

Jhabvala, F.: Declarations by Judges of the ICJ. AJIL 72 (1978) 830-855.

Jhabvala, F.: The development and scope of individual opinions in the ICJ. Thesis 1977. Ann Arbor, Mi., Univ. Microfilms International, 1985.

Jhabvala, F.: Individual opinions under the new rules of Court. AJIL 73 (1979) 661-668.

Jiménez de Aréchaga, E.: Judges *ad hoc* in advisory proceedings. ZaöRV 31 (1971) 697-711.

Jiménez de Aréchaga, E.: The participation of international organizations in advisory proceedings before the ICJ. In: Il processo internazionale. Studi Gaetano Morelli. Communicazioni e Studi 14, 1975.

Lachs, M.: Evidence in the procedure of the ICJ: The role of the Court. In: Hacia un nuevo orden internacional y europeo. Estudios Manuel Díez de Velasco, 1993, 427-437.

Lachs, M.: La preuve et la CIJ. In: La preuve en droit. Ed. Ch. Perelman, P. Foriers, 1981, 109-122.

Lachs, M.: The revised procedure of the ICJ. In: Essays on the development of the international legal order in memory of Haro F. van Panhuys, 1980, 21-52.

Lillich, R., G. E. White: The deliberative process of the ICJ. A preliminary critique and some possible reforms. AJIL 70 (1976) 28-40.

Malintoppi, A.: Plaidoiries davanti alla Corte internazionale di Giustizia, 1989.

Mani, V. S.: International adjudication: Procedural aspects, 1980.

Nafziger, J. A. R.: Some remarks on the writing style of the ICJ. In: Contemporary issues in international law. Essays Louis B. Sohn, 1984, 325-345.

Niyungeko, G.: La preuve devant les juridictions internationales, 2 vols. Thèse Bruxelles, 1988.

Oellers-Frahm, K.: Die Verfahrensordnung des IGHs vom 14 April 1978. AVR 18 (1979/80) 309-320.

Plender, R: Rules of procedure in the International Court and the European Court. EJIL 2 (1991) 1-30.

Prott, L. V.: Role, consensus and opinion analysis at the ICJ. NYIL 14 (1983) 69-85.

Rosenne, S.: The agent in litigation in the ICJ. In: Law, policy, and international justice: Essays Maxwell Cohen, ed. W. Kaplan, D. McRae, 1993.

Rosenne, S.: Procedure in the International Court. A commentary on the 1978 Rules of the International Court of Justice, 1983.

Rosenne, S.: Some reflections on the 1978 Revised Rules of the ICJ. CJTL 19 (1981) 235-253.

Salvioli, G.: Problèmes de procédure dans la jurisprudence internationale. RDC 91 (1957/1) 553-617.

Schwarzenberger, G.: International law as applied by international Courts and Tribunals, 4: International Judicial Law, 1986.

Schwebel, S. M.: The docket and decisionmaking process of the International Court of Justice. STLJ 13 (1990) 543-567.

Schwebel, S. M.: Three cases of fact-finding by the ICJ. In: Fact-finding before international Tribunals. 11th Sokol Colloquium, ed. R. B. Lillich, 1992, 1-17.

Scobbie, I.: Discontinuance in the International Court: The enigma of the 'Nuclear Tests' Cases. ICLQ 41 (1992) 808-840.

Scobbie, I.: The presence of an absent third: procedural aspects of the East Timor case. In: International law and the

question of East Timor, 1995, 223-242.
Sekino, S.: New Rules of the ICJ, adopted on 14 April 1978. Kokusaiho Gaiko Zassi 80 (1981) 86-114. [In Japanese]
Stillmunkes, P.: La 'forum prorogatum' devant la CPJI et la CIJ. RGDIP 68 (1964) 665-686.
Stuyt, A.M.: 'Contre-mémoire' ou 'Livre blanc'? Nouvelles tendances à la CIJ. RGDIP 82 (1978) 401-433.
Thirlway, H.: The law and procedure of the International Court of Justice 1960-1989: I-V. BYBIL 60 (1989) 1-157; 61 (1990) 1-133; 62 (1991)1-75; 63 (1992) 1-96; 64 (1993) 1-54 [To be continued].
Thirlway, H. W. A.: Procedure of international Courts and Tribunals. In: EPIL 1 (1981) 183-187.
Torres Bernárdez, S.: A propos de l'interprétation et de la revision des arrêts de la CIJ. In: Le droit international à l'heure de sa codification. Etudes Roberto Ago, vol. 3, 1987, 443-496.
Visscher, Ch. de: Aspects récents du droit procédural de la CIJ, 1966.
Wegen, G.: Discontinuance of international proceedings: The hostages case. AJIL 76 (1982) 717-736.
Wegen, G.: Vergleich und Klagerücknahme im internationalen Prozess, 1987.
Witenberg, J. C.: L'organisation judiciaire. La procédure et la sentence internationales. Traité pratique, 1937.
Witenberg, J. C.: La recevabilité des réclamations devant les juridictions internationales. RDC 41 (1932/3) 1-136.

Preliminary Objections

Abi-Saab, G.: Les exceptions préliminaires dans la procédure de la CIJ. Etude des notions fondamentales de procédure et des moyens de leur mise en œuvre, 1967.
Ago, R.: Eccezioni 'non esclusivamente preliminari'. In: Il processo internazionale. Studi Gaetano Morelli, 1975, 1-16.
Ammoun, F.: La jonction des exceptions préliminaires au fond en droit international public. In: Il processo internazionale. Studi Gaetano Morelli, 1975, 17-39.
Ciobanu, D.: Preliminary objections related to the jurisdiction of the UN political organs, 1975.
Gerber, F.: Le consentement de l'état à la juridiction de la CIJ, 1980.
Grisel, E.: Les exceptions d'incompétence et d'irrecevabilité dans la procédure de la CIJ, 1968.
Johnson, D. H. N.: The case of the Monetary Gold Removed from Rome in 1943. ICLQ 4 (1955) 93-115.
Mabrouk, M.: Les exceptions de procédure devant les juridictions internationales, 1966.
Malloy, M. P.: Objections to adjudication in contentious cases before the ICJ. BJIL 5 (1979) 262-347.
Morelli, G.: Eccezioni preliminari di merito? RDI 58 (1975) 5-11.
Rosenne, S.: The reconceptualization of objections in the ICJ. In: Il processo internazionale. Studi Gaetano Morelli, 1975, 735-761.
Salvioli, G.: Problèmes de procédure dans la jurisprudence internationale. RDC 91 (1957/1) 553-617.
Sperduti, G.: Ancora sulle eccezioni preliminari di merito. RDI 58 (1975) 657-665.
Thirlway, H. W. A.: Preliminary objections. EPIL 1 (1981) 179-183.
Villani, U.: Preliminary objections in the New Rules of the ICJ. IYBIL 1 (1975) 206-221.

Non-Appearance

Abou-el-Wafa, A.: La non-comparution devant la CIJ, 1986.
Arangio-Ruiz, G.: Non-appearance before the ICJ / La non-comparution devant la CIJ. AIDI 64/1 (1991) 193-376.
Colliard, C.-A.: La non-comparution. In: La juridiction internationale permanente. Colloque de Lyon, 1987, 167-190. [See also at 257-273].
Eisemann, P. M.: Les effets de la non comparution devant la CIJ. AFDI 19 (1973) 351-375.
Elkind, J. B.: Non-appearance before the ICJ. Functional and comparative analysis, 1984.
Fitzmaurice, G.: The problem of the 'non-appearing' defendant government. BYBIL 51 (1980) 89-122.
Grasern, L.: Verfahrensboykott vor dem Internationalen Gerichtshof: Sachvermittlung und Beweiswürdigung. AV 25 (1987) 460-483.
Lamm, V.: Some remarks about non-appearance before the ICJ. In: Questions of international law, 3: Hungarian perspectives, ed. H. Bokor-Szegö, 1986, 111-131.
Lanz, M.: Le défaut des parties devant les juridictions internationales, 1986.
Mangoldt, H. von: Versäumnisverfahren in der internationalen (Schieds-) Gerichtsbarkeit und souveräne Gleichheit. In: Völkerrecht als Rechtsordnung. Festschrift Hermann Mosler, 1983, 503-528.
Mosler, H.: Nichtteilnahme einer Partei am Verfahren vor dem IGH. In: Staatsrecht - Völkerrecht - Europarecht. Festschrift Hans-Jurgen Schlochauer, 1981, 439-456.
Non-appearance before the ICJ / La non-comparution devant la CIJ. Rapporteur: M. G. Arangio-Ruiz. AIDI 64/II (1991) 339-381.
Stanczyk, J.: The equality of Parties before the ICJ in cases of non-appearing respondent States. In: Forty years ICJ: Jurisdiction, equity and equality, ed. A. Bloed
Thirlway, H. W. A.: Non-appearance before the ICJ, 1985.
Thirlway, H. W. A.: Normative surrender and the 'duty' to appear before the ICJ: MJIL 11 (1989-1990) 912-925.

Interim Measures of Protection

Adede, A. O.: The rule on interlocutory injunctions under domestic law and the interim measures of protection under international law: Some critical differences. SJILC 4 (1976-1977) 277-301.
Arbour, J. M: Quelques réflexions sur les mesures conservatoires indiquées par la CIJ. Les cahiers de droit, Québec 16 (1975) 571-573.
Barile G.: Osservazioni sulla indicazione di misure cautelari nei procedimenti davanti la Corte internazionale de Giustizia. Comunicazioni e Studi 4 (1952) 145-156.
Beirlaen, A.: De bindende kracht en de afdwingbaarheid van de door het Internationale Hof van Justitie aangeduide conservatoire maatregelen. RBDI 18 (1984-1985) 739-775.
Beirlaen, A.: De ordonnantie van 11-9-1976, gewezen in de zaak Plateau continental de la mer Egée en de bevoegdheidsproblematiek in de fase der conservatoire maatregelen van het Internationaal Hof van Justitie. RBDI 14 (1978-1979) 425-459.
Bernhardt, J. P. A.: The provisional measures procedure of the ICJ through US Staff in Teheran: 'Fiat Iustitia, Pereat Curia?' VJIL 20 (1980) 557-613.
Bettati, M.: L'affaire du plateau continental de la mer Egée devant la CIJ: Demande en indication de mesures con-

servatoires, ordonnance du 11 septembre 1976. AFDI 22 (1976) 99-115.
Caron, D. D.: Interim measures of protection: Theory and practice in light of the Iran-United States Claims Tribunal. ZaoRV 46 (1986) 465-518.
Cocatre-Zilgien, A.: Les mesures conservatoires décidées par le juge ou par l'arbitre international. RGDIP 70 (1966) 5-48.
Cot, J.-P.: Affaires des essais nucléaires (Australie c. France et Nouvelle Zélande c. France): Demandes en indication des mesures conservatoires: ordonnances du 22 juin 1973. AFDI 19 (1973) 252-271.
Crockett, C. H.: The effects of interim measures of protection in the ICJ. CWILJ 7 (1977) 348-384.
Daniele, L.: Le misure cautelari nel processo dinanzi alla Corte internazionale di Giustizia, 1993.
Dumbauld, E.: Interim measures of protection in international controversies, 1932.
Dumbauld, E.: Relief 'pendente lite' in the ICJ. PBAQ 33 (1962) 265-277.
Dumbauld, E.: Relief 'pendente lite' in the PCIJ. AJIL 39 (1945) 391-405.
El-Ashaal A.: Non compliance with the provisional measures of ICJ. REgDI 34 (1978) 313-331.
Elias, T. O.: The ICJ and the indication of provisional measures of protection. Gilberto Amado Memorial Lecture, 1978.
Elkind, J. B.: Interim protection: A functional approach, 1981.
Elkind, J. B.: French nuclear testing and Article 41: Another blow to the authority of the Court? VJTL 8 (1975) 39-84.
Evans, M. D.: Provisional measures, the arbitral award of 31 July 1989 (Guinea Bissau v. Senegal) and maritime delimitation. RHDI 45 (1993) 9-32.
Fabri, F.: Le misure provisorie nel sistema di securezza della Nazioni Unite. RDI 47 (1964) 186-230.
Frankel K. D.: ICJ has preliminary jurisdiction to indicate interim measures of protection: The Nuclear Tests Cases. NYUJILP 7 (1974) 163-176.
Goldsworthy, P. J.: Interim measures of protection in the ICJ. AJIL 68 (1974) 258-277.
Gross, L.: Some observations on provisional measures. In: International law at a time of perplexity: Essays Shabtai Rosenne, ed. Y. Dinstein, 1989, 307-323.
Guggenheim, P.: Les mesures conservatoires dans la procédure arbitrale et judiciaire. RDC 40 (1932/2) 649-763.
Guggenheim, P.: Les mesures provisoires de procédure internationale et l'influence sur le développement du droit des gens, 1931.
Hambro, E.: The binding character of the provisional measures of protection indicated by the ICJ. In: Rechtsfragen der internationalen Organization. Festschrift Hans Wehberg, 1956, 152-171.
Hammarskjøld, Å.: Quelques aspects de la question des mesures conservatoires en droit international positif. ZaoRV 1935, 5-33.
Haver, P.: The status of interim measures of the ICJ after the Iranian-hostage crisis. CWILJ 11 (1981) 515-542.
Lagoni, R.: Interim measures pending maritime delimitation agreements. AJIL 78 (1984) 345-368.
Mani, V. S.: On interim measures of protection: ICJ practice. IJIL 13 (1973) 262-272.
Mendelson, M.: Interim measures of protection in cases of contested jurisdiction. BYBIL 46 (1972-1973) 259-322.
Mendelson, M.: Interim measures of protection and the use of force by States. In: The current legal regulation of the use of force, ed. A. Cassese, 1986, 337-360.
Merrills, J. G.: Interim measures of protection and the substantive jurisdiction of the ICJ. CLJ 36 (1977) 86-109.
Merrills, J.G.: The justiciability of international disputes. CBR 47 (1969) 241-269.
Niemeyer, H. G.: Einstweilige Verfügungen des Weltgerichtshofs: Ihr Wesen und ihre Grenzen, 1932.
Oda, S., T. Sugihara: Interim measures of protection of the World Court. Kokusaiho Gaiko Zassi 67 (1968-1969) 777-791. [In Japanese]
Oda, S., T. Sugihara: Provisional measures of the ICJ - 1970s. Kokusaiho Gaiko Zassi 78 (1979-1980) 604-622. [In Japanese]
Oellers-Frahm, K.: Die einstweilige Anordnung in der internationalen Gerichtsbarkeit, 1975.
Oellers-Frahm, K.: Interim measures of protection. EPIL 1 (1981) 69-72.
Oxman, B. H.: Jurisdiction and the power to indicate provisional measures. In: The ICJ at a crossroads, ed. L. F. Damrosch, 1987, 323-354.
Perrin, G.: Les mesures conservatoires dans les affaires relatives à la compétence en matière des pêcheries. RGDIP 77 (1973) 16-34.
Pescatore, P.: Les mesures conservatoires et les référés. In: La juridiction internationale permanente. Colloque de Lyon, 1986, 315-362.
Rucz , C.: L'indication de mesures conservatoires par la CIJ dans l'affaire des activités militaires et paramilitaires au Nicaragua et contre celui-ci. RGDIP 89 (1985) 83-111.
Salkiewicz, S. A.: Les mesures conservatoires dans la procédure des deux Cours de La Haye, 1984.
Sztucki, J.: Interim measures in the Hague Court: An attempt at a scrutiny, 1983.
Takane, S.: Interim measures of protection in the ICJ. HLR 31 (1981) 1681-1702.
Tama, N. M.: Nicaragua v. United States: The power of the ICJ to indicate interim measures in political disputes. DJIL 4 (1985) 65-87.
Tesauro, G.: Le misure cautelari della CIG. In: Il processo internazionale. Studi Gaetano Morelli, 1975, 873-901.
Thirlway, H. W. A.: The indication of provisional measures by the ICJ. In: Interim measures indicated by international Courts, ed. R. Bernhardt, 1994, 1-36. [See also Discussion, 119-152]
Toraldo-Serra, N. M.: Le misure provisorie internazionali: Ricerca storico-giuridica, 1973.
Venturini, G.: Le misure cautelari nel diritto internazionale. Archivio giuridico 'Filippo Serafini', 1938, 40-89, 152-182.
Villani, U.: In tema di indicazione di misure cautelari da parte della Corte internazionale di Giustizia. RDI 57 (1974) 657-681.
Villani, U.: Le misure cautelari nell'affare della Piattaforma continentale del mare Egeo. RDI 60 (1977) 128-138.
Wortley, B. A.: Interim reflections on procedures for interim measures of protection in the ICJ. In: Il processo internazionale. Studi Gaetano Morelli, 1975, 1009-1019.

Intervention

Cellamare, G.: Le forme di intervento nel processo dinanzi alla Corte internazionale di Giustizia, 1991.
Chinkin, C. M.: Third-party intervention before the ICJ. AJIL 80 (1986) 495-531.

Collier, J. G.: Intervention in the International Court: A slight breakthrough. CLJ 50 (1991) 216-218.
Davì, A.: L'intervento davanti alla Corte internazionale di Giustizia, 1984.
Decaux, E.: L'intervention. In: La juridiction internationale permanente. Colloque de Lyon, 1987, 219-255. [See also 257-273]
Elias, T. O.: The limits of the right of intervention in a case before the ICJ. In: Völkerrecht als Rechtsordnung. Festschrift Hermann Mosler, 1983, 159-172.
Fritzemeyer, W.: Die Intervention vor dem IGH Eine international-verfahrensrechtliche Untersuchung auf rechtsvergleichender Grundlage, 1984.
Fritzemeyer, W.: Intervention in the ICJ, 1983.
Greig, D. W.: Third-party rights and intervention before the ICJ. VJIL 32 (1991-1992) 285-376.
Günther, K.: Zulässigkeit und Grenzen der Intervention bei Streitigkeiten vor dem IGH: Rechtsfragen zu Artikel 62 und 63 des IGH-Statuts. GYBIL 34 (1991) 254-295.
Hoogh, A. J. J. de: Intervention under Article 62 of the Statute and the quest for incidental jurisdiction without the consent of the principal Parties. LJIL 6 (1993) 17-46.
Jessup, Ph. C.: Intervention in the ICJ. AJIL 75 (1981) 903-909.
Jiménez de Arechaga, Ed.: Intervention under Article 62 of the Statute of the ICJ. In: Völkerrecht als Rechtsordnung. Festschrift Hermann Mosler, 1983, 453-465.
Licari, T.: Intervention under Article 62 of the Statute of the ICJ. BJIL 8 (1982) 267-287.
Macdonald, R. St. J., V. Hughes: Intervention before the ICJ. AJICL 5 (1993) 1-33.
Madakou, A.: Intervention before the ICJ. Mémoire Institut Universitaire de Hautes Études Internationales, 1988.
Morelli, G.: Sul controllo della Corte internazionale di Giustizia circa l'ammissibilità dell'intervento in causa. RDI 67 (1984) 7-15.
Morelli, G.: Fonction et objet de l'intervention dans le procès international. In: Essays Manfred Lachs, 1984, 403-408.
Morelli, G.: Note sull'intervento nel processo internazionale. RDI 65 (1982) 805-815.
Oda, S.: Intervention in the ICJ: Articles 62 and 63 of the Statute. In: Völkerrecht als Rechtsordnung. Festschrift Hermann Mosler, 1983, 629-648.
Oda, S.: Intervention in the ICJ. Kokusaiho Gaiko Zassi 84 (1985) 1-28. [In Japanese]
Rey Caro, E. J.: El principio de no intervención en la jurisprudencia de la Corte internacional de Justicia. AHLADI 9 (1991) 339-358.
Rosenne, S.: Some reflections on intervention in the ICJ. NILR 34 (1987) 75-90.
Rosenne, S.: Intervention in the ICJ, 1993.
Sperduti, G.: Etude sur l'intervention dans le procès international. In: Hacia un nuevo orden internacional y europeo. Estudios Manuel Díez de Velasco, 1993, 713-717.
Sperduti, G.: L'intervention de l'Etat tiers dans le procès international: Une nouvelle orientation. AFDI 31 (1985) 286-293.
Sperduti, G.: Notes sur l'intervention dans le procès international. AFDI 30 (1984) 273-281.
Stanczyk, J.: Permissibility of intervention under Article 62 of the Statute before the ICJ. PYBIL 16 (1987) 121-142.

Execution of Judgments

Anand, R. P.: Execution of international judicial awards: Experience since 1945. World Rule of Law Booklet Series 33, squf.
Brown, C.: Enforcement of ICJ decisions in United States Courts. MJILT 11 (1987) 73-92.
Compliance with judgments of international courts, ed. M. K. Bulterman, M. Kuijer, 1996.
Condorelli, L.: Rapport: L'autorité de la décision des juridictions internationales permanentes. In: La juridiction internationale permanente. Colloque de Lyon, 1987.
Deutsch, E. P.: Problems of enforcement of decrees of international Tribunals. ABAJ 50 (1964) 1135-1139.
El Ouali, A.: Effets juridiques de la sentence internationale: Contribution à l'étude de l'exécution des normes internationales, 1984.
Fitzmaurice, G.: The foundation of the authority of international law and the problem of enforcement. MLR 19 (1956).
Ioannou, K. M.: Some problems of enforcement of the judgments of the ICJ. International institutional mechanisms and domestic procedures, 1971.
Nantwi, E. K.: The enforcement of international decisions and arbitral awards in public international law, 1966.
Oellers-Frahm, K.: Zur Vollstreckung der Entscheidungen internationaler Gerichte im Völkerrecht. ZaöRV 36 (1976) 654-679.
Ouali, A. E.: Effets juridiques de la sentence internationale: Contribution à l'étude de l'exécution des normes internationales, 1984.
Reisman, W. M.: Nullity and revision: The review and enforcement of international judgments and awards, 1971.
Reisman, W. M.: The enforcement of international judgments. AJIL 63 (1969) 4-27.
Reismann, J.: L'exécution des décisions de la CIJ et de la CJCE: Une comparaison. Thesaurus Acroasium 18 (1991) 573-581.
Rosenne, S.: L'exécution et la mise en vigeur des décisions de la CIJ. RGDIP 57 (1953) 532-583.
Schachter, O.: The enforcement of international judicial and arbitral decisions. AJIL 54 (1960) 1-24.
Tanzi, A.: Problems of enforcement of decisions of the ICJ and the law of the UN. EJIL 6 (1995) 539-572.
Tuncel, E.: L'exécution des décisions de la CIJ selon la Charte des Nations Unies, 1960.
Vulcan, C.: L'exécution des décisions de la CIJ d'après la Charte des Nations Unies. RGDIP 51 (1947) 193-205.

Jurisprudence

Basak, A.: Decisions of the UN organs in the judgments and opinions of the ICJ, 1969.
Bastid, S.: La jurisprudence de la CIJ. RDC 78 (1951/1) 575-686.
Bermejo, R.: Les principes équitables et les délimitations des zones maritimes: Analyse des affaires Tunisie/Jamahiriya arabe libyenne et du Golfe du Maine. HYBIL 1 (1988) 59-110.
Bernhardt, R.: Homogenität, Kontinuität und Dissonanzen in der Rechtsprechung des IGHs. ZaöRV (1973) 1-37.
Cassese, A.: The concept of 'legal dispute' in the jurisprudence of the ICJ. In: Il processo internazionale. Studi Gaetano Morelli, 1975, 173-200.
Digest of the decisions of the ICJ / Répertoire des décisions de

la CIJ / Handbuch der Entscheidungen des IGH 1976-1985; 1990.

Eisemann, P. M., V. Coussirat-Coustère, P. Hur: Petit manuel de la jurisprudence de la CIJ, 1980.

Fife, R. E.: Den internasjonale domstol i Haag: Rettspraksis 1946-1993; 1994.

Fontes Juris Gentium, Series A, Section I, vols. 5-6: Handbuch der Entscheidungen des IGHs / Répertoire des Décisions / Digest of the Decisions (1947-1975), 1961-1978.

Green, L. C.: International law through the cases, 1978.

Hambro, E., A. W. Rovine: The case law of the ICJ: A repertoire of the judgments, advisory opinions and orders of the ICJ, 8 vols., 1952-1976.

Harris, D. J.: Cases and materials on international law, 1979.

Henkin, L., R. C. Pugh, O. Schachter, and H. Smit: International law: Cases and materials, 1993.

Hoenderkamp, E.: The Danube: Damned or dammed? The dispute between Hungary and Slovakia concerning the Gabčíkovo-Nagymaros Project. LJIL 8 (1995) 287-309.

International law in transition: Essays Nagendra Singh, ed. R. S. Pathak, R. P. Dhokalia, 1992.

Isaja, H.: Les opinions dissidentes des juges socialistes dans la jurisprudence de la CIJ. RGDIP 79 (1975) 657-718.

Jiménez de Aréchaga, Ed.: The work and the jurisprudence of the ICJ 1947-1986. BYBIL 58 (1987) 1-38.

Jiménez de Aréchaga, Ed.: La teoria general del derecho internacional publico en la jurisprudencia de la CIJ. Anuario juridico interamericano, 1979, 117-130.

Lachs, M.: Thoughts on the recent jurisprudence of the ICJ. EJIDS 4 (1990) 77-94.

Lailach, M.: The General Assembly's request for an Advisory Opinion from the ICJ on the Legality of the Threat or Use of Nuclear Weapons. LJIL 8 (1995) 401-429.

Lalive, J.-F.: La jurisprudence de la CIJ. SJIR 6 (1949) 163-202; 9 (1952) 193-236.

Malintoppi, A.: Plaidoiries davanti alla Corte internazionale di Giustizia, 1989.

Malloy, M. P.: An analysis of the jurisprudence of the ICJ in cases concerning boundaries. Thesaurus acroasium 14 (1985 271-393.

Pirotte, O.: La notion d'équité dans la jurisprudence récente de la CIJ. RGDIP 77 (1973) 92-135.

Précis de la jurisprudence de la CIJ, ed. K. Marek, vol. 1, 1974.

Résumé des arrêts, avis consultatifs et ordonnances de la CIJ 1948-1991, ed. Nations Unies, 1992.

Röben, V.: Le précédent dans la jurisprudence de la CIJ. GYBIL 32 (1989) 382-407.

Singh, J. N.: International justice: Jurisprudence of the World Courts (PCIJ & ICJ), 1991.

Sohn, L. B.: The role of equity in the jurisprudence of the ICJ. In: Mélanges Georges Perrin, 1984, 303-312.

Summaries of judgments, advisory opinions and orders of the ICJ 1948-1991, ed. United Nations, 1992.

Syatauw, J. J. G.: Decisions of the ICJ, A digest, 1969.

Verzijl. J. H. W.: The jurisprudence of the World Court. A case by case commentary; vol. 2: The ICJ (1947-1965), 1967.

World Court digest, vol. 1, 1986-1990, ed. R. Hofmann, et al., 1993

The ICJ and International Law

Akehurst, M.: Custom as a source of international law. BYIL 47 (1974/75) 1-53.

Akehurst, M.: A modern introduction to international law, 1987.

Alvarez, A.: Le Droit international nouveau dans ses rapports avec la vie actuelle des peuples, 1959.

Anand, R. P.: International law and the developing countries: Confrontation or cooperation, 1987.

Anand, R. P.: New states and international law, 1972.

Annacker, C.: Die Durchsetzung von erga omnes Verpflichtungen vor dem Internationalen Gerichtshof, 1994.

Anzilotti, D.: Corso di Diritto Internazionale, 1928.

Anzilotti, D.: Teoria generale della responsibilita dello Stato nel diritto internazionale, 1902.

Arbour, J.-M.: Droit international public, 1985.

Bauer, H.: Der Satz 'pacta sunt servanda' im heutigen Völkerrecht, 1934.

Berlia, G.: Essai sur la portée de la clause de jugement en équité en droit des gens, 1937.

Encyclopedia of public international law, 12 vols., ed. R. Bernhardt, 1981-1990.

Blum, Y. Z.: Historic titles in international law, 1962.

Brierly, J. L.: The Law of Nations, 1928.

Briggs, H. W.: Reflections on the codification of international law by the ILC and other Agencies. RDC 126 (1969/1) 233-316.

Brownlie, I.: International law and the use of force by States, 1981.

Brownlie, I.: Principles of public international law, 1990.

Bürgenthal, Th. H. G. Maier: Public international law in a nutshell, 1985.

Butler, W. E.: Comparative approaches to international law. RDC 190 (1985/1) 9-90.

Cahier, Ph.: Changements et continuité du droit international. RDC 195 (1985/6) 9-374.

Cambridge essays in international law. Essays Lord McNair, 1965.

Carillo Salcedo, J. A.: El derecho internacional en perspectiva histórica, 1991.

Carreau, D.: Droit international, 1986.

Cassese, A.: International law in a divided world, 1986.

Castren, E. J. S: Traité de droit international, 1938.

Chen, L.: An introduction to contemporary international law: A policy oriented perspective, 1989.

Cheng, B.: General principles of law as applied by international Courts and Tribunals, 1987.

Collins, L.: Essays in international litigation and the conflict of laws, 1994.

Combacau, J., S. Sur: Droit international public, 1993.

D'Amato, A.: The concept of custom in international law, 1971.

D'Amato, A.: Good faith. EPIL 7 (1984) 107-109.

Degan, V. D.: L'équité en le droit international, 1970.

Díez de Velasco Vallejo, M.: Instituciones de derecho internacional público 1, 1993.

Dokhalia, R. P.: The codification of public international law, 1970.

Droit international: Bilan et perspectives, ed. M. Bedjaoui, 2 vols., 1991.

Dupuy, P.-M.: Droit international public, 1993.

El-Erian, A.: The ICJ and the concept of universality. CJTL 19 (1981) 197-211.

Elias, T. O.: Africa before the World Court. Gandhi Memorial Lectures, 1981.

Elias, T. O.: New horizons in international law, 1992.

Elias, T. O.: The modern law of treaties, 1974.

Encyclopaedic dictionary of international law, ed. C. Parry, 1986.
Equity in the world's legal system: A comparative study, ed. R. A. Newman, 1973.
Falk, R. A.: The status of law in interational society, 1970.
Franck, Th. M.: Fairness in the international legal and institutional system. RDC 240 (1993/3) 9-498.
Fauchille, P.: Traité de droit international public, 1921-1926.
Gidel, G.: Cours de droit international, 1929.
Gormley, W.: The codification of 'pacta sunt servanda' by the ILC: The preservation of classical norms of moral force and good faith. Saint Louis ULJ 14 (1970) 367-428.
Green, L. C.: International law: A Canadian perspective, 1984.
Gross, L.: Selected essays on international law and organization, 1993
Grzybowski, K.: Soviet public international law, 1970.
Gutiérrez Espada, C.: Derecho internacional público, 1: Introducción y fuentes, 1993.
Haggenmacher, P.: La doctrine des deux éléments du droit coutumier dans la pratique de la CIJ. RGDIP 90 (1986) 5-125.
Hassan, T.: Good faith in treaty formation. VJIL 21 (1981) 443-481.
Herczegh, G.: General principles of law and the international legal order, 1968.
Higgins, R.: Problems and process: International law and how we use it, 1994.
Hoof, G. J. H. van: Rethinking the sources of international law, 1983
International law in transition: Essays Judge Nagendra Singh, ed. R. S. Pathak, R. P. Dhokalia, 1992.
International law: Achievements and prospects, ed. M. Bedjaoui, 1991.
Janis, M. W.: An introduction to international law, 1988.
Jenks, C. W.: The common law of mankind, 1958.
Jenks, C. W.: Principles of international law, 1966.
Jennings, R. Y.: The acquisition of territory in international law, 1963.
Jennings, R. Y.: International law. EPIL 7 (1984) 278-297.
Jiménez de Aréchaga, Ed.: El derecho internacional contemporaneo, 1980.
Jiménez de Aréchaga, Ed.: International law in the past third of a century. RDC 159 (1978/1) 1-343.
Jouve, Ed.: Le droit des peuples, 1986.
Kapoor, S. K.: International law, 1992.
Kelsen, H.: Reine Rechtslehre, 1934.
Kelsen, H.: Peace through law, 1944.
Kimminich, O.: Einführung in das Völkerrecht, 1984.
Koskenniemi, M.: Theory: Implications for the practitioner. In: Theory and international law: An Introduction, 1991, 3-45.
Krylov, S. B.: Les notions principales du droit des gens. La doctrine soviétique du droit international. RDC 70 (1947/1) 407-476.
Kunz, J. L.: The meaning and the range of the norm 'pacta sunt servanda'. AJIL 39 (1945) 180-197.
Kwiatkowska, B.: The ICJ doctrine of equitable principles applicable to maritime boundary delimitation and its impact on the international law of the sea. In: Forty years ICJ: Jurisdiction, 1988, 119-158.
Lachs, M.: Pacta sunt servanda. EPIL 7 (1984) 364-371.
Lachs, M.: Some thoughts on the role of good faith in international law. In: Declarations on principles, ed. R. J. Akkerman et al., 1977, 47-55.
Lapenna, L.: Conception soviétiques de droit international public, 1954.
Latham Brown, D. J.: Public international law, 1970.
Lauterpacht, H.: The function of law in the international community, 1933.
McNair, A. D.: The law of treaties, 1961.
McWhinney, E.: Conflit idéologique et ordre public, 1970.
Mani, V. S.: Basic principles of modern international law, 1993.
O'Connell, D. P.: International law, 2 vols., 1965-1970.
O'Connor, J. F.: Good faith in international law, 1991.
Oppenheim's International law, 9th ed., vol. I [in two vols., 4 parts]: Peace. Ed. R. Jennings, A. Watts, 1992.
Papacostas, B. G.: Le principe 'pacta sunt servanda' et l'Organisation des Nations Unies. RHDI 6 (1953) 231-238.
Paul, Vl.: The abuse of rights and bona fides in international law. ÖZöRV 28 (1977) 107-130.
Pellet, A.: Droit international public, 1981.
Perestroika and international law, ed. W. E. Butler, 1990.
Quintana Aranguren, J. J.: Instituciones basicas de derecho internacional publico, 1994.
Reuter, P.: Droit international public, 1983.
Rogoff, M. A.: International politics and the rule of law: The United States and the ICJ. BUILJ 7 (1989-1990) 267-299.
Rosenne, S.: An international law miscellany, 1993.
Rosenne, S.: The position of the ICJ on the foundations of the principle of equity in international law. In: Forty years ICJ: Jurisdiction, equity and equality, ed. A. Bloed, P. van Dijk, 1988.
Rosenne, S.: Documents on the ICJ / Documents relatifs à la CIJ, 1991
Rossi, Ch. R.: Equity and international law: A legal realist approach to international decision-making, 1993.
Rousseau, Ch.: Droit international public, 1987.
Ruda, J. M.: Some of the contributions of the ICJ to the development of international law. NYUJILP 24 (1991-1992) 35-68.
Ruzié, D.: Droit international public, 1991.
Schachter, O.: International law in theory and practice, 1991.
Schwarzenberger, G.: The fundamental principles of international law. RDC 87 (1955/1) 191-385.
Schwebel, S. M.: Human rights in the World Court. VJTL 24 (1991) 945-970.
Schwebel, S. M.: Relations between the ICJ and the UN. In: Le droit international au service de la paix. Mélanges Michel Virally, 1991, 431-443.
Schweisfurth, T.: Socialist conceptions of international law. EPIL 7 (1984) 417-424.
Shahabuddeen, M.: Developing countries and the idea of international law. In: Essays Wang Tieya, ed. R. St. John Macdonald, 1994, 721-736.
Shearer, I. A.: Starke's International law, 1994.
Starke, J. G.: Introduction to international law, 1989.
Steiner, H. J.: International law, doctrine and schools of thought in the twentieth century. EPIL 7 (1984) 297-309.
Strupp, K.: Les règles générales du droit de la paix. RDC 47 (1934/1) 258-595.
Sturgess, G., Ph. Chubb: Judging the world: Law and politics in the world's leading Courts, 1988.
Thierry, H., J. Combacau, S. Sur, et al.: Droit international public, 1981.
Third World attitudes toward international law: An introduction, ed. F. E. Snyder, S. Sathirathai, 1987.
Thirlway, H. W. A.: International customary law and codification, 1972

Tunkin, G. I.: International law in the international system. RDC 147 (1975/4) 1-218.
Tunkin, G. I.: Theory of international law, ed. W. E. Butler, 1974.
Valencia-Ospina, E.: The ICJ and international environmental law. AYIL 2 (1992) 1-10.
Verdross, A., B. Simma: Universelles Völkerrecht: Theorie und Praxis, 1984.
Virally, M.: Le droit international en devenir: Essais écrits au fil des ans, 1990.
Visscher, Ch. de: De l'équité dans le règlement arbitral ou judiciaire des litiges du droit international public, 1972.
Visscher, Ch. de: Théories et réalités en droit international, 1955.
White, G.: The principle of good faith. In: The United Nations and the principles of international law: Essays Michael Akehurst, ed. V. Lowe, C. Warbrick, 1994, 230-255.
Whiteman, M. M.: Digest of international law, 1963.
Whitton, J. B.: La règle 'pacta sunt servanda'. RDC 49 (1934/3) 147-276.
Zoller, E.: La bonne foi en droit international public, 1977.

Indices

HISTORICAL EVENTS

Index of Names

Subject Index

Index of Cases

Acknowledgments of Photographs

The illustrations contained in this book come from various sources. The author expresses his gratitude to all institutions and private persons who have been instrumental in the assembling and reproduction of photographs. He wishes to express his indebtedness to the following institutions and private persons in particular: Royal Library (The Hague); Library Africa Study Centre (Leiden University); University of Virginia Library; Bibliotheca Rosenthaliana (University of Amsterdam); Ir. E. W. Leeuwin (Amsterdam); Mrs Janny van Wezel (The Hague); Tom Verhaar (The Hague); Willem Vermeij (The Hague).

Photographs of decorative elements were produced by D-Vorm (Bert & Lilian Mellink); a few exceptions are acknowledged below. Photographs of public sessions of the Court were produced over the years by Max Koot (The Hague) and Studio Van der Plas (Wassenaar); a few additional photographs and the front cover photograph were supplied by D-Vorm.

The official photographs of Judges appearing in Chapter Nine were for the greater part produced by Max Koot (The Hague); in a few cases additional photographs were supplied by D-Vorm. The official photographs of the Members of the Court and the Staff of the Registry, appearing on pp. v, vi, 104, 340 were produced by D-Vorm.

Virtually all historical documents, early prints and engravings reproduced throughout this book are from the Peace Palace Library collection. Acknowledgments are due to Mr. D. Lugthart and Mr. C. de Man for their generous support in the selection of items. Pictures from the collections of the Peace Palace Library, taken for the greater part from the 'Pictures Catalogue' and 'Catalogue of Portraits' arranged by J. Ter Meulen and P. J. J. Diermanse, appear on the following pages: 1-14, 18, 21-30, 33-38, 41-43, 45, 46, 48, 49, 51, 53, 57, 61, 65-71, 74, 98, 114-116, 118, 128, 130, 180-186, 191, 192, 195, 196, 198, 200, 205, 213, 222-233, 236, 241, 242. Pictures appearing on pp. 38, 40, 46, 53 (2x), 58, 66, 67, 71, 114, 124 are from the photo-collection of the Carnegie Foundation (photographs Jan den Hengst; copyright Carnegie Foundation, 1988). Pictures appearing on pp. 27, 115, 116, 128 were kindly supplied by D. Brouwer, The Hague; copyright Carnegie Foundation.

Pictures appearing on pp. 123, 135, 163, 208, 251, 252 and most photographs appearing on pp. 258-339 were kindly supplied by Max Koot (The Hague).

Pictures appearing on pp. 133, 139, 151, 363, 365 were kindly supplied by Studio Van der Plas.

Pictures appearing on pp. 244-247 were kindly supplied by the Africa Study Centre at Leiden University.

The pictures of historical maps to be found on pp. 178, 201, 221, 235, 244, 256 are taken from the *Monumenta Cartographica Portugaliae* (Lisboa, 1987), a copy of which was presented to the ICJ by the Portuguese Government.

Pictures appearing on pp. 183, 190 are from the collections of the Academic Historical Museum of Leiden University.

Pictures appearing on p. 354 were kindly supplied by Judge C. G. Weeramantry.

The picture appearing on p. 96 was kindly supplied by Virginia University Library, Special Collections Department. Edward R. Stettinius Papers (Mss. 2723)

The picture appearing on p. 198 is copyright Harris & Ewing (1938).

The picture appearing on p. 219 was kindly supplied by Kluwer Academic Publishers.

SERBIE
GEORGE WASHINGTON
TURQUIE
RUSSIE
· COMMÉMORATION ·
· de la Conférence de la PAIX ·
la HAYE · mai-Juillet · 1899 ·
FRANCE